Law Librarianship Practice

Law Librarianship Practice

Challenges and Opportunities in Law Firm, Government, and Academic Law Libraries

Edited by Ellyssa Kroski

BLOOMSBURY ACADEMIC
NEW YORK • LONDON • OXFORD • NEW DELHI • SYDNEY

BLOOMSBURY ACADEMIC
Bloomsbury Publishing Inc
1359 Broadway, New York, NY 10018, USA
50 Bedford Square, London, WC1B 3DP, UK
29 Earlsfort Terrace, Dublin 2, Ireland

BLOOMSBURY, BLOOMSBURY ACADEMIC and the Diana logo are trademarks of Bloomsbury Publishing Plc

First published in the United States of America 2026

Cover design: Diana Nuhn
Cover image © iStock.com/Pitiphothivichit

Library of Congress Cataloging-in-Publication Data

ISBN: HB: 978-1-5381-9973-2
PB: 978-1-5381-9974-9
ePDF: 978-1-5381-9975-6
eBook: 979-8-7651-5459-5

Typeset by Deanta Global Publishing Services, Chennai, India

To find out more about our authors and books visit www.bloomsbury.com and sign up for our newsletters.

Contents

Preface

Ellyssa Kroski

Law librarianship is a constantly evolving field that has seen major shifts in practice over the past several years, including the post-pandemic trend toward remote and hybrid work, the increased prominence of virtual services, the outsourcing of library staff, burgeoning cybersecurity risks, and the advent of generative artificial intelligence (AI). Law librarians have adroitly adapted to all of these changes and have once again proven their resilience.

Law Librarianship Practice is a cutting-edge book that provides insights into the latest emerging trends and technologies in academic, government, and law firm librarianship. This book offers guidance from forward-thinking library leaders on how they are tackling the challenges of law librarianship today, including managing remote workforces, negotiating with vendors, navigating outsourcing services, planning for emergencies, riding out law firm mergers, succession planning, and more. Experts working in the field provide practical applications of new technologies and opportunities, such as how librarians are conducting AI-informed competitive intelligence, using big data for decision-making, and what's happening in AI. The book also covers innovative initiatives in the areas of diversity, equity, and inclusion, Access to Justice, and more.

Law Librarianship Practice serves as a comprehensive manual of modern-day law library practices, providing invaluable resources for law librarians. Readers will gain inspiration from nearly thirty chapters contributed by distinguished academic, government, and law firm librarians as well as library consultants who share their experiences along with a combination of researched data, contract excerpts, surveys, and other real-world intelligence.

Divided into three segments, readers will be led through twenty-eight chapters in the areas of Law Library Management, Law Library Technologies, and Law Library Challenges and Opportunities.

The Law Library Management part includes chapters on Policy Development; Budgeting for the Law Library; Negotiating Contracts; The Business of Running a Law Library; Managing Remote and Hybrid Workers; Vendor Relations: Navigating Challenges and Opportunities with Collaboration, Negotiation, and Implementation; Institutional Knowledge Management and Succession Planning; How to Create a Strategic Plan and Prove the ROI of the Library; Law Firm Libraries: Organizational Structure, Positioning of the Library, and Law Firm Mergers; Digital Leases and Lost Legacies: The Quest for Sustainable Access; and Risk Management in Law Libraries.

Part II of the book covers **Law Library Technologies** and features the chapters: The Law Library Website; The Law Library Intranet; Cybersecurity Issues and Training; AI and Machine Learning in Law Libraries; Generative AI in Law Libraries; AI-Driven Competitive Intelligence; Big Data and Law Libraries; and Data on the Horizon: Involvement and Impact of Law Librarians in Big Data Projects.

The final segment of the book is dedicated to discussing **Law Library Challenges and Opportunities** and includes the chapters Advancing the Impact of Legal Information: Challenges and Opportunities in Law Firm Libraries; Challenges and Opportunities in Government Law Libraries; Using Scenario

Planning to Discover Challenges and Opportunities in Academic Law Libraries; How Law Libraries Can Reimagine Diversity, Equity, and Inclusion (DEI) in an Anti-DEI Climate; Access to Justice (A2J); Law Library Partnerships, Working in the Field without an MLIS; The Professional Law Librarian Today; and The Law Library as a Center for Innovation.

This book will inspire and guide library leaders to be at the forefront of law libraries today.

Foreword

Ronald E Wheeler

Why have I been tasked with creating this foreword? Perhaps it is because I have been a practicing law librarian for almost twenty-four years. It could be the numerous leadership roles I took on or was elected to over the years, including serving as president of the American Association of Law Libraries (AALL)[1] during 2016–2017. My having received the Distinguished Alumnus Award from the Wayne State University School of Library and Information Science in 2016 may also have factored into the equation. Then again, it might be my compulsion to show up and to speak up at law library-related events wherever and whenever I possibly can, with the goals of sharing useful information with others and learning from the many brilliant minds present at these law library events. It could very well be my resolve to demonstrate the kind of open-hearted kindness and empathy that I have always received from my professional coworkers, mentors, and peers. More than anything, however, I think my love for our profession, a love that I am told shines through every law library-related interaction I have, may have helped our Editor choose me to create a foreword. Even if none of these factors influenced the decision to choose me to pen this foreword, these factors are nonetheless the building blocks of my professional reputation, and they are the things I value most about my work even more than publications, commendations, or academic titles.[2]

It is June of the year 2024. I am sitting and thinking, but no words are coming. I am attempting to pen a meaningful foreword for this exciting and truly cutting-edge book, which describes the contemporary practice of law librarianship. Yet even I must acknowledge that most people, even most librarians from other types of libraries, have little knowledge of how truly different law librarianship is from any other branch of librarianship. Law librarianship is a profession that may have as many unique traits as it does traits in common with other professional librarians. What excites me most about this book is that it will finally articulate a detailed, nuanced, expansive, and long-overdue explanation of my noble profession. The explanation found within these pages will transcend any single practitioner's perspective.

How can I be so sure about these ambitious predictions? I am sure because, unlike most others, this book calls upon numerous law librarians, working in wildly different settings and with different levels of experience, to collectively describe our profession. Each contributing author is guaranteed to approach their description from a slightly different angle. I say that with confidence because contributing authors have each been given only one topic or one singular facet of law librarianship about which to offer their views. Therefore, when collected within this volume, a multifaceted yet complete picture will take shape for the reader. This revolutionary volume will then finally shed light on the essential work that law librarians do, and it will illuminate the profession from as many different angles as there are contributors. It will describe a cohesive profession, but it will also reveal how varied and diverse we law librarians and our law libraries really are. It will explain what has until now remained unexplained. It will solve an ongoing mystery. It will create knowledge in an area that has to date been largely unknowable.

Surprisingly, however, I am acquainted with—and in some cases, I am close friends with—many of the contributors to this text. Law librarianship really is quite a small profession, and we North American law librarians end up knowing or "knowing of" each other because of the collaborative nature of our work and the reality that the size of our profession leaves only about two degrees of separation between any of us. Moreover, thanks to organizations like the AALL, [3] the International Association of Law Libraries (IALL),[4] the Canadian Association of Law Libraries (CALL),[5] the British and Irish Association of Law Libraries (BIALL),[6] and the Australian Library Association (ALA),[7] my network of professional colleagues, friends, and acquaintances extends quite literally all across the globe.[8] Thus, I have worked with, conferenced with, spoken with, corresponded with, or hung out with most of the contributors to this work. As for the rest, I most certainly have done so with one of their coworkers, mentors, or professors. These fine information professionals are not strangers to me. They are my heroes. Thus, my confidence in the innovative and revolutionary nature of what is written within these pages flows from my personal connections to the contributing authors, their work, their workplaces, and the ways they continue to shape the future of the information professions.

A final and perhaps the most important feature making law librarianship unique is the nature and uses of U.S. Law itself. Author Philippe Sands writes that "the law is a bridge that connects us to our shared past and guides us toward a more just and equitable future." J. William Fulbright wrote that "law is the essential foundation of stability and order both within societies and in international relations." Henry Adams spoke of the law in the following way. He said, "chaos was the law of nature; order was the dream of man." With that, he asserted that law is what helps us to make that dream a reality. I will give Aristotle the final comment here with his decree that, "At his best, man is the noblest of all animals; separated from the law and justice he is the worst."[9] Taken in total, these opinions underscore the belief that it is the law that has the potential to give the world order, justice, and peace. If we agree with that assertion, then law librarians do, indeed, have a venerable task.

Law librarians, then, are charged with tasks that buttress and support the very foundations of societies and governments of contradistinct types. In government law libraries, those libraries created to be a presence in state, county, court, government agency, and other arms of U.S. government, law librarians work to guarantee the public accessibility of the law for the citizens of the United States of America, noncitizens living within the U.S. borders, and the many souls interested in our laws and living beyond our borders. These law librarians hold a special place in my heart because they must sometimes literally fight to maintain access to our laws for people suffering economic challenges and those subject to oppression, disability, language barriers, lack of education, and various other woes. Even when the law is theoretically accessible, without expert guidance, appropriate technology infrastructure, and other help, our body of U.S. Law can be unintelligible to those without legal training. In law firm and corporate law libraries, where law librarians support attorneys charged with using our laws to serve clients with varying specialized interests, their role helps to define—sometimes expanding and at other times narrowing—how law may be used by clients as wide-ranging as individual citizens, small businesses, start-ups, multinational corporations, and foreigners seeking asylum as they flee oppressive governments, ideologies, or individuals worldwide. Finally, in academe, law librarians serve dual yet vital missions. Their importance is evinced by the fact that every accredited U.S. law school is required by their accrediting body—the American Bar Association—to have a law library meeting certain minimum specifications with respect to the quality and accessibility of their materials. First, academic law libraries are instrumental in assisting the legal academy in its pursuit of truth and justice through academic scholarship, service, teaching, and the representation of the oppressed and the indigent. Second, they are vital conduits ensuring the effective flow of legal knowledge and information from law school faculties and other sources of legal knowledge to the students that are our future lawyers and our hope for a brighter and more just future to be governed by the rule of law. Thus, the most important and distinct work undertaken by professional law librarians can be characterized as authenticating, preserving, guaranteeing the accessibility and free use of legal information by all who desire such access, and teaching legal research techniques and processes to our nation's future lawyers.

Most forewords include a description of the foreword author's relationship with the book's author. In this case, due to the large number of contributing authors, many of whom I know well and others whom I merely know tangentially, I instead give you a description of my relationship with our profession. By doing so, I endeavor to impart the deep and abiding love I have for law librarianship that has developed throughout my twenty-plus-year relationship with both the profession and its practitioners. In the same way that personal knowledge of a single author creates certainty about her scholarship, my knowledge of and love for this profession have produced my absolute certainty in the value of the academic work you are about to read.

One often hears a hackneyed adage asserting, "time flies when you're having fun." My sense is that most people have encountered this statement somewhere. Well, much to my dismay, after spending years with my head in the sand, working hard in various roles in numerous academic law libraries while navigating life's ups and downs; joys and sorrows; beginnings and endings, I find that when I do look out at the world around me, what I see confirms that, indeed, time has flown. And I really have been having more fun than I would ever have imagined possible.

This I declare with both earnestness and dismay as I reflect on the arc of my career that is yet a work in progress. It is a career that has given me my proudest moments and my greatest achievements. A career during which many of my professional colleagues became, unexpectedly, the most significant friendships of my life. This career has gifted me opportunities to travel the world. It presented me with challenges from which I learned many of life's most important lessons. This career of mine has allowed me to live and work in every region of the United States, experiencing an array of cultures, climates, regional cuisines, and many social realities that were unimaginable to the person I was when I left my hometown of Detroit.[10] It is a career that has nurtured my ambitions, encouraged me to achieve, required me to set aside my naïve notions of reality and truth, and to make room for understanding the lived experiences of so many others. When I say others, I mean people whose lives are dramatically different from mine, yet filled with the same human desires, hopes, fears, pain, and most importantly, the joys that we experience as part of our shared human condition. My career has given me a rich, full, colorful, often difficult, yet simultaneously wonderful working life. These are the things I am most grateful for, and I owe them all to the people that make up the profession of law librarianship.

I have described for you the length and breadth of my career, and I have even shared my feelings about my work. Yet, I have said very little about exactly what made my career so unique, so special, and so rewarding that twenty-four years passed by in what seems like the blink of an eye. Luckily, I do not have to try to answer that question. The pages that follow this foreword will provide the answers for all of us. What I will say is that my belief in the accuracy of the words written here and my absolute confidence in the wisdom this text provides flow directly from the respect I have for the authors of the chapters contained within.

It is only now, as I close this foreword, that I see with clarity how significant are these words of mine reflecting on the importance of the Law, the Rule of Law, and the accessibility of the Law to the people whose lives are governed by it. Only yesterday, July 14, 2024, I inadvertently witnessed, while scrolling through channels on television, the alleged attempted assassination of former U.S. president and current presidential candidate Donald J. Trump. I then watched as the President of the United States, Joseph R. Biden Jr., took the podium at a press conference to denounce political violence of any kind and to offer his prayers and well-wishes to his political opponent, Mr. Trump. These heart-rending events offer perhaps the best justification for the continued and essential work of law librarians in North America and throughout the world. For, what good is the law without free and universal access to it? Without access, the law becomes like the tree that falls in a forest when no one is around to hear it. Does that tree make a sound? Similarly, do those inaccessible laws have their desired impact? Do they have any impact at all?

It is with the most sincere, heartfelt love and respect for my country, the United States of America, and for ordinary people, the citizens of our world; for the profession of law librarianship and all of the practicing law librarians worldwide; and with an abiding and intense yearning for peace that I close this foreword.

Peace!
Ronald E Wheeler
Associate Dean of Law Libraries
Associate Professor of Law & Legal Research
Boston University School of Law

NOTES

1. AALL is the premier professional association serving the profession of law librarianship in the United States. It is also the organization for which I served as president in 2016.
2. Ronald E. Wheeler serves as the Associate Dean of Law Libraries and Associate Professor of Law & Legal Research at the Fineman & Pappas Law Libraries of Boston University School of Law. He has served in these roles since 2016.
3. The website for the American Association of Law Libraries; accessed July 15, 2024, https://www.aallnet.org/.
4. The website for the International Association of Law Libraries; accessed July 15, 2024, https://iall.org/.
5. The website for the Canadian Association of Law Libraries/Association Canadienne Des Bibliothèques De Droit; accessed July 15, 2024, https://www.callacbd.ca/.
6. The website for the British and Irish Association of Law Libraries; accessed July 15, 2024, https://biall.org.uk/.
7. The website for the Australian Law Librarians' Association, accessed July 15, 2024, https://www.austlawlib.org/.
8. I penned this paragraph while sitting in a pub in Oslo, Norway, where I was attending the IALL conference in June 2024.
9. Philippe Sands, East West Street (New York: Alfred A. Knopf, 2016). J. William Fulbright, The Arrogance of Power (New York: Random House, 1966), 96. Henry Adams, The Education of Henry Adams, ed. Ira Nadel (New York: Oxford University Press USA, 2009), 377.W. D. Ross, ed., The Works of Aristotle, trans. Benjamin Jowett (Oxford: The Clarendon Press, 1921), 1253.
10. I began my career in law librarianship at the University of New Mexico School of Law in Albuquerque, NM. I then served as Associate Director at the Georgia State University College of Law Library in Atlanta, GA. My first law library directorship was at the University of San Francisco School of Law Library, and from there I took on the directorship at Suffolk University Law School in Boston before moving to the Boston University School of Law and its Fineman & Pappas Law Libraries.

Part I

Law Library Management

1

Policy Development in Law Libraries

Sheri H. Lewis

Law libraries are complicated entities embedded in even more complex academic, governmental, or corporate institutions. In librarianship practice, managers and staff guide the direction of their operations, programs, and services in informal and formal ways. Law library organizations may have norms and customs that offer accepted informal practices for their communities. However, law libraries require well-defined and adopted guidance to ensure efficiency and success. Policies are a formal method for articulating the scope and parameters of how a law library conducts its enterprise. This chapter will explore and offer applications of policy development in law libraries. It also draws from practical experience and studies in policy development from the broader library community. While the focus is on library-created and managed policies, the discussion also considers existing policies of parent institutions and outside entities as they intersect with and affect library policy development. This chapter begins by defining policies in law libraries and their scope, continues with categories and context for policies, offers approaches to policy formulation and development, and concludes with further considerations for the care and maintenance of a law library's policies. The author also lists resources for further study on this topic.

WHAT IS LAW LIBRARY POLICY?

Policies are fundamental principles for planning and managing libraries[1] as they regulate and control organizational actions.[2] *Policy* is "an officially accepted set of rules or ideas about what should be done" and "an idea or belief that guides the way you live or behave."[3] Policies should clearly state how a library organization intends to conduct its services, actions, or business.[4] Ideally, a law library's policies clarify "how the library will act in various situations."[5]

Policies exist for all audiences in a law library community. From a user's perspective, they might explain "the organization's stand on a subject and why there's a rule about it" and communicate to "the reader how the organization intends to operate."[6] For managers and staff, "policies also may act as the instruction manuals to how a law library functions."[7] Clear and effective policies offer a consistent and well-conceived framework for a law library organization's activities and actions.

Policies are one aspect of how libraries explain and guide how they function. A law library may also have *norms* that develop and serve as informal and unwritten ways of understanding how the community functions and the expectations within it. Policy development may be unnecessary, inappropriate, or even counterproductive for such norms,[8] as they may represent culture but not operations. Moreover, law libraries may also have *procedures* that are "the customary methods of handling things"[9] and *guidelines* that provide interpretative direction. Policies are distinguishable from other policy-like documents, such as procedures[10] and guidelines.[11] A law library should not create a policy when it does not represent an official articulation of how it conducts its enterprise.

A law library does not develop all existing policies applicable to its organization. External entities, including parent institutions, oversight bodies, and the government, create policies and laws[12] directing the work of law libraries. Law library managers should avoid creating policies that are not in alignment with or conflict with those more appropriately produced by external partners or entities. As discussed in this chapter, law libraries may derive their policies from oversight bodies or parent institutions. In such instances, a library may apply an existing directive or develop its specific application of that policy in a library context.

LAW LIBRARY POLICIES AND THEIR CONTEXT

Law library policy may cover a wide range of operations, services, and activities in an institution. Some policies guide patrons in using law library spaces, services, and resources. Other policies are staff-focused and centered on operational matters. Law libraries create and adopt policies directly or through external directives. This chapter does not explore law library policy in any specific area,[13] although it does offer common examples. Instead, it presents two useful distinctions for policy creation and application—internal or external in origin and public or staff-facing in focus.

Policies may originate from the law library (internal) or an external entity.[14] Internal policies are created and controlled by a library and rescinded or revised as circumstances change in operations, community needs, and expectations. Externally created policies may stem from parental organizational oversight or existing federal, state, or local laws applicable to libraries, their governing institutions, or the general population.[15] In this context, library policy development may also be hybrid, where an institution applies an external rule or law to create a local application through policy.

State patron privacy[16] and federal copyright laws[17] provide good examples for considering external and hybrid policy origin in law libraries. Most state statutes have a law protecting the confidentiality of library records.[18] Such laws provide an external source of policy. However, a library may develop its policy statements by acknowledging state law and articulating specific applications for the institution. For instance, a law library policy might clarify the specific information covered by the privacy law (a borrower's circulation records) and exceptions not covered (patron computing and database use). Similarly, for copyright law, a law library may develop local policies for copying and scanning materials to ensure or at least encourage compliance.[19]

Library Codes of Conduct, research support, access services, and collection development policies are helpful examples of internal policy creation. *Codes of Conduct* typically communicate an organization's expectations for interaction in library spaces, including activities, equipment use, and resources, and generally define what people are allowed to do when using a library.[20] *Codes of Conduct* may be patron or staff-focused or broadly intended for all members of a law library community. Reference or research assistance offers a unique example of policy development in law libraries where an institution articulates limits to avoid the unauthorized practice of law.[21] Access to library facilities and collection development policies[22] are two areas where policy formulation may be internal or hybrid, as parental or external entities often determine or direct policy with implications for space and budget.

The origin and focus of a law library's policies provide essential context for policy developers. The four categories—external, internal, patron-focused, and staff-focused—offer a helpful, albeit simple, rubric for considering broad aspects of policy formulation. As the above examples illustrate, law library policies are often complex and reflect aspects of their internal and broader institutional operations.

Table 1.1 lists many areas of policy development in law libraries, with examples from the literature in academic library settings.[23] The table includes patron-focused and internal and staff-focused policies. While most policy areas in these lists are internal, others are hybrid or externally derived.

Table 1.1 Categories for Law Library Policies

Categories for Patron-Focused Policies	
Access	• Patrons: community members, affiliates, public • Membership, fees • Minors, animals • Hours: building, study, service, regular, special
Facilities	• Noise: talking, equipment, mobile phones • Study spaces: collaborative, quiet, zones • Specific locations: rooms, desks, carrels • Activities: eating and drinking, sleeping, tobacco use, advertising, signage, taking photographs, video recording
Equipment	• Computers, printers, copiers, scanners • Lockers • Supplies
Circulation Services	• Borrowing: loan periods, renewals, recalls • Patron accounts: confidentiality of records, fines, blocks • Resource sharing, interlibrary loan • Special collections: reserves, rare items • Circulation of supplies, equipment
Collections/Resources	• Use of rare, fragile items • Copyright: copying, printing scanning • Electronic resources: downloading, distributing content • Licenses, use restrictions
General Patron Services	• Document delivery services: paging, scanning • Reference, research support • Providing legal advice • Service delivery: patron categories • Training, instruction
Categories for Internal and Staff-Focused Policies	
Facilities	• Staff work areas, noise • Maintenance, repairs • Equipment, furniture • Security, cameras
Personnel	• Work schedules, time off • Performance reviews • Compensation, benefits • Professional development, training
Financial	• Budget • Expenditures, reimbursement • Fundraising, donors • Payments, fees, cash management
Operational	• Supplies • Committees, groups • Statistics • Technology: equipment, software, networks, systems • Internal document management, intranets • Programs: events, exhibits, displays

(*Continued*)

Table 1.1 (Continued)

Categories for Internal and Staff-Focused Policies	
Collections/Resources	• Collection development • Acquisitions, renewal, cancellation • Gifts, donations • Retention, weeding • Storage • Archives, special collections
Emergency	• Evacuation • Closing the library • Specific situations: active shooter, flood, fire • Notification system: staff and patrons

These lists are not exhaustive or prescriptive of all matters to be addressed by library policy. The table provides examples to accompany this chapter's policy formulation and development discussion.

LAW LIBRARY POLICY FORMULATION AND DEVELOPMENT

Motivation for policy development varies across institutions and is a helpful consideration when beginning the process. Law libraries should avoid policy articulation solely from a problem-solving perspective. While managers may focus on creating or revising their policies only when something has gone wrong, a sound policy development strategy addresses known issues and anticipates challenges before they occur. Policy development may focus on a single instance where a law library creates a new policy or reevaluates an existing one. A library may also engage in a programmatic and more ambitious effort through a policy audit by inventorying, collecting, assessing, and revising its existing policy statements.[24] Policymakers should approach their work systematically and with an approach ensuring careful assessment of needs and desired outcomes.

A law library should initiate policy development positively and proactively by explaining and clarifying its intentions from an engagement perspective. This first stage, or policy formulation, is guided by the SAID rubric—state, assess, identify, determine. The SAID model presents a series of threshold questions to help law library managers determine the landscape for policy creation. While SAID envisions individual policy development, it also applies to a systematic review and revision of many library policies through an audit process. Upon completion of the SAID rubric, a law library is ready to begin the drafting stage of policy development.

SAID RUBRIC

State the Purpose—What is the problem to be solved? What is the goal to be achieved? Is policy the appropriate vehicle for addressing the problem or goal?

Assess the Landscape—Is there a current policy or model to draw on? Can the library determine and direct policy development on the matter? Do policymakers have the information necessary to proceed?

Identify the Stakeholders—Who should be involved in policy development? Who will be affected? Who will implement, direct, and oversee the policy? Who needs to approve a policy statement?

Determine the Output—What is the desired format for the product? What should be included (or not) in the policy? Is this policy related to other policies or plans?

Policies are not necessary or appropriate for every aspect of a law library's operations, programs, and services. Accordingly, law libraries should not create policies without an expressed need. Therefore, an essential initial step in the development process is to *state the purpose* of a policy. Policies should only exist if necessary to achieve a particular goal or to address a known or anticipated issue. Policymakers should avoid developing solutions for problems that do not exist or creating organizational principles absent a need for them. As discussed at the outset, policies are one vehicle for explaining how an organization functions. Libraries should not choose policy formulation when the matter is better explained with procedures or is an accepted norm that is not mandatory for the community. By stating the purpose at the outset, law library managers will ensure that policies successfully meet the needs of their organization.

An information-gathering exercise is valuable for many managerial tasks, and policy development is no exception. By *assessing the landscape* and having essential information known at the outset of a process, law libraries will be better equipped to create sound and well-informed policy statements. Pre-development assessment includes considering the status quo and gathering information to inform policy formulation. Policymakers should first identify any current policies in the library and any related governing laws, rules, or relevant policies from external or parent institutions. Law library managers may also be interested in examples of best practices from other law libraries.[25] Finally, developers should conduct sound policy research to gather information, facts, and data. They should also conduct surveys, focus groups, or other formal or informal assessment activities to inform their work. Policy development relies on a sound understanding of the library and its needs. Policymakers should ensure they have all the facts necessary to make informed decisions and proceed thoughtfully with their work.

Policies affect people, and engaging with the individuals who will live with the outcome is essential. By *identifying and incorporating stakeholders* into the process, policymakers will set the stage for successful policy development and implementation. Stakeholders include those who create, comply with, oversee, and approve policy statements. Policymakers should incorporate perspectives from those different vantage points to consider the range of future policy experiences. Since it is impossible to include all stakeholders in policy creation, law library managers should identify representative individuals and embrace diverse viewpoints.[26] By incorporating cultural competency in developing policies, law libraries will reflect marginalized communities within them.[27] The identification of stakeholders is, of course, only a first step. Policy developers also must consider and employ effective engagement with those stakeholders from the initial steps of formulation to the drafting and implementation stages of policy development.

Law librarians will be more efficient in policy development by *determining the output* at the outset. Policy documents exist in different forms—from brief, individual policy statements to lengthy, detailed policy manuals with related forms and procedures. Policymakers should ascertain the desired product, including identifying the essential content and determining if the policy is part of or alongside other organizational documents. Policy statements are not the only products of policy development. Good policymakers generate a paper trail of materials that guide and assist their work: checklists, timelines, workflow charts, assessments, research, and data. Such outputs are part of a library's institutional memory and a helpful reference when revisiting policies. After determining all outputs for policy development, law librarians can proceed to the writing stage with a clear plan for their work.

Good policy writing uses simple and succinct language but with sufficient content to communicate effectively.[28] Law libraries should carefully and thoughtfully approach policy drafting, perhaps especially given the strong writers and thinkers in their patron communities. The scope of a policy should be broad and flexible enough for a range of situations but with sufficient specificity to cover typical activities and circumstances. While predicting every situation a policy may address is difficult, one should anticipate common occurrences and include any parameters and limitations. Policy authors should write for an inclusive, gender-neutral community, avoiding jargon that requires expertise while ensuring that policy statements are accurate and consistent.[29] While law library users may have law and library expertise (or both), law library managers should not assume that is the case for everyone in the community. Law library policies should speak to and communicate effectively with all readers (not just the experts!).

A valuable strategy for effective organizational policy is consistency across documentation. Ideally, law libraries should use an established format and standard content for all policy statements. The two *T's and four P's* guide below provides a baseline for the essential policy elements. The first four—*title, time, purpose,* and *policy*—are fundamental and perhaps apparent components. Policy statements should also identify the *people* involved, especially policymakers and overseers,[30] and the library's *plan* for how a policy fits within others for greater transparency in the organization.

THE TWO T'S AND FOUR P'S GUIDE

Title: The name of the policy and the name of the library adopting it
Time: The date adopted or last modified
Purpose: The reason for the policy and its alignment with the library's mission or goals
Policy: The policy statement with accompanying use cases or definitions
People: The audience for the policy and the names of policymakers and overseers
Plan: Related documents or resources—forms, procedures, guidance, or other policies

Producing a final written policy may be the most exciting stage in policy development. However, several finalizing norms are necessary before completing the writing stage. In addition to thorough editing, managers should set aside time for verification, validation, and approval.[31] During verification, policymakers compare the final version with earlier drafts and project notes as an accuracy check using the documentation created in the process. Validation is another critical finalizing step for policymakers when they ask stakeholders for a final review and seek input from trusted colleagues not involved in developing the policy. The final sign-off stage of policy development should be uneventful when policymakers communicate and address approver expectations and concerns during the process. Nonetheless, policymakers should plan for additional time between approval and adoption for unexpected matters before implementation.

Policy work is challenging, and success is due to dedication to the process. As law libraries move from policy development to adoption, managers should acknowledge and celebrate the efforts of those involved. Recognizing policymakers' time and commitment is appropriate and helps pave the way for effective policy implementation and acceptance in the law library community.

PRESENT AND FUTURE CONSIDERATIONS: CARING FOR AND MAINTAINING POLICY

The policy development process does not conclude with a written policy statement. Policies succeed with implementation and ongoing maintenance. Law library managers should implement new or revised policies with effective communication and training. They also should regularly review policies to determine whether they remain valid and valuable and to identify areas for improvement in the policy or its application. Law library policies require care and maintenance to continue to serve as effective vehicles for their organizations. Policies are not static but are living institutional documents that change with a law library's environment.

Communication and training are vital and complementary components for implementing policy change. Communication should address both internal (managers, staff) and external (users, other departments)[32] members of a law library community and use various methods (online, print) and locations (library, parent organization) for easy access.[33] Training is also vital for a law library's internal and external members. However, the library's approach to communication and training varies for different stakeholders depending on their engagement with the new policy. Communication and training for law library patrons may be more informational, focusing on the policy's purpose, departures from previous policies, and specific use cases. Staff and managers must have the same information conveyed to patrons and additional training on communicating and enforcing the new policy, including departures from it. A law library's communication and training plans may vary with different policy implementations. New policies representing significant organizational changes will require more extensive efforts to communicate and train than those making minor modifications to existing policies. Law library managers who anticipate considerable adjustments with new policies may find that sharing the policy documents early and adopting transition periods are helpful strategies[34] for managing policy change in their organization.

"Policies are like housework—never truly done."[35] Law library policies require oversight and regular assessment on a meaningful cycle[36] to ensure they remain relevant and valuable organizational tools. Oversight and assessment represent the last policy development stage when policymakers hand off their work to law library managers and staff. Typically, managers oversee library policy and should develop an ongoing and regular plan for conducting that work. Managerial oversight duties include monitoring the application of the policy to gauge its effectiveness and gathering input from stakeholders through formal or informal assessments. Assessment sits at the core of policy oversight, and a critical inquiry is the consistency of policy application. If a law library observes frequent departures or exceptions to an existing policy, it may need to consider revising it or rethinking communication and training. Accordingly, oversight may result in a new policy development process as the cycle begins again.

Policy maintenance offers another opportunity to acknowledge library managers and staff. As law libraries become aware of success stories due to new policies, they should use such awareness to recognize policy developers and library team members who effectively implement policies. Policy success stories may encourage and help routinize policy development in law libraries as they tout the benefits and rewards of that essential work to the organization.

CONCLUSION

Policy development presents an opportunity for a law library. It benefits all members of a law library community, including managers, staff, and users.[37] Law libraries developing and maintaining clear and current policies will promote consistency in decision-making, support team members in learning and performing their work, and create transparency in operations and service delivery. Law libraries with well-crafted policies offer clarity for interactions within and with their environments and signal value for open communication with their communities. While managers may experience policy work as time-consuming and challenging (and it can be), they also may find satisfaction, enrichment, and value in an effort that supports and enhances their library and its mission, vision, and goals.

NOTES

1. M. Fahimeh Ahmadian, Chandrashekara, and Seyedhadi Marjaei, "Study of Library Policies in Universities," *Library Philosophy and Practice* (March 2019), https://digitalcommons.unl.edu/libphilprac/2324/.
2. Nancy J. Campbell, *Writing Effective Policies and Procedures: A Step-by-Step Resource for Clear Communication* (New York: American Management Association, 1998), 1–13.
3. "Definition of 'Policy,'" *The Britannica Dictionary Online* (2024), https://www.britannica.com/dictionary/policy.

4. Marie Keen Shaw and Hali R. Keeler, *Supervision and Management: An Introduction for Support Staff* (Lanham, MD: Rowman & Littlefield, 2019), 97-113, 99.
5. Nathan A. Delmar and Theresa K. Tarves, "Policy Development & Strategic Planning," *Introduction to Law Librarianship* 1 (2021): 49-62, 50.
6. Campbell, *Writing Effective Policies and Procedures*, 1.
7. Delmar and Tarves, "Policy Development & Strategic Planning," 49-62, 50.
8. Campbell, *Writing Effective Policies and Procedures*, 8-10.
9. Campbell, *Writing Effective Policies and Procedures*, 1-13.
10. Shaw and Keeler, *Supervision and Management*, 100-101.
11. "Is it a Policy, Procedure, or Guideline?," UW-Madison Policy Library, last modified June 1, 2022, https://development.policy.wisc.edu/2022/06/01/is-it-a-policy-procedure-or-guideline/.
12. For a general discussion of laws related to library environments, see Mary Minow, *The Library's Legal Answer Book* (Chicago, IL: American Library Association, 2003) and Tomas A. Lipinski, ed., *Libraries, Museums, and Archives: Legal Issues and Ethical Challenges in the New Information Era* (Lanham, MD: Scarecrow Press, 2002).
13. Law library managers have a variety of resources available for policy development in specific areas. Websites include patron-facing policies and are helpful resources for best practices from other institutions, especially for access and reference services.
14. Robert D. Stueart and Barbara B. Moran, *Library and Information Center Management*, 7th ed. (Westport, CT: Libraries Unlimited, 2007), 65-92, 83.
15. Campbell, *Writing Effective Policies and Procedures*, 57-81.
16. "State Privacy Laws Regarding Library Records," American Library Association, last updated November 2021, https://www.ala.org/advocacy/privacy/statelaws.
17. "Resource Guides Copyright for Libraries: General Information," American Library Association, last modified May 29, 2024, https://libguides.ala.org/copyright.
18. Bruce M. Kennedy, "Confidentiality of Library Records: A Survey of Problems, Policies, and Laws," *Law Library Journal* 81, no. 4 (Fall 1989): 733-768.
19. "Resource Guides Copyright for Libraries: Special Topics," American Library Association, last modified May 29, 2024, https://libguides.ala.org/copyright/special-topics.
20. For an example of a *Code of Conduct*, see "Conduct on Library Premises," Library of Congress, https://www.loc.gov/rr/conduct.html.
21. Charles J. Condon, "How to Avoid the Unauthorized Practice of Law at the Reference Desk," *Legal Reference Services Quarterly* 19, no. 1-2 (2001): 165-180; Wendi Arant and Brian Carpenter, "Where is the Line? Legal Reference Service and the Unauthorized Practice of Law (UPL)—Some Guides That Might Help," *Reference & User Services Quarterly* 38, no. 3 (Spring 1999): 235-239.
22. For discussion of law library collection development policies, see Jasmin Hollingum, "Collection Development Policies in Law Firm Libraries: Do We Need Them?," *Legal Information Management* 13, no. 1 (2013): 62-65, https://doi.org/10.1017/S147266961300011X; "Collection Development Policies," American Association of Law Libraries (AALL) Academic Law Libraries Special Interest Section, accessed July 28, 2024, https://www.aallnet.org/allsis/resources-publications/academiclawlibcoldevpolicies/; "Collection Development Policies," American Association of Law Libraries (AALL) Government Documents Special Interest Section, accessed July 28, 2024, https://www.aallnet.org/gllsis/resources-publications/toolkit/collection-development/.
23. Ahmadian, Chandrashekara, and Marjaei, "Study of Library Policies in Universities."
24. For an extensive discussion about the design for a library policy audit, see Sandra Nelson and June Garcia for the Public Library Association, *Creating Policies for Results: From Chaos to Clarity* (Chicago, IL: American Library Association, 2003), 22-70.
25. Delmar and Tarves, "Policy Development & Strategic Planning," 49-62.
26. "Cultural Proficiencies for Racial Equity: A Framework - 2.4 Policies, Procedures and Norms," Joint ALA/ARL Building Cultural Proficiencies for Racial Equity Framework Task Force, last updated August 2022, https://www.ala.org/sites/default/files/advocacy/content/diversity/ALA%20ARL%20Cultural%20Proficiencies%20for%20Racial%20Equity%20Framework.pdf.
27. Id.

28. Campbell, *Writing Effective Policies and Procedures,* 82–134.
29. Id.
30. "Guidelines for Policy Development at UW-Madison," *UW-Madison Policy Library,* University of Wisconsin-Madison, accessed July 28, 2024, https://development.policy.wisc.edu/.
31. Campbell, *Writing Effective Policies and Procedures,* 264–296.
32. Nelson and Garcia, *Creating Policies for Results,* 105–131.
33. Delmar and Tarves, "Policy Development & Strategic Planning," 49–62.
34. Campbell, *Writing Effective Policies and Procedures,* 318–342.
35. Nelson and Garcia, *Creating Policies for Results,* 127.
36. Aaron Schmidt and Amanda Etches, *Useful, Usable, Desirable: Applying User Experience Design to Your Library* (Chicago: American Library Association, 2014): 49–70.
37. Shaw and Keeler, *Supervision and Management,* 99–100.

RECOMMENDED RESOURCES

American Association of Law Libraries. Academic Law Libraries Special Interest Section. *Collection Development Policies.* Accessed July 28, 2024. https://www.aallnet.org/allsis/resources-publications/academiclawlibcoldevpolicies/.

American Association of Law Libraries. Government Documents Special Interest Section. *Collection Development Policies.* Accessed July 28, 2024. https://www.aallnet.org/gllsis/resources-publications/toolkit/collection-development/.

Ahmadian, Fahimeh, M. Chandrashekara, and Seyedhadi Marjaei. 2019. "Study of Library Policies in Universities." *Library Philosophy and Practice.* Last modified March 20, 2019. https://digitalcommons.unl.edu/libphilprac/2324/.

American Library Association. *Library Bill of Rights.* Accessed July 28, 2024. https://www.ala.org/advocacy/intfreedom/librarybill.

American Library Association. *Resource Guides: Copyright for Libraries.* Last modified May 29, 2024. https://libguides.ala.org/copyright.

American Library Association. *Resource Guides, Library Policy Development: General.* Last modified April 30, 2024. https://libguides.ala.org/librarypolicy.

American Library Association. *State Privacy Laws regarding Library Records.* Last modified November 2021. https://www.ala.org/advocacy/privacy/statelaws.

American Library Association, and the Joint ALA/ARL Building Cultural Proficiencies for Racial Equity Framework Task Force. 2022. *Cultural Proficiencies for Racial Equity: A Framework.* https://www.ala.org/pla/initiatives/edi/racialequityframework.

Arant, Wendi, and Brian Carpenter. 1999. "Where is the Line? Legal Reference Service and the Unauthorized Practice of Law (UPL)—Some Guides That Might Help." *Reference & User Services Quarterly* 38, no. 3 (Spring): 235–239.

Campbell, Nancy J. 1998. *Writing Effective Policies and Procedures: A Step-by-Step Resource for Clear Communication.* New York: American Management Association.

Condon, Charles J. 2001. "How to Avoid the Unauthorized Practice of Law at the Reference Desk." *Legal Reference Services Quarterly* 19, no. 1-2: 165–180.

Delmar, Nathan A., and Theresa K. Tarves. 2021. "Policy Development & Strategic Planning." In *Introduction to Law Librarianship*, edited by Zanada Joyner and Cas Laskowski, 49–62. Tucson, AZ: Daniel F. Cracchiolo Law Library.

Encyclopedia Britannica, Inc. 2024. *The Britannica Dictionary Online*. "Policy." Accessed July 28, 2024. https://www.britannica.com/dictionary/policy.

Hollingum, Jasmin. 2013. "Collection Development Policies in Law Firm Libraries: Do We Need Them?" *Legal Information Management* 13, no. 1 (March): 62–65.

Kennedy, Bruce M. 1989. "Confidentiality of Library Records: A Survey of Problems, Policies, and Laws." *Law Library Journal* 81, no. 4 (Fall): 733–768.

Kotch, Marianne. 2002. *Policymaking for Vermont Public Librarians and Trustees*. Washington, DC: Institute of Museum and Library Services.
Lipinski, Tomas A., ed. 2002. *Libraries, Museums, and Archives: Legal Issues and Ethical Challenges in the New Information Era*. Lanham, MD: Scarecrow Press.
Mann, Emily Zoe, Stephanie A. Jacobs, Kirsten M. Kinsley, and Laura I. Spears. 2023. "Tracking Transparency: An Exploratory Review of Florida Academic Library Privacy Policies." *Information and Learning Sciences* 124, no. 9/10 (January): 285–305.
Minow, Mary. 2003. *The Library's Legal Answer Book*. Chicago: American Library Association.
Nelson, Sandra, June Garcia, and the Public Library Association. 2003. *Creating Policies for Results: From Chaos to Clarity*. Chicago: American Library Association.
OCLC. *WebJunction: Policies*. Accessed July 28, 2024. https://www.webjunction.org/explore-topics/policies-procedures.html.
Schmidt, Aaron and Amanda Etches. 2014. "Chapter 5: Policies and Customer Service." In *Useful, Usable, Desirable: Applying User Experience Design to Your Library*. Chicago: American Library Association.
Shaw, Marie Keen Shaw and Hali R. Keeler. 2019. "Chapter 6: Policies and Procedures." In *Supervision and Management: An Introduction for Support Staff*. Lanham, MD: Rowman & Littlefield.
Stueart, Robert D. and Barbara B. Moran. 2007. "Chapter 4: Planning Information Services and Systems." In *Library and Information Center Management*. 7th edition. Westport, CT: Libraries Unlimited.
University of Wisconsin-Madison. *UW-Madison Policy Library: Guidelines for Policy Development at UW-Madison.* Accessed July 28, 2024. https://development.policy.wisc.edu/

2

Budgeting for the Law Library

Justin Huckaby

Law libraries today deal with many different facets within their operations. One of the main components of law library management is the art of budgeting. Law library budgets can be complicated or simplified depending on the type of law library in question, that is, academic, government, or law firm. When budgeting, law libraries must consider many different factors, including today's needs as well as the future needs of the collection.

This chapter will discuss the methodical approach to budgeting. It will include several case studies of individual libraries and their budgeting practices. The chapter will also include several suggestions on how law libraries might approach budgeting within their respective organizations as they follow the three-step process described throughout this chapter.

Hopefully, by the end of this chapter, law librarians will have gained an insightful understanding of the complexities of budgeting through the various suggestions and real-world experiences. It is my hope that a newcomer to law library budgeting will be able to delve into this facet of law libraries with better knowledge and confidence to adequately serve their constituent communities.

Budgeting can be a long and drawn-out process, but it is something that is easily managed. The basic process of budgeting within a fiscal year can best be described through a three-step process that can be repeated each year.

STEP ONE—STUDY THE LIBRARY'S BUDGETARY NEEDS

Most law libraries utilize a budgeting method known as incremental budgeting, which is sometimes referred to as traditional budgeting. This budgetary concept is based on the notion that costs will always increase. The process is simple in application.

Several months before the next fiscal year is to begin, law librarians will start the budgeting process for the next period. Most law libraries will start with the current budget allocations from the current fiscal year.[1]

As most resources will increase in cost each subscription year, law libraries will need to account for the increase in cost in the next fiscal year. This can be done in several ways. Some law libraries will approach this issue by adding a 3–5 percent increase in funding for that particular resource or cost center. Other law libraries will reach out to the vendor to determine what the increase will actually be. When this is done, a law library will then be able to accept that stated increase or negotiate with the vendor to have the vendor lower the amount of the upcoming increase.[2]

During this period of time, law libraries will also evaluate their various resources to determine if the return on investment is actually worth the cost. Librarians will look at usage statistics of the various databases. They might also look at circulation statistics of physical materials to see if a certain type of loose-leaf or monograph collection is being utilized. If it is not being utilized enough, the law library might decide to cancel that standing order or not renew an electronic resource.[3] It should be noted that the various vendors will have terms and conditions associated with cancellation processes. Some vendors require a thirty-day notice of an intention to cancel or not renew.

Some vendor terms and conditions will not be honored in public academic law libraries and government law libraries. As divisions of a sovereign organization, these institutions must follow state law, which results in certain terms being considered null and void as it applies to public institutions. These public academic law libraries and government law libraries will have the vendors sign a contract addendum detailing these conditions. An example of an addendum is below.

VENDOR CONTRACT ADDENDUM

Mandatory Addendum

This addendum is between _________________ (state institution) and _____________ (vendor). Vendor acknowledges that _____________ is a state institution and is subject to the law of the State governing actions of state entities. Vendor further acknowledges that the state institution does not waive, relinquish, or forfeit any of the rights, benefits, protections, guaranties, or prohibitions that may be provided under any law, statute, regulation, or policy. The parties agree that this Addendum is incorporated into the contract and agree that should any provision of the contract conflict with this Addendum, the terms of the Addendum control.

1. State institution contracts are governed by the law of the State. Any provision that purports to set the venue outside of the State is deleted.
2. The state institution does not waive its sovereign immunity.
3. Any provisions limiting the time for the state institution to pursue legal action are deleted.
4. Any references to the state institution waiving any cause of action it may have against the vendor are deleted.
5. Any references to the state institution limiting damages or remedies are deleted.
6. The state institution will deliver payments to the vendor no later than forty-five days after receipt of the invoice and goods or services.
7. The continuance of any state institution contract is based on the availability of funds. Should there be no funds available for any succeeding funding period, the contract will be canceled as of the end of the current funding period. The contract is cancelable with thirty days' notice to the vendor.
8. Any reference to an automatic renewal of the contract or the contract term is deleted.

Vendor

By: __________________________ (Signature)
Name and Title: ________________________
Date: ______________________________

State Institution

By: __________________________ (Signature)
Name and Title: ________________________
Date: ______________________________

When law libraries are conducting these evaluations in the budget preparation process, it should be noted that just because they decide to cancel a resource does not mean that they will eliminate that amount of funding from their new proposed budget. That money might be moved and allocated somewhere else, or a new resource of the same caliber could be bought or licensed in its place. These decisions are not always easy. With that said, when presented with budget cuts, these decisions do become easier.

Academic Law Libraries

Academic law libraries will approach Step One in similar ways. With that said, not all academic law libraries conduct their budgeting process directly. A Midwestern Public Law School Library is not directly involved in the Step One process. Their law school has a dedicated business professional who conducts this process. The business professional will reach out to the law library director to learn of the law library's needs. The business professional will then quantify those needs into a proposed budget, including a hefty inflationary rate increase on top of the prior fiscal year's allocations.

In comparison, a Northeastern Private Law School Library does not participate in the process with budget discussions at all. The law school might consult with the law library about its budgetary needs, but this does not always occur in the Step One process.

Government Law Libraries

Government and court law libraries can approach Step One in vastly different ways. Some institutions are governed by local courts and judicial systems. Others are governed by an appointed board of trustees. A Southwestern County Law Library handles the entire process in-house. Each department within the law library handles Step One for their respective departments. They evaluate their own work product, usage, and costs. They propose their own budget that will then be combined into the law library's overall budget.

In comparison, a Southeastern Court Law Library does not participate in the Step One process at all. Their budget is managed and produced by the Court's Finance Office. The law library is considered a small department in the overall Court's operations. Generally, the prior year's budget allocation is the same budget allocation for the next year. The law library might be requested to justify its expenses from the current year in order to continue to receive the same level of funding. Increases are usually never on the table.

Law Firm Libraries

Law firm libraries will approach Step One in several different ways as well. It should be noted that law firm libraries will each operate on different models. Some law firms have a centralized library that serves the entire law firm. Other law firms will have smaller libraries that only serve specific attorneys or practice groups. A Midwestern Law Firm Library handles its budgeting and services as one centralized library. They handle all library services for the entire firm including its satellite offices. The director works closely with their e-resources analyst and their technical services specialist for Step One. Together, they will go through each line item and vendor to check planned spending as part of multi-year agreements, or they will contact the vendors directly for an estimated cost. They start meeting monthly in Step One until all resources and vendors have been evaluated and determined.

In comparison, a Southeastern Law Firm Library is organized in such a way that the law library is divided into small units that work directly for specific attorneys and practice groups. The Step One process is similar in that the small unit will evaluate its resources and expenditures to develop a proposed budget. However, the budget is not combined with the other small units. Instead, the proposed budget is attributed to the practice group. This also means that the attorneys within the practice group are more heavily involved in the Step One process. The attorneys will inform the small units of their needs and satisfaction with the currently available resources.

STEP TWO—NEGOTIATION

Step Two involves the art of negotiation. At this point, most law libraries have developed a proposed budget. It is time for the negotiation and approval process. This process will generally occur one to two months prior to the start of the new fiscal year. A lot of considerations go into this process.

Law libraries will need excellent marketing skills for the negotiation process. This is the part where law libraries have to sell their services and abilities to the higher-ups. This can be handled by the law library itself or its parent organization.[4] Generally, the powers that be are only concerned with the bottom line when it comes to finances. Therefore, law libraries have to convince the approvers that they provide value to the institution and that the requested funding is necessary to provide the needed services to the respective patron population.

Academic Law Libraries

Academic law libraries might participate in this process, but that is not always the case. In fact, most academic law libraries do not participate in the Step Two process. In a Midwestern Public Law School Library, Step One is somewhat combined with Step Two. When the director meets with the law school's business professional, the director has to justify the needs at that time. The majority of Step Two is handled by the law school itself. The law school will submit the proposed budget to the university and advocate on behalf of the law library for the requested funds. Hopefully, the director did a great job advocating on behalf of the library when meeting with the business professional. Justifications made during that process in Step One will be used in negotiating with the university by the law school in Step Two.

The Northeastern Private Law School Library operates in a similar manner to the Midwestern Public Law School Library when working through Step Two. The law library will advocate for its needs with justifications during the Step One process. The law school will then submit the proposed budget to the university in order to seek approval. The law school will utilize the justifications provided by the law library in Step One during the negotiation process with the university.

Government Law Libraries

Government and court law libraries will conduct Step Two in different ways as well. For instance, the Southwestern County Law Library conducts Step Two entirely by itself, after completing Step One and compiling a proposed budget. The law library will submit the proposed budget to its board of trustees. In the negotiation process, the director will then negotiate on behalf of the various units regarding their needs and wants. Sometimes the unit heads might be asked to speak before the board of trustees regarding certain matters pertaining to the budget. Usually, the unit heads will have prepared their justifications and given them to the director to speak on their behalf before the board of trustees.

In comparison, the Southeastern Court Library does not participate in Step Two at all. By this point, the Court's Finance Office has already compiled the proposed budget, which is normally the same amount of funding as the previous fiscal year. As the law library's budget is just a small portion of the overall Court's budget, the negotiation process generally does not involve much negotiation specifically regarding the law library's portion of the budget. With that said, expected large purchases might require some marketing in this process. The Court will submit the proposed budget to the Legislature for approval. It is rare, but the law library might be asked to appear before the Legislature's

Appropriations Committees to testify and provide justifications for the expected large purchases previously alluded to. However, generally, the Court's representatives will handle the testimony portion of Step Two before the Appropriations Committees.

Law Firm Libraries

Law firm libraries will approach Step Two in a few ways. It will depend on how the law firm operates its law library. A centralized law firm library will have an easier path in the approval process as opposed to a law firm that has small unit libraries for the various practice groups. In the Midwestern Law Firm Library, they try to maintain multi-year contracts so that Step Two is an easier process. The director will submit the proposed budget to law firm management. As the budget is already encumbered due to the multi-year contracts, the law firm management will generally approve the budget without much negotiation. However, new funding will take extra work. Generally, the director will make a business case to law firm management regarding purchasing new resources, and so on. However, even if law firm management approves the new funding, it will not always allow the library to actually spend the funding or make the new purchases. It will allocate the funds, but they will only release the funds if the law firm is having a profitable year, which will not be determined until well into the next fiscal year for the firm.

Step Two for the Southeastern Law Firm Library is slightly different. The first phase requires the small units to submit their finalized proposed budgets to the lead attorney for the practice group. Assuming the practice group approves the budget, they will submit the overall practice group budget to the law firm management for approval. This process actually can be better for the small unit libraries because they have an attorney advocating on behalf of the practice group to the other attorneys. As most practice group leaders are on the same equity partnership level as the law firm management (or might be on law firm management themselves), requests or increases, and so on, usually are granted as long as the law firm is maintaining its profitability.

STEP THREE—FINALIZATION AND IMPLEMENTATION

Step Three is the final step in the yearly budgeting process. After consideration by the approving entity, a finalized budget will be sent back to the law libraries for implementation. This step will occur within the month prior to the start of the next fiscal year. Assuming a hardy negotiation has taken place, law libraries should not be entirely surprised when the finalized budget is finally sent to them. At a minimum, the hope is that the approvers have sent the law library a budget set at least to the current fiscal year's appropriation amounts. However, if the approvers send back a budget that has decreased, the law library must then begin the cutting process. Cutting subscriptions is never easy. Assuming the law library did a robust study in Step One, the cutting process should be slightly easier. At this point, the law library will already have decided to cut some things based on usage statistics, and so on. Now the law library will need to determine what resources can be cut that do receive some usage.[5] Another option some law libraries will have is to decide if they need to move some resources to being paid out of any endowments the law library might have.

Academic Law Libraries

Academic law libraries will usually have a good bit of work to do once Step Three is ending. At this point, the University has approved a budget for the next year. If increases were provided by the University, the law library will now decide how to spend the new monies or will encumber the new monies to cover the inflationary price increases of existing subscriptions. If decreases were made by the University, the law library will have to reevaluate the resources that made it through Step One as more cuts will be necessary.

A positive aspect of academic law libraries is that most have some form of endowment or fundraising mechanism. Therefore, the law library will possibly have the option to pay for the resources out of endowment funds as opposed to the official university approved funds. This is extremely helpful when budgets are decreased due to drops in enrollment, and so on. Both the Midwestern Public Law School Library and the Northeastern Private Law School Library have endowments. Therefore, if their respective universities make cuts during the Step Three process, both law school libraries have the opportunity to pay for resources out of their endowments.[6]

The finalized budgets for academic law libraries can range from small to very large. These factors depend on the size of the school, size of enrollment, private versus public, and so on. Public institutions usually have more room to shift to endowments or receive more funding from the sovereign as entities of the state. Private institutions will be more tuition-dependent and will undergo more periods of financial exigency. A model finalized academic budget utilizing percentages is below. These percentages were developed through studying both the Midwestern Public Law School Library and the Northeastern Private Law School Library budgets.

EXAMPLE ACADEMIC LAW LIBRARY BUDGET

Salaries/Benefits—50%
Print Resources—5%
Electronic Resources—33%
Professional Development—3%[7]
Professional Membership Dues—1%
Systems and Commodities—8%

Government Law Libraries

Government and court law libraries will usually not have a lot of work to complete at the conclusion of Step Three. Depending on who the approving entity is for these law libraries, it will determine if more work will need to be done. These libraries will generally not receive many increases each fiscal year due to the funding processes. However, decreases are likely to occur if anything outside of the normal process of appropriating the same amounts as the prior fiscal year.

The Southwestern County Law Library will not have a lot of work to do in this process. Because the law library is governed by a board of trustees, it has been directly involved with each step of the budgeting process. Therefore, there will likely be no surprises when the budget is officially approved and finalized. If a decrease does occur, the law library might have the option to shift some costs to an endowment managed by a Friends of the Library organization. This will be more likely for county law libraries than court law libraries.

Since the Southeastern Court Law Library is fully reliant on the Court in this budgeting process, there is not much the law library can do during Step Three. Since the Court generally tries to appropriate money at the same levels each year, new resources will likely not be added to the available resources for the patrons. Also, the Court has to convince the Legislature that at least the same level of funding is necessary. If the Legislature decides to cut some of the Court's funding, the law library will share in the pain. It is at this point that the law library will have to consider cutting more resources over the resources already cut in Step One. Since the court law library does not have an endowment, it will have no other option but to actually cancel existing resources.

Finalized budgets for government and court law libraries will depend on the size of the institution. A county law library might be large or small depending on the size of the county. A court law library will depend on the level of the court itself. A trial court library will usually be smaller than an appellate court library. Therefore, this will be reflected in the finalized budgets. Model finalized budgets, utilizing percentages, for both a county law library and a court law library are below. The percentages were determined after studying both the Southwestern County Law Library and the Southeastern Court Law Library budgets.

EXAMPLE COUNTY LAW LIBRARY BUDGET

Salaries/Benefits—50%
Print Resources—25%
Electronic Resources—10%
Systems and Commodities—15%

EXAMPLE COURT LAW LIBRARY BUDGET

Salaries/Benefits—50%
Print Resources—44%[8]
Electronic Resources—3%
Commodities—2%

Law Firm Libraries

Step Three for law firm libraries is generally the easiest process out of all the law libraries. Since the law libraries are heavily involved with both Step One and Step Two, they already have a good idea of what to expect from the approval process and the receipt of the finalized budget.

If the law firm has a centralized library for the entire firm, the law library might have some work to do at the conclusion of Step Three. Since the approved budget was presented by the library director, law firm management may decide to make some cuts to the requested budget. In the example of the Midwestern Law Firm Library, it is possible that law firm management will not necessarily cut the funding completely out of the budget. Most of the resources are obtained through multi-year agreements, and since these are purely private institutions, the extra protections of the sovereign-funded academic and government law libraries will not exist. They will be purely bound by the agreements and be required to pay the agreed-upon multi-year pricing. If funding needs to be decreased, law firm libraries will have the option to move some monies into that special fund only to be spent after evaluation of the law firm's revenue for the year. Assuming business picks up, the funds might be released, resulting in no funding decreases for the law library.

If the law firm utilizes the small unit practice group model, then the law library's workload at the conclusion of Step Three will most likely not be as involved. In the example of the Southeastern Law Firm Library, the lead attorney for the practice group presented the budget to law firm management. As the involved attorneys would consider themselves and the law firm management as peers, requests will more than likely be granted. It is possible some cuts would be necessary, but the practice group will be more involved in the cancellation process than in other types of law firms. It should be noted that even the small unit libraries heavily utilize multi-year agreements, so cancellations may be off the table temporarily.

Finalized budgets for law firm libraries will also vary depending on the size of the firm. Does the firm have multiple offices? Does one library serve all offices? Does the firm utilize the small unit model? Does the firm pass the cost onto the client? All these questions will contribute to the size of the approved finalized budget. A model finalized budget for a law firm library utilizing percentages is provided below. As small unit libraries are hard to model as they vary greatly among various practice groups, the model is based on studying the Midwestern Law Firm Library that serves the entire firm.

EXAMPLE LAW FIRM LIBRARY BUDGET

Salaries/Benefits—50%
Print Resources—0%[9]
Electronic Resources—45%
Commodities—5%

Mid-Year Considerations

Regardless of the type of law library, mid-year evaluations of resources should always be taking place. They are necessary for several reasons. Law libraries want to make sure that they are staying within the allocated budget.

As a reminder, the finalized budgets were just estimations of what the law library would actually need to cover its yearly expenses. Academic and government law libraries will sometimes underestimate. The inflationary price increases were more than originally expected. Law firm libraries utilize multi-year agreements more often than not, so their price estimations are usually accurate. For most academic law libraries and county law libraries, they can rely on some of their endowment funds when this occurs. If not, law libraries will have to make mid-year cuts. Since subscriptions will begin and end throughout the year, there is normally something law libraries can cut when this happens. It is rare for the law library to have all their subscriptions start at the beginning of the fiscal year. They will most likely have some options. Right around the time these decisions are being made, the next fiscal year's budgeting process will begin. It is possible to do a little mid-year budgeting at the same time as you begin Step One of the next year's process.[10]

CONCLUSION

Budgeting in law libraries can be very complicated, but not necessarily a daunting task with a little background knowledge. We can see that most law libraries utilize a similar process when developing a yearly budget. Most law libraries utilize the incremental budgeting process. They start with their current year's expenditures and account for inflation/price increases.

Academic law libraries and county law libraries are similar in their budgeting functions. They have their base funding, but they also have endowments and fundraising to rely on when necessary. Fundraising can be essential for some extra expenditures not already appropriated. However, we also see that court law libraries and law firm libraries do not actively fundraise or have endowments. They rely primarily on their parent organization or sovereign for funding.

The budgeting process should be meticulous when planning for the next fiscal year. Incremental budgeting allows the law library to have a place to start. Stakeholders should be involved and allowed to express their needs and wants. It is not best practice to allow the parent organization to have full control over the process. Law libraries should be allowed to advocate for themselves. Law librarians know best when it comes to utility, usage, and vendor intricacies.

However a law library conducts its budget process, mid-year check-ins should be mandatory. When unexpected things happen, the law library must be able to adapt to a large unforeseen expense and pivot its priorities for the rest of the fiscal year. Sometimes that means cutting a treasured but unused resource. It may also mean switching to borrowing resources from other law libraries through interlibrary loan. Regardless, the law library patrons should see no change in service if at all possible.

In the end, budgeting is its own art form. With a little preparation and education, any librarian should be able to tackle the process. Remember, always start early and always be able to pivot!

NOTES

1. Aliyu Nasiru Muhammad, Rufai Clis Misau, and Yerima Muhammad, "Budgeting in Public Libraries," *Journal of Accounting and Financial Management* 3, no. 1 (2017): 2–3.
2. Sheila S. Intner and Peggy Johnson, *Fundamentals of Technical Services Management* (Chicago, IL: American Library Association, 2008), 90.
3. Peggy Johnson, *Fundamentals of Collection Development and Management*, 2nd ed. (Chicago, IL: American Library Association, 2009), 91.
4. Vicki L. Gregory, *Collection Development and Management For 21st Century Library Collections: An Introduction*, 2nd ed. (Chicago, IL: ALA Neal-Schuman, 2019), 95.
5. Intner and Johnson, *Fundamentals of Technical Services Management*, 95.
6. George Pike, "The Academic Law Library Budget," in *Academic Law Libraries Within the Changing Landscape of Legal Education: A Primer for Deans and Provosts*, eds. Michelle Wu, Scott B. Pagel, and Joan S. Howland (Getsville, NY: William S. Hein & Co., Inc., 2020), 20–21.
7. Academic law libraries also budget for professional development and professional memberships. Other types might do this as well, but it is always a factor within academic law libraries.
8. Court libraries will provide resources in the formats that their respective judges have requested. Most court libraries in the Southeast still rely heavily on print resources.
9. Though it is not a hard rule, most law firm libraries have moved to strictly electronic resources. Very few continue to obtain resources in print.
10. Pike, "The Academic Law Library Budget," 26.

REFERENCES

Gregory, Vicki L. *Collection Development and Management For 21st Century Library Collections: An Introduction*, 2nd ed. Chicago, IL: ALA Neal-Schuman, 2019.

Intner, Sheila S., and Peggy Johnson. *Fundamentals of Technical Services Management.* Chicago, IL: American Library Association, 2008.

Johnson, Peggy. *Fundamentals of Collection Development and Management*, 2nd ed. Chicago, IL: American Library Association, 2009.

Muhammad, Aliyu Nasiru, Rufai Clis Misau, and Yerima Muhammad. "Budgeting in Public Libraries." *Journal of Accounting and Financial Management* 3, no. 1 (2017): 2–3.

Pike, George. "The Academic Law Library Budget." In *Academic Law Libraries Within the Changing Landscape of Legal Education: A Primer for Deans and Provosts*, edited by Michelle Wu, Scott B. Pagel, and Joan S. Howland, 20–21. Getsville, NY: William S. Hein & Co., Inc., 2020.

3

Negotiating Contracts

Suzanne Darais and Kerry Lohmeier

Negotiating contracts with vendors varies in complexity, ranging from straightforward agreements to intricate and time-consuming negotiations. Vendors may adopt different pricing models based on the size of the library, bundling resources, or other factors, and may or may not allow modifications to contract wording. Additionally, while some vendors permit the selection of individual titles, others may only offer bundled packages. These variations present both challenges and opportunities in the negotiation process. Knowing how to navigate these negotiations is crucial to securing the best pricing for your firm, court, or institution and ensuring the contract meets the library's specific needs.

To gather information for this chapter, we surveyed law firm, government, academic, and other types of law librarians to collect data. There were 111 respondents. Fifty-six were from academic libraries, sixteen were from firm libraries, thirty-six were from government libraries, and three were from other types of law libraries. This chapter will identify trends gleaned from the survey along with practical insights into the process of negotiating contracts.

BEST PRACTICES FOR NEGOTIATIONS

Numerous factors must be evaluated when negotiating contracts. The importance of each factor will depend on the specific needs of the library. Key considerations include pricing, additional charges, subscription versus ownership models, licensing terms, confidentiality clauses, and termination provisions. General steps and issues that arise during the negotiation process follow.

Identify the Need

There are several steps involved in contract negotiations for goods and services. The negotiation process typically begins when the library identifies a need. It is advantageous for the library to have a clear vision of a successful outcome before entering negotiations. The process will vary based on the outcome; examples include renewing a subscription, expanding a current subscription, and subscribing to a new database or service. Initial research and inquiries to vendors provide the foundation for negotiations. Information gathered may be leveraged to improve negotiations. The library works toward a deal that includes everything it needs in the contract, even if all wish list items are ultimately not met.

Gather Organizational Requirements

Librarians need to evaluate their institution's collection needs, collection development policies, and current usage patterns. Stakeholder needs evolve over time. For example, many public libraries were not accessible to the public during COVID-19, and some have retained this policy going forward. Users in a particular library may prefer or only need electronic materials as there have been cultural shifts in the way we work and learn. Firms may change practice area emphasis, public libraries may change their stance on which materials need to be publicly accessible, and academic library standards are changing. This evolution provides an opportunity to reassess the library's offerings and engage stakeholders in discussions about priorities. Public libraries with a mission to preserve information may have less flexibility when engaging in such analysis.

If the library already subscribes to a database, usage statistics can offer insight into the value of the product when preparing for a renewal. Costs can be calculated per use if the product is not being used often. Ask questions if the statistics are unclear or don't provide a complete picture. Compare usage across comparable products when possible. A vendor may think usage is high compared to other similarly situated libraries. A library's unique data across similar products may tell a different story. This data may also be useful if products are shared across libraries and part of the negotiation involves reaching an agreement with another library on cost sharing.

This background information may provide leverage during negotiations for better pricing or terms. Leverage doesn't always work with a vendor. Just as library priorities change, vendor priorities may change over time. This can impact pricing and other contract terms.

Many directors and others negotiating contracts know vendor pricing from working at other libraries. However, bringing that knowledge to the negotiation may not move the needle on pricing. Vendors may provide preferential pricing for early adopters of a product for a library they want to list as a customer, or for other reasons.

Know the budget, needs, wants, and constraints before negotiating. The library should go into the negotiation with priorities set, a plan, and a list of objectives. This helps if the decision-maker for the library needs to make a quick decision. Part of this preparation includes determining the terms and pricing needed and being prepared to walk away if goals are unmet. Know the organizational rules and preferences around multi-year contracts, special terms required by the organization, and any terms required by state or federal law.

Gather Market Intelligence

Prior to negotiations, it is crucial for libraries to conduct thorough research to understand the vendor landscape. Identifying the major players, their pricing structures, and the popularity of their products will inform decision-making and strengthen the library's negotiating position. For new products or services, in-depth research and comparisons with available alternatives are necessary. Colleagues' experiences, listserv inquiries, and, where applicable, public records requests can provide additional insights, particularly regarding pricing, which is often confidential.[1] While this approach may not be feasible for all negotiations due to time constraints, it can be valuable in complex cases.

Vet Vendors

Gather information about the vendor's financial position and plans. Negotiation options may change if the vendor is merging with another entity, acquiring a product, or suffering financial hardship. Knowing a vendor has steady or increasing profits may also help with negotiations. This information is less useful when dealing with a vendor that provides the same pricing to everyone and is transparent about that pricing.

Ask about the backup services and cybersecurity measures. Does the vendor use Amazon Web Services to secure the library's information in the cloud, or will it reside on a server under someone's desk? Has the vendor been hacked or lost client data before? Inquire about the vendor about their recovery plans in the event data is lost through human error, system failure, or a cyberattack.

Discover Pricing Models

Pricing models vary widely. There are potential discounts for up-front payments versus ongoing periodic payments. Better pricing may be available through consortia, by signing a multi-year agreement, or for discounts based on prior purchases. Seasonal discounts may also be available. A current trend among large vendors is to package materials together, requiring the purchase of entire packages to access specific items, without the option to license or purchase individual titles. An additional factor influencing the contract amount is the availability of discounted rates for bundling print and digital resources. It is important to note that not all vendors offer reduced rates for bundled materials. Additionally, the option to purchase specific titles individually may not always be available.

When licensing materials, vendors generally use a flat fee, base pricing on the number of users, or base pricing on the number of simultaneous users. Pricing for academic libraries typically is based on the number of full-time equivalent (FTE) students. Court pricing may include the number of full-time employees. Firm pricing may be based on the number of full-time attorneys or the number of attorneys using the product.

Libraries should thoroughly explore these options to determine the most cost-effective approach, considering both immediate and long-term financial implications. Evaluating whether to subscribe to or purchase resources outright requires careful consideration of budget constraints, access needs, and the frequency of updates.

Look for Additional Charges

Contracts may include unexpected additional charges. To avoid surprises, it is essential to clarify these potential fees up front. For instance, some vendors might include service charges not initially quoted. Others may impose access fees for ongoing use of purchased materials within a database. To ensure transparency and avoid unforeseen expenses, consider the following steps:

- Request a detailed breakdown: Ask the vendor to provide a comprehensive list of any potential additional charges up front.
- Review the Contract Carefully: Examine the contract terms thoroughly to identify any clauses related to extra fees.
- Consult with the Vendor: Have a detailed discussion with the vendor to clarify any ambiguous terms or charges that might arise.

Examples of Additional Charges:

- Service Charge: A fee for the maintenance or support services provided by the vendor.
- Access Fee: A recurring fee required to maintain access to purchased materials in the vendor's database.
- Installation or Setup Fees: Costs associated with the initial setup or installation of the vendor's system or service.

Subscription versus Ownership

Vendors may offer the option to subscribe to a database or purchase the material outright. With a subscription, the library pays a recurring fee to access the vendor's database. This fee grants the library temporary access to the materials for the duration of the subscription period. This contract model has lower up-front costs and often includes regular updates and access to the latest materials. However, this model has ongoing expenses, and there is a loss of access to the materials if the subscription isn't renewed.

There are higher up-front costs when a contract is for ownership of materials or a database. If a database is purchased, there is often an annual fee to continue accessing the materials on the vendor's platform. This model provides permanent access, assuming the platform doesn't become obsolete. Traditionally, libraries have been concerned with current access for patrons along with the preservation of library materials. Ownership or perpetual access costs more but may be the preferred option to ensure patrons have continuous access to materials. If a library anticipates needing access to materials for several years, the librarian should forecast access costs versus ownership costs to see which makes the most sense. Some vendors, like Docuseek, provide pricing for a range of streaming licenses as well as the life-of-file license to help make that calculation. Part of the negotiation may include working with the vendor to set pricing for multiple years to determine if access or ownership is the best route for the library.

When deciding between subscription and ownership, consider budget, access needs, and update frequency. Budget analysis should include an evaluation of immediate and long-term expenses. Determine whether patrons need continuous access to the most current materials or if a one-time purchase suffices. Consider how frequently the materials are updated and if staying current is crucial for the library's needs.

If the library cannot achieve its requirements, the negotiation should end even though it may be tough to walk away. Only 18 percent of survey respondents (50 percent of firm respondents, 16.7 percent of government respondents, and 10.7 percent of academic library respondents) stated they were often able to negotiate pricing, so in an era of shrinking or flat budgets and rising costs, walking away may become more common.

Requesting Proposals

Once the search has been narrowed to two or three top vendors, a Request for Proposals (RFP) may be issued. This will clarify items such as feature sets, hidden fees, included services, installation times, staff training costs, and so on. If this step isn't necessary, the library may reach out to the vendor to initiate a trial or to more informally request a quote. Public academic libraries may be exempt from RFP rules based on policy exceptions.

Some vendors with multiple products package materials for quotes. This can make it challenging to determine what the individual items in the package cost. Don't be afraid to press the vendor. Ask for the products the library needs individually or have them repackaged into a deal that works for the library. Pricing still may not be as transparent as desired, but it will provide more information to see if the library can get the product(s) needed at a price that works for it. One survey respondent noted a vendor offered three tiers of product access. Rather than each tier including everything from the previous tier plus additional products, each tier contained a different assortment. None of the tiers met the library's needs. The vendor wasn't forthcoming about what products within each tier cost during meetings or in written communications. To feel more comfortable with the package that was eventually negotiated, the respondent spent time evaluating the three tiers, trying to estimate pricing, tracking down some information through advertised consortia deals, and speaking with colleagues.

Starting the Negotiations

Start negotiations early. It takes time for both sides to get answers. Negotiations with large legal services providers tend to involve multiple layers of people beyond assigned representatives. Negotiations may involve several parties on each side. For example, 77 percent of survey respondents have another person who reviews contracts before they can be signed. The reviewer may be an attorney or general counsel for the organization. While library directors may be involved in contract negotiations and be responsible for overall budget management, only 36 percent of directors sign contracts. Five percent of contracts are signed by the librarian negotiating the deal, 23 percent are signed by the Director of Purchasing/Finance, 6 percent are signed by an attorney, and 29 percent of respondents selected 'other'.: Several respondents who selected 'other' indicated that the amount of the contract dictates who signs the contract. Other responses included, but were not limited to, the law school dean, provost, court administrator, county administrator, trial court administrator, chief information officer, library chair, contracting officer, chief finance officer, executive vice president of finance and administration, managing partner, or a county judge along with at least one county administrator.

For complex negotiations, it's beneficial to request direct communication with the decision-maker at the vendor's organization. Although this request is often declined, success in securing this contact can streamline the negotiation process. It's crucial to follow up on any verbal discussions—whether by phone or in person—with a detailed email that summarizes key points and outstanding questions. This ensures that objectives and concerns are clearly communicated and understood by all parties involved. Initiating the negotiation process early avoids rushed decisions as the negotiation unfolds.

Selecting the Contract Term

When negotiating or renewing a contract, price increases can be significant. Some vendors exclusively offer annual pricing, while others provide contracts ranging from one to five years, with prices adjusted based on the contract length. Many vendors increase prices by 2–7 percent annually, but these rates are sometimes only available with a multi-year contract. Multi-year contracts not only lock in modest price increases but also save significant time by eliminating the need to renegotiate each year. However, it's important to consider that budgets and collection needs can change, and being locked into a multi-year contract may pose challenges.

The survey revealed trends across library types regarding contract terms. Ninety-four percent indicated that multi-year contracts are permitted at their library. Of those entering multi-year agreements, 32 percent always sign multi-year contracts, 21 percent sign them about half the time, 45 percent sign sometimes, and 2 percent never sign multi-year contracts when vendors offer them. A large academic law library respondent indicated that even though multi-year contracts are allowed, they are frowned upon unless there is a strong reason to enter into them.

Contract terms may include evergreen provisions. Contracts containing this clause state that a contract will automatically renew for a set period unless one party provides the other with notice of cancellation before the end of the contract term. The notice of non-renewal must comply with the terms in the agreement, which typically include how to send the notice, who to send it to, the length of notice required, and so on. The clause may be straightforward or may be hidden within other terms. To avoid automatic renewal, negotiate for the removal of this clause. If that isn't successful, a calendar reminder about the evergreen clause can serve as a reminder to review the contract and send in a non-renewal notice that complies with the terms of the contract. Alternatively, look for a vendor with a comparable product that doesn't include an evergreen clause to avoid being stuck in a contract for a service that isn't useful for the library. State law may have additional requirements for evergreen clauses.

Reviewing Contract Terminology

Carefully reviewing all terms—whether for licensing, service, or purchase agreements—is essential. Updates to terms may be missed in the final deal after prolonged negotiations. Keeping notes as the negotiation progresses will provide a list to cross-check and verify during the final review of the contract. For license agreements, this includes ensuring that definitions are correct, understanding who can access the material, knowing the restrictions on sharing or copying the material, and so on. As noted earlier, 77 percent of survey respondents have an additional person who reviews contracts before they can be signed. This provides an extra safeguard but doesn't remove the duty to check terms carefully. This may not alleviate all issues as one survey respondent noted, "I feel contracts have become increasingly difficult to understand[,] especially our digital library one."

Additional Services

Vendors may include additional materials that make the contract more appealing. These services can range from training and serials tracking to enhanced customer support. When evaluating these extras, consider their relevance and potential benefits to the organization. For instance, if enhanced customer service is included, research the vendor's track record in delivering this service to assess its true value as part of the cost-benefit analysis.

Licensing

Contract terms often include protections for the vendors so the vendor feels secure in licensing copyrighted works. These terms include who can use the material, permitted uses (sharing, printing, downloading), unauthorized use, cost, method of access, and the license duration. Changing the vendor's standard terms may involve concessions on pricing or other contract provisions, so it is important to carefully weigh the implications of any changes.

Confidential Information

If the product or service collects personal information about patrons, the contract should include terms about what happens to personally identifiable patron information. Start by identifying the types of personal data collected and understanding how the vendor intends to use and protect it. Ensure the contract includes provisions for securing personal data against unauthorized access and breaches. Specify how long the vendor will retain personal data and the process for its deletion upon the termination of the contract or upon request. Ensure the contract complies with data protection regulations relevant to the library.

Terminating the Contract

Contracts typically include terms for termination, which might cover scenarios such as breach of contract, financial hardship, refunds, dispute resolution, and the required notice period for non-renewal. The contract should identify the specific circumstances under which either party can terminate the contract, such as breach of terms or financial difficulties. Libraries with fluctuating budgets may need to negotiate more flexible terms to accommodate potential changes in financial conditions. If the library and vendor engage in conversations about termination, it is best to follow up on the discussion with an email to restate what both parties agreed upon.

Communicating with Stakeholders When Negotiations Fail

Despite thorough preparation, some negotiations fail. Academic libraries have seen steep price increases for products that used to offer more favorable discounts for educational use. One notable case involved a vendor tripling the price of study aids, leading many libraries to discontinue their subscriptions. Rising costs, particularly for products incorporating new technologies like generative AI, may exceed the library's budgetary limits. In such cases, early engagement with stakeholders is crucial. Gather insights on their usage patterns, priorities, and what they might be willing to forgo. This information will help the library explore alternative products, set priorities for negotiations, and prepare for the possibility of discontinuing a product or service.

Transparent communication is key when a negotiation does not succeed, and the library needs to walk away. How these conversations are managed can significantly impact stakeholder perception of the situation. While many stakeholders understand the financial constraints that might prevent renewing or purchasing a product, academic libraries might find it more challenging to explain such decisions to students, who may be less aware of the broader range of resources required to support educational objectives. In these cases, consider engaging with student representatives, like the Student Bar Association president, to explain the process and constraints. This approach may help clarify priorities, gain buy-in for alternative solutions, and ease the transition when a favored resource is no longer available. Direct communication with stakeholders also provides valuable data for selecting new products for trials or demos, leading to more informed decisions about future vendor contracts.

ISSUES WITH NEGOTIATING CONTRACTS

When navigating a contract negotiation, various issues may arise. Higher-than-expected pricing and opaque pricing algorithms that are difficult to understand may be encountered. Additionally, the inability to negotiate directly with decision-makers can complicate efforts to adjust pricing and modify contract language, leading to time-consuming negotiations. Securing access for all library users can also be challenging. These issues will be discussed in more detail.

When survey respondents were asked about their concerns regarding contract negotiations, the top three issues were the lack of power in negotiations, lack of transparency, and uncertainty about their annual budget. Respondents were also concerned with rising costs, vendor relations, customer support, form contract language, and lack of market competition.

Transparency, Budget, and Pricing

When considering whether to sign up for a multi-year contract, it is essential to assess if the budget will remain relatively stable and if the subscription item is essential and unlikely to be cut, even in the event of unanticipated budget reductions. One survey respondent shared that when COVID hit, their library was initially told to cut 20 percent from their budget. They had signed two large contracts that were not due for renewal for two more years, which forced them to cancel items they wanted to keep while retaining titles (included in the multi-year contracts) they wanted to cancel. Additionally, shortly after entering into one of those large contracts, the library decided to cancel some items during a collection review but had to wait over two years for the subscription to expire.

Be aware that hidden costs in a contract can cause the total amount paid to exceed the original stated price. For example, in a contract for leasing and purchasing titles in both digital and print formats, one vendor included a clause stating, "shipping costs for matching print editions will be charged separately."

When negotiating or renegotiating large contracts, some vendors' pricing algorithms lack transparency. The specifics of how the algorithm operates are often not disclosed, complicating the negotiation process for large contracts involving hundreds of bundled titles, both electronic and in print. In fact, the subscription price may increase as more titles are cut from the subscription. It is not possible to immediately determine the new subscription price after making cuts to materials in the package. The vendor sales representative acts as an intermediary for the pricing team. After the desired cuts are submitted, the representative will consult with the pricing team to determine the new prices and then relay this information back to the client.

A more recent trend affecting library budgets is when a library is required to purchase a package of materials when it only needs a few specific titles. One survey respondent expressed their concern about this, stating they were troubled by "the constant repackaging of resources into packages that contain a considerable amount of irrelevant resources." Another respondent highlighted the "difficulty in getting particular databases because they are part of a group and you must get the whole group."

Another respondent expressed concern about market consolidation, which has the effect of reducing competition. Consolidation can result in fewer options and substantial price increases. For example, materials previously accessible through Lexis or Westlaw may become unavailable when a new company, now owning the materials, cancels contracts with these vendors. Consequently, the materials can only be accessed through the new company and must be paid for separately if continued access is desired.

Contract Clauses

To avoid common issues in contract clauses, it is crucial to thoroughly read through the contract. Some clauses may contain requirements that the library cannot meet. One survey respondent discovered that a contract required the library to track all database users and collect their names and email addresses. Even if the library had been interested in collecting this information (which it was not), as a public library open in the evening with minimal staffing, there was no way they could ensure this information would be collected. When the librarian informed the vendor representative that it would be impossible for the library to adhere to that clause and requested its removal from the contract, the representative stated that their legal department would not permit it. When the librarian asked to speak directly with someone in the vendor's legal department and was denied, the library decided it would not be able to contract with that vendor.

Another survey respondent from a public library pointed out that one vendor used a form contract geared toward law firms, which contained wording that would have prevented public library patrons from using the resource. When asked, the vendor was not willing to modify the contract.

Companies are now including clauses in their contracts pertaining to Artificial Intelligence (AI). One such clause, which may be difficult for libraries to enforce, states that users cannot take materials from the database and use them in an AI large language model. Another clause outlines who owns the content generated by AI if generative AI is supplied and used in the database the library is leasing. If a clause like this is present, make sure the library has sufficient rights to use, modify, and distribute AI-generated content.

Some vendors will accommodate changes to contract wording. Government libraries, in particular, may be required by law to include specific legal provisions in their contracts. One survey respondent noted that "multi-year contracts in their library are prohibited by state law unless there are terms in the contract that allow the library to cancel the contract for essentially any reason." The respondent added that they were surprised that one of their vendors always accepted this modification. It never hurts to ask for changes to the contract wording, so don't hesitate to request adjustments if necessary.

Canceling contracts is usually straightforward, with most contracts containing a clause outlining the cancellation process. Be sure to locate and understand this clause. When canceling a contract, it is important to have a written record of the cancellation request. An email is typically sufficient, especially for smaller contracts. A survey respondent shared their experience of requesting the cancellation of a database subscription when the contract came up for renewal, only to be billed for the database for the next three years. Each time the library was contacted about delinquent payment, the librarian sent the original cancellation email as proof. After three long years, the company finally stopped the billing.

When signing a contract for more than one year, make sure to see how easy it would be to terminate the agreement. An issue that often arises in relation to canceling a contract is the clause addressing early termination for financial exigency. This clause allows the licensee to terminate the agreement without penalty if they do not have sufficient funds to continue with the contract. Many multi-year contracts include a financial exigency clause. However, when asked if they felt exigency clauses would be honored by the vendor, 44 percent of survey respondents answered yes, 54 percent were unsure, and 2 percent said no. Even with an exigency clause, the library may not want to use it. For example, a university may hesitate to invoke this clause to avoid signaling a significant problem within the institution.

Negotiating access for all user groups can sometimes be challenging. Court libraries might be able to secure access for court personnel but not for public patrons, or vice versa. Similarly, firm librarians may need to purchase separate contracts for each office in different states. Academic librarians often try to negotiate campus-wide access to databases to leverage their purchase for university-wide benefit. However, some vendors will only allow access on a single terminal in the law library, refuse to permit remote access, or require the law library to pay separately for a subscription even after the main campus library has paid for campus-wide access. While many vendors are reasonable in allowing campus-wide and remote access, some create pricing structures and access policies that are not beneficial to all user groups within an institution.

Who Negotiates

Larger vendors typically have multiple representatives involved in contract negotiations. While this approach can facilitate more timely and effective responses to inquiries, it can also add pressure, especially if these representatives push the library to take advantage of a time-sensitive offer. There may be a feeling of consuming a significant amount of the representatives' time when asking questions, which can lead to pressure to make a quick decision. However, it is important to remain firm. Consider involving colleagues in the negotiations to balance the numbers on each side and to support the library's position.

Another issue is the inability to work directly with someone in the company who can make decisions. When negotiating pricing or trying to modify a contract, it is often frustrating to be unable to speak directly with a decision-maker. This lack of direct communication prevents the librarian from obtaining information about why certain modifications cannot be made. In expressing concerns about the negotiation process, one survey respondent described this experience as "negotiating at a distance with all the people involved in the process."

The process of having to negotiate through an intermediary introduces another issue: negotiating large contracts can be more time-consuming than desired. Time must be allocated to inform the vendor of the titles to be cut and then wait for the pricing team to provide the final contract price through your representative. As the price often increases, it may be necessary to reassess the cuts and make further adjustments. This involves continual back and forth with multiple vendor representatives. Given the lack of transparency in pricing, one strategy to save time is to inform the representative of the amount the library desires to pay for the renewal. The representative can then consult with their pricing team to determine how much needs to be cut from the retail price list to meet the budget. Additionally, prices will vary depending on whether a one-year, two-year, or longer contract is signed, so obtaining numbers for each option can also be time-consuming as requests route through vendor representatives. Fortunately, some vendors are very transparent with their pricing, offering fixed prices that apply to any type of library that subscribes.

When discussing vendor relations, one respondent felt that some vendors try to treat different types of libraries with different needs "in a cookie-cutter fashion." Another respondent highlighted increased turnover among vendor representatives, noting that new representatives often lack familiarity with the client's situation and seem less invested in the outcomes sought. This can exacerbate timing and other issues.

A final concern expressed by some respondents is the lack of formal training in contract negotiations. Many possess theoretical knowledge from their education or work experience, but this knowledge may not translate into practical strategies for negotiating with vendors. Collaborating with colleagues within the organization or institution can help a librarian gain knowledge and confidence in negotiations, and reaching out to an extended professional network may be beneficial. It is likely that someone within the network has had similar experiences and is willing to share information. This is an area where professional organizations could step in and provide free training and materials.

In conclusion, negotiating contracts with vendors is a complex process that requires careful planning, thorough research, and strategic negotiation skills. The diverse range of vendor practices—such as varying pricing models, contract modification policies, and bundling options—makes it essential for librarians to be well-prepared and knowledgeable about both their own needs and the specific offerings and policies of each vendor. To navigate these negotiations successfully, libraries should:

1. *Research Extensively*: Understand the product, vendor, and market conditions. Gather information from colleagues, listservs, and public records when possible.
2. *Assess Needs and Priorities*: Evaluate collection needs, usage statistics, and stakeholder priorities. This helps in setting clear objectives and making informed decisions.
3. *Plan and Strategize*: Enter negotiations with a clear plan, know budget constraints, and be prepared to walk away if terms are unfavorable. Start negotiations early to avoid rushed decisions.
4. *Engage Stakeholders*: Communicate with stakeholders, especially when negotiations fail or when significant changes to services are anticipated. This builds trust and demonstrates the library's commitment to finding the best possible resolution.
5. *Be Persistent and Clear*: Seek transparency in pricing and contract terms, and follow up on all communications. Understand the fine print, particularly regarding licensing, additional charges, and termination clauses.

Despite best efforts, some negotiations may not yield the desired outcomes. Exploring alternative solutions or finding new vendors to work with can help mitigate the impact of an unsuccessful negotiation. Additionally, reflecting on the process and identifying areas for improvement can strengthen future negotiation strategies, ensuring better results over time.

Ultimately, successful contract negotiation is about finding a balance between securing necessary resources at a reasonable cost and maintaining the flexibility to adapt to evolving needs. This involves understanding the library's specific needs and being aware of the various pricing models, contract terms, and bundling options offered by different vendors. Libraries can effectively navigate the complexities of vendor negotiations by employing the strategies and considerations discussed, such as thorough research, clear communication, and strategic planning. Approaching negotiations as described enables librarians to make informed decisions that align with long-term goals and budgetary constraints, ensuring that the best possible outcome for the institution is obtained. Additionally, fostering good relationships with vendors and staying updated on market trends can further enhance the negotiation process, allowing for more favorable terms and conditions in future agreements.

NOTE

1. John Eye, "Improving Contract Negotiations for Library Collections through Open Records Requests," *College & Research Libraries* 84, no. 6 (2023), accessed June 28, 2024, https://crl.acrl.org/index.php/crl/article/view/26101/34023.

4

The Business of Law Librarianship

Abigail Ross

A librarian's job description has remained fundamentally the same for many years: collect, organize, catalog, research, and analyze information, and make it accessible for others' use. Though that piece remains the same, the format the data and information come in and how those tasks are accomplished have changed drastically—and continue to change in the twenty-first century. Librarians are now, more than ever, information brokers: putting people in touch with the information they need to do their jobs.[1] Annoy a librarian and one will find their library re-cataloged (both print and online) to Lewis Carroll's *Jabberwocky* with all passwords changed, for what a librarian makes accessible can also be made inaccessible. All joking aside, this ability to provide or to hide, gives librarians a great deal of power and influence.

In the business world, this power is often minimized, overlooked, or the credit is given to others. Historically, the C-suite (the C-level or C-suite refers to the group of managers and executives who lead businesses; they oftentimes hold titles that begin with C such as CEO, CIO, CFO, etc.) has talked about the importance of information but didn't like rewarding those who provide it. That is changing. As the world becomes more connected and the ability to find and recall, information has become more important to provide an edge, the role of the information broker has increased in both visibility and importance.

This also means that librarians have to plant one foot in the library side of work, and one foot in the business side, or the concept of the business of law librarianship. The phrase "The Business of {BLANK INDUSTRY}" refers to the commercial and operational aspects of that industry. For example, a law firm is in the business of providing legal advice, but the law firm itself has to be managed, hence the Business of law. A law library is in the business of providing and archiving information, but the library itself has to be managed in such a way as to remain "profitable."[2] It is not enough to run the library efficiently or cost-effectively; it has to be run in a way that contributes to the profitability and efficiency of the overall organization they serve by controlling costs, leveraging technology, and aligning services with strategic goals. Libraries, in a nutshell, have to actively contribute to increasing shareholder value. This is what the Business of law librarianship refers to—the idea that the library cannot just provide information for information's sake, it has to be evaluated by the same metrics as any business unit. Most law libraries have a symbiotic relationship with a parent organization. They provide a piece of the overall product that the organization produces. They cannot exist without the larger organization—the organization cannot provide their product without information.

Law librarians, therefore, must have expertise not just in traditional collection, classification, access, recall, and research of legal content, but also in data analysis, competitive intelligence, market research, finance, and other traditionally business-focused services. They must focus on fact-based decision-making, tracking metrics, efficiency, cost management, and potentially even generating revenue, in addition to providing research and reference services, negotiating vendor contracts, managing budgets, implementing new technologies, and training users on legal research tools.

LEADERSHIP AND THE IMPORTANCE OF TITLES

This is not a new concept. Librarians in general have always worn many hats, and managing space, resources, and technologies in a cost-effective manner has always been part of the job description, even if it wasn't labeled as a business skill or taught in library schools. The literature is full of advice on How To Run Your Library Like A Business.[3] This trend has gathered speed over the last decade or so and is being accelerated by the demand for information at all levels of an organization—and the recognition that information brokers are vital to an organization's success.

Titles are important, and the law library leadership needs to reflect this. Librarians know they operate at the C-level, but outsiders often do not, and respect is often only given when the official title appears after a name or department. That respect may feel like it's been slow in coming, but it is coming. This is analogous to a sea-change in accounting departments in the 1970s and 1980s, when many of them dropped the word "accounting" in favor of "finance." That rebrand emphasized how the profession had expanded beyond traditional accounting to include higher-level financial analysis, business partnering, and strategic advisory services. CFOs became a thing in the 1980s—and the idea of promoting those CFOs to executive positions (CEO, etc.) has become much more common since then.

Law librarians could use those lessons to bring about the same type of change in their profession. Two things that make the capitalist world go round are money and information. Librarians control that latter piece, and that is reflected in the rising number of C-level information managers—Chief Information Officers (CIOs), Chief Knowledge Officers (CKOs), or equivalent. These people need to be well-trained in all aspects of information—where to find it, how to analyze it, the technology used to store it and shape it, and how to wield it effectively. These are skills librarians already have.

The trick is convincing the Powers-That-Be to give librarians a seat at the table in order to leverage that knowledge into C-level positions. As Greg Lambert famously wrote, "If law librarians don't find themselves a seat at the table, they will find themselves on the menu."[4] This starts with proper titles and leadership roles. There has long been a discussion in the law library world on what to call librarians. Fancy terms such as "Knowledge Manager," "Research Analyst," or "Information Broker" sound impressive—and may assist in the goal of C-suite ascension, but they don't always make clear what librarians do, nor do they encompass *all* they do.

There is no agreement yet on the perfect title in the library profession, but it is important to give some thought to personnel titles and how they play into people/s perception of librarians and their path to the C-level. Business leaders put a great deal of thought into their titles as a way to demonstrate what they do, showcase their skills, detail hierarchies, and even reflect where they want to go in their careers. The librarian path to the C-suite needs to start with leaders whose outward-facing business names and trappings showcase equal footing. That may mean a transition to multiple-adjective titles, such as Information Broker/Analyst or Managing Information Partner. Most business positions cannot be summarized in one word the way "librarian" can, and so utilize a phrase that captures strategic importance, core values and/or organizational structure, and yet still conveys an actual skillset to the average person. Some suggestions for librarians include Chief Information Officer (CIO), Chief Knowledge Officer (CKO), or Chief Research Services Officer (CRSO).

BUSINESS SKILLS

Asking law librarians to pick up additional skills is always a bit ironic. Librarians are naturally curious people who pursue information just for the fun of it, so on the one hand, they tend to do these things naturally. On the other hand, who has the time to go back to school for another three degrees? Most librarians would probably love to be perpetual students. An MLIS fits nicely with an international MBA and a finance/accounting degree(s). Skills taught on the job and on the fly in law libraries often overlap with those other degrees.

Though not taught in library degree programs, those types of skills are essential. Librarians can often be at a disadvantage when they come up against others who do have them—who went to school for them or attended month-long training sessions to acquire them. The skill librarians most commonly lack is negotiation. Advocating persuasively for one's self, one's department, or one's organization is needed on an almost daily basis, and yet it isn't taught in Library Science degree programs. Such skills are necessary for arranging resource access and relationships in the form of licensing and vendor contracts, but also for setting internal salaries, titles, and obtaining that all-important seat at the table.

This is closely related to marketing. Librarians are not historically known for their sophisticated marketing skills. Stereotypically, they tend to be more introverted, less likely to trowel makeup on work product (for reasons of time, money, or even just disinterest), and more focused on the content of the work than the outside perception. This means librarians are laser-focused and competent, but it can also be a glaring issue when coming up against more sophisticated marketers and the results they can attain. Many law librarians can tell stories of working on a project or initiative, only to have the credit given to a marketing team who, at least to outside eyes, simply put their name on the front page and presented it in a flashy meeting.

This can affect law librarians not just when doing their research, but also when it comes to evaluating services or demonstrating user engagement—what the rest of the world refers to as market research. A combination of marketing, gentle interrogation, creative writing, and data analysis, market research is necessary to justify expenditures, show ROI (return on investment) and/or VOI (value on investment). It isn't enough to ask patrons if they are happy with a service or resource; one must quantify consumer behavior and analyze market trends to benchmark department progress.

Strategic planning and project management—often two sides of the same coin—are taught in limited ways in library degree programs. Too many people get caught in the day-to-day activity traps, without being able to manage projects and simultaneously see the big picture. Knowing how to craft realistic and obtainable goals and manage them effectively keeps any organization running smoothly.

Data analysis exploded on the library scene years ago as metric-driven decisions became the norm, not only as a way to defend decisions but also to eliminate bias. Librarians are being asked to do far more statistical analysis than previously, and almost all of that isn't for external patron-facing research projects but rather internal quantitative analysis. Numerical insights are a required management tool, even for those departments that don't normally hire people with mathematics backgrounds.

Good management also encompasses organizational behavior. Law librarians not only manage data, books, space, and databases, but also people. Minimizing conflicts among disparate employees while spearheading individual motivation requires diplomacy and delicacy. Good communication is key to keeping a library functioning and patrons happy.

And not just communication with staff, but with everyone within an organization. It could be argued that the majority of emails written by law librarians are mini-treatises (research results), use cases (convincing someone to give us money or resources for something), or case studies (showing why the money spent on a particular project yielded results or increased organizational value). Business writing skills help translate data into persuasive arguments and continued funding.

None of this can be accomplished without sophisticated budgeting skills. From the basics of Excel and accounting programs to ROI and VOI components and calculations, to resource and staff allocation, no business runs without a thrifty, financially disciplined money manager at the helm. Good financial management of a law library gives one financial control and greater flexibility and allows for project prioritization and better-informed decision-making. As with one's personal finances, more financial freedom awaits when every penny is accounted for and justified. Understanding all of that gives a library manager an edge over other departments in any organization.

All of those skills taken together are how librarians prove to the C-level MBAs in any organization that they are increasing value or return on investment. In short, a law librarian has to be as meticulous as a NASA Mission Controller; as media-savvy as a TikTok influencer; as data-filled as an actuary; as experienced in animal behavior as a zookeeper; as linguistically gifted as a professional emoji translator; and as astute as the contributors to the *Harvard Business Review*. Law librarians need all of these skills to ensure maximum chaos is not only contained but cataloged.

Take heart because this is not as daunting as it may first appear. Just as no law librarian can be an expert in all areas of research, neither does an office filled with MBAs expect any one person to master all of these skill sets. That amazingly innovative CEO in the papers on any given day isn't an expert in all of these skills, only in some, and she delegates the rest. What she *does* have, and doesn't delegate, is awareness of these skills, respect for what is required to master them, and the adaptability to deploy them.

What, then, does a library run like a business look like? How can librarians be crack researchers and sophisticated, business-savvy, corporate tacticians at the same time without spending even more years in school?

How to Think Like a Marketer

Law librarians always have to think about these skills in relation to their jobs. During every action taken, every resource explored, every patron question answered, the following questions should be asked: How can this be marketed? How can this be tracked? How can this be quantified? How will the personnel be managed to get the most out of this? How will it be written about? How can this be utilized to show ROI? Management is holistic—there is no action taken that does not reverberate across all of these topics. A good CEO leads from the front by constantly asking all of these questions to keep abreast of what is happening all around them—and how they can use that to their advantage.

Customer Service Excellence

Law librarians need to play to their strengths. Ask around, and the number one characteristic of any librarian anyone has ever met is excellent customer service. Librarians genuinely want to help patrons find their information, analyze their judicial data, or win their case. Librarians dig through dark archives, scour the web, and actually pick up the phone to talk to people to find the information someone is looking for. Librarians are helpful and take pride in their willingness to assist anyone with any questions on any topic.

This same skill can be applied up the chain, with true commercial shrewdness. C-levels like positive, proactive problem-solving. Don't say "no" to any proposal or new idea just for the sake of saying "no." Telling people "no," even when justified, is a conversation stopper. It causes people to double down and dig in, rather than trying to find solutions. It often leads to the person saying "no" to shut down their own thinking—they dwell on all the challenges and ways they can't do something instead of trying to find the way(s) they can. When someone says "yes," or even just "let me think about how we can make that happen," magic happens: Concessions are made, new relationships are forged, and goodwill is created. Sometimes processes or procedures will have to be changed or new methods will have to be created. Librarians will have to be adaptable in order to provide assistance and get the job done. A good CEO sees the (the possibility) of solutions, not impediments.

Professional Development

Librarians need to obtain, and then advertise, any official certifications or degrees or credit needed to prove competency. There may not be enough hours in the day to pursue an MBA, but there might be enough time for a local seminar or training that gives certifications, CLE credit, or something concrete to point to. This can be difficult as it feels as if professional development budgets are constantly being cut, and many law librarians, particularly those in the private sector, are not given time to participate in such trainings and often have to take vacation days to attend. Look at how other departments, particularly Marketing departments, are doing this.

For example, a Marketing coordinator at a previous firm always seemed to have unlimited travel and professional development funds, while the library struggled even to get the registration fee paid for a local one-day training for a new librarian. When asked about this, she replied that they don't call it professional development but instead focus on specific skills. In other words: spin. They weren't asking for money to spend four days frolicking in Chicago. They would phrase their requests with specifics: they would ask to attend a conference in Alsip, Illinois and learn about [insert specific topic(s) here from the conference program]. They would also make sure there was at least one client or partner meeting included. Then they would add those topics or meeting results to their resumés. Librarians may not have that kind of flexibility in arrangements, but the idea is a good one: don't be humble and put a little spin in your life.

Also, pursue these opportunities outside the usual library-related areas. Learn basic accounting and budget visualization tools. Work on the so-called "soft skills" such as leading with emotional intelligence, leveraging relationships, and networking. Take a class on change management or impactful leadership. Add all of that to the toolkit and shout it from the rooftops. A good CEO would sit through that three-day conference on AI search strategies and proudly add Prompt Engineer to her signature line, without a whiff of self-consciousness.

Outsourcing

Librarians must continue to think outside the box. Librarians are good at this—they must be able to find creative ways to track down information or compile analytics using resources that don't track numbers in the format needed. Or find a way to stretch that small budget to accommodate all the resources our patrons are asking for. One way to do this is "outsourcing," a word that is often viewed negatively, but is really a way to elevate the concept of certain functions beyond "support."[5]

The concept of outsourcing is not new: adjunct professors are a form of outsourcing, as are the copy cataloging or full cataloging and filing services many libraries have used for decades. There are some libraries that have outsourced their entire operations, usually under pressure from administration that looks at the idea of commoditizing information services the way they do office services. These arrangements have mixed success—they often do end up as a cost-saving measure, but often diminish the role of the library in the operations of the organization because there's no on-site full-time advocate. More than one firm has gone this route, downgrading the library, then realizing the arrangement isn't providing the competitive information needed, and starting up a whole "new, innovative" department to fill the gap. This new department isn't called a library because there is more client-facing work or data analytics than "just pulling cases." Ironically, librarians let go earlier when their jobs were outsourced are hired back. There are horror stories of lawsuits for breach of contract or subpar or plain unusable research work product. Many librarians feel they have to double-check everything, negating any potential cost savings. Many of these relationships have soured due to lack of engagement with patrons/users/attorneys, low familiarity with specialty practice areas, or just peculiarities of the hiring organization.

These are the extreme examples. A more recent trend is to find a happy medium in outsourcing day-to-day research and reference or special projects. This is usually due to economies of scale, that is, taking advantage of expensive online resources by collaborating with other libraries. But more recently these efforts have been focused on access to talent or subject specialists. Could any random librarian master a particular skill or area of expertise? Of course—librarians are brilliant! But do they have the time and/or inclination and/or support to do so? Often not. Few organizations can afford to keep their own librarians *and* subject-area expertise on staff at all times. A librarian's work is valuable—and one has to pay for value—and hence can also be perceived as expensive when compared to other professions. Yet information services are needed, and there have been bidding wars over expert witness librarians, IP librarians, and other specialists in their fields. Outsourcing specific projects to research consultants can be a way to keep the costs down and still answer those odd questions that come up, without pulling the full-time staff away from their important duties. It makes it easier to keep a wide variety of subject specialists at the ready.

Such relationships have to be well-managed, just as with any outside vendor. An organization must choose someone with a good reputation, someone trusted—which is often the easiest part as there are many librarians who work in the industry for decades before leaving to start their own companies. Give that person the tools they need to succeed: access to resources, direct access to people who can answer their questions, enough time to understand not just the project but internal policies and procedures, and articulated, clear expectations. A good CEO knows that the library-as-a-service model is perfect for an outsourcing relationship, and there is plenty of evidence that over the long term, outsourcing can stabilize costs, but only if the organization emotionally invests in the arrangement the way it would with an employee.

Patron Retention and Outreach

Libraries must focus on keeping current customers (patrons) and attracting new ones. Every business in the history of the world thinks about outreach: market expansion and/or identifying new markets, building customer loyalty, and lead generation. Research can be done to gather insight on demographics, interests, pain points, and purchasing behavior (or request behavior). Start thinking about utilizing market segmentation strategies when building or marketing services. Librarians cannot be all things to all people, so focus on being some great things to some people. That is, tailor the message and services to certain groups. A law library often caters to closed or select groups already (attorneys at a firm, employees of a court, attorneys in a local community, enrolled law students) but those groups can be further subdivided. Look at what each of those groups needs and create services—or at least messages about those services—to speak to those specific needs. A good CEO knows that a business is only successful when a steady stream of customers is coming in the door.

Statistics and ROI

Libraries need to find a way to quantify everything above. Keep statistics on requests answered (and tag them by type so the information can be sliced and diced), resources utilized in a year, complaints or compliments given, database usage, streaming media views, e-book usage, and staff utilization. Calculate market penetration rate: What percentage of the total customer base utilizes the library services in any way?[6] How many of those people come back? Take the time to calculate ROI and also VOI. Take those assessments, evaluations, and metrics and combine them with the unique context only librarians can provide. An organization can measure resource usage through clicks—but librarians know that if that resource is delivered via email with full-text articles then clicks aren't telling the whole story. That one metric doesn't demonstrate how well existing workflow meets a need. A good CEO knows that decisions need to be as data-driven as possible.

Information Literacy in an AI-Driven World

Librarians need to continue to act as information gatekeepers and literacy trainers, just as they have for centuries. Despite the gleeful articles written in the early 1900s and again in the 1990s, librarians did not die with the advent of loose-leaf filings or the internet.[7] On the contrary, those new technologies were incorporated into current workflows, and librarians became leaders in innovative ways to use them, and teachers on how to use them effectively. This will come in handy again as the world faces the Artificial Intelligence (AI) revolution. Librarians can be gatekeepers, guides, and interpreters of all the information going into and coming out of AI products. They can utilize all those semantic and syntactic search skills and strategies and redeploy as prompt engineers. They can remind all those inside and outside the legal profession of the importance of ethical usage. Librarians *are* the intelligence behind AI as they provide users with predictive research, generate queries, and craft prompts. Librarians provide the real AI: *actionable intelligence*. But none of that can be accomplished without the foundations of information access: collecting materials and resources, reviewing and classifying those resources, negotiating and managing access to those resources, tailoring searches to retrieve data from those resources, analyzing the data that is found to make it usable, archiving those efforts for future use, and so on. A great CEO knows that the real secret to running a business is adaptability in incorporating evolving technologies or market changes or new revenue streams and making it look like they've been doing that all along.

CONCLUSION

Contrary to popular opinion, most of these skills are not taught; they're learned. That is, they're sought out by motivated people on the job or through independent reading or training. This means that anyone can learn them. Look internally and think about which of these skills can be pursued. Look around at what other businesses are doing (libraries or not). Read the literature.[8] Start looking at the library as a business with unique and quantifiable revenue streams and talk about it as a revenue-supporting function that can leverage patrons' time.

Talk the talk—use business terms to refer to services. Correct anyone who doesn't use those same terms. Law librarians don't "provide information to a patron so they can create work product for a client." Rather, they "leverage data-driven insights to empower customers and drive operational efficiency by proactively delivering tailored information resources that directly address the pain points and workflow requirements of the target clientele. By providing this value-added intelligence, librarians enable patrons to optimize their productivity, make more informed decisions, and achieve their strategic objectives in a competitive business landscape."

This may feel like the old Dilbert-inspired Corporate B.S. Generator,[9] but using the correct vernacular, so to speak, is one way to show clients/administrators/oversight boards that librarians mean business. Data, information, and knowledge *drive* all of these organizations—and librarians are the ones who provide it. Doing so with the know-how and confidence of a CEO is what will propel librarians into leadership roles and business influencers.

NOTES

1. If we were brokering anything else under the sun—real estate, executives, heck, even old books—we'd make more money. But add the word "librarian," and stand back and watch the dollar signs decrease.
2. That word is in quotes for the moment because measuring the profit of a law library is tricky.
3. See one of my favorites from 2006: Joseph Esposito, *What if Walmart Ran a Library*, https://quod.lib.umich.edu/j/jep/3336451.0009.104?view=text;rgn=main.
4. Greg Lambert, "Who Leads the Law Library? How About Law Librarians?," 3 *Geeks and A Law Blog*, https://www.geeklawblog.com/2017/03/who-leads-law-library-how-about-law.html.
5. See George Bradt, "Why You Should Outsource All Your Support Functions," *Forbes*, 2017, https://www.forbes.com/sites/georgebradt/2017/07/03/why-you-should-outsource-all-your-support-functions/.
6. A "good" market penetration rate in most industries is 30 percent—I bet most libraries are higher.
7. See Fredlund Ingeborg, "Loose Leaf Law Reports," *Law Library Journal* 3 (1911): 44.

8. See reading lists: Independent Information Professionals Reads, https://aiip.org/Discover/IIP-Reading-List; "The 62 Books People in Power Found Essential This Year," an abbreviated version, https://www.bloomberg.com/news/newsletters/2023-12-14/best-books-of-2023-picked-by-ceos-and-wall-street-leaders. I particularly enjoyed Bob Iger's, *The Ride of a Lifetime: Lessons Learned from 15 Years as CEO of the Walt Disney Company*.
9. Feel free to use some of those generated phrases—I suspect others do: https://www.atrixnet.com/bs-generator.html.

5

Managing Remote and Hybrid Workers

John DiGilio

It is often said that necessity is the mother of invention. Well, when it comes to the business of law, few things scream necessity with the same urgency as a slowdown or even a stoppage in productivity. Thus, it was during the most desperate days of the recent pandemic that human ingenuity and perseverance combined to accomplish something that had only previously been talked about as something of a pipe dream in law firms. Work for attorneys and staff alike went fully and perhaps even irreversibly remote. The change was so swift, so seamless, and so successful that even now we marvel at what we accomplished almost overnight and nervously ponder what it means for the future of practice. What we have seen from experience so far is that with proper and skillful management, remote work can be a major benefit to both the firm and its employees. This is as true of law firm libraries as it is of the firms themselves.

DEFINING REMOTE AND HYBRID WORK

Perhaps we should start with some definitions. What exactly does it mean to work remotely? A quick survey of business media demonstrates that the definitions of "remote work" are fairly uniform. One of the largest and most active online hiring sites, Indeed.com, sums it up quite nicely, stating that "[r]emote work is work done outside of a traditional office environment."[1] The site goes further, mentioning that it can include both working from one's own home as well as using technology to work from other diverse spaces beyond even that. While there is some debate as to the latter, for the purposes of this chapter, any work performed outside the traditional office as "remote work" will be included. This includes legal research, reference services, and, of course, managing digital resources.

During the height of the pandemic, most of us were working remotely all the time. Others divided their time between off-site locations and the office. This is what we shall refer to in this chapter as "hybrid work" or "hybrid working." Referring back to Indeed.com, the site and many other sources also refer to this as "flexible working." This term is easily confused with other types of non-traditional work arrangements beyond mere location.[2] Now that the COVID crisis has significantly abated, an increasing number of firms are bringing their employees back into the office in a hybrid form that mandates in-office time while allowing for a set number of remote days. Remote and hybrid working trends might be irreversible. Last December's Survey of Business Uncertainty, conducted by the Federal Reserve Bank of Atlanta, Stanford University, and the University of Chicago Booth School of Business, found that a quarter of the panelist companies were allowing either fully remote or hybrid work arrangements.[3] Of that group, almost 70 percent reported that these allowances had a positive impact on the recruitment and retention of talent.[4] It is no wonder that respected business publications such as Forbes and others have predicted that remote working is here to stay.[5]

THE IMPORTANCE OF EFFECTIVE MANAGEMENT

Whether your firm or organization is offering fully remote working opportunities or utilizing the hybrid work model, the key to the success of your library or information service offerings depends on the effective management of your staff regardless of where they are working, when, or how often. Any degree of out-of-office working changes the administrative, social, and collaborative dynamics of the job significantly. Early studies on the effects of remote working on everything from productivity to work habits produced confusing and seemingly contradictory results. One investigation, for instance, found that remote workers were almost 8 percent more productive than those required to be in the office all the time.[6] Another determined that productivity actually went down, while the hours that workers were actually putting in had increased significantly.[7] Talk about work-life balance issues in the making! Only with effective management can we hope to maintain and maybe even increase staff productivity and morale, while reducing miscommunication, inefficiency, and employee attrition.

CHAPTER GOALS

The purpose of this chapter, however, is not to debate the impact of remote working on a firm's bottom line. Rather, it is to look at what department leaders can do to support their teams under this new model. This chapter is about best practices and practical considerations for managers, directors, and all who lead library teams in this emerging, ever-newer "normal." We will look at strategies for setting clear expectations for our departments, building trust among dispersed teams, leveraging technology for communication and connection, and supporting the well-being of our staff. In the end, our library and information departments still have services to provide, and capable leadership can make all the difference in whether those deliverables are met or exceeded despite the team being remote, hybrid, on-site, or any combination thereof.

THE DYNAMICS OF REMOTE WORK

Advantages of Remote Work

There are many benefits offered by remote and hybrid working arrangements. What may appeal to one group of employees may not provide the same motivation to others. Some of the big incentives include increased flexibility in scheduling, a reduction in commute times and commuter stress, and a more satisfying overall work-life balance. Flexible scheduling gives employees more opportunities to work life's little interruptions into the workday. From scheduling necessary appointments for things like healthcare to taking on split or off-hour shifts to provide for family care or handling special projects, team members can get their hours in while saving hard-earned leave hours for more relaxing pursuits. When it comes to the time it takes to get to and from work, long commute times have proven to be more than just an annoyance. Studies have shown that longer commutes take a real toll on employee health and well-being![8] Work-life balance is often a misunderstood concept. While it does not necessarily mean some set ratio of work hours to personal hours, it does call into question whether a person's work energizes them for their time away and vice versa. The ability to conduct both work and play in such close proximity while being afforded the flexibility to more spontaneously move between both can lead to a maximization of each.

Remote Working Challenges

There are two sides to this coin, however. With opportunities come challenges, and there are several here of which team leaders should take note, including decreased team collaboration and cohesion, the potential lack of access to on-site resources, and a significant reduction in meaningful visibility. Effective collaboration and cohesiveness can be challenging enough to build when people with diverse interests and skills are physically present together. For those in firms with multiple locations, the dynamic is even trickier, with camaraderie beginning in the local offices first. But the stakes are especially high when you are trying to hold together a team in which every individual is potentially off on their own. Not only can collaboration take a hit, but loneliness itself can become a force to be reckoned with. Not only can workers become cut off from one another and from management, but they can find themselves separated from resources that have traditionally been available only on-site. The potential effect this lack of access can have on the efficiency and satisfaction of the research process—not to mention the quality of the results and end-user experience—cannot be overstated. Of course, all of this is compounded by the fact that it could be happening well out of sight and proximal control of leaders and mentors.

Remote Working: Key Misconceptions

While effective management—proactive and reactive—is key to tackling the situations mentioned above, managers must also be ready to contend with two major misconceptions that currently muddy the remote work waters. In a way, they have become challenges in and of themselves, if for no other reason than our need to dispel these myths from the start. The first of these has already been mentioned. It is the notion that remote workers are somehow inherently less productive than on-site employees. As noted, the studies conducted to date have drawn differing conclusions here, and much is actually dependent on the nature of the remote working program and how it is managed. Anecdotally, many law firm library managers and directors have observed that the productivity of their teams jumped with the introduction of remote and hybrid working. This, of course, feeds into the second major misconception, which is that remote management is also made inherently less effective by lack of physical oversight. The reality is that most of us in leadership positions have long been dealing with teams that are geographically dispersed. If anything, having more of our employees working remotely or virtually has given us the opportunity to up our managerial game and really demonstrate just how effective we can be.

MANAGEMENT STRATEGIES FOR EFFECTIVE REMOTE WORK

The key differences between managing in-office and remote teams are substantially the same for law firm libraries. While there are myriad approaches to the actual management of remote and hybrid teams, four major issues face us all as team leaders. These are establishing clear expectations for staff, building team trust and communication, managing team and individual performance, supporting the well-being of employees, and leveraging the technology needed to make it all happen. The sections that follow include strategies for bridging these gaps and thus the distances that stand between us and a successful remote working program.

Establishing Clear Expectations at Sidley Austin, LLP

I still vividly remember those last few days before my own firm went into pandemic lockdown. We knew that some kind of "work from home" pivot was needed, and everyone was looking to the department leaders to come up with workable plans for their teams. Knowing the professionalism and skills of my staff, I determined that the crucial step in our plan was simply to communicate exactly what I and the firm expected of them in what we had hoped would only be the few weeks ahead. Of course, we had not contemplated at the time that we would be working fully remote for a whole year, but this step proved especially critical once the length of the lockdown became evident. This meant that roles and responsibilities had to be clearly defined and communicated to the team. While we already had strong job descriptions and skill expectations for each of our departmental roles, remote working added new nuances to each function that we had not previously contemplated. We needed to be sure we not only knew what everyone was doing, but that we had a way to track and report on it. Job descriptions were immediately revisited and revised as needed to include aspects of remote work. Four years later, these on-the-spot changes have become permanent considerations for all new hires. Remote work is now factored in from the start!

It is important to note that these new expectations not only involved redefining the roles of the team members but also revising our existing departmental goals and setting new ones to handle the changes. While we still needed to focus on raising the annual bar on our services and output, we suddenly also had to factor in the potential effects of remote working. For example, could we still expect the same degree of growth, or did we need to factor in an additional upswing of "how do I do this from home" requests from attorneys and others? What could such an uptick mean for staffing numbers and workload balance? We needed to be ready to act should we find ourselves deluged and stretched too thin. Another example involves how we interacted as a team. In addition to the standard online monthly team meetings we had planned for the year, we also had to create new goals focusing on things like virtual check-ins with managers and teammates. New internal communication protocols and tools had to be mandated to ensure that everyone on the team stayed connected. Setting these and other expectations not only got us through the lockdown successfully but continues to be an integral part of how I manage my team of hybrid workers today.

Building Team Trust and Communication

While newly established expectations and revised goals are a step in the right direction, they will go unfulfilled without the understanding, support, and ultimately, the collaboration of the library staff. None of that is possible without two things—trust and communication—among the whole team. Trust and communication are developed more easily as a consequence of people working together in person, and they are certainly easier to measure and manage in that situation. But while remote working arrangements may change the dynamic, they do not take away from their importance. In many ways, trust and communication become of even greater importance when your staff members are all working on their own.

The importance of trust in the workplace cannot be understated. Not only is it essential for getting the best work out of your people and for fostering good relationships, but without it, there can be no collaboration or innovation. People will not work well with others they feel are unreliable or uncaring. They also will not get behind change that they suspect was created without their best interests having been factored in. It is also important to remember that trust is both a two-way street and multidimensional. Your team members need to trust and respect one another, and they need to be able to trust—and know that they themselves are trusted by—you and the rest of your firm's leadership. When real trust is lacking, you can bet that employee morale and job satisfaction are but a shadow of what they could be. This, of course, goes back to what I said at the start of the paragraph. Employees who are unhappy or frustrated or who feel under-respected do not produce their best work. It's an ugly cycle that can hurt the department and even the firm as a whole.

The best way to develop and nurture that kind of trust in teams is to keep the lines of communication wide open and flowing. Getting busy, remote professionals to take time out of their workday to simply communicate takes patience, persistence, and creativity. This may entail a lot of virtual team meetings for both business and pleasure, digital departmental newsletters and updates that focus on both news and fun, one-on-one check-ins, and regular reminders that we are all here for one another. This could include virtual holiday gatherings complete with contests and singing, monthly all-department meetings to let everyone know what's going on in both our library and the firm, and to celebrate the successes (individual and team) from the previous month. Staff may be incentivized to offer training or deep-dive sessions for their teammates so that they get to know one another and each other's skills. Your library may even publish an annual digital cookbook of favorite recipes to share with colleagues in other departments as we have done at Sidley Austin, LLP. The key considerations here are that it is essential everyone participates, team members are kept informed, and that these interactions are not always only about business.

There are a few other tips and tricks for truly effective communication and trust-building worth sharing here. First is the importance of remembering that variety really is the spice of life. By diversifying the types of communication you and your department share, you will engage a wider audience. Too many meetings on the schedule can quickly become taxing, and too many email messages are an annoyance to most folks. Switch it up and spread those "touches" out. Second, it is also important to offer a variety of methods for your team's communications and to integrate them into the ways they already interact. Email and virtual meeting platforms like Zoom, Webex, and others are a given. But what about instant messaging built into your request/ticketing platform? Or app-based communications tools like Messenger, WhatsApp, and others that can reside on smartphones and mobile technology? Of course, it depends on what your firm's policies allow, but again, that variety is the spice of remote work life. Just be careful not to overdo it or to create situations where not everyone can access the tools you make available!

MANAGING PERFORMANCE AND PRODUCTIVITY

It does not matter whether your staff is in the office, fully remote, or some hybrid form of the two; the need for tracking and reporting on the good work your department is doing is essential to showing its return on the firm's investment. What makes the ROI process unique for remote and hybrid teams, however, is the fact that you may not have a real clue as to where your folks are actually working or when. You cannot just pop your head into their office or workroom. Regardless of what it means when your employees are working "remotely," the success of your library will be determined in large part by its productivity and the metrics you use to demonstrate it. It is a three-part process that involves monitoring, measuring, and maintaining—the "Three Ms."

Monitoring and Measuring Remote Performance

Monitoring the productivity of your team means establishing a key set of meaningful performance metrics that can be called upon consistently and reliably to show the depth and breadth of both the work and the effort your team is putting forth. The importance of having some sort of system that tracks your department's activities from multiple angles cannot be emphasized enough. Whether you buy such a platform from one of the many vendors that offer ticket/request and time tracking or build something in-house, you need those numbers to show your ROI and justify things like the need for more support for current staff, restructured responsibilities, and new tools to alleviate workload or increase efficiency. There is a lot you can do with good numbers to back you up. You can even use those results to show your team just how integral they are to your firm's overall success. They can come in handy during performance reviews (a *must* for remote workers) and goal setting. They can also make for a quick and definite morale boost!

Regardless of the type of system you use to monitor your team's workload and productivity, the key is to produce metrics that are truly meaningful to the firm's leadership and which capture the true breadth of your library's contributions. The days of simply reporting on the number of requests your department receives are long gone. While statistics are helpful to have, they paint an incomplete picture. They do not speak to the nature or complexity of the work your team is being asked to do. They do not tell the real story of just how much work was required to make sure the attorneys and requestors got what they needed. And what about the team members who do not work on requests? How are you capturing their hard work and contributions? There is so much more this singular statistic leaves off the table. With your remote team out of sight, having a robust and diverse suite of measures is what will keep them from also being out of mind when it comes to the firm's decision-makers.

Library management teams can, with some effort, quantify and qualify the productivity of their departments. Statistics can be kept, counting every request that comes in and capturing the hours that the research team spends working on those requests. For the non-researchers who manage collections and access to the library's resources, their tasks and the time they take can also be logged. Libraries may consider tracking the various groups for whom the work is being done, looking for usage patterns and outreach opportunities. Where and when possible, libraries can even record the level of satisfaction of the people who are receiving the work product that is generated. This is a lot of data, and the library can report on all of it. Monthly reports to the library team and firm or organizational leadership that compare year-over-year performance and usage can be designed as well as annual comprehensive, customized reports to the firm's leaders and the head of every practice group and department. These reports may focus on the ways attorneys and others in the organization are making use of the library's services and may offer suggestions for resources and offerings that are being underutilized.

Another argument for expanding the types of data points captured serves as both a callback to the aforementioned goal setting and a segue to the next section on the well-being of the team. Robust, expositive metrics can be a real boon in the quest to maintain and even increase the productivity of your team. There is a great deal of discussion these days regarding the burnout of remote workers. Working from home, for example, apparently increases the likelihood that employees will work more hours daily, skip necessary breaks, and feel obligated to take on more work to ensure job security. These metrics should provide you with the insight you need to get ahead of these situations and make a case for either bringing on more staff, rebalancing the workload, or simply reminding your staff about the importance of work-life balance.

SUPPORTING REMOTE TEAM WELL-BEING

Work-life balance is every bit as important to remote and hybrid workers as it is to those who spend their days in the office. While the idea of working from home or a cozy coffee shop may sound relaxing, work is work regardless of where it is being done. It can just as easily cause burnout and become overwhelming at home as it does when a person is on-site. Just like the importance of productivity, what makes it uniquely challenging in a remote situation is the fact that you are unlikely to actually see its physical and mental manifestations. Compounding the problem is the fact that remote workers are far more likely to find themselves without someone to talk to and feeling isolated and alone. To inspire and maintain the productivity discussed in the previous section, you have got to ensure that proper support for the well-being of your team members is available in ways that meet them where they are and that they know this support is available.

Recognizing and Addressing Isolation and Loneliness

Even the most introverted of humans are still social creatures by nature. When in the office, we at least have the option of avoiding opportunities to socialize with teammates and coworkers. Remote work, however, can lack those traditional interactions. Even with family or friends at home, the inability to easily connect with work colleagues can lead one to feel isolated or lonely. The best way to ascertain whether any of your team members are experiencing these feelings, and to help prevent them from manifesting, is to encourage regular social interactions (even if virtual) and to provide plenty of opportunities for team bonding. Managers should be checking in on their reports on a regularly scheduled basis. These do not have to be long meetings, just enough to ask how someone is doing. In fact, team members should also be encouraged to check in on one another. It beats always having to talk to your boss and is great for building teamwork and trust.

In large library settings, or even small ones, groups of team members with similar professional interests may be encouraged to schedule their own meetings to chat. Staff members may also be randomly paired up for virtual coffee breaks in which no work is done, but instead the goal is to get to know one another. Be creative in developing the opportunities, and let our social, human nature do the rest.

Promoting Work-Life Balance

Work-life balance is something that we often talk about, but how many of us know what it actually is? Author and productivity consultant Julie Morgenstern says that "work-life balance is not about the amount of time you spend working versus not working. It's more about how you spend your time working and relaxing, recognizing that what you do in one fuels your energy for the other."[9] The problem when it comes to remote working is where to draw those lines when it is highly likely that work and relaxation are happening in the same place. New lines must be drawn to make up for the ones that working from home has blurred.

An important part of managing a remote team is ensuring that your team understands the importance of relaxing as well as putting in a hard day's work. There are two ways to do that. The first is personal accountability. It is important that you, as a manager, both encourage your staff members to set boundaries and take care of themselves, as well as demonstrate how to do this yourself. Leading by example is a powerful motivator here. What is meant by boundaries? One example is setting a cut-off time for all work-related activities. At the designated hour, the laptop gets put away, and work communications are silenced. Another is making mealtime an email-free period with no calls or virtual meetings allowed. Again, it is important that managers do the same here and set a good example. The second way to accomplish this goal is to remind your team that firm policies and benefits apply whether they are in the office or at home. That means taking the required breaks, utilizing time off, and keeping overtime to a reasonable minimum. It also entails making sure your staff is aware of any resources your firm might provide for getting mental health support. They are there for a reason! Happy, healthy, and energized employees are productive, high-performing employees.

LEVERAGING TECHNOLOGY FOR REMOTE MANAGEMENT

It is no secret that the business world is awash with tools and resources to make managing remote teams easier and more effective. In fact, this was the case for on-site management long before telecommuting even became a thing. Project management, team communication, video conferencing, real-time document collaboration—you name it and there is a software package or application that promises to streamline what you are doing. The real considerations here are not what is available, but rather how you make your buying decisions and how you implement and integrate those tools into your team's workflows.

Selecting Technology for Remote Working

A three-pronged approach is recommended for selecting the right technology to support your remote or hybrid team. The first step is to assess what technology you already have. What is going to work at a distance, and what will be of no use if your people are not in the office? The second is to consider the needs of your team when it comes to additional tech to replace the tools that did not make the cut above or to fill any gaps. And third, you are going to want to look for tools and resources that play nice in both situations.

Taken together, this means conducting a meaningful needs assessment for your team and not just looking for what is cool or might be nice to have. What you choose needs to be user-friendly and should either complement or work with existing tools. No one wants to break either the bank or tried-and-true workflows. Remember what we said about creating frustration, confusion, and extra work when it comes to building trust and supporting the well-being of your people.

Integrating Technology into Remote Work Processes

Effectively integrating new resources for remote working into your established workflows and processes is where the proverbial rubber hits the road when it comes to technology. Part of getting tech to work well is to use it well. This too is a triple front. It involves setting rules, providing training, and continuous evaluation to make sure you are getting the most bang for your buck and not compromising the work quality or client relationships with your shiny new toys.

Establishing rules for the usage of the new tech entails setting and communicating the intended or appropriate use cases. It also means considering hot-button issues that can harm your firm or its clients, like data security, file sharing, and licensing. These too are all things that need to be communicated to your team. That is where training comes in. Not only do you want folks to get up to speed quickly on how to use the newly acquired technology, but you also want to empower them to feel confident about doing so. Creating or having good user support guides on hand will go a long way in helping you and your team achieve this goal. Finally, be sure to check in with staff to get their feedback, questions, or concerns regarding the technology. Ultimately, it is the quality and efficiency of their work that are affected. They are on the front lines and will let you know whether your chosen tools are making their jobs easier or causing consternation. It is a great way to both ensure you have the right resources for the job and to show your team that you are doing your best to set them up for success.

Adapting to Change and Future Trends

The future of this remote working juggernaut is still a bit of an unknown. During the recent pandemic, it became a reluctant—very reluctant in the case of some firms—necessity. But with the easing of the lockdown and distancing restrictions, we have also seen firms begin to claw back some of those generous work-from-home allowances. Yes, there are still many firms whose staff are fully remote. But the numbers that are limiting remote working or establishing in-office minimums are on the rise. So too is the number of law shops that have gone back to being fully in-office. The consensus seems to be that generally some form of remote working is here to stay. As such, library managers and leaders need to be thinking about what comes next and how to be ready for it. No one wants to be caught off-guard again!

As library managers, we need to stay on top of emerging trends in this area. The news is chock full of speculation and studies into the remote option, and best practices are emerging and evolving continuously. Encourage team members to attend webinars and conference sessions on remote work. And remind staff that nothing is a given and that flexibility is key to our future in this industry. The more we do to make remote working a smooth experience for all at our libraries, and the more we work to show its actual benefits, the less chance that it will be taken away as an option! We have not even yet begun to see the impact of Artificial Intelligence on remote working. I have little doubt, however, that we soon will. We need to be ready.

We are still in the early days of this remote work trend. As we saw when COVID brought the world to a halt, change can and will come quickly. It may have been the flexibility and openness to change inherent in our profession that got our libraries through so smoothly and successfully. These are traits that we will need to keep calling upon as we brace for whatever comes next. It is critical that we take the time to regularly review and update our management practices. We need to ensure that they remain effective and relevant no matter what life may throw at us. That's why we are here, after all.

FINAL THOUGHTS FOR MANAGERS OF REMOTE TEAMS

In this chapter, we discussed some of the key issues facing those of us who manage remote and hybrid workers. We also covered some strategies for best supporting our teams, thus making our own jobs more successful in that regard. From team- and trust-building to effective communication, technology concerns, and even support for employee well-being, we have looked at ways to meet and overcome the challenges of remote working. It really comes down to doing what we can to set our teams up for continued success in this changing landscape. As remote and hybrid working becomes more common in law firms, effective management skills and approaches too are becoming more critical than ever. The strategies herein are shared in the hope of helping all law firm library managers and leaders design and implement work environments that are productive for their firms and supportive of their teams. As we have learned in recent years and continue to demonstrate today, remote library teams can drive the overall success of their firms.

NOTES

1. "Q&A: What Is Remote Work?," Indeed, updated May 31, 2024, https://www.indeed.com/career-advice/finding-a-job/remote-work.
2. Indeed, "Q&A: What is Remote Work?"
3. "Survey of Business Uncertainty, Monthly Report: December 2023," Federal Reserve Bank of Atlanta, released December 2023, https://www.atlantafed.org/-/media/documents/datafiles/research/surveys/business-uncertainty/chart-pack/2023/2023-12.pdf.
4. Federal Reserve Bank of Atlanta, "Survey of Business Uncertainty, Monthly Report: December 2023." "Survey of Business Uncertainty, Monthly Report: December 2023," Federal Reserve Bank of Atlanta, released December 2023, https://www.atlantafed.org/-/media/documents/datafiles/research/surveys/business-uncertainty/chart-pack/2023/2023-12.pdf.
5. Dr. Gleb Tsipursky, "Is The End Of Remote Work Jobs Approaching?," *Forbes*, Updated February 6, 2023, https://www.forbes.com/sites/glebtsipursky/2023/02/06/the-future-of-remote-work-is-here-to-stay/.
6. "Does Working From Home Make Employees More Productive?," *The Economist*, December 27, 2020, https://www.economist.com/graphic-detail/2020/12/27/does-working-from-home-make-employees-more-productive?.
7. "Remote Workers Work Longer, Not More Efficiently," *The Economist*, June 10, 2021, https://www.economist.com/business/2021/06/10/remote-workers-work-longer-not-more-efficiently?.
8. Libin Han et al., "The Effect of Commuting Time on Quality of Life: Evidence from China," *International Journal of Environmental Research and Public Health* 20(1): 573, https://www.ncbi.nlm.nih.gov/pmc/articles/PMC9819363/.
9. https://www.juliemorgenstern.com/.

6

Vendor Relations

Navigating Challenges and Opportunities with Collaboration, Negotiation, and Implementation

Crystal Alberthal and Pearl McCrea

In law librarianship, ensuring access to information is vital for the pursuit of justice. Within this context, cultivating robust vendor relationships emerges as a key strategy for optimizing operational efficiency and facilitating the acquisition of information and resources essential for advancing and accessing justice. Regardless of the type of law library—whether academic, private, or governmental—and irrespective of one's position, effective vendor relations are fundamental to the organization's success. The products provided by vendors are crucial for supporting the curriculum, scholarship, and practice of law. As library collections and services increasingly transition to electronic, virtual, cloud-based, and vendor-hosted formats, libraries must invest more in these relationships.[1] Such investments are crucial for overcoming the challenges faced by law libraries, ultimately enhancing their effectiveness and reducing associated difficulties.

Librarians and vendors have been writing about the importance of library—vendor relationships for decades.[2] In 2006, Sam Brooks, executive vice president of Marketing, Sales, Publisher Relations & Strategic Partnerships at EBSCO Information Services, wrote that as library staff are advocates for end-users, and are end-users themselves, they can provide the best services "if vendors can better equip the libraries to do so. In order for vendors to accomplish this task, they often rely heavily upon libraries for insight and direction to improve products and services. Thus, dependence is evident in this circular pattern, and forging strong relationships is key to the continued development of products and services for use by librarians and patrons."[3] Just short of two decades later, it continues to hold true.

Through strategic collaboration, negotiation, and implementation of resources with vendors, law libraries create space to invest in high-impact services and endeavors. This chapter underscores the significance of such partnerships through the lens of an academic law library. It provides examples, research, advice, and strategies to navigate the challenges and embrace the opportunities that amplify access to pivotal legal materials, vital for navigating both historical legal precedents and contemporary legal challenges.

COLLABORATION

Encountering a paywall when trying to access content can be extremely frustrating. This frustration is compounded when it's unclear who to contact for access or by not knowing how much it will cost. Trying to understand the available services a vendor offers, the cost, or what their product can do for a library can feel similarly frustrating but should not be unclear or full of roadblocks for would-be adopters.[4] Building relationships with vendors has the potential to change this experience significantly. While vendors do have a vested interest in selling their services and products, many of them, especially those specializing in library services, genuinely care about helping libraries improve their services and expand access to information.

Collaborative efforts with vendors are beneficial as they provide a direct line of communication and support. When librarians and vendors establish strong relationships, there is the potential to access a wealth of knowledge and resources that can demystify complex product offerings and pricing structures. This ongoing partnership and dialogue help librarians stay informed about new products, updates, and features that can enhance library services. Clear and transparent communication with a vendor about what the library needs or what the problem is, and asking what services they have that could meet it, is often the best approach to starting and building a collaborative relationship.

One example of this is when the University of Washington Gallagher Law Library (hereafter, Gallagher Law Library) began working more closely with EBSCO's GOBI Library Solutions.[5] GOBI is a global library book vendor specializing in print and electronic resources for academic, research, and special libraries. Initially, the Gallagher Law Library used GOBI strictly as a purchasing tool, like Amazon. However, through ongoing dialogue and collaboration, the law library discovered that GOBI offers a wealth of additional services, many of which are included in the existing payment structure or provided as courtesy services to their customers. This realization allowed the law library to improve its collection development workflows and acquisitions. As Maaike Oldemans and Jennifer Kronenbitter note, "the use of electronic tools as well as electronically available methods from vendors like EBSCO's GOBI Library Solutions and Amazon has made acquisition and collection development more efficient."[6] By maintaining clear and transparent communications with vendors, libraries can stay informed and take advantage of all their offerings. This approach can even lead to the creation of custom products or services, which has the potential to benefit other libraries, too.

Barbara Kawecki, director of sales, U.S. and Canada at GOBI Library Solutions, wrote that "a successful partnership provides mutual benefits for both the library and the vendor. The library benefits from the expertise, resources and economies of scale that a vendor can offer, while the vendor benefits from the perspective and workflow knowledge that the library can provide."[7] Partnerships and collaboration with vendors can help vendors understand the unique needs of the library better. When a vendor has a better understanding of operations and services, it has the potential to inform changes to their products, which lead to custom solutions tailored to a specific library's needs, or better yet, benefit all libraries they do business with.[8]

Vendors' solicitations are very common, especially from those with whom libraries don't already do business. Many of these solicitations may seem irrelevant or unwelcome, but it can be worth considering them. Taking the time to schedule a call or video conference could reveal ways the vendor can help. Just as it's important to be clear and transparent with existing vendors about the library's needs, it's equally important to approach new vendors with the same level of communication and openness, as they may present valuable opportunities the library hadn't anticipated.

Mutually Beneficial Digitization Projects

One example of these collaborative partnerships is the ability to work on specialized digitization projects with vendors like William S. Hein & Co., Inc. (hereafter, Hein).[9] Hein is a legal publisher, periodical subscription agent, and distributor of legal periodicals that has been in business for over one hundred years. They started as a legal publishing firm in the 1920s and have grown their online research platform to create multidisciplinary databases going beyond law and bringing together worldwide primary and secondary sources. Libraries that work with Hein to digitize legal material participate in the positive impact of contributing to the preservation and accessibility of legal materials.

Faced with space constraints, libraries may see this as a viable solution to weeding their print collection while maintaining digital access and ownership of the content. When print material is damaged or destroyed in the digitization process, Hein is often willing to provide libraries with digital ownership of a scan of the print. Provided these materials fall outside of copyright, libraries are then permitted to make them digitally available via their catalog or digital repositories. This enhances open access to historical legal content by making it available online, so people can access these materials without needing to visit the library in person. This is especially beneficial for libraries that might not have the resources to provide physical access to these documents.

Law libraries that contribute significant portions of the content for new databases with a vendor like Hein are typically offered a substantial discount on a subscription or perpetual access. This level of contribution can look different depending on the library and vendor preferences. In some instances, a library only needs to loan their physical content to the vendor for digitization and can expect to receive it back upon completion. In other arrangements, it's not possible to digitize the print material without unbinding it or causing damage to the print during the digitization process, so the library must consider the value of print versus digital ownership and access for their collection. Libraries can work with the vendor to find a solution that works for them and their collection.

The Gallagher Law Library has participated in multiple mutually beneficial digitization projects. Most recently, it was one of the primary contributors to the HeinOnline West Academic Casebooks Archive[10] project, with over two thousand titles contributed. These were titles that the library determined it did not need to retain in print, so this effectively helped it weed crowded areas of the collection in addition to receiving perpetual digital access to the materials provided to Hein for digitization. As part of this collaboration and agreement, it received a discount on its first year of the online subscription.

Law Library Microform Consortium (LLMC) Digital[11] (hereafter LLMC) is another organization that is active in collaborating on digitization projects with law libraries. LLMC is a nonprofit cooperative of libraries working toward "saving the law" by preserving legal titles and print resources and in the process has started an Open Access Initiative.[12] Open access (OA) materials are another positive possibility of collaborating with vendors. Specialized digitization projects can contribute to OA legal materials and a more equitable digital landscape. Once content is digitized by LLMC, it sends the material to a salt mine to be preserved as an eventual last copy. Building a relationship with multiple vendors all working toward similar goals is a good strategy for libraries to use to diversify their access and participate in preservation initiatives.

Financial Benefits, Cooperative Agreements, and Shared Resources

Collaborating with vendors can lead to significant financial benefits for libraries, allowing them to stretch budgets further. This can often include discounts, bundled services, or cooperative agreements that can result in cost savings. Although this may not be a possibility for firm libraries, for academic and government libraries, forming or joining alliances or consortia, whether within their own organization or at the local, regional, or national level, has benefits. The power of critical mass has the potential for negotiating better terms, distributing the cost, and can lead to better offerings for library users.[13]

The University of Washington Libraries (hereafter UW Libraries) and the Gallagher Law Library illustrate how collaboration with each other and shared vendors can lead to significant cost savings and an increase in available resources for users across the institution. The Gallagher Law Library is autonomous from UW Libraries in every way, *and* they share an Integrated Library System (ILS), as well as the University of Washington's (hereafter UW) financial and procurement systems that require and encourage internal partnerships. By using common vendors, these libraries streamline some of their procurement processes and avoid unnecessary or duplicative vendor negotiations for shared tools and resources such as their ILS, Springshare Applications[14] (a platform for libraries that includes subject guides, calendars, chat services, e-reserves, etc.) and OCLC products[15] (a global nonprofit library organization that provides library metadata, resource sharing, and discovery and interface products and services). Perhaps not an option for firm libraries, for academic libraries like UW Libraries and the Gallagher Law Library, this institutional collaboration allows them to build relationships with vendors who are already familiar with UW procurement and finance processes and are approved by UW vendor control, reducing redundancy.

Additionally, cooperative agreements with alliances, consortia, and university-wide licenses with vendors for things like e-book platforms (like ProQuest, De Gruyter, EBSCO, Cambridge, and Elgar), self-check-out solutions like Meescan,[16] and serials subscriptions (Wiley, Taylor & Francis, Cambridge, Oxford) enable these libraries to access significant discounts, bundled services, and more favorable terms. In 2018, George Machovec, executive director of the Colorado Alliance of Research Libraries, wrote, "many consortia now talk about 'deep collaboration' with new opportunities provided by multi-tenant cloud-based library managements systems."[17] The Orbis Cascade Alliance[18] is an example of such a consortium where its member libraries have benefited from collective negotiations, leading to enhanced offerings for library users while stretching limited budgets through cost savings and efficient resource management. Susanne Markgren, when talking about the opportunities and advantages born out of alliances such as WALDO (Westchester Academic Library Director's Organization),[19] now Lyrasis,[20] states, "Together we are stronger and more empowered to make suggestions (or demands) of publishers, vendors, and the consortium itself. And they are more apt to listen. The more we share with one another, the more informed and energized we become."[21]

Accessibility

Collaborating with vendors that include built-in accessibility features enables libraries to align with accessibility standards more easily. If a librarian doesn't know whether a particular vendor meets required accessibility standards, often they are discoverable on a vendor's website, but libraries should also feel empowered to reach out to the vendor's customer service or their representative to find out. This partnership helps libraries provide content and services that are more inclusive and user-friendly, even if they don't have specialized expertise. For digital collections, this approach enhances libraries' capability to reach and support a diverse range of users effectively. The following are examples of built-in accessibility features in vendor products and services:

- Springshare's LibApps platform is designed for all types of libraries with accessibility at the forefront. These apps include built-in accessibility features, such as screen reader compatibility, keyboard navigation, and alt-text functionalities. Springshare offers phenomenal customer service and user documentation to support their products. They also continuously evaluate their tools for compliance with current accessibility regulations and standards.[22]
- Vendors like EBSCO, ProQuest, and JSTOR have integrated their e-book platforms with popular e-readers and screen reader capabilities. These features allow visually impaired users to access and navigate digital content more easily.
- Digitization projects with vendors like Hein and LLMC can have Optical Character Recognition (OCR) applied to documents, making them both searchable and readable by screen readers. This added benefit of digitized content ensures print is accessible to those who use assistive technology.

- Libraries can build digital repositories by creating their own or subscribe to one like Bepress's Digital Commons, which adheres to accessibility standards, allowing users to benefit from access to the content.

NEGOTIATION

The landscape of negotiating with vendors has evolved significantly and touches nearly every aspect of the functions and services of law libraries, reflecting changes in the prioritization of collection format, technology, market dynamics, and institutional priorities. Vendor contracts have evolved from traditional, one-size-fits-all legacy agreements to complex modern contracts. Legacy agreements often lack detailed provisions for technology integration, data security, and compliance. Modern contracts are more comprehensive and reflective of the organization's unique needs, addressing issues such as data protection, service levels, compliance with specific regulations, and technological requirements.

Managing vendor relationships and negotiating contracts and licenses for various services, resources, tools, and products involve a multifaceted set of challenges and opportunities. These days, negotiating a print library maintenance agreement (LMA) seems clear and seamless compared to embarking on licensing annual maintenance fees, electronic content, databases, or services. In addition to budget considerations, institutions must navigate a complex landscape to ensure they secure favorable contracts while complying with state and federal laws, privacy regulations, and guidelines. For some institutions, particularly public academic universities, licensing and privacy regulations and policies can be more restrictive than state and federal laws. This brings up unique challenges when working with vendors who are not legally required to agree to terms and conditions that are not enforceable. The negotiation process for private institutions or law firm libraries, which have more autonomy in negotiating and assuming liability, might be less complex and lengthy.

Negotiating with vendors presents several challenges:

- Complex Terms and Conditions: Vendor contracts often include legal terms that can be difficult to understand and negotiate. Institutions must have staff, or access to their legal department, with the expertise and skill to ensure agreements align with their specific needs and comply with applicable laws and regulations.
- Budget Constraints: Institutions facing budget challenges may be limited in their ability to secure optimal terms. Negotiating favorable pricing while adhering to budgetary constraints requires strategic planning and flexibility.
- Contractual Obligations: Institutions must carefully review contractual obligations to avoid potential liabilities. This includes understanding renewal terms, service level agreements, and exit clauses.
- Data Security and Privacy: Ensuring that vendor agreements comply with privacy regulations, particularly regarding Personally Identifiable Information (PII) and Family Educational Rights and Privacy Act (FERPA)[23] is crucial. Contracts should stipulate how vendors handle data, storage, and security protocols.
- Technology Integration: Vendors provide tools and systems that must be able to integrate with existing infrastructure and systems. The challenge lies in testing compatibility and minimizing accessibility and service disruptions during and after implementation.

Consider the negotiation process with major legal research database vendors such as Westlaw, LexisNexis, and Bloomberg Law, where each of the stated challenges above needs careful consideration. Additionally, each vendor offers unique features and pricing models, which can complicate comparisons and decision-making. When it comes to legal databases such as these, institutions must weigh the benefits of comprehensive databases against the costs, considering both immediate needs and long-term value.

In addition to the universal challenges already stated, unique challenges can arise depending on memberships your institution is part of, such as consortia or alliances, and other factors such as academic institutions with multiple libraries that share one ILS. Unique challenges arose when the Gallagher Law Library negotiated terms with OCLC to license Tipasa,[24] a library management resource-sharing service. The process was lengthy and required careful vendor negotiations with OCLC, the University Privacy and Procurement Offices, and the IT department to address issues such as user access, privacy, data sharing, and system integration. Because UW Libraries and the Gallagher Law Library have a shared ILS but separate resource-sharing services to meet the needs of unique patron groups (law vs. non-law), full integration of Tipasa into the ILS was not possible. Additionally, some of the tools and features of Tipasa were in violation of the institution's privacy guidelines. Careful consideration of these circumstances and guidelines necessitated that Gallagher Law Library opt out of some features of Tipasa, and they were unable to integrate others due to system limitations and potentially unwanted effects in a shared ILS environment. Institutions must be able to guarantee compliance with privacy and data security standards and be flexible and adaptive to provide the services needed to ensure access to information.

LaptopsAnytime[25] is a manufacturer of customizable kiosks that dispense laptops and chargers to meet libraries' specific needs. Their support includes on-site setup, annual maintenance and service contracts, as well as ongoing communication and adaptation to ensure the kiosks continue to meet institutional needs and requirements. When embarking on acquiring these kiosks, the Gallagher Law Library and UW Privacy Office identified a specific concern regarding the camera feature on these kiosks that can capture PII. Through negotiations with UW Privacy, Law IT, and LaptopsAnytime, they were able to create a customized cover that blocked access to the camera and disabled it and included this in the contract. Institutions must evaluate how equipment and services like these handle data, including camera footage, and comply with privacy regulations. Clear policies and agreements should address data security and user privacy concerns.

Vendor relations, licensing negotiations, and privacy concerns represent significant and continually growing areas of focus for academic institutions. This is especially important with the integration of AI into many legal databases and resources already licensed by law libraries. By understanding the continually changing landscape, addressing challenges, and leveraging the skills and expertise of law librarians and other units within the organization, institutions can ensure compliance and navigate these complexities effectively. The evolution of vendor contracts, from legacy to modern agreements, reflects the growing sophistication and demands of academic environments. Alerting the vendor to specific processes and/or policy requirements of your institution at the beginning of the negotiation process will benefit both parties, help your vendor better understand the landscape at your institution, and hopefully avoid delays in service. Through careful management and negotiation, institutions can secure favorable agreements and uphold their commitment to privacy and data security.

IMPLEMENTATION

Implementing vendor solutions effectively is essential for optimizing library operations and improving user experience. Finding vendors that offer collaborative and flexible onboarding services can significantly improve law libraries' offerings and use of those services. Positive indications from vendors of collaborative and flexible onboarding services include frequent communication, a clear invitation to hear what the library's needs are, a desire to know specific limitations, and a willingness to collaborate with libraries' IT departments.[26] A lack of these indicators is a red flag that the vendor may not be a good fit for your institution.

Transitioning to a new service always presents challenges and requires a period of adjustment. Choosing vendors that can help law librarians with hands-on onboarding can drastically improve this process and experience. Vendors like OCLC offer onboarding cohorts for their cloud-based resource-sharing solution, OCLC Tipasa. Having a cohort of librarians experiencing a similar transition can be extremely helpful. This makes the work more manageable for the vendor, as they're able to batch training, and it creates a support system for librarians.

To determine whether a service might benefit from this reimagining and new technology, employing the "5 Whys and the 5 Hows" can be a helpful strategy for getting to the heart of a problem and identifying whether it can be solved in a different way. This strategy was originally developed by Sakichi Toyoda to find the nature of a problem and its solution.[27] A library should begin by asking a series of "why" and "how" questions before approaching a solution, see table 6.1. When manual workflows are in place, there's often an automated solution available; it's just a matter of asking around until you find the right vendor. Modernizing and automating services like resource sharing or aspects of collection development not only enhance efficiency, but also empower libraries to better serve their user's needs.

Automation Technology

Automation technology in a law library refers to the use of software and hardware systems to streamline tasks like cataloging, circulation, and data management. By automating processes such as checkouts, the physical processing of materials, and aspects of collection management, law libraries can improve efficiency and provide expanded access to their resources. The two examples covered here illustrate the value that can be added from a collection development perspective.

GOBI

Collaborating with vendors like GOBI allows libraries to explore solutions that automate aspects of collection development. Library-specific vendors such as GOBI offer a wide range of custom solutions that can help automate and expedite library workflows. Collection assessments and GOBIAlerts are some of their underutilized services that libraries should absolutely take full advantage of. They also offer shelf-ready solutions, electronic data interchange (EDI) invoicing, demand-driven or evidence-based acquisitions (DDA and EBA), different levels of cataloging services, and approval plans.

Table 6.1 The 5 Whys and the 5 Hows

Example of 5 Whys Strategy: *Issue: Spending too much time on resource-sharing requests*	
Due date reminders sent manually via email	Why?
There's no automation for this process	Why?
The current platform lacks this feature	Why?
Other platforms offer this service	Why?
Lack of exploration of alternative platforms	Why?
Example of 5 Hows Strategy:	
Automate reminders and notifications	How?
Integrate more workflow automations	How?
Evaluate other platforms	How?
Leverage vendor relations to find better solutions	How?
Implement a streamlined system	How?

GOBI can conduct collection assessments to examine specific subjects within a library's collection to fill in any gaps. For example, a library could conduct a collection assessment to identify whether there are gaps in a specific subject matter of strong interest to the law library. This is particularly useful for identifying gaps in diversity, equity, and inclusion subject matter or if the library has a particular focus, such as Native American Law. Some libraries even use these assessments to help spend gift funds when faced with restrictive collecting parameters associated with the fund. Time frames can be set around the assessment, and the vendor can work with a library to ensure the content they're providing is within the specifications the library assigns. Some libraries may not want to purchase content published outside of the past five years, as an example of a specification GOBI can filter.

There are many positive outcomes from working with a vendor and paying for the service that would otherwise be conducted by a librarian. Having a vendor assess collection gaps can lead to improvements in slip plans and collection development policies and create a more well-represented collection. Sometimes these assessments can also reaffirm that the library is purchasing all published content in an area. This is a good way for a law library to confirm that its current collecting practices are in line with where it would like them to be.

Another advantage to partnering with GOBI is the ability to create and utilize GOBIAlerts. This feature within GOBI lets libraries set up tailored profiles for selection librarians or faculty. While the setup is labor-intensive, it then creates a way for faculty and librarians to recommend titles for purchase directly to the collection management librarian, who can evaluate them for purchase. These customizable features can be tailored to meet libraries' unique needs and allow them to do more with a smaller staff. These profiles are a result of ongoing dialogues and understanding between the librarians and the vendor.

OCLC GreenGlass

Periodically revisiting and reinvestigating what a vendor's services can do for a library is worthwhile. Libraries and the services vendors offer change quickly. Just because a vendor didn't seem like the right solution to a problem four years ago doesn't mean they aren't now. Maintaining open communication with the vendor and consortia partners can lead to meeting library needs in unexpected ways. Sometimes a misunderstanding about services can lead a library to years of doing manual work that could be automated with the help of a vendor.

OCLC GreenGlass is a web-based application that provides libraries with insights into their collections, including the number of copies, holdings of other libraries, and online duplication. In 2021, the UW Libraries procured GreenGlass to assess their collection. The Gallagher Law Library was hesitant to participate due to a misunderstanding about the product's capabilities, deciding it wasn't worth the effort or time investment. However, several years later in 2024, after following up with the vendor and consulting with their counterparts at UW Libraries, Gallagher law librarians learned that the product met the law library's needs.

The platform's ability to sort collections by factors like uniqueness or duplication, whether in print, through a partner library, or electronically proves particularly helpful for collection management. These features can assist libraries interested in moving unique and rare materials that they wish to preserve out of circulation. These are also useful metrics when weeding the collection. While it is possible to perform this work manually using OCLC WorldShare and searching title by title, it is incredibly time-consuming. Maintaining relationships with vendors and consortia, continuously attending trainings as services evolve, and staying curious about improving workflows and services are essential tools in a librarian's toolbox.

CONCLUSION

Vendor relationships play a pivotal role in modern law librarianship. They provide opportunities to improve access to information, optimize operations, and offer innovative services. Through collaboration, negotiation, and effective implementation of vendor services, products, and solutions, law libraries can overcome numerous challenges and seize opportunities for growth and improvement.

For law libraries to stay relevant and effective, they must prioritize accessibility and improve efficiency by leveraging vendor partnerships. Georgie Donovan, Associate Dean for Collections and Content Services at William & Mary Libraries from 2015 to 2020, asserts that "creativity, flexibility, listening, and trying to understand the vendor's goals helps lead not only to a positive long-term relationship, but to better pricing and terms."[28] Vendors should be viewed as strategic allies in enhancing access to justice through improved access to information. By continuously exploring and revisiting vendor offerings, libraries can maximize the benefits of these partnerships. Embracing innovation and outsourcing where appropriate can significantly improve accessibility, operational efficiency, and quality of service. Adopting automated solutions and fostering effective vendor relationships will ultimately benefit the entire library community, ensuring that law libraries remain vital collaborators, innovators, and stakeholders in their roles, and within their legal community.

NOTES

1. Kirsten Ostergaard and Doralyn Rossmann, "There's Work to Be Done: Exploring Library-Vendor Relations," *Technical Services Quarterly* 34, no. 1 (2017): 13
2. J. Michael Thompson and Carol Seiler, "Library-Vendor Partnerships - An Overview of Our Symbiotic Relationships," *Against the Grain* 30, no. 2 (2018): 16.
   Keith Courtney, "Library/Vendor Relations: An Academic Publisher's Perspective: Library/Vendor Relationships," *Journal of Library Administration* 44, no. 3-4 (2006): 57-58.
3. Sam Brooks, "Introduction: The Importance of Open Communication Between Libraries and Vendors," *Journal of Library Administration* 44, no. 3-4 (October 2006): 1-2.
4. Laurel Sammonds Crawford and Allyson Rodriguez, "Evolving Ethos and Etiquette: Why and How We Altered Our Library-Vendor Relationships," in S. Marien ed., *Library technical services: Adapting to the changing environment* (Purdue University Press, 2020), 402.
5. EBSCO, "GOBI Library Solutions," accessed August 9, 2024, https://www.ebsco.com/products/gobi-library-solutions.
6. Maaike Oldemans and Jennifer Kronenbitter, "Technical Metamorphosis by Design," in S. Marien ed., *Library technical services: Adapting to the changing environment* (Purdue University Press, 2020), 325.
7. Barbara Kawecki, "Transforming Library Vendor Relations: Turning Relationships into Partnerships," *Against the Grain* 30, no. 2 (2018): 14.
8. Rhonda Y. Kauffman and Martina S. Anderson, "Diversity, Inclusion, and Social Justice in Library Technical Services," in S. Marien ed., *Library technical services: Adapting to the changing environment* (Purdue University Press, 2020), 227.
9. HeinOnline, "The Fastest-Growing Multidisciplinary Research Platform," accessed August 9, 2024, https://home.heinonline.org/.
10. HeinOnline, "West academic Casebooks Archive," accessed August 9, 2024, https://home.heinonline.org/content/west-academic-casebooks-archive/.
11. LLMC, "LLMC Digital," accessed August 9, 2024, https://llmc.com/.
12. LLMC, "LLMC Digital Open Access," accessed August 9, 2024, https://llmc.com/openaccess/search.aspx.
13. George Machovec, "Consortial Partnerships with Libraries and Vendors," *Against the Grain* 30, no. 2 (2018): 26.
14. Springshare, "We Help Libraries Thrive in a Digital-First World," accessed August 9, 2024, https://www.springshare.com/.
15. OCLC, "Get the Tools You Need Now," accessed August 9, 2024, https://www.oclc.org/en/home.html.
16. Meescan, "Meescan Self-Checkout," accessed August 9, 2024, https://meescan.com/.
17. George Machovec, "Consortial Partnerships with Libraries and Vendors," *Against the Grain* 30, no. 2 (2018): 27.

18. Orbis Cascade Alliance, "About the Alliance," accessed August 9, 2024, https://www.orbiscascade.org/about/.
19. Waldo, "WALDO: Westchester Academic Library Directors Organization," accessed August 12, 2024, https://waldo.lyrasis.org/index.html.
20. Lyrasis, "About Lyrasis," accessed August 12, 2024, https://www.lyrasis.org/about/Pages/default.aspx.
21. Susanne Markgren, "Challenging the Status Quo: Collaboration and Creativity in Small Academic Libraries," in *Marien, S. (2020). Library technical services : adapting to the changing environment. Purdue University Press.* 303.
22. Springshare, "Springshare is Committed to Access for Everyone!," accessed August 9, 2024, https://www.springshare.com/accessibility.html.
23. U.S. Department of Education, "Family Educational Rights and Privacy Act (FERPA)," accessed August 9, 2024, https://www2.ed.gov/policy/gen/guid/fpco/ferpa/index.html.
24. OCLC, "Tipasa," accessed August 12, 2024, https://www.oclc.org/en/tipasa.html.
25. LaptopsAnytime, "Automated Checkout Kiosks," accessed August 9, 2024, https://www.laptopsanytime.com/.
26. Kirsten Ostergaard and Doralyn Rossmann, "There's Work to Be Done: Exploring Library-Vendor Relations," *Technical Services Quarterly* 34, no. 1 (2017): 13–33.
27. American Society for Quality, "Five Whys and Five Hows," accessed August 12, 2024, https://asq.org/quality-resources/five-whys.
28. Georgie Donovan, "The Myth of the Tough Negotiator," *Against the Grain* 30, no. (2018): 22.

7

Institutional Knowledge Management and Succession Planning

Amy Carr and Sabrina Sondhi

The buzz-phrases "institutional knowledge" and "succession planning" are not new concepts. People generally agree that these ideas are important and that organizations and workplaces should be pursuing these goals. However, many libraries and workplaces do not spend the necessary time to create and implement succession plans, which backfires and creates crises when employees retire, change jobs, or go on extended leave.

One of the ways to think about institutional knowledge is to consider it as recorded or unrecorded information that explains how the workplace functions. It often includes historical and financial records of the institution, but for the purposes of this chapter, think of it as the collected wisdom of how the organization operates. This can include common knowledge, such as where a certain person's desk is located and where copier paper is stored. But it can also include things you don't necessarily need daily and likely were not a part of onboarding, for example, what paperwork is needed to add a new vendor, how to requisition a new desk chair, and how to make the computer system generate a year-end report. When these infrequent issues come up, there is most likely a specific person who can get them resolved. These are all straightforward tasks but can pose significant productivity challenges if that specific person is not present.

Succession planning, at its most basic level, is "any effort designed to ensure the continued effective performance of an organization, division, department, or work group by providing for the development, replacement, and strategic application of key people over time."[1] Succession plans draw upon recorded institutional knowledge and can take many forms, but most often come into play when an organization goes through personnel changes. Particularly when workers have specialized functions or duties, with little overlap, personnel changes can cause a gap in your workforce, which poses problems for everyone. However, a succession plan can prevent these problems. A succession plan acts as a "[s]ystematic effort by the library to ensure continuity in key positions, retain and develop intellectual and knowledge capital for the future, and encourage individual advancement."[2]

WHY IS SUCCESSION PLANNING NECESSARY AND BENEFICIAL?

When an employee leaves for a new job elsewhere, there is a negative impact on their former workplace. Replacing an employee takes both time and money; meanwhile, their work duties may not be getting done efficiently or at all. Studies show that completing an external hire usually takes one to three months.[3] During that time, workflows may stall, tasks may pile up, and your remaining employees are often ineffectively shouldering additional burdens. That extra work and stress can lead to burnout and more employees leaving. A study on LinkedIn showed that 59 percent of respondents considered leaving their job as a direct result of a colleague's resignation.[4]

Having a succession plan won't stop an employee from leaving their job for new opportunities, but it will make the transition smoother and create a stable environment for the remaining employees while a new hire is brought on board. A good succession plan will also help identify and develop talented employees who already have leadership roles for internal promotion. This can create a culture of learning and growth that aids in employee retention. Reviewing and recording workflows helps employees understand how their tasks contribute to the organization's end goals. This often boosts individual employee motivation and group morale. Finally, succession planning is an excellent tool for furthering DEI. Due to its focus on objective processes and competencies, succession planning tends to reduce conscious and unconscious bias when it comes to providing opportunities and developmental support to employees.

HOW TO GET STARTED MAKING A SUCCESSION PLAN

If the idea of a succession plan seems daunting, it can be helpful to break it down into smaller elements and frame it as an extension of existing activities. Consider that staff development encompasses succession planning. Thinking about critical roles and cross-training to ensure coverage is engaging in staff development in a very intentional way. It involves committing to creating redundancy of specialized skills among your staff. However, to do this successfully, there need to be well-defined job descriptions.

Beginning a succession plan is an excellent time to review and revise job descriptions. Generally, staff should have a clear understanding of their tasks, and those tasks should be accurately reflected in their job descriptions. It is good practice to review and update these descriptions annually because they are imperative for succession planning. Accurate job descriptions become a valuable tool for assessing how potential absences could be covered and by whom. Solo librarians and library directors will need to engage senior leaders in understanding library duties and determining who can step in as needed.

Intuitively, we all know how important the preservation of institutional knowledge is, but how often do we take the necessary steps to ensure we're capturing it? A succession plan is a wonderful impetus for setting up an in-house repository. This can also create an opportunity for staff to showcase their expertise as you have them write instructions and deliver training related to their roles. Including staff in this way has multiple benefits—ensuring task instructions are accurate, creating buy-in for the plan itself, and strengthening intra- and interdepartmental relationships.

Here are the steps for forming a strong succession plan:

- Communicate the value of a plan and create buy-in.
- Identify workflows and positions that need a plan; update job descriptions.
- Identify which of your staff can develop and grow for the future.
- Record the plan in a shared space and include measurable goals for implementation.
- Implement the plan immediately, for example, cross-training, development, etc.
- Periodic reassessment as your goals, needs, and personnel change.

Over the course of this chapter, we will cover each in detail and share some examples of how to implement them in your workplace.

COMMUNICATION

It is critical in any succession planning effort to provide clear and comprehensive communication about the plan. You need to engage your staff so they understand the reason behind the plan, how it will be implemented, and its value to them individually as well as to the department and organization. It's also important that senior leadership be aware of and (ideally) supportive of the effort. Especially for solo or small staff organizations, it's a given that you'll need to rely on and include staff from other departments to ensure continuity of service in the event of staff absences.

Creating and implementing a succession plan can feel destabilizing if staff don't fully understand the rationale for the initiative. Putting the plan together takes time and effort. It's natural for people to feel proud of, and perhaps even a little territorial about, their contributions to the organization. Staff may be reluctant to participate, either as trainers or trainees. They may believe succession planning will make them or their roles superfluous. This may hinder the development of the plan as individuals slow down or actively sabotage the process.

However, even if only to cover absences, a succession plan can be enormously helpful. Therefore, a key first step is to explain to the staff how this plan will produce competency in people who are willing and able to step in and assist when others are out. Cross-training also increases individual employees' value to the organization and gives them the opportunity to develop additional skill sets. Finally, succession planning can help staff to better understand how individual roles fit together, leading to synergies in problem-solving and workflow improvements.

Another way to communicate the benefit of creating a plan is to highlight real problems that your department or library has experienced due to siloed knowledge. For example, the time when no one knew how to issue a new Lexis password to a visiting faculty member during the week your senior reference librarian was on vacation. Or the time when your firm library was charged for a print treatise that had been mistakenly delivered but no one realized until after the return period had passed because your processing librarian was on maternity leave. You can use real-life examples to explain why succession planning is valuable even if your workforce remains stable.

Communicating the value of succession planning to your senior leadership is essential, particularly if you're a solo practitioner or have such a small staff that you'll need to rely on people outside the department for assistance. In this case, a frank discussion about department responsibilities and their importance to the organization is crucial. Focus on the aspects of service that are most essential so you can ensure coverage at least at that level.

For example, the solo librarian at a midsize firm was out for a medical procedure. The firm knew this would happen and felt like they had planned for it. However, her anticipated two-week absence turned into an unexpected two-month leave. Staff weren't equipped to fill in at all the necessary levels and work went undone. When she returned, she spent most of her time resolving mistakes and addressing issues that fell through the cracks, which put her behind in keeping up with current tasks. This forced the firm to realize the importance of having a true succession plan.

Once you have senior leadership buy-in and have identified the interdepartmental staff who can fill in as needed, it's critical that you open lines of communication with those individuals to explain the plan. It can be difficult to ask people to assume additional responsibilities, especially if they aren't related to their primary role. This is why clearly identifying the essential services and their organizational importance will be key to success. In an ideal world, all the groundwork for the plan is laid *before* you need it!

GATHER AND REFINE INFORMATION

Succession planning lets us imagine our department in the future. It allows us to consider what our office or library will look like in five or ten years and what skills will be needed. It also gives us an opportunity to evaluate our staff's strengths and weaknesses. We're all familiar with the scenario of a high performer with no possibility of immediate promotion. Succession planning can provide substantive professional development for individuals—challenging them and allowing them to broaden their skills now rather than letting them stagnate. Building these skills and competencies can benefit the individual and the organization over time.

Initiating the succession plan itself can provide opportunities for staff development. For instance, in a law firm with a large library staff, the director asked one of her high-performing direct reports to head up the succession planning effort. This not only preserved the director's time so she could focus on other pressing issues, but it also gave the staff member a chance to spearhead a major departmental initiative. Regular check-in meetings were scheduled with the director to confirm the staff member was on track, and the director could provide guidance as needed.

Begin by assessing the roles in your department. Ask yourself these questions: What are your workflows and how do individuals contribute to those workflows? Are your workflows documented? Do job descriptions accurately reflect what your staff actually do on a regular basis? Even though developing a succession plan provides an excellent opportunity to review and revise *all* job descriptions, don't get bogged down in the details at this point. Not every role or task needs to be included in your plan. Instead, consider those individuals who perform key tasks that must be done to support the department's work. This is where you'll focus your initial efforts on building documentation and providing training. You can return to revising additional job descriptions later.

For example, when the acquisitions librarian at a large academic library was scheduled to go on three months of planned maternity leave, she asked herself, "What tasks do I do that cannot wait for my return?" She narrowed her many duties down to three time-sensitive tasks: unsolicited items needed to be returned, a staff member's timesheets needed to be approved, and a report showing declining fund balances needed to be run weekly for the selectors. These three tasks didn't need to be performed by the same person, but they did need to happen! In consultation with the library director, these tasks were written up in a step-by-step fashion by the acquisitions librarian, and the assignees had the opportunity to shadow the librarian before she went on leave. Since the library could plan for this event, everything went smoothly. Furthermore, creating that plan also meant that the following year, when that same librarian went on a two-week vacation, staff already knew what needed to be done in her absence and had a system in place to keep things moving.

While a succession plan is ostensibly for replacing staff who retire or take a new job, it can also help in those instances when staff are out unexpectedly, especially when those absences will be longer than a few days. The time and effort you and your staff spend documenting work processes, training substitutes or replacements, and developing cross-department relationships will pay dividends in these situations as you're able to seamlessly shift duties and responsibilities. It also means the individuals who step in to help will feel confident about their ability to successfully handle that temporary task.

DEVELOP YOUR STAFF

Reviewing job descriptions, identifying key tasks, and cross-training staff for key roles are all good opportunities to support and reward your high performers. If you have employees whose skills are underutilized or who are at risk of seeking a more senior position elsewhere, now is your chance to create a culture of learning and growth so they can have internal opportunities. Objectively identifying essential tasks that have organizational importance and then cross-training helps employees understand their value to your organization and confirms to them that their performance is trusted.

For example, at a large academic library, a member of the collections maintenance staff volunteered to be cross-trained to cover absences in other library departments. Due to her familiarity with multiple workflows, over the next six years she was hired as a serials processing clerk, and then, after completing her MLS degree, as a cataloger. Her deep knowledge of how these multiple departments and workflows functioned gave her an advantage over outside candidates. This meant that the library was able to retain a valued employee, whereas otherwise she might have sought promotion elsewhere.

At a large law firm, several individuals who felt stagnant in their roles were reenergized and reengaged by participating in the succession planning initiative. One of the technical services staff members proved extremely adept at teaching others. When the process began, he hadn't even known he'd enjoy teaching, let alone excel at it. This person wasn't necessarily at risk of leaving the organization; however, he was becoming increasingly dissatisfied. Feelings like this can lead to people underperforming over time. Identifying ways to provide both personal and professional growth makes it more likely that they will remain and continue to be solid contributors. In this case, the director worked with the staff member and his manager to incorporate this new skill set into his responsibilities, benefiting him and the department.

WRITE IT DOWN

All the work of revising job descriptions, identifying crucial roles and work processes, and cross-training will be for naught if you don't record the plan. Be sure this documentation is in a place where others can find it and that they know where that is—especially if you're relying on staff outside your department. A shared drive is ideal.

Instructions should be written by the primary task holder, and workflows should be detailed enough to allow someone with little to no experience to step in and get to work. It may be helpful to have a separate document that explains why a workflow or policy is the way it is. Decisions that seem obvious to you may be mysterious to others. Someone who is doing a single task in isolation to help out will have an easier time and likely do a better job if they understand why it's done a certain way.

For example, after a small academic library's processing clerk retired, the librarian who temporarily took on the task of monograph processing considered the multitude of steps too finicky and unnecessary. They thought: Why take the time to write the processing date on the verso when not doing so would save lots of time? A few months later, the interlibrary loan librarian discovered that new books didn't include this handwritten date, which affected efficiency for her role! She could no longer quickly determine whether her library had held the book for at least a year, which was an internal rule designed to give their patrons a first chance at new purchases before allowing them to be lent to other libraries. So that "time-wasting" processing step was necessary after all and for a reason that the new processing librarian could not have guessed.

Similarly, in a midsize firm, local office staff were assigned to file library materials without an appropriate understanding of the need for timeliness in completing this task. This is a great example of the primary library staff member intuitively realizing this necessity but forgetting to impart that in the instructions and training provided.

Having thorough and readily available documentation relating to both workflows and employees' responsibilities will help cover potential absences ahead of time. It also helps ensure coverage of vital, specialized tasks during a hiring timeline. This is when written documentation really shines.

You won't be able to do all of this by yourself, even if you're a solo librarian. No one works completely alone and, even if you are very familiar with your institution, you still may not know all the details that go into a good succession plan. When possible, have the staff who perform the tasks in question write down the instructions and cross-train their colleagues. If you encounter resistance, for example, a staff member doesn't explain a workflow in enough detail for others to understand it, remember that a person who performs a specific task repeatedly may consider it obvious or straightforward. Take the time to walk through the steps with them and ask questions. If need be, take notes and edit the written workflow to the necessary level of detail yourself; then your staff member can simply confirm that it is correct.

Different organizations use different approaches to capture their succession plan documentation. A small legal tech company relied on a productivity and note-taking web application. This was an easy way to assemble information in a location that was accessible to all and could be updated as needed. A large law firm's library staff used their document management system. Each workgroup had its own folder with nested subfolders that were viewable by everyone. A midsize law firm with a solo librarian set up space on a shared drive. This allowed for greater flexibility with folder structure than the more locked-down document management system.

Each option has pros and cons. You'll need to determine the right approach for your organization.

IMPLEMENT IT

The next step in the journey is to implement the succession plan. Speak to your staff about the nuts and bolts of this process. Be sure to cover the basics. Who is being cross-trained? Who will provide the training? What are the goals of this implementation phase?

It's understandable to feel like the hardest part has been accomplished by the time you reach implementation. You've set up lines of communication and gotten buy-in, you've identified roles and responsibilities, you've assembled documentation and created a repository for it. However, implementation is what matters most. Don't undo all that hard work by stumbling now!

Implementation is critical to successfully handling unanticipated absences and stepping in when someone leaves the organization. Staff need to know what they'll be responsible for and why and how to find the instructions for their tasks. Success in this area really relies on the strength and clarity of your documentation and goal-setting. For example, if "Nora" is going on vacation for two weeks, it should be straightforward and easy for her supervisor and colleagues to check the documentation, see what tasks must continue to be performed, and know who has *already* been cross-trained to perform them. Similarly, if "David" has a family emergency and will be away for an unspecified extended period of time, the same process applies.

Goal setting means that you should have a checklist of what your implementation phase includes. Your checklist should cover what cross-training needs to occur, what documentation needs to be expanded, and whether any problems or concerns have arisen that need to be addressed. Only when all these tasks have been completed can you say that you have a succession plan in place!

A staff member at a large law firm tasked with succession planning used project management software and held regular meetings with workgroup managers to ensure training was completed. This was also wrapped into the annual review process with the expectation that everyone participated in the effort. Although the process was informal for a midsized firm, a checklist helped to keep the project on track. In both cases, substitutes shadowed the staff they'd be covering for and then did the work themselves, with the primary staff member confirming for accuracy.

Often, firms require staff to complete a certain number of professional development hours each year. Speak to your HR or staff development department to see if this cross-training would qualify. This option may make trainees more enthusiastic about participating.

ONGOING ASSESSMENT

A good succession plan is an iterative process. It's important to periodically reassess job descriptions, roles and responsibilities, documentation, and assigned substitutes. It can help to play out scenarios, imagining what would happen if someone were absent or unavailable. How will needed tasks get done? Who knows how to do them? Where is the documentation to assist them? Do you need to update your plan to reflect any changes? Considering these questions allows you to be proactive rather than reactive.

Ongoing improvement allows you to continue to include your staff in the succession planning process, which furthers their individual and collective development, builds morale, and fosters a workplace that is centered on shared purpose and respect.

Both a large and a midsize law firm decided to make this assessment part of their annual review process each year. It was an obvious time to reevaluate job descriptions and assigned responsibilities and to make any changes or updates to the plan. A legal tech company also opted for an annual review, but they decoupled it from staff reviews. Instead, they decided to do this at the end of the fourth quarter when they had more time to focus on reassessing and updating the plan.

WHAT IF I'M A SOLO LIBRARIAN?

Thus far, our discussion of succession planning has focused on departments with multiple staff members. If you're a solo librarian or in a very small department, this is for you! Remember that you're not alone. While you may need to look to staff in other departments to fill out your succession plan, the good news is this is very doable and normal practice. It can also be a wonderful opportunity to build strong, mutually beneficial interdepartmental relationships and increase the visibility of the library and its services.

Generally, the steps in succession planning for solo or small staff libraries are similar to those for larger libraries. Execution is where the plans differ, and it's important to factor that into your process.

Communication/Information Gathering. In a solo or small staff situation, getting buy-in and support from senior leaders and individuals in other departments is critical. You must identify people who can continue to provide service in the event of an absence, and you want to set them up for success. You may need to involve multiple people to ensure coverage while respecting primary responsibilities.

Who will you need to speak with to get this process started? Is there someone in the C-suite who can approve and champion this initiative, which may be necessary to get help from other departments?

Think about the services offered by your department. Which are essential? It may help to prioritize all your responsibilities so you can clearly determine what tasks must be done versus those that can be sidelined temporarily. For example, after assessing, you may decide your essential services are getting research questions answered, library invoices paid, and materials checked in.

Before taking this list to senior leaders, consider how these services affect the organization. What would the impact be if tasks weren't completed or service was suspended? Who would be most affected? These are the points that will be meaningful to the organization's decision-makers.

Another question you'll need to be able to answer is how much time it will take someone to complete these tasks. It's difficult to ask someone to fill in if they don't understand what that commitment will look like when added to their other work responsibilities.

Your priority list may also make it easier to decide which staff members outside your department can be most helpful. For example, if paying library invoices is a critical task, someone in the accounting department might be a natural fit to take on that responsibility.

Documenting. This step becomes even more important when you are relying on people outside the library. Earlier, we mentioned providing the rationale for tasks, perhaps in a separate document if that makes sense. This is very helpful for staff who work in other departments, particularly if they're being asked to take on a responsibility that is different from their primary role. Instructions should be clear and concise. Meet with the individuals who might need to fill in and have them review the instructions to identify any areas of confusion. Then, correct the document to ensure clarity.

Another key element is storing this documentation in an easily accessible location. This might be your document management system with viewable folders or perhaps a shared drive. Ensure all staff, not just senior leaders, can access the repository.

Implementing. As with the documentation step, implementation is critically important when staff from other departments are part of your succession plan. Remember that these staff may not have the same understanding of processes and procedures as library staff do. Help them see the value in what you're asking them to do and how it affects the organization more broadly.

It is possible that staff may feel anxious about needing to provide library services. You can increase their confidence by giving them an opportunity to shadow you as you complete the tasks you'll be asking them to do. It's even better if you can give them the chance to walk through the instructions and complete the task themselves. Finding time to schedule this training may be challenging, but it's essential to the success of your plan. Here is where your relationship with the C-suite may prove helpful in breaking through logjams.

Earlier we mentioned that it might be possible for your HR or staff development department to award professional development credits for this cross-training. If your firm requires staff to earn a specific number of professional development credits each year, this can be a great way to get more enthusiastic participation. Approach them and see if they'd be willing to assign credits to the training.

Finally, be sure to thank staff from other departments for their willingness to take on this additional responsibility. This simple acknowledgment can do a lot to build a collegial and supportive environment.

Assessment. The need for periodic assessment of the succession plan is the same for solo or small staff libraries as for those with larger staff.

In addition to monitoring any changes to your processes or services, you'll want to keep an eye on staff changes in the departments listed in your plan. If substitute staff leave the organization, you'll need to identify a new person who can help. Then you must work through the training process with them so they're ready to go when an absence occurs. Even if there is no turnover, it makes sense to revisit the instructions and the substitutes' understanding of the process periodically. A refresher session may be advisable, perhaps on an annual basis.

These steps should get you started on your own succession plan. Don't be afraid to tweak them to fit your environment. You know what will work best for your organization. The important takeaway is how essential a succession plan is to maintaining service. The work you put in up-front will be more than worth it when you need to implement the plan.

CONCLUSION

By now, we hope you recognize the value of developing a succession plan and feel empowered to create one for your own library. Use the steps above as a guide while honoring the uniqueness of your organization. Adjust this process as needed to suit your particular situation.

Remember, the plan doesn't need to be immensely detailed on your first attempt. Prioritize the most important tasks and begin there. It's better to have a rough plan in place and a checklist of improvements to add rather than no implemented plan at all. A good succession plan lets you prepare for the future while improving the present.

Keep in mind that you don't have to be the only one creating a plan. Engage others in the process and distribute tasks when you can. Bringing your department together to work on this initiative can result in a greater sense of shared purpose and will promote buy-in.

Succession planning can often result in surprising benefits for you, your department, and your organization. Examining individuals' contributions to the whole may lead to implementing workflow changes and process improvements. Discovering new abilities in your staff allows you to reimagine roles and responsibilities. You may develop or strengthen relationships both within your department and with other departments in your organization. Ultimately, everyone benefits when a good succession plan is in place.

NOTES

1. William J. Rothwell, *Effective Succession Planning* (New York: Amacom, 2010), 6.
2. Paula M. Singer, with Gail Griffith, *Succession Planning in the Library: Developing Leaders, Managing Change* (New York: ALA, 2010), 1.
3. Jennifer Soper, "Internal vs. External Recruitment: A Guide for Small Businesses," last modified August 23, 2016, https://fitsmallbusiness.com/internal-vs-external-recruiting/.
4. Cathy Anderson, "Is 'The Great Resignation' Contagious?," *LinkedIn News*, 2022, https://www.linkedin.com/posts/linkedin-news_is-the-great-resignation-contagious-activity6889270475533381632-WzTU?utm_source=share&utm_medium=member_desktop.

8

How to Create a Strategic Plan and Prove the ROI of the Library

Rachel Gordon and Marci Wilding

In today's dynamic legal landscape, law libraries are experiencing profound transformations driven by technological advancements, evolving user expectations, and the imperative for cost-effective operations. As key players in legal research and knowledge management, law libraries must navigate these changes strategically to remain relevant and impactful. This chapter explores the crucial role of strategic planning in guiding law libraries through these challenges and seizing new opportunities, focusing on the need for alignment with user needs, stakeholder expectations, and the demonstration of Return on Investment (ROI).

Strategic planning is crucial for law libraries to define their mission, set clear goals, and allocate resources effectively. Law libraries are often perceived as cost centers within organizations, viewed primarily in terms of the resources they consume rather than the value they generate in access, privacy, democracy, diversity, education, and intellectual freedom.[1] This perception underscores the importance of strategic planning, which can help law libraries demonstrate their value by aligning their services with organizational goals and measuring their impact in terms of ROI.

In an era of budget constraints and increasing demands for transparency and accountability, strategic planning enables law libraries to demonstrate their value to stakeholders. For instance, higher education has transformed from focusing on programs and departments unable to offer a ROI to focusing on the needs of the job market and the acquisition of discreet skills.[2] Law libraries need to use strategic planning to help identify key performance indicators (KPIs) and metrics for measuring their impact. By tracking these metrics and communicating their achievements, law libraries can build trust and secure support from stakeholders, ensuring their continued relevance and success.

CRAFTING A STRATEGIC PLAN FOR YOUR LAW LIBRARY

Strategic planning is a fundamental process for law librarians, enabling libraries to align their resources and services with the evolving needs of their patrons and the broader legal community. Strategic planning is also a systematic process that involves envisioning a desired future for the library, setting achievable goals, and outlining the steps needed to reach those goals. It requires a deep understanding of the library's mission, vision, and values, as well as the external and internal factors that influence its operations.

Begin by assessing the current state of the library and its operations. Do this by conducting a SWOT analysis, identifying the library's current situation as reflected by its Strengths, Weaknesses, Opportunities, and Threats. This analysis provides a comprehensive view of where the library stands and what challenges and opportunities lie ahead. Collect quantitative and qualitative data on library usage, patron satisfaction, collection usage, and other relevant metrics. This data will inform your understanding of current performance and areas needing improvement. Involve key stakeholders—library staff, faculty, students, legal professionals, and administration—in the assessment process. Their insights and feedback are crucial for an accurate understanding of the library's status and needs.

Next, define the library's mission and vision. To draft the library's mission statement, articulate the library's purpose and core functions. The mission statement should reflect the library's commitment to serving its patrons and supporting the institution's broader goals. Craft a vision statement that describes the future state of the library. This should be an aspirational description of what the library aims to achieve in the long term.

Based on the assessment and the mission and vision statements, identify key strategic priorities. These are broad areas where the library needs to focus its efforts to achieve its vision. The American Library Association (ALA) has a list of trends/future trends listed on their website that can inform discussions about what may be a focus for your library.[3] Common strategic priorities for law libraries might include enhancing access to legal information, improving technological infrastructure, expanding outreach and community engagement, supporting legal research and education, and promoting digital equity and inclusion.

Define and set your goals and objectives under each strategic priority. For each strategic priority, set specific, measurable, achievable, relevant, and time-bound (SMART) goals. Break down these goals into actionable objectives that provide clear directions on how to achieve them.

Example: *Strategic Priority:* Enhancing access to legal information. *Goal:* Increase online access to legal resources by 30 percent over the next three years. *Objectives:*

- Digitize five hundred key legal documents annually.
- Partner with legal databases to provide remote access to patrons.

Implement a user-friendly digital catalog.

For each objective, create detailed action plans. These plans should outline the specific steps required, assign responsibilities, set timelines, and identify necessary resources.

Example Action Plan for Digitization Objective:

- Step 1: Conduct a needs assessment to identify priority documents for digitization.
- Step 2: Secure funding for digitization equipment and software.
- Step 3: Train staff on digitization processes and best practices.
- Step 4: Begin digitizing documents, starting with those identified as high priority.
- Step 5: Regularly review and assess progress, making adjustments as needed.

Next, implement the action plans, ensuring that all staff members are aware of their roles and responsibilities. Regularly monitor progress toward achieving the objectives and goals, using metrics and feedback mechanisms to assess performance. Having regular staff meetings where the status of the action plan is discussed, and responsible parties can provide feedback and express their needs, is a way to keep everyone knowledgeable and included in the plan as a living process.

Lastly, evaluate and revise your plan as an ongoing process. Periodically evaluate the effectiveness of the strategic plan and make necessary revisions to address new challenges and opportunities. This should be done at least annually and as needed when new events or challenges arise.

THE DIFFERENCES IN STRATEGIC PLANNING IN ACADEMIC, GOVERNMENT, AND LAW FIRM LIBRARIES

While the foundational elements of strategic planning—such as setting goals, defining objectives, and creating action plans—are similar across different types of libraries, the specific focus areas and creation process for law library strategic plans are tailored to address the unique needs and challenges of legal information services. By understanding these distinctions, law librarians can develop strategic plans that effectively support their patrons and align with the broader goals of their institutions.

GOVERNMENT LAW LIBRARIES

Mission and Objectives:

- *Public Access and Transparency*: Government law libraries often aim to provide access to legal information for the public, promoting transparency and informed citizenship. Their mission includes ensuring that citizens, government officials, and legal professionals can access and understand legal materials.
- *Supporting Government Agencies*: They also support the legal research needs of government agencies, legislative bodies, and public officials. This involves providing timely and accurate legal information to assist in policymaking, legislation, and government operations.

Key Stakeholders:

- *General Public*: Unlike academic and law firm libraries, government law libraries serve a broader audience, including the public. Strategic planning must account for public access and education.
- *Government Officials and Employees*: These libraries support the research needs of government officials, legal advisors, and public employees. Understanding their requirements is crucial for strategic planning.
- *Judicial System*: Government law libraries often serve courts and judges, requiring specialized legal collections and research support.

Collections and Services:

- *Legal Documents and Public Records*: They maintain extensive collections of legal documents, public records, legislative histories, and government publications. Strategic planning should focus on preserving and providing access to these materials.
- *Public Legal Education*: They may offer educational programs, workshops, and resources to help the public understand legal issues and navigate the legal system.

Technology and Infrastructure:

- *Digital Access and Equity*: Ensuring digital access to legal information is a key priority. Government law libraries often emphasize digital equity, providing resources and tools to underserved communities.
- *Preservation of Legal Documents*: They focus on preserving historical legal documents and ensuring long-term access. Strategic plans should include digitization and archiving initiatives.

Compliance and Regulations:

- *Adherence to Government Policies*: Strategic planning must align with government policies, regulations, and ethical standards. Compliance with public information and privacy laws is critical.

Academic Law Libraries

Mission and Objectives:

- *Support for Legal Education*: The primary mission is to support the teaching, research, and learning needs of law students and faculty. This includes providing access to a wide range of legal resources and research support.
- *Scholarly Contributions*: They support faculty research and scholarship, contributing to the academic output of the law school.

Key Stakeholders:

- *Law Students and Faculty*: The primary users are law students and faculty, requiring collections and services that support legal education and academic research.
- *Academic Community*: They also serve the broader academic community, including other departments and researchers.

Collections and Services:

- *Curriculum-Aligned Resources*: Collections are tailored to the law school's curriculum and research interests. Strategic plans should address the acquisition and management of these specialized resources.
- *Research Support Services*: They offer advanced legal research training and one-on-one consultations, emphasizing support for academic research.

Technology and Infrastructure:

- *Study and Collaboration Spaces*: Academic law libraries focus on providing study spaces, technology labs, and collaborative work environments. Strategic plans should consider space utilization and technological needs.
- *Integration with Academic Systems*: They need to integrate with the institution's academic systems and platforms, supporting seamless access to resources and services.

Compliance and Regulations:

- *Academic Policies*: Strategic planning must align with the law school's policies, accreditation standards, state regulations, and academic regulations.

Law Firm Libraries

Mission and Objectives:

- *Support for Legal Practice*: The primary mission is to support the legal practice needs of the firm's attorneys and staff. This includes providing access to practical legal resources and research services.
- *Efficiency and Cost-Effectiveness*: Emphasis on cost-effective resource management and efficient service delivery to support the firm's business objectives.

Key Stakeholders:

- *Attorneys and Legal Staff*: The main users are the firm's attorneys, paralegals, and legal assistants. Understanding their practice areas and information needs is essential for strategic planning.
- *Clients*: Indirectly, the library also supports the firm's clients by enabling high-quality legal work.

Collections and Services:

- *Practice-Specific Resources*: Collections are tailored to the firm's practice areas, with a focus on current and practical legal materials. Strategic plans should prioritize acquiring and maintaining these resources.
- *Efficient Research Services*: They offer rapid and accurate legal research services, emphasizing efficiency and productivity.

Technology and Infrastructure:

- *Legal Databases and Tools*: Heavy reliance on specialized legal databases and tools (e.g., Westlaw, LexisNexis) is common. Strategic plans should address budgeting for these resources and training staff.
- *Integration with Firm Systems*: They need to integrate with the firm's practice management and document management systems, ensuring seamless access to information.

Compliance and Regulations:

- *Professional and Ethical Standards*: Strategic planning must ensure compliance with professional conduct rules, confidentiality requirements, and other legal industry standards, including the use of AI software.

EXAMPLE OF A STRATEGIC PLAN FOR A GOVERNMENT LIBRARY:

Yoknapatawpha Falls Government Law Library Strategic Plan (2024–2029)

Mission Statement: The Yoknapatawpha Falls Government Law Library is committed to providing comprehensive legal information and research services to government officials, legal professionals, and the public. We aim to support informed decision-making, promote public access to legal resources, and uphold the principles of justice and transparency.

Vision Statement: To be a premier legal information center that empowers users with accessible, accurate, and up-to-date legal resources and fosters a well-informed community.

Strategic Priorities and Goals

Strategic Priority 1: Enhance Access to Legal Information

Goal 1: Expand digital access to legal resources by 50 percent within five years.

- Objective 1.1: Digitize historical legal documents and public records.
- Action Plan:
  - Step 1: Conduct an audit of existing physical collections to identify digitization priorities (Q1 2024).
  - Step 2: Secure funding through government grants and partnerships (Q2 2024).
  - Step 3: Collaborate with digitization experts to convert documents into digital formats (Q3 2024).
  - Step 4: Develop an online repository for public access (Q4 2024).
- Objective 1.2: Improve the usability of the online catalog.
- Action Plan:
  - Step 1: Gather user feedback through surveys and focus groups to identify usability issues (Q1 2025).
  - Step 2: Work with IT to redesign the online catalog interface (Q2 2025).
  - Step 3: Implement advanced search features and user-friendly navigation (Q3 2025).
  - Step 4: Conduct training sessions for users on how to navigate the new catalog (Q4 2025).
- Objective 1.3: Increase public awareness of digital resources.
- Action Plan:
  - Step 1: Launch a marketing campaign highlighting new digital resources (Q1 2026).
  - Step 2: Partner with community organizations to promote digital access (Q2 2026).
  - Step 3: Host webinars and workshops on using digital legal resources (Q3 2026).

Strategic Priority 2: Strengthen Research Support Services

Goal 2: Improve research support services for government officials and the public by 30 percent over five years.

- Objective 2.1: Develop specialized research guides on key legal topics.
- Action Plan:
  - Step 1: Identify high-demand legal topics through user inquiries and trends analysis (Q1 2024).
  - Step 2: Assign librarians to create detailed research guides (Q2 2024).
  - Step 3: Publish guides on the library's website and promote their use (Q3 2024).
- Objective 2.2: Enhance training programs for legal research skills.
- Action Plan:
  - Step 1: Design a comprehensive training curriculum for government officials and public users (Q4 2024).
  - Step 2: Schedule regular workshops and online training sessions (Q1 2025).
  - Step 3: Develop on-demand video tutorials and online courses (Q2 2025).
- Objective 2.3: Increase the availability of one-on-one research consultations.
- Action Plan:
  - Step 1: Promote consultation services through the library's communication channels (Q3 2025).
  - Step 2: Implement an online booking system for easy appointment scheduling (Q4 2025).
  - Step 3: Monitor usage and gather feedback to continuously improve services (Q1 2026 onward).

Strategic Priority 3: Upgrade Technology and Infrastructure

Goal 3: Modernize the library's technology infrastructure to support advanced legal research and public access.

- Objective 3.1: Improve internet speed and connectivity throughout the library.
- Action Plan:
  - Step 1: Assess current internet infrastructure and identify areas for improvement (Q1 2024).
  - Step 2: Collaborate with IT departments to upgrade network systems (Q2 2024).
  - Step 3: Test and ensure reliable internet access in all library areas (Q3 2024).
- Objective 3.2: Implement state-of-the-art legal research tools and databases.
- Action Plan:
  - Step 1: Identify and evaluate new legal research tools and databases (Q1 2025).
  - Step 2: Secure funding and negotiate subscriptions with vendors (Q2 2025).
  - Step 3: Integrate tools into the library's digital platform and provide training for users (Q3 2025).
- Objective 3.3: Develop a comprehensive digital preservation strategy.
- Action Plan:
  - Step 1: Conduct a needs assessment for digital preservation (Q1 2025).
  - Step 2: Research and implement best practices for digital preservation (Q2 2025).
  - Step 3: Establish regular reviews and updates to ensure long-term preservation (Q3 2025 onward).

Strategic Priority 4: Foster Community Engagement and Outreach

Goal 4: Increase community engagement and public outreach activities by 40 percent over five years.

- Objective 4.1: Develop partnerships with local organizations and educational institutions.
- Action Plan:
  - Step 1: Identify potential partners and collaborative opportunities (Q1 2024).
  - Step 2: Establish formal agreements for joint events and programs (Q2 2024).
  - Step 3: Organize community-focused legal information sessions and workshops (Q3 2024 onward).
- Objective 4.2: Enhance the library's social media presence and online engagement.
- Action Plan:
  - Step 1: Develop a social media strategy to highlight library services and resources (Q1 2025).
  - Step 2: Create engaging content and schedule regular posts (Q2 2025).
  - Step 3: Monitor and analyze engagement metrics to refine the strategy (Q3 2025 onward).
- Objective 4.3: Launch public legal education initiatives.
- Action Plan:
  - Step 1: Identify key legal issues of interest to the public (Q4 2024).
  - Step 2: Partner with legal experts to develop educational content (Q1 2025).
  - Step 3: Host quarterly public legal education seminars and evaluate participant feedback (Q2 2025 onward).

Implementation and Monitoring

The strategic plan will be implemented in phases, with regular monitoring and assessment to ensure progress toward goals. A dedicated strategic planning committee will oversee the implementation, review progress reports quarterly, and make necessary adjustments.

RETURN ON INVESTMENT

ROI is an economic measurement used to determine the value of output based on financial input. Law libraries receive set budgets, making it easy to quantify the input. The difficult part is determining the value of the output when there is no monetary return. How can a law library demonstrate value to key stakeholders, especially those with budgetary oversight who may not be members of the core patron group/use services? As non-revenue-generating units, law library budgets are often scrutinized as an easy place to make cuts.[4] Law librarians must justify their resource and personnel needs and convey the needs of patrons to institutions with fiduciary duties of their own.

Law libraries can leverage both quantitative and qualitative data to convey value to their institution. Quantitative data includes required reporting and institutional assessments, which includes budget reports, patron surveys, and instructional feedback. Qualitative data can also come from patron surveys, as well as focus groups, informal check-ins, and feedback submitted online and at points of service.

Lower visibility libraries may have a lower priority in the eyes of officials responsible for budgeting and resource allocation. It is up to law library leadership to seek out and leverage opportunities to spotlight library services, resources, and personnel to stakeholders. This includes being present for in-person visitors, supporting the institution in non-library endeavors, and providing high-quality, responsive services.

QUANTITATIVE ASSESSMENT

Defining and utilizing performance metrics is essential for gauging success and ensuring continuous improvement in strategic planning. For government law libraries, success is measured through metrics such as public access rates, user satisfaction levels, and the library's impact on government initiatives and support for government functions. These metrics help ensure that the library is effectively serving the public and supporting the operational needs of government agencies. In academic law libraries, performance metrics are closely tied to academic support, research impact, and the satisfaction of students and faculty. These indicators provide insight into how well the library is enhancing the educational and research environment, contributing to academic achievements, and meeting the needs of its primary users. Meanwhile, law firm libraries focus on metrics related to efficiency, the speed of service delivery, and cost-effectiveness. By prioritizing these areas, law firm libraries can demonstrate their value in providing quick, accurate legal information and supporting the firm's overall operational efficiency.

QUALITATIVE ASSESSMENT

Law library assessments are often qualitative in nature. Maintaining positive relations with key stakeholders is critical to law library success, especially in an age where library services involve curating information and providing seamless database access. Negative word-of-mouth can erode the law library's brand, lower trust, and impact customer relationships.[5] Qualitative feedback comes in a variety of forms, both solicited and unsolicited. Surveys are one important mode of collecting qualitative feedback. The Maryland State Law Library inserts a survey link in the signature of all outgoing emails as well as on its website.[6] Comment cards, email feedback, and verbal feedback are other modes of qualitative feedback. It is important to develop a narrative around qualitative feedback to provide context and impact to key stakeholders.[7]

COMMUNICATION

Communication is critical to conveying ROI in any law library. Key stakeholders need information distilled into manageable and understandable formats. Tailoring the format and content to the key stakeholder's preferred communication style can result in a stronger message. Similarly, generic messages may be dismissed or ignored and thus lack the desired impact. Graphics and tables may convey information better than text, making a stronger impact. Other best practices include simplifying the message, appealing to the self-interest of the intended audience, presenting the message with confidence, and personalizing the message.[8] The 2015 *Economic Value of Law Libraries Report* includes a section on communication best practices that include working with stakeholders to determine delivery preferences, creating a schedule of reporting aligned with the institution's decision-making cycle, refraining from using library jargon, finding opportunities to present in formal meeting settings, and determining the communication styles that match organizational preferences.[9]

Government Law Libraries

Government law libraries vary in type, including agency and court libraries. Even among libraries of the same type, key stakeholders vary, and missions and strategic priorities may not be clearly enumerated. The Maryland State Law Library operates the state's main self-help legal website using pro bono and low-cost student staff to maintain updated legal information targeted to self-represented parties.[10]

Government law libraries are publicly funded and are accountable to the government and public for expenditures. In this type of library, qualitative feedback from patron compliments could be persuasive to decision-makers. Government law libraries might consider a worst-case-scenario framing to convey the impact on the community if the library were to close. Tracking metrics, like the number of self-represented parties served over time, can show the effectiveness and necessity of the law library in the access to justice context.[11]

Academic Law Libraries

Academic law librarians must navigate a complex and frequently changing set of rankings and reporting requirements to demonstrate minimum ROI. These include reporting to the ABA and other accrediting bodies, *U.S. News & World Report*, and consortial groups.[12] Outside of formal reporting, scholarly impact metrics demonstrate how the library supports faculty scholarship, publication, and recruitment.

There are a variety of ways that academic law librarians contribute to their institutions. They may teach and sometimes hold faculty appointments. Formal instructional contributions are measured in terms of enrollment and student evaluations. Informal instructional contributions are reported annually to the Association of Research Libraries, but could also be spotlighted on the library's website, in a newsletter, and/or in the annual report. Academic law librarians' service and support to the law school and university communities are difficult to quantify but are significant contributions that can impact perceptions of the library.

ROI is evaluated differently depending on institutional priorities and opportunities to increase visibility. Some possible priorities and ways to show ROI include the following:

- Faculty scholarly impact
- Librarian instructional impact
- Support for faculty working in niche areas of law
- Support for interdisciplinary and empirical research
- Technology competence and incorporating emerging technology in the classroom
- Student support, including bar preparation/passage, career development, and wellness
- Service to the law school and the university (committee membership, support for faculty search committees)
- Access to justice initiatives and clinic support
- Receipt of grants and awards

Communicating value is key to demonstrating ROI and is often overlooked. Standard reporting does not convey true return, and some legal education reporting has come under scrutiny, with some law schools declining to submit data to U.S. News & World Report.[13] In order to convey ROI, law libraries should consider communicating value using annual reports,[14] newsletters,[15] website content and blogs, social media, and promotional items.[16] The messaging utilized needs to be tailored to the specific institution, its mission, and strategic priorities. Messaging should be timed to reach stakeholders at key moments, like the beginning of each academic semester to reach new patrons. The law library strategic plan should have been developed with institutional priorities in mind, but these represent static points in time, and librarians need to convey the story of how the library continues to meet the evolving needs of the institution.

Law Firm Libraries

Firm librarians must maintain different sets of metrics to communicate the value of their services to partners and administrators. Law firms generally utilize billable hours to generate revenue with some exceptions for alternative fee arrangement formats. Despite this difference and having different key stakeholders than academic law libraries, many of the same best practices apply, including aligning the library's strategic plan and operations with the firm's strategic priorities. These could include traditional research support, resource sharing, knowledge management, conflicts checks, and client development. Firm library billing practices should maximize efficiency by parsing administrative work from librarians to staff.[17] Librarians should review electronic resource usage and tailor subscriptions narrowly based on actual usage.[18] By demonstrating both value added by librarian output and savings realized by effective resource management, firm librarians can communicate the true value of their services to the firm.

Creating a strategic plan for a law library is a dynamic and collaborative process that requires careful assessment, clear goal-setting, and flexible implementation. By following the steps outlined in this chapter and adhering to best practices, law librarians can develop strategic plans that not only address current challenges but also position their libraries for future success. Utilizing the strategic plan to plan, implement, and assess is critical to conveying ROI in a way that creates value and leads to sustained resource allocation and positive patron experiences. Communicating effectively with key stakeholders is the final, critical component necessary to convey ROI and ensure ongoing institutional support for law libraries.

NOTES

1. Steven Bell, Lorcan Dempsey, Barbara Fister, and Nancy Allen, eds., *New Roles for the Road Ahead: Essays Commissioned for ACRL's 75th Anniversary*, ed. N. Allen (Association of Research Libraries, 2015), 11, https://alair.ala.org/bitstream/handle/11213/17196/new_roles_75th.pdf?sequence=1&isAllowed=y
2. Malcolm Brown, et al., *2020 Educause Horizon Report Teaching and Learning Edition* (Louisville, CO: EDUCAUSE, 2020), 6, https://www.learntechlib.org/p/215670/.
3. "Trends," American Library Association, last modified August 8, 2014, accessed June 27, 2024, https://www.ala.org/future/trends.
4. Law library budgets, personnel, collections, and physical spaces have been sliced and diced in the name of modernization, based on this false understanding of what it is that makes a good law library. Amanda Watson, Amanda Karel, Amanda Runyon, and Leslie Street, "Demonstrating Law Library Value Through Mission-Centered Assessment," *Law Library Journal* 115, no. 40 (2023): 10.
5. See Dahlia Allwyn Ribeiro and Arti D. Kalro, "Four decades of negative word-of-mouth and negative electronic word-of-mouth: A morphological analysis," *International Journal of Consumer Studies* 47, no. 6 (2023): 2528–2552.

6. Steven P. Anderson, "ROI for Government Law Libraries," AALL Digital White Paper. Defining ROI: Law Library Best Practices, 2016, https://www.aallnet.org/wp-content/uploads/2016/01/AALL-ROI-Whitepaper-2016_FINAL.pdf.
7. See AALL Digital White Paper, Defining ROI: Law Library Best Practices, https://www.aallnet.org/wp-content/uploads/2016/01/AALL-ROI-Whitepaper-2016_FINAL.pdf.
8. Amanda B. Albert, "Communicating Library Value - The Missing Piece of the Assessment Puzzle," *Journal of Academic Librarianship* 40 (2014): 634-637.
9. American Association of Law Libraries, "The Economic Value of Law Libraries," 2015, last visited June 27, 2024, https://www.aallnet.org/wp-content/uploads/2018/01/EconomicValue-ofLawLibrariesFinalReport.pdf.
10. Steven P. Anderson, "ROI for Government Law Libraries," AALL Digital White Paper. Defining ROI: Law Library Best Practices, 2016, https://www.aallnet.org/wp-content/uploads/2016/01/AALL-ROI-Whitepaper-2016_FINAL.pdf.
11. Jean M. Wegner, Montell Davenport, Carolyn Hayes, and David Sanborne, "Using Metrics to Showcase Value," AALL Digital White Paper. Defining ROI: Law Library Best Practices, 2016, https://www.aallnet.org/wp-content/uploads/2016/01/AALL-ROI-Whitepaper-2016_FINAL.pdf.
12. For example, NELLCO's ALLStAR, https://www.nellco.org/page/allstar#:~:text=Allstar%20is%20NELLCO's%20data%2Dsharing,analyze%20data%20about%20their%20libraries.
13. Anemona Hartocollis, "Yale and Harvard Law Schools Withdraw From the U.S. News Rankings," *The New York Times*, November 16, 2022.
14. "Annual Reports," AALL Marketing and Outreach Toolkit, last visited June 26, 2024, https://www.aallnet.org/allsis/resources-publications/marketing-outreach-toolkit/mktgtools/.
15. "Newsletters," AALL Marketing and Outreach Toolkit, last visited June 26, 2024, https://www.aallnet.org/allsis/resources-publications/marketing-outreach-toolkit/mktgtools/.
16. "Promotional Items," AALL Marketing and Outreach Toolkit, last visited June 26, 2024, https://www.aallnet.org/allsis/resources-publications/marketing-outreach-toolkit/mktgtools/.
17. Steve Lastres, "Law Libraries . . . By the Numbers: Demonstrate the Value of Your Library to Drive Optimal Legal Services," AALL Digital White Paper. Defining ROI: Law Library Best Practices, 2016, https://www.aallnet.org/wp-content/uploads/2016/01/AALL-ROI-Whitepaper-2016_FINAL.pdf.
18. Steve Lastres, "Law Libraries . . . By the Numbers: Demonstrate the Value of Your Library to Drive Optimal Legal Services."

9

Law Firm Libraries

Organizational Structure, Positioning of the Library, and Law Firm Mergers

Marcia Burris

Law libraries within law firms serve a fundamental role as facilitators of access to legal and other information resources. The ways in which this core function plays out, however, are as myriad and unique as each law firm. Even the name of the department varies between firms, as different facets of library, information, research, and knowledge services are emphasized. This chapter explores the evolving roles played by law firm libraries, whatever they may be called, in providing a wide range of services to the firm and the corresponding evolution of the library's placement within the firm's organizational structure. In addition to these organic structural changes within law firms, we'll look at an increasingly common occurrence—the law firm merger—and the logistical challenges, impacts, and opportunities such an event presents for the library.

INSIDE THE LAW FIRM LIBRARY

Law firm library and information departments support both the legal practices and business of their firms, notably by providing research services along with access and training support related to information products used by attorneys and legal staff. However, the applicability of the information professional skill set to a variety of functions across the business creates a range of opportunities which are realized in different ways across different firms. With skills in research and analysis, training, information management, product evaluation and contract management, and even project management, the library team may be called upon to support business development, conflicts and intake, knowledge management, or other business functions, or tasked with contributing to or even leading technology initiatives as dictated by firm needs. With such an array of potential contributions, law firm libraries show remarkable diversity in the combination of services they provide, how their teams are staffed, and where the library or research department is situated within the overall organization.

Research functions of the library can also differ widely between firms. Direct research support is typically offered to support legal matters and business needs such as client development, but the balance of legal and business development research varies widely. In some firms the library provides a higher proportion of business development research, while in others the library is more focused on performing research in support of client legal matters. In addition to providing research in response to a variety of requests, the library may also be involved in initiatives to proactively deliver curated information to the firm. Where libraries are involved in the delivery of proactive research work products such as new litigation or current awareness services, the focus and scope of these initiatives also vary according to firm needs and priorities.

Where similar services are provided within different firms, such as traditional legal research related to client matters, differences are also seen in the ways each firm approaches the library as a driver of firm and client value. For example, law firms vary in their use of the library for traditional legal research in support of client matters, and even within a single firm, individual attorneys may utilize the library differently. Some treat the library as a resource to be deployed strategically when special needs arise that require unusual expertise. Other attorneys and practice groups may utilize the library when it is preferable for research to be provided efficiently by a timekeeper with lower rates, to ensure better value to the client. Still, others consider librarians members of their practice teams and routinely request research across a variety of matters, resulting in the library team performing a high volume of client-related, billable research and becoming a profit center within the firm. Additionally, some firms may utilize library teams for in-depth specialized research to support their corporate, medical, labor, or other practices. The research services model of each firm will inform its staffing decisions and team structure. Firms with higher research volume will necessarily have larger library teams, but configuration and reporting of these groups can differ. For example, some firms maintain large, centralized research teams, while in other firms, library team members who provide dedicated support to specific functions may be embedded within other administrative departments or legal teams.

In addition to traditional research, the research and analysis skills of librarians can be leveraged in diverse law firm functions such as business development, conflicts and intake, and records management. With strength in organizing information and the ability to apply technology to users' needs, the library team may be involved in ongoing knowledge management functions, such as maintaining the firm intranet or managing technology applications used by practice groups or administrative teams. The library may also be tapped to participate in or lead projects such as intranet development or the implementation of conflict systems or practice technology solutions such as drafting tools or closing binder applications.

Organizational Structure

With law firm libraries often undertaking wide-ranging responsibilities, many firms wonder where their library should fit in the organizational structure. However, the answer is as specific to each firm as is the unique set of research services and other functions the library department provides to support the firm's needs. While some patterns are apparent across the legal marketplace, there is no one singular "best practice" around law firm library structure, and each firm must evaluate its own needs and resources to most effectively align its information professionals within the organization. In addition, even within a single firm, reporting alignment may change over time as library department services and responsibilities evolve.

The head of the library department most often reports to the law firm's Chief Operating Officer, but may also report to the Chief Information or Technology Officer, Chief Administrative Officer, Chief Knowledge Officer, or other C-level executives. The variety of reporting structures seems to include nearly every alignment imaginable. In fact, according to data from consulting firm Harbor Global, LLC, no single line of reporting is used within a majority of law firms. The Harbor 2023 Benchmarking Library & Information Services Survey posed the question: "To whom does the top-ranking employee of the Research & Information Services department ultimately report?" Among eighty-five responding firms, a wide range of reporting verticals were reported. The leading response was the Chief Operating Officer, with 22 percent of all participating firms and 19 percent of firms ranked in the Am Law 100 reporting that their library is aligned under the COO. However, in smaller firms, with correspondingly smaller C-suites, the research or library function is more likely to report directly to the COO or other firm executive than is the case in larger firms. Alignment of the library under the COO is most common among the smallest law firms, with 40 percent of firms below the Am Law 200 (unranked firms) reporting up through the COO, according to the Harbor survey, a rate double that reported by the larger firms surveyed. On the other hand, in the largest firms, which typically also have correspondingly larger C-suites, the library is most likely to report to another firm officer.[1]

According to Harbor, the second most common reporting structure across all firm libraries is to the Chief Information Officer, with 16 percent of firms reporting this alignment. Other responses include reporting to the Chief Knowledge Officer, Chief Administrative Officer, Chief Financial Officer, Executive Director, Chief Innovation Officer, Chief Marketing Officer, Chief Technology Officer, Managing Partner, or General Counsel. However, even with so many different reporting alignment options listed in the survey, the second most frequent response among all participants was that they report to a C-level or other firm leader not anticipated in the survey question, with 18 percent of all firms selecting "Other," further illustrating the diversity of reporting structures in place.[2]

Libraries are somewhat unique among law firm departments, notes Colleen Cable, a director with Harbor's Research + Intelligence Advisory team, in that they do so many different things in support of both front-office legal practice needs and back-office administrative functions. This uniqueness and diversity of functions mean that libraries don't naturally fit into a consistent place within law firms, as illustrated by the Harbor survey results. Cable has seen libraries report to virtually every C-level role, including Technology, Marketing, Knowledge Management, and Training. More recently, she has noted an increase in libraries reporting to Innovation and Practice Services officers as those functions are added to firms.[3]

Aligning the library with newly created administrative functions continues a long-standing pattern of law library placement in law firms evolving along with each firm's unique business structure. Lori Martin, Director of Library and Research Services at Bradley Arant Boult Cummings LLP for many years, has led her department through several such organizational changes. First hired by a library committee composed of firm partners, Martin subsequently reported to leaders in new positions added to the firm over the years, including a firm administrator, a director of administration, and finally a chief operating officer, as Bradley followed the progression typical of many firms that increasingly embraced the role of non-attorney business professionals during the 1990s and early 2000s. As the firm continued to grow and new administrative functions were added in the 2010s, the Bradley library team realigned under the newly created Practice Support area, a multifaceted administrative division which also encompasses practice group business management and e-discovery. Today, while formally aligned within Practice Support, Martin also works closely with the firm's Chief Information Officer, particularly on projects related to artificial intelligence and innovation, where the library's expertise in evaluating new products and strong focus on the end-user experience are assets. These projects highlight the library's ability to collaborate effectively across business functions well beyond the administrative vertical in which it is positioned.[4]

New and Expanding Roles

In addition to collaborating with other firm teams on specific projects, library departments often formally assume broader responsibilities across a variety of functional areas. In many law firms, the library supports firm intranets, records or information management, and/or conflicts and new business intake. These functions, while outside the traditional library and research role, nevertheless present opportunities to utilize foundational library and information professional skills, such as research and organization of information. Such diverse responsibilities are often added to established library teams over time as firm needs evolve.

Nancy Rine, Director of Research Services and Conflicts at Fried, Frank, Harris, Shriver & Jacobson LLP, has seen the addition of several non-traditional functions to her library team over the years.

Table 9.1 Law Firm Library Skills and Experience

General Skills *Supporting Diverse Use of Library or Research Team*	**Specific Prior Experience** *Supporting Diverse Use of Library or Research Team Members*
Research skills Organization of information Project management Ability to collaborate across departments Ability to apply user perspective to technology implementation	Experience with a specific product or technology category Experience supporting a specific practice area or business team within the firm

Originally hired in a function that was "straight library," Rine gradually saw her team's scope expand to include conflicts research, followed by other aspects of new business intake including oversight of the firm's intake software. With her team aligned under the firm's technology department, Rine also assumed responsibility for records management as the records function increasingly focused on electronic content rather than paper files. For a time, Rine even managed the firm's technology helpdesk team. Rine attributes the alignment of each of these functions with her team to a combination of the right skills at the right time to meet the firm's evolving needs, as well as a willingness to ask questions about firm processes and explore possibilities with the firm. Rine notes that the reassignment of various areas of responsibility has also been prompted by changes in firm personnel over the years, with each change presenting the opportunity to evaluate and reconfigure firm functions to meet current and future needs. In each instance, traditional library skills such as research, organization of information, and support for the end-user experience were important aspects contributing to Rine's team's success in these roles.[5]

Across firms, the decision to add new areas of responsibility to the library or research team is often prompted by the identification of a specific business need that is currently unmet, along with a recognition of skills and aptitude within the existing library team suitable to the need. The opportunity to assume new roles may be presented by existing skills and prior experience of the library department's members or leader, such as a general facility with research, organization of information, project management, ability to collaborate across firm departments, and ability to apply user perspective to technology implementations. Prior demonstrated success, such as experience with a prior technology implementation or even a successful non-technology project, can position the library to be tapped for new opportunities. As new responsibilities and roles are added, the extent of the library's involvement may range from contributing to leading different initiatives. Where additional projects and functions are successful, the result is often a virtuous cycle where the experience gained adds value to future initiatives, creating new opportunities for the team and the firm.

CHANGES IN LAW FIRM STRUCTURE AND OR REALIGNMENT OF RESEARCH SERVICES

Just as the services provided by the library may change over time, so may the best reporting alignment within the firm. The implementation or discontinuation of various services offered by the library or other business teams, changes in personnel across the library and other departments, or a change in firm administrative structure may all precipitate a reassessment and potential realignment of the research services team within the organization. Teams may also shift alignment as firm business practices evolve. For example, an increased emphasis on research in support of business development may correspond with merging the library and business development functions. Growth of skills or greater specialization among team members may result in functions being parsed into new subgroups, such as medical, corporate, or client quality research teams. Changes in personnel, such as the hiring of an individual with unique skills and background, may create previously unforeseen opportunities to deploy those skills to the firm's advantage. The development of entirely new functions within the firm, such as practice services or innovation departments, presents additional opportunities for strategically repositioning the library. As demonstrated by the great variety of reporting structures and service offerings in law firms today, it is clear that libraries can be effective in any number of configurations and are adaptable to numerous existing and emerging firm functions.

Law Firm Mergers

One of the biggest changes that can occur in the life of a law firm is a merger with another firm. Mergers create unique opportunities and challenges for all involved, including the research and knowledge teams. However, just as each research department and law firm is unique, not all mergers are the same, and the process of integrating two firms can differ widely according to the unique circumstances of the combining organizations.

Perhaps the most significant factor affecting the merger process and outcome is the relative sizes of the combining firms. In a "tuck-in acquisition," a larger firm typically absorbs a smaller firm. The greater the size differential, the more likely it is for the smaller firm to be absorbed into the larger firm in a manner that closely resembles the experience of lateral hires, with the acquired firm adopting the technology, resources, and policies of the more predominant firm. In a "merger of equals," two firms that are fairly similar in size combine, often creating a new firm identity. (Logistically, the new firm may retain and rename an existing business entity of one of the legacy firms as part of the merger process, but the end result is a new brand reflecting the joining of the two firms.) In a merger of relative equals, firms may go through an intensive process of evaluating which systems, resources, and policies and procedures should be adopted by the combined firm, sometimes picking one of the legacy firm's systems over the other, and sometimes developing entirely new systems that are built to best suit the future needs of the combined firm. A distinct type of merger often seen in the combining of global firms is the formation of (or joining an existing) Swiss *verein*. Under the *verein* model, firms not only join to associate with each other under one brand, but also maintain separate legal entities with their own legal and financial liability, as well as distinct operational systems. Apart from mergers, firms may also experience significant "organic growth" or decline, as individual attorneys or groups of lawyers make lateral moves from one firm to another. This type of growth can also impact the library and other firm departments, but to a lesser degree than a merger.

Combining firms cite many reasons for merging, including an improved firm geographic footprint, stronger brand identity, deeper bench strength, and the addition of teams in strategically important practice areas. In a successful merger, the impact to the firms' business is more than strictly additive, as the new footprint and practice strength lead to new client and business opportunities, including entirely new work. An additional key merger goal, which is often unstated, is to achieve improved economies of scale in operations, including more efficient administrative staffing and better pricing in vendor contracts. Along with the opportunities presented by the merger, firms face the challenge of integrating attorneys from different legacy firms into a new cohesive practice and of supporting attorneys and staff who may need to adapt to new firm technology, resources, and processes.

A library or research department of a firm undertaking a merger should work to support both the stated and unstated goals of the merger, ideally in a way that demonstrates the library's capabilities to the leadership of the new combined firm and shows alignment with the organizational goals and priorities of the firm. In other words, the library should help support a positive outcome from the merger while positioning the research team to support the new firm going forward post-merger.

Practical Aspects and Considerations in Mergers

In any merger, the library plays an important role, both in the process of combining the research resources and operations of the two merging entities, and in supporting the combining legal practices. In practical terms, many of the same steps apply for all mergers, regardless of size or type. Research subscriptions must be evaluated and potentially merged, renegotiated, or, if appropriate, canceled or lapsed. Services provided by library and research teams, and the teams themselves, perhaps historically operating under different reporting structures, must be aligned for the new firm's needs. Much of this work must be done in advance of the actual merger date, often while maintaining a high degree of confidentiality prior to the public announcement of the merger.

MERGER CHECKLIST QUESTIONS

Entity

What is the merger type: tuck-in acquisition, merger of equals, other combination?

Will a new business entity be formed, or will an existing entity be updated?

Which of the combining firms will be predominant?

Will the predominant or surviving firm adopt a new name?

If an acquisition occurs, will 100 percent of the acquired firm's attorneys be joining the new firm? If not all attorneys are joining the combined firm, does the number of departures affect the status of the legacy firm or change how the combination will be implemented?

Will the merger result in any new practice groups or realignment of practice teams within the firm?

Staffing

Do both of the combining firms have library or research services teams?

Who do these groups report to within the firm (COO, CIO, other)?

What is the scope of responsibility for each team? Do they support functions beyond traditional library services?

Who leads each respective team? What are the background, experience, and skill level of each leader and team member? What responsibilities are assigned to each individual?

If a combining firm does not have a formal library or research services department, who in the firm is responsible for negotiating online contracts, print collection management, processing print materials, payment of library invoices, assigning online research access, and other functions?

Which individuals will be responsible for sharing information in preparation for the merger, and with whom?

If both combining firms have directors or managers, who will lead the department post-merger? Who will the selected department leader report to in the new firm's organizational structure? Will their responsibilities change in any way? Will some responsibilities continue to be handled by the other leader or others in the firm?

If both combining firms have research librarians or technical service staff, how are these groups historically organized? Do researchers support all attorneys firm-wide or are they associated with specific offices or practice groups?

Should any roles or responsibilities be realigned post-merger?

Will the overall level of staffing within the department be appropriate to the future needs of the combined firm?

How can the combined department come together as a group and effectively collaborate going forward?

Resources

What technology resources are used by each of the combining law firm libraries (catalog or ILS, request tracking system, research usage monitoring, etc.)?

What processes and procedures are in place regarding print and online collection management?

What subscriptions does each combining firm maintain?

How will the geographic footprint of the combined firm or change in headcount in specific locations affect any site-specific or jurisdiction-based subscriptions?

For major online resources:

- When do subscriptions expire/renew?
- Are subscriptions firm-wide or assigned to designated users or teams?
- What product versions and/or content sets are included?
- Are any research subscriptions bundled with other products?
- What language is included in each subscription regarding mergers, changes of circumstance, firm growth/decline, assignment, cancellation, and other key terms?
- Who are the vendor representatives or contacts for each subscription?
- Who is historically responsible for each contract within the combining firms?
- Who will take the lead role in any vendor discussions related to the merger? Who else will be included in discussions?

Checklist

Confirm the nature of merger and the future firm name and entity.

Confirm the scope of the merger/acquisition, including whether the combination includes all attorneys from the legacy firms.

Confirm the timing of preliminary disclosure of existing subscriptions and contractual agreements to the other firm, subject to appropriate confidentiality.

Exchange information about existing staffing and organizational structure, subject to confidentiality.

Develop a strategy for team integration and schedule team calls as appropriate.

Create a merger project management or collaboration site, if appropriate.

Identify subscriptions and vendor contacts.

Identify individuals in the firm responsible for each contract.

Review subscription agreements, including clauses related to mergers and changes of circumstance. Note contract expiration dates, product versions, and any other differences.

Establish a communication plan for notifying vendors of the merger and initiating negotiations as needed.

Schedule internal project management touchpoint calls with individuals collaborating on contract review and negotiation.

Review the scope of services provided by each library, including non-traditional research and other types of services performed for the firm. Confirm the status of each area of responsibility within the combined firm.

As needed, prepare user guidance regarding changes in resource access or research services. Prepare or coordinate training on upgraded research platforms as needed.

Saskia Mehlhorn, director, Knowledge and Research Services at Norton Rose Fulbright US LLP, has experienced a variety of law firm mergers. Mehlhorn was with the law firm of Fulbright & Jaworski, at the time one of the largest law firms in the United States, when Fulbright combined with the international law firm Norton Rose, to form Norton Rose Fulbright. Other mergers followed as several international and United States firms joined with Norton Rose Fulbright, which is organized as a verein.

Mehlhorn recommends that any library leader whose firm is involved in a merger obtain as much information as possible, as early as possible in the process. As merging firms work toward combining library staff, operations, and subscriptions, early steps in the process include identifying the primary library contacts in the other merging entity and determining what resource subscriptions the other firm maintains.

Mehlhorn stresses the importance of carefully reviewing contracts ahead of the merger, in preparation for eventual discussions with vendors. Copies of existing subscription agreements should be shared between the combining firms for comparison, and each contract should be reviewed for pricing, content, and terms. Where each firm in the merger has existing subscriptions with a common vendor or resource, Mehlhorn, who is also an attorney, likes to use redlining to compare contract language. She also coordinates contract review with the firm's vendor relations office or in-house counsel. Additionally, Mehlhorn recommends preparing draft communications to be ready to send to vendor contacts as soon as possible once the merger is announced and confidentiality is no longer required. Discussions with each vendor can then proceed at a pace that makes sense for the specific circumstances. For any resources to which merging firms subscribe on a firm-wide (enterprise) or practice group basis, the relevant contracts may need to be combined in due course.

Combining the existing library personnel of merging firms is also an important step in the merger and often an ongoing process. Mehlhorn, who has been involved with mergers where each combining firm had an existing library team, notes that combining library teams can also be a very different experience depending on the nature of the merger. In an international merger, especially under the verein model, the combining firms' libraries may continue to function independently within their own jurisdictions. In these instances, library groups from the legacy firms can become available to each other as collaborative resources going forward, supporting occasional needs for cross-jurisdictional assistance. Mehlhorn has used introductory conference calls to enable such teams to get acquainted with each other and says the teams welcome the addition of cross-border support.

In mergers where library teams from different firms must be integrated within a single entity, this process can be challenging due to the potential differences in library service models and reporting structures of the legacy firm libraries, as well as the unique personalities, aptitudes, and interests of each individual employee. In mergers involving larger firms with well-established administrative structures and processes, the scale of the merger may pose additional challenges, as many, if not all, firm administrative departments will be undergoing similar integration, leading to additional uncertainty regarding the future organization of the firm. In addition, most administrative teams experience a surge in workload related to activities surrounding the merger, while individual employees likely feel some uncertainty about their future roles in the new firm.

Mehlhorn notes that in many mergers, the combining firms approach the combination desiring to protect current employees from potential job loss. However, some individual responsibilities could change, since, as with other types of organizational change, mergers may present an opportunity to realign library services and staff. During the sensitive process of integrating departments, Mehlhorn recommends working to find common ground among the merging teams and opening dialogue so that each employee has the opportunity to feel heard. On a practical level, these conversations should also include steps to learn about each team member's current role and abilities. As plans are made for the newly combined department, attention should also be paid to the historical differences in library functions between the legacy firms, so that individual personnel and the overall library structure can be aligned to most effectively serve the new firm.[6]

Many firms involved in mergers, especially smaller firms, may not have a professional library department. In a merger where one of the combining law firms does not have a library team, discussions must still take place to determine where various responsibilities related to the library currently reside. For example, online research subscriptions may be managed by a "library attorney" or a member of the finance team. Access to online resources may be assigned through the technology or human resources team as part of the attorney onboarding process. Print subscriptions may be overseen by an office administrator or another designated individual. In the midst of a merger with a firm where the management of library resources is decentralized, it can be challenging to uncover the different stakeholders who should be included in discussions about library matters. Once identified, though, many firm personnel who have been tasked with some aspect of library services in addition to their primary role will be delighted to hand over responsibility for these areas to the library team of the combined firm.

An additional challenge that arises in a merger where one firm lacks a formal library function is that, depending on the growth in the number of attorneys the library team may be called upon to support as a result of the merger, it may be difficult for existing staff to meet the increased workload as attorneys of the acquired firm discover the benefit of working with the library department for research resources and support.

Many newly merged firms, in addition to seeing increased business opportunities across the combined firm, experience an additional surge in lateral growth post-merger, as the expanded firm platform attracts both additional client business and new attorneys. The potential increase in business due to the combined effects of the merger, along with subsequent lateral growth, may contribute further increases in library utilization and could indicate a need for additional library staff to support the growing legal practice.

Consolidating Print and Online Collections

Merging law firm libraries must also address their separate print and online resource collections. This process includes consolidating vendor accounts and assigning ongoing print and electronic subscriptions to the new firm entity, and, as appropriate to the merger circumstances, combining or renegotiating contracts for online research platforms.

While the use of print libraries has declined dramatically, most firms still have some print materials on subscription. A merger presents the need to not only review and merge the legacy firms' print collections and subscriptions but also to compare and normalize the acquisition strategies and policies of the combining firms. The merger may provide an opportunity to further reduce print materials, especially where similar resources are maintained by the combining firms. Even where direct duplication of content is not a factor, some firms may use the merger as an opportunity to revise their collection policies in favor of future savings. For example, if one of the merging firms has a policy of not purchasing any print treatises available through an existing online subscription, members of the other legacy firm may be open to also discontinuing duplicative print in the spirit of creating a more consistent approach to resource spending across the combined firm.

Most firms subscribe to a number of online research platforms, ranging from single-user licenses for niche products to practice group subscriptions or site licenses for other specific resources, to firm-wide (enterprise) subscriptions for major research platforms. Merging firms should review existing subscriptions across the two combining firms, noting the various resources, vendors, types of licensing, expiration dates, costs, and key contract terms regarding renewal or cancellation, assignment, and mergers or change of circumstance. Potential duplicative resources should be noted, including any resources which might be subject to reevaluation at a future date.

The process of updating or combining subscriptions will vary according to the merger circumstances and details of existing contracts. The number of users on each account and the expiration date for each legacy subscription are key considerations, as are the specific terms and conditions of the existing agreements. Changes in circumstance and merger language in any existing agreements should be carefully reviewed, as the application of these terms may vary depending on the specifics of the merger. For example, if some firm members decline to join the newly combined firm, or if a smaller firm dissolves prior to the effective merger date, the combination might be treated as "organic" growth.

In addition to these important contract terms, special attention should be paid to subscription content sets and product versions. For some major research subscriptions which offer occasional "upgrades" to the newest version, merging firms may not be on the same version. In another common scenario, two combining firms may have subscriptions to the same online platform but include very different content sets due to the vendor supporting a high degree of content customization. The approach to combining subscriptions such as these may vary depending on the vendor, subscription renewal timeline, extent of account differences, and other factors. In any instance, the library should proactively gather as much information as possible and be prepared to address subscription differences with vendors and firm leaders, as they work toward the best resource allocation going forward. Even with advance preparation, for large and complex subscriptions, the process of renegotiating contracts for the merged firm can take some time, and legacy subscriptions may need to run in parallel for some time while terms of a new agreement are finalized.

Efficient access to any subscribed online resources is a key consideration, and even while contract discussions continue, attention must be given to this aspect of the user experience. For firms that have enabled Single Sign-On (SSO), changes in firm networks and email addresses post-merger can affect the SSO process. This is especially challenging in a situation where separate legacy subscriptions remain in place after a merger, while users are on a new single email domain. In such a scenario, unless steps are taken to address the new firm technology environment, existing SSO may break, or users may be inadvertently signed on to a research platform from the same vendor, but which has a different content set than they are accustomed to using. Library teams should work with their vendors and technology teams to ensure each subscription will be accessible to any assigned users.

A unified approach should also be taken toward client matter number validation or other logon requirements to ensure that any resources which require a client matter number are configured to the combined firm's correct matter number format. Any changes in login procedure should be communicated to affected users, along with clear guidance regarding the firm's policies regarding online research costs.

Additional Opportunities

Throughout the process of a law firm merger, it is often necessary to reach "across the aisle" to get things done, as the library and other teams collaborate with a variety of stakeholders from each firm to gather necessary current state information and prepare to meet the requirements and goals of the new firm. With law firm libraries known for their ability to effectively collaborate with other groups, as well as their proficiency in analyzing and organizing information, mergers can present additional opportunities for the library and knowledge team to provide additional value to the firm by supporting the merger efforts of firm administration and other departments. The library's contributions may extend throughout the merger, from initial groundwork to integration.

As a firm first considers merger opportunities, the library may conduct research to identify potential merger targets or to support the strategic evaluation of merger opportunities. This includes investigating the litigation and transaction background of other firms, identifying firm footprint and practice area alignment between firms, researching key law firm performance indicators such as published financial data, and providing background profiles on law firms or individual attorneys, including coverage in local and legal news sources.

When a potential merger appears to be beneficial, the firms' management teams will begin to exchange private information to further explore whether the combination would be a good fit. As these conversations among leadership progress, the library can continue to contribute through additional research as needed. If the knowledge team hosts collaboration sites or client extranets, it may consider offering a similar platform enabling leadership of the two firms to securely and conveniently exchange information. Hosting a merger site demonstrates the research department's expertise in this valuable area, while collecting contracts and other key documents in advance of the merger enables greater access and efficiency in combining accounts post-merger. As with any site containing sensitive information, the knowledge team should ensure that proper security is applied to the merger collaboration site to prevent disclosure of confidential information beyond those with authorization and a need to know.

Once firm leaders have come to an agreement, the work of combining firm systems may begin, even while a formal vote of firm partners or members is pending. At this stage in the merger process, the library and knowledge teams may begin supporting combination efforts within their own areas and across the firm. Teams with strong project experience may be tapped to help facilitate the combination of other departments, leveraging the team's expertise in subscription management, collaboration, and process evaluation and improvement.

As merger-related activity increases the workload across firm administrative teams, some firm departments may benefit from additional support with contract renewals or contract integration, so that they can focus on their core areas of expertise. For example, while the IT team prioritizes technical aspects of the merger, they might welcome support for collecting and comparing various technology subscriptions. In addition, with many vendors providing a variety of legal information and technology products which are used across many departments, firms often subscribe to multiple resources from major vendors. Where a number of contracts are in place and may have historically been managed by different teams, there may be a benefit to centralizing discussions with each of these major vendors. In some instances, it may be helpful to pair a librarian or knowledge management leader with a colleague from the finance or administrative team to facilitate these vendor discussions.

In some mergers, knowledge departments may be tapped to support not only subscription management, but even the processes of other functional groups. Some firm departments may require interim solutions to support efficient functioning during the merger process. For example, during the time leading up to the official combination or integration of firm systems, the two combining firms' conflicts and intake teams may need to run conflicts in separate systems and require a process to share results with their counterparts at the other firm. Where administrative processes differ widely between legacy teams, a member of the knowledge group with experience in process improvement and project management may act as a neutral party to help the subject-matter experts within conflicts or other administrative teams develop interim and future processes.

Just as the configuration of library services varies between firms, the role of library and knowledge teams in a merger will differ according to the needs of the combining firms and the backgrounds of the individuals involved. Openness to exploring ways in which the team can support the firm during this crucial time can lead to additional opportunities for the library and beneficial outcomes for the firm.

Once the merger is completed, contracts have been successfully renegotiated, teams and technologies have been integrated, and new processes have been implemented and operationalized, the library's role in supporting other departments may subside, but the team's contributions will help position the library for future success.

ONGOING EVOLUTION

With change as a constant within law firms and the legal industry overall, the core function of library and information professionals in facilitating access to information remains timeless and relevant. Indeed, the current diversity among law firm library departments as they successfully meet numerous distinct needs across the business of their firms also suggests the adaptability of these skilled teams to future needs which have not yet emerged.

Whether affected by mergers, organic growth, or other organizational changes, or simply subject to gradual shifts as the legal environment continues to evolve, the dynamic nature of law firm libraries points to ongoing opportunities to meet the research and information needs of their firms for years to come.

NOTES

1. Harbor, "The Harbor 2023 Benchmarking Library & Information Services Survey," 2023, https://harborglobal.com/services/community-insights/benchmarking-surveys/information-services-survey.
2. Ibid.
3. Interview with Colleen Cable, Director, Harbor's Research + Intelligence, July 18, 2024 via email.
4. Interview with Lori Martin, Director of Library and Research Services at Bradley Arant Boult Cummings LLP, July 1, 2024, via email.
5. Interview with Nancy Rine, Director of Research Services and Conflicts, Fried Frank Harris Shriver & Jacobson, LLP, July 3, 2024, via email.
6. Interview with Saskia Mehlhorn, Director, Knowledge and Research Services, Norton Rose Fulbright, LLP, interviewed on July 14, 2024, via email.

10

Digital Leases and Lost Legacies

The Quest for Sustainable Access

Sabrina Sondhi

Both academic and law firm libraries have been transitioning from print to digital for many years.[1] We rely on treatises in Westlaw and Lexis, looseleaf content in VitalLaw, and periodical material in HeinOnline. Digital material fulfills patron needs and fosters the possibility of remote work. It also accommodates the trend of shrinking library spaces and shrinking library budgets[2] and can reduce the amount of staff time needed to maintain a collection, for example, filing looseleafs, and stamping and shelving. In addition, certain resources are more efficient to use digitally rather than in print, for example, Shepard's. The transition from print collections to digital alternatives is sensible, so this chapter is by no means advocating that we return to a majority print-collection model. However, as we collectively move in the direction of primarily digital, we need to keep certain drawbacks and concerns in mind and minimize those negative aspects where possible.

This chapter collectively refers to "legal publishers," most often in a less than positive light due to their collective failure to address preservation and access goals. However, it's important to recognize that not all publishers behave alike. Some are more supportive of preservation and access goals than others. Aspects of this will be discussed below.

DRAWBACKS AND CONCERNS RELATED TO DIGITAL CONTENT

Our prior practice of collecting in print has led to certain assumptions about the role of libraries in preserving information. As Michelle Wu expressed twenty years ago, "[o]nce purchased, print materials belong to a library, which then has access to the material in perpetuity."[3] Given that reality, librarians as selectors have focused on the growth of a collection. "For decades, the formula for developing collections . . . was fairly clear: acquire the core primary and secondary materials,"[4] and supplement for specific local practice groups or curricular needs. Once the money was found to acquire something, that acquisition *stayed* in the collection and was available to patrons. Ending a print subscription meant that only future publications were sacrificed; the material already purchased remained available on the shelf and no one could take it away from us unless and until we *chose* to withdraw it.[5]

However, licensed digital collections turn that assumption on its head. No one truly owns digital property, except the publishers and copyright owners.[6] Digital licenses must be paid for each year, with the cost at the publisher's discretion. That payment by the library is only for temporary access to both the old and any newly added content. Termination of the subscription, due to budget constraints or otherwise, results in the library losing access to *all* of the content *and* having nothing to show for its previous annual payments. Given that draconian penalty to subscribing libraries, publishers are empowered to raise annual costs and disincentivized to produce more than the bare minimum of new content. Therefore, switching from purchased print materials to licensed digital content is not an even trade. So, digital leasing must be considered in a new light. We must consider these questions: How much is this specific resource worth to us and our patrons over time, and will it remain valuable to us in the long term?

We also hold many assumptions about how libraries (and librarians) support one another to fulfill patron needs. However, digital holdings, particularly leased titles, can restrict or counteract all of these supportive past practices. For example, interlibrary loan allows a library access to content by connecting with another library that possesses that content. Once the borrowing library acquired that content, they could provide it to their patron just like a normal loan of owned material. Unfortunately, many database licenses restrict a library's ability to share content with non-subscribers, including through interlibrary loan.[7] At first, the advantages of digital material may seem to outweigh this concern—a library can have most of what it needs and allow others to fill its gaps with their print holdings. However, as a library's digital holdings grow, that library will find itself in the position of being a net borrower for those gaps in its collection, meaning they borrow more than they lend. Over time, as more libraries use digital leasing, fewer and fewer lenders will be available. Thus, it weakens the interlibrary loan system as a whole and reduces the likelihood that a future borrower's needs can be met.

Relying on the assumption that "someone else" will hold an item in print is dangerous. It dates from a time when many of our print holdings overlapped, and there was a multitude of redundancies among libraries. When we weed our print collections, many libraries double-check WorldCat to confirm they are not discarding the last copy available in the shared ecosystem. However, when we switch to a digital leasing model and an individual library thereby gives up ownership of an item, that judgment call of whether or not to retain an item has *already* been made at the outset: it has already been discarded as the library does not own the item. Down the road, once everyone individually makes this choice, the decision becomes permanent—no library holds the item, and it potentially ceases to exist. That collective decision to discard may not become apparent for many years, at which point it is impossible to correct the error.[8]

Finally, we tend to hold assumptions about the stability of the content we pay for. For example, if we purchase a print treatise, we know that two months from now the content printed on the pages will remain the same—we're unlikely to discover a chapter ripped out or a section of material magically replaced with blank pages. But that fraught possibility is exactly what we sign up for when we license digital materials. Vendors are profit-driven, and maintenance of older or less-used digital materials still costs money. It is not unusual for a vendor to stop providing or offering less profitable content for sale.[9] Database vendors also license certain content to host in their product; when those licenses change, the content available in the database also changes. Sometimes these changes are announced, and other times the treatise or resource in question simply vanishes. Before, when libraries selected in print, publishers chose to make certain items available and libraries influenced that market by purchasing or not purchasing. Even if a publisher chose to let a title go out of print for profit reasons, multiple libraries held copies and remained willing to circulate them. Thus, in the past, we all had certainty that specific information would continue to be available. Libraries no longer control that outcome; publishers do.

Similarly, when we look to purchase or lease individual monographs, many libraries follow a purchase-on-demand or PDA model. The idea is that we can pay a small fee up-front to have the item in our catalog and we don't have to pay more unless and until a patron wants to use it. The previous print model relied upon a librarian selector, someone who could use their judgment to purchase items "just in case" a patron was likely to want them.[10] The choice of materials that a library held was meaningful; it often helped shape the research that its patrons did. However, a digital PDA "just-in-time" model puts the answer to the question "what should libraries hold" in the hands of publishers. Any remaining collection development decision-making is given to the patron, who may or may not be knowledgeable. Dangerously, the PDA model also relies "on the assumption that materials, once created, may always be acquired and purchased."[11] When a library purchases and holds a physical volume, it has made a choice. Now, whether or not a digital volume will be available for purchase in the future is a choice left in the hands of the publishers.

MORE POWER IN THE HANDS OF PUBLISHERS (IS BAD FOR LIBRARIES)

Over the past twenty years, we've also seen rapid consolidation of legal publishers. Where once there were over a dozen robust companies, we've shrunk to a handful as Lexis, Westlaw, Wolters Kluwer, and Bloomberg absorbed smaller companies.[12] Where once we had multiple providers covering a specific area of law, we now may be reduced to only one or two. As with any monopolistic system, this lack of competition has led to higher prices being charged for materials as libraries and researchers have fewer alternatives.

Unlike general publishers who must continually convince buyers to purchase new material, law publishers know that we *cannot* opt out of collecting certain material. There is a reason why a large part of law library budgets has been devoted to serials rather than monographs: we're locked in by the nature of legal information. If we are not purchasing a key treatise in print, we have to have the database that contains it. We must have a source of statutes and cases covering our jurisdictions—almost certainly digital, because using those sources in print was not an efficient process. These purchases are not optional for our patrons—practicing attorneys, law professors, and students—and the law publishers know this fact and use it against libraries ruthlessly with ever-rising prices for those products. This results in libraries having to make hard choices each year, made even more difficult by their flat or declining budgets.

So why do publishers continually raise prices when they know we don't have more money to spend? The simple answer is that they are fighting each other over the currently available income and the future market for legal publishing. Consider how some publishers have wooed law students—future attorneys—in the past: point systems, coffee mugs, and pizza during vendor presentations. Many students who begin law school with no preference between one database or another casually choose the vendor they'll prefer for the rest of their career based on this initial bribery. But many academic librarians have noted the drop-off of bribery attempts in recent years. Bloomberg Law no longer assigns reps to most law schools, and Westlaw's academic reps have seen an expansion of their service territories, resulting in fewer, if any, visits to the schools within their territories.

This withdrawal from the student market may be due to a shift in the publishers' focus. Big law firms were once more likely to subscribe to multiple databases and multiple publishers' material. If the incoming associates skewed in favor of one publisher's material, for example, Westlaw, then that could have major implications for the firm's future subscription choices and collection practices. However, with rising costs, there is a greater likelihood that a law firm will only subscribe to one database among the "big three." The attorneys' preference and each database's coverage will be factors, but the subtle choice of which database is chosen often falls to the librarian—and law librarians continue to be wooed by the legal publishers with free lunches, conference swag, and sponsorship of library associations. This speculative model indicates that attorneys have less ability to express their preference between multiple options because the choice will have already been made for them.

YOU HAVE (SOME) POWER: THINGS YOUR LIBRARY CAN DO

So how do we combat these concerns? We have no choice but to switch to digital options due to cost, lack of physical space, and our patrons' evolving needs. But those digital holdings can be ephemeral and yield too much power into the hands of the publishers. Happily, though, you still have some options for protecting the integrity of your library's and the larger legal community's long-term holdings.

One way to ameliorate some of these harms is to consider purchasing digital content instead of only leasing it. In your license agreement, this will be referred to as a "perpetual access model" rather than an "annual access model." Under a perpetual access model, if you decide to stop paying for the digital content in the future, you lose only the new content, not the old content. In other words, it's the equivalent of retaining the older issues of the print journal you paid for.

A perpetual access model has a steep initial cost. For example, a recent quote the author received for a database covering thirty years of digitized legal and political journals offered a perpetual access model for a $50,000 initial fee with a $3,000 annual fee for new content. That same database charged $7,000/year under an annual access model, that is, temporary leasing of the content. That differential may seem off-putting at first, but if there are valuable titles that are likely to be used long-term, meaning your patrons' research areas or practice groups won't shift away from them, the initial higher cost of perpetual access will even out over time. Plus, your library will have the ongoing benefit of ownership of that material.

Likewise, if there are valuable titles in your collection needs that don't require frequent updating, you should consider purchasing matching print materials in addition to leasing the digital content, that is, creating redundancy. Then, if your digital access ends, you'll still own that content and be able to make it available to your patrons. This will give you greater bargaining power with your digital content provider and ensure that your patrons are not bereft if you end up losing access to or cutting leased digital material.

Consider banding together with similarly sized libraries and sharing the collection development costs as a consortium. A classic example of this among academic law libraries is the PALMPrint archive, developed by the NELLCO law library consortium and the Legal Information Preservation Alliance (LIPA).[13] This archive collects and preserves federal and state primary legal materials and is jointly owned by its members. In exchange for an annual fee and shipping costs, member libraries may borrow print items. There is no comparably sized archive of secondary legal materials, but the creation of a smaller version among law libraries with shared collection needs would be relatively straightforward. A shared collecting agreement also need not cover your entire collection; it can be narrow in scope. For example, for many years, two large academic libraries in New York City informally agreed to purchase alternating editions of casebooks. This meant that collectively they each had access to an unbroken run of textbooks if their faculty wanted to use them, but each library bore only half the cost.

Another alternative to leasing digital material that you need less frequently is to allocate a portion of your budget to a membership at a subscription library that collects content in print. Like database leasing, subscription fees don't bestow ownership, but they grant access to a wider range of legal materials while supporting a library that is purchasing materials. Most legal subscription services are marketed to lawyers and law firms. They typically assess an annual fee and then may charge for research and/or retrieval services. Most will scan material and email digital content to the requestor. They also lend print-legal material. Examples of such providers include Columbia Law School in New York City, Jenkins Law Library in Philadelphia, and the LA Law Library in Los Angeles.[14]

POTENTIAL OPTIONS WHEN NEGOTIATING CONTRACTS

Finally, we must always keep in mind that licenses for digital content are *contracts*—which means that you as the purchaser can negotiate. Sometimes this won't work, particularly when monopolistic publishers know that you have few alternatives. But even the largest vendors have been known to agree to additional terms or to changes to boilerplate clauses in their agreements.

One potential change to ask for is to strike out any licensing provisions that prohibit the use of a database for interlibrary loan purposes.[15] After all, if you were purchasing a print copy, you would have the ability to make copies for certain purposes under copyright fair use. Retaining those equivalent rights when the copy is digital is something for which you can negotiate. Also discussed above concerning leased digital content is the specter of content removed by the publisher. Whether and how you will be notified of that content removal is something that you can request in the contract.

When purchasing digital content through a perpetual access model rather than leasing, reading your proposed contract carefully is even more important. Look ahead to what types of problems or concerns might arise, not only during the life of the contract but also in the future if you were to end the contract. In that possible future, how would you and your patrons be able to access the content you still own? Will you be able to use the publisher's database? Will the publisher provide the digital content to you on CD-ROM or on portable hard drives? During the life of the contract, can you upload the content you own to your intranet?

As for the usage of leased digital content, which patrons are permitted access? Is it only your students and faculty? Employees of your law firm? An enumerated list of attorneys in the practice group? Anyone who visits your library in person? Can your authorized users use this data for any purpose? Can it be redistributed in a course packet? Sold as part of a print binder for a CLE? None of these are new questions, but you should not assume the answers. You won't know the answers in your particular situation until you ask. If you are hesitant to negotiate and want more guidance, there are many books and resources available.[16]

One last thing to keep in mind when negotiating for digital content is the potential for future collective action by libraries against unfair dealings. Such possibilities require data, so when negotiating for digital content, librarians should document their requests and the publishers' responses. For example, make note of whether a publisher denies requests for purchase rather than licensing of digital content packages, whether a library is permitted to purchase or lease free-standing titles rather than an entire digital package, or pricing disparities for digital material if a library is seeking to pay for it rather than an individual purchaser. This type of information, collected by libraries, would potentially support and make possible collective anticompetitive and antitrust claims against publishers in the future.[17]

HOW TO PAY FOR IT

The major drawback of many of these strategies is that they cost money! Routinely purchasing print as well as digital content and joining subscription libraries both have ongoing, modestly higher costs. Purchasing digital content under a perpetual access model has a high initial cost but then a lower annual cost. Depending on the amount at issue, your library's budget may be able to absorb these costs. However, you can think of larger expenditures, like purchasing instead of leasing the content of a database, as a long-term investment for your institution. You may then have more success pitching these as one-time or unusual costs upward to your finance unit, law school dean, or managing partner.

When a purchase opportunity like this comes along, take some time to think about how it would fit into your institution's overall goals. Maybe the digital content would support certain tenured faculty or an established practice group in your firm. If so, would the lower perpetual access fee help the library guarantee that they can retain this subscription in the future? If you purchase matching print alongside digital material, would this result in teaching opportunities for your faculty? Will it allow you to pass along research charges to your firm's clients? If you pay the fee to join a subscription library, would you have greater access to materials you don't currently collect but that might support a foray into an additional practice area?

One key strategy is to think about how what *you* want for your library can be framed as a benefit to your decisionmaker and *their* priorities. For example, if you want to acquire perpetual access to a database full of Chinese law materials, you might argue to your Dean that having this collection would help your international programs department create exchange student opportunities with institutions in East Asia. Therefore, the initial high cost would benefit the law school's revenue over time. At a law firm, in order to argue for buying duplicative print materials such as court rules, you might point to the ever-increasing annual cost of the relevant database and argue against the firm's dependence upon a single vendor for its most basic research needs. If you can translate library purchases into metrics that matter for your institution—billable hours, reduced complaints, better retention of faculty, a larger number of student applicants—you are more likely to gain support from supervisors who may prioritize organizational rather than departmental goals.

CONCLUSION

The primary takeaway of this chapter is that we, as librarians, need to be deliberate in our choices. When we select digital content instead of print, we need to consider how that affects our library's long-term value and the broader health of our ecosystem as legal information providers. If your library does not already have a collection development policy that sets out parameters for print versus digital collecting priorities, you should consider creating one. If you already have one, take the time to review it annually and assess whether it still accurately reflects your library's and patrons' needs and realities.

The shift toward digital resources is inevitable, but it must be balanced with a commitment to preserving the integrity and accessibility of our collections. As stewards of legal information, we must ensure that our decisions today do not compromise the resources available to future generations. By being proactive, we can maintain the essential role of law libraries as reliable and comprehensive sources of legal knowledge.

NOTES

1. Claire M. Germain, "Digital Legal Information: Here Today, Gone Tomorrow?" *AALL Spectrum 2*, no. 8 (May 1998): 27.
2. Christine Bowersox and Sheri H. Lewis, "Collection Building in the Twenty-First Century: Law Firm and Academic Perspectives," *AALL Spectrum* 21, no. 6 (July/August 2017): 48–52.
3. Michelle M. Wu, "Why Print and Electronic Resources Are Essential to the Academic Law Library," *Law Library Journal* 97, no. 2 (Spring 2005): 233, 242.
4. Bowersox and Lewis, *Collection Building*, 50.
5. Wu, *Why Print and Electronic Resources Are Essential*, 243.
6. See, e.g., Joshua A. T. Fairfield, *Owned: Property, Privacy, and the New Digital Serfdom* (New York: Cambridge University Press, 2017).
7. Wu, *Why Print and Electronic Resources Are Essential*, 242.
8. This is the major argument for dark archives: to avert collective results stemming from individual actions, for example, everyone independently decides to weed "Book X." However, most dark archives for legal information have focused on primary material. There is little or no safety net for much of the secondary material we routinely discard or now subscribe to in digital form.
9. Wilhelmina Randtke, "Long Term Financial Costs of Maintaining a Digital Collection," *Technical Services Law Librarian* 43, no. 3 (March 2018): 11, 12.
10. *Id.* at 11.
11. *Id.*
12. See James Heller, "Do Androids Dream of Electric Books? Thoughts on Legal Content Dissemination and Consumption in the Digital Environment," *AALL Spectrum* 18, no. 1 (September/October 2013): 23, 24. Providing a description of some of these acquisitions by other legal publishers.

13. See "PALMPrint Law Library Consortium, Inc.," *NELLCO*, accessed August 18, 2024, https://www.nellco.org/page/palmprint.
14. See "Fee-Based Services," *Columbia Law School*, last modified January 9, 2024, accessed August 18, 2024, https://guides.law.columbia.edu/fbs/subscriptionservice/faqs; "Overview," *Jenkins Law Library*, accessed August 18, 2024, https://www.jenkinslaw.org/membership/overview; "Members Program Borrowing Rules," *LALAWLIBRARY*, last modified November 1, 2021, accessed August 18, 2024, https://www.lalawlibrary.org/pdfs/Members%20Borrowing%20Rules%2012_1_2021.pdf.
15. Wu, *Why Print and Electronic Resources Are Essential*, 242.
16. See, e.g., Lesley Ellen Harris, "Licensing Digital Content for Your Library," *AALL Spectrum* 5, no. 5 (February 2001): 28–30; Lesley Ellen Harris, *Licensing Digital Content: A Practical Guide for Librarians* (Chicago, IL: American Library Association, 2002).
17. See Michelle M. Wu, "Restoring the Balance of Copyright: Antitrust, Misuse, and Other Possible Paths to Challenge Inequitable Licensing Practices," *Law Library Journal* 114, no. 2 (Spring 2022): 131, 152–153.

11

Risk Management in Law Libraries

Marci Wilding

The pivotal role that libraries serve in supporting legal professionals and scholars comes with a unique set of risks that must be managed effectively to ensure libraries can continue to fulfill their mission. Libraries face a broad spectrum of risks, including legal, financial, operational, and reputational challenges. Legal risks may arise from issues such as copyright infringement, breaches of confidentiality, or failure to comply with regulatory requirements. Financial risks can stem from budget cuts, misallocation of funds, or economic downturns that affect funding sources. Operational risks encompass disruptions to library services due to natural disasters, technological failures, or staffing shortages. Additionally, reputational risks may result from negative public perception, data breaches, or controversial content.

Effective risk management is crucial for libraries to navigate these challenges and achieve their mission. "Risk management can be defined as a systematic process of identifying, analyzing, and quantifying the risks of human, physical, and financial loss to preserve the assets of the library by selecting the most appropriate method of managing those risks through avoidance, prevention, reduction, knowing assumption, transfer of the risk of loss to others, or by the purchase of insurance."[1] By proactively identifying, assessing, and mitigating risks, libraries can safeguard their assets, ensure the continuity of services, and maintain the trust and confidence of their users and stakeholders.

UNDERSTANDING RISK IN LIBRARIES

Risks are inherent in any organization, and for libraries, they can manifest in various forms such as legal, financial, operational, and reputational risks. Legal risks in libraries often involve issues related to compliance with laws and regulations. For example, failing to adhere to copyright laws can result in legal disputes and fines, while noncompliance with privacy regulations can lead to breaches of confidentiality and potential lawsuits. Libraries must navigate a complex legal landscape to ensure they operate within the bounds of the law, protecting both their collections and their users' rights.

Financial risks are another critical concern. Libraries, particularly those in law firms and academic institutions, often operate under tight budget constraints. Risks in this category include funding cuts, economic downturns, and financial mismanagement. For instance, unexpected budget reductions can force libraries to curtail services, reduce staff, or delay important projects, impacting their ability to support their users adequately.

Operational risks pertain to the day-to-day functioning of the library. These can include staff shortages, technology failures, and service disruptions. For example, a library might face operational risks when key staff members retire or leave the organization, resulting in a loss of expertise and institutional knowledge. Similarly, reliance on outdated technology can lead to system failures, impeding access to digital resources and hindering library operations.

Reputational risks involve the potential for damage to the library's public image and credibility. Negative publicity, whether due to controversial acquisitions, data breaches, or stakeholder dissatisfaction, can tarnish a library's reputation. For instance, a high-profile data breach could not only compromise sensitive information but also erode trust among patrons and stakeholders, affecting the library's long-term reputation and effectiveness.

The sources of risks in libraries are varied and can be both internal and external. Internal sources of risk often stem from within the organization. Staff turnover and competency gaps pose significant internal risks. When experienced staff members leave, they take with them valuable knowledge and skills, creating gaps that can affect service quality. Inadequate policies and procedures, as well as a lack of training and awareness among staff, can further exacerbate these risks. For example, if staff members are not well-versed in cybersecurity best practices, the library becomes more vulnerable to cyber threats.

External sources of risk originate outside the organization and can include changes in legislation and regulations, economic instability, and technological advancements. For instance, new legislation might impose additional compliance requirements, increasing the administrative burden on the library. Economic instability can lead to funding cuts, while rapid technological advancements pose continuous challenges in terms of keeping up with new tools and protecting against cybersecurity threats.

The interconnectedness of these sources of risk is an important consideration. Internal and external risks often reinforce each other, creating a complex web of challenges. For example, economic instability (an external factor) can lead to budget cuts, which may result in staff layoffs (an internal factor), subsequently increasing operational risks due to a reduced workforce and expertise. The impact of these risks on libraries can be profound.

Understanding the types and sources of risks that libraries face is the first step in developing effective risk management strategies. By recognizing the potential operational, financial, and reputational impacts of these risks, libraries can better prepare to address and mitigate them, ensuring they continue to fulfill their mission and serve their communities effectively.

LEGAL FRAMEWORK FOR RISK MANAGEMENT

Libraries, whether in law firms, government agencies, or academic institutions, must adhere to a variety of laws and regulations that govern their operations. Understanding these legal requirements and implementing robust compliance measures are critical steps in mitigating legal risks and ensuring that libraries can continue to serve their patrons effectively and lawfully.

One of the fundamental areas of concern is copyright law. Libraries play a pivotal role in providing access to a vast array of copyrighted materials, making adherence to copyright regulations crucial. Copyright laws protect the intellectual property rights of creators, and libraries must ensure that they do not infringe upon these rights.[2] This involves careful management of digital and physical collections, adherence to licensing agreements, and educating staff and patrons about the limitations and allowances under copyright law. Failure to comply can result in legal disputes, financial penalties, and reputational damage.

Privacy laws, such as the General Data Protection Regulation (GDPR) and the Health Insurance Portability and Accountability Act (HIPAA), impose stringent requirements on how libraries collect, store, and use personal data. Libraries must implement comprehensive data privacy policies to protect patron information from unauthorized access and breaches.[3] This includes securing digital records, controlling access to sensitive information, and ensuring that data handling practices comply with legal standards. Libraries must also be transparent about their data practices, providing patrons with clear information on how their data is used and protected.

The Freedom of Information Act (FOIA) is another significant regulation that impacts libraries, particularly those in the government sector.[4] FOIA mandates that libraries provide access to public records upon request, promoting transparency and accountability. Libraries must establish procedures for handling FOIA requests efficiently and ensure that they comply with legal timelines and confidentiality requirements. This can be challenging, especially when balancing the need for openness with the protection of sensitive information.

Accessibility laws, such as the Americans with Disabilities Act (ADA), require libraries to make their resources and services accessible to individuals with disabilities. This includes providing alternative formats for materials, ensuring the physical accessibility of library spaces, and offering assistive technologies. Compliance with these laws is not only a legal obligation but also a moral imperative to ensure equitable access to information for all patrons. Libraries must regularly assess their accessibility measures and make necessary adjustments to accommodate the diverse needs of their users.

In addition to these specific regulations, libraries must also uphold the principles of intellectual freedom, which are central to their mission. Intellectual freedom encompasses the right to access information without censorship and the protection of patrons' rights to read, view, and inquire freely. Libraries must resist external pressures to censor materials and ensure that their collections reflect a wide range of viewpoints. This commitment to intellectual freedom can sometimes lead to legal challenges, especially when controversial materials are involved, but it is a fundamental aspect of a library's role in a democratic society.

RISK ASSESSMENT IN LIBRARIES

Risk assessment is a critical element of the risk management process in libraries, serving as the foundation for identifying, analyzing, and prioritizing potential threats that could impact library operations. In the context of libraries, risk assessment involves a systematic approach to identifying vulnerabilities and implementing strategies to mitigate these risks, ensuring that libraries can continue to fulfill their mission effectively and sustainably. This involves a thorough examination of both internal and external factors that could pose risks.

Conducting regular risk assessments offers several benefits. It enables libraries to improve decision-making by providing a clear understanding of potential risks and their implications. This knowledge allows library managers to allocate resources more effectively, prioritizing areas that require immediate attention. Additionally, regular risk assessments foster a culture of awareness and preparedness, encouraging staff to remain vigilant and proactive in identifying and addressing potential issues.

The risk assessment process in libraries comprises several key components. The first step is risk identification, which involves identifying potential risks. Brainstorming sessions with staff can generate a wide range of potential risks, while SWOT analysis (assessing strengths, weaknesses, opportunities, and threats) provides a structured approach to identifying vulnerabilities. Reviewing historical data and incident reports also helps in identifying recurring issues and potential risks based on past experiences.

Once risks are identified, the next step is risk analysis, which involves assessing the likelihood of each risk occurring and its potential impact on library operations. This analysis helps in understanding the severity of each risk and its potential consequences, allowing for more informed decision-making. Following risk analysis is risk evaluation, where identified risks are evaluated as to their significance. This involves prioritizing risks according to their potential impact and likelihood, which helps libraries focus on the most critical threats. Prioritization is essential in ensuring that resources are allocated effectively to mitigate the most significant risks.[5]

Several methods and tools can facilitate the risk assessment process. A risk matrix/heat map is a valuable tool for assessing and prioritizing risks based on their likelihood and impact, as you can see in figure 11.1.[6] Note how your matrix is structured in terms of number, severity and likelihood headings, and determination of risk level depends on the risk appetite of your organization. Risk appetite is "the types and amount of risk, on a broad level, an organization is willing to accept in pursuit of value."[7] Therefore, the structure of the matrix and the ultimate determinations of the risks therein will vary from library to library and over time. By plotting risks on a matrix, libraries can visually identify which risks require immediate attention and which can be monitored over time. You can describe the risk as high, medium, or minimal risk or numerically with number ranges that you set as an organization.

Risk registers are another valuable tool, providing a structured way to document identified risks, their potential consequences, and proposed mitigation strategies, which you can see in figure 11.2.[8] These registers serve as a central repository for tracking risks and their management over time. When assessing which risks to address first, you will need to determine what risk mitigation intervention would have the greatest impact. When allocating resources for risk mitigation, if the risk level for a specific identified risk has increased since your last evaluation, it is wise to investigate and address this risk promptly, as it is active and has the potential to escalate further.

Technology solutions, such as risk management software, can streamline the risk assessment process by automating data collection, analysis, and reporting. These tools offer real-time insights into potential risks, enabling libraries to respond more quickly and effectively. They also facilitate ongoing monitoring and review, ensuring that risk management efforts remain dynamic and responsive to changing conditions.

	Likelihood	5-Very Likely	4-Likely	3-Possible	2-Unlikely	1-Highly Unlikely
Severity	5-Very serious-financial loss, increased training, loss of resources, immediate action needed	25	20	15	10	5
	4-Significant-resources lost or increased resources needed	20	16	12	8	4
	3-Moderate-action needed to prevent loss or injury	15	12	9	6	3
	2-Minor-some effects on resource allocation	10	8	6	4	2
	1-Negligible-dedicating resources to risk needs evaluation	5	4	3	2	1

High Risk Medium Risk Low Risk

Figure 11.1 Library Risk Matrix-Heat Map. *Source*: Created by author.

Risk Description	Possible Consequences	Likelihood	Severity	Risk Rating	Goal Rating	Date	Owner	Mitigation Strategy
Legal								
Copyright Infringement	Monetary penalties and reputational damage	2	3	6	1	5/1/2024	Mary Edwards	Create guidelines for copying with training
Financial								
Budget Cut	Reduced services and resource availability	4	4	16	10	1/1/2025	Tim Smith	Obtain admin projections. Evaluate use of subscription services
Operational								
Power Outage	Disrupted operations and service	4	3	12	10	3/1/2024	Pam Sage	Create map of generator supplied power with tech.
Reputational								
Controversial Content	Public backlash, censorship	4	3	12	6	5/1/204	Mary Edwards	Create policy for content complaints. Create public notice

High Risk **Medium Risk** **Low Risk**

Figure 11.2 Library Risk Register. *Source*: Created by author.

The risk assessment process in libraries can be broken down into a step-by-step approach. First, establish the context by understanding the library's operating environment and objectives, keeping your organization's individualized risk appetite in mind. Next, identify risks through brainstorming, SWOT analysis, and reviewing historical data. Then, analyze and evaluate the identified risks, assessing their likelihood and impact. Develop risk mitigation strategies based on this evaluation, focusing on the most significant risks. Finally, implement a system for monitoring and reviewing risks, ensuring that the library remains prepared to address new and evolving threats.

Roles and responsibilities in the risk assessment process should be clearly defined. Library leadership should oversee the process, ensuring that risk management efforts align with the library's strategic goals. Staff at all levels should be involved in identifying risks and implementing mitigation strategies, fostering a collaborative approach to risk management. In order to identify risks, keep in mind that staff need risk training.

RISK MITIGATION STRATEGIES

Risk mitigation is a fundamental aspect of risk management in libraries, playing a crucial role in minimizing or eliminating potential threats that could disrupt operations, damage reputations, or incur financial losses. Risk mitigation is defined as "the reduction of the likelihood that a risk event will occur and/or reduction of the effect of the risk event if it does occur."[9] This proactive approach is essential for libraries to operate smoothly and efficiently, as it helps prevent or minimize the negative consequences of various threats.

Several types of risk mitigation strategies can be employed in libraries, each tailored to address specific risks effectively. One common strategy is risk avoidance, which involves refraining from activities or decisions that could lead to potential risks. For example, a library may choose not to acquire certain rare or fragile materials that could be easily damaged or stolen, thereby avoiding the associated risks altogether.

Another effective strategy is risk reduction, which aims to minimize the likelihood or impact of risks through proactive measures. Libraries can reduce risks by implementing robust policies and procedures, upgrading technology, and enhancing physical security. For instance, installing surveillance cameras and access control systems can significantly reduce the risk of theft and vandalism, while regular maintenance and updates of IT systems can mitigate the risk of technology failures.

Risk transfer is a strategy that involves shifting the potential consequences of risks to third parties, such as insurance companies or service providers. By purchasing insurance coverage, libraries can transfer the financial burden of certain risks, such as property damage or liability claims, to the insurer. This not only provides financial protection but also allows libraries to focus on their core mission without the constant worry of catastrophic losses. There is also the option to share the risk in partnerships or co-ownerships.

In some cases, libraries may decide to accept certain risks without taking further action. This strategy, known as risk acceptance, is appropriate when the cost of mitigating a risk outweighs the potential impact of the risk itself. For example, a library may accept the risk of occasional equipment malfunctions if the cost of acquiring redundant systems is prohibitive. However, this decision should be made carefully, with a clear understanding of the potential consequences and a plan for managing them if they arise.

Implementing risk mitigation strategies involves developing detailed risk treatment plans that outline the specific actions to be taken to address identified risks, as shown in table 11.1.[10] These plans should include clear objectives, timelines, and responsibilities, ensuring that all staff members understand their roles in the risk mitigation process. Regular monitoring and review of these plans are essential to assess their effectiveness and make necessary adjustments.

By fostering a culture of continuous improvement, libraries can stay ahead of emerging threats and adapt to changing circumstances. This involves regularly reviewing risk assessments, updating policies and procedures, and incorporating feedback from staff and patrons. One potential schedule would be to review your heat map settings once a year with your strategic plan. This will align your work with your organization's work. Create the risk register using the updated risk matrix and formulate the risk treatment plans for the top 5–10 risks prioritized and identified. These treatment plans should be updated at the intervals you define: monthly, quarterly, or biannually.

CRISIS MANAGEMENT AND BUSINESS CONTINUITY PLANNING

In the realm of law librarianship, where the stability and accessibility of information are paramount, crisis management and business continuity planning emerge as critical components of risk management in order to prepare libraries to withstand and recover from unexpected disruptions. Crisis management involves preparing for, responding to, and recovering from events that threaten the normal operations of a library[11] ranging from natural disasters to security breaches and public relations issues. Effective crisis management ensures that libraries can continue to serve their communities even in the face of significant challenges.[12]

Identifying the types of crises that libraries might face is the first step in developing robust crisis management plans. Natural disasters can devastate physical infrastructure and collections. Security breaches, whether physical or cyber, pose risks to the confidentiality and integrity of library resources and patron data. Public relations crises can tarnish a library's reputation and erode public trust. Libraries should also prepare for power outages, cyberattacks, pandemics, fires, water damage, technological failures, staff shortages, economic downturns, and censorship challenges.

Table 11.1 Library Risk Treatment Plan

Budget Cuts for 2025–2026 Fiscal Year			*Risk Level 16*	*Goal Level 10*
Initiative	*Mitigation Strategy*	*Owner*	*Evaluation*	*Date*
Review library services and programs to identify those essential	Reduce avoidance	Mary Edwards	Focus on core functions, less critical programs identified to scale back	Completed 2/1/2024; list located 2025 Risk box folder "Prioritization List"
Develop alternative revenue streams	Reduce	Obhed Guthrie	Grand awards, paid events, premium services, donations	In process—2 grants applied for on 2/1/2024, contacts with known alumni made 3/1/2024
Form strategic partnerships and cost-sharing opportunities	Share	Obhed Guthrie	Shared resources, co-hosted events	In process—contact to chamber on 2/1/2025, partnership with the main library for a speaker series 3/1/2024
Optimize operational efficiency	Reduce	Lisa Jones	Vendor negotiations streamlined workflows	In process—opened negotiations with vendors on 2/1/2024, 3 vendors successful negotiations estimated savings 12K next year on 3/1/2024, Mapping circulation and ILL workflows

A well-prepared library has a designated crisis response team of trained staff members. This team coordinates the response, establishes clear communication protocols, and ensures all stakeholders are informed. Effective communication is crucial during a crisis, as timely and accurate information can mitigate the impact and facilitate recovery. Prevention is critical. Regular risk assessments can identify vulnerabilities and develop strategies to mitigate them. Training programs ensure staff are aware of potential risks and know how to respond effectively, significantly reducing the likelihood of a crisis.

Preparedness involves developing comprehensive crisis management plans and conducting regular drills. These plans outline specific actions for different types of crises, ensuring all team members are familiar with their roles. Drills help test these plans, providing opportunities to identify weaknesses and make adjustments. During a crisis, the response phase is activated. The crisis response team implements the crisis management plan, focusing on minimizing harm and restoring normal operations quickly. Clear and consistent communication with stakeholders is essential to maintain trust and provide reassurance.

The recovery phase involves assessing the crisis's impact, restoring library operations, and evaluating the response's effectiveness. This phase is critical for learning and improvement, providing insights into what worked well and what could be improved for future crises. Libraries should document these lessons and incorporate them into their crisis management plans.

Business continuity planning ensures the continuity of library operations during and after a crisis. Key components of a business continuity plan include identifying critical functions and resources, such as core services, essential staff, and critical technology systems. Establishing alternative facilities and systems ensures the library can continue operations even if the primary location is compromised.

Effective communication procedures keep all stakeholders informed and engaged during a crisis. This plan serves as a roadmap for maintaining essential services and minimizing disruptions. Regular drills and simulations help identify weaknesses and provide opportunities for improvement. Continuous monitoring and updating ensure the plan remains relevant and effective against evolving risks.

The relationship between crisis management and business continuity planning is interconnected. While crisis management focuses on the immediate response, business continuity planning ensures long-term resilience. Together, these practices provide a comprehensive framework for maintaining stability and continuity in the face of adversity.

STAFF TRAINING AND DEVELOPMENT

Ensuring library professionals are well-prepared to manage potential risks safeguards the institution and enhances the quality of service provided to patrons. The first step in developing an effective training program is a training needs assessment, identifying the specific requirements of library staff concerning risk management. Conducting a thorough needs assessment ensures that training is relevant and targeted. Methods include surveys to gather broad data on staff perceptions, interviews for in-depth discussions, and observations to highlight areas where additional training is required. Combining these methods creates a comprehensive picture of training needs.

Key areas of staff training in risk management include risk awareness, compliance training, emergency response training, and cybersecurity training. Risk awareness training educates staff on identifying and reporting risks, such as suspicious activities or potential hazards. Compliance training covers legal requirements like copyright laws and data privacy regulations. Emergency response training includes procedures for evacuations, crisis communication, and first aid. Cybersecurity training focuses on protecting against data breaches and cyberattacks.

Developing a successful training program involves defining clear and measurable objectives, selecting effective training methods, and creating supporting materials. Workshops and seminars offer interactive learning, while online courses provide flexibility. Effective materials, such as presentations and videos, enhance understanding and serve as valuable references.

Careful implementation of training programs is necessary, including scheduling to accommodate staff availability and minimizing disruptions to library operations. Engaging staff through interactive elements, such as discussions and hands-on activities, enhances understanding and retention. Evaluating the effectiveness of training programs through assessments, surveys, and participant feedback ensures continuous improvement. By prioritizing staff training and development, libraries build a resilient workforce capable of managing risks proactively, contributing to a safer and more secure environment for all patrons.

CASE STUDIES IN CRISIS MANAGEMENT AND BUSINESS CONTINUITY PLANNING

Case Study 1—Natural Disaster in Academic Library

Background

The University Law Library, located in a region prone to severe weather, serves as a critical resource for law students, faculty, and legal researchers. The library houses an extensive collection of legal texts, digital resources, and archival materials. With a dedicated staff of twenty-five professionals, the library supports a wide range of academic and research activities.

Crisis Scenario

In September 2023, a Category 4 hurricane, Hurricane Lydia, was forecasted to make landfall near the university. The impending storm posed significant risks, including potential flooding, power outages, and physical damage to the library building and its collections.

Crisis Management Plan Activation

Preparation Phase:

1. Risk Assessment: The library had conducted a risk assessment the previous year, identifying hurricanes as a high-probability, high-impact risk. Consequently, the library had developed a comprehensive crisis management plan.
2. Crisis Response Team: The library's crisis response team, led by the Head Librarian, included representatives from IT, facilities, collections management, and public relations.
3. Preventive Measures: In anticipation of the hurricane, the team took several preventive measures:
   - Moved rare and valuable materials to higher floors.
   - Secured windows and doors with storm shutters.
   - Backed up all digital data to an off-site location.
   - Instructed staff to unplug electronic equipment and cover it with waterproof materials.

Response Phase:

1. Evacuation and Safety: Two days before the hurricane's landfall, the university announced a mandatory evacuation. The crisis response team ensured all staff and patrons were safely evacuated and provided clear instructions for personal safety.
2. Communication: The team established a communication protocol using email, social media, and the university's emergency alert system to keep stakeholders informed. Updates included the library's closure status, safety tips, and expected timelines for reopening.
3. Monitoring: Throughout the storm, team members monitored the situation remotely using weather updates and reports from the university's emergency management team.

Recovery Phase:

1. Damage Assessment: Once the storm passed, the crisis response team conducted a damage assessment. They found minor flooding on the ground floor, broken windows, and some water damage to materials that were not moved.
2. Restoration: The team implemented the recovery plan.
   - Engaged a professional restoration company to address water damage and mold prevention.
   - Collaborated with the university's facilities management to repair broken windows and ensure structural safety.
   - Worked with IT to verify the integrity of digital systems and restore services.
3. Communication with Stakeholders: Regular updates were provided to staff, students, and faculty regarding the progress of restoration efforts and timelines for reopening.

Business Continuity Plan Implementation

Critical Functions and Resources:

1. Alternative Facilities: The business continuity plan identified a temporary location in another building on campus where critical library services could continue. This facility had backup power and internet connectivity.
2. Essential Services: The plan prioritized maintaining digital access to legal databases and e-resources, essential for students and faculty continuing their studies and research remotely.
3. Staff Reassignment: Staff were reassigned to the temporary facility and worked remotely where possible. Duties included processing digital requests, virtual reference services, and maintaining online resources.

Communication and Notification Procedures:

1. Notification System: The business continuity plan included an automated notification system to inform staff and patrons about the relocation and available services.
2. Stakeholder Engagement: Regular meetings via video conferencing were held with staff to coordinate efforts and provide updates. Social media and the library's website were continuously updated to keep patrons informed.

Testing and Maintenance:

1. Drills and Simulations: Prior to Hurricane Lydia, the library had conducted regular drills simulating various crises, including hurricanes. These drills helped refine the crisis management and business continuity plans, ensuring staff were familiar with their roles.
2. Continuous Improvement: Post-crisis, the team conducted a thorough review of the response and recovery efforts. Lessons learned were documented, and plans were updated to address identified gaps and improve future readiness.

Case Study 2—Leadership Transition in Government Library

"About 5 months after I started this job in 2022, our chief financial officer died. The knowledge of our internal controls, our income flow, and many other financial functions died with them. It will be obvious the risk this creates in any organization. Law libraries tend to be hierarchically shallow, so the loss of any key employee may mean an entire function is eliminated. We had no financial analysts or support staff.

Government law libraries have some particular challenges when it comes to money. We tend to be funded almost wholly by public funds. Usually, we are funded by fees received by the courts when a case is filed. The spending of that money is constrained, usually by a governance oversight like a board of trustees and is audited. Any interruption in the oversight and management of those funds can be an existential risk.

The initial focus was to ensure that our statutorily mandated monthly governance meetings continued to provide our governance board with accurate financial information. Due to the number of uncertainties, we switched to reports generated directly from our accounting software. In this way, I could be sure that there were not any errors in transposition or any undocumented provenance for where the money was coming from or going to.

We then had to determine what to do with the role. We decided to professionalize the financial function. The CFO had not had an accounting degree or background but, like many organizations, had been promoted into the role from an adjacent one. I contracted with an external accountant who would take on our monthly financial reporting and reconciliation to ensure continuity. And I postponed the decision about whether to hire a new financial staff person.

All of this was contemporaneous with our annual government oversight audit. In a way, it was extremely helpful. There were huge knowledge gaps, but the auditor had some of our historical knowledge. The new accountant was quickly able to identify issues or challenges that might be coming based on historical financial data. As we worked through the audit, more gaps appeared and were closed.

Some of these were small things. We shifted from only one person having access to the bank account or the accounting software to having multiple people. It did not mean they could move money around but there was greater transparency. Now, if one of our management team wants to see invoices charged to their department, they can do so directly. And if the person responsible for the financial reporting leaves or is incapacitated, other staff can immediately pick-up the responsibility.

We also shifted our bill payment process to improve transparency. As you know, there have been cases of law librarians embezzling from their libraries. We took this moment to make as many processes as transparent as possible. Just as with our banking, our management team approves invoices in a central online application and the approval process is transparent to everyone involved.

An important reason for choosing online tools, for accounting and for expense payment, was to enable the accountant and the auditor to also be able to access those systems directly. On previous audits, we had provided data or images to them, but they could not see the source. We have eliminated that opaqueness by giving them direct access to apps so they can view transactions and any associated audit trail.

The one area that we could not automate or professionalize was our internal controls. More than 95 percent of our income is deposited in our bank account by the Administrative Office of the Courts. This means our staff does not handle a lot of cash or checks or other payments. At the suggestion of our auditor, though, we engaged a second auditor to look at our internal controls for handling money.

It was a long process. It has been nearly 2 years since our CFO's death. All of our process changes and the internal controls review happened within a single fiscal year. We have had only one complete fiscal year since then, to assess whether the changes we have made worked or not and to tweak those that needed improvement.

In a way, having a significant risk arise was good for the organization. Our governance board was more aware of what they may not know or need to ask about. We had an opportunity to professionalize a key, perhaps the key, operational function. We decided to stay with an outsourced accountant to help with continuity and resilience. Our reporting is clearer and more improved. As the director, I feel as though I know much more, and I am confident that my management team knows much more, about how the money flows through our law library, even when they are not involved in receiving or spending it."[13]

WHAT DOES RISK MANAGEMENT MEAN FOR US?

Effective risk management is crucial for the sustainability and resilience of libraries, especially in law firm, government, and academic law library settings. Throughout our exploration, we have highlighted the criticality of identifying and mitigating risks to shield libraries from harm and guarantee uninterrupted services. Regular risk assessments and effective mitigation strategies are key to proactively managing risks and fortifying resilience.

Best practices in risk management include deploying robust data security measures, providing comprehensive staff training, and formulating meticulous crisis management plans. However, libraries often face challenges such as financial constraints and lack of awareness, which can impede the implementation of these practices.

Looking ahead, libraries must continually refine their risk management practices through regular assessments, ongoing training, and adaptability to evolving risks. Future research in risk management within libraries could explore the impacts of emerging technologies on risk management practices. This exploration could yield valuable insights into how libraries can adapt and evolve their practices to mitigate risks effectively in a rapidly changing environment.

NOTES

1. Sally Alexander, Mary Breighner, and Jeanne Drewes, eds., *Risk Management and Insurance Manual for Libraries* (ALA Editions, Core Publishing), Chap. 1, Page 3, 2021, https://alastore.ala.org/sites/default/files/book_samples/9780838948019_sample.pdf.
2. Kenneth Crews, *Copyright Law for Librarians and Educators* (Chicago: American Library Association, 2020), 9-10.
3. ALA, *Library Privacy Guidelines for Library Management Systems,* https://www.ala.org/advocacy/privacy/guidelines/library-management-systems.
4. E. Shepherd, A. Stevenson, and A. Flinn, "The Impact of Freedom of Information on Records Management and Record Use in Local Government: A Literature Review," *Journal of the Society of Archivists* 30(2), 227-248, https://doi.org/10.1080/00379810903445000.
5. A. H. Kuzucuoglu, "Risk Management in Libraries, Archives and Museums," *IIB International Refereed Academic Social Sciences Journal* 5, no. 15 (2014): 277-294, https://www.proquest.com/scholarly-journals/risk-management-libraries-archives-museums/docview/1647083539/se-2.
6. Full-color PDF editable figures may be found here:

   Marci Wilding, "Figure 11-1, 11-2, 11-3," in *Law Librarianship Practice: Challenges and Opportunities in Law Firm, Government, and Academic Law Libraries,* ed. Ellyssa Kroski (Rowman & Littlefield Publishers, 2025), 1, https://archive.org/details/figures-11-1-11-2-11-3-color-law-librarianship-practice.
7. Frank Martens and Larry Rittenberg, *Risk Appetite-Critical to Success: Using Risk Appetite to Thrive in a Changing World*" (Research, COSO, 2020), 1. https://www.worldcomplianceassociation.com/noticias/noticia_doc_wca__seg_220520_243166.pdf.
8. Wilding, "Figure 11-1, 11-2, 11-3", 2, https://archive.org/details/figures-11-1-11-2-11-3-color-law-librarianship-practice.
9. National Academies Sciences, Engineering, & Medicine, *The Owner's Role in Project Risk Management.* (Consensus Study Report, Washington, DC: National Academies Press, 2005), 41.
10. Wilding, "Figure 11-1, 11-2, 11-3," 3, https://archive.org/details/figures-11-1-11-2-11-3-color-law-librarianship-practice.
11. Example of Physical Disaster Response plan: University of Washington Libraries, "Disaster Response Plan for Library Collections," https://www.lib.washington.edu/preservation/disaster/unit-plan.
12. ALA, *Resource Guide for Library Safety and Preparedness,* https://www.ala.org/advocacy/resource-guide-library-safety-and-preparedness.
13. David Whelan, "Risk Management in Libraries" interview by Marci Wilding, unpublished, June 18, 2024, email.

Part II

Law Library Technologies

12

The Law Library Website

Jingwei Zhang and Syd Stephenson

A library website is an integral part of the law library, a virtual space that extends a patron's library experience beyond using the physical location. Being a 24/7 online presence, a website can be used as an access point to the library's collections, databases, and research tools. A well-designed law library website can benefit the overall branding of its institution and strengthen the bond with its patrons. From academic law libraries, to government, law firms, and private law libraries, the role and functions of websites have undergone significant changes to meet the evolving needs of law students, faculty, legal professionals, and the general public.

This chapter begins with the changing roles and functions of different types of law libraries and a discussion of the common elements found on law library websites. Then we delve into the critical foundations for creating and maintaining robust and inclusive websites, examining the usability and accessibility concerns and principles of website design. The chapter concludes with practical guidance on the project planning and management of website design, along with a discussion of the launch, maintenance, and life cycle of a website, providing a comprehensive overview of law library website development and management.

EVOLVING ROLES OF LAW LIBRARY WEBSITES

Virtual Extension of the Physical Library Space

The website, as the virtual side of the library, has become increasingly important, especially in times when physical access is limited. The COVID-19 pandemic highlighted the importance of robust library websites, as many law libraries had to temporarily close or restrict in-person operations. During that time, websites became the primary means for patrons to access digital collections, research guides, and virtual reference services. Many law libraries chose to use the Springshare LibGuides platform to create subject and instructional guides that provided the most updated information about the library operation status, links to all kinds of virtual library services, and access points for electronic resources.[1] Compared to updating the library website itself, which many times involves working with IT departments, creating and updating LibGuides is more flexible and can ensure the timely delivery of the latest information to library patrons, especially during times like the pandemic. LibGuides can be used as extensions to the main library website(s).

Websites as Marketing Tools

Another notable function of law library websites is to use them as marketing tools to promote library services and resources. A well-organized library website can increase the library's visibility and leave a good first impression on new patrons. Particularly for an academic law library that is autonomous from the university library system and nestled under the law school, the website contributes to the overall branding and outreach efforts of the law school. The library website can be a deciding factor for prospective law students, as it can demonstrate the depth and breadth of available resources, research support, and library facilities. For public law libraries, as they stand at the frontline to meet legal needs and bridge the gap to justice, library websites can be used to promote services, increase awareness, and collaborate with community partners.

Access to Justice

Law library websites are also online platforms that provide access to authoritative legal information to their diverse user communities, regardless of socioeconomic status or legal expertise.[2] Federal Depository Library Program (FDLP) is a good example of how law library websites can achieve this goal.[3] Through this program, libraries across the country serve as official repositories for government publications, including essential primary legal materials like the United States Code and Code of Federal Regulations. Law library websites can also provide plain-language legal information, self-help resources, and referral services, making the law more accessible to the public. Particularly, this can support pro se litigants in exercising their rights and seeking due process.

CONTENT OF LAW LIBRARY WEBSITE

Website Functions by Library Types

The content and functions of a law library website vary greatly depending on the library type, as each serves different patron groups. The top priority for an academic law library is to serve the law school community it affiliates with. For those that are open to the public, they also serve public patrons, such as local bar members. Many U.S. academic law libraries maintain autonomous websites that are separate from the university library system, operating under the law school's online presence. The physical location of a law library is usually within its affiliated law school. It is both an information hub and a social gathering space for the law school community. The website mirrors these purposes. Most law library websites can be accessed through the law school website, usually under the "Academic" tab or "Student Life" tab on the law school homepage.[4] That also applies to law libraries that are non-autonomous from the law schools, despite the site domain of the law library website being under the university library website.[5] A typical academic law library website includes information on library services such as reference and circulation hours, research guides, links to electronic resources, course reserves and study room reservation systems for law students, and law school repositories. For faculty members, law library websites provide information about the research assistance specifically offered to them, such as the faculty liaison program. For public patrons, the website may highlight library hours and provide access to free online legal resources curated by the library.

Government law libraries serve a wide variety of patrons, including the general public, self-represented litigants, attorneys, government employees, members of the judiciary, and more. The information available on government law library websites is typically structured with these distinctions in mind. For example, there may be subsections that specifically label resources for each patron type. Resources for attorneys often include information about CLEs, legal reference assistance, and access to databases such as Lexis and Westlaw. Subsections for pro se patrons and other members of the general public may include links to basic legal forms, websites to help find a lawyer, or tutorials on conducting basic legal research.[6]

Generally, law firm libraries don't have a traditional, public-facing website. Instead, information about their services, print collections, and electronic resources is shared internally—via their intranet. The reason for this is that the patrons of a law firm library are typically attorneys and other law firm staff, and access is restricted to law firm employees only.[7]

Other types of law library websites include those belonging to bar association libraries and non-profit law libraries such as private membership law libraries. These libraries will often charge a fee for accessing some or all of their services. Services available to the public may be extremely limited or broad—it varies across individual libraries. These types of libraries will generally have websites that are structured similarly to government law firm websites.[8]

Understanding Your Patrons

To make a library website more usable for patrons, it is necessary to understand their information needs. The more diverse patron groups a law library serves, the broader content a library website should maintain. Online course reserves, exam archives, online study guides, and tutorials are popular content for academic law libraries. Public law libraries, such as court libraries, are used by many self-represented litigants who need access to forms and practical guidance. Self-help resources like court forms, guides on legal research methodology, lists of primary sources, and information on legal clinics, pro bono services, and community legal education are common content found on these library websites. Content is curated based on the information needs of the library's patrons. Just like maintaining a library collection, a library website also needs regular "weeding" of its content and structure to better assist its patrons. This can be achieved by studying the usability of the website to make adjustments, which will be discussed in a later section of this chapter.

A law library website can be used as a "one-stop shopping place" for library patrons, whether it is to find the operation status of the library, consult with a reference librarian using the chat reference tool, access the link to a database subscribed to by the law library, or access the legal research resources hosted on the library website. Regardless of the types of law libraries, the most common categories of content on law library websites are information about the library, online guides and tutorials, and legal research resources.

Information About the Library

This is the online "bulletin board" of a law library and is usually displayed in the most prominent place on a website. It provides the most basic information a patron needs to know before using the library, such as the hours, directions, contact information, staff directories, library policies, and so on. Patrons can also use this information as an access point for the various services provided by the law library. For example, for law libraries that offer online chat reference, patrons can use the websites to get connected with reference librarians while getting information on the operation hours and coverage of that service at the same time.

In addition to presenting these types of library information on the website, libraries can also create social media accounts as additions to the main library websites. Specifically, information like the hours and operation status of the library, which are subject to constant changes, special library events, or the promotion of newly acquired library resources, can be easily edited as social media posts and pushed to a broader range of audiences.[9]

Online Guides and Tutorials

Library guides and tutorials are important value-added services provided by law librarians that can be found on library websites across all kinds of law libraries. The most popular platform for library guides used by academic law libraries is Springshare's LibGuides. The platform provides templates for creating topical guides, A–Z lists of databases, or even creating a library website itself that matches the institution's branding and domain. Some law libraries use self-developed platforms to create research guides that can be tailored to meet the institution's specific needs and aesthetic styles.[10] In addition to text-based research guides, libraries can also consider using online video tutorials to enhance interactions with patrons and provide multiple ways for content delivery.[11]

Subject-Specific Guides and Tutorials

For academic law libraries, these guides can cover topics as broad as a doctrinal course in law school curriculums, such as research guides on constitutional law, or as specific as the law enacted during COVID-19. They are also used by many government and non-profit law libraries, especially on legal topics that are frequently consulted by public patrons, like family law issues, landlord and tenant issues, veteran affairs, and so on.[12] The content of a subject-specific guide is similar to an annotated bibliography. It usually includes a brief introduction to the subject and lists resources available in the library that are relevant to this subject, arranged by content types. Librarians can insert direct catalog links to monographs or journals and links to databases subscribed to or owned by the law libraries, making it easy for patrons to access these resources from one centralized guide.

Instructional or Process-Oriented Guides and Tutorials

Instructional or process-oriented guides provide step-by-step instructions and practical examples for using specific legal resources and tools. The goal is to provide targeted training so patrons can effectively utilize library resources. Examples include guides on the formatting of appellate briefs or tips for student journal editors to check citations. Many court law libraries create this type of guide to help self-represented patrons navigate the litigation process.[13]

Informational Guides and Tutorials

These types of guides serve important administrative functions, helping patrons understand and stay current with the library's services, policies, events, and resources. Examples of these guides are:

- New Student/Patron Guides: introduce new users to the library's layout, collections, services, and policies.
- Resource/Service Guides: highlight specific resources, databases, special library events, and so on.
- Policy Documentation Guides: provide details on circulation policies, facility use guidelines, research instruction procedures, and so on.

These guides can be particularly effective during emergencies or disruptions as they are easier to create and update than changing the website itself. During the COVID-19 pandemic, many law libraries created guides outlining changes to operations, remote access details, temporary policies, and virtual support options. These guides can be effective ways to reach out to patrons and keep them informed about the constant changes in library services and operations during special times.

Legal Research Resources

A core function of any law library website is to serve as a centralized gateway to essential legal research resources. Through the OCLC EZProxy and other authentication systems, the website enables secure remote access for authorized patrons to access the library's online collection. In addition to paid databases, law library websites frequently maintain a curated list of free internet resources for legal research. This may include links to government websites, open-access repositories, and research guides from trusted institutions, which can be particularly valuable for public patrons to get legal research assistance. Some law libraries also maintain digital repositories or integrate platform access for primary legal sources.[14]

Content Organization

Tabs can be used to organize the content on library websites to increase findability. Libraries serving a diverse patron group can use tabs by patron types to present specific content tailored to that group while displaying information that is applicable to all patrons on the homepage. For other libraries, content can be organized by the types of resources or the subject matter of resources.

The homepage of the Gallagher Law Library of the University of Washington School of Law divides its "Services" section into four patron groups, with each linking to a separate LibGuides page that highlights the services available to that patron group.[15]

Another example is the Sacramento County Law Library, which primarily serves the local community. On the library's homepage, while displaying popular content such as the catalog search, access to e-books, and "lawyers in the library" service, it also lists the library resources by common legal topics so patrons can access the content that is most relevant to them in one click.[16]

USABILITY

Usability is the foundation of website design and development, as well as the foundation for our practice as librarians. As information professionals, our ultimate goal is to assist our patrons in finding the information they need using the website, whether it is to find a database to conduct legal research or a directional question about the location of a study room in the law library. The key question on the usability of a law library website is: Does it provide what your patrons need and can they find it efficiently? The information presented on a law library website should be relevant and effective to satisfy the information needs of the various patron groups served by your law library. In the meantime, how this information is presented and delivered to your patrons is also crucial to enhancing the usability of a website. To ensure a website is usable, the library should consider the user experience of its patrons, adopt a user-centered design model, and ensure the accessibility of the website.

User Experience

User experience (UX) is a crucial aspect of ensuring the usability of law library websites. Your websites should be engaging, efficient, and accessible for patrons who use the website to seek information. The core concept of UX is to re-approach the design of a product from the user's perspective. For law librarians, that means you need to empathize with your patrons and understand what their experiences and expectations are with using the library website. For example, many academic law libraries offer online study room reservations. Since this type of service is usually available to current law students only, instead of putting the reservation link on the homepage of the law library, a better place is under tabs like "Library Services for Students." Considering that not all students are familiar with the location of the study rooms, it would be helpful to include some navigation information for the study rooms on the reservation page. Also, if there is any library policy on the usage of study rooms, it should be presented on the reservation page as well. In this example, all the relevant information for students to reserve and use study rooms is placed on the same web page, so that they don't need to navigate through different parts of the library website to complete this task.

User-Centered Design

A user-centered design approach means that you need to actively engage your patrons throughout the design process to ensure that the website meets their needs, expectations, and workflows effectively. It can maximize the UX of a law library website, which ultimately promotes usability. To achieve this goal, the first and most important step is to understand your patrons. You can conduct user studies to gather insights about the different patron groups that interact with the law library website, whether they are law students, faculty members, local bar members, or the general public. There are typically three stages of user studies: investigating the current usage of the library website, identifying places for improvement, and, after the redesign of the website, reevaluating the user experiences. User studies can be done through surveys, interviews, focus group sessions, usability testing, and so on.

Evaluation of Usability

User surveys are probably the most popular and commonly used tools to evaluate the usability of library websites. These surveys can have a combination of open-ended questions and rating scales that can assess satisfaction levels with various website elements like navigation of content, accessibility of online resources, and the currentness and accuracy of information. Many academic law libraries have conducted general user surveys that include the usability of library websites as part of the surveys.[17]

Some typical questions to ask about the usability of a law library website can include the following examples:

- How often do you use the law library website? (answers with rating scale)
- How often do you use the law library website to find announcements from the library? (answers with rating scale)
- What types of research instruction do you find the most helpful on the library website? (multiple choices)
- When you search for information in the library, how do you begin your search? (multiple choices)
- How easy is it to find what you need on the library's website? (answers with rating scale)
- Do you feel comfortable/confident navigating the library website without knowing the "library terms"?
- How do you like the font, color, and layout of the library website?

Usability testing is the observation of real users as they use the website to perform typical tasks under different scenarios. This hands-on approach can reveal usability issues such as confusing layouts or unclear information. For libraries that serve diverse patron groups, it is important to perform usability testing with users representing all potential patron groups. Usability testing can be conducted remotely using online collaboration tools like Zoom or Webex. For example, you can design tasks that ask the patrons to find specific research resources or services using the law library website. In that process, you can then record and observe how patrons interact with the web content and study the screen mouse movements they use to complete those tasks.

Other than inviting and observing patrons performing certain tasks using the law library website, card sorting is another effective usability testing method.[18] Librarians can invite patrons to work with cards containing topics, content categories, or functionality labels found on the website. Participants will organize these cards into logical groups and hierarchies based on their expectations and experiences. For example, a card sorting could include cards labeled "Databases List," "Study Aids," "Research Guides," "Library Policies," "Interlibrary Loan," and more. Law students may group these very differently than local bar members based on their distinct research goals and workflows.

If participants consistently struggle to group certain content items together during the study, it may indicate confusing labeling or a content mismatch that needs to be redesigned.

Besides formal user surveys and usability testing, you can also use in-house data from the public services department that reflects the daily usage of the library services to identify the needs of your patrons. By combining survey data, usability test findings, and in-house data, you can make informed design decisions, reduce design assumptions, and construct a website that maps closely to the expectations of your diverse patrons.

ACCESSIBILITY

Web Content Accessibility Guidelines

Another important aspect to increase the usability of a law library website is to ensure the website is accessible to people of all abilities. In addition to the legal requirements such as Section 504 and 508 of the Rehabilitation Act and Title II of the Americans with Disabilities Act, there are also accessibility guidelines for libraries to follow. The Web Content Accessibility Guidelines (WCAG) developed by the World Wide Web Consortium (W3C) are the most widely recognized standards and guidelines for web accessibility.[19] WCAG provides a set of technical requirements and recommendations. The current version, WCAG 2.2, outlines four main principles for web accessibility:

1. Perceivable: Websites should provide text alternatives for non-text content (images, videos, audio), captions or transcripts for multimedia, and options for adjusting the visual presentation (contrast, text resizing).
2. Operable: Websites should ensure keyboard accessibility, provide sufficient time for users to read and interact, avoid design elements that may cause seizures, and offer navigational aids like skip links, back-to-top links, and headings.
3. Understandable: Content should be clear and concise, with consistent navigation and labeling. Websites should also support input assistance like spell-checking.
4. Robust: Web pages and applications must be compatible with assistive technologies (screen readers, voice recognition) and capable of interpreting the web-page layout accurately.

Website Accessibility for Neurodivergent Patrons

The discussion of the accessibility of library websites has been primarily focused on accommodating patrons with more "visible" disability needs, such as those with physical impairments. However, it is crucial to recognize that accessibility extends beyond these evident challenges. In recent years, librarians have been paying more attention to the needs of neurodivergent patrons. These are patrons who have cognitive or neurological differences, including those on the autism spectrum or with ADHD, dyslexia, or other neurodivergent conditions. You can accommodate neurodivergent patrons by implementing features like adjustable font sizes, color schemes, and layouts to reduce visual overstimulation. Clear, consistent navigation and labeling also help minimize cognitive overload.

Law libraries can use the universal design principles to evaluate how inclusive their websites are. The core value is to create products and environments that are user-friendly to the widest range of people. The seven principles of universal design are equitable use, flexibility, simplicity, perceptible information, tolerance for error, low physical effort, and appropriate size and space. When designing or evaluating your website, the universal design principles can be used in conjunction with WCAG 2.2 guidelines. For example, while WCAG 2.2 may require providing text alternatives for non-text content, universal design principles would encourage presenting information in multiple formats (text, audio, video) to accommodate different cognitive processing styles.

Make Your Library Website More Inclusive

Below are some recommendations on the content and layout of websites to make them more inclusive, especially for neurodivergent patrons.

Concise and Clear Information

- Present information in a concise and straightforward way to avoid cognitive overload.
- Choose clean, readable fonts and ensure appropriate font sizes for optimal legibility. Some studies have suggested that sans-serif fonts are more visually appealing and can enhance the browsing experience.[20]
- Avoid excessive and unnecessary use of images and graphics, as they can be visually overwhelming for some users. Make sure you provide alternative text descriptions for all non-text elements to ensure accessibility for users with visual impairments or neurodivergent conditions that affect visual processing.

Simple and Organized Layout

- Maintain a simple and well-organized layout with a clear hierarchy.
- Implement effective search functionality to increase findability.
- Make sure the layout also works well on mobile devices.

Multiple Ways of Content Delivery

- Provide multiple formats to present information, such as text, audio, video, and downloadable documents in various formats (e.g., PDF, Word, HTML) to satisfy different preferences and assistive technologies.
- Using social media platforms to distribute information and engage with users through different channels.

Empowerment

- Include an accessibility statement on the law library website, outlining the library's commitment to equity and inclusion.[21]
- Provide clear guidelines and resources on how users can request accommodations, report issues, or provide feedback on the website's accessibility.
- Offer accessibility training for librarians and staff and create educational guides for patrons. Foster a culture of continuous improvement by regularly seeking input from patrons and conducting accessibility evaluations.

PRINCIPLES OF WEBSITE DESIGN

Most law libraries are not going to code their websites from scratch. Rather, many libraries will customize and publish their websites on a platform known as a Content Management System (otherwise shortened as a CMS). Though most CMS systems provide users with access to pre-coded, customizable web design templates and assets, there should still be at least some thought and planning put into the design and layout of your library's website. Your website's design should feel unique and representative of your library, while maintaining ease of use. There are three principles that you should be familiar with as you plan and design your website: branding, web-page layout conventions, and how to create various assets for your web pages.

Branding

Branding refers to the identity of a website created through consistent, recognizable features that are representative of your institution. A branding kit is useful no matter the size of your library or library staff. If your library has several staff members who are publishing web content—or even if it's just one person pushing out content—it is important to have documented standards for your website's content. Your library's branding kit should be made available to all members of your staff and include clear guidelines on how it should be implemented on the website.

The typography for your website should include no more than one to two fonts for headings and one to two fonts for body text to maintain consistency throughout each individual page.[22] Your choice of fonts is a critical decision, as the wrong font can make your website look dated, or, even worse, not accessible to potential users. Certain fonts, like scripts, may not be easily readable or may come across to users as unprofessional. Additionally, web design best practices are changing constantly. So, a font that may look trendy and unique today could be very dated within a few years. Another guideline that may be helpful to include in a branding kit is the font sizes that your staff should be using depending on where the text is located. For example, at the OCU Law Library, staff are instructed to use a 16 px font for body text. Standards for heading sizes will vary, since there are six possible heading structures within HTML (H1-H6).[23]

Color palettes are a little more challenging to put together. While there are many platforms available that will generate color palettes for free, it is recommended that you utilize color theory concepts in your website's color palettes, along with neutrals like white and black. If you select colors at random, chances are that they will not look very pleasing to your users. Can you imagine a library website that uses bright pink and bright yellow as its primary colors? It would be quite distracting! Color theory concepts that generally result in a strong color palette for a branding kit are complementary colors, monochromatic colors, and analogous colors. Complementary colors are a pair of colors that face opposite each other on a color wheel. Monochromatic colors are varieties of the same slice on a color wheel. Monochromatic colors will vary in tint, shade, and tone. Lastly, analogous colors are a pair of colors that are situated next to each other on a color wheel. You will also want to provide guidance on acceptable alternate colors that would fit within your institution's branding guidelines.

Typically, libraries will use their own institution's logo on their website. Branding kits will include multiple alternates of a logo to fit a variety of box sizes and remain viewable on multiple background colors. For instance, at Oklahoma City University School of Law, there are six logo variants that can be used on website pages. There are two full-sized, navy-blue logos to be used on a white background, two smaller navy-blue logos to be used on a white background, and two white logos to be used on a navy-blue background. Law libraries that belong to universities or already established library systems may already have logos in place that you can use for your website. For law libraries that do not have institutional logos to rely on (or libraries that would prefer to create their own), there are a few options. One option is to create a logo internally using graphic design software. Platforms such as Canva and Adobe Photoshop are very popular choices for logo design. While this route may be more challenging if your team does not have much graphic design experience, it is more cost-effective than hiring an outside entity to design a logo for your library.

Web-Page Layout

There are several elements that make up the layout of a typical web page: a header, navigation, body, and a footer. These elements are also typically arranged in a specific order. On a desktop, the header directly at the top of the page, a navigation bar is directly underneath or located on the side of the web page, the body is filled with the page's primary content, and a footer is at the bottom of the page. On a mobile device or tablet, the layout order will be mostly the same, but certain elements may compress to fit the screen size. For instance, a navigation bar that spans a web page horizontally on a desktop will often compress to a hidden hamburger menu on mobile. Additionally, a row of three images on a desktop should convert to one column of images on mobile.[24] Keep in mind that there's no need to reinvent the wheel here! Website users expect a web page to be laid out this way, so there's no need to confuse them in the name of being creative.

The *header* of a web page typically includes a banner image, the website title, and the website's logo. The *navigation bar* will typically be located in or just below the header, or on the side of the page. Additionally, a well-structured navigation bar will organize the pages on a library website into intuitive, sensical lists where applicable. The *body* of the page is where the content is located. Each web page will have unique body content specific to the purpose of the page. Lastly, the footer of a website usually includes secondary navigation links, contact information, hours and library address, and website copyright. Secondary navigation found in a website footer will often include links to pages like a privacy policy, contact, accessibility, site maps, and more.[25]

CMS Assets versus Coding

Depending on which content management system/website platform is used, it may be necessary to use only CMS assets, only utilize coding, or a combination of the two. Customizable CMS assets typically include rich-text boxes, media embed options (images, videos, galleries, etc.), content and design blocks, and more. These are essentially pre-coded assets that are made customizable by the CMS platform. Depending on which platform you use (Squarespace, WordPress, LibGuides CMS, etc.), you will have a variety of customization options available. A popular CMS for academic libraries is Springshare's LibGuides CMS.[26] This content management system is the most basic of basic and provides access to a limited number of pre-coded customization options. LibGuides CMS is a popular platform among librarians due to its ease of use and a shallow learning curve. LibGuides CMS users do not need to have any traditional website development platform experience to create a website or research guide, and research librarians can be set up with individual accounts under an institution so that they may create and publish guides and web pages on their own schedule, without the need to involve an institution's IT department. To give a LibGuides CMS website a more traditional website feel, librarians can use HTML, CSS, and a little bit of JavaScript.

HTML, or Hypertext Markup Language, is essentially the skeleton of a web page. HTML uses tags to determine the structure of a web page, and the text and media included within that structure. Using HTML, you can add text content, embed media, link to emails or website URLs, complete basic text styling, and more. This is accomplished through the use of tags. For instance, to structure a primary heading, one would use the <h1></h1> tags, including the text for the heading between the starting

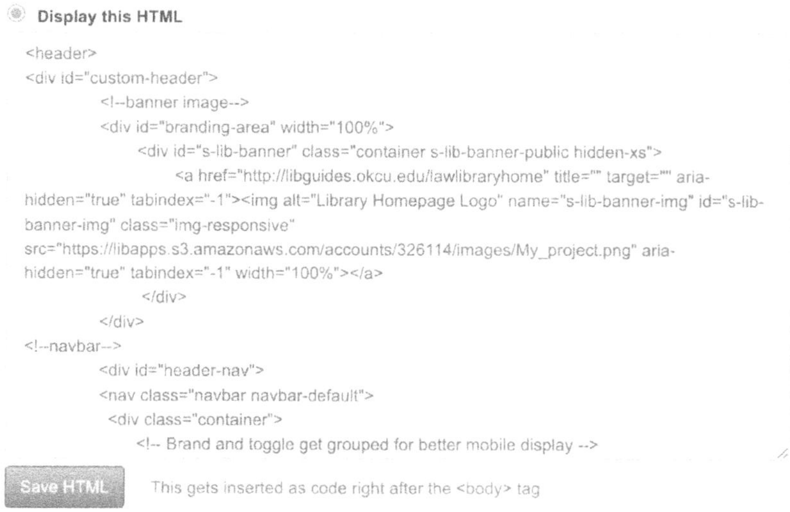


```
<header>
<div id="custom-header">
        <!--banner image-->
        <div id="branding-area" width="100%">
            <div id="s-lib-banner" class="container s-lib-banner-public hidden-xs">
                <a href="http://libguides.okcu.edu/lawlibraryhome" title="" target="" aria-
hidden="true" tabindex="-1"><img alt="Library Homepage Logo" name="s-lib-banner-img" id="s-lib-
banner-img" class="img-responsive"
src="https://libapps.s3.amazonaws.com/accounts/326114/images/My_project.png" aria-
hidden="true" tabindex="-1" width="100%"></a>
            </div>
        </div>
<!--navbar-->
        <div id="header-nav">
        <nav class="navbar navbar-default">
          <div class="container">
            <!-- Brand and toggle get grouped for better mobile display -->
```

Figure 12.1 Header HTML Snippet from the Oklahoma City University Law Library Website.

Group JS/CSS Code

```
body {
      padding: 0px 0px;
      font-family: 'Verdana', sans-serif;
      color: #222222;
      font-size: 16px;
      background-color: #FFFFFF;}

.s-lib-side-borders {
      padding: 0px 15px;}

#s-lg-public-skiplink {
      top: -70px;}

#menu-text {
      padding-right: 5px;
      font-size: 14px;
      font-family: 'Tahoma', sans-serif;
```

Inserted into the <HEAD> section of all pages

Add custom META / STYLE / SCRIPT code and/or include CSS / JS files here. If adding custom code, remember to wrap your code in <style> or <script> tags.

Need a place to upload CSS / JS files related to your customization? Go to Admin > Look & Feel > Custom JS/CSS > Upload Customization Files.

Figure 12.2 CSS Snippet from Oklahoma City University Law Library Website.

and ending tag: <h1>Chickasaw Nation Law Library</h1>. CSS, or cascading style sheets, is the language that adds the actual design and layout rules to a web page. CSS takes the skeleton created with HTML and turns it into what you see on a live website. JavaScript is another common language used in web design, and its purpose is to dictate the behavior of web pages and their features.[27] Bootstrap is a framework that utilizes HTML, CSS, and JavaScript in such a way that is more responsive and easier to develop.[28] Figures 12.1 and 12.2 provide a sample of HTML and CSS code used to create the header for the Oklahoma City University Law Library website.

CREATING A LIBRARY WEBSITE

For many libraries, outsourcing the design and maintenance of a website is not an affordable option. The task of creating or redesigning a library website may be completed by multiple staff members, but more often than not, it is left to one librarian. This can be a challenging task to take on, as many law librarians likely do not have backgrounds in web design and web development. This is a very broad topic that could likely be covered in a stand-alone book, but the following sections will at the very least give readers a starting map for creating or revamping their own library website. The website creation or redesign process typically includes three stages. The first stage is the project planning stage, followed by production, and ending with the launch of the new or updated website.

Project Planning and Management

Web development and design projects tend to be highly variable and can encounter a variety of issues that can delay project completion. For this reason, it is important to follow project management and project planning best practices. This will keep your website design project (fingers crossed) organized and on time. *Project management* is the practice of organizing and delegating a project with the goal of completing the project in an efficient, timely, and cost-effective manner. Project managers for website design projects will often use project management software such as Trello to track project progress and assign tasks/packages to project team members. Project teams will also often utilize project management frameworks such as Agile, Waterfall, and Kanban to organize how objectives are being completed during each part of the production stage.[29]

Project planning is an aspect of project management that focuses on dictating how the project will unfold and setting expectations for your project team.[30] To better visualize how a project will be organized and structured, it is recommended to create a project planning document or a project outline. A project planning document for a website design project typically includes a project overview, detailing the purpose of the project; a timeline of major milestones for the project; a definition of project roles and responsibilities; project goals and objectives; and any sample designs or content matrices. Below is a sample project planning document.

SAMPLE WEB DESIGN PROJECT OUTLINE

Sample Project Planning Document—Academic Law Library Website Redesign

Website Improvement Project Outline

Prepared by: Author Name

Project Overview

This section of a project planning document should include a short paragraph outlining the scope and purpose of the project.

For example:

"The goal of this project is to update the design and user interface of the LibGuides currently serving as the law library's website. Content on this website will also be updated to reflect current library resources and staffing. Additionally, this project will improve the accessibility of the library's website."

Goals and Objectives

This section should include 3–5 project goals along with their corresponding objectives.

For example:

- Goal 1: Improve the layout and design of the library website.
- Goal 2: Update website content to reflect accurate and up-to-date information.
  - Objective 2.1: Update the Databases A–Z list to reflect current electronic resources and information on how these resources can be accessed.
  - Objective 2.2: Update website to reflect current staffing, library information, and available library resources and services.
  - Objective 2.3: Create a schedule for content updates.
- Goal 3: Ensure all aspects of the library's website adhere to web accessibility best practices and follow Rehabilitation Act Section 504 and 508 guidelines.
  - Objective 3.1: Create a maintenance schedule for site accessibility and content functionality.

Identified Needs

This section should include a list of specific needs for your library's website. For example: The law library website needs improvements to the content, design, and accessibility of the website.

Project Roles and Responsibilities

This section should be used to identify the members of your project team, their roles, and their responsibilities.

Project Timeline

Under this section, list out your milestones and anticipated due dates in a table, similarly to the sample table 12.1.

Table 12.1 Sample Project Timeline

Date Due By:	*Milestone:*
09/19/2025	Request access to law school website branding kit.
09/20/2025	Send out a website wish list email to library staff.
09/26/2025	Begin testing design upgrades on unpublished library sandbox.
09/26/2025	Create unpublished duplicates of current website pages on sandbox.
10/07/2025	Finish draft site map and send for approval.
10/31/2025	Finalize project task lists.
12/09/2025	Submit new library website banner for approval.
01/06/2026	Finish drafts of Home and About the Library pages and submit for feedback.
02/06/2026	Finish drafts of Students pages and Collections pages and submit for feedback.
03/17/2026	Finish Law Practice Technology Certification page and submit for feedback.
05/05/2026	Make requested changes to pages and design, send final draft for review.
05/12/2026	Complete user testing.
05/16/2026	Complete final accessibility and content checks, and modifications.
05/17/2026	Publish updated library web pages to live site.

Technology Considerations

Use this section to outline or list any technology being used for your website project. You can list any website platforms, programming languages, or project management software you may be using, for example.

Sample Designs

This is an optional section, but it will be helpful to include some sample designs/mockups for the pages on your website. These will likely be very different from the final product, but it will be helpful to have a rough draft of what the project outcome should be available in the document for all project team members to view.

Content Matrices

Use this section of your project planning document to outline what content you anticipate will be located on each page. You can do this through a table or a list.

Production

The production stage of a website project involves the actual design and content creation for your library's website. During this stage, members of the website project team will rely on the project documentation (including the project planning document) and any project management software or frameworks being utilized to stay on track. This will likely be the longest stage of the website design process, as you (and your team, if staffing permits) will be creating the content and assets that will go on your website. Depending on which CMS you are using—and if you are creating an entire website from scratch or simply overhauling existing pages—production can take place in a few different ways. For an overhaul of an existing library website, it may be most efficient to set up an unpublished development sandbox on the back end of your CMS. For example, on LibGuides CMS, admin users may create an unpublished group. In the settings for this unedited group, users can add HTML for the header and footer, as well as CSS and JavaScript that command all LibGuides and subpages included under the group. Once pages are ready to be set live, the HTML, CSS, and JavaScript can be pasted into the live group's settings, and new pages can be regrouped to the live group.

For more traditional CMS such as Squarespace or WordPress, you can create an entire unpublished website as one unit during production if you are creating a website from scratch. Similar to the unpublished sandbox that can be created on LibGuides, you can also use a development server to serve as your sandbox during the production stage of your website's overhaul. This will allow you to make changes to site design and content without affecting what is shown on the live site. Changing the design of your website as a whole will be a little different, as these platforms usually have you select from a list of design templates and then customize certain aspects of the template to adhere to your institution's branding standards. A rich-text editor for HTML, CSS, and JavaScript may or may not be available to further customize your site's design—it will depend on the platform. As milestones of the project are met, completed packages (i.e., pages or groups of pages) should be sent to key project stakeholders for feedback. During production, you will also want to preview or test how your pages will look as a live website on desktop, tablet, and mobile screens as well as on all of the major web browsers. This testing should be done as you go, as adding elements to pages during the design process can drastically alter how a web page will look on different screen sizes and what might not work on different browsers.

Launching a Website and Continued Maintenance

For most content management systems, setting your library's website live will be relatively simple, but you will likely need to work with your institution's IT department as well as your internet service provider to complete a few technical tasks. This may involve configuring the URL for your website, moving a site from a development server over to the live URL, or uploading any additional files and assets that are needed. In tandem with this, your website project team will need to complete a few tasks before launch. First, your team will need to conduct a full audit of your unpublished website or unpublished website pages. This includes checking content for accuracy, completeness, spelling, and grammar. Next, you will need to complete user testing. After user testing is complete, take time to review any feedback and implement that feedback (if possible) into a final draft of your website. After final revisions have been made, the website can be set live.

Website Maintenance Schedule

Before launching your website, you should assign a website maintenance schedule for upkeep on accessibility, site content, and website features. All three of these aspects should be checked on a regular basis. A website maintenance schedule is necessary because it is important to be proactive about any access issues that your website can experience, rather than reactive. Links can "break" at any time, and for a multitude of reasons. For instance, at Oklahoma City University School of Law, the library website hosts hundreds of links. Many of these links are to proxied databases, electronic resources that require single sign-on, and links to external resources. When links break, patrons lose access to important resources—students can lose access to digital study aids, or pro se patrons could lose access to important self-help resources.

Additionally, it is prudent to keep an accessibility maintenance schedule because best practices can and will change over time. It may be useful to go through each page with an accessibility checklist on a regular basis. There are also browser extensions you can utilize that will run individual web pages through an accessibility checker. It may also be a good idea to occasionally test your website's

Table 12.2 Sample Website Maintenance Schedule

Task	*Timeline*	*Responsibility*
Accessibility Checks	Weekly	Electronic Services Librarian
Link Checks	Weekly	Electronic Services Librarian
Content Checks	Weekly/As Needed	Access Services Librarian

accessibility by using a screen reader. Screen readers are useful accessibility testing tools because it will let you test functionalities such as alternative text and tab ordering. Content can be updated as needed, and the frequency of content checks will depend on what information is available on your website. For instance, if your website includes multiple calendars or information about weekly/monthly events, then you may need to conduct content checks on a daily or weekly basis. A sample website maintenance schedule can be found in table 12.2.

THE WEBSITE LIFECYCLE

The most important thing to keep in mind is that a website is a living thing. Your library's website will need continuous attention and, eventually, another redesign. It is recommended that libraries reevaluate their website on an annual or semi-annual basis. A complete overhaul of a library website will likely be needed every three to five years. What may make a website usable and designed in a way that looks good now will likely not be the case three to five years from now. Additionally, library websites contain a particularly unique aspect of the website lifecycle in that pieces of the site will need overhauls at different times than others. For instance, A–Z database lists may need regular redesigns and overhauls based on the needs of patrons and based on what the library is subscribing to at the time. Legal research guides and tutorials may also need dedicated overhauls outside of a general website redesign. If staffing permits, it may also be helpful to assemble a law library website committee composed of staff and community members. Part of the website lifecycle is making improvements to the library's website based on the information needs of your patrons.

CONCLUSION

A law library website is more than an online information bulletin board for its physical location. It is the digital gateway to provide essential resources and services to its diverse patron groups. A user-friendly library website contributes to the overall outreach efforts of the law library and the institution it is affiliated with. Whether a library uses CMS assets or coding to build the website, it is important to consider the branding elements used to represent the institution. The content and layout of the web pages should also be carefully designed to be accessible and enhance user experiences. Through project planning and management, librarians can ensure the website continues to remain valuable and adaptable to the evolving needs of your patrons.

NOTES

1. Thomas Sneed, "The Effect of COVID-19 on Law Libraries: Are These Changes Temporary or a Sign of the Future?," *Washburn Law Journal* 60, no. 1 (2020): 107–129, 111.
2. American Association of Law Libraries Special Committee on Access to Justice, "Law Libraries and Access to Justice," American Association of Law Libraries, accessed June 25, 2024, https://www.aallnet.org/wp-content/uploads/2018/01/AccessToJusticeSpecialCommittee2014LawLibrariesAndAccessToJustice.pdf.

3. "FDLP: Free Document Dissemination through the Federal Depository Library Program," U.S. Government Printing Office, accessed June 25, 2024, https://www.gpo.gov/how-to-work-with-us/agency/services-for-agencies/federal-depository-library-program.
4. Elizabeth G. Adelman et al., "Academic Law Library Director Status since the Great Recession: Strengthened, Maintained, or Degraded?," *Law Library Journal* 112, no. 1 (Winter 2020): 117–134. See also the survey on the usage of chat reference among academic law libraries in 2022, Jingwei Zhang, Survey of chat reference ABA Law Schools (updated 08_2022), https://doi.org/10.7282/00000413.
5. "Law Library," Cornell University Library, accessed June 26, 2024, https://law.library.cornell.edu/.
6. Syd Stephenson, "Government/Non-Profit Law Library Website Survey Data," accessed July 11, 2024, https://scholarship.law.okcu.edu/work/ns/bfe58409-eb2e-4040-9972-39bcf8406d69.
7. "Types of Law Libraries," American Association of Law Libraries, accessed June 27, 2024, https://www.aallnet.org/careers/about-the-profession/types-of-law-libraries/.
8. Syd Stephenson, "Government/Non-Profit Law Library Website Survey Data," accessed July 11, 2024, https://scholarship.law.okcu.edu/work/ns/bfe58409-eb2e-4040-9972-39bcf8406d69.
9. Jessica Almeida and Nicole P. Dyszlewski, "Marketing and Outreach," in Zanada Joyner, and Casandra M. Laskowski, eds. *Introduction to Law Librarianship* (Mountain View, CA: Pressbooks, 2021).
10. "Research Guides & Videos," Harvard Law School, accessed June 26, 2024, https://hls.harvard.edu/library/research-services/research-guides-videos/.
11. "Tutorials," Georgetown Law Library, accessed June 26, 2024, https://guides.ll.georgetown.edu/home/tutorials. See also "Videos and Tutorials," Alameda County Bernard E. Witkin Law Library, accessed June 26, 2024, https://lawlibrary.acgov.org/videos-and-tutorials/#.
12. "Start Here: Quick Guides to Library Resources and Websites on a Given Topic," Wisconsin State Law Library, accessed June 28, 2024, https://wilawlibrary.gov/learn/starthere/index.html.
13. "Self-Represented Litigant Guide to Legal Research," Harris County Robert W. Hainsworth Law Library, accessed June 26, 2024, https://www.harriscountylawlibrary.org/self-represented-litigant-guide-to-legal-resources.
14. "Digital Collections," Rutgers Law School, accessed June 26, 2024, https://njlaw.rutgers.edu/.
15. "Homepage," University of Washington Gallagher Law Library, accessed June 26, 2024, https://lib.law.uw.edu/home.
16. "Homepage," Sacramento County Public Law Library, accessed June 26, 2024, https://saclaw.org/.
17. "Usability and User Studies," American Association of Law Libraries, accessed June 26, 2024, https://www.aallnet.org/allsis/resources-publications/marketing-outreach-toolkit/usability-user/.
18. Ellyssa Kroski, "Card Sorting," PB Works, accessed July 15, 2024, http://cardsorting.pbworks.com/w/page/14591705/FrontPage.
19. "Web Content Accessibility Guidelines (WCAG) 2.2," World Wide Web Consortium, accessed July 19, 2024, https://www.w3.org/TR/WCAG22/.
20. Devorah Kletenik et al., "From Awareness to Action: Teaching Software Accessibility for Neurodiverse Users," *SIGCSE 2024: Proceedings of the 55th ACM Technical Symposium on Computer Science Education* 1 (March 2024): 687, 691, https://doi.org/10.1145/3626252.3630859.
21. "Accessibility Statement," Boston University School of Law, accessed June 26, 2024, https://www.bu.edu/law/libraries/about/accessibility-statement/.
22. Michael Mendez, "Website Design," in *The Missing Link: An Introduction to Web Development and Programming* (Geneseo, NY: Open SUNY Textbook, 2014), 25–37. https://torl.biblioboard.com/content/417626ca-ced4-4bad-8291-5f16e13e52e7.
23. "HTML Basics," MDN Web Docs, accessed June 10, 2024, https://developer.mozilla.org/en-US/docs/Learn/Getting_started_with_the_web/HTML_basics.
24. Patrick J. Lynch and Sarah Horton, "Page Structure," in *Web Style Guide*, 4th ed. (New Haven, CT: Yale University Press, 2016), 174–206, https://webstyleguide.com/6-page-structure.html.
25. Lynch and Horton. "Page Structure," 174–206.
26. "LibGuides & LibGuides CMS," Springshare, accessed June 26, 2024, https://springshare.com/libguides/. For examples of using Springshare LibGuides to create law library websites, see "Chickasaw Nation Law Library," Oklahoma City University School of Law, accessed June 26, 2024, https://libguides.okcu.edu/lawlibraryhome/home. See also "Charles N. and Hilda H.M. Mason Law Library,"

University of the District of Columbia David A. Clarke School of Law, accessed June 26, 2024, https://udclaw.libguides.com/home.
27. "JavaScript Tutorial," W3 Schools, accessed June 24, 2024, https://www.w3schools.com/js/default.asp.
28. "Bootstrap Get Started," W3 Schools, accessed June 25, 2024, https://www.w3schools.com/bootstrap/bootstrap_get_started.asp.
29. Adrienne Watt, *Project Management* (BCcampus Open Education, 2014), https://opentextbc.ca/projectmanagement/.
30. Watt, *Project Management*.

FURTHER READING

Benedetti, Allison R. "Promoting Library Services with User-Centered Language." *portal: Libraries and the Academy* 17, no. 2 (2017): 217–234.

Bignoli, Callan and Lauren Stara. *Responding to Rapid Change in Libraries: A User Experience Approach*. Chicago, IL: ALA Editions, 2021.

Khawaja, Paul. "Accessibility of Public Library Websites in the United States." *Universal Access in the Information Society* 22, no. 3 (2022): 1047–1057.

Lindahl, David. "Organizing the Library for User-Centered Design," in *Participatory Design in Academic Libraries: New Reports and Findings*, edited by Nancy Fried Foster, 7–20. Washington, DC: Council on Library and Information Resources, 2014. https://www.clir.org/wp-content/uploads/sites/6/pub161.pdf.

Lynch, Patrick J. and Sarah Horton. *Web Style Guide*. 4th ed. New Haven, CT: Yale University Press, 2016. https://webstyleguide.com/index.html.

Mendez, Michael. *The Missing Link: An Introduction to Web Development and Programming*. Geneseo, NY: Open SUNY Textbooks, 2014. https://milneopentextbooks.org/the-missing-link-an-introduction-to-web-development-and-programming/.

Spina, Carli. "WCAG 2.1 and the Current State of Web Accessibility in Libraries." *Journal of Library User Experiences* 2, no. 2 (2019). https://doi.org/10.3998/weave.12535642.0002.202.

Uhl, Scott. "Applying User-centered Design to Discovery Layer Evaluation in the Law Library." *Legal Reference Services Quarterly* 38, no. 1–2 (2019): 30–63.

Watt, Adrienne. *Project Management*, 2nd ed. BCcampus Open Education, 2014. https://opentextbc.ca/projectmanagement/.

WebAIM. "Cognitive Disabilities Part 1: We Still Know Too Little, and We Do Even Less." Accessed June 28, 2024. https://webaim.org/articles/cognitive/cognitive_too_little/.

WebAIM. "Web Accessibility Evaluation Guide." Accessed June 28, 2024. https://webaim.org/articles/evaluationguide/.

13

The Law Library Intranet

Iain Barksdale, Erik Adams, and Kristen Naik

Librarianship is built upon the study of information. Finding this information is what we pride ourselves on, not only as individuals, but as a profession. But sharing this information is an increasingly inconsistent endeavor plaguing many in this profession. Technology's rapid evolution has eased this sharing in some cases but also complicated it in many others. Intranets help simplify this essential role of the librarian by allowing for a static sharing of important materials in an all-encompassing site.

Intranets provide a crucial tool in any library toolbox but are particularly useful for the legal field, where nuances and specialties reign supreme. For law librarians, intranets often serve the purpose of organizing and sharing resources. But they can do so much more when leveraged appropriately. Below you will find the information and tools essential for law librarians to best serve their institutions, whether that be public, academic, or private.

This chapter outlines what an intranet is, requirements for an intranet at your institution, types and components of intranets, common intranet products, how to choose the appropriate intranet for your institution, as well as evaluating and maintaining your intranet instance(s).

WHAT IS AN INTRANET?

The term "intranet" has various definitions based on source and context. Simplistically and etymologically, it is the converse of the Internet, an open and "unowned" system, whereas an intranet is a computer network that is internal and private. However, just as the term "Internet" has come to encompass more than its core definition, so has the term "intranet." So just what have these tools evolved into over the years and what definition can we use to encompass the changes over the years?

A BRIEF HISTORY

We cannot define the term "intranet" without first discussing another term and entity, which by now we all take for granted and has expanded beyond its original definition, the Internet, as intranets are an extension of this technology. From its beginnings as the ARPAnet in the late sixties, the pieces of the modern Internet were slowly added over time to become the fully-fledged conglomeration of services we use today and refer to as the Internet. Platform-agnostic access to all forms of information is now the norm, afforded to us by technologies based on standard internet protocols. We have swiftly moved from a system consisting mainly of accessing information via text, hyperlinks, and tables. The Internet now offers database access, file transfers, email, hyperlinking, static images, animated images, streaming audio and video, telephony, forums and message boards, blogs, and social media. These are now served up to us via web browsers using World Wide Web protocols, frameworks, and dedicated apps. All of these tools that make up the Internet can also be used within an intranet.

So, if an intranet is more than just an internal, private network, then what is it? According to *Merriam-Webster*'s dictionary, it is, "a network operating like the World Wide Web but having access restricted to a limited group of authorized users (such as employees of a company)."[1] In Tyson Greer's *Understanding Intranets,* it is defined as "a private computer network that uses Internet standards and protocols to enable members of an organization to communicate and collaborate more efficiently with one another, thereby increasing productivity."[2]

Greer also posits five core functions of an intranet, which help further one's understanding of an intranet's functions.

1. Email: interpersonal and intergroup communication
2. File sharing: sharing knowledge, information, and ideas
3. Directories: management of information and user access
4. Searches: finding what you need, when you need it
5. Network management: maintenance and intranet modifications

It is the combining of these functions that leads to a fully-fledged intranet, although not all are required to be present in the final product in order to have a product we will call an intranet, as email is often accessed via a fully featured stand-alone client and email web clients do not always offer full features. However, a full-service intranet is meant to be a one-stop shop for private information, leading to increased productivity and user satisfaction. You can think of an intranet in library terms as a discovery layer. As a discovery layer allows patrons to access disparate resource data in a singular interface, an intranet does the same for internal information. All of these tools for accessing information will be presented to users in a web-based format owned by an institution with access limited to members of the institution.

NEED ANALYSIS

Now that we have a basic understanding of what an intranet is, how do we know if our department or institution can benefit from implementing an intranet? Do you need an intranet to help boost productivity related to your online information and increase user satisfaction? Do you have important institutional information that is difficult to access, or needs to be migrated to a digital format? Do you simply want to consolidate your print policies and procedures into an easy to edit and maintain form?

There are many ways to perform a needs analysis, which often consists of one or more of the following: professional observation, surveys, and focus groups. This process helps balance the strengths and weaknesses of each tool and offers the data needed to create a highly defensible needs analysis and project proposal. Decisions at this level should not be made just based on professional observation; you will also need to gather some objective data using the other methods. This is just a data-gathering starting point. One does not need all three methods for needs analysis; decisions could be made based solely on a survey or a focus group. Focus groups in particular will help to generate user buy-in, which will be crucial for success in a project of this type.

Professional Observation

As information professionals, we have the training, skills, and experience to observe how individuals in our institution are consuming and processing the information required to do their respective work. We are conduits for the use of much of this information, and often we are direct suppliers of this information as well. As we go about our work in our institutions, what are we seeing and hearing? What are our patrons saying directly to us?

This stage of information gathering may be active or passive. Firm librarians can engage in both brief, informal conversations with attorneys as well as scheduled meetings. During these conversations, it is important to attend to how participants speak about accessing the various types of information used in the firm. For academic librarians, one can "walk the faculty offices" for faculty input and talk to individual students to get a basic idea of how they are accessing the information they need to use. If the intranet is solely for the library, this process will be streamlined since you will have a much smaller and more familiar user base with which to work.

This informal stage of information gathering helps to set the next stage of needs analysis, the survey. With the information in hand, gathered from professional observation, one can build a survey with questions that are pertinent to our individual institution's information usage and culture.

Surveys

Once exploratory information is gathered, it is best to follow up with a more formal data gathering that can be objective and quantified. This "hard data," obtained via surveys will be easier to analyze and present in a visual manner. These surveys will help determine if an intranet would be beneficial, and also provide the tools for making a case if it is determined that an intranet would be beneficial.

Surveys help gather information at this stage; however, surveys are not without their drawbacks. Without a method to enforce compliance in responding to surveys, they are self-selecting, as only those most interested in the topic will respond. This can lead to small sample sizes and skewed results in relation to the institution or library as a whole. It is also difficult to draft a good survey, so plan on taking some time to draft one to ensure you are gathering the data that you need. Also, be aware of bias when creating surveys. You may be predisposed to wanting an intranet, so take care not to create leading questions in any surveys.

In general, the survey should reduce responses to numerical data and also allow for open commentary at some point. Likert scales are a favorite among survey designers, for they allow the respondent to gauge their response on a 5-point scale. A Not Applicable option should be incorporated into the Likert responses as a sixth option when necessary. Alternatively, a combination of Likert scale questions with a free text box allows for maximum data gathering.[3]

Questions should not only focus on gathering how individuals are accessing and using institutional data, but also on how individuals feel about how they are accessing the data. User satisfaction with a system can ultimately determine whether they use it or not. Is your current system user-friendly, and do your users feel confident in how they access the data that they require on a daily basis? How easily is archival data accessed? Is all the required data even in digital form? Despite the subjectivity of feelings, they are still important in determining the initial needs of users for a particular solution or product and later, how it will be implemented.

Focus Groups

Should your survey responses reveal the need for an intranet, the next step before deciding on a software solution would be conducting stakeholder focus groups. Not all institutions or departments will have the same needs or feelings about how an intranet will be utilized. Focus groups help determine how stakeholders currently interact with the information they require on a day-to-day basis.[4] It is very helpful to have a projection on a whiteboard or smart board for intranet focus groups to capture markup for your current tools, as this will help in making the designs for which product will work best for your users. Whether you decide on purchasing a solution or creating your own intranet, this is a good time to ask questions about current interface issues. In the end, your intranet will be a compromise of user wants and needs; appropriately tailored focus groups will help build the best overall system and help generate user buy-in.

TURNKEY OR SELF-DEVELOPED?

Once the decision has been made that your library would benefit from having an intranet, the next step will be determining whether you will acquire a turnkey system or develop your intranet in-house. Your user needs, budget, and on-site IT support will be the prime determiners for which solution you will pursue. This decision point has many trade-offs and will also require a long-range implementation plan to avoid any issues down the road, regardless of which solution you end up choosing.

Definitions

A turnkey system, sometimes referred to as an out-of-the-box system, is a fully developed software solution that will only require installation and setup, although there are some hosted solutions that only require setup. Depending on the software and where the application server resides, this may be completed by the product vendor or your IT unit. A self-developed, or in-house, solution will be created by your own staff. A self-developed solution may be created from the ground up and completely custom, or created with preexisting tools.

Turnkey

There are several benefits to turnkey systems. Implementation is usually quick and relatively issue-free. The vendor activates an instance of the software on their servers for your library. Upon completion, they provide a customized link to access your instance, and then institutional customization can begin. The software has been developed, tested, and field-proven; system maintenance and upgrades are usually completed by the vendor. Vendors usually have a procedure to solicit input for feature suggestions from customers to add to their upgrade cycle. If you do not already have dedicated IT staff available, a turnkey system can be more financially feasible than a self-developed intranet. Turnkey systems can usually be branded for an institution, but full integration into an existing institutional web framework may not always be possible.

However, turnkey systems are not a single purchase. They usually involve an initial purchase cost followed by an ongoing support subscription. Yet, there are vendors that have moved to subscription-based plans with the cost based on activated features, user counts, and/or volume of data. Often it is possible to customize both functionality and cost on a subscription-based turnkey solution to suit your library's needs. Based on the feedback from the evaluations listed above, the required features should be apparent.

Self-Developed

If your institution has the talent and time available in-house, then it may be a better option to self-develop your intranet. Self-development allows for full control over the layout and the look and feel. This can be a boon if your institution has a required template for web pages, whether they are internal or external. Keep in mind, although there are many DIY website tools available, building an interface from scratch does require more User Interface and Experience (UIX) than these DIY website tools can offer.

One of the main drawbacks of a self-developed system is ongoing support and development. Building your own intranet is a long-term commitment from the beginning to the final product and beyond to maintenance and improvement. As such, an internal long-range plan is required to both evaluate new features and overcome technical issues. A self-developed system may take longer to implement, which may be a negative to decision-makers.

FREE, OPEN-SOURCE, OR COMMERCIAL SOLUTIONS?

Free

For those with budgetary concerns, free intranet software components are available. Building an intranet based on free software is similar to building your own computer. While the services is free, it requires gathering intranet components from several different sources, putting them all together, and turn the components into a usable intranet. This requires a technological savvy that many law librarians may lack—understanding interoperability, coding, and software configuration are musts.

There are free products available for all aspects of an intranet, including discussion board software, wikis, calendars, contact management, and file sharing. When evaluating a free product, consideration must be given to many technical factors, including the hardware requirements to run the software, what operating systems are supported, and whether the institution has expertise available to support the software. It will likely be difficult to secure approval for a product that only runs on a Unix-like operating system like Linux if every other computer in the organization is running a version of Windows.

That said, below is a short list of free products that could be used to build an intranet:

Table 13.1 Free Intranet Components Overview

Product	*Name*	*URL (as of publication)*
Forum or Discussion Board	phpBB	https://www.phpbb.com
	MyBB	https://mybb.com
	Simple Machines	https://www.simplemachines.org
Wiki Tool	MediaWiki	https://www.mediawiki.org/wiki/MediaWiki
	Wiki.JS	https://js.wiki/
	BookStack	https://www.bookstackapp.com/
Calendars and Directory	Sabre/DAV	https://sabre.io/
	Baikal	https://sabre.io/baikal/
	Xandikos	https://pypi.org/project/xandikos/

Without readily available and skilled IT staff, predicted cost savings may not come to fruition. With free software, more time is spent on installation, configuration, and maintenance as compared to single vendor solutions. This support can take up an enormous amount of time, which, after all, is not a free resource.

Open-Source

Open-Source software, like free software, may also offer tempting solutions for building an intranet. It is provided with the original code, which theoretically empowers users to make changes to the software to suit local needs, though significant skill is required to make changes. One popular combination of Open-Source software that can be used as a foundation for building an intranet is called "LAMP"—an acronym for Linux (an operating system), Apache (web server software), MySQL (a database system), and PHP (a scripting language for creating web pages). Open-Source products often have active communities that work together using various development and versioning platforms. There are also several vendors that provide paid support for some Open-Source products, such as Red Hat (which supports Linux), Oracle (which offers support plans for MySQL), and many smaller businesses. Because ongoing development is generally provided by the user community, third-party support for Open-Source solutions is often less expensive than a proprietary solution. Still, it is often said that Open Source is only free if your time has no value, and cost savings may prove elusive.

It is also worth mentioning that most of the free products listed in the previous section are also Open-Source. For example, MediaWiki has a robust developer community; the developer website (https://developer.wikimedia.org/) has links to developer documentation.

Commercial Solutions

Another option is the purchase or subscription model offered by vendors of turnkey intranet solutions. See the above sections for a more detailed overview of turnkey solutions. Pricing options can range from several dollars per user per month to thousands of dollars per year. Paid subscriptions usually include ongoing support and regular updates. Because vendors often have large paying client bases, outages are rare, and when they occur, they are usually swiftly remedied. Be aware, when it comes to soliciting client suggestions for changes and additions, some vendors are more transparent and supportive than others.

VENDORS

There are many vendors that provide different options for intranets, some very generalized and some library-specific. There will be a trade-off between library-specific features and price. Instead of attempting to simply offer a laundry list of intranet software vendors, we will focus on three, one that offers library-specific intranet functionality and two that offer general intranet functionality. Springshare, which many academic libraries already use at varying levels; Guru Technologies, which offers a robust enterprise-level intranet solution; and Microsoft SharePoint, which is very popular in law firms and corporate environments.

Springshare

Springshare is a vendor familiar to many law librarians, particularly those in academic spaces. It is a subscription-based, hosted software solution. Although the Springshare suite might not fit our definition or expectations of a fully-fledged intranet (it lacks a fully integrated email server/client functionality), its tools are tailored for libraries and offer features that make up for the lack of an integrated email component.

The core Springshare components required for creating an intranet are LibGuides & CMS (the core intranet module), LibApps, LibCal, and LibStaffer. LibGuides & CMS is marketed as Springshare's library internet solution. With these components active, you have a singular solution for file sharing, directories, searches, and network management. LibGuides & CMS covers file sharing and searches. It is an expansion of LibGuides that offers an internal version of LibGuides and scalable management of your internal information. It is basically Springshare's version of a wiki and allows you to tailor access to your information in how it is created and accessed. LibCal and LibStaffer cover directories and searches. Offering easy access to both general calendars and staff schedules, these tools allow you to keep track of work schedules, appointments, and events. LibApps covers network management, although all the modules have context-specific administrative sections.

Following along the lines of integrating different tools, LibApps offers varying degrees of integration with ILS solutions, Microsoft Exchange, and Google web apps. There are also other library-specific tools offered by Springshare, apart from their intranet solutions, which makes LibApps a very robust intranet solution for libraries.

It is very simple to brand and customize LibApps as they utilize the popular web framework Bootstrap, a "powerful, extensible, and feature-packed frontend toolkit."[5] Many institutions use Bootstrap, making branding and customization even easier as a library can leverage work already done.

Guru Technologies

Guru Technologies offers Guru AI Intranet, a product that features a custom interface and third-party product integration. It consists of three tools: Enterprise AI, Intranet, and Wiki. Guru AI Intranet is a hosted solution that offers per-user subscription-based pricing, which can be very cost-effective for smaller libraries. It meets all the requirements of our definition, backed by AI integration of your important data.

Enterprise AI Search covers file sharing, directories, and searches. The AI search interface connects many different tools, such as Microsoft Teams, OneDrive, Slack, Box, and others. Intranet covers file sharing, directory searches, and network management. This consolidation of information sources lends itself to increased productivity—a main draw of intranets. Intranet is the homepage portal that consolidates the Guru tools and offers a one-stop dashboard for your vital information. Wiki covers file sharing and searches. Like a traditional wiki, Wiki is a tool used to capture important institutional knowledge and offer tools to easily organize and access your information. Guru also offers simple customization and branding for their intranet solution.

While Guru may be an affordable intranet solution, it is a generalized enterprise intranet solution. It will provide all the services needed in an intranet, but without any specialized library tools. However, for smaller non-academic libraries, this might be a cost-effective solution.

Microsoft SharePoint

In many law firms, the choice of intranet software is SharePoint. In an informal survey of ten of the largest law firms in the United States, nine out of ten surveyed were using SharePoint either as their primary intranet site or as part of a complex intranet solution. SharePoint is available both as a software package that can be installed on-premises and as a completely hosted solution (For more, see https://www.microsoft.com/en-us/microsoft-365/sharepoint/sharepoint-licensing-overview). Pricing varies depending on options and the number of users, and SharePoint is available from Microsoft bundled with other products like Microsoft Office 365.

SharePoint is not an email or messaging system, though it can be integrated into Microsoft's Exchange email system as well as the Teams messaging platform. It includes facilities for sharing a variety of file types, including word-processing documents, PDFs, spreadsheets, and others, though notably excluding key data file types including Tableau workbooks, flows, and data. These accepted file types can be saved in document libraries and custom-shared databases (lists in SharePoint parlance). It comes with templates for a variety of types of sites, including team, project, and community, all of which can easily be customized to meet organizational and ad hoc needs. SharePoint also allows for custom privacy settings even within organizations, granting administrators more specialized control over these intranets. In addition to its offerings out of the box, there are countless websites with instructions on how to create wikis, shared calendars, simple request management systems, project management, RSS readers, and more.

Besides the features SharePoint provides out of the box, many third-party vendors make it possible to integrate their systems easily into a SharePoint site. Lucidea's Sydney Digital (https://lucidea.com/sydneydigital/), SirsiDynix EOS.Web (https://www.sirsidynix.com/eos-web-web-services/), and Softlink Liberty (https://ic.softlinkint.com/library-management-system/) all boast of their ability to integrate with existing SharePoint sites. Popular document management systems (DMS) like iManage and NetDocuments have partnered with third-party vendors to integrate their products with SharePoint (i.e., https://imanage.com/technology-partners/aderant/aderant-handshake/, https://www.netdocuments.com/partner-app-integrations). SharePoint can even be integrated with Springshare's Libguides and Guru Technologies (discussed previously), opening another avenue for publishing content.

SharePoint Online also integrates with Microsoft's no-code product, Power Automate (https://learn.microsoft.com/en-us/power-automate/sharepoint-overview), which makes it possible to create event-based automations. For example, you can use a SharePoint site to not only create a form but have form submissions fill in a custom list and be notified via email when a new item is added to said list. Microsoft has lists of similar projects on their website (https://make.powerautomate.com/templates/) with instructions on how to set them up. Additionally, SharePoint also connects to One-Drive, creating a seamless integration with both OneDrive and Microsoft 365 products.

With its bundling with other Microsoft products, SharePoint is an easy choice for many firms that are already supporting the Microsoft ecosystem. Its customizable options allow for many different uses across departments. However, to fully leverage these solutions, an understanding and training in Microsoft products are required to truly maximize its operability.

LOCAL OR HOSTED?

Definitions

A local system is installed on a web server that your institution has purchased and is usually located on-site, although not necessarily in your building. A hosted system is a remote web server that is provided by your turnkey software vendor. The server will be part of a group of servers, known as a server farm, that may be owned and maintained by the vendor, or it may be part of a cloud service. Either way, support and maintenance will be provided by the vendor.

Local

A local system will be set up and maintained by institutional staff. This will consist of a server, web server software, and any tools required for building your intranet. The needs analysis should include considerations of the cost and capacity of a local server. Servers are more robust than desktop computers and can often be used for years before replacement is required; thus, the cost can be amortized. A local system may result in faster response times for both hardware and software issues, as the staff responding to issues will have firsthand knowledge of the code and server setup.

Of course, the downside of a locally hosted intranet is that there is no vendor to blame when there are problems. Responsibility for maintaining all aspects of a locally hosted intranet server will fall on institutional IT staff.

Hosted

It is possible to have the web server aspects of your intranet hosted by a third-party service such as HostGator, GoDaddy, Amazon, or Microsoft. Most institutions will have either a local web server or a hosted account administered by IT. Always check with your IT staff, as many institutions will no longer allow third-party hosting of institutional websites for security reasons.

A hosted turnkey system will be completely managed by your software vendor, as it is becoming less common for turnkey vendors to install a product on a local server. It may be necessary to engage in some initial management and customization of software or provide a security certificate, but web server maintenance and software updates are traditionally handled by the software vendor. Hosted systems are relatively hands-off and are highly beneficial if there is a small number of local staff or if IT staff are unavailable for this level of service.

EVALUATING ROI

Introduction to ROI

Evaluating return on investment (ROI) should be part of any intranet project. Effort should be made to measure and determine what impact an intranet has had on an organization's productivity, whether it has improved collaboration and communication, simplified finding and sharing of knowledge, and the effort to maintain and update an intranet should all be factors. Measuring ROI will make it possible to justify the cost of creating and running an intranet. The techniques discussed below can also be used to identify strengths and weaknesses of an intranet, identify opportunities and challenges, and opportunities for improvement.

Surveys

In evaluating the ROI of the intranet, you come full circle back to two of the techniques we used to determine if an intranet was needed and what solution to choose. However, having an existing intranet adds a new source of data to analyze how users are interacting with the intranet via web analytics. Most librarians have had the experience of being told that a treatise is essential to their work, while circulation statistics suggest that the book has never actually left the shelf. Web analytics can be used in a method similar to circulation statistics: users may say that a feature of an intranet is important, but web analytics can show just how often it is actually used. User surveys, follow-up focus groups, and web analytics can all be used to determine the worth of one's efforts in implementing an intranet.

As outlined in the previous survey section, Likert scale surveys can once again be used to gather information on generalized changes in user productivity and attitudes. The ROI surveys should be based, as closely as possible, on the original language in the needs analysis surveys. This will enable you to quickly visualize comparisons of changing data. Although your main focus is to evaluate the success of our intranet, you can also use this stage to gather system improvement data.

Focus Groups

The follow-up focus groups are run in a similar manner to the ROI surveys. The follow-up focus groups grant the opportunity to review the questions asked earlier and see if there have been any perceived improvements from your users. Having users engage in information retrieval assignments can highlight UIX issues you may not have predicted from earlier data gathering. Timed information retrieval assignments allow the assessor to compare how individuals access the information. There is not always just one way to navigate to information. If, during day-to-day use, a user has discovered an efficient way to access information, the interface can be modified to steer other users toward that process. Any issues may also be addressed at this time and noted for future improvements. These improvements to the system will now be based on actual usage in the workplace.

Web Analytics

Web analytics are the final piece of the ROI analysis puzzle. Self-developed intranets may require the installation of a web analytics solution such as Google Analytics. With a turnkey system, web analytics are usually part of the system. The tools Research Monitor (from TRG) and Onelog (from iTS aka Info Technology Supply Limited) also allow for tracking of web usage and other analytics, though these require a subscription, which can be a deterrent to some institutions. Turnkey systems often have web analytics pre-installed and can often offer a more customized picture of usage. These analytics allow for assessment of top users, uses, and time spent on the intranet. This may seem like a large amount of data, but analytic solutions often offer dashboards for data visualization. This usage data can inform the questions to pose to the focus group, allowing for targeted improvements.

Further Improvements

After completing ROI analysis, evaluate the data and use the "Start Stop Continue" (SSC) model to improve the user experience. In short, individual features of a website can be evaluated for which new features should be added (or "started"), which features are not meeting expectations and can be discontinued (or "stopped"), and which features are meeting expectations and should continue. The SSC model can also be used to evaluate the processes and procedures used to maintain a website: what tasks need to be started, which processes are inefficient or ineffective and need to stop, and which processes are working and can continue.

One point of review at this stage would be your information architecture. Are users able to efficiently navigate your intranet to access the information they are seeking? What refinements can you make to page navigation? Are user expectations being met? Did you remember to offer a persistent site-wide search bar for accessing information?

MAINTAINING YOUR INTRANET

Whether a self-developed or turnkey intranet, managing the information and interface is an iterative process. The boring reality is that the work of keeping an intranet fresh and useful is never done. In addition to constant improvements and modifications to the tools themselves, our understanding and application of these technologies also develop over time. As such, it is best to audit and update your intranet on a regular schedule to maintain currency. One of the authors regularly updates their intranet every two years.

If there is a significant technological update between routine maintenance, assess the costs and benefits by evaluating the ROI (as outlined above) for an unscheduled update. In addition to the ROI, one should also consider if the update will require additional staff time or knowledge for the initial upgrade as well as future maintenance.

CONCLUSION

Intranets can help collect, organize, and share critical information with your patrons. Not only that, but they can create a workspace for you and your team to effectively collaborate. Whether you are building your intranet from scratch, purchasing an out-of-the-box product, or a combination of the two, challenges will arise when implementing your own instance. Hopefully, the information presented in this chapter will provide a foundation for overcoming obstacles as they arise on your intranet journey. A well-thought-out and implemented law library intranet can immensely increase not only library productivity, but also user satisfaction.

NOTES

1. "Intranet," Merriam-Webster, 2024, accessed June 6, 2024, https://www.merriam-webster.com/dictionary/intranet.
2. Tyson Greer, *Understanding Intranets* (Redmond, WA: Microsoft Press, 1998).
3. Laura South, David Saffo, Olga Vitek, Cody Dunne, and Michelle A. Borkin, "Effective Use of Likert Scales in Visualization Evaluations: A Systematic Review," *Computer Graphics Forum* 41, no. 3 (2022): 43–55.
4. Mona J. E. Danner et al., *Using Focus Groups to Listen, Learn, and Lead in Higher Education*, 1st ed. (Sterling, VA: Routledge, 2018).
5. Bootstrap, "Bootstrap Homepage," accessed August 15, 2024, https://getbootstrap.com.

14

Cybersecurity Issues and Training

Susan Boland

Once upon a time, security in law libraries meant security gates, locked doors, tattle tape, and maybe a security guard. Now, law libraries need to protect their digital spaces as much as their physical ones. As our systems and tools become more complex, law libraries, our partners, and our parent institutions become more vulnerable to cyberattacks. Law librarians face increased challenges and opportunities to protect ourselves, our parent institutions, and our patrons when it comes to cybersecurity.

WHAT IS CYBERSECURITY

There is no standardized definition of cybersecurity, but the Cybersecurity & Infrastructure Security Agency (CISA) tells us it is "the art of protecting networks, devices, from unauthorized access or criminal use and the practice of ensuring confidentiality, integrity, and availability of information."[1] Law libraries are all about confidentiality, integrity, and availability of information, so integrating cybersecurity into our everyday practices aligns perfectly with our values. Common cybersecurity threats include misconfigurations; denial-of-service (DoS) and distributed-denial-of-service (DDoS) attacks; phishing; stolen or compromised credentials; zero-day and unpatched vulnerabilities; malware and ransomware; and malicious insider actions.

A misconfiguration is "an incorrect or suboptimal configuration of an information system or system component that may lead to vulnerabilities."[2] Misconfigurations can be present in many places such as hardware, software, databases, applications, and networks. These may or may not be under your library's control and are often not even within the parent institution's control. Examples of misconfigurations include not changing the default configurations that come with software or applications, improper privilege and access controls, lack of network segmentation, and insecure credentials.[3] More and more organizations have moved or are moving to the cloud. This means cloud misconfiguration has become a growing cybersecurity issue. IBM's *Cost of a Data Breach Report 2023* found that 11 percent of attacks leading to a data breach succeeded due to a cloud misconfiguration.[4]

DoS and DDoS attacks deny legitimate users access to a service, system, or device. The most well-known type of DoS attack is when bad actors overload a network with traffic and crash it.[5] Can't get to your favorite website or network? They might be suffering from a DoS or DDoS attack. Amazon, Google, Meta, and Microsoft all have had service interruptions due to attacks. Another common cybersecurity issue that most of us unfortunately have encountered is phishing attempts, where bad actors target people through email, texts, phone, or other methods to obtain sensitive data or install malicious software. Stolen or compromised credentials allow unauthorized access to devices and systems and are sometimes obtained through phishing. They are used in other cybercrimes such as data breaches and ransomware attacks. Verizon's *2024 Data Breach Investigations Report* found that since 2013, stolen credentials appeared in 31 percent of reported data breaches.[6]

Our devices and systems often require updating, remediation, or modification to improve their operation, fix issues, or address security vulnerabilities. This is done through patching. An unpatched vulnerability is a flaw or weakness that allows attackers to exploit a known issue. CISA maintains a catalog of known vulnerabilities.[7] Unfortunately, knowing about a vulnerability and patching it are two different things. One study found that once the patches were available, it took most organizations fifty-five days to remediate 50 percent of critical vulnerabilities found in the CISA Known Exploited Vulnerabilities Catalog.[8] Why do known vulnerabilities sometimes remain unpatched? Patching is a Sisyphean task. Organizations of all sizes struggle with patching, and there are reasons that vulnerabilities may not be immediately, or ever, patched. Patching takes time, money, and skill; it can often break something vital; it may not even be possible due to the age of a product, interdependencies, or other reasons; or the thing needing patching isn't owned by your organization or is inaccessible by your organization.[9] Known vulnerabilities are difficult enough to keep up with, but organizations also face zero-day vulnerabilities. A zero-day vulnerability is unknown or one where there is no fix yet.[10] In 2023, Google identified ninety-seven exploited zero-day vulnerabilities, sixty-one of them targeted end-user platforms and products, and thirty-six targeted enterprise technology.[11]

Malware is a catch-all for malicious hardware, software, or firmware of all types, intended to harm systems and devices.[12] Ransomware is a type of malware that encrypts files so that users and systems cannot access or use them, and then attackers demand a ransom in exchange for decrypting them. They may also threaten to destroy or release the data.[13] Ransomware attacks are becoming increasingly common, with 2023 seeing 32 percent of data breaches involving ransomware or extortion.[14] Cybersecurity threats caused by malicious insiders are situations where an insider, such as an employee, contractor, vendor, or other person with access to facilities, equipment, or networks, uses their access or knowledge for harm.[15]

A potential new threat in cybersecurity is artificial intelligence (AI). AI is not yet showing up as a significant cause of cybersecurity incidents.[16] Current information suggests that bad actors are exploring the use of AI for learning more about potential victims, improving phishing and social engineering campaigns, and improving scripting and coding.[17] AI has also been flagged for privacy issues. ChatGPT has leaked portions of chat history and payment information.[18] Many employees using AI in the workplace do not seem to realize that sensitive data should not be put into public Large Language Models.[19] Certain AI tools have now been banned by some organizations.[20]

UNDERSTANDING THE COSTS OF A CYBERSECURITY INCIDENT

When an organization experiences a cybersecurity incident, the costs involve more than just money, although a cybersecurity incident can be extremely expensive in that regard. In 2023, the average cost of a data breach was $4.45 million.[21] The cost of notifying people, regulators, and other third parties about a data breach was $370,000.[22] Lost business costs added up to $1.30 million.[23] Ransomware demands vary. One survey found that the median initial ransom demand for legal and government organizations was $1,000,000.[24] Although law enforcement and cybersecurity experts advise organizations not to pay ransomware, many organizations do. Fifty-six percent of higher education institutions that reported a ransomware attack paid the ransom.[25] Costs of cyberattacks also include business interruptions and staff time. The average time to contain a data breach was seventy-three days.[26] The average time to identify and contain a ransomware attack can be even longer. Many in law libraries would view the highest costs of a cybersecurity incident to be its impacts on our patrons and the loss of trust. As more and more of our services and resources are digital in nature, losing access to those services and resources due to a cybersecurity incident can be devastating. Having patron data stolen and sold or released may lead to irrevocable damage to goodwill and trust.

Law firms, libraries, courts, government, and academic institutions have all fallen victim to cybersecurity incidents and had to pay these costs. Law firms, which make particularly juicy targets of cyberattacks that involve data exfiltration, have been the victims of high-profile breaches including the firms Appleby (Paradise Papers); Cravath, Swaine & Moore; DLA Piper; Orrick, Herrington & Sutcliffe; Jenner & Block; and Mossack Fonseca (Panama Papers).[27] As this chapter was being written, Seattle Public Library became a victim of a ransomware attack and services went down.[28] Before that, the British Library and Toronto Public Library were attacked.[29] The Pennsylvania Courts experienced a DoS attack that took their e-filing system, e-pay systems, and website down.[30] Beyond the courts and public libraries, state, federal, and local governments have been attacked.[31] Even CISA has been a victim![32] Institutions of higher education have also not been immune, with major attacks that have hit California universities, University of Georgia, Ohio State, and many more.[33]

WHY LAW LIBRARIES AND THEIR PARENT INSTITUTIONS ATTRACT BAD ACTORS

Law libraries collect, preserve, and make accessible data which makes them an attractive target for bad actors. While the type of information collected may vary by library, most libraries do some sort of recording of reference interactions, instruction or workshop attendance, resource usage, website usage, and facilities usage. Bad actors could gain personally identifiable information and borrowing histories from our ILS. Tracking reference interactions may include details such as dates, the specific questions asked and research projects requested, along with who was asking the questions, what client it was for, and billing information. Instruction or workshop attendance may include personally identifiable information. Resource usage can encompass everything from user credentials and personally identifiable information to searches used and materials viewed or downloaded. Website or intranet usage can track visitors, their IP addresses, technology used to access the site, referral URLs, other sites visited, and more. Facilities usage may cover who enters the building or library, at what times, and on what dates. In addition to this type of data, employment records, sensitive emails, research data, and attorney work products stored in library systems may also be targets. Federal, state, and local governments; law firms; courts; and academic institutions all keep sensitive and valuable data and provide important services so even if the law library itself is not a target, their parent institution is.

Aside from the data and services provided, bad actors also target libraries and their parent institutions due to lack of resources, lack of staff, lack of cybersecurity expertise, legacy systems, and reliance on third parties. For example, in the review of the cyberattack on it, the British Library cited legacy infrastructure as one of the security vulnerabilities that increased the severity of the attack; third-party providers within their network; and lack of Multi-Factor Authentication (MFA) for domain access due to costs and inconvenience.[34] While higher education institutions increased their spending on cybersecurity from 2019 to 2023, their budget allocation was lower than the global average.[35] There is a global shortage of cybersecurity professionals, and a survey of legal technology decision-makers found that although 58 percent of respondents said there was at least one full-time dedicated information security employee, 27 percent had no specialized employees for cybersecurity, and 10 percent responded that they had no one.[36] Even well-known, well-funded, and widely trusted third-party providers can provide bad actors access to our most sensitive data. Vulnerabilities in Microsoft products and services, which are widely used across our organizations, have resulted in serious cyberattacks. In its review of a 2023 cyberattack by a Chinese nation-state actor group that exploited a vulnerability in Microsoft Exchange, the Cyber Safety Review Board noted that "Microsoft's ubiquitous and critical products, which underpin essential services that support national security, the foundations of our economy, and public health and safety, require the company to demonstrate the highest standards of security, accountability, and transparency" but concluded that "Microsoft's security culture was inadequate."[37]

STAKEHOLDER CONFIDENCE SURROUNDING CYBERSECURITY

Law firm clients have become much more cognizant of the risks surrounding law firm security of their sensitive data. According to the 2023 ABA Legal Technology Survey, 14 percent of clients requested a security audit or review, and 22 percent of respondents reported clients had requested the firm answer a security questionnaire.[38] Law firms themselves lack confidence in their ability to prepare, detect, and respond to cyberattacks.[39] Many students do not feel confident in their college or university's ability to keep their data safe and to use that data in an ethical manner.[40] Americans do not trust the government to keep their data safe.[41]

CYBERSECURITY, LIBRARY VALUES, AND PROFESSIONAL RESPONSIBILITY

At the heart of library values are the privacy, security, and integrity of information. *The American Association of Law Libraries Ethical Principles* state that "[w]e create and implement service policies for the protection of patron confidentiality, privacy, and personal data."[42] *The American Library Association (ALA) Code of Ethics* similarly requires libraries to protect library users' privacy and confidentiality.[43] The *ALA Library Bill of Rights* further tasks libraries with advocating for, and educating about, privacy and the safeguarding of library data.[44] The *Interpretations of the Library Bill of Rights* incorporate cybersecurity and cite the *NISO Consensus Principles on Users' Digital Privacy in Library, Publisher, and Software-Provider Systems* with guidance that includes being transparent with users as to how data is collected, used, and retained; allowing users as much control as possible over data collection; not collecting beyond what is necessary; anonymizing and aggregating data; complying with state and national standards; encrypting data; updating systems to address vulnerabilities; using appropriate access control methods for sensitive data; establishing procedures for security training, breach reporting, incident response, and system configuration and auditing; not sharing users' personally identifiable information with third parties or without explicit permission from the user; and retaining ownership of library data and auditing vendor data practices.[45] The International Federation of Library Associations and Institutions (IFLA) also incorporates privacy and security into their code of ethics.[46] Furthermore, IFLA issued a policy statement on cybersecurity that recognizes that while libraries may not have control over everything in their information systems, they can incorporate cybersecurity practices in the "selection, administration, education, and management of the library systems and services provided"; by advocating for cybersecurity measures within their institutions and with vendors; through the development and publishing of policies around cybersecurity and privacy; by educating and training library personnel in cybersecurity fundamentals; through teaching digital and cybersecurity literacy to their users; and conforming to International Organization for Standardization (ISO) standards for cyber and information security.[47]

In addition to being part of library values, cybersecurity is also present in the rules of professional responsibility. ABA Model Rule 1.1 requires competent representation, and in the comments, competent representation includes knowing the "benefits and risks associated with relevant technology."[48] ABA Model Rule 1.6 makes explicit the duty to make reasonable efforts to safeguard client information and the comments provide guidance on factors to be considered in determining the reasonableness of those efforts.[49] ABA Model Rule 1.9 outlines duties to former clients, and the comments make clear that an attorney has a continuing duty to preserve confidentiality.[50] ABA Model Rule 1.15 addresses safeguarding the property of clients and third parties, which may include data.[51] ABA Model Rule 5.3 maintains that when using third-party vendors, lawyers must ensure those vendors provide services in a way consistent with the lawyers' professional obligations, which means the vendor must also make reasonable efforts to safeguard client information.[52] Various ethics opinions have reinforced lawyer cybersecurity obligations.[53]

THE LEGAL AND REGULATORY LANDSCAPE

Securing our law library digital spaces is not a choice. Cybersecurity has become increasingly regulated, but it has been regulated in a patchwork manner with new laws being proposed and passed every day. This creates a challenge for any law library to comply with cybersecurity laws and regulations. Highlighted here is a high-level overview of the legal and regulatory landscape, but this is in no way a comprehensive discussion of the legal and regulatory landscape.

There is no single federal law regarding cybersecurity. Law libraries or their parent institutions that are federal agencies, state agencies administering federal programs, and organizations supporting federal programs, receiving federal grants, or selling services to the federal government must comply with the Federal Information Security Modernization Act (FISMA), which defines a framework to protect government information resources from threats.[54] FISMA delegates the development of information security standards and guidelines to the National Institute of Standards and Technology (NIST).[55] The Federal Risk and Authorization Management Program (FedRAMP) applies to security and risk assessment for cloud technologies.[56] Depending on the type of information handled by an organization, other federal laws and regulations may also apply. For example, a law firm qualifying as a financial institution is subject to the Gramm-Leach-Bliley Act and the Federal Trade Commission's standards for safeguarding customer information and for data breach notification.[57] Higher education institutions participating in federal student loan programs must also protect student financial aid information under the Gramm-Leach-Bliley Act.[58] Law firms handling records of publicly traded companies may be subject to the Sarbanes-Oxley Act and the Securities and Exchange Commission's rules.[59] The Health Insurance Portability and Accountability Act and Health and Human Services' regulations would apply to organizations and their business associates that handle health information or provide legal services for covered entities.[60] For law libraries associated with higher education, the Family Educational Rights and Privacy Act of 1974 (FERPA) and the Department of Education regulations implementing FERPA, which protect the privacy of student education records, apply.[61] Section 5 of the Federal Trade Commission Act, which bars unfair and deceptive acts and practices in or affecting commerce, is now interpreted to cover misrepresentation of security protections and unreasonable security practices.[62] Paying ransomware may fall under the prohibition of making or facilitating ransomware payments to an attacker on the Office of Foreign Assets Control's Specially Designated Nationals and Blocked Persons List.[63]

States have their own laws that impact law libraries. According to the American Library Association, forty-eight states and the District of Columbia have laws protecting the confidentiality of library records, while Kentucky and Hawaii have attorney generals' opinions protecting library users' privacy.[64] Most of these statutes apply only to libraries that are public, so most do not apply to private libraries. Also, the statutes are all different. Most cover at least directory-type information and circulation records, but other types of data collection may not be covered by these statutes. The penalties for violating these statutes also vary from state to state. Interlibrary loan, consortium activities, and other library services that cross state lines may open up potential liability under more than one state's laws.

As of 2020, the National Conference of State Legislatures reports that at least thirty-two states had statutes that require state government agencies to have security measures in place to ensure the security of the data they hold.[65] At least twenty-five states also have data security laws that apply to private entities as well.[66] These statutes often do not contain details on what types of security measures or standards are to be used, utilizing generic language such as "reasonable" security measures and practices. All fifty states, the District of Columbia, Guam, Puerto Rico, and the Virgin Islands have enacted data breach notification laws that require companies and government agencies to notify consumers, regulators, and credit bureaus about data breaches.[67] Again, these statutes vary from state to state. There are differences regarding when notification is required (not every data breach requires notification and the personal information covered by the laws is defined differently), the timing of notices (some states require notification within a certain number of days whereas others are more vague), their form (some states allow email notification, telephone, fax, or substitute notification), their content (some states require certain content be included while other states have no requirements regarding what must be included in the notification), and their penalties for noncompliance (some states allow for private causes of action, and others have fines or injunctions).[68] Because the laws apply to information released about state residents and are not dependent on where an organization is physically located, organizations may need to comply with multiple data breach laws when a data breach occurs. Florida, Indiana, Louisiana, and North Dakota also require public entities to report ransomware incidents; and when a ransomware attack does occur, Florida and North Carolina prohibit state and local governments from paying the ransom.[69]

A growing number of states have general, comprehensive data privacy laws: California, Colorado, Connecticut, Delaware, Indiana, Iowa, Kentucky, Maryland, Minnesota, Montana, Nebraska, New Hampshire, New Jersey, Oregon, Tennessee, Texas, Utah, and Virginia have enacted a general privacy, data protection, or data security law.[70] The one most people are familiar with is the California Consumer Privacy Act, or the CCPA.[71] The content of the laws varies, but most of these are tied to businesses or commercial products and services and exempt state and local governments or state institutions of higher education.

While law libraries based in the United States may need to be most concerned with federal and state cybersecurity laws, law libraries and our parent institutions operate in a globally interconnected fashion. This means that law libraries also need to pay attention to the laws of other nations. If a law library processes the personal data of European Union citizens or residents, or offers goods or services to them, then the General Data Protection Regulation (GDPR) applies. Under the GDPR, personal data is any information that relates to an individual who can be directly or indirectly identified.[72] The GDPR requires that organizations ensure the security of personal data and use appropriate methods to safeguard it.[73] The GDPR also contains provisions related to required data breach notifications.[74] China's Personal Information Protection Law of the People's Republic of China (PIPL) is similar to the GDPR. It also applies to organizations processing the personal data of citizens regardless of whether they are located outside of China and requires this data to be protected from unauthorized access.[75] According to the UN Trade and Development (UNCTAD), 137 countries have enacted laws to protect data and privacy.[76] Depending on the people law libraries and their parent institutions serve or collect data on, these laws of other nations specifying security and privacy may apply. Forty-six countries have signed The International Counter Ransomware Initiative, pledging that "institutions under the authority of our national government should not pay ransomware."[77] Finally, while not a law or regulation, organizations that accept or use credit or debit cards must comply with the PCI Data Security Standards developed and maintained by the PCI Security Standards Council to protect payment data.[78]

BASIC CYBERSECURITY PRACTICES FOR EVERYONE

Every challenge offers an opportunity, and cybersecurity is no different. Cybersecurity is the responsibility of everyone in the law library, so what can individuals who are not IT professionals do? Practice everyday cybersecurity hygiene and teach our patrons about everyday cybersecurity as well. Individuals, through phishing, malware, or other methods, can be the vector for a cybersecurity incident. CISA's *Secure Our World* is a great starting place for basic cybersecurity practices, and it focuses on just four steps: (1) recognize and report phishing, (2) use strong passwords, (3) turn on multifactor authentication, and (4) update software.[79]

NIST has developed a Phish Scale that organizations can use when engaging in embedded phishing awareness training programs (simulated phishing emails are sent to users to combat real-world phishing scenarios), but this is also a useful tool to teach and learn about the type of details to look for in order to identify a phishing email. Common ways to identify a phishing email are to look for spelling and grammar errors; inspect for errors or inconsistencies in visual cues such as branding, logos, design, and formatting; examine the language used such as a generic greeting, lack of detail in the signature, a sense of urgency, threatened consequences for inaction, and requests for sensitive information; technical indicators such as domain spoofing, incorrect URL when you hover your cursor over the hyperlink, a display name hiding the real sender, or email address in the sender's name or email address fields; an executable or downloadable attachment type; and common tactics such as "too good to be true" offers, limited time offers, unusual requests from a friend or authority, things that appear to be work-related but not necessarily expected, or from an expected source, appeals to the heartstrings, and so on.[80] When a phishing email, text, or call is received, while you do not want to respond or click on things, or download things, you also should not just delete and ignore it. Report phishing attempts to information security in your organization; forward phishing emails to reportphishing@apwg.org (the Anti-Phishing Working Group, which is an international coalition of counter-cybercrime responders, forensic investigators, law enforcement agencies, technology companies, financial services firms, university researchers, NGOs, and multilateral treaty organizations); forward phishing texts to 7726 (SPAM) and they will automatically be sent to wireless providers; and report any phishing attempts to the FTC at FTC.gov/Complaint. If you fall for a phishing attempt (and they are getting more and more sophisticated), report it immediately and notify any potentially affected parties; disconnect from the network if you might have been infected with malware; and change any potentially compromised passwords.

CISA provides guidance on creating strong passwords and suggests making passwords at least sixteen characters long; using a random string of upper- and lower-case letters, numbers, and symbols or a passphrase of four to seven unrelated words; and using unique, strong passwords for each account rather than reusing passwords.[81] Longer passwords are stronger, and passwords using random strings or words, mixed-case letters, numbers, and symbols are harder and take longer to brute force (brute force attacks use computing power to discover a password by trying every combination of letters, numbers, and symbols).[82] CISA also suggests using a password manager, which does not require users to memorize every password for every account and also means users do not need to write passwords down and keep them in insecure places.[83] No more Post-it notes stuck to computers! If your password is compromised, it is easier to change one password than to have to change the same password on multiple accounts. Users can see if their current passwords have appeared in a data breach by using the website Have I Been Pwned.[84]

Strong passwords are not enough, so use multi-factor authentication (MFA) whenever it is available. MFA is something you know (a password or pin) along with something you have and/or something you are (biometrics such as a fingerprint). MFA means just what it says—you supply two or more methods of different types to verify your identity; for example, a password (something you know) and a text confirmation sent to your phone (something you have). Many organizations use authenticator apps as the something you have for MFA. Authenticator apps, such as Duo, Microsoft's authenticator app, and Google's authenticator app, generate time-based, one-time passcodes that refresh every thirty seconds to complete the login.[85] MFA is not foolproof, and some methods of MFA offer more security than others. The most secure forms of MFA are FIDO (Fast Identity Online) authentication and PKI-based authentication.[86] FIDO uses public/private key cryptography where a user's device retains a private cryptographic key and registers the public key with an online service so that when the user visits a site and is prompted to sign in, they verify with the passkey associated with their device and it signs the online service's challenge.[87] Physical security tokens such as Yubikeys use FIDO. PKI-based authentication also uses public/private key cryptography but the key pair is obtained and shared through a trusted public or an internal Certificate Authority (an entity that issues digital certificates for verification purposes).[88] Government entities employ widespread PKI-based authentication through the use of Personal Identity Verification Cards (PIV cards) or Common Access Cards (CAC cards).[89] PKI-authentication is also used with Virtual Private Networks (VPN).

The fourth step for everyday cybersecurity is to make sure any software is kept up to date. CISA recommends turning on automatic updates, only downloading updates from trusted vendor websites (don't click on that email link), and replacing discontinued or unsupported software.[90]

ENTERPRISE-WIDE CYBERSECURITY BEST PRACTICES

Organization-wide cybersecurity for the handling of data that is not otherwise specially regulated (such as health or financial data) and that complies with the Federal Trade Act's Section 5 requirement of "reasonable" measures to protect consumer data should at a minimum follow the FTC's *Cybersecurity for Small Businesses* guidance, which provides resources developed by NIST, the U.S. Small Business Administration, and the Department of Homeland Security.[91] Some of the cybersecurity basics are similar to everyday cybersecurity practices, just on an organization-wide level: update software, require strong passwords, and use MFA.[92] Additionally, the FTC recommends securing data, backing up files off-site or to the cloud whether paper or digital, encrypting devices and systems that contain sensitive information, securing routers by changing default credentials, turning off remote management, and logging out as an administrator, using WPA2 or WPA3 encryption for wireless networks, training and updating staff on cybersecurity, and having a plan for when the worst happens, including what to do if your organization suffers a data breach.[93] These recommendations are also good practices to follow in your own home where possible.

As far as organizations are concerned, best practices also mean looking beyond the immediate organization and working with third-party vendors on their cybersecurity as well. This is often referred to as supply chain security, and it is another issue where the FTC provides guidance. Since law libraries rely so much on third-party vendors for many of our services, this is very pertinent to us. The FTC recommends security provisions be spelled out in your vendor contracts; that you have processes to confirm that the security provisions are being followed; that you control vendor access to sensitive information; that you encrypt sensitive data and make sure vendors encrypt sensitive information; that if a vendor accesses your systems, make sure they create strong passwords and use MFA; and realize that if a vendor has a cybersecurity incident, you will need to report the attack and notify customers as well as ensure recovery.[94]

NIST provides guidance on standards that those associated with the federal government must follow, but it is also useful guidance for other organizations. Following NIST standards is a way for organizations to make sure they are compliant with state and federal laws governing privacy and security. The NIST Cybersecurity Framework 2.0 provides a technology-neutral structure for cybersecurity with the core functions of govern, identify, protect, detect, respond, and recover.[95] Through govern, organizations need to establish oversight, strategy, policies, priorities, and expectations when it comes to cybersecurity.[96] Identify consists of inventorying the assets involved in cybersecurity, such as the data, software, hardware, systems, people, and third-party vendors.[97] Protect covers the prevention and planned mitigation aspects of cybersecurity such as authentication and access control, data security, and platform security.[98] Detect involves finding and analyzing attacks and intrusions.[99] Respond encompasses containing, reporting, and communicating incidents.[100] Finally, recover includes the restoration of operations and communication of recovery efforts.[101] *FIPS Publication 200: Minimum Security Requirements for Federal Information and Information Systems* lays out the current safeguards and practices required for government systems, covering seventeen security-related areas.[102] *NIST Special Publication 800-53* provides a list of suggested security controls for FISMA compliance.[103] NIST cybersecurity standards can get very technical and not every standard will be applicable to law libraries. NIST recognizes the challenges for smaller organizations and has created the NIST Cybersecurity Framework 2.0: Small Business Quick-Start Guide Overview to help.[104] The NIST Computer Security Resource Center provides access to NIST projects, news and updates, the glossary, and standards and guidance.[105]

NIST is not the only source for cybersecurity frameworks and standards that law libraries and their parent institutions can use. Another resource for cybersecurity standards is the Center for Internet Security (CIS), a nonprofit that publishes CIS Critical Security Controls and CIS Benchmarks. The *CIS Critical Security Controls V.8.1* provides eighteen controls, then procedures and tools to implement those controls, and then safeguards that fall under each control with the safeguards prioritized for different levels of enterprise implementation groups: (1) inventory and control of enterprise assets; (2) inventory and control of software assets; (3) data protection; (4) security configuration of assets and software; (5) account management; (6) continuous vulnerability management; (7) audit log management; (8) email and web browser protections; (9) malware defenses; (10) data recovery; (11) network infrastructure management; (12) network monitoring and defense; (13) security awareness and skills training; (14) service provider management; (15) application software security; (16) incident response management; and (17) penetration testing.[106] The CIS Benchmarks provide security configuration recommendations for vendor products.[107] The ISO also has a series of cybersecurity standards that the *IFLA Statement on Cybersecurity* refers to: *ISO/IEC 27001: Information Security Management System – Requirements*, *ISO/IEC 27002: Code of Practice for Information Security Management*, and *ISO/IEC 27032: Information Technology – Security Techniques – Guidelines for Cybersecurity* as standards libraries should follow.[108] The ISO standards are not open access, but the NIST materials are available to anyone, and Center for Information Security materials are available under a Creative Commons license.

OPPORTUNITIES FOR NEW AND OLD ROLES

Cybersecurity offers extreme challenges for law libraries but also opportunities for law librarians to take on new roles and adapt old roles to address the new challenges. Law librarians have always been at the forefront of technology adoption in their organizations, and cybersecurity is no different. There is a global shortage of cybersecurity professionals. Librarians serving in a Systems Librarian role must necessarily take on cybersecurity responsibilities. They maintain servers, run backups, patch and upgrade systems and services, run firewalls, manage the website, deal with hardware and software issues, and more. None of this can be done without taking cybersecurity into account. As we increase our reliance on digital collections and services, librarians will have to incorporate best practices for cybersecurity into our workflow so that we can ensure the integrity of our information as well as continued access to our services. We are already experienced with authority control, access management, data management, and disaster planning and recovery. Incorporating cybersecurity best practices is just adding another layer to these tasks.

Librarians often serve as gatekeepers of technology in their organizations, particularly when it comes to dealing with vendors. Investigating the security of vendor products, building cybersecurity into contracts, and holding vendors accountable are other opportunities for librarians to take an active role in cybersecurity for their organizations. Librarians are also guardians of our patrons' privacy, and this creates an advocacy role for librarians when it comes to cybersecurity. Sometimes librarians are the only ones raising privacy issues when others are blinded by the shiny new technology. In addition to being advocates, librarians also teach and train their users. The cybersecurity challenges that everyone faces, no matter their role, offer us a tremendous opportunity to educate. Cybersecurity literacy is particularly important for law students, attorneys, judges, and others working in the legal field because of the type of information they access and store and their ability to set current and future cybersecurity policy.

Cybersecurity presents challenges to law librarianship but opportunities as well. By embracing these challenges and opportunities, law librarianship continues to be future-proof and to cherish our values of privacy, security, and integrity of information.

NOTES

1. "What Is Cybersecurity?," *Cybersecurity & Infrastructure Security Agency Blog*, February 1, 2021, https://www.cisa.gov/news-events/news/what-cybersecurity [https://perma.cc/7QF2-X53X].
2. "Glossary: Misconfiguration," NIST Computer Security Resource Center, accessed June 18, 2024, https://csrc.nist.gov/glossary/term/misconfiguration [https://perma.cc/WVN2-AJC4].
3. For a list of the top ten cybersecurity misconfigurations, see "NISA and CISA Red and Blue Teams Share Top Ten Cybersecurity Misconfigurations," Cybersecurity & Infrastructure Security Agency Cybersecurity Advisory, October 5, 2023, https://www.cisa.gov/news-events/cybersecurity-advisories/aa23-278a [https://perma.cc/8QXD-2DZL].
4. "Cost of a Data Breach Report 2023," IBM, 2023, 20, https://www.ibm.com/reports/data-breach [https://perma.cc/6RVF-J3SL].
5. For more on common DoS attacks, see "Understanding Denial-of-Service Attacks," *Cybersecurity & Infrastructure Security Agency Blog*, February 1, 2021, https://www.cisa.gov/news-events/news/understanding-denial-service-attacks [https://perma.cc/MYT5-LARM].
6. "2024 Data Breach Investigations Report," Verizon, 2024, 43, https://www.verizon.com/business/resources/reports/dbir/2024/dbir-report/ [https://perma.cc/2C6V-XQTL].
7. "Known Exploited Vulnerabilities Catalog," Cybersecurity & Infrastructure Security Agency, accessed June 18, 2024, https://www.cisa.gov/known-exploited-vulnerabilities-catalog.
8. "2024 Data Breach Investigations Report," Verizon, 21.
9. Emma W., "The Problems with Patching," *National Cyber Security Centre Blog*, July 10, 2019, https://www.ncsc.gov.uk/blog-post/the-problems-with-patching [https://perma.cc/Q43C-QYFM].
10. "Glossary: Zero Day Attack," NIST Computer Security Resource Center, accessed June 18, 2024, https://csrc.nist.gov/glossary/term/zero_day_attack [https://perma.cc/A5QU-3V8B].
11. "We're All in this Together: A Year in Review of Zero-Days Exploited In-the-Wild in 2023," *Google*, March 2024, 4, https://storage.googleapis.com/gweb-uniblog-publish-prod/documents/Year_in_Review_of_ZeroDays.pdf [https://perma.cc/4C8B-KM72].
12. "Glossary: Malware," NIST Computer Security Resource Center, accessed June 18, 2024, https://csrc.nist.gov/glossary/term/malware [https://perma.cc/8CZN-DCPA].
13. "Ransomware: What It Is & What to Do About It," CISA, accessed June 18, 2024, https://www.cisa.gov/sites/default/files/2021-01/NCIJTF%20Ransomware_Fact_Sheet.pdf [https://perma.cc/82JT-2ZGZ].
14. "2024 Data Breach Investigations Report," Verizon, 7.
15. "Defining Insider Threats," CISA, accessed June 18, 2024, https://www.cisa.gov/topics/physical-security/insider-threat-mitigation/defining-insider-threats [https://perma.cc/MHG9-G8KC].
16. "X-Force Threat Intelligence Index 2024," IBM, 2024, 4, https://www.ibm.com/reports/threat-intelligence [https://perma.cc/PAC5-EAKF].
17. "Navigating Cyberthreats and Strengthening Defenses in the Era of AI," Microsoft Threat Intelligence Cyber Signals, February 2024, 4–5, https://www.microsoft.com/en-us/security/business/security-insider/wp-content/uploads/2024/02/cyber-signals-issue-6.pdf [https://perma.cc/Y2F8-273K].
18. OpenAI, "March 20 Chat GPT Outage: Here's What Happened," March 24, 2023, https://openai.com/index/march-20-chatgpt-outage/.
19. "AI Adoption and Risk Report," Cyberhaven Labs, Q2 2024, 9–10, https://www.cyberhaven.com/lp/lp-eb-data-report-q2-2024 [https://perma.cc/5L5J-DVSW].
20. Greg Noone, "Generative AI Banned at Over a Quarter Of Firms, While Two-Thirds Have Imposed Stringent Guardrails," Tech Monitor 30, updated January 26, 2024, https://techmonitor.ai/technology/ai-and-automation/firms-generative-ai-ban [https://perma.cc/U6V5-K6FJ].
21. "Cost of a Data Breach Report 2023," IBM, 5.

22. "Cost of a Data Breach Report 2023," IBM, 15.
23. "Cost of a Data Breach Report 2023," IBM, 15.
24. 2024 Threat Report, Arctic Wolf Labs, 2024, 10, https://arcticwolf.com/resource/aw/arctic-wolf-labs-2024-threat-report?lb-mode=overlay [https://perma.cc/7AYF-75XP].
25. "The State of Ransomware in Education 2023," SOPHOS, July 2023, 7, https://assets.sophos.com/X24WTUEQ/at/j74v496cfwh4qsvgqhs4pmw/sophos-state-of-ransomware-education-2023-wp.pdf [https://perma.cc/PZ8Q-UUHL].
26. "Cost of a Data Breach Report 2023," IBM, 14.
27. See "The Top 11 Legal Industry Cyber Attacks," *Artic Wolf Blog*, April 30, 2024, https://arcticwolf.com/resources/blog/top-legal-industry-cyber-attacks/ [https://perma.cc/H8FT-MN5M].
28. The Seattle Public Library, "Statement on Ransomware Event Impacting Library Services," *Shelf Talk Blog*, May 28, 2024, last updated June 7, 2024, https://shelftalkblog.wordpress.com/statement/ [https://perma.cc/F54P-HH6D].
29. Marshall Breeding, "Libraries Under Cyberattack," *Computers in Libraries* 44, no. 2 (March 2024), https://librarytechnology.org/document/29866/library-tech-trends-2024.
30. "Pennsylvania Courts' Cyber Attack Update," *The Unified Judicial System of Pennsylvania News*, February 12, 2024, https://www.pacourts.us/news-and-statistics/news/news-detail/1166/pennsylvania-courts-cyber-attack-update [https://perma.cc/Z9YQ-NE23].
31. See Paul Bischoff, "A Recent History of US Government Breaches - Can You Trust Them with Your Data?" Comparitech, November 28, 2023, https://www.comparitech.com/blog/vpn-privacy/us-government-breaches/ [https://perma.cc/PU6C-4B3G].
32. Jonathan Greig and Suzanne Smalley, "CISA Forced to Take Two Systems Offline Last Month After Ivanti Compromise," *The Record*, March 8, 2024, https://therecord.media/cisa-takes-two-systems-offline-following-ivanti-compromise [https://perma.cc/Z8HY-2U64].
33. See Sam Cook, "US Schools Leaked 37.6 Million Records in 3,713 Data Breaches," *Comparitech*, May 14, 2024, https://www.comparitech.com/blog/vpn-privacy/us-schools-data-breaches/ [https://perma.cc/XL6J-9DVU].
34. "Learning Lessons from the Cyber-Attack: British Library Cyber Incident Review," British Library, March 8, 2024, 6, 14, https://www.bl.uk/home/british-library-cyber-incident-review-8-march-2024.pdf [https://perma.cc/AK7J-ZEXY].
35. Lauren Coffee, "Universities Boost Spending to Curb Cyber Attacks," *Inside Higher Ed.*, April 25, 2024, https://www.insidehighered.com/news/quick-takes/2024/04/25/colleges-spending-more-ever-cybersecurity-efforts# [https://perma.cc/79Z8-228S].
36. Above the Law & Arctic Wolf, "Law Firm Cybersecurity in the New Reality," 8, 2024, https://info.abovethelaw.com/hubfs/2024%20Artic%20Wolf%20Report/ATL_ArticWolf_LawFirm_Cybersecurity_Report_2023.pdf [https://perma.cc/4HUT-HNJP].
37. Cyber Safety Review Board, "Review of the Summer 2023 Microsoft Exchange Online Intrusion," *Cybersecurity & Infrastructure Agency*, March 20, 2024, 17, https://www.cisa.gov/sites/default/files/2024-04/CSRB_Review_of_the_Summer_2023_MEO_Intrusion_Final_508c.pdf [https://perma.cc/P3SJ-2K7M].
38. John Simek, "2023 Cybersecurity TechReport," *ABA TechReport 2023*, December 18, 2023, https://www.americanbar.org/groups/law_practice/resources/tech-report/2023/2023-cybersecurity-techreport/
39. See Above the Law & Arctic Wolf, "Law Firm Cybersecurity in the New Reality," 7.
40. See Jenay Robert, "Student Data Privacy and Security: A Call for Transparent Practices," Educause, October 3, 2022, https://www.educause.edu/ecar/research-publications/2022/student-data-privacy-and-security-a-call-for-transparent-practices/trusting-institutions [https://perma.cc/BZ2T-4Z7F].
41. See "2022 Americans on Cybersecurity," PC Matic, 2022, https://www.pcmatic.com/news/USACyberSurvey/ [https://perma.cc/G86H-VGE2]; Edward Segal, "Must Surveyed Americans Lack Confidence in Government to Protect them from Cyberattacks," August 12, 2021, https://www.forbes.com/sites/edwardsegal/2021/08/12/most-surveyed-americans-lack-confidence

-in-government-to-protect-them-from-cyberattacks/ [https://perma.cc/6XNA-2A6N]; Kenneth Olmstead and Aaron Smith, "Americans and Cybersecurity," Pew Research Center, January 26, 2017, https://www.pewresearch.org/internet/wp-content/uploads/sites/9/2017/01/Americans-and-Cyber-Security-final.pdf [https://perma.cc/SZ2K-34C3].
42. American Association of Law Libraries (AALL), "Ethical Principles," approved by the AALL membership August 30, 2019, https://www.aallnet.org/advocacy/government-relations/recommended-guidelines/aall-ethical-principles/ [https://perma.cc/VER3-82TS].
43. American Library Association (ALA), "ALA Code of Ethics," adopted 1939 and last amended June 29, 2021, https://www.ala.org/tools/ethics [https://perma.cc/3737-RTMQ].
44. ALA, "Library Bill of Rights," adopted June 19, 1939, and last amended January 29, 2019, https://www.ala.org/advocacy/intfreedom/librarybill [https://perma.cc/L9F2-2SCP].
45. ALA Intellectual Freedom Committee, "Privacy: An Interpretation of the Library Bill of Rights," adopted June 19, 2002 and last amended June 24, 2019, https://www.ala.org/advocacy/intfreedom/librarybill/interpretations/privacy [https://perma.cc/X5U5-LAG6].
46. International Federation of Library Associations and Institutions (IFLA), "IFLA Code of Ethics for Librarians and other Information Workers (Full Version)," approved August 2012, https://repository.ifla.org/handle/123456789/1850.
47. IFLA, "IFLA Statement on Cybersecurity," February 2022, https://repository.ifla.org/handle/123456789/1912.
48. American Bar Association (ABA), "Model Rules of Professional Conduct Rule 1.1, Comment [8]," accessed June 24, 2024, https://www.americanbar.org/groups/professional_responsibility/publications/model_rules_of_professional_conduct/rule_1_1_competence/comment_on_rule_1_1/.
49. ABA, "Model Rules of Professional Conduct Rule 1.6, Comment [18]," accessed June 24, 2024, https://www.americanbar.org/groups/professional_responsibility/publications/model_rules_of_professional_conduct/rule_1_6_confidentiality_of_information/comment_on_rule_1_6/.
50. ABA, "Model Rules of Professional Conduct Rule 1.9, Comment [7]," accessed June 24, 2024, https://www.americanbar.org/groups/professional_responsibility/publications/model_rules_of_professional_conduct/rule_1_9_duties_of_former_clients/comment_on_rule_1_9/.
51. ABA, "Model Rules of Professional Conduct Rule 1.15," accessed June 24, 2024, https://www.americanbar.org/groups/professional_responsibility/publications/model_rules_of_professional_conduct/rule_1_15_safekeeping_property/.
52. ABA, "Model Rules of Professional Conduct Rule 5.3, Comment [3]," accessed June 24, 2024, https://www.americanbar.org/groups/professional_responsibility/publications/model_rules_of_professional_conduct/rule_5_3_responsibilities_regarding_nonlawyer_assistant/comment_on_rule_5_3/.
53. See Joshua Lenon, "A List of All the Ethics Opinions on Cloud Computing for Lawyers," *CLIO Blog*, accessed June 24, 2024, https://www.clio.com/blog/cloud-computing-lawyers-ethics-opinions/ [https://perma.cc/3DPE-YG8W]; ABA Committee on Ethics & Professional Responsibility, Formal Opinion 498, March 10, 2021, https://www.americanbar.org/content/dam/aba/administrative/professional_responsibility/ethics-opinions/aba-formal-opinion-498.pdf; ABA Committee on Ethics & Professional Responsibility, Formal Opinion 483, October 17, 2018, https://www.americanbar.org/content/dam/aba/administrative/professional_responsibility/ethics-opinions/aba-formal-op-483.pdf; ABA Committee on Ethics & Professional Responsibility, Formal Opinion 477R, revised May 22, 2017, https://www.americanbar.org/content/dam/aba/administrative/professional_responsibility/ethics-opinions/aba-formal-opinion-477.pdf.
54. Federal Information Security Modernization Act of 2014, Pub. L. No. 113-283, 128 Stat. 3073 (2014).
55. See "Federal Information Processing Standards Publications (FIPS Pubs)," NIST Information Technology Laboratory, accessed June 18, 2024, https://www.nist.gov/itl/publications-0/federal-information-processing-standards-fips [https://perma.cc/TPG2-FBBU]; "Current Publications - SP 800," NIST Computer Security Resource Center, accessed June 18, 2024, https://csrc.nist.gov/publications/sp800 [https://perma.cc/7N55-Q3Y4].
56. "Program Basics," FedRAMP, accessed June 25, 2024, https://www.fedramp.gov/program-basics/ [https://perma.cc/BUP4-DX9Q].

57. See 16 C.F.R. § 314.1 (2024); Federal Trade Commission, Bureau of Consumer Protection, Advisory Opinion on Application of Title V, Subtitle A, of the G-L-B Act, and of the Commission's Privacy Rule to Attorneys at Law," April 8, 2002, https://www.ftc.gov/sites/default/files/documents/advisory_opinions/application-title-v-subtitle-g-l-b-act-and-commissions-privacy-rule-attorneys-law/hirshon-beales020408.pdf [https://perma.cc/DT7V-RVWN].
58. "(General-23-09) Updates to the Gramm-Leach-Bliley Act Cybersecurity Requirements," Federal Student Aid, February 9, 2023, https://fsapartners.ed.gov/knowledge-center/library/electronic-announcements/2023-02-09/updates-gramm-leach-bliley-act-cybersecurity-requirements [https://perma.cc/YGN6-5BGL].
59. See Cybersecurity Risk Management, Strategy, Governance, and Incident Disclosure, 88 Fed. Reg. 51896, August 4, 2023.
60. See 45 C.F.R. § 160.103(1)(ii) (2023).
61. See 20 U.S.C. § 1232g; 34 C.F.R. pt. 99 (2023).
62. See F.T.C. v. Wyndham Worldwide Corp., 799 F.3d 236 (3d Cir. 2015).
63. "Updated Advisory on Potential Sanctions Risks for Facilitating Ransomware Payments," United States Department of the Treasury, September 21, 2021, https://ofac.treasury.gov/media/912981/download [https://perma.cc/NC2M-TQ4E].
64. American Library Association, "State Privacy Laws Regarding Library Records," ALA Privacy, last updated November 2021, https://www.ala.org/advocacy/privacy/statelaws [https://perma.cc/C7FL-6G89].
65. "Data Security Laws: State Government," National Conference of State Legislatures, https://www.ncsl.org/technology-and-communication/data-security-laws-state-government [https://perma.cc/M4JZ-6EKA].
66. Jeff Kosseff, *Cybersecurity Law*, 3rd ed. (Hoboken, NJ: John Wiley & Sons, Inc., 2023), 52–54.
67. Kosseff, *Cybersecurity Law*, 46, Appendix B; "Security Breach Notification Laws," National Conference of State Legislatures, updated January 17, 2022, https://www.ncsl.org/technology-and-communication/security-breach-notification-laws [https://perma.cc/7BFF-ZUEN].
68. Kosseff, *Cybersecurity Law*, 50–52.
69. Jonathan Greig, "An Inside Look into States' Efforts to Ban Gov't Ransomware Payments," August 22, 2022, https://therecord.media/an-inside-look-into-states-efforts-to-ban-govt-ransomware-payments [https://perma.cc/BG3T-AAKV].
70. Andrew Folks, "US State Privacy Legislation Tracker," International Association of Privacy Professionals' Research Center, June 17, 2024, https://iapp.org/resources/article/us-state-privacy-legislation-tracker/# [https://perma.cc/49XK-7GC6].
71. Cal. Civil Code §§ 1798.100 to 1798.199.100 (Deering, Lexis current through 2024 Reg. Sess. Ch. 22).
72. Kosseff, *Cybersecurity Law*, 410–412.
73. Regulation 2016/679 of The European Parliament and of the Council of 27 April 2016 on the Protection of Natural Persons with Regard to the Processing of Personal Data and on the Free Movement of such Data (GDPR), 2016 O.J. (L 119), art. 5, https://eur-lex.europa.eu/legal-content/EN/TXT/PDF/?uri=CELEX:32016R0679.
74. GDPR arts. 33, 34, https://eur-lex.europa.eu/legal-content/EN/TXT/PDF/?uri=CELEX:32016R0679.
75. See Personal Information Protection Law of the People's Republic of China, arts. 3, 51, updated December 29, 2021, http://en.npc.gov.cn.cdurl.cn/2021-12/29/c_694559.htm [https://perma.cc/68D4-AESC] (unofficial translation).
76. "Data Protection and Privacy Legislation Worldwide," UNCTAD, accessed June 20, 2024, https://unctad.org/page/data-protection-and-privacy-legislation-worldwide [https://perma.cc/72QJ-7LXM].
77. "International Counter Ransomware Initiative Members Come Together to Strongly Discourage Ransomware Payments," Singapore National Police Force, January 29, 2024, https://counter-ransomware.org/briefingroom/8ed7d1de-1a74-4a36-a2df-d5950624ebd8.
78. "PCI Security Standards Overview," PCI Security Standards Council, accessed June 18, 2024, https://www.pcisecuritystandards.org/standards/ [https://perma.cc/W8P5-QEFZ].

79. "Secure Our World," Cybersecurity & Infrastructure Security Agency Cybersecurity Best Practices, accessed June 24, 2024, https://www.cisa.gov/secure-our-world [https://perma.cc/5ZB6-RDDE].
80. Shanee Dawkins and Jody Jacobs, "NIST Phish Scale User Guide," NIST, November 2023, https://doi.org/10.6028/NIST.TN.2276.
81. "Use Strong Passwords," Cybersecurity & Infrastructure Security Agency Secure Our World, accessed June 24, 2024, https://www.cisa.gov/secure-our-world/use-strong-passwords [https://perma.cc/27T3-8B29].
82. See HIVE Systems, "Are Your Passwords in the Green?," *HIVE Blog*, accessed June 24, 2024, https://www.hivesystems.com/blog/are-your-passwords-in-the-green [https://perma.cc/NN93-F2LH].
83. "Use Strong Passwords," Cybersecurity & Infrastructure Security Agency Secure Our World.
84. Have I Been Pwned, accessed June 24, 2024, https://haveibeenpwned.com/.
85. Max Eddy and Thorin Klosowski, "The Best Two-Factor Authentication App," *New York Times Wirecutter*, updated April 12, 2024, https://www.nytimes.com/wirecutter/reviews/best-two-factor-authentication-app/ [https://perma.cc/6FDP-MHUD].
86. "Implementing Phishing-Resistant MFA," Cybersecurity & Infrastructure Security Agency, October 2022, https://www.cisa.gov/sites/default/files/2023-01/fact-sheet-implementing-phishing-resistant-mfa-508c.pdf [https://perma.cc/XRX2-AL2J].
87. "How Passkeys Work," FIDO Alliance, accessed June 24, 2024, https://fidoalliance.org/how-fido-works/ [https://perma.cc/U52K-EFS5].
88. Jerome Becquart, "PKI and FIDO2: The Dynamic Duo of Authentication," *Axiad Blog*, accessed June 24, 2024, https://www.axiad.com/blog/pki-and-fido2/ [https://perma.cc/H8JS-GXRK].
89. "Personal Identity Verification Card 101," IDManagement, accessed June 24, 2024, https://www.idmanagement.gov/university/piv/ [https://perma.cc/L4ZZ-H3ZY].
90. "Understanding Patches and Software Updates," *Cybersecurity & Infrastructure Security Agency Blog*, February 23, 2023, https://www.cisa.gov/news-events/news/understanding-patches-and-software-updates [https://perma.cc/53H6-8SJ4].
91. "Cybersecurity for Small Business," Protecting Small Businesses, Federal Trade Commission, accessed June 24, 2024, https://www.ftc.gov/business-guidance/small-businesses/cybersecurity [https://perma.cc/24A2-TDDX].
92. "Cybersecurity Basics," Federal Trade Commission Cybersecurity for Small Business, accessed June 24, 2024, https://www.ftc.gov/business-guidance/small-businesses/cybersecurity/basics [https://perma.cc/822M-3BAP].
93. "Cybersecurity Basics," Federal Trade Commission Cybersecurity for Small Business.
94. "Vendor Security," Federal Trade Commission Cybersecurity for Small Business, accessed June 24, 2024, https://www.ftc.gov/business-guidance/small-businesses/cybersecurity/vendor-security [https://perma.cc/J5NT-B2VA].
95. The NIST Cybersecurity Framework (CSF) 2.0, National Institute of Standards and Technology, February 26, 2024, https://doi.org/10.6028/NIST.CSWP.29.
96. "The NIST Cybersecurity Framework (CSF) 2.0," 3.
97. "The NIST Cybersecurity Framework (CSF) 2.0," 3.
98. "The NIST Cybersecurity Framework (CSF) 2.0," 4.
99. "The NIST Cybersecurity Framework (CSF) 2.0," 4.
100. "The NIST Cybersecurity Framework (CSF) 2.0," 4.
101. "The NIST Cybersecurity Framework (CSF) 2.0," 4.
102. "FIPS 200: Minimum Security Requirements for Federal Information and Information Systems," National Institute of Standards and Technology Computer Security Resource Center, March 2006, https://doi.org/10.6028/NIST.FIPS.200.
103. "SP 800-53 Rev. 5: Security and Privacy Controls for Information Systems and Organizations," September 2020, https://doi.org/10.6028/NIST.SP.800-53r5.
104. "NIST Cybersecurity Framework 2.0: Small Business Quick-Start Guide Overview," National Institute of Standards and Technology, February 2024, https://doi.org/10.6028/NIST.SP.1300.
105. "Computer Security Resource Center," National Institute of Standards and Technology, accessed June 24, 2024, https://csrc.nist.gov/ [https://perma.cc/QL5B-26DY].

106. "CIS Critical Security Controls® Version 8.1," Center for Internet Security, June 2024, https://learn.cisecurity.org/cis-controls-download-v8 [https://perma.cc/2B4E-YLCY].
107. "CIS Benchmarks," Center for Internet Security, https://www.cisecurity.org/cis-benchmarks-overview [https://perma.cc/D48Q-HEWG].
108. "IFLA Statement on Cybersecurity."

15

Artificial Intelligence and Machine Learning in Law Libraries

Sarah Ryan and Cas Laskowski

Artificial Intelligence (AI) and Machine Learning (ML) are disruptive technologies that are changing routine information seeking, drafting, and workflows. These legal informatics tools have the power to transform our profession. In this chapter, you will learn how AI/ML grew out of libraries and has interested law librarians for more than sixty years. You will gain a succinct primer on AI/ML, including terms, processes, and decision points for library leaders. You will consider how AI/ML affects reference services, legal research instruction, access and technical services, library spaces, staffing, and more. Finally, this chapter will encourage you to leverage AI/ML to achieve your broad goals, such as increased access to legal information for citizens, a nationally coordinated legal information system, or simply more funding for the cutting-edge work that your librarians are already doing. For today's law library leaders, the growth of AI/ML suggests six questions addressed by this chapter:

1. What should individual library leaders know about AI and ML?
2. What should staff and patrons know about AI and ML processes, models, and frameworks?
3. How do we adjust reference services and legal research instruction for AI and ML?
4. How do AI and ML affect access and technical services?
5. How might AI and ML affect library fundamentals, like spaces and staffing?
6. How can we leverage AI/ML to achieve broader goals in our libraries and profession?

GLOSSARY

This is not a comprehensive list of every machine learning term. It is meant as a supplemental glossary and explanation for this chapter.

Adversarial Attacks—Attempts to fool AI systems by leveraging known vulnerabilities in the models.

Algorithms—Step-by-step procedures for calculations: procedures implemented in code and run on data (e.g., clustering is an unsupervised machine-learning algorithm).

Catastrophic Forgetting—The tendency of a machine learning model to adjust to new training data in such a way that it fails to perform as effectively on the initial data it was trained on.

Hallucinations—The label applied to generative AI outputs that do not comport with truth.

Hyperparameters—machine learning algorithmic settings set by the developer to create a model external to the model (e.g., in the clustering algorithm, a hyperparameter is the minimum number of items a cluster must have before the model identifies it as a cluster. A cluster size of two will result in many more clusters in a complex dataset, resulting in over-specification, whereas a cluster size of ten might increase inaccuracy by making the clusters too large to be meaningfully representative).

Models—the output of a machine learning algorithm run on data (e.g., the clustering model maps the central value of each cluster [a centroid]. It might then predict to which cluster a new piece of data belongs by calculating distance to different centroids and assigning it to the closest cluster).

Parameters—machine learning model settings learned by the model from the data, internal to the model (e.g., the centroids of the clusters are the parameters of the cluster model. These centroids will be different depending on the training data and are not set by the developer).

Weights—a parameter within a neural network; they convey the importance of a variable; coefficients of the model equation.

- E.g., we might create a model to determine if we want to go out with friends on the weekend. We might weigh travel time more heavily than food cost.
- E.g., calculating the price of a car using the following formula (model) where weight 1 would be positive (a newer car makes for higher value) and weight 2 would be negative (more miles decrease value).
    - Price of car = ($w_1 \times$ YEAR + $w_2 \times$ MILES)

SIXTY YEARS OF LAW LIBRARIAN INTEREST IN AI/ML

Law librarians have been concerned with AI and ML for more than sixty years. The developments in legal informatics that we are seeing today were made possible by early library projects. For instance, in the early 1960s, a physicist named Myer M. Kessler was named director of MIT's Technical Information Program (TIP),[1] and then Associate Director of the MIT Libraries.[2] Kessler aimed to make physics journals searchable and retrievable from online consoles.[3] He worked with librarians to develop and test the new system.[4] Across campus, Kessler worked with an interdisciplinary group, including Robert Fano and F. J. Corbató, on the MAC, or Machine-Aided Cognition and Multiple-Access Computer systems, project.[5] The MAC project overlapped with the TIP program,[6] but had broader aims, including AI.[7] Law librarians were invested in these developments.[8]

In 1962, the *Law Library Journal* (*LLJ*) reported on a major investment by the Council on Library Resources to investigate computerized storage and retrieval, human-computer communication, and AI.[9] In the early 1970s, the Chicago Association of Law Libraries held a seminar on library automation, and *LLJ* published nearly twenty of those papers in a special issue on technology.[10] In the introduction to the special issue, David Badertscher noted a thirteen-year trend in librarianship literature covering developments ranging from KWIC (Key-Word-In-Context) to COBOL (Common Business Oriented Language).[11] The *LLJ* issue also contained timeless wisdom, such as Morris Cohen's advice that technological exploration is a duty of every law librarian, not just specialized committees,[12] and Frederick Smith's reminder that we embrace technological change for the sake of improving justice.[13] In that same issue, Peter Nycum outlined a training program for law students and librarians, including mathematics, computing languages, hardware and software knowledge, simulation and model-building, and more.[14] Several law librarian and industry contributors to the *LLJ* issue advocated for national standards and coordination of new technologies--from the Library of Congress, American Bar Association, American Bar Foundation, and so on--[15] including work on the simple question: "What are the needs of . . . law libraries in particular?"[16] National coordination did not happen.

Following the conversations of the 1970s, law librarians continued to advocate for national leadership on legal information. Law librarians went to the White House in 1979, established a committee on public legal information services in 1981, and pushed for nationwide information access and training.[17] But no federal agency answered the call, and legal information vendors fought even statewide access efforts.[18] So, the work of building frameworks for legal information dissemination, systems evaluation, and training fell to volunteer-led committees[19] and individual law libraries, educators, and researchers.[20] As we move into a new legal informatics era, we have yet another opportunity to coordinate our efforts. The first step is to ensure that we have a shared vocabulary and understanding of advances in AI/ML.

ML PROCESSES

ML is a subfield of AI that develops data-driven models to accomplish various tasks. ML models result from applying a particular algorithm, or method, to a dataset. For example, you can use the linear regression algorithm on a set of real estate pricing data—the training data—to develop a model that will predict the likely price of a property based on its features (e.g., number of rooms). Simple linear regression is the method; the model is the line that represents the pattern in the data and allows you to predict the likely price of another property (*y*) by mapping the number of rooms that property has (*x*).

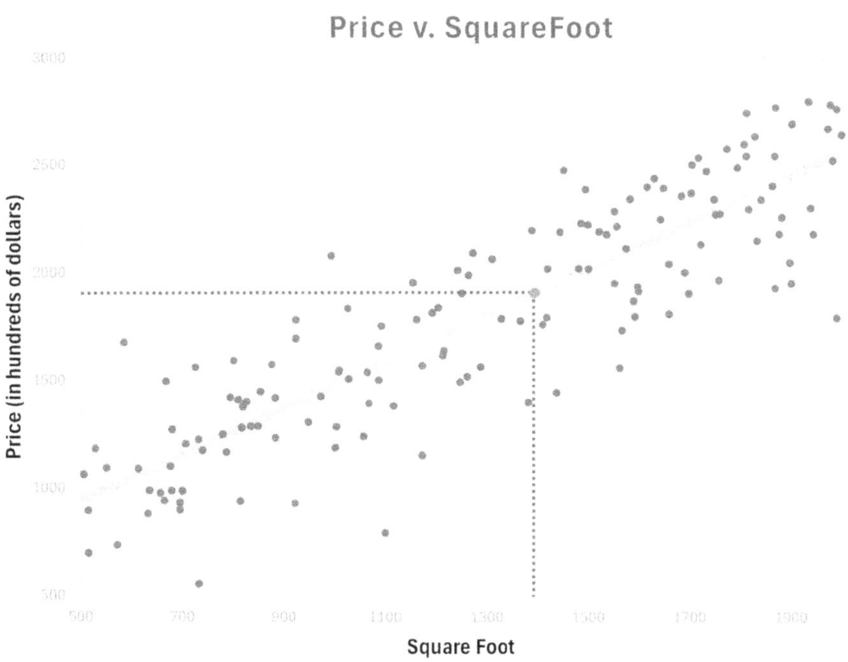

Figure 15.1 This Scatter Plot Shows the Linear Regression Analysis for Housing Data with the Light Blue Line Representing the Predictive Model. The Red Dot Represents the Prediction for a House of 1,375 SQFT with an Approximate Price of $191,200. (Data is synthetic for demonstrative purposes only.) *Source*: Created by author.

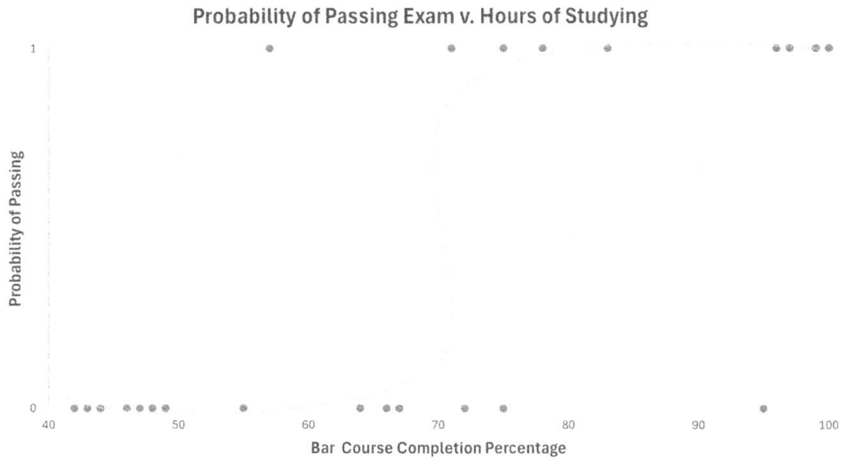

Figure 15.2 This Logistic Regression Shows the Probability that Someone Will Pass the Bar Exam Based on How Much of Their Bar Prep Course They Completed. (Data is synthetic for demonstrative purposes only.) *Source*: Created by author.

Linear regression—which maps linear relationships and predicts continuous outputs—is a subset of supervised ML regression algorithms that include logistic regression—often used to determine binary outputs—and polynomial regression—capturing nonlinear relationships.

Creating an ML model is not a sequential process. It involves multiple stages of exploration, experimentation, and evaluation. This iterative nature is important for librarians to understand, as it allows them to critically engage with the various decision points and examine any proposed model with a keen eye for potential pitfalls.

Creating and Utilizing ML Models

At its most basic elements, ML development involves four phases: (1) data collection and preparation, (2) algorithm selection, (3) model training and evaluation, and (4) production and adaptation.[21] This is not a linear process, as any stage might provide feedback or results that require us to revisit an earlier stage in the development process or require us to contemplate steps ahead.

For example, suppose we want to forecast when certain materials will be requested and how to adjust staffing to meet higher service demands. We might collect a complex dataset of item use records, active cases or classes or court schedules, reference requests, and other data relevant to the workflows and needs of our patrons. We could then use this data to build a model, likely the result of several smaller models, to help predict future use of resources and support requirements.

Or, suppose we want to enhance the acceptance rates of faculty or attorney scholarship. In that case, we would need a dataset of various article metadata that we would supply as training data to create a model that predicts the likelihood of acceptance into certain bar journals, law journals, or other legal periodicals. Each of these would use tabular data.

Or, if we were hoping to facilitate the digitization of historic documents, be it for preservation or to comply with record retention, we might initially create a training dataset out of a subset of image PDFs tagged by staff with relevant classifications (e.g., briefs versus complaints, or invoices versus client communication). We can then input that data into a convolutional neural network to create an image classification model that can predict the type of document so they can be sorted more quickly sorted for the next stages of the digitization process. In any of these cases, it would be critical to collect a substantial amount of data for development as the data would be split into a subset to train the model and a subset to test the resulting model.

Understanding the tasks we hope to accomplish elucidates the data we need to compile to complete said tasks. Poor data selection—deciding what facets and metadata to include in the dataset—or engineering—cleaning the data and handling errors in the dataset—can lead to bias and erroneous predictions in the final model. With the journal prediction model, there is likely to be some aspect of the decision-making process, like student editor preferences, that we cannot capture with the data available to us. Neither will our model be able to accurately predict the likelihood of acceptance of an article on an emerging topic absent from the training data. So, we must be forethoughtful in both the data we decide to compile and in implementing the resulting model in light of those factors.

Then we need to decide on the algorithmic method we will use to input our training data and create our model through training. Part of this decision will depend on the available dataset and the goal we hope to accomplish. If our dataset is a structured set of data, as with tabular data or images with items in the image highlighted and tagged, then we can use a supervised model. That is to say, a model is trained on what factors to weigh in its decision. For the image example, highlighting the individual items in the picture tells the model to focus on the pattern of those pixels to learn to identify a chair, table, dog, and so on.

If, however, our dataset is unstructured, as in full-text documents or images that simply get accompanied by tags, we would use an unsupervised model. Unsupervised models try to identify the simplest corollary pattern in the data, resulting in the most accurate output. Imagine that we simply have a set of animal images that are either tagged husky or wolf. In that scenario, the model will try to discern what pixels seem to correlate with the expected output, husky or wolf. These models reduce the work required at the data preparation stage but are prone to their own shortfalls. With the husky and wolf model—a real-world example—researchers hypothesized and confirmed that the model was not accurately predicting the dog in the model but rather the existence or absence of snow in the pictures.[22] So, while the model was predicting with high accuracy the cause of that accuracy was a flaw in the data where most wolf pictures had snow and most husky pictures did not.[23]

It is not always clear which algorithm might best suit our particular goal, so many ML efforts try to create multiple models using different algorithms to identify the most efficient, useful, and accurate algorithm for their purpose. For a journal prediction model, we can use a recurrent neural network or a random forest algorithm. For image classification, we can use a convolutional neural network or a random forest algorithm.

It is not critical for the purposes of this chapter that librarians recognize every algorithm listed above, just that selecting a method is not an objective process. During this stage, developers will evaluate the model to determine which performs best. This evaluation exposes issues in the models, such as overfitting on the training data, similar to memorizing answers to a test but not learning the subject matter. This evaluation is limited to the data collected in stage one and subject to the same biases.

As such, the initial evaluation results are not a definite indicator of model performance on real-world data, which is why the final stage is production and adaptation. This stage seeks to deploy the model and assess how it performs on real-world data, data that was unseen by the model during development. Ideally, there should be a great deal of oversight and limited reliance on the model at this stage. However, there is no shortage of examples of models that were prematurely released to their users' detriment.[24] To avoid that fate, we should plan for the human effort needed for production and adaptation. For instance, our aforementioned digitization of historic documents model would only provide a percentage likelihood that any document fits any classification. For that reason, part of our implementation process must include human oversight to review documents that do not fall within high enough confidence levels (e.g., 90 percent likelihood or above). That threshold is set by us, so we must decide if we want to keep a high threshold that might require more documents flagged for manual review or if we want a lower threshold with a higher chance that documents are misclassified. As in other parts of the workflow, errors might be easily caught and corrected or extremely disruptive.

ML MODELS AND FRAMEWORKS

As we consider employing AI models in our libraries, knowing the types of models available is helpful. While there are many ways to classify ML models, this section will group them by their aim and briefly summarize what they can accomplish.

Computer vision models enable computers to process input images and provide a resulting decision based on the visual data. Computer vision algorithms include convolutional neural networks (CNNs) and random forest algorithms. In libraries, they are used to extract text from images using optical character recognition (OCR), a feature now present on many book scanners. They can also be used in digitization to automatically categorize documents or tag images.

Natural language processing (NLP) models can identify semantically meaningful patterns in text data, allowing them to interpret and analyze text with varying degrees of accuracy. NLP algorithms include recurrent neural networks (RNNs) and transformers. Transformers are the algorithms used in popular generative AI models like ChatGPT. Relevant uses include document summarization or topic modeling.

Recommender systems provide personalized recommendations based on historic user behavior data. There are two types of recommendations: content-based and collaborative filtering. Content-based systems recommend new items that are similar to other items the user has selected previously. Collaborative filtering systems recommend new items that were selected by other users who historically behaved like the user receiving the recommendation. Some library service platforms and knowledge management systems already integrate these models.

Other models include anomaly detection systems, which try to identify outliers in data and are often used in cybersecurity to spot malicious network traffic; time series analysis, which attempts to track temporal patterns in data such as weather; and knowledge graphs, which leverage the relationships between entries to provide predictions. These models might be used to identify outliers

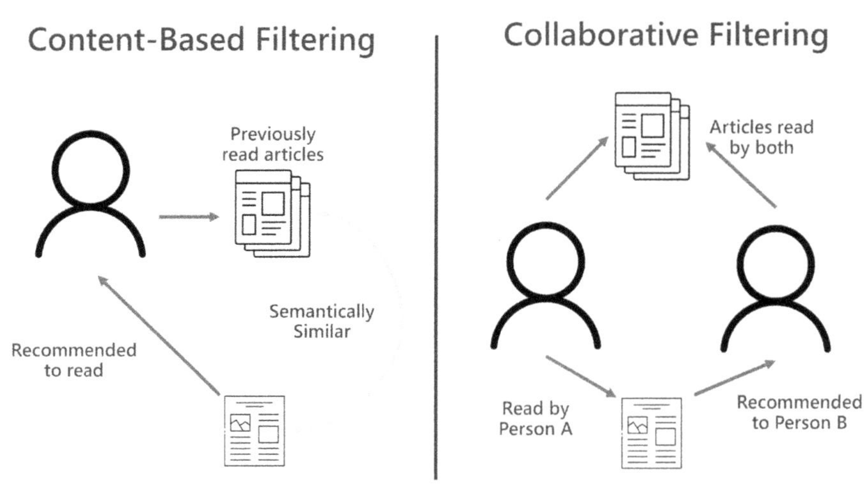

Figure 15.3 This Image Demonstrates the Different Ways Recommender Systems Determine Relevant Suggestions. Content-based Filtering Provides Suggestions That Are Related to a User's Previous Selections, Such as If They Are Semantically Similar. Collaborative Filtering Provides Suggestions That Are New to You but Were Selected Previously by Other Users Who Behave as You Do. *Source*: Created by author.

in library usage statistics to improve services, predict library foot traffic based on historical usage patterns, and enhance search algorithms by incorporating the network structure of citations and references, respectively.

Generative AI models can create text, images, music, and so on, from input text prompts. Algorithms include generative adversarial networks (GANs) and variational autoencoders (VAEs). Libraries are already using these to generate website text more swiftly and assist with drafts. They can also create synthetic legal documents for training and testing purposes and generate summaries and recommendations for legal research.

Even well-staffed libraries are grappling with increasing AI applications, whether appended to existing databases and systems or released as new offerings, while also investigating ways to leverage these technologies to enhance workflows or innovate services. As such, information science researchers are attempting to develop frameworks for AI adoption and creation for libraries.[25] To date, no one system has fully emerged as the solution for all AI/ML needs.

AI IN REFERENCE SERVICES

Implementing AI at different stages of our service model can make our reference services better and more efficient. AI can triage requests, answer common questions, assist with resource identification and research, and draft initial language for communication or policy.

NLP is not without error, but the current models are exceptional at learning and mapping semantic similarity. If we train a model in a few different ways to ask when the library is open, the models can often identify unseen alternative queries as semantically similar. This ability to relate new information to learned historical data can be applied in triaging requests and answering questions.

Libraries can leverage NLP to analyze the content of incoming requests and route them to the appropriate individual. This can reduce the need for patrons to remember multiple emails and for library staff to monitor and route emails manually. This same capability can be used to create reference chatbots. Librarians can craft answers to common questions and train a model to identify the questions related to the specific answers. In doing so, librarians can more efficiently spend their time on more complex patron questions and other services.

The most advanced way to leverage AI in library services is to support research that utilizes AI. This may seem like a large task as few law librarians are sufficiently trained in developing these systems, but the same was once said about providing empirical research and data analytic support.[26] For example, the University of North Carolina Law Library has been part of an AI research project examining Jim Crow legislation.[27] That project digitized North Carolina session laws and used OCR to create text files of the law, creating a machine-readable dataset of historic North Carolina laws. The project team then created a subset of that data comprised of known Jim Crow legislation and other laws, as they needed both to train the system and create an ML model using a bag of words algorithm (BOW). BOW breaks down the law into a list of all the words in that legislation, and the model learns what words tend to be present when it is a Jim Crow law (e.g., Black or White). The resulting model can provide a prediction of the likelihood that a law is a Jim Crow law. They then fed the remaining set of session laws into the model, reviewed its predictions, and published a set of identified Jim Crow laws.

The UNC Law Library assisted initially with legal information training for the research team and resource acquisition. Based on their 2023 presentation at the AALL Annual Conference, librarians have been increasingly involved in the overall project. The classification work has also been expanded to several other law libraries through additional grant funding. Of course, some law libraries might not be able to provide the bespoke ML model development and support that UNC did. But through strategic planning and collaboration, we can create scaffolded models of support and maybe even consortia-level support to expand access and services.

AI AND LEGAL RESEARCH INSTRUCTION

Adding AI to legal research platforms means that all legal research instruction is now AI literacy instruction as well. To prepare our patrons to engage with these new offerings, it is critical that we not only sound warning bells but also acknowledge the potential of AI tools. Doing otherwise will reduce our credibility and alienate us from those we are trying to train. By embracing the balance, we can instruct our patrons on low-risk use cases and teach them to employ caution appropriately.

As evidence of this, many academic libraries have published LibGuides for faculty and students on the implications and uses of generative AI University of Arizona (UA) Libraries created a Student Guide to ChatGPT,[28] which has a tab for professors, and the UA Law Library created a more specific guide for legal research titled the ChatGPT and Generative AI Legal Research Guide.[29] These guides are vital resources for teaching communities to balance awareness with information literacy training.

Weaving AI literacy into our existing courses and training programs need not be onerous. We need only create reflection points within our existing scaffold to reflect on these new systems. When covering approaches to legal research, for example, we often teach students to find a useful secondary authority as a first research step. When teaching this step, we can encourage our students and trainees to engage with AI systems to answer preliminary research questions or identify potentially helpful secondary authorities. For instance, a July 21, 2024, query to ChatGPT 3.5 of "what should I read to learn about health law" yielded a two-book recommendation: "'Health Law: Cases, Materials, and Problems' by Barry R. Furrow et al. . . . [and] 'Health Care Law and Ethics' by Mark A. Hall et al." Students could compare these recommendations with secondary sources suggested by law library database searches, library guides, and Amazon recommendations,[30] and more. At later research stages, we often challenge students to critically engage with a more complex research question and evaluate how changes to their query affect the results. This is especially helpful if they can compare with others to see the range of language in queries and responses. So, in addition to having them share their search strings and results with fellow classmates, students can now compare their strategies and outcomes to AI results. Further, we can introduce the vernacular of "prompt engineering" or crafting prompts for AI systems, which respond best to context-rich, precise queries written in the form of tasks. In amending our existing strategies to incorporate AI, we are calling on students to utilize the same analytical skills used generally in legal research and to add new skills like prompt engineering.

Specialized Legal Research Instruction

While basic and advanced legal research courses are necessarily AI/ML courses now, academic and law firm law libraries should also prepare to support additional training in four legal areas heavily affected by emerging technologies and regulations: (1) intellectual property, (2) privacy, human rights, and democracy, (3) business law, and (4) state AI/ML laws.

Intellectual Property

AI has introduced a host of intellectual property problems, and the U.S. Copyright Office, courts, and legislators have been slow to respond to emerging issues of authorship and ownership.[31] On one hand, generative AI creations, such as an AI-generated painting, challenge traditional notions of what *can* be protected because they may be initiated by humans or machines (i.e., authorship), emerge in physical or electronic forms (e.g., non-fungible tokens), and draw extensively or minimally from existing works (i.e., originality).[32] On the other hand, ML corpora challenge normative assumptions about what *should* be protected (e.g., copyright v. fair use) because advancements in ML and ML-generated AI tools require large, inexpensive datasets for learning.[33] Beyond specific copyright and fair use issues, legal scholars worry that our current theories and systems have failed to properly determine human accountability and property rights in the creation and management of AI/ML products, processes, and outcomes.[34]

Privacy, Human Rights, and Democracy

Emerging technologies and AI systems can threaten individual privacy, human rights, and democracy. In an influential 2019 article, Karl Manheim and Lyric Kaplan described AI as "the most disruptive technology of the modern era."[35] They argue that AI poses unique threats to privacy through new forms of surveillance and diminished anonymity,[36] and new threats to elections and democratic institutions via a host of intended and unintended violations of transparency, accountability, and fairness.[37] Within the broad AI framework, legal scholars are concerned with specific threats to privacy and human rights such as photographic and videographic "deepfakes,"[38] AI evidence admission in criminal cases,[39] and unregulated algorithms that threaten humans (e.g., autonomous vehicles that kill).[40] In keeping with the concerns of intellectual property scholars, rights and privacy scholars are concerned with holding individual humans and government institutions accountable for the outcomes and effects of AI.[41]

Business Law

On the flip side of privacy losses are the businesses profiting from AI/ML. In a highly regarded 2017 article, Julie Cohen argued that the platform-driven economy is more than a new business model, social technology, or infrastructure; it is an "emerging informational economy."[42] In the new platform economy, companies like Google develop AI tools that reach into every facet of human life, use ML and AI in ways that are difficult to explain to the public, and openly resist government regulation.[43] This new economy requires new approaches to banking,[44] employment,[45] trade,[46] and other constituents of business law.

State AI/ML Laws

As usual, state law remains a relevant concern for legal researchers. The National Conference of State Legislatures (NCSL) has tracked hundreds of proposed and enacted state laws related to general and specific AI issues (e.g., autonomous vehicles, deepfakes, facial recognition).[47] The NCSL tracked more than forty bills in the first six months of 2024.[48] The Council of State Governments,[49] Brennan Center for Justice,[50] and numerous law firms are also tracking the development of state AI laws. Law librarians should ensure that our patrons have access to this information.

ACCESS AND TECHNICAL SERVICES

Arguably, no units of the library have been more affected by AI and ML than access and technical services. For years, these units have been dealing with three truths at the heart of AI/ML: (1) texts are data, (2) machines are often our readers/patrons, and (3) computers must do some of the work because funding for librarians has not proliferated like information has.[51]

As AI and ML advance and Automated Library Information Systems (ALIS)[52] continue to improve, many access and technical services units could confront another reality: they do not make sense as separate departments.[53] With remote users accessing library data/resources through tools that retrieve cataloged materials,[54] suggest and request complementary resources,[55] and create new texts,[56] the distinctions between facilitating access and managing resources are likely to diminish. Some academic libraries have already created positions and functional units that provide access-technical services.[57] Long-term, institutions will likely hire broadly skilled librarians to troubleshoot access-technical services issues. These librarians will conceive of their work, at least in part, as data services.

Texts Are Data

While there is intellectual, cultural, and aesthetic value to every library resource,[58] more and more researchers view library collections as data. When texts are seen as data, users expect to be able to mine them.[59] When datasets are seen as texts, users expect libraries to manage them as they would any other collected resource.[60] In 2020, Isaiah Michael Omame and Juliet C. Alex-Nmecha described a host of texts-as-data library applications, including the use of OCR to automatically catalog and quickly retrieve texts, the use of NLP tools to automatically translate texts, and automatic indexing using Expert Systems.[61] Omame and Alex-Nmecha predict that AI systems will both minimize certain technical and circulation services work and increase specialized text-as-data system design work.[62] Some of this work involves managing collections as data for machines, a task that requires the collection, data, and metadata management skills found in contemporary access and technical services departments.[63]

Machines Are Readers

While libraries exist to serve humans, machines have long been our patrons too. Decades have passed since a typical human library user discovered resources via paper catalog cards or a single library database. Rather, human patrons have increasingly used federated search tools. Federated searching involves a unified machine interface interacting with underlying databases and electronic resources; that is, a machine patron speaking to machine applications and machine-readable documents to yield useful results for a human end user.[64] In our transition to federated searching, we gained insight into user search behaviors and metadata issues.[65] Then, we developed modern metadata standards and data governance procedures.[66] This has paved the way for systems that assume that a machine—not a human—is the first-level reader.[67]

These new tools facilitate machine-driven discovery of images and audio materials,[68] text mining,[69] data creation, feedback, and suggestions for improvements.[70] Libraries are leading the development of such systems. For instance, the University of North Texas Libraries, in partnership with the University of Illinois Computer Science Department, is training ML models to discover and label individual items within large state government materials collections. If successful, the project will harness the power of machine reading to preserve and disseminate individual state government documents at risk of being lost to large, loosely structured web archives. The project reflects an uncomfortable truth: libraries lack the human resources to manually manage many individual documents.

Computers Shoulder Work

Librarians have been navigating the exponential growth in unstructured data with AI and ML tools, both homegrown and vendor-developed.[71] Library systems, cooperatives, and vendors are using AI for cataloging, resource sharing, and other access-technical services tasks. For instance, OCLC's *WorldShare AI* uses AI to suggest subject headings and enrich metadata.[72] Ex Libris's *Rapido* automates and simplifies parts of the interlibrary loan process, such as identifying the best lender for an item.[73] The British Library, University of North Texas Libraries, and others are using AI to search and tag historical documents.[74]

While access and technical services librarians have led the development of AI tools, they have often done so from a position of resource scarcity and cost-cutting.[75] Many technical services units have been asked to economize their work and increase efficiency for years. As Edward M. Corrado, Associate University Librarian at the Naval Postgraduate School, observed, some of these innovative library units are now asking whether they have reached near-maximum efficiency through minimal human processing.[76] From that vantage point, new AI and ML tools could offer few benefits.

LIBRARY SPACE

Librarians have been at the forefront of accessibility and "design for learning" conversations that have revolutionized academic spaces for decades.[77] Since the 1970s, federal law has prompted law libraries to consider the needs of disabled students, attorneys, and clients.[78] As a result, most libraries have retrofitted or designed spaces to accommodate diverse patrons.[79] Barrier-free and universal design principles have prompted small changes at most law libraries,[80] however, whereas learning-centered design has had far-reaching effects on the look and functionality of academic law libraries.

The learning-centered approach to space planning starts with questions about desired student experiences and outcomes, including social and interactive learning.[81] Using this framework, libraries have moved or reduced physical collections and repurposed existing rooms to offer space for active, group, and experiential learning.[82] In 2014, Lee E. Peoples, Director of the Law Library at the Oklahoma City University School of Law[83] developed a list of learning-centered space planning questions.[84] We should revisit those questions to determine how advances in legal informatics might further alter our library spaces (see table 15.1).

Table 15.1 Peoples' 2014 Learning-Centered Space Planning Questions, Adapted for AI/ML

2014 Learning-Centered Space Planning Questions	*AI/ML Learning-Centered Space Planning Questions*
1. How important to your success as a student is the learning behavior of working with classmates outside of class to prepare for class, complete class assignments, or to study for final exams?	1. How much will future students' success hinge on having collaborative learning spaces for AI/ML coursework or projects (e.g., including augmented reality (AR), virtual reality (VR) work)?
2. How important to your success as a student is the learning behavior of studying alone outside of class?	2. How much will students' success hinge on having new/more independent learning spaces for AI/ML coursework or projects (e.g., more servers in library?)
3. How important to your success as a student is the learning behavior of studying alone but in proximity to other students who are also working alone?	3. How much will future students' success hinge on being able to do AI/ML alone but in proximity to other students who are also working alone?
4. How important to your success as a student is the learning behavior of discussing ideas from readings or classes with other students outside of class?	4. How much will future students' success hinge on being able to do AI/ML work in conversation with other students?
5. How important to your success as a student is discussing ideas from your readings or classes with faculty members or librarians outside of class?	5. How much will future students' success hinge on being able to do AI/ML work in conversation with faculty or librarians outside of class?
6. How important to your success as a student is discussing the law, your career, or related topics with students, librarians, or faculty members outside of class?	6. How much will future students' success hinge on being able to discuss AI/ML, or related careers with other students, librarians, or faculty members outside of class?
7. How important to your success as a student is working with a faculty member or librarian outside of class on a research project, paper, or other activity?	8. How much will future students' success hinge on being able to do AI/ML projects with faculty members or librarians outside of class?

The beauty of the learning-centered design questions is that they require discussions of the future of legal education and practice, including the library's role as an AI innovation incubator.

Libraries are increasingly offering designated AI incubation spaces. In 2018, the University of Rhode Island (URI) libraries in Kingston opened one of the first AI laboratories in an academic library.[85] In the years since, numerous university libraries have followed suit. In 2021, for instance, the Hale Library at Kansas State University in Manhattan opened its AI Studio. Patrons can use the studio's basic computers to access generative AI platforms such as ChatGPT and Dall·E, or the studio's more powerful computers to run generative models and tools such as Stable Diffusion and Alpaca.[86] Law students were among the first to discover such spaces. Harvard Law School students used the university's innovation lab (i-lab), housed in the business school complex, to develop the Evisort contract AI tool.[87] In the past few years, more than two dozen law schools have developed AI and emerging technologies centers, with law libraries running some of these labs and studio spaces.[88]

Of course, just as with the COVID-19 pandemic, library leaders need to consider if AI/ML-driven space usage and design is temporary or permanent.[89] Just as with spaces for early mainframe computers, designated AI/ML spaces could be underutilized in the future or rendered obsolete by further advances. Regardless of these possibilities, the opportunity to redesign library spaces to accommodate new learning goals could also help us reevaluate our broader efforts to support the varied educational needs of diverse patrons.

AI AND THE LIBRARY STAFF

Key to any of these efforts is a knowledgeable and resourced staff. Every member should have a foundational understanding of AI systems necessary to critically engage with the systems they use, creatively consider where they might leverage AI for better workflows or services, and teach and train about these systems. Having sufficiently prepared staff will require investment in training for current staff and careful job crafting and hiring for future positions.

There is no shortage of training options for ML, but trying to find training at the right level or with the right aim is often trickier. Reading this chapter is a good foundation on which to build. Training targeted at library staff, like the AI for GLAM model from The Library Carpentries,[90] is often a good introduction to the material. There are also professional development programs, like the IDEA Institute on Artificial Intelligence at the University of Tennessee, Knoxville. Still, these are more difficult to attend due to the small cohort size.[91]

When staff desire to expand upon this foundational knowledge, it will be best to connect with library communities engaged in this work to identify the best training resources, like AI4LAM, at this time.[92] To assist with these conversations, below is a non-comprehensive list of possible learning topics in AI for Libraries, some of which are covered briefly in this chapter.

- AI foundations: What are these systems, and how do they work?
- ML models: How are they created, and what can they do?
- Ethical considerations in ML: What are the ethical concerns that arise from ML models, and how can you reduce the risk of them?
- Data engineering and mining: cleaning and preparing data for ML projects and performing initial data analysis and exploration.
- No-code ML: using ML platforms and services that don't require any coding expertise.
- Employing existing ML models: identifying applicable models built by others and utilizing them in your work.
- Developing basic ML models: train your own ML models and explore different model types; this will require knowledge of a coding language.
- Developing neural network models: expanding on the above to explore and develop models using neural network architectures.

Along with this learning, library leaders should embrace the current moment to engage their staff in conversations about the future of their libraries, law librarianship, and legal informatics. To aid in those discussions, we offer the following questions to consider.

1. How might AI/ML reinvigorate efforts to create a nationally coordinated legal information system?
2. What existing platforms and consortial arrangements could be leveraged to support ML model development and other AI projects?
3. How can we effectively explain the limits of AI/ML—that is, poor prediction of emerging/novel trends—to patrons, staff, and others?
4. How can we train our patrons and staff to be sophisticated AI users?
5. How will law libraries be organized and staffed in the coming decades?
6. How do we secure resources for our own development of AI tools?
7. How do we advocate for the space needed for future patrons and librarians?

NOTES

1. M. M. Kessler, *TIP System Report* (Cambridge, MA: Massachusetts Institute of Technology, Technical Information Project, 1967); Massachusetts Institute of Technology Libraries, *Collection Overview, Myer M. Kessler Papers* (Cambridge, MA: MIT Libraries), https://archivesspace.mit.edu/repositories/2/resources/1008.
2. Massachusetts Institute of Technology, *Press Release* (Cambridge, MA: Office of Public Relations of the Massachusetts Institute of Technology, 1964, December 11); Massachusetts Institute of Technology, *News Office Records* (AC-0069) (Cambridge, MA: Massachusetts Institute of Technology), https://cdn.libraries.mit.edu/dissemination/diponline/AC0069_NewReleases/NewsRelease_1960/AC0069_1964/AC0069_196412_012.pdf; Trudi Bellardo Hahn, "Pioneers of the Online Age," *Information Processing & Management* 32, no. 1 (1996): 33-48.
3. Kessler, *TIP System Report*, preface.
4. Oscar M. Trelles, "Automation in Law Libraries: The State of the Art," *Law Library Journal* 68, no. 3 (August 1975): 209-233.
5. Robert M. Fano, *Project MAC Progress Report V, July 1967-1968* (Cambridge, MA: Massachusetts Institute of Technology, 1968); Massachusetts Institute of Technology Libraries, *Collection Overview, Fernando J. Corbató Papers* (Cambridge, MA: MIT Libraries), https://archivesspace.mit.edu/repositories/2/resources/866.
6. Fano, *Project MAC Progress Report V*, 141-154.
7. Fano, *Project MAC Progress Report V*, ii-iii.
8. E.g., Peter Nycum, "Looking Ahead - Law and the New Technology," *Law Library Journal* 64, no. 2 (May 1974): 123 ("The National Science Foundation is a sponsor of 17 different regional computing networks.").
9. *Law Library Journal*, "Current Comments," *Law Library Journal* 55, no. 2 (May 1962): 123 ("The Council has allocated $162,258 for the study, the initial phase of which is expected to be completed in October 1962.").
10. David Badertscher, "Introduction," *Law Library Journal* 64, no. 2 (May 1974): 113.
11. Badertscher, "Introduction," 113.
12. Morris L. Cohen, "President's Page: Technology and Law Librarianship," *Law Library Journal* 64, no. 2 (May 1974): 111-112 ("It is terribly important to law librarianship that law librarians concern themselves with these developments and begin serious exploration of possible improvements in their libraries. . . . With all this, however, we must beware of the danger of adopting change for the sake of change.")
13. Frederick E. Smith, "Computer Application to Legal Documentation: What Is Not Being Done," *Law Library Journal* 64, no. 2 (May 1974): 114 ("When there is criticism of the whole system of administration of justice . . . as well as the unavailability of adequate representation to all levels of society, can we afford to accept anything less than the most efficient system we can devise for the

storage and dissemination of legal documentation? Only . . . when problems in the administration of justice are not substantially affected by access to legal documentation, can we expect success from such a program.")
14. Nycum, "Looking Ahead—Law and the New Technology," 124.
15. Smith, "Computer Application to Legal Documentation," 117–118 (decrying a lack of leadership from the Library of Congress, American Bar Association, American Bar Foundation, and others in creating a national legal information system.); Cohen, "President's Page," 111 ("It is terribly important to law librarianship that law librarians concern themselves with these developments and begin serious exploration of possible improvements in their libraries. We have not always kept abreast of the best thinking and latest developments in general librarianship. Our Committee on Automation and Scientific Development cannot do the job alone; they can only stimulate and lead."); Carlos A. Cuadra, "Are Computer Service Agencies Responding to the Needs of Libraries," *Law Library Journal* 64, no. 2 (May 1974): 126.
16. Cuadra, "Are Computer Service Agencies Responding to the Needs of Libraries," 126.
17. Richard A. Danner, "From the Editor: Public Access to the Law," *Law Library Journal* 79, no. 2 (Spring 1987): 163 (describing the foundations of the current American Association of Law Libraries Legal Information Services to the Public Special Interest Section).
18. Peter W. Martin, "Neutral Citation, Court Web Sites, and Access to Authoritative Case Law," *Law Library Journal* 99, no. 2 (Spring 2007): 329–330 (describing the defeat of a joint effort by the Wisconsin Bar Association and the Wisconsin Judicial Council to encourage the Wisconsin Supreme Court to establish a digital archive of judicial decisions, and other changes).
19. See, e.g., M. Kathleen Price, "Setting the Legal Information Agenda for the Year 2000: Preliminary Report of the National Legal Resources Committee," *Law Library Journal* 81, no. 2 (1989): 349.
20. Scott F. Burson, "A Reconstruction of Thamus: Comments on the Evaluation of Legal Information Retrieval Systems," *Law Library Journal* 79, no. 1 (1987): 133–144. (from a loosely structured *LLJ* special issue on public access to legal information, responding to a 1986 article by Daniel Dabney, and furthering a normative conversation on what users should expect from computerized research platforms); see also, Michele I. Dalehite, "Vendor-Supplied Automated Authority Control: What It Is and How to Get It," *Law Library Journal* 81, no. 1 (1989): 117–130; Sheilla E. Desert, "WESTLAW Is Natural v. Boolean Searching: A Performance Study," *Law Library Journal* 85, no. 4 (1993): 713; Kelly Kunsch, "Natural Born Killers: An Argument against Teaching Natural Language Searching," *AALL Spectrum* 1, no. 2 (1996): 16;
Margaret Maher Krause, "Look Beyond LEXIS and WESTLAW: Other Computer Applications in the Practice of Law," *Law Library Journal* 85, no. 3 (1993): 575.
21. For a detailed description of the machine learning model development process, *see* David Lehr and Paul Ohm, "Playing with the Data: What Legal Scholars Should Learn About Machine Learning," *U.C. Davis Law Review* 51, no. 2 (2017): 653.
22. Marco Tulio Ribeiro, Sameer Singh, and Carlos Guestrin, "'Why Should I Trust You?' Explaining the Predictions of Any Classifier," in *International Conference on Knowledge Discovery & Data Mining* (San Francisco, CA. 2016); Balaji Krishnapuram, "ACM Digital Library, Association for Computing Machinery Special Interest Group on Management of Data, and Association for Computing Machinery Special Interest Group on Knowledge Discovery & Data Mining," In *KDD'16 : Proceedings of the 22nd ACM SIGKDD International Conference on Knowledge Discovery and Data Mining : August 13–17, 2016* (San Francisco, CA, New York: Association for Computing Machinery, 2016), 1135.
23. Ribeiro, Singh, and Guestrin, "Why Should I Trust You?," 1135.
24. Eating disorder model. Benefits model.
25. *See* Rifqah Olufunmilayo Okunlaya, Norris Syed Abdullah, and Rose Alinda Alias, "Artificial Intelligence (AI) Library Services Innovative Conceptual Framework for the Digital Transformation of University Education," *Library Hi Tech* 40, no. 6 (2022): 1869.
26. Teresa M. Miguel-Stearns and Sarah E. Ryan, "The Empirical Research Law Librarian Part 1: Making the Case and Filling the Role," *Trends in Law Library Management & Technology* 24, no. 1 (2014): 1.
27. UNC-Chapel Hill Law Libraries, "On the Books: Jim Crow and the Algorithms of Resistance," https://onthebooks.lib.unc.edu/.

28. https://libguides.library.arizona.edu/students-chatgpt.
29. https://law-arizona.libguides.com/c.php?g=1301273&p=9750816.
30. In his Opening Grand Session speech at the 2024 AALL Annual Conference, Cory Doctorow argued that Amazon algorithms sort more expensive and less relevant results to the top and that the best product for a search is often at approximately result 17. As purchasers of legal information products, our students should evaluate marketing and sales platforms such as Amazon.
31. Kalin Hristov, "Artificial Intelligence and the Copyright Dilemma," *IDEA: The Journal of the Franklin Pierce Center for Intellectual Property* 57, no. 3 (2017): 431; Daryl Lim, "AI & IP: Innovation & Creativity in an Age of Accelerated Change," *Akron Law Review* 52, no. 3 (2018): 813; Michael D. Murray, "Generative and AI Authored Artworks and Copyright Law," *Hastings Communications and Entertainment Law Journal* 45, no. 1 (Winter 2023): 27.
32. Murray, "Generative and AI Authored Artworks."
33. Benjamin L. W. Sobel, "Artificial Intelligence's Fair Use Crisis," *Columbia Journal of Law & the Arts* 41, no. 1 (2017): 45.
34. Margot E. Kaminski, "Authorship, Disrupted: AI Authors in Copyright and FirstAmendment Law," *U.C. Davis Law Review* 51, no. 2 (December 2017): 589; W. Michael Schuster, "Artificial Intelligence and Patent Ownership," *Washington and Lee Law Review* 75, no. 4 (Fall 2018): 1945; Shlomit Yanisky-Ravid, "Generating Rembrandt: Artificial Intelligence, Copyright, and Accountability in the 3A Era: The Human-like Authors Are Already Here: A New Model," *Michigan State Law Review* 2017, no. 4 (2017): 659.
35. Karl Manheim and Lyric Kaplan, "Artificial Intelligence: Risks to Privacy and Democracy," *Yale Journal of Law and Technology* 21 (2019): 108.
36. Manheim and Kaplan, "Artificial Intelligence," 119–132.
37. Manheim and Kaplan, "Artificial Intelligence," 133, et seq.
38. Matthew B. Kugler and Carly Pace, "Deepfake Privacy: Attitudes and Regulation," *Northwestern University Law Review* 116, no. 3 (2021): 611.
39. Paul W. Grimm, Maura R. Grossman, and Gordon V. Cormack, "Artificial Intelligence as Evidence," *Northwestern Journal of Technology and Intellectual Property* 19, no. 1 (2021): 9.
40. Alicia Solow-Niederman, "Administering Artificial Intelligence," *Southern California Law Review* 93, no. 4 (2020): 633.
41. Solow-Niederman, "Administering Artificial Intelligence," 641, 695.
42. Julie E. Cohen, "Law for the Platform Economy," *U.C. Davis Law Review* 51, no. 1 (2017): 133.
43. Cohen, "Law for the Platform Economy," 190, 194.
44. Kevin Werbach, "Trust, but Verify: Why the Blockchain Needs the Law," *Berkeley Technology Law Journal* 33, no. 2 (2018): 487.
45. Ifeoma Ajunwa, "The Paradox of Automation as Anti-Bias Intervention," *Cardozo Law Review* 41, no. 5 (2020): 1671.
46. Rory Van Loo, "The Missing Regulatory State: Monitoring Businesses in an Age of Surveillance," *Vanderbilt Law Review* 72, no. 5 (2019): 1563.
47. National Conference of State Legislatures, *Artificial Intelligence 2024 Legislation* (Washington, DC, 2024, June 3), https://www.ncsl.org/technology-and-communication/artificial-intelligence-2024-legislation.
48. National Conference of State Legislatures, *Artificial Intelligence 2024 Legislation.*
49. The Council of State Governments, *Artificial Intelligence in the States: Emerging Legislation* (Washington, DC, 2023, December 6), https://www.csg.org/2023/12/06/artificial-intelligence-in-the-states-emerging-legislation/.
50. Brennan Center for Justice, *States Take the Lead on Regulating Artificial Intelligence* (Washington, DC, 2023, November 6), https://www.brennancenter.org/our-work/research-reports/states-take-lead-regulating-artificial-intelligence.
51. Andrew M. Cox, Stephen Pinfield, and Sophie Rutter, "The Intelligent Library: Thought Leaders' Views on the Likely Impact of Artificial Intelligence on Academic Libraries," *Library Hi Tech* 37, no. 3 (2019): 418 (featuring library leaders' opinions and predictions on the future of resource access as AI-mediated and including AI-created metadata); Jean Godby, Karen Smith-Yoshimura, Bruce Washburn, Kalan

Knudson Davis, Karen Detling, Christine Fernsebner Eslao, Steven Folsom, Xiaoli Li, Marc McGee, Karen Miller, Honor Moody, Craig Thomas, and Holly Tomren, *Creating Library Linked Data with Wikibase: Lessons Learned from Project Passage* (Dublin, OH: OCLC Research, 2019), https://doi.org/10.25333/faq3-ax08 (explaining that MARC and other library standards assumed human readers and that the future could revolve around linked open data that presumes machines as the primary readers); see, e.g., University of North Texas Libraries, "Leveraging Existing Bibliographic Metadata to Improve Automatic Document Identification in Web Archives," *Institute of Museum and Library Services* [Grant LG-252349-OLS-22], last accessed June 17, 2024, https://www.imls.gov/sites/default/files/project-proposals/LG-252349-OLS-22-preliminary-proposal.pdf (arguing that supervised machine learning models are necessary for processing large tranches of government and legal documents as data, for direct access to users through the web, because there is simply not sufficient human effort to process all of the documents and testing methods for this work).

52. See, e.g., Arnold Hirshon, *Integrated Library Information Systems in ARL Libraries* (Washington, DC: Association of Research Libraries, 1983); Ex Libris [Clarivate], *Aleph*, accessed June 17, 2024, https://exlibrisgroup.com/products/aleph-integrated-library-system/ (i.e., integrated library system that can handle both cataloging and circulation).
53. Megan Lounsberry, "Troubleshooting Electronic Resources from an Interlibrary Loan Perspective," *Technical Services Quarterly* 37, no. 3 (2020): 223.
54. See, e.g., Godby et al., *Creating Library Linked Data with Wikibase* (explaining how retrieval will center around resource entities that will be connected by machines to other similar entities); Loida Garcia-Febo, "Exploring AI," *American Libraries Magazine*, March 1, 2019, (explaining how Chris Bourg, director of the MIT Libraries, is encouraging the development of an infrastructure that would make MIT collections accessible by APIs and ML algorithms).
55. Ex Libris [Clarivate], *Change is the Name of the Interlibrary Loan Game. Are You Ready?*, accessed June 17, 2024, https://exlibrisgroup.com/blog/change-is-the-name-of-the-interlibrary-loan-game-are-you-ready/; IFLA Document Delivery and Resource Sharing (DDRS) Section, "Can Artificial Intelligence Lead Us to a Smarter ILL Future or Other Library Services?" [Webinar Description], last accessed June 17, 2024, https://www.ifla.org/news/can-artificial-intelligence-lead-us-to-a-smarter-ill-future-or-other-library-services/.
56. Hao Yu, "Reflection on Whether Chat GPT Should be Banned by academia from the Perspective of Education and Teaching," *Frontiers in Psychology* 14 (2023): 1181712 (on how ChatGPT can create texts, including textbooks); see also, a large and interesting body of research on user-created content in gaming, e.g., Gabriele Aroni, "Games as Authorial Platforms? An Exploration of the Legal Status of User-created Content from Digital Games," *International Journal for the Semiotics of Law-Revue* 36, no. 5 (2023): 2021; Marc Schubhan, Maximilian Altmeyer, Dominic Buchheit, and Pascal Lessel, "Investigating User-created Gamification in an Image Tagging Task," in *CHI Conference Online*, 2020; Regina Bernhaupt, Florian Mueller, Joanna McGrenere, Andy Cockburn, SIGCHI (Group: U.S.), and Association for Computing Machinery, In *CHI'20: Proceedings of the 2020 CHI Conference on Human Factors in Computing Systems: April 25–30, 2020* (Honolulu, HI, New York: Association for Computing Machinery, 2020), 1.
57. Lounsberry, "Troubleshooting Electronic Resources," 223; see also Margaret A. Leary, "Creating One Library at the University of Michigan Law Library," *Trends in Law Library Management and Technology* 18 (2008): 12 (on a reorganization to functional service units).
58. Susan Gaultier, Teresa Miguel-Stearns, Sarah Ryan, and Fang Wang, "More than a Bunch of Old Books: Perspectives from Rare Book School," *AALL Spectrum* 19, no. 5 (March 2015): 27.
59. Leo Appleton, "AI and Academic Libraries: What's All the Fuss About?," *New Review of Academic Librarianship* 30, no. 1 (2024): 1.
60. Andrew Cox, "How Artificial Intelligence Might Change Academic Library Work: Applying the Competencies Literature and the Theory of the Professions," *Journal of the Association for Information Science and Technology* 74, no. 3 (2023): 367.
61. Isaiah Michael Omame and Juliet C. Alex-Nmecha, "Artificial Intelligence in Libraries," in *Managing and Adapting Library Information Services for Future Users*, ed. Nkem Ekene Osuigwe (Hershey, PA: IGI Global, 2020), 129, https://doi.org/10.4018/978-1-7998-1116-9.

62. Omame and Alex-Nmecha, "Artificial Intelligence in Libraries," 136–137.
63. Cox, "How Artificial Intelligence Might Change Academic Library Work," 374.
64. Yumin Jiang and Georgia Briscoe, "The Wise Researcher: One Library's Experience Implementing a Federated Search Product," *AALL Spectrum,* November 2008.
65. Helen Georgas, "Google vs. the Library (Part II): Student Search Patterns and Behaviors When using Google and a Federated Search Tool," *portal: Libraries and the Academy* 14, no. 4 (2014): 503.
66. Etai Mizrahi, "4 Common Metadata Standards To Follow," *Seconda,* May 2, 2024, https://www.secoda.co/blog/4-common-metadata-standards-to-follow.
67. Cox, Pinfield, and Rutter, "The Intelligent Library," 423.
68. Cox, "How Artificial Intelligence Might Change Academic Library Work," 373.
69. Cox, Pinfield, and Rutter, "The Intelligent Library," 423.
70. Cox, "How Artificial Intelligence Might Change Academic Library Work," 373; Cox, Pinfield, and Rutter, "The Intelligent Library," 422–423.
71. Edward M. Corrado, "Artificial Intelligence: The Possibilities for Metadata Creation," *Technical Services Quarterly* 38, no. 4 (2021): 395.
72. LibLime, "Revolutionizing Library Cataloging with Artificial Intelligence (AI)," *LinkedIn,* December 4, 2023, https://www.linkedin.com/pulse/revolutionizing-library-cataloging-artificial-intelligence-ai-coo9c/.
73. Ex Libris [Clarivate], *Rapido,* accessed June 17, 2024, https://exlibrisgroup.com/products/rapido-library-resource-sharing/.
74. LibLime, "Revolutionizing Library Cataloging"; University of North Texas Libraries, "Leveraging Existing Bibliographic Metadata," 1.
75. Corrado, "Artificial Intelligence," 396.
76. Corrado, "Artificial Intelligence," 397.
77. Jessica de Perio Wittman, "Moving Beyond the Basics of the ADA and Section 504: Opportunities for Equitable and Inclusive Access to Law Libraries, Collections, and Services," *Legal Reference Services Quarterly* 42, no. 3–4 (2023): 272; Lee F. Peoples, "Designing a Law Library to Encourage Learning," *Journal of Legal Education* 63, no. 4 (May 2014): 612; see, e.g., Scott Bennett, *Libraries Designed for Learning* (Washington, DC: Council on Library and Information Resources, 2003), 3; Scott Bennett, *Righting the Balance, in Library as Place: Rethinking Roles, Rethinking Space* (Washington, DC: Council on Library and Information Resources, 2005), II.
78. de Perio Wittman, "Moving beyond the Basics," 275–277 (discussing the promise and ultimately weak results of Section 504 of the Rehabilitation Act of 1973, which at least prevented law schools from denying admission to students with disabilities).
79. de Perio Wittman, "Moving beyond the Basics," 289.
80. de Perio Wittman, "Moving beyond the Basics," 289.
81. Peoples, "Designing a Law Library to Encourage Learning," 616–617.
82. Peoples, "Designing a Law Library to Encourage Learning," 616.
83. In 2024, Lee Peoples is the Associate Dean of Library and Technology of the Chickasaw Nation Law Library at Oklahoma City University School of Law.
84. Peoples, "Designing a Law Library to Encourage Learning," 621.
85. George M. Eberhart, "Why Artificial Intelligence Matters," *American Libraries,* June 26, 2018, https://americanlibrariesmagazine.org/blogs/the-scoop/ai-lab-library/.
86. American Libraries, "Realizing Potential," *American Libraries,* March 1, 2024, https://americanlibrariesmagazine.org/2024/03/01/realizing-potential/.
87. <Elaine McArdle, "HLS Students Harness Artificial Intelligence to Revolutionize How Lawyers Draft and Manage Contracts," *Harvard Law Today,* December 20, 2017, https://hls.harvard.edu/today/evisort/.>
88. Tawnya K. Plumb, "Access to Justice in the Age of AI," in *Law Librarianship in the Age of AI,* ed. E. Kroski (Chicago, IL: ALA Editions, 2019), 125
89. See Thomas Sneed, "The Effect of COVID-19 on Law Libraries: Are These Changes Temporary or a Sign of the Future?," *Washburn Law Journal* 60, no. 1 (Fall 2020): 107.
90. https://carpentries-incubator.github.io/machine-learning-librarians-archivists/01-welcome/index.html.
91. https://idea.infosci.utk.edu/.
92. https://github.com/AI4LAM.

16

Generative AI in Law Libraries

Michelle Rodenburg and Jennifer Wondracek

Today, it is hard to imagine what law libraries looked like before the internet. The ways in which new attorneys learn both the law itself and how to practice it revolve around tools like online legal research tools, Zoom meetings, metadata, eDiscovery, and analytics. Not since the introduction of the internet have we faced such a dramatic change in the way that law libraries may function, until the introduction of Generative AI (GAI). In this chapter, we look at the way GAI functions, the strengths and weaknesses of GAI, the ways GAI has already impacted law librarianship, and the ways in which GAI may continue to impact the field of law librarianship.

Traditional AI, sometimes referred to as "simple AI," "classic AI," or even "weak AI," has long been used in legal research and differs greatly from GAI. We often find these terms used interchangeably, which leads to confusion and misunderstanding regarding the capabilities of these two distinct technologies. Our judicial system itself continues to perpetuate this misunderstanding, as judges have penned standing orders on the use of AI, attempting to control the use of these tools in the courtroom. One such orders came from Judge Michael Baylson of the Eastern District of Pennsylvania, which specified that the use of AI in the drafting of filings must be documented and disclosed. This standing order simply stated that the use of "Artificial Intelligence" in the preparation of a filing must be disclosed—it did not differentiate between traditional AI and GAI. With the long-term and prevalent use of traditional AI in legal research, one must question if all queries presented to Westlaw or Lexis in the preparation of a filing in Judge Baylson's court must be disclosed.[1]

When lawyers are told of the capabilities of GAI, they often rightfully respond that they have been using AI in their legal research for many years. As stated by the senior director of Westlaw Product Management at Thomson Reuters, "we've used AI to serve up editor-created answers for over a decade."[2] In fact, AI has been fully integrated into Westlaw and Lexis for over twenty years. So why, given the longevity we have already experienced with AI in the legal research process, are we hearing so much lately about the changes GAI will bring to the practice of law?

It is important to understand the differing capabilities of traditional AI and GAI. Traditional AI was designed to deal with certain tasks, responding to relevant prompt input. The capabilities of traditional AI are limited to the specific task it was created to perform—whether that task be optimized search results, watching recommendations, or voice assistance. On the other hand, GAI is designed to take its assistance further by actually creating a new expression of information. GAI is trained with large datasets—meaning huge amounts of data are input into GAI tools, also referred to as large language models (LLMs), in order to "train" the tool. The GAI tool then combs through the massive amounts of data that it is trained on in order to identify structures and patterns within the training data. The GAI tool then uses those structures and patterns that it has identified in order to create answers that best reflect what it has learned. GAI goes even further by incorporating retrieval-augmented generation (RAG). RAG specifically addresses the weaknesses of LLMs (like giving false answers when the answer can't be found, relying on out-of-date training data, or relying on resources it shouldn't) by pointing LLMs to authoritative and updated knowledge sources. In this way, GAI can take its training data, while expanding on it through RAG, and respond to prompts by creating images, language, videos, audios, code, and more. It is important to note, though, that while RAG mitigates the weaknesses of LLMs, it does not eliminate them—all LLMs, which will be discussed later.

In creating this new data, GAI tools search to create the best answer to the question presented—not necessarily the correct answer. It is important to understand that when a GAI tool answers a prompt, it does not have its entire answer planned out from the beginning. These GAI tools simply locate the next word in their response while pulling from the structures and patterns they have identified from their training data.

A good example of this process, originally provided by Joe Regalia, involves the game of golf. He found that when asked who, between a player with a higher score and a player with a lower score, won a round of golf, GAI would consistently say the player with the higher score won.[3] For those not familiar with golf—it is the player with the lower score (or fewer strokes) who wins. GAI came to the answer that the higher score won because it was simply looking for the best answer to the question presented. Looking through its training data, GAI found that in most games, the higher scorer wins. It extrapolated this presumption, concluding that saying the higher scorer wins was the best answer.[4] When this author presented this experiment to their students, they mostly received the correct answer from GAI—that the lower scorer in golf wins. However, there was one notable exception—one student (using ChatGPT 3.0) found that while GAI told her the correct rule (that the lower score in golf wins), it still came to the incorrect conclusion (that the higher score in this situation is the winner).

UNDERSTANDING CHATGPT AND SIMILAR NON-LEGAL TECHNOLOGIES

There are many GAI products available today that perform a wide variety of tasks, such as assisting in writing quiz questions, starting MARC records, drafting onboarding checklists, summarizing cases, drafting contract clauses, and generating social media posts, including text, images, and hashtags that are customized to the specified social media platform.[5] Due to their ability to recognize patterns, this technology is even being used to create new and personalized medical treatments for diseases.[6] While LLMs will not replace law librarians or lawyers, they will likely become essential tools that increase our efficiency. For instance, how long do you agonize over an important email, rereading it for grammar, wondering if it is in the correct tone, and similar concerns? Using an LLM, like ChatGPT, can help you polish your message, adjust the tone if needed, and help you finalize that email in seconds rather than dwelling on it for an hour.

Although there are thousands of products, there is a relatively small number of GAI models on which most of those products are run. The reason for this is that these tools require training on an enormous amount of data, which gives them the designation of LLMs.

LLMs are generally trained with two types of data: targeted source and web crawl. "Targeted sources are relatively small individually, relatively well defined, and chosen because they are considered 'high quality' and diverse to help the LLM imitate various styles of language."[7] Examples include respected repositories, like arXiv, Project Gutenberg, and many Bepress Digital Commons repositories.

Web crawl data is data that is collected when a robot crawls the internet, collecting data from internet websites. For instance, Common Crawl, an open repository, currently contains approximately 250 billion pages of internet data collected through web crawling.[8] Common Crawl is unfiltered, so it collects all data it can, regardless of the category and acceptability to polite society. Alphabet has filtered the data from Common Crawl to eliminate objectionable content, such as hate speech, and published this 15.7 million website collection as their "Colossal Clean Crawled Corpus" or C4, as has EleutherAI's "Pile-CC" dataset.[9] C4 was the subject of a *Washington Post* investigation, and interested readers can search the C4 dataset through the *Washington Post*'s website to delve into the data.[10]

Many companies have tried to filter their training data to avoid objectionable content. This can reduce outputs such as Nazi propaganda. Reducing objectionable content does not, however, ensure unbiased outputs. Data bias has been an issue discussed in computing circles for decades. There is even a popular saying, "garbage in, garbage out." Algorithmic bias also exists, where the AI system has a built-in bias acquired during programming or builds one through user feedback and machine learning. They are unable to distinguish correlation from causation.

Bias in AI systems can lead to unexpected issues. In 2016, ProPublica ran a story about AI-generated risk assessment scores from the COMPAS assessment.[11] These scores look at a variety of factors, including prior criminal records, to try to predict recidivism and are often used by judges determining pre-trial release. According to ProPublica, the COMPAS assessment "correctly predicts recidivism 61 percent of the time. But blacks are almost twice as likely as whites to be labeled a higher risk but not actually re-offend. It makes the opposite mistake among whites: They are much more likely than blacks to be labeled lower risk but go on to commit other crimes." To avoid unexpected outcomes, it is always a good idea to question the underlying data and algorithms when possible.

LLMs are often costly to train due to information gathering, content filtering, and the processing time and power of the actual ingestion of the information. While the exact costs are often not provided by the companies, the estimated costs often go into the millions and sometimes well beyond. Google's Gemini Ultra cost approximately $191.4 million to train.[12]

Some companies, such as OpenAI, creator of ChatGPT, also claim to use licensed content[13] in their training materials, which increases the cost. Due to training costs, GAI products often use one or more of these relatively small numbers of models. For instance, Lexis+ AI uses models from both OpenAI and Anthropic, creator of Claude, switching between models for different tasks based on the model's strengths and costs.

Once LLMs are provided access to training materials, they are able to process these materials to identify connections between words, sentences, and paragraphs, thereby recognizing patterns and structures. LLMs are particularly impressive at understanding and replicating complex patterns, such as English grammar. While the exact process occurring inside an LLM is not known, even to its creators, the general process is understood. An LLM takes a user-provided prompt that requests it to create or answer something, and compares the prompt to its known patterns and data. Using statistical analysis, it predicts the most likely desired string of words and generates a unique output.[14]

As an example of how this might work, consider the following question: How would you complete this sentence? "The man breached the _____." There are many possible options for this missing word or phrase. If no other information is provided, the LLM will look to see what the most common options are with this string of words and provide you with a possible answer that may be far from the desired response. When the user provides more information with the prompt, the LLM will be able to provide a more probable answer to the question. For instance, if the user provides context in their prompt about a landlord-tenant dispute based on the lack of heat, the LLM might finish the sentence with contract, lease, or warranty of habitability. If, however, the user adds information to the prompt about medieval warfare, the LLM is more likely to provide a response such as castle or wall. The LLM may even be able to pull details from articles on specific battles from its training data to provide better responses based on the level of context provided by the user. Thus, it is best to provide LLMs with context when drafting a prompt to obtain the most relevant and complete response.

Some of the mainstream GAI products, such as ChatGPT, run on LLMs with just their basic training data. This data may be time-limited. For instance, GPT-4 was released with training data through

September 2021, meaning events such as the decision in *Dobbs v. Jackson Women's Health Organization, 597 U.S. 215* (2022), were unknown to the LLM. GPT-4 has since been given web browsing capabilities, opening the date range on the data it can access.

Web browsing is not the only capability of ChatGPT. A wide variety of features have been released, and more are scheduled for release. ChatGPT can, among other things,

- allow users to select a model;
- generate and revise text;
- summarize long documents;
- generate and edit images;
- read files that are uploaded from your computer hard drive, OneDrive, or Google Drive, treating them as an additional layer of data to use in their response, similar to RAG;
- translate text between languages;
- analyze data;
- draft computer code in multiple languages;
- design presentation outlines and content;
- create educational training materials and lesson plans; and
- create custom GPTs.

Not all mainstream GAIs have all of these features, and ChatGPT does not have all of the features other AI products may offer. For instance, Perplexity AI Pro allows the user to select from different vendors' models, including GPT-4 Omni, Claude 3 Sonnet/Opus, and Sonar Large 32k.[15] Each of these models has its own pros and cons that can affect the output. Allowing for selection gives the user more precise control over the AI response. The free version of Perplexity also incorporates the ability to focus a response using specific sources of information, such as academic papers, Wolfram|Alpha, Reddit, and so on. This selection helps Perplexity build its RAG.

RAG layers a more specific layer of data on top of the training data.[16] For instance, Perplexity AI converts the user prompt into a more traditional search string for use in a search engine. After running the search string, the AI creates a corpus of data from the search results. The AI model then uses this data to help refine its generated output, improving its accuracy and mitigating hallucinations. Perplexity AI then provides links to some of the sources that it relied on when generating its response to allow the user to validate or expand the AI response. Perplexity creates a new RAG corpus with each new thread.

The features of these AIs are regularly updated, often without notice. For example, as this author was writing about Perplexity AI's RAG abilities, ChatGPT began offering the author outputs with links attached. After some investigation, it appears that ChatGPT's list of features now includes RAG.

Some other mainstream GAI text products include the following:

- Anthropic's Claude: Advertised as the ethical AI system. It does not allow its models to train on user input; it filters its training data to attempt to avoid bias, and its model is restricted from participating in illegal or harmful activities. Currently, it is one of the best performing AI models on benchmarking tests.
- Google Gemini: Formerly Bard, Gemini Advanced is the most robust of Google's AI models at the moment. Google is working to integrate its AI models into many Google products, including Gmail, Docs, Sheets, Search, Photos, and similar applications.
- Microsoft Copilot: Formerly Bing Chat, Copilot is the current Microsoft chatbot. It utilizes OpenAI models. Microsoft has begun offering AI integrations to Microsoft Office 365 for an additional charge.

- Pi AI: Created by Inflection AI, Pi is designed to be more emotional and empathetic than other AI systems. Consider it an AI companion who can support your mental health, and do not expect it to be as productive as other AI systems.
- Poe: Poe provides access to a variety of third-party AI models, including Claude, GPT, Gemini, Llama, Mistral, Pika, and many others. It allows users to create bots with a variety of models.

It should be noted that these tools advance quickly, and new models and products will likely be out before this book is published.

This list is not exhaustive by far. In addition to publicly available resources like those listed above, many firms have or are in the process of developing in-house GAI workflows, such as Baker-Hostetler LLP's custom LLM "Baker Brain." It should also be noted that GAIs exist for images, videos, code scripting, and audio. These products often can both produce and "read" these types of formats, allowing the GAIs to add new content to their creative processes and output. For this chapter, we are focusing on text generators and multimodal GAIs, such as ChatGPT, which can "read" and create a variety of types of outputs.

THE DEVELOPMENT OF LEGAL GAI

Those who open their own law firms will often lament the sheer amount of administrative work required to keep an office running smoothly. Between scheduling client meetings, answering the phone, and setting calendar reminders, much of a lawyer's time may be spent on tasks that do not require legal thinking. The use of GAI could cut down on the time spent on the administrative side of lawyering—which, in turn can cut down time and cost for clients.

The large variety of tasks in which GAI can be effectively used in law librarianship and legal practice necessitates a large variety of tools. These tools can include chatbots, drafting tools, contract review tools, eDiscovery tools, and more.

Currently, the tool that users are most familiar with is ChatGPT. Developed by OpenAI, ChatGPT is free and easy to use—standing to revolutionize the ability for all people to interact with GAI. OpenAI has two different types of ChatGPT—the free and non-limited usage ChatGPT 3.5 and ChatGPT 4.0, which is currently also free to use but limits usage without purchase. ChatGPT 4, along with being a partially paid resource, promises more accurate answers, has an expanded conversation memory, and can respond to visual and audio input.[17] On the Uniform Bar Exam, ChatGPT 3.5 passed the exam with a score in the 10th percentile.[18] ChatGPT 4.0, on the other hand, reportedly also passed but earned a score that ranked in the 90th percentile of test takers.[19] While impressive, there are doubts as to whether the reported 90th percentile passage is an accurate reflection of ChatGPT 4.0's actual performance on the Uniform Bar Exam.[20] ChatGPT continues to be an extremely influential tool in making GAI accessible to a broader audience, but it is also facing issues that question its ability to continue operating—namely, litigation such as the *New York Times* case discussed later in this chapter.

Other GAI technologies that are relevant to law librarianship and legal practice will be reviewed below:

Thomson Reuters CoCounsel—Developed by CaseText, CoCounsel dubs itself "the world's first reliable AI legal assistant, powered by GPT-4."[21] This legal assistant tool seeks to aid practitioners in deposition preparation, legal research, creating timelines, summarizing datasets, and contract review and compliance.

Relativity aiR—Formerly oppressive amounts of ESI (electronically stored information) can now be better stored, reviewed, and produced via tools that implement GAI. Relativity uses GAI for document review, case strategy, investigation, and legal hold automation.[22]

DISCO Cecilia AI—Cecilia AI platform promises that confidential data input into the tool will not be sent to train another company's model.[23] It advertises itself as helping attorneys with timelines, auto-review, deposition summaries, and features a Q&A that allows you to interrogate your evidence.

Lexis+AI—This tool within Lexis uses chat AI technology to function similarly to ChatGPT but addresses some of the major issues that users face with ChatGPT in legal uses—like functioning in a closed data environment (addressing confidential information concerns), extra training on legal tools, and using up-to-date information.[24]

Thomson Reuters Westlaw's AI-Assisted Research and Ask Practical Law AI—Westlaw's Precision allows users to type in a legal question or issue and receive results and summaries based completely upon trusted Westlaw content.[25] Ask Practical Law AI enhances the Practical Law platform to allow users to ask questions directly to the platform and receive a single, tailored response with citations.[26]

LawDroid—LawDroid Copilot is designed to function as an AI legal assistant, assisting lawyers with legal research, correspondence drafting, and document summaries. LawDroid Builder is a no-code AI creation platform designed to answer calls, capture leads, and build scalable tools.[27]

Harvey—Harvey is designed to address many of the concerns that lawyers have over the use of GAI—including enhanced security and confidentiality methods and using a custom-trained case law model. Built on OpenAI, Harvey looks to assist lawyers in managing workflows, answering complex research questions, and drafting, analyzing, and comparing legal documents.[28]

EVALUATING GAI TOOLS

As GAI tools become available to attorneys, it is increasingly important to establish criteria for evaluating these tools. Using GAI wisely includes analyzing what these tools are good at, as well as what they are not so good at. A general rule of thumb while using GAI is that the more concise the question, the better the answer will be. GAI is typically not very good at answering questions that are broad or leave room for interpretation or assumptions. On the other hand, GAI is generally good at things like analyzing, summarizing, drafting and brainstorming, writing or editing for tone or audience, and client and case management.

Overall, GAI provides accurate answers. According to a 2023 Goldman Sachs study, the accuracy of AI versus human benchmarks has continually improved, to the point that AI far outperforms the accuracy of its human counterparts in image classification and reading comprehension.[29]

While overall accurate, GAI is known to create false answers, known as hallucinations. This is not unexpected, as all LLMs hallucinate, and GAI hallucinations are inevitable.[30] There are serious limitations to meet responsible integration, supervision, and accurate oversight of legal GAI models, as there remains a need for transparent and in-depth benchmarking and public evaluations.[31] As discussed earlier in this chapter, these models are designed to create the "best" answer—which is not always the correct answer. A Stanford study published in 2024 found that GAI tools (ChatGPT, PaLM 2, and Llama 2) hallucinated at least 75 percent of the time when asked about a Court's core ruling.[32] While commonplace, lawyers have seen the serious implications of these hallucinations. One of the most famous examples of this is the *Mata v. Avianca Inc.* case in the Southern District of New York.[33] In this case, filed in 2022, two attorneys submitted a motion that cited hallucinated cases.[34] When the judge requested that the attorneys produce the text of the hallucinated cases, ChatGPT provided the full text of eight hallucinated cases that included internal citations and false quotes.[35] Both attorneys were sanctioned.[36] In another instance, a lawyer in Colorado was fired from his firm and suspended from practice after using ChatGPT to write a motion with hallucinated case citations.[37] In Missouri, a client was fined after an appeal brief was found to contain only two genuine case citations—while the other twenty-two citations were hallucinations.[38] This came after the client found that hiring a "legal consultant" out of California would cost less than 1 percent of hiring an attorney in Missouri.[39] The legal consultant, without the client's knowledge, had relied on GAI to create the faulty brief.[40]

Under ABA Rule 3.3 (a), a lawyer shall not knowingly make a false statement of fact or law to a tribunal or fail to correct a false statement of material fact or law previously made to the tribunal by the lawyer.[41] Additionally, Federal Rule of Civil Procedure 11 requires that "attorneys read, and thereby conform the existence and validity of, the legal authorities on which they rely."[42] When using GAI tools, students and practitioners must be aware of the risk of hallucinations and take precautions to ensure that they do not become a GAI horror story. At the very least, students and practitioners should cite check any cases, statutes, rules, or any assumptions contained in GAI-created materials.

Another possible issue with the widespread usage of GAI tools within the legal profession is a possible lack of reliability. If using GAI, it is advisable to become acquainted with multiple tools. The use of multiple tools can help mitigate risks of system outages, as well as maximize cost efficiency. It is advisable to analyze the dataset contents found in each different tool, and then use the tool that best fits your query.

It is also important to consider ease of use and system limitations when using a GAI tool. Different tools allow users to construct different types of queries in different capacities. Notably, tools such as Lexis+ AI limit the number of times you can revise a query or conversation or request conversational turns, while others require users to create a new conversation for each query. Some tools remember and store conversations to revisit later, while others "forget" and delete previous conversations.

While considering which tool to use and how to use it, one should also consider the logistics of the question they would like answered by the GAI tool. If looking to answer a multi-jurisdictional question, one would once have avoided a tool like Lexis+ AI, which originally allowed only one jurisdiction to be searched at a time—users could not even search an issue in both state and federal fields simultaneously. Lexis+ AI has now removed this limitation. Complex issues require additional care when utilizing GAI, as they may need to be broken down into smaller queries to reduce the risk of assumptions or misunderstandings on the part of the GAI tool. Another thing to keep in mind when assessing GAI are the parameters that come pre-baked into the tools. These parameters define how the model utilizes its training data to create output data and dictate how the model makes decisions and provides data back to you based on the queries that you provide.

CONCERNS SURROUNDING THE USE OF GAI

According to ABA Rule 1.6 (a), a lawyer shall not reveal information relating to the representation of a client unless the client gives informed consent, the disclosure is impliedly authorized in order to carry out the representation, or the disclosure is permitted by paragraph (b).[43] The use of GAI tools understandably makes a lot of students and practitioners uncomfortable when it comes to confidentiality concerns. Confidentiality generally stands in contrast to the way that LLMs function—using prompts to continue to learn and provide information to other users. ChatGPT is open about using prompts input by users as training data to improve services, that conversations with ChatGPT may be reviewed by human trainers as well, and that conversations with ChatGPT cannot be permanently deleted.

Students and practitioners should take care to not provide confidential client information while using GAI. As explained elsewhere in this chapter, there are many valuable uses of GAI in the practice of law that do not warrant the disclosure of client information. For those who do wish to use GAI for tasks that include confidentiality concerns, there are promising movements in this area, in GAI tools designed specifically for lawyers. For example, Lexis + AI functions in a closed conversation environment—where information input into the tool is protected, and information learned in conversations is not shared with other users. At the very least, while the use of GAI is not an accepted and routine part of legal representation, lawyers should retain informed consent from their clients (with a detailed description of how GAI will be used and associated billing practices) before using GAI in client representation.

Additionally, ABA Rule 5.5 (a) states that "a lawyer shall not practice law in a jurisdiction in violation of the regulation of the legal profession in that jurisdiction or assist another in doing so," while ABA Rule 5.3 (b) states that "a lawyer having direct supervisory authority over" a nonlawyer must make "reasonable efforts" to ensure that the conduct is compatible with professional obligations—and the Rule goes on to assign responsibility for such conduct of the nonlawyer to the lawyer.[44] Just as a lawyer must monitor to make sure that a paralegal in their firm is not engaging in the unauthorized practice of law, the same must be done with the use of GAI tools in client representation. As GAI tools continue to be developed to aid attorneys, clients, and pro se litigants, we continue to see uses of GAI that test the limits of the unauthorized practice of law. For example, DoNotPay, an online legal service chatbot, developed smart glasses to be worn by users in court proceedings to offer real-time legal advice, branding itself the "world's first robot lawyer."[45] Quickly, state bar associations, clients, and attorneys reacted and filed suits against DoNotPay for the unauthorized practice of law.[46] In some states, the unauthorized practice of law rises to a misdemeanor.[47] In June 2024, DoNotPay reached a settlement with an individual who said that he would not have used the service "had he known that DoNotPay was not actually a lawyer" after he used the service to draft demand letters, a small claims court filing, and an LLC operating agreement.[48] Other sites, such as AI.Law, which says it is designed to be used by lawyers to "make the most of their time," promise to write pleadings in two minutes.[49]

In addition to the issues already discussed, the future of GAI continues to be plagued with questions of ownership. Famously, the *New York Times* sued OpenAI for copyright infringement over the use of published work in the training of GAI. The crux of the *Times'* argument is that after millions of published articles were used to train OpenAI, it now directly competes with the *Times* as a reliable source of information.[50] Further, uncertainty still surrounds who has the right to own (and use) information put into a GAI tool, as well as the output created by GAI output.[51]

While capable of great computing power, GAI still reflects something unfortunately found throughout human decision-making: bias. This bias can be found throughout the GAI decision-making, including training data, algorithms, and predictions. A high-stakes example of how bias may be perpetuated through AI comes in the case of the use of COMPAS, discussed earlier in this chapter.

Another growing concern among attorneys and clients is the impact of GAI on billing. Specifically, there is concern about billing clients fairly, as the use of GAI by attorneys will cut down time spent by lawyers on research matters. There is a fear that this reduced time will not be accurately reflected in client bills. Practitioners should be cautioned to accurately keep track of time spent serving their clients—even when this time is used highly effectively with the aid of GAI. Overbilling is not the only concern that practitioners should keep in mind regarding billing and GAI—a federal judge in New York reduced a law firm's requested fee after the firm used ChatGPT-4 to calculate their fees.[52]

While GAI technologies promise to have a large impact in many industries—including the legal industry—there are some serious drawbacks to consider. To help combat tendencies of ChatGPT offering violent, sexist, or racist remarks, OpenAI sought to hire human workers to help label (to then eliminate) toxic language found in training data through an "ethical AI" company in Kenya called Sama.[53] The large labor force supplied by Sama was tasked with reviewing exorbitant amounts of very troubling materials while earning a meager take-home wage of $1.32-$2 per hour.[54]

An additional concern when discussing the value of GAI technologies is the general lack of transparency in the way that these tools make decisions. Much of the behind-the-scenes work of LLMs are protected—these tools do not want everyone to know how they work, so that others cannot simply replicate these tools.[55] This secrecy creates a serious lack of transparency. Without transparency, we as users are unable to identify and address issues like bias within the systems.

Impact on the climate is another concern that must be discussed in the context of GAI. The development and use of LLMs like ChatGPT use a staggering amount of electricity—it is estimated that you would have to watch 1,625,000 hours of Netflix in order to consume the amount of power it takes to train ChatGPT 3.[56] According to an article in *Nature*, ChatGPT alone is currently using the equivalent energy of 33,000 residential homes. While these technologies continue to develop and could potentially become more energy efficient, they will also be used at a higher frequency. By one calculation, by 2027, the global AI sector could consume about the same amount of annual energy demand as the Netherlands.[57] The lack of transparency in the GAI field means that we do not have a clear idea of how much energy is consumed in different GAI functions. There are calls to require that AI developers submit energy use disclosures.[58] At the World Economic Forum's annual meeting, OpenAI chief executive Sam Altman warned that the next wave of GAI will require so much more power than expected that our existing energy systems will struggle to cope.[59] In addition to the draw on electricity, GAI requires large amounts of fresh water in order to cool processors and generators.[60] Local residents in West Des Moines filed a lawsuit stating that Microsoft used around 6 percent, or 11.5 million gallons, of water in its training of GPT-4.[61] By 2027, estimates say that the rate of global demand for water for AI could rise to approximately the equivalent of 50 percent of the total water used in the United Kingdom.[62]

METHODS FOR ASSESSING THE IMPACT OF THESE TOOLS ON LIBRARY SERVICES AND OPERATIONS

Any assessment of the impact of GAI tools on library services and operations is likely anecdotal at this point, as we have yet to see the full potential of how these technologies can be used. Likely, the clearest impact of GAI in this area can be found in instruction. As with past technologies, today's law students are expected to be fluent in the use of GAI when they enter the job market.

In reference, law librarians have already seen GAI citation hallucinations appearing in reference questions and law review cite checks. As students become more accustomed to the use of GAI, reference librarians must keep in mind that reference requests will likely already have been addressed to a GAI tool before coming to the reference desk. Additionally, public-serving reference librarians will likely see a rise in public patrons and pro se litigants who seek advice from GAI for legal research tools. These tools hold great potential for access to justice for many people, particularly considering that tools like ChatGPT are free, easily accessible, and allow users to search "conversationally" with or without the use of legal jargon. According to Sateesh Nori, who is testing GAI as a component of an eviction defense and tenant protection clinic at the New York University School of Law, the impact of GAI in clinics and bringing legal aid to underrepresented people has such huge potential that it "is like the invention of fire."[63]

In addition to the growing role GAI has, and will likely continue to have, in the ways that librarians, practitioners, students, pro se litigants, and public patrons learn about and interact with the law, it also stands to benefit law libraries in the streamlining of technical and administrative tasks. As discussed earlier in this chapter, one of the most promising and reliable areas of use of GAI is assisting in predictable or routine tasks. Technical services stand to benefit from LLMs and the ability to process, analyze, and track language usage in large datasets (including large library holdings). Tasks like drafting correspondence, scheduling, and employee training could be streamlined for library administrative staff through the adoption of GAI tools.

TECHNOLOGY IMPLEMENTATION AND INTEGRATION

Most library AI literature focuses on research and instruction. Other areas of the library may also see improved productivity and efficiencies with the use of GAI. Other tasks that GAI may assist with include the following:

- Administrative Tasks
  - Drafting job descriptions
  - Creating onboarding checklists
  - Creating tabletop simulations to work through emergency plans for situations like active shooters, natural disasters, or cyber breaches.
  - Developing employee training lists

    - Drafting policies and procedures
    - Answering questions about uploaded PDFs, such as policy manuals, open enrollment data, etc. (Can turn into a custom GPT for multiple users)
- Public Services
    - Creating presentations, including slides
    - Drafting scripts
    - Editing recordings
    - Converting written scripts to audio
    - Converting citations into specified format
    - Answering basic questions
    - Tutoring with custom GPTs
- Technical Services
    - Creating and correcting cataloging records
        - This is already occurring with CatalogerGPT,[64] a custom OpenAI GPT that can create MARC records from pasted data or links.
    - Answering questions about LMS tasks and processes
    - Subject Heading Selection
        - See OpenAI Custom GPT Subject Cataloger, which specializes in Library of Congress subject headings.[65]
    - Translating foreign language metadata
    - Creating material descriptions for LibGuides
- Department independent
    - Data entry and conversion
    - Creating training documentation
    - Learning new skills
    - Social media post creation, including text, images, and hashtags
    - Data analysis
    - Advertising materials and signage generation
    - Troubleshooting technology
    - Creating alt-text for images
    - Checking websites against web accessibility guidelines
    - Custom GPTs for topic of choice
    - Analyze and streamline workflows

The key to determining how AI may assist in the library is to look for digital pain points. For instance, perhaps you need to create order records for book orders. An AI system may be able to take your invoice from your purchases and convert the information into the format your accounting system requires. It may also be able to take the data from the invoice, look up the purchased items online, collect metadata about the purchases, and format the metadata into MARC record format. Some of these would require multiple steps, but the tasks are all basically pattern recognition and data collection and formatting tasks.

It may sound like a Herculean task to review a library's processes and procedures, but remember that you do not need to change everything at once and the task does not need to fall solely on one person. You may also find that trial and error will guide you in what tasks your particular library is ready for.

BEFORE YOU JUMP IN—INITIAL CONSIDERATIONS

While AI enthusiasm is a great thing, there are several considerations to think about before making the decision to use GAI in the library.

Existing Restrictions

Many companies restrict employees' access to GAI products. It was quickly discovered that without proper training, employees could easily misuse AI products and cause breaches of data and security. For instance, Samsung implemented a ban on mainstream GAI use in May 2023 after employees leaked internal source code to ChatGPT.[66] Before using a new GAI product, you should check to see if there are any existing internal restrictions on the technology.

If you do not have a policy in place already, your organization should consider adding a policy or guidelines to assist employees with how they can ethically and responsibly use GAI in their work. Different entities will have different needs. For instance, educational institutions in the United States must protect certain student records under the Family Educational Rights & Privacy Act (FERPA),[67] whereas a global law firm may need to protect information covered by the European Union's General Data Protection Regulation (GDPR).[68] Due to these varying needs, it is advisable to have a knowledgeable lawyer involved in the policy creation and approval process. There are many entities that offer advice and sample language on GAI policy drafting. Select a reputable source for your organization type, such as the Association of Research Libraries,[69] the International Federation of Library Associations and Institutions,[70] or a legal database with vetted policy recommendations, such as LexisNexis Practical Guidance's Artificial Intelligence (AI) Driven Tools in the Workplace Policy.[71]

Just as there may be restrictions on GAI product use within your company, there may be restrictions in your government or local industry. For instance, as of May 6, 2024, the National Archives and Records Administration (NARA) prohibits its employees from accessing ChatGPT on its network and NARA-issued devices due to security concerns.[72] The State of New Jersey issued guidance that establishes guardrails for state employees using GAI products, such as exploring different methods of prompting, fact-checking output, disclosing use in content, and avoiding the release of sensitive information.[73] In the legal field, many courts are issuing rules and standing orders regarding the use of GAI in court filings.[74]

Other businesses and governments may have already acquired access to GAI products that they have vetted and approved for employee use. As many companies already use Microsoft Office products, adding a Copilot subscription has been an easier decision than starting with a new company. Check with your IT department, which will likely know if there is a company/government-wide approved GAI product.

Questions to Ask

If you do not have restrictions or a previously approved GAI, there are several questions to ask before signing a contract:

1. Are there specific features that you need to accomplish the tasks you have?
2. Have you reviewed the terms of service for the products you are considering? Look at the clauses for
   a. confidentiality and privacy;
   b. input use;
   c. output use and ownership;
   d. similarity of outputs with others;
   e. copyrighted content; and
   f. abuse or other clauses that may call for your data to be held for a limited period to assure compliance with product use.
3. Have you run the contract past your internal legal counsel?
4. What is the projected cost of use?

a. Is it more cost-effective to build your own LLM? (A possibility for larger entities that create large amounts of content)
    i. Training
    ii. Hardware
    iii. Electricity/Utilities
    iv. Maintenance
    v. Support staff
b. Do you have the capacity to build a hybrid system that uses an existing model through an API that does not allow your data to be kept?
c. Is a subscription to a model cost-effective? If yes, are you able to afford a level with stronger privacy protections, such as enterprise levels?

5. Who will be responsible for creating the curriculum and training users?

When you have the answers to these questions, you should be able to move forward with selecting the right GAI model for your library.

HOW TO APPROACH TEACHING GAI

While teaching GAI to law students, it is helpful to start by positioning GAI tools in the wider context of how law students complete their research and legal tasks. Generally, GAI is useful to law students to help them think, not think for them. GAI can be a useful tool, while the student or attorney remains in a position of control.

We cannot deny that GAI will change the way we perform legal research and work in law. We must now function under the understanding that both clients, as well as law students, are putting their legal queries into GAI tools before consulting other resources—a far cry from the traditional method of legal research that involved licensing, huge paywalls, or hours of research in a local law library.

For example, the Law Practice Technologies course at UNC School of Law is designed to prepare students to work effectively in law post-graduation. Historically, this and other courses like it have included instruction on Word styles, eDiscovery software, and document automation. Now, GAI plays a prominent role in these courses. New graduates are often expected to be fluent in GAI. As a legal technology professor, this author has been approached by a local practitioner specifically looking to hire an "AI attorney" to address the AI needs of the firm, including identifying areas of improvement and implementing GAI workflows to enhance the firm's productivity and accuracy. Law students are often eager to learn how to ethically and efficiently use GAI, and the ability to use GAI tools is becoming an increasingly marketable skill.

With law schools creating rules for students on the use of GAI (often limiting the use of GAI by students) in their academic work, it is important for students to have the opportunity to use GAI tools while in school and receive training on prompt generation. Specifically, it is important for law students to learn their ethical obligations in relation to GAI so that they are equipped to address when the use of AI will be appropriate and allowed, in their future practice.

More and more law schools across the country are adopting policies on GAI, further impacting the ways that students are limited or encouraged in their use of GAI. An overarching theme of these policies is a prohibition on the use of GAI on papers and exams.[75] Many of these policies also provide authority to instructors to dictate the use of GAI in their classes—including parameters on documenting use of GAI in permissible uses.[76] Additionally, some law schools have adopted policies regarding admission essays—the University of Michigan School of Law has asked that prospective students not use GAI in any part of their application drafting process, while Arizona State's Sandra Day O'Connor College of Law explicitly permits the use of GAI in the application process.[77]

TALES FROM THE TRENCHES

This technology is still new enough that there are no written case studies on library implementation of GAI. Several tactics of note have been mentioned at conferences and in conversations that may be helpful when planning an implementation.

One large firm library has adopted a method used by HR and IT for compliance training. The firm library has created a one-hour training program on their AI legal research tools. Anyone, partners included, who has not completed the training program by the set date will lose access to the GAI tools and will be unable to access them again until the training is completed. Firms and entities with the ability to turn off access to portions of their research systems by person may make good use of this tactic. Academic accounts do not generally have the same administrative tools for individual access, so other methods will need to be employed.

The same large firm has relayed that some clients will not allow the use of AI on their cases. Unfortunately, the research systems are currently unable to limit AI access by client, only by user. The firm library is utilizing a tool called Research Monitor. This tool tracks and analyzes research subscription usage and allows for pop-up messages, such as reminders to check if the client allows AI tools to be used on their matters. While not the perfect solution, it does allow the firm to keep track of the research and potentially redirect forgetful attorneys and summer associates to the correct tools for the client.

The Library of Congress has been experimenting with traditional artificial intelligence and machine learning for years, creating the Library of Congress (LC) Labs program in 2016. In 2023, LC Labs released its Artificial Intelligence Planning Framework[78] that advocates for three phases: (1) understand, (2) experiment, and (3) implement. Each of these phases looks at the elements of data, models, and people. The full framework, with worksheets and other helpful tools, is available in the LC Labs AI Planning GitHub Repository.[79] Perhaps the most important lesson to take from the LC Labs project is that implementation should not be rushed. It is the end stage, not the beginning, and it takes careful planning and testing.

Law schools and their libraries are still finding their way in implementation. Many teachers were concerned about academic integrity with GAI, and many schools reacted by putting restrictions on GAI use, such as honor code violations. Others left it to the individual professor to decide whether and how GAI should be used. With the release of Lexis+ AI and Practical Law AI in the spring of 2024, law schools can no longer delay dealing with the issue. Many librarians have stepped up to train law students in legal research and legal technology courses or in non-credit-bearing sessions.

HOW TO USE GAI

There are major differences in using GAI to address legal versus non-legal questions, which must be considered when addressing how to write efficient prompts. When using GAI for legal purposes, the prompt writer must answer certain questions (like jurisdiction) before writing a prompt—answering these questions can often require advanced legal knowledge. Providing education on prompt writing is a new form of the classic legal writing classes.

Generally, when writing a GAI prompt, there are a number of areas to address in the prompt in order to yield a meaningful, helpful result. For more information and a fillable worksheet to use while crafting a prompt, you can visit https://law-capital.libguides.com/Jennys_AI_Resources/AI_Prompt_Worksheets.

Below are areas to address when crafting a prompt:

Tone—It is helpful to tell GAI exactly who the intended recipient of the output should be, the more specific the better. Tell GAI if the output should be written formally, professionally, informally, for attorneys, for a law school class, or for a 6th grade class.

Role—Provide a persona for GAI to play to help it understand how to present information—like a prosecutor, defense attorney, professor, first-year associate, client, or judge.

Output—Tell GAI exactly what you would like the final product to look like. Tell GAI if you would like a letter, email, outline, presentation, or table.

Purpose—Why are you asking this? Let GAI know if you are providing background to a client, trying to convince a client to hire your firm, etc.

Issue—What do you want included in the output? Give as much information as possible!

Refinement—How can you provide more information to get a better-tailored result? Do not be afraid to provide follow-ups to your prompt to yield an optimal result.

In addition to these general guidelines, there are other things to keep in mind while creating prompts that could impact the output you receive. Microsoft has released guidance saying that using a polite tone in creating your prompt yields different (often better) results.[80] In one prompt writing study, it was found that a GAI model was better at answering math problems when it was told to approach the problem as if it were a computer on *Star Trek*.[81]

It is recommended that law students use a research log for documenting the use of GAI that abides by University and Court rules on documenting any use of GAI. Suggested column titles to use in this log are: Purpose (purpose of using the GAI tool/research question presented/etc.), GAI Tool (the name of the actual tool used), Prompts or Queries (the questions presented to the tool, tracking also helps us get better at constructing and identifying prompts yielded helpful or unhelpful results), Uses of the Output (how the answer given by the GAI tool was used by the researcher), and Conversation Link (a place to put the link to the conversation itself).

DEEP DIVE: HANDLING HALLUCINATIONS AND MISINFORMATION

According to *Merriam-Webster*, a hallucination is "a plausibly but false or misleading response generated by an artificial intelligence algorithm." The word hallucination made it out of medical and drug cases into the mainstream legal language after the attorneys representing Roberto Mata in the case of *Mata v. Avianca. Inc.* submitted a brief with cases that neither opposing counsel nor the judge could locate, discussed earlier in this chapter. This case would likely not have made the stir that it did, but for three things: (1) ChatGPT had been released to the public only a few months before the attorneys exercised poor judgment in its use, (2) the attorneys doubled down and had ChatGPT generate the missing cases, providing these fake "judicial opinions" to the judge, and (3) the media, including the *New York Times*, took note and news stories began popping up at an alarming rate.

In 2023, we began to see legal companies integrating GAI into their products. And shortly thereafter, we began seeing marketing campaigns claiming that outputs from these products were "hallucination-free." Unfortunately, these claims were embellished. Due to the reliance on probability and poor-quality and outdated data, GAI LLMs are incapable of being hallucination-free. Hallucinations may arise in multiple ways, including misinformation in the training data, bias in the training data or algorithm, outdated information, or AI architectural issues that affect the training data or learning process.

In law and libraries, citation hallucinations have become more common. *Mata v. Avianca, Inc.* included six incorrect citations from ChatGPT. In another instance, Professor Paul McGreal posted on social media platform X in February 2024 about Lexis+ AI returning case citations from 2025 and 2026. When looking at the case names provided, such as "Doe v. State University (2025)" and "Smith v. City of Chicago (2026)," one can almost see the LLM using a statistical analysis to generate case names to answer the question "What cases have applied Students for Fair Admissions, Inc. v Harvard College to the use of race in government decision making?" The Lexis+ AI response was to state that the product was being adjusted and any citations that were not hyperlinked likely indicate a hallucinated case.

Anecdotally, librarians across the country are seeing an influx of patrons looking for materials by citations only to discover that they do not exist. Some of these citations are coming from faculty or students who have directly used the AI product without realizing that it can hallucinate. Others are being given the citations by a third party who insists the cited document exists. One common time this third-party provision appears is during journal citation checks when reviewers are attempting to verify the existence and authenticity of the cited material.

In addition to nonexistent information, some hallucinations are rooted in existing material. Potential causes of this type of hallucination include an incorrect interpretation of the cited material, use of material from the wrong jurisdiction, or old information that is no longer accurate. The latter may be particularly predisposed to hallucination when there is a long history of use of the old law and a relatively recent change, due to the frequency of use and the statistical nature of an LLM. When an appeal landed in the Second Circuit Court of Appeals where the plaintiff's attorney had used ChatGPT to identify a case after a fruitless traditional legal research process failed to locate one, the Court was unimpressed. The Court determined "[a]t the very least, the duties imposed by Rule 11 require that attorneys read, and thereby confirm the existence and validity of, the legal authorities on which they rely." This includes verifying the interpretation of the case law and the currentness of the law.

On June 4, 2024, a team of Stanford researchers released an updated study on the reliability of AI legal research tools. This study asked 200 legal questions of three legal research and one mainstream AI product. The researchers then reviewed the answers based on correctness and groundedness, which looked at whether the output propositions were relevant and a correct interpretation of the law. The researchers reported hallucination rates ranging from 17 percent to 43 percent. While there are obvious benefits to the accuracy of some systems over others, even a 17 percent hallucination rate gives one pause considering the effects that these inaccuracies may have on a client's case and life. All of the legal GAI products far exceed the mainstream non-legal products, however. For instance, as mentioned above, a different study found that the mainstream tools hallucinated at a 75 percent rate when queried about judicial opinions.[82]

While the rates seem high, it is worth pointing out that the study used the same questions for all systems, regardless of the information available to the GAI product. For instance, one of the products questioned was Westlaw's Practical Law AI, which focuses on materials from Practical Law. Practical Law is a conglomeration of secondary source materials, such as checklists, practice notes, and other practitioner-oriented materials regarding a narrow range of legal topics, with an emphasis on business law and related issues. The database contains no case law and does not cover the topics of constitutional law or family law. Yet, the practitioners claimed that a poor result from this database regarding a question on the dissent in the same-sex marriage case *Obergefell v. Hodges* is a hallucination. This author disputes this label of hallucination but would rather label it the result of a poor prompt that did not consider what information the AI product has available to use in its answer.

All of the legal research GAI products are also using other methods of mitigating, but not fully eliminating, the hallucinations. For instance, all of the products are using RAG with different legal information products being included in the products' RAG. For instance, Practical Law is mostly a secondary source, whereas Lexis+ AI includes federal and state case law, statutes, constitutions, regulations, some administrative opinions, and Matthew Bender treatises.

HOW TO TACKLE RESEARCH GENERATED BY GAI PRODUCTS

There are several approaches that researchers should consider when using GAI.

First, researchers should know the product and its underlying data before undertaking research. If the information is not included in the RAG or training data, at best the researcher is going to be frustrated by a lack of results. At worst, the researcher is going to get inaccurate or misinterpreted results from a system that is very confident in its answers. This confidence can be hard to shake the

AI out of. For instance, this author once asked ChatGPT about a legal issue that resulted in the system citing a hallucinated case. After nine interactions, where the author kept insisting that the case did not exist, ChatGPT once again verified the case's existence and told the author to consult an attorney or a law librarian or look the case up in a research system such as Westlaw or Lexis. It was not until the author verified that she met all of these qualifications and had looked it up in both recommended research systems with no results that ChatGPT admitted its mistake.

Part of knowing your system is also knowing its prompt limitations. Is there a character limit on input or output? Are there a limited number of follow-up interactions? Does the system use a guided prompt, an open prompt without restrictions on the entry method, or a hybrid? Are there limitations on how many jurisdictions you may search at once? Will the output generate a downloadable file? If yes, what types of files? And similar questions.

Second, if your use of the GAI output has high stakes, you need to verify all information. For instance, any information used with legal clients should be vetted for accuracy and interpretation before use, as recommended by *Park v. Kim*. Lower-stakes activities, such as trivia games, may not carry the same imperative to verify the information.

Next, ethical considerations that librarians should consider include those discussed earlier in this chapter: patron privacy, academic integrity, the bias of AI detectors, and moral issues such as the methods of reducing bias in training models and the climate impact.

Fourth, the American Library Association first affirmed a patron's right to privacy in 1939. This right extends to all library patrons, regardless of the library type. Before entering confidential or proprietary information into a GAI system, the librarian should know the contract terms regarding privacy and confidentiality clauses as well as vendor and product uses and ownership of user inputs and outputs.

Fifth, academic librarians and professors have likely heard an "end of the world" scenario regarding students cheating using GAI and never turning in their own work product again, thus causing the dumbing down of society. It is true that some students cheat, and some cheaters use GAI products. However, the Turnitin AI detection software reports that of 200 million reviewed papers in the last year, 10 percent contained some evidence of AI use, but only 3 percent "were generated mostly by AI."

AI detectors themselves raise potential issues as well. Research shows that these systems can carry a bias against English language learners and neurodiverse individuals, causing a high rate of false positives. Due to this research and some anecdotes, such as the Texas A&M University professor who failed his entire class for AI use based on false reports, many people have called for a ban on the technology outright. Others have called for responsible faculty use where the technology is not determinative but only a tool that flags language for human review.

Finally, GAI is here to stay. The technology is already being integrated into standard business platforms like Microsoft Office and Google Workplace. Individuals who refuse to use the technology are likely to be surpassed in their careers by those who are willing to ethically and responsibly embrace the technology.

EDUCATING YOURSELF ON GAI

There are many ways to learn about GAI and how to use it. If you learn best by practicing, you may benefit from a class. Many entities are offering classes, both for-credit and non-credit bearing. These classes teach you the basics and then give you the opportunity to test the products out in a controlled, supervised manner.

If you are a self-learner, there are plenty of materials to teach yourself how to use the technology, from short tutorials to massive treatises. You may also want to take advantage of online materials, such as LibGuides or LinkedIn Learning coursework. For the adventurous, you can even ask ChatGPT to create a curriculum for you, including exercises.

CONCLUSION AND LOOKING AHEAD

GAI has rapidly expanded and improved in less than two years since its release to the public. This trajectory does not appear to be slowing down anytime soon, and law libraries need to prepare and take advantage of some of the new opportunities. The technology is going to be integrated into more and more applications. For example, as the first draft of this chapter was being finalized, Ex Libris announced a new AI feature in its discovery layer product, Primo. Expansion is planned for other vendors as well. While the authors do not envision GAI replacing law librarians, those who are comfortable using the technology may replace those who refuse to do so.

We are not new to the sort of crossroads in technology that we see today. In 1999, LexisNexis announced the online version of Shepard's Citation Service,[83] and the print was quickly abandoned by most. Not many librarians will argue that online citators were a bad advancement. GAI has the potential to be a similar game-changing technology. Perhaps rather than fear or be intimidated by this change, we should party like it's 1999 while stepping into a new era.

NOTES

1. U.S. District Court for the Eastern District of Pennsylvania, *Standing Order Re: Artificial Intelligence ("AI") in Cases Assigned to Judge Baylson*, June 6, 2023, https://www.paed.uscourts.gov/sites/paed/files/documents/procedures/Standing%2520Order%2520Re%2520Artificial%2520Intelligence%25206.6.pdf.
2. "AI-Powered Legal Research: Where Legal Research Meets Generative AI," *Thomson Reuters Law Blog*, December 1, 2023, https://legal.thomsonreuters.com/blog/legal-research-meets-generative-ai/.
3. Joe Regalia, "ChatGPT and Legal Writing: The Perfect Union?" *Write.law*, accessed June 17, 2024, https://write.law/blog/chatgpt-and-legal-writing-the-perfect-union.
4. Regalia, "ChatGPT and Legal Writing."
5. According to TheresAnAIForThat.com, which tracks active AI products, as of June 23, 2024, the website was tracking 12,892 AIs. TheresAnAIForThat.com, accessed June 23, 2024, https://theresanaiforthat.com/.
6. See example, Young Sam Cho, "From Code to Cure: Unleashing the Power of Generative Artificial Intelligence in Medicine," *International Neurourology Journal* 27, no. 4 (December 2023): 225-226, https://doi.org/10.5213/inj.2323edi06.
7. Stefan Baack, "A Critical Analysis of the Largest Source for Generative AI Training Data: Common Crawl," in *FAccT '24: Proceedings of the 2024 ACM Conference on Fairness, Accountability, and Transparency*, June 2024, pp. 2199–2208, https://doi.org/10.1145/3630106.3659033.
8. Common Crawl, accessed June 23, 2024, https://commoncrawl.org/.
9. Baack, "A Critical Analysis."
10. Kevin Schaul, Szu Yu Chen, and Nitasha Tiku, "Inside the Secret List of Websites That Make AI Like ChatGPT Sound Smart," *Washington Post*, April 19, 2023, https://www.washingtonpost.com/technology/interactive/2023/ai-chatbot-learning/.
11. Julia Angwin, Jeff Larson, Surya Mattu, and Lauren Kirchner, "Machine Bias," *ProPublica*, May 23, 2016, https://www.propublica.org/article/machine-bias-risk-assessments-in-criminal-sentencing.
12. Stanford University Human Centered Artificial Intelligence, "Artificial Intelligence Index Report 2024," 64, https://aiindex.stanford.edu/wp-content/uploads/2024/04/HAI_AI-Index-Report-2024.pdf.
13. OpenAI, "GPT-4," March 14, 2023, https://openai.com/index/gpt-4-research/.
14. Microsoft Learn, "Understanding LLMs," May 9, 2024, https://learn.microsoft.com/en-us/ai/playbook/technology-guidance/generative-ai/getting-started/use-case-recommend.
15. Perplexity, "What is Perplexity Pro?" accessed June 23, 2024, https://www.perplexity.ai/hub/faq/what-is-perplexity-pro.

16. Perplexity, "How Does Perplexity Work?" accessed June 23, 2024, https://www.perplexity.ai/hub/faq/how-does-perplexity-work.
17. Coursera Staff, "CHATGPT-3.5 vs. 4: What's the Difference?" *Coursera,* accessed June 17, 2024, https://www.coursera.org/articles/chat-gpt-3-vs-4.
18. Coursera Staff, "CHATGPT-3.5 vs. 4"
19. OpenAI, "Introducing GPT-4O and More Tools to ChatGPT Free Users," accessed June 17, 2024, https://openai.com/index/gpt-4o-and-more-tools-to-chatgpt-free/.
20. Eric Martínez, "Re-Evaluating GPT-4's Bar Exam Performance," *Artificial Intelligence and Law*, March 30, 2024, https://doi.org/10.1007/s10506-024-09396-9.
21. "Cocounsel," *Casetext*, December 22, 2023, https://casetext.com/.
22. Relativity, "Relativity Announces Expansions to Relativity Air Its Suite of Generative AI Solutions at Legalweek 2024," *PR Newswire*, January 29, 2024, https://www.prnewswire.com/news-releases/relativity-announces-expansions-to-relativity-air-its-suite-of-generative-ai-solutions-at-legalweek-2024-302046049.html.
23. "Cecilia AI," *DISCO's Generative AI-Powered Legal Solutions,* accessed June 17, 2024, https://csdisco.com/offerings/cecilia.
24. LexisNexis, "Lexis+ Ai: Ai Legal Assistant by LexisNexis," *Lexis+ AI | AI Legal Assistant by LexisNexis,* accessed June 17, 2024, https://www.lexisnexis.com/en-us/products/lexis-plus-ai.page.
25. Thomson Reuters, "Westlaw Precision Now Has Generative AI," *Thomson Reuters,* accessed June 22, 2024, https://legal.thomsonreuters.com/en/c/westlaw/westlaw-precision-now-with-generative-ai.
26. Kristin Delaney, "Introducing Ask Practical Law AI on Practical Law: Generative AI Meets Legal How-to," *Thomson Reuters Law Blog*, January 24, 2024, https://legal.thomsonreuters.com/blog/legal-how-to-meets-generative-ai/.
27. "Work Smarter with Ai Legal Assistants," *LawDroid*, June 14, 2024, https://lawdroid.com/.
28. "Generative AI for Professional Services," Harvey, accessed June 17, 2024, https://www.harvey.ai/.
29. Jan Hatzius, Joseph Briggs, Devesh Kodnani, and Griovanni Pierdomenico, "The Potentially Large Effects of Artificial Intelligence on Economic Growth," *Global Economics Analyst*, March 25, 2023, https://www.gspublishing.com/content/research/en/reports/2023/03/27/d64e052b-0f6e-45d7-967b-d7be35fabd16.html.
30. Ziwei Xu, Sanjay Jain, and Mohan Kankanhalli, "Hallucination Is Inevitable: An Innate Limitation of Large Language Models," *arXiv.org*, January 22, 2024, https://arxiv.org/abs/2401.11817.
31. Varun Magesh, Faiz Surani, Matthew Dahl, Mirac Suzgun, Christopher D. Manning, and Daniel E. Ho, "Hallucination-Free? Assessing the Reliability of Leading AI Legal Research Tools," May 30, 2024, https://dho.stanford.edu/wp-content/uploads/Legal_RAG_Hallucinations.pdf.
32. Matthew Dahl, Varun Magesh, Mirac Suzgun, and Daniel E. Ho, "Hallucinating Law: Legal Mistakes with Large Language Models Are Pervasive," *Law Regulation and Policy*, January 11, 2024, https://hai.stanford.edu/news/hallucinating-law-legal-mistakes-large-language-models-are-pervasive.
33. *Mata v. Avianca, Inc.* (United States District Court Southern District of New York June 22, 2023) No. 1:2022cv01461 - Document 54.
34. Benjamin Weiser, "Here's What Happens When Your Lawyer Uses ChatGPT," *The New York Times*, May 27, 2023, https://www.nytimes.com/2023/05/27/nyregion/avianca-airline-lawsuit-chatgpt.html.
35. Weiser, "Here's What Happens When Your Lawyer Uses ChatGPT."
36. Ramishah Maruf, "Lawyer Apologizes for Fake Court Citations from ChatGPT," *CNN Business,* May 28, 2023, https://www.cnn.com/2023/05/27/business/chat-gpt-avianca-mata-lawyers/index.html.
37. Aaron Mok, "A Stressed Out Rookie Lawyer Says He Got Fired after He Used ChatGPT to Do His Job," *Business Insider,* accessed June 17, 2024, https://www.businessinsider.com/young-lawyer-fired-using-chatgpt-job-work-hallucinations-errors-2023-11.
38. Rudi Keller, "Missouri Appeals Court Fines Litigant after Finding Fake AI-Generated Cases Cited in Filings," *Missouri Independent*, February 13, 2024, https://missouriindependent.com/2024/02/13/missouri-appeals-court-fines-litigant-after-finding-fake-ai-generated-cases-cited-in-filings.
39. Keller, "Missouri Appeals Court Fines Litigant after Finding Fake AI-Generated Cases."
40. Keller, "Missouri Appeals Court Fines Litigant after Finding Fake AI-Generated Cases."

41. "Rule 3.3: Candor Toward the Tribunal" in Center for Professional Responsibility (American Bar Association). 2013. "Model Rules of Professional Conduct." https://www.americanbar.org/groups/professional_responsibility/publications/model_rules_of_professional_conduct/.
42. *Park v. Kim*, No. 22-2057 (2d Cir. 2024).
43. "Rule 1.6: Confidentiality of Information" in Center for Professional Responsibility (American Bar Association), 2013. "Model Rules of Professional Conduct." https://www.americanbar.org/groups/professional_responsibility/publications/model_rules_of_professional_conduct/.
44. "Rules 5.3: Responsibilities Regarding Nonlawyer Assistance and 5.5: Unauthorized Practice of Law" in Center for Professional Responsibility (American Bar Association), 2013. "Model Rules of Professional Conduct." https://www.americanbar.org/groups/professional_responsibility/publications/model_rules_of_professional_conduct/.
45. "Save Time and Money with Donotpay!" *DoNotPay*, accessed June 17, 2024, https://donotpay.com/.
46. Sara Merken, "Legal AI Startup Donotpay Reaches Settlement in Customer Class Action," *Reuters*, June 6, 2024, https://www.reuters.com/legal/legalindustry/legal-ai-startup-donotpay-reaches-settlement-customer-class-action-2024-06-06.
47. "Unauthorized Practice of Law," *Eisner Gorin LLP*, accessed June 17, 2024, https://www.egattorneys.com/unauthorized-practice-of-law-bpc-6125.
48. Merken, "Legal AI Startup Donotpay Reaches Settlement in Customer Class Action."
49. AI.Law, "Legal AI Like Nothing Else on the Market." *AI.Law*, June 8, 2024, https://www.ai.law/.
50. Michael M. Grynbaum and Ryan Mac, "The Times Sues OpenAI and Microsoft over AI Use of Copyrighted Work," *The New York Times*, December 27, 2023, https://www.nytimes.com/2023/12/27/business/media/new-york-times-open-ai-microsoft-lawsuit.html.
51. William Morriss, "Who Owns AI Created Content? The Surprising Answer and What to Do about It," *Reuters*, December 14, 2023, https://www.reuters.com/legal/legalindustry/who-owns-ai-created-content-surprising-answer-what-do-about-it-2023-12-14/.
52. Debra Cassens Weiss, "Use of ChatGPT to Support Fee Bid Is 'Utterly and Unusually Unpersuasive' Federal Judge Says," *ABA Journal*, February 27, 2024, https://www.abajournal.com/news/article/use-of-chatgpt-to-support-fee-bid-is-utterly-and-unusually-unpersuasive-federal-judge-says#google_vignette.
53. Billy Perrigo, "OpenAI Used Kenyan Workers on Less than $2 per Hour: Exclusive," *Time*, January 18, 2023, https://time.com/6247678/openai-chatgpt-kenya-workers/.
54. Perrigo, "OpenAI Used Kenyan Workers on Less than $2 per Hour."
55. Manasi Vartak, "Responsible AI Explained," *Built In*, May 18, 2023, https://builtin.com/artificial-intelligence/responsible-ai.
56. James Vincent, "How Much Electricity Does AI Consume?," *The Verge*, February 16, 2024, https://www.theverge.com/24066646/ai-electricity-energy-watts-generative-consumption.
57. Vincent, "How Much Electricity Does AI Consume?"
58. Lauren Leffer, "The AI Boom Could Use a Shocking Amount of Electricity," *Scientific American*, October 13, 2023, https://www.scientificamerican.com/article/the-ai-boom-could-use-a-shocking-amount-of-electricity/.
59. Kate Crawford, "Generative AI's Environmental Costs Are Soaring - and Mostly Secret," *Nature News*, February 20, 2024, https://www.nature.com/articles/d41586-024-00478-x.
60. Crawford, "Generative AI's Environmental Costs Are Soaring - and Mostly Secret."
61. Matt O'Brien and Hannah Fingerhut, "Artificial Intelligence Technology behind ChatGPT Was Built in Iowa - With a Lot of Water," *AP News*, September 9, 2023, https://apnews.com/article/chatgpt-gpt4-iowa-ai-water-consumption-microsoft-f551fde98083d17a7e8d904f8be822c4.
62. Crawford, "Generative AI's Environmental Costs Are Soaring - and Mostly Secret."
63. -Marco Poggio, "Gen AI Shows Promise - and Peril - for Pro Se Litigants," *Law360*, May 3, 2024, https://www.law360.com/articles/1812918/gen-ai-shows-promise-and-peril-for-pro-se-litigants.
64. CatalogerGPT, accessed June 17, 2024, https://chatgpt.com/g/g-8ymg1Ftwo-catalogergpt.
65. Subject Cataloger, accessed June 17, 2024, https://chatgpt.com/g/g-Eg4pSebTH-subject-cataloger.

66. Sawdah Bhaimiya, "Samsung Bans Employees from Using AI Tools like ChatGPT and Google Bard after an Accidental Data Leak Report Says," *Business Insider*, May 2, 2023, https://www.businessinsider.com/samsung-chatgpt-bard-data-leak-bans-employee-use-report-2023-5.
67. Family Educational Rights & Privacy Act, 20 U.S.C. § 1232g.
68. General Data Protection Regulation, Regulation (EU) 2016/679.
69. "Research Libraries Guiding Principles for Artificial Intelligence," Association of Research Libraries, April 2024, https://doi.org/10.29242/principles.ai2024.
70. "Generative AI for Library and Information Professionals," International Federation of Library Associations and Institutions Artificial Intelligence Special Interest Group, April 1, 2024, https://www.ifla.org/g/ai/generative-ai/.
71. LexisNexis Practical Guidance, 2023. *Policy on AI Use*. LexisNexis Practical Guidance. https://www.lexisnexis.com/pdf/practical-guidance/ai/pgexpert-annotated-form-ai-driven-tools-in-the-workplace.pdf]
72. Keith Day, "ChatGPT Blocked for NARA Usage," *National Archives Employee Communications*, May 1, 2024, https://www.archives.gov/files/foia/2024.05.01-nara-employee-communications-blocking-chatgpt.docx.pdf.
73. State of New Jersey, "Interim Guidance on Responsible Use of Generative AI," 2023, https://www.nj.gov/circulars/23-oit-007.pdf.
74. Responsible AI in Legal Services, "AI Use in Courts Tracker," April 3, 2024, https://airtable.com/appKUCriCQDI1BxIV/shrflAPpNKaNMnacR/tblNmp6mff8CzLuQD.
75. See example: Joseph Landau, "School of Law Memorandum on Academic Integrity," *Fordham University*, accessed June 25, 2024, https://www.fordham.edu/school-of-law/life-at-fordham-law/student-life/office-of-student-affairs/conduct-and-grievance-policy/academic-integrity/; Provost & Chief Academic Officer, "Student Generative AI Usage Guidance," *UNC Chapel Hill*, February 13, 2024, https://provost.unc.edu/student-generative-ai-usage-guidance/; "Generative AI Resources," *Berkeley Law Library*, last updated June 24, 2024, https://www.law.berkeley.edu/library/legal-research/chatgpt/; University of Washington School of Law, "Honor Code" *UW School of Law – Academic Policies*, accessed June 25, 2024, https://www.law.washington.edu/students/academics/honorcode.aspx; "Honor Code and Procedure for Law Students," *Washburn University School of Law*, accessed June 25, 2024, https://www.washburnlaw.edu/policies/honorcode.html.
76. See example: "4.9 Law School Policy on Generative AI," *University of Chicago Law School*, November 8, 2023, https://www.law.uchicago.edu/students/handbook/academicmatters/generative-ai; Provost & Chief Academic Officer, "Student Generative AI Usage Guidance," *UNC Chapel Hill*, February 13, 2024, https://provost.unc.edu/student-generative-ai-usage-guidance/.
77. "ASU Law to Permit Use of Generative AI in Applications," *ASU*, July 27, 2023, https://law.asu.edu/newsroom/asu-law-permit-use-generative-ai-applications; "Apply to the JD Program," *University of Michigan Law School*, accessed June 25, 2024, https://michigan.law.umich.edu/admissions/apply-jd-program#.
78. Abigail Potter, "Introducing the LC Labs Artificial Intelligence Planning Framework," *The Signal*, November 15, 2023, https://blogs.loc.gov/thesignal/2023/11/introducing-the-lc-labs-artificial-intelligence-planning-framework/.
79. GitHub, "Library of Congress AI Framework," accessed June 17, 2024, https://github.com/LibraryOfCongress/labs-ai-framework/tree/main.
80. "Why Using a Polite Tone with AI Matters," *Microsoft*, accessed June 17, 2024, https://www.microsoft.com/en-us/worklab/why-using-a-polite-tone-with-ai-matters.
81. Rick Battle and Teja Gollapudi, "The Unreasonable Effectiveness of Eccentric Automatic Prompts," *arXiv.org*, February 20, 2024, https://arxiv.org/abs/2402.10949.
82. Dahl, Magesh, Suzgun, and Ho, "Hallucinating Law."
83. Robyn Rebollo, "One More Look at Shepard's Citation Service: A Private Law Librarian's Perspective," *LLRX.com*, September 1, 1999, https://web.archive.org/web/20160321204657/http://www.llrx.com/features/shepards.htm.

17

AI-Driven Competitive Intelligence

Jim Currie, Josh Farley, and Victoria Swindle

A panicked and apologetic business development manager is on the line. She just found out that a top partner in her practice has a meeting with a promising prospect tomorrow and needs a briefing. However, you calmly reassure her that you will have a report for her by the end of the day. You are confident in your team's ability to deliver incisive and actionable intelligence to help win new business. Your group is leaner than you'd like (of course it is!), but you've got instantaneous access to vast stores of information, a defined and flexible process, and cutting-edge tools to magnify your team's capabilities.

The above represents a typical moment in the life of a competitive intelligence (CI) practitioner at a law firm. CI takes the challenges facing organizations—a highly competitive environment, fragmented markets, industry consolidations, and internal cost pressures—and treats them as its subject matter.

What do CI practitioners do? They aggregate, summarize, and emphasize information to help stakeholders understand the current situation and potential opportunities. They also interpret data and draw meaningful conclusions.

While some may see their primary role as that of a facts reporter, CI practitioners recognize their role in driving competitive advantage for their organization. CI can increase library visibility and organizational impact by further positioning librarians as trusted advisors. And what was once a highly labor-intensive process is now more achievable than ever, thanks to widely available artificial intelligence (AI) tools.

IN THE BEGINNING . . .

In 1966, Bill Fair of Fair, Isaac and Company, Inc., now known as Fair Isaac Corporation (FICO), predicted "that within five years the gathering of intelligence as currently practiced by governments in both military and diplomatic affairs [would] become a formal, recognized activity in corporate management." Fair referred to these intelligence-gathering units within private corporations as the "Corporate CIA."[1] Today, members of these intelligence-gathering units are known as CI practitioners, and their employment is not limited to companies and law firms, as CI may also be practiced in academic and government settings. Among Fair's reasons for predicting the genesis of the "Corporate CIA" were evolutions in technology, which included "the development of computers" and their "capacity to store and retrieve information at a far lower cost than heretofore possible."[2] As new advances in technology during the mid- to late-twentieth century contributed to the creation of CI as a discipline, the recent emergence of widely available large language models (LLMs) represents the next technological evolution in CI.

WHAT IS COMPETITIVE INTELLIGENCE?

Competitive Intelligence is information gathered and analyzed by an organization to gain a competitive advantage. CI can be further broken down into two broad categories: *tactical intelligence* and *strategic intelligence*. *Tactical intelligence* is gathered and analyzed to assist with short-term opportunities and initiatives, such as responding to a Request for Proposal (RFP), a formal document used to solicit bids from service providers, or preparing for a meeting with a prospective client. *Strategic intelligence* is aimed at the long term and includes activities such as horizon scanning or determining the number of existing clients in a region where an organization is considering opening a new office. Good CI functions incorporate both tactical and strategic intelligence into their workflow and tailor their work product to fit the needs of their stakeholders.[3]

WORK PRODUCT

The work product produced by CI functions operating in legal services organizations can be broadly grouped into three categories. The first, often making up the largest share of CI work product, is *existing and prospective client research*. Research on existing and prospective clients can include company reports (also known as company dossiers or taxicab reports), the location of their global or regional operations, and your company's historical relationship with the client. The second category, *competitor research*, includes research on topics such as the location of competitor operations, their service offerings, and their go-to-market strategy. Often, existing and prospective client research is used hand-in-hand with competitor research when formulating a plan of attack for winning new business. Organizations need to see where they can differentiate their client offerings from those of their competitors. The third category, *industry and other macro trends*, may include recent trends in a legal practice area, trends within a client's industry, or broader market trends.

Focus on Driving Revenue and Profitability

Understanding market trends, customer preferences, and competitive dynamics better equips organizations to make decisions that will lead to increased business and market share. By providing insight into cost efficiencies related to resource allocation and risk management, which will further support decisions benefiting the financial health of an organization, CI functions help drive revenue and profitability, increasing the company's competitive advantage.

THE COMPETITIVE INTELLIGENCE PROCESS

Understanding what CI is, it is also necessary to understand the CI process. CI functions with an established process allow the quality and credibility of their research to be repeatable. In their 2023 review of CI literature, Maungwa and Laughton proposed a six-phase competitive intelligence process.[4] For the purposes of this chapter, the CI process should be understood to encapsulate these six phases: Phase 1: Articulating and Defining, Phase 2: Information Resource Gathering, Phase 3: Information Processing and Collation, Phase 4: Analysis, Phase 5: Reporting, Phase 6: Feedback and Evaluation.

Phase 1: Articulating and Defining

CI professionals work with attorneys, business development colleagues, and other stakeholders to identify their specific needs. This might involve understanding client pain points, competitor strengths, pricing strategies, pulling cases, evidence, and so on. In this phase, they would ask questions like, "What information is needed?" "How do our services align with the client's needs?" and "Who are the competitors to securing work in this area?" Define the relevant competitors in the legal market, considering practice areas, firm size, and geography.

Phase 2: Information Resource Gathering

CI professionals begin by brainstorming relevant keywords and phrases related to the client or competitor, their practice areas, and potential areas of interest. They consider synonyms, legal terminology, and industry-specific jargon to ensure comprehensive coverage by starting with a broad search and gradually refining it based on initial results. Relevant terms are used in retrieved documents to develop the search strategy further. Search terms and strategies are tracked for future reference and to share with colleagues. Legal subscription research databases like LexisNexis, Westlaw, Bloomberg Law, TLO, and so on, provide access to court cases, legal precedents, previous legal service providers, and regulatory filings, offering insights into client legal challenges and competitor strategies. Market and financial intelligence tools like S&P Capital IQ, D&B Hoovers, EMIS, and PitchBook can help bring up to speed on a company and its recent activity. Industry publications, such as trade journals and market research reports, reveal trends, best practices, and innovations within the industry. News aggregators and publishers such as Law360, Google News, and Manzama will inform about the latest issues affecting the subject of the research. By leveraging these varied resources, businesses can develop a well-rounded understanding of their clients and competitors, enabling them to make informed decisions.

Phase 3: Information Processing and Collation

Once information is collected from disparate sources, it needs to be systematically organized. This involves categorizing the data by relevance, source, and type and storing it in a structured format using tools like spreadsheets, databases, or dedicated software. Raw data at times contains inconsistencies, duplicates, or errors that can skew the analysis. Data cleaning involves removing these inaccuracies to ensure the dataset's integrity. This step includes verifying facts, correcting errors, and standardizing formats. Ensuring the credibility of the collected data is paramount. CI practitioners must cross-check information from multiple sources to verify its accuracy. This step might involve consulting primary sources, cross-referencing with authoritative publications, or confirming data through reputable third-party verifications.

Phase 4: Analysis

With the data organized, cleaned, and verified, the next step is to analyze the information. Contrary to most facets of librarianship, where librarians usually refrain from interpreting, CI depends on the analyst's ability to interpret data and connect previously unconnected dots, highlighting only the most pertinent details. A researcher may conduct tasks such as a review of a potential client's 10-K risk statement and recent news to identify current pain points, utilize LexisNexis Intelligize or S&P Capital IQ's blackline tool to compare recent and past public filings for significant changes, or assess historical legal representation data of a company to gauge their commitment to certain law firms. CI practitioners then take the next step, using their skills and knowledge to infer actionable insights, such as how their firm can assist the prospective client with their pain points, determining which updates to a company's public filings are of consequence and their implications, and deducing conclusions about a company's selection processes for legal counsel based on previous hiring patterns. Such analysis can help librarians provide valuable insights and recommendations to their stakeholders and demonstrate the impact of CI on strategic decision-making.

Phase 5: Reporting

Generating reports that successfully summarize the processed information can make or break the CI process. These reports should be clear, concise, and tailored to the needs of the intended audience, whether they are senior management, legal teams, or other stakeholders. Reports should highlight significant findings, trends, and actionable insights derived from the data. Effective reporting includes not only a summary of significant findings and trends but also a detailed analysis of how these insights can impact strategic decisions. Additionally, the reports should highlight any potential risks, opportunities, and recommendations for action, providing a roadmap for informed decision-making. Reporting may involve the creation of visualizations such as charts, graphs, and tables that facilitate easy understanding and interpretation. Tools like Microsoft Power BI can be invaluable at this stage, enabling the creation of interactive dashboards that highlight key insights. Visual aids such as charts, graphs, and tables should be utilized to enhance clarity and facilitate easy interpretation of complex data. The final report to a CI stakeholder could vary widely, potentially being as brief as an email summary or as extensive as a thirty-page document with multiple sections, featuring in-depth text and visual data. By presenting data in an organized and engaging format, these reports ensure that the valuable insights derived from competitive intelligence are effectively communicated and utilized to drive strategic initiatives within the organization.

Phase 6: Feedback and Evaluation

Gaining feedback and evaluating the deliverable is a crucial phase in the competitive intelligence process for law librarians, focusing on assessing the effectiveness of the gathered and analyzed information. This phase involves soliciting feedback from key stakeholders, such as legal professionals and decision-makers, to gauge the relevance and utility of the insights provided. By reviewing how well the information met their needs and supported their decision-making, law librarians can identify strengths and areas for improvement in their intelligence processes. Evaluation also includes assessing the accuracy and timeliness of the data, ensuring that the methods used were effective and that the insights were actionable. This feedback loop enables continuous refinement of research methods and tools, ensuring that the competitive intelligence efforts remain aligned with evolving needs.

TRADITIONAL CHALLENGES IN CI

As described above, CI involves some difficulties for information professionals in areas such as information gathering, analysis, and scalability. A brief overview of these difficulties will help prepare people for using AI to solve them.

Unstructured Data

Structured data consists of distinct elements, such as numbers or short text strings with a well-defined schema, such as a table. The CI practitioner can do a lot with structured data. For example, a well-structured list of firm contacts at a specific company can be summarized to show the number of possible decision-makers in different locations.

When relying on online sources for information, much of the data one encounters will be unstructured, either embedded in prose or presented in pseudo-tables that are not easily converted to distinct tabular format. When faced with unstructured data, the CI practitioner has two main options: analyze using qualitative approaches or structure the data oneself. Both approaches can be very time-consuming.

Domain Specificity

While some librarians may be tax lawyers, knowledgeable about current controversies around climate reporting, or understand the competitive landscape among employment and labor law firms, no researcher can be an expert in all areas relevant to their organization's quest for competitive advantage. The need to "get up to speed" on a topic by reviewing primers and background documents on a subject before even beginning the actual project to research each unfamiliar acronym or jargon word, or to differentiate between accepted facts versus the assumptions or opinions of the author all pose barriers to running a fully scaled CI function.

Data Dump

Law librarians face significant challenges when converting a data dump—a large volume of unstructured, unfiltered, or raw data—into a more manageable and digestible format. Data dumps challenge law librarians in terms of management and organization. The data is typically unstructured or unindexed, requiring time to sift through and locate relevant information. However, the most crucial aspect is maintaining the integrity and confidentiality of data, especially sensitive or personal information. Law librarians can transform a data dump into a valuable resource by applying their categorization, indexing, and database management skills, playing a pivotal role in this process. By organizing the data effectively, they can make it accessible and useful for legal research and practice.

Scalability

The prospect of growing a CI function faces hurdles beyond just messy source data and special knowledge requirements. The whole endeavor of summarizing and contextualizing information in response to a CI request is inherently resource-intensive. Libraries building a CI function must often navigate a narrow channel between the Scylla of thorough, thoughtful analysis, and the Charybdis of multiple diverse and time-sensitive requests.

Promise of AI

While AI will not eliminate all of these difficulties in the near future, its use can address many of them. The rest of the chapter will focus on tools and research techniques to help provide valuable insights within an organization, allow CI professionals to spend more time in the analysis and presentation phases of the CI cycle, and supercharge the CI function.

BACKGROUND ON AND INTRODUCTION TO GENERATIVE AI

With the public debut of OpenAI's ChatGPT in November 2022, the availability of large language models built on neural networks trained on enormous datasets has transformed the AI landscape. Let's look at some of the strengths and limitations of these models in the context of CI.

Strengths

Text Summarization: Summarization automatically condenses lengthy documents into concise blocks of text, preserving the core information while eliminating extraneous details. This technology enables law librarians to rapidly process and disseminate critical information, improving efficiency and productivity. The algorithms can distill complex judicial opinions into brief, readable abstracts highlighting key legal arguments and outcomes, making it easier for legal professionals to stay informed without wading through dense texts.

Translation: While machine translation has been available online for nearly two decades, LLM models allow for more accurate and efficient language translation. For example, analyzing a foreign-language company filing need not include an entirely separate translation step, and contextual translation issues are less likely to hinder the analysis.

Structuring data: LLM models can summarize data in a tabular format, addressing a major CI challenge. We will examine this in detail in our first case study.

Forecasting: Forecasting is transforming how law librarians analyze past legal inquiry patterns, enabling them to predict future information needs. This foresight allows for a more efficient allocation of resources, ensuring that the most relevant and up-to-date information is readily available. Examining the frequency and context of previous requests allows librarians to preemptively curate resources and update collections. It can digest vast amounts of case law and then identify trends and predict rulings, thereby enhancing the advisory role of law librarians.

Limitations

When thinking about AI-driven research strategies, it is helpful to keep in mind the limitations of LLMs. Because the margin for error is greater in CI, as compared to legal research, thoughtful prompt design can mitigate these shortcomings and occasionally parlay them into strengths. According to Amatrian and others, LLMs exhibit the following limitations.[5]

Transient State: The lack of persistent memory in LLMs means that they do not retain information from previous interactions, a hurdle in maintaining continuity in research. In fact, most commercially available generative AI (GenAI) chatbots employ systems that manage limited context retention, and this will likely only improve as development continues.

Probabilistic Nature: LLMs are essentially language probability generators, choosing each next word based on probabilities assigned based on training data. This stochastic nature can be expected to generate slight variations in responses to identical prompts. While this could pose a challenge to consistency, it also presents an opportunity for researchers to explore a range of perspectives and insights, enriching the research process.

Outdated Information: LLMs rely on historical data from their training set, many of which are 2–3 years old.

Content Fabrication: The phenomenon of "hallucination," where LLMs generate plausible but incorrect information, is particularly concerning in legal research. It is essential to verify the information provided by GenAI with authoritative legal sources to maintain the integrity of research findings.

Resource Intensity: The significant computational resources required for LLMs translate to financial costs that may be prohibitive for some organizations. However, the investment in GenAI can be justified by the efficiency gains and depth of analysis it enables, which can be particularly beneficial in complex qualitative research. A Fall 2023 study published by Harvard Business School and Boston Consulting Group (BCG) found that BCG consultants using generative AI produced work 25 percent faster with 40 percent higher quality than those not using GenAI.[6]

Domain Specificity: While LLMs are generalist in nature, they often require domain-specific data to excel. Pointing the AI to specific sources will form part of most sound prompt strategies. Understanding and addressing the limitations of LLMs are critical for effective prompt design and maximizing the potential of GenAI for CI research. In the next section, we will discuss prompt strategies to do just that.

PROMPT DESIGN BASICS

What Is a Prompt?

In generative AI models, a "prompt" refers to the text-based input provided by the user to steer the model's output. This input can vary greatly, from straightforward queries to intricate task instructions or comprehensive descriptions. For LLMs, basic prompts could be as uncomplicated as posing a question directly or using one word to outline a particular task, for example, "Summarize."[7]

Prompt Design versus Prompt Engineering

Shortly after ChatGPT was launched in November 2022, Prompt Design and Prompt Engineering were used interchangeably to describe an LLM user's purposeful construction of a textual input to elicit a refined output. While Prompt Design and Prompt Engineering do share commonalities, the why, where, and who is involved with their deployment differ.

- *Prompt Design*: Involves creating textual inputs that guide the output of generative AI models. It's about crafting the initial instructions, questions, or tasks to elicit a specific response from the model.[8]
- *Prompt Engineering*: Is a more advanced discipline that not only includes prompt design but also encompasses understanding the model's capabilities, limitations, and iteratively refining prompts to improve the model's performance for specific goals. It's akin to traditional software engineering practices applied to AI model interaction.[9]

For the purposes of a CI practitioner, we will focus on prompt design.

Questions versus Instructions

A prompt consists of various components, such as instructions, questions, input data, and examples. A prompt that lacks either instructions or questions will not elicit a desired response from an AI model, while the other components are optional.[10]

Prompts posed as questions are best used for:

- *Research and exploration*: for example, "What are the main causes of litigation in the pharmaceuticals industry during the last six months?"
- *Opinion and discussion*: for example, "Do you believe business development teams at AmLaw 100 firms would benefit from increasing the size of their embedded research function?"
- *Problem-solving*: for example, "How would you find the root cause of a decrease in net promoter score within the hospitality industry during the last twelve months?"

Prompts provided as instructions are used for:

- *Specific actions*: for example, "Summarize this report in five sentences or fewer."
- *Educational purposes*: for example, "Explain the legal tactic known as the 'Texas Two-Step.'"
- *Creative tasks*: for example, "Generate a SWOT analysis for ABC Corp."

Prompts can also use both questions and instructions in a single input to direct and refine the model's response.

Use of Natural Language—Specific, True, Clear, and Conclusive

A prompt's use of natural language is one of its main characteristics. Natural language, the language that humans use to communicate with each other, is different from formal languages, such as programming or mathematical languages. Formal languages have strict rules and syntax, while natural language is more flexible, expressive, and diverse, but also more ambiguous, complex, and variable.

When designing a prompt, it is important to use natural language that is specific, true, clear, and conclusive.

For example, consider the following prompt:

e.g., "Write a report on the latest trends in the automotive industry."

This prompt, while it does not lack truth, is not clear, specific, or conclusive. It does not specify what kind of report, what aspects of the industry, what time frame, what sources, or what format.

A better prompt would be:

e.g., "Write a one-page executive summary of the key trends and challenges in the global automotive industry during the past twelve months, based on the data from the attached spreadsheet. Use bullet points and bold headings to highlight the main points."

The first prompt leaves much of the output to the AI model's interpretation of the context surrounding the instruction; the second prompt provides more context to direct the output.

Designing a Basic Prompt

Observing an improvement in the relevance of a model's output following consistent exposure to similar inputs, authoritative voices on GenAI advocate standardizing natural language prompt structures.[11] Below, we provide the structure of a basic prompt, intended to be repeatable and efficient, to be used by CI practitioners or more broadly:

- Step 1. *Define the purpose:* Why are you constructing a prompt, and what is the desired output?

  Before the CI practitioner can craft an effective prompt, it is important to specify the intention behind the creation of said prompt.[12] Here, the idea of Problem Formulation can be used. Introduced in an article published in the Harvard Business Review by Oguz A. Acar in 2023, Problem formulation involves clearly establishing the problem's focus, scope, and limitations. Without a properly defined problem, even the most advanced prompts are inadequate.[13]

  Among the elements that encapsulate Problem Formulation, problem diagnosis, and decomposition are useful in defining the purpose or goal of your prompt:
- *Problem diagnosis*: Identify the main issue for the model to solve. What is the main thing you want the model to achieve?
- *Problem decomposition*: Decompose multiplex challenges into more approachable, bite-sized tasks.
- *Construct a prompt:* There are different ways to classify prompts, but we suggest that each prompt consider the elements: *persona, task, constraint, format, and context.*

  a *Persona:* Modulates voice and perspective.

     e.g., "You are a marketing analyst at a global law firm."

     Providing a persona will allow the model to contextualize what information may or may not be relevant in its output.

  b. *Task:* Declare the *core objective* of the prompt.

     e.g., "please *summarize* the legal issues and trends affecting technology companies"

     By declaring a task for the model to execute, the user is more likely to receive results in line with their expectations. Without a definite task, the model is left to assume what the user is asking it to do.

  c. *Constraints:* Limit scope, inputs or other parameters.

     e.g., "using only the information from this current web page and no other sources."

     Designing constraints for a prompt involves establishing clear limits by specifying the permissible inputs, the processes involved, and the restrictions on the potential outputs while exploring potential solutions.[14]

d. *Format:* Directs the presentation of results.

e.g., "Answer using brief bullet points"

It is important to tell the model how you would like the output presented.

e. *Context*: Provides background to hone the response.

e.g., "to inform your partner colleagues."

LLMs can generate responses that are generally coherent and pertinent when no specific context is given. However, these models may deliver inaccurate information where context is ambiguous or not well represented in training datasets. Providing context allows for a more nuanced understanding by the LLM, enabling it to produce a response that aligns more closely with the intended outcome.[15]

- Below is the complete prompt, where the user wants to summarize a law firm legal update to help with spotting trends. We can look at a CI prompt using this framework:

  e.g., "As a partner at a global law firm *[persona]*, please summarize the legal issues and trends affecting technology companies *[task]* using only the information from this current web page and no other sources *[constraint]*. Answer using brief bullet points *[format]* to inform your partner colleagues *[context]*."

  Breaking this down further, let's consider each element and its functions. Not all prompts will require the use of each element. However, considering each will generally make prompts more effective and help tailor the results.

Step 2. *Review your prompt*: Look to enhance the probability of receiving the desired output and ensure the prompt is clear, specific, true, and conclusive.

Step 3. *Record results*: Record the prompt and the model's output. While the stochasticity of a model's output will create variances in response to an identical prompt, some commonalities and patterns will emerge to the observer as prompts are tweaked.

Table 17.1 Basic Elements of a Prompt

Prompt Element	*Function*	*Format/Examples*
Persona	Modulates voice and perspective	• Experienced law librarian • Law firm partner • Regulatory lawyer
Task	Core objective of the prompt	• Summarize/synthesize • Extract • *[Implicit]* Who/what/why/where/when/how?
Constraint	Limits scope, inputs, or other parameters	• Include only results from 2023 or later • Using only the content in this 10-K risk statement • Only reference cases listed on this page
Format	Directs presentation of results	• Concise bullets • 200 words or less • An attractive and professional report
Context	Provides background to hone response	• to inform your colleagues • to support our law firm's strategy

Step 4. *Iterate*: Testing, refining, and reframing the problem will allow the user to improve their prompt design skills by allowing the user to see which prompts work best for specific tasks and questions.[16]

Other helpful prompt tips to keep in mind:

- *Give examples*: "include sections for each specific jurisdiction mentioned (for example, United States of America, United Kingdom, European Union, Canada, Australia, California, etc.)"
- *Tone*: "Use a conversational tone to make your prompts more approachable."[17] "Language models do not always react well to nice, friendly language. If you REALLY want them to follow some instructions, you might want to use forceful language. Believe it or not, all caps and exclamation marks work!"[18]
- *Use advanced prompting frameworks, such as Chain-of-thought (CoT)*: CoT makes the model explain its reasoning. Advanced prompting techniques are discussed in depth in the following section on *Advanced Prompt Strategies*.

Case Studies

We will present two case studies exploring the utility of GenAI to improve CI work and the life of the practitioner tasked with doing it. We will also explain the benefits of using GenAI for the task, as well as the drawbacks. In case study 1, we present a scenario where the CI practitioner is tasked with gathering data on top executives and formatting them into a table using Microsoft Copilot. In case study 2, we use ChatGPT-4o to conduct a Win/Loss Analysis of a "winning" and "losing" response to an RFQ (Request for Qualifications/Quote). Like an RFP, an RFQ is a formal document used to solicit bids from service providers. RFQs are often employed to obtain bids from pre-qualified vendors for projects with a clearly defined scope, wherein cost is the primary criterion for selection (i.e., engineering and design, manufacturing, IT procurement, and construction). Conversely, RFPs often relate to projects with more broadly outlined goals that can be achieved through various innovative solutions, placing greater emphasis on value beyond just price (i.e., law firms, consulting firms, marketing and advertising agencies, etc.). For the context of this chapter, both terms will be treated as interchangeable.

Case Study 1—Making a Table

Background

CI practitioners are often tasked with wrangling unstructured data. Often, this involves manually scraping data and placing it in an Excel table for further analysis or presenting the information in a more digestible format.

In our first case study, a partner in the transportation practice of a global law firm has tasked the CI team with compiling a list of executive profiles of targets for a business development initiative.

Methodology

Prior to prompting the GenAI tool, we used search results from an online resume database to apply company, industry, location, and keyword filters, resulting in a list of twenty-five individuals in leadership positions at major United States-based airlines.

To establish a baseline, we manually scraped the data into an Excel file, noting the time taken to accomplish the task. The task was repeated five times.

Remaining on the same results page, we then prompted Microsoft Copilot with a basic prompt designed to produce a four-column table with each individual's name, title, company, and location, noting the time taken from input to final output. The task was repeated five times.

Following the collection process, the final results were manually checked for accuracy.

Table 17.2 Microsoft Copilot—Making a Table from Popular Online Resume Database

Name	*Title*	*Company*	*Location*
John Doe	Executive Vice President, Chief Regulatory and Corporate Affairs Officer	Southwest Airlines	Dallas, Texas, United States

Source: Microsoft Copilot.
The output provided by Microsoft Copilot included twenty-five rows. For the purpose of illustration, the table has been condensed to a single row. Additionally, names were anonymized to maintain the individual's privacy.

Results

On average, it took the individual performing the manual extraction eight minutes and fifty-two seconds to take the data from the webpage and organize it into Excel.

After prompting Microsoft Copilot with the basic prompt provided in quotes under "User Input": Copilot produced a table with the desired results (see table 17.2) in 42.71 seconds on the first attempt. However, on subsequent attempts, Copilot could not duplicate the output provided on the first attempt. On attempts two, three, and four, Copilot only provided the name, title, company, and location of the first six individuals appearing on the page. On the fifth attempt, Copilot provided the correct title, company, and location but listed the user's name as the name for each individual.

User Input:
"Please create a four-column table listing the individuals from this page with the following columns: Name, Title, Company, Location."

GenAI (Microsoft Copilot) Output:
"Certainly! Here's a table listing the individuals from the page:

This table includes the name, title, company, and location of the individuals mentioned on the page. If you need more details or additional entries, please let me know!

Lessons Learned

- *Timesaver*: On our first attempt, Copilot cut the time spent extracting this data manually by approximately 92 percent.
- *Stochasticity can be variably unpredictable*: Only the first attempt produced the desired output. While stochasticity is at play when working with GenAI, it appears variable depending on the *task* of the prompt presented to the model.
- *Iteration is important*: Following five attempts with Copilot, we changed elements of the prompt in an effort to entice Copilot to replicate the output provided during the first attempt. After fourteen reattempts, each with a change made to an element of the prompt, Copilot once again produced the desired output.
- *Not all elements of a basic prompt are (always) essential*: We recommend using persona, task, constraint, format, and context for basic prompts, but all elements are not always necessary. For example, the prompt in this case study lacked persona and context. We added them in later iterations, but the output did not change.

Case Study 2—Win/Loss Analysis: Comparing Request for Proposals (RFP) or Request for Qualifications (RFQ) Responses

Background

CI practitioners can help their employer gain a competitive advantage by analyzing past winning responses to RFPs or RFQs against those that lost. This is often referred to as Win/Loss Analysis or

Post-Mortem Review. Typically, a proposal is evaluated against those of competitors for the same opportunity. However, if there are no competitor proposals available for comparison, it can be insightful to analyze the company's past proposals—both successful and unsuccessful—submitted to the same client. GenAI can be most effectively utilized in the Win/Loss Analysis process, which also includes activities such as post-opportunity buyer interviews, by comparing past proposals.

In our second case study, a CI team is tasked with conducting a win/loss analysis on a winning proposal and a losing proposal for an airport construction and architecture firm (Company B) following an unfavorable decision by a prospective buyer.

Methodology

Due to privacy and confidentiality constraints surrounding the use of internal company RFP responses, we obtained two RFQ responses for the development of a new airport terminal at a major Florida airport, obtained through Florida's "Sunshine" law. One response was the "winning" response, which we reference as "Company A Response," and the other was a second or third runner-up, which we reference as "Company B Response." Company A's response was 342 pages and Company B's response was 354 pages. In addition, we also gathered the solicitation documents from the airport authority, which, when audio, video, and attendance files were removed, were bound together to form an 850-page document which we reference as "Solicitation Material."

Prior to prompting GenAI, we manually conducted a win/loss analysis using the documents. A meticulous review and summarization of both responses took roughly twenty-six hours for one team member to complete.

Next, we prompted ChatGPT-4o to conduct a win/loss analysis of the responses.

Finally, we manually checked the output from ChatGPT-4o for accuracy.

Results

In addition to the prompt below, we uploaded PDF files titled "Solicitation Material," "Company A Response," and "Company B Response" to ChatGPT-4o. ChatGPT-4o took approximately 52.40 seconds to produce the output that appears under "GenAI (ChatGPT-4o) Output."

User Input:
"You are a business development professional at an airport engineering and architecture firm conducting a review of past RFQ responses aimed at identifying what sets winning proposals apart from losing ones. Referencing the document titled "Solicitation Material," compare the documents titled "Company A Response" and "Company B Response." Identify and analyze the differences and similarities between the two responses. Be as specific as possible. Present your comparison in a table with the following columns: Criteria, Company A, Company B, and Winner. Include specific examples illustrating the key differences between the two responses. Base your analysis solely on the referenced files. Once you have analyzed all material, provide your best guess as to which company was successful in getting selected for the work outlined in the "Solicitation Material." Provide specific reasons why."

GenAI (ChatGPT 4o) Output:
"Based on the extracted text, here's a comparison of the responses from Company A and Company B using specific criteria relevant to the RFQ.

Analysis and Conclusion

Based on the comparison, Company A has an edge over Company B.

While Company B has relevant experience specifically with the soliciting airport, the broader and more detailed achievements and capabilities presented by Company A likely make them the preferred choice for the project.

Table 17.3 ChatGPT-4o—RFQ Comparison Matrix

Criteria	*Company A*	*Company B*	*Winner*
Team Composition	Mentioned partners: Company A, Partner 1, Partner 2, Partner 3	Mentioned team: Company B and team members	Tie
Experience	Highlighted $8B in projects, top national awards, and resumes of key personnel	Notable projects, specific awards not mentioned	A
Relevance to Project	Emphasized past projects and success at the soliciting Airport and similar airports	Mentioned history with the soliciting airport	A
Design and Innovation	Detailed innovative design aspects by Partner 2	General mention of design capabilities	A
Commitment to Inclusion	Specific awards for inclusion	No specific mention of inclusion awards	A
Client Testimonials	Strong references from previous clients, with similar documented successes	Adequate references, but fewer documented successes	A
Financial Stability	Mentioned $8B in projects, showcasing financial strength	No specific financial figures mentioned	A
Safety Record	Fully compliant with detailed safety records and certifications listed	Compliant, but less detailed on safety records	A
Cost Proposal	Competitive, includes real-time cost estimating and trend analysis	Competitive, detailed but less emphasis on real-time updates	A
Schedule Management	Detailed, proactive approach with real-time updates	Structured, focus on milestone tracking	A
Stakeholder Communication	Regular, detailed updates, and on-site decision-making authority	Emphasis on communication but less detail on processes	A

Source: ChatGPT-4o.
Table shortened by removing rows comparing *Introduction, Project Understanding,* and *Technical Approach,* listed as "Tie" in the *Winner* column without notable analysis. Airport, Company, and Partner names were anonymized.

Best Guess for Selected Company*: Company A*

The selection committee would likely be impressed by Company A's extensive experience, financial strength, innovative design capabilities, competitive yet transparent cost proposal, strong references, and commitment to inclusion, making them a strong candidate for the project.

Lessons Learned

- *Summarization and comparison*: GenAI tools excel at summarization and comparison. ChatGPT-4o summarized and compared over 1,500 pages in less than sixty seconds.
- *When it comes to prompt design, "basic" does not necessarily mean "short"*: The prompt used to elicit the output in this case study was 132 words. While on the longer side of prompts, the five basic elements were used without relying on advanced prompting.

- *Eliminating analytical bias*: An expert carrying out a win/loss analysis or post-mortem is typically aware of the results, which can inadvertently influence their evaluation. Provided that the GenAI tool has not been trained with data containing the results of the RFP or RFQ in question, it's possible to attain an analysis free from bias.
- *Critical thinking*: ChatGPT 4.0 identified the winning proposal without prior knowledge.
- *Room for iteration*: ChatGPT 4o's first attempt at an output did not include specific examples from the extracted texts despite being prompted by the user to do so. In this instance, follow-up prompts would be necessary to obtain more detailed examples.

Advanced Prompt Strategies

Going beyond these core strategies, the prompt designer can also employ sophisticated methods to provide (1) the model with more specific context using examples or (2) request the model to justify its answer to enhance LLM responses. The approaches are not fixed, but the techniques of Few-shot Learning, Chain-of-Thought, Thread-of-Thought, and Self-Reflection and Self-Consistency can help the prompt designer in adapting queries to particular situations.

Few-Shot Learning (FSL)

Few-shot learning is a prompting technique in which the user presents an LLM with examples, allowing it to generalize beyond the knowledge domains of the original training set and reduces the risk of content fabrication.

To use FSL for prompt design, researchers need to only provide the model with a few examples of the desired input-output pairs, followed by a query or a task. Examples should be representative of the domain, task, and format that the user wants the model to emulate. When then presented with a clear and specific query analogous in structure, the model can infer the pattern and generate a response that matches.

Case study: Generate a list of potential legal issues for a technology sector client based on a brief description of their situation.

The librarian could use FSL to design a prompt like this:

> e.g., "A semiconductor firm is considering a merger with another firm in the same industry. Potential legal issues: Department of Justice (DOJ) and Federal Trade Commission (FTC) merger review; Antitrust and competition laws; Intellectual property rights and licensing agreements; Corporate governance and due diligence."

Chain-of-Thought

Chain-of-thought techniques "endow language models with the ability to generate . . . a coherent series of intermediate reasoning steps that lead to the final answer for a problem (Wei et al., 2022)." While many CoT use cases apply to word-math or symbolic reasoning problems, the technique can enhance model response to many complex reasoning tasks, improving relevancy and reducing hallucination by increasing the transparency of reasoning.

Used in a prompt, CoT instructs the model to think step-by-step to generate a response that shows its steps and explanations. The simplest type of CoT prompting is Zero-shot CoT, which, following Kojima et al. (2022), simply appends the phrase "Let's think step-by-step" to improve model performance on logical reasoning tasks.

Thread-of Thought (ThOT)

While CoT serves to make the model's reasoning more explicit, a variation of CoT called ThOT can improve the completeness and relevance of responses when the subject matter is particularly complicated. Instead of "Let's think step-by-step," the prompt strategy employs phrasing meant to elicit a clear and coherent response from the model.

To identify multiple potential business development opportunities for a client or prospect, a law firm researcher might use the following ThOT prompt to direct the model to explore the topic thoroughly:

> e.g., "As a partner at a global law firm and using the provided excerpts from Company X's 10-K risk statement, address each company risk one-by-one in sequence and discuss relevant and actionable law firm business development opportunities in a report for your colleagues."

In the example, the user directs the model to follow a specified "thread" in its response.

Ethical Considerations

Competitive intelligence thrives on uncovering valuable information about clients and competitors, but the line between ethical research and unethical practices can be blurry, especially with AI in the mix.

AI systems can analyze vast amounts of data swiftly, but they can also produce erroneous or biased results. Law librarians must critically assess the outputs of AI tools, ensuring that the information used for CI is accurate and trustworthy. AI systems learn from historical data, which can include biases that reflect existing societal inequalities. Law librarians must be vigilant about the risk of these biases influencing CI outcomes.

Privacy and Security

Confidentiality and data privacy are also significant ethical concerns. Law librarians often handle sensitive information that, if improperly managed, could lead to breaches of confidentiality. When using AI tools, it is crucial to ensure that data privacy is maintained and that the AI systems comply with relevant legal and ethical standards regarding data protection.

Unpaid resources may monetize use by ad targeting and tend to offer fewer data control options. Such tools may also recycle user-generated prompts and system responses to further refine their model using real-world examples. For example, it was widely reported in early 2023 that Samsung employees had uploaded confidential company information including source code and meeting transcripts to ChatGPT. This data was added to ChatGPT's knowledge base and was then freely available to anyone who asked. Also, since LLM models are based on distributed neural network architectures, there is no easy way to delete such data once it is "in the wild."

In general, paid premium or enterprise services will offer more control over data, including opting-out of data collection. OpenAI's ChatGPT, Anthropic's Claude, and Meta's MetaAI offer premium services, as do Google Gemini (Claude) and Microsoft Copilot (GPT). However, it is still necessary to understand the terms of service regarding privacy and security.

If budget is a concern, DuckDuckGo offers an anonymized chat that promises not to reuse prompts and responses to train the model. Users can select from multiple LLM models to power the chat including GPT, Claude, and open-source models like Llama and Mixtral.

Looking Forward

The legal profession is currently experiencing a significant shift due to the increasing prevalence of artificial intelligence technology. This transformation has far-reaching implications for law librarians, presenting both challenges and opportunities. In CI, as in all research, it is important to recognize that while AI "can assist in streamlining routine tasks and improving efficiency, it is important to ensure that the technology complements human expertise rather than replacing it."[19] Regardless of the platform used for research, it should be seen as a valuable steppingstone in finalizing the end result.

In the fast-paced world of law libraries, there is often a pressure to deliver top-notch service efficiently and cost-effectively. Integrating AI tools can significantly enhance workflows, making research more precise and expeditious. Embracing AI as a resource can empower law librarians to enhance their competencies, improve organizational competitiveness, and contribute to the future of legal services. By honing their expertise in AI tools, prioritizing strategic thinking and knowledge management, and continuously refining their research methods, law librarians can play a pivotal role in fostering adept, efficient, and strategic research in the age of AI.

NOTES

1. William R. Fair, "The Corporate CIA—A Prediction of Things to Come," *Management Science* 12, no. 10 (June 1, 1966): B-503, https://doi.org/10.1287/mnsc.12.10.b489.
2. Fair, "The Corporate CIA."
3. Josh Farley, "The Thinker & the Doer," *AALL Spectrum* 28, no. 3 (January 2024), https://aallspectrum.aallnet.org/html5/reader/production/default.aspx?pubname=&edid=e43d1447-80e9-4753-9db1-ff7f18c86736&pnum=43.
4. Maungwa and Laughton, "The Use of Theories in Competitive Intelligence: A Systematic Literature Review," *Journal of Intelligence Studies in Business* 13, no. 2 (2023), https://repository.up.ac.za/bitstream/handle/2263/95327/Maungwa_Use_2023.pdf?sequence=1&isAllowed=y(up.ac.za).
5. Gao Linna, "The Impact of ChatGPT on Enterprise Competitive Intelligence Systems," *Information Systems and Economics* 4, no. 9 (January 1, 2023), https://doi.org/10.23977/infse.2023.040909.; Xavier Amatriain, "Prompt Design and Engineering: Introduction and Advanced Methods," arXiv.org, January 24, 2024, https://arxiv.org/abs/2401.14423.
6. Camilla J. Martinez and Tiffani A. Mezitis, "Harvard Business School Partners With BCG on AI Productivity Study," *News | the Harvard Crimson*, October 13, 2023, https://www.thecrimson.com/article/2023/10/13/jagged-edge-ai-bcg/.
7. Amatriain, "Prompt Design and Engineering."
8. Amatriain, "Prompt Design and Engineering."
9. Amatriain, "Prompt Design and Engineering."
10. Amatrian, "Prompt Design and Engineering."
11. Krishna Ronanki, Beatriz Cabrero-Daniel, and Christian Berger, "Prompt Smells: An Omen for Undesirable Generative AI Outputs," January 23, 2024, https://doi.org/10.1145/3644815.3644982.
12. Ggaliwango Marvin, Nakayiza Hellen, Daudi Jjingo, and Joyce Nakatumba-Nabende, "Prompt Engineering in Large Language Models," in *Algorithms for Intelligent Systems*, 2024, pp. 387–402, https://doi.org/10.1007/978-981-99-7962-2_30.
13. Oguz A. Acar, "AI Prompt Engineering Isn't the Future," *Harvard Business Review*, June 8, 2023, https://hbr.org/2023/06/ai-prompt-engineering-isnt-the-future.
14. Acar, "AI Prompt Engineering Isn't the Future."
15. Marvin et al., "Prompt Engineering in Large Language Models."
16. Marvin et al., "Prompt Engineering in Large Language Models"; Acar, "AI Prompt Engineering Isn't the Future."
17. Marvin et al., "Prompt Engineering in Large Language Models."
18. Amatriain, "Prompt Design and Engineering: Introduction and Advanced Methods."
19. Anne Robbins, "LibGuides: AI and Law Teaching: Introduction," *libguides.law.illinois.edu*, November 28, 2023, https://libguides.law.illinois.edu/AILegalTeaching.

18

Big Data and Law Libraries

Monique Gonzalez

Libraries today are using big data in geospatial mapping, metadata consultation, text and data mining, data visualizations, preservation, data management planning, and more. Big data may evoke images of massive stacks of information, but its significance extends beyond volume. The gathering, preservation, and processing of vast amounts of data to gain insights, make informed decisions, and foster innovation all fall under the umbrella of big data.[1] Big data is being used in many industries. The retail industry provides personalized recommendations through its use of big data. The travel industry uses big data to enhance customer experiences.[2] In healthcare, big data is laying the foundation for advancements in genomic research and personalized medicine.[3] The time is ripe for law libraries to use big data to improve operational efficiencies and user services.

WHAT IS BIG DATA?

It is important to begin with a clear definition of big data, as used in this chapter, to go beyond its voluminous nature to capture its potential strategic use in law libraries. Four characteristics should be considered when defining big data in the context of law libraries: volume, velocity, variety, and veracity—the Four Vs of Big Data.[4]

One aspect of big data is the immense volume of information that is generated and collected daily. In 2021, an estimated 2.5 quintillion bytes of data were created by individuals daily compared to the 44 zettabytes of information produced in the previous decade combined.[5]

Mobile devices such as smartphones, which most people use both personally and professionally, have fueled much of this growth. Data at the organizational level has experienced similar trends in growth, but on a smaller scale. As a result, traditional data storage and processing methods do not handle the vast amount of information created and stored in a way that makes it readily accessible for making data-driven business decisions. Many companies are looking to cloud and third-party providers to manage the sheer volume of data. Cloud storage is projected to hold at least 200 zettabytes of data by the year 2025.[6]

The speed at which data is being created has catapulted big data trends. Additionally, this velocity has led to the need for sophisticated data analysis and management tools to keep pace with ever-increasing information. To ensure that libraries can effectively process and utilize this information, it is important to invest in a data science platform to automate data analysis and management, enabling them to make more informed and timely decisions.

To properly analyze big data, it is imperative to consider the variety of data sources that will be used, as this can impact the accuracy and reliability of the resulting insights. Big data may be unstructured, semi-structured, or structured in various formats such as audio, video, text, and images. Structured data, such as a spreadsheet, is highly formatted and organized in a way that makes it easily accessible for quantitative analysis. Unstructured data lacks formatting and organization but may be suitable for qualitative analysis. Social media content, text files, videos, and audio recordings are examples of unstructured data. Semi-structured data may have both structured and unstructured characteristics that are commonly observed in web development.[7] Big data can come from various sources in a law library, and it may be structured, unstructured, or semi-structured. The library management system (LMS) is one of the best sources of big data. These systems handle day-to-day operations such as cataloging, circulation, and inventory management. They generate vast amounts of data such as checkouts, reservations, and renewals. User statistics for electronic resources is another valuable source of information. User interactions with the library's website, social media, and catalog also provide a wealth of information. Using advanced analytics techniques, this data may be analyzed collectively to enhance operations and tailor collections more closely to user needs.

Finally, it is important to consider veracity when defining big data. Is the data reliable? The omission of one of the Four Vs of Big Data often occurs when determining big data, and veracity appears to be the most frequently overlooked. Information professionals recognize the critical nature of considering the quality of data because inaccurate, incomplete, or misleading information can lead to incorrect conclusions and decisions.[8]

At a time when deepfakes and mistrust are all-time high, the basic tenets of information literacy should not be set aside when assessing big data. The ability to identify the need for information, locate it, assess it, and utilize it remains unchanged.[9]

BIG DATA IN THE LEGAL INDUSTRY

The use of big data is prevalent in industries such as retail, healthcare, and media and entertainment.[10] The legal field is catching up with the big data trend, and more applications are being implemented. Law firms are increasingly using big data to improve various aspects of their operations, including billing, marketing, and customer service.[11] Data analytics platforms may also aid in predicting the outcome of certain cases based on jurisdiction, arguments, trier of fact, and counsel. Legal analytics can also assist with better allocation of resources for complex cases. Oatley discusses the application of big data in crime analytics, including predictive policing, which highlights the growing intersection of big data and legal practice.[12] In summary, law firms increasingly use big data to streamline operations, make informed decisions, and gain a competitive advantage.

As the legal industry increasingly embraces big data, it is important that law librarians are not only informed about big data and data analytics but are also equipped to assist law students, summer associates, faculty, or attorneys. Law librarians are often the first line of inquiry when users seek datasets, engage in research, or look for an answer that requires data analytics. John Bailey, of Dell Company, is quoted as saying, "Institutions that fail to embrace big data as an opportunity will be left behind by those that do as the power of data-informed strategic decision fuels them forward in the league tables."[13] Law libraries have been robustly evaluating "small data" for many years due to limited technology and experience in this area.[14] Unlocking knowledge within big data can enable law libraries to create new and more helpful services for users and make better data-informed decisions.

HOW LIBRARIES ARE USING BIG DATA

The University of Michigan Library offers a Data Services department that supports the discovery, access, organization, visualization, and preservation of data. Their expertise includes geospatial data and mapping, data management planning, metadata consultation, text and data mining, data visualization, preservation, and data sharing. They also provide workshops and training in these areas.[15]

In 2019, the National Library Board of Singapore (NLB) adopted Amazon Personalize, a cloud-based machine learning recommendation service, for its new recommendation system.[16]

The NLB had a data warehouse with transactional data that the team used to record patrons and their borrowing patterns. As a result, their focus was on training the model to improve recommendation accuracy. The service was integrated into the NLB's website and mobile app, allowing for personalized recommendations for its book and eBook collections. By leveraging a fully managed cloud-based service, NLB avoided the burden of maintaining its own infrastructure while also enabling the implementation of new algorithms and product enhancements without additional investments, resulting in reduced capital expenditures.[17]

The Brooklyn Public Library (BPL) currently utilizes Tableau to visualize its data. According to Selvon Smith, CIO, Tableau effectively communicates the library's operations in a manner that anecdotes cannot match.[18] Through Tableau, the library can track the number of individuals entering each branch, monitor program attendance, and track public computer and Wi-Fi usage, among other data points. All employees have access to this information, which is used to inform decisions at both the system-wide and branch levels. This transparency ensures that everyone in the organization understands the factors considered when making decisions.

Tableau's data visualization has had a profound impact on library operations. While some information was previously available in reports, working with the data and interpreting it was a challenge. Visualization of data has made it easier for individuals to understand the results, and reporting has become more effective. This allows individuals who are unfamiliar with analyzing data to easily comprehend what is happening and determine the necessary actions to take.[19]

THE CHALLENGES OF BIG DATA

After exploring some of the innovative ways libraries are using big data, it is equally important to consider the challenges of big data, such as data privacy, security, ethics and bias, and data mining. Librarians are often the champions of data privacy. This role may need to evolve to one of data ethics advocates, guiding patrons not only on privacy but also on the responsible use of data and understanding the implications of digital footprints.

Big data presents a risk of data being stolen, especially when using external software, hardware, vendors, or consultants that may have security vulnerabilities.[20]

An example of data theft is the high-profile case of Edward Snowden, which exposed how internet giants, such as Facebook and Google, provided the U.S. government with access to user data. However, this risk also exists outside of big data.[21]

Personal identity data is often stored on computer networks of various organizations used in daily transactions such as banking, shopping, visiting a doctor, attending school, and so on. Even internet browsing and search history is stored and used for various purposes, including advertising. Big data analysis can be used to collect extensive personal information, including identity, behavior, and preferences. This information can be used in harmful ways if it lands in the wrong hands. Identity theft, financial fraud, harassment, and discrimination are just a few ways in which personal data use might be detrimental.

The collection, storage, and analysis of large amounts of data also come with ethical concerns. As technology advances, a lot of personal data is collected without the owner's express consent or a clear understanding of how their information is being used and shared. Neglecting privacy settings, biometric tagging for facial recognition, and GPS location on smartphones are just a few of the ways an extensive digital footprint is being created, often with little or no conscious consideration by users.[22] Although there are many ethical gray areas when it comes to big data and data mining, there are a few guiding principles that most experts agree on which are as follows:

1. Personal information and identities must remain private.
2. Private information must be shared confidentially.
3. Users should have a clear understanding of how their data is used.
4. Big data should not interfere with free will.
5. Big data must not institutionalize unfair bias.[23]

Using these guiding principles is a good starting point for big data projects in law libraries.

DATA MINING FOR BUSINESS INTELLIGENCE

After an extensive look at how big data is defined, created, and stored, the next consideration is how law libraries might effectively use data mining to uncover business intelligence hidden in big data. Law libraries can identify trends, predict outcomes, better understand behaviors, and make recommendations that were not previously available to them.

Cross-Industry Standard Process for Data Mining (CRISP-DM) framework is a widely accepted approach to data mining which includes planning, implementing, and managing projects. This six-part process includes organizational understanding, data understanding, data preparation, modeling, evaluation, and deployment.[24]

The most important part of the process is understanding the questions that you would like to answer for the organization. Some examples include:

- Which resources are most frequently accessed?
- When is peak usage?
- Which search terms are most often used to search the catalog?

Identifying the relevant data and determining its location and accessibility presents the next challenge after establishing clear objectives. Once data is collected, it must be cleaned, or data that isn't needed or usable must be omitted. The remaining data must be presented in a consistent format, such as columns and rows. Once the relevant data is both clean and consistent, the analysis can begin. Models apply algorithms to analyze datasets by classifying or predicting their outcomes. In the evaluation phase, the usefulness of the model is evaluated. During deployment, the model is automated and fine-tuned, and results are shared with stakeholders.[25]

BEST PRACTICES FOR IMPLEMENTING A SUCCESSFUL BIG DATA STRATEGY

Change management in libraries involves the application of structured approaches to guide the transition from current practices to desired ones. The emphasis on change impact and stakeholder assessment within academic libraries suggests formal change management practices can lead to a measurable increase in the adoption of new systems.[26] Sucozhañay highlights the need for library managers to act as change agents, employing transformational leadership and stakeholder management to overcome implementation challenges.[27]

Undertaking a data mining project necessitates close coordination between the law library, information technology, and data analysts. Librarians are responsible for identifying and locating the requisite big data while ensuring its proper utilization. The IT department ensures that appropriate technology solutions are in place, and data analysts analyze the big data.

Traditional education and training for law librarians do not prepare them to handle big data. Library Science programs increasingly offer courses covering big data analysis and management. San Jose State University's School of Information offers a data science focus within their MLIS program.[28] Similarly, Catholic University offers a data science course of study for MSLIS students.[29] The University of Pittsburgh, School of Computing and Information, provides an elective Applied Data-Driven Methods certificate as part of the MLIS degree program.[30] There are also numerous professional training opportunities focused on data science that law librarians can take advantage of to acquire data science skills.

Although privacy and security were discussed in *The Challenges of Big Data* section, the importance of these issues warrants mentioning them again in the context of best practices. There is a need to establish appropriate policies about privacy, security, access control, and governance, which are crucial components of a comprehensive big data strategy. Organizations can implement several safeguards to protect data, ensure its confidentiality, and protect its integrity and availability.

Encryption transforms readable data into a coded format that can only be accessed or decrypted by authorized individuals who have a decryption key. This safeguard is essential for protecting sensitive information stored or transmitted over networks. It mitigates the risk of data breaches by making the information unreadable to unauthorized users.[31]

Threat detection and defense systems monitor networks for threats and prevent threats from carrying out intended actions. Antivirus/anti-malware software can be used to detect and eliminate malicious software. Firewalls act as barriers between secure internal networks and untrusted external networks. They control incoming and outgoing network traffic based on an organization's security policies.[32]

Data minimization involves collecting data necessary for a specific purpose. By limiting the amount of personal information collected, organizations reduce the risk associated with data breaches because there is less valuable information for attackers to steal. Anonymization removes personally identifiable information when it is not needed. Anonymized data ensures that personal details cannot be linked back to any individual without additional information that is kept separately.[33]

RapidMiner and Dataiku are two commonly used data analytics platforms. Both platforms can be used for preparing data, text mining, characterization, and predictive analysis.[34] Working with third-party vendors or consultants who provide big data management services can limit the law library staff's involvement required if using data analytics platforms. This becomes especially important if the requisite skills are not present to use a data analytics platform. For example, Apache Hadoop is an open-source framework used to store and process large datasets.[35] Several big data analytics companies, such as Amazon's AWS Elastic MapReduce, are meeting the needs of companies using Hadoop. AWS Elastic MapReduce is among the top commercial Hadoop distributors and may be best suited for organizations who do not want to manage all the necessary servers for big data analysis. Alpha Apex Group is a leading big data consultant providing comprehensive data management services.[36]

Microsoft's PowerBI and Tableau are two powerful data visualization tools. After analyzing data, it is important to effectively communicate the business intelligence gleaned from the data. These tools enable users to transform complex information into visual representations that can tell a story about an organization based on the underlying data. Once the story is told, practical steps can be developed and implemented to solve real-world business problems.

UTILIZING BIG DATA FOR COLLECTION MANAGEMENT

Collection development is usually delegated in one of three ways: one person is responsible for collection development decisions; several selectors are responsible for specific geographic or subject areas; multiple selectors function as a committee; or several selectors make independent collection decisions that are not restricted by subject or geographic area. Regardless of the collection development approach, selectors traditionally make decisions based on a few core interests.[37]

Budget constraints are paramount in collection development decisions. Other factors include the institutional mission and goals, curriculum and scholarly needs of faculty and students, recent legal developments, accreditation standards, user data and feedback, legal developments, new and updated publications, and collection development services such as GOBI.

A modern approach to collection development using big data can optimize processes. Data analytics can help librarians understand patterns and trends within current collections, such as what materials are most frequently used or underutilized. This insight can inform future purchase decisions, awareness activities, and weeding efforts. Observing borrowing patterns, search behaviors within the catalog, and ILL requests can reveal the material patrons are most interested in to predict emerging trends.[38] This information could be used for individuals, certain groups, and collectively. Data analytics can also be used to forecast trends by analyzing prominent current events, social media trends, and academic research areas. This information can then be used in collection development. By analyzing data on resource usage patterns, libraries can determine if users prefer electronic or print resources for various subjects or types of materials.

Preparing big data for analysis can be challenging when using disparate data sources that gather different information. Data must be standardized, which includes tasks such as removing duplicate information, correcting errors, and checking accuracy. The use of outdated systems may impede the data cleaning process due to differences in format or structure. In many cases, migrating to a more advanced platform that is better equipped to handle large amounts of data may be necessary. If someone on staff doesn't have the skills to clean data, it presents another hurdle to be overcome by using someone outside the organization or making sure staff have proper data science training.

An example of a modern approach to collection development was presented at the 2022 International Federation of Library Associations and Institutions (IFLA) World Library and Information Congress (WLIC) conference in Dublin, Ireland. The Library of Congress gathered and analyzed physical, chemical, and optical data to make informed choices about whether to keep or remove certain books, with the goal of maintaining the cultural heritage strength of the collections assessed. To address gaps in knowledge and conduct an unbiased evaluation, a data analytics method was needed to identify materials that may be in danger and distinguish between high-quality and low-quality copies of books.

The study analyzed the physical, chemical, and optical traits of over 500 similar books from the period of 1840–1940. The books were sourced from five major research libraries across the United States. A system was established to collect and store information such as tensile strength and acidity. This information, along with other non-scientific details for each book, was organized in JavaScript Object Notation (JSON), a data-interchange language, and stored in CouchDB, a database management system, to keep everything well organized so it could be easily retrieved and analyzed later.[39] JSON can represent structured data in a way that is easy for humans to read and write while machines can easily parse and generate.[40] The team used a query tool to evaluate individual data points in real time and a comparison tool that utilized an open-source International Image Interoperability Framework (IIIF) viewer to closely examine photo documentation between books.[41]

When thinking about preservation, it is important to look at how materials, surroundings, and usage can affect items. The research team found that the original properties of the paper used to make the books were the most important factor in determining their condition later. This project showed that being able to gather, save, and analyze datasets can significantly improve an organization's ability to make unbiased collection development decisions.[42]

THE WAY FORWARD WITH BIG DATA

Advanced data analytics involving machine learning models can help predict individual user preferences based on past behavior, leading to highly personalized recommendations similar to services like those seen on commercial platforms such as Amazon and Netflix.

Data analytics makes collaboration between libraries easier. Resources can be acquired based on broader community interests across geographical regions or subject area specializations. Libraries can better coordinate collection development efforts beyond their own libraries and consider the collection efforts of other libraries. This is especially appealing when it comes to expensive resources that might otherwise be out of reach for individual library budgets.

Law librarians have an opportunity to be change agents and embrace big data to make data-driven decisions, improve patron services, and ensure that libraries remain relevant as knowledge centers in an increasingly digital world and that librarians position themselves as leaders in this area, as the availability of big data opens the door for more technological advances.

As law libraries become more reliant on big data to make informed decisions and improve patron services, policies on big data should be implemented to ensure the proper management and protection of data. The policy should reflect the mission and goals of the library while ensuring critical elements addressed in this chapter are included in the policy. Detailed guidelines are provided below.

DESIGN A LAW LIBRARY BIG DATA POLICY[42]

1. Purpose
   Establish guidelines for the collection, storage, analysis, and use of big data to improve library services and operations.
2. Data Collection
   Detail the types of data that will be collected and stored. This may include information on library users such as borrowing history, search queries, and facility usage. Collection methods might include website analytics, surveys and other automated systems. Patrons should be informed that relevant and necessary data will be collected, and sensitive information such as financial data will not be stored.
3. Data Analysis
   Address the analytics tools and techniques used to process and interpret data collected. Discuss reports generated and how the information is used.
4. Privacy and Security
   Clarify data security measures. Libraries must ensure data collected is secure from unauthorized access, accidental loss, or misuse. This can be achieved by implementing encryption protocols, regular security audits, access controls for staff members who handle data, etc.
5. Data Usage
   Explain how the library leverages collection information to enhance services and operations. For example, data may be used to inform collection development, optimize resource allocation or enhance user experiences with the library.
6. Data Sharing
   Include guidelines for data sharing and transparency. Law libraries should be transparent about how they use and share data with third parties and obtain consent from users before sharing their information. Additionally, libraries should have clear procedures in place for responding to data breaches or requests for data access from law enforcement authorities.
7. Retention and Disposal
   Develop a clear data retention policy that addresses how long the data will be stored and how it is deleted considering any legal and institutional requirements.

8. Staff Training
   Ensure that staff understand the importance of big data in library operations. Staff should develop and maintain competencies in data handling, analysis and interpretation as appropriate through professional development. Promote a data-driven culture throughout the organization by leading with choices based on quantitative and qualitative information.
9. Policy Review
   Review the policy annually and address new technologies and regulations. Outlining the types of data collected, security measures implemented, guidelines established for data sharing and general transparency can help maintain the trust of patrons and confidence of staff that ethical standards for big data usage will be upheld.

NOTES

1. Dr. Ajay Lala and Pinkal Jain, "Investigating the Ethics of Big Data and Data Mining," *Data Science: Practical Approach with Python & R* (2023): 85, https://doi.org/10.58532/nbennurch293.
2. "Big Data Analytics in the Tourism and Travel Industry," Epam, accessed July 14, 2024, https://startups.epam.com/blog/big-data-in-tourism-and-travel.
3. Mubashir Hassan et al., "Innovations in Genomics and Big Data Analytics for Personalized Medicine and Health Care: A Review," *International Journal of Molecular Science* (April 22, 2022): 23, https://doi.org/10.3390/ijms23094645.
4. Vishnu Pendyala, *Veracity of Big Data: Machine Learning and Other Approaches to Verifying Truthfulness* (San Jose, CA: Apress, 2018), 5–9.
5. "How Much Data is Created Every Day in 2024?," *TechJury*, accessed July 1, 2024, https://techjury.net/blog/how-much-data-is-created-every-day/.
6. "How Much Data is Created Every Day in 2024?"
7. "Structured and Unstructured Data," *Imperva*, accessed July 1, 2024, https://www.imperva.com/learn/data-security/structured-and-unstructured-data/#:~:text=Structured%20data%20is%20usually%20easier,it%20in%20a%20relational%20database.
8. Vishnu Pendyala, *Veracity of Big Data: Machine Learning and Other Approaches to Verifying Truthfulness* (San Jose, CA: Apress, 2018), 10.
9. "Research Foundations: Information Literacy," Seminole State College of Florida, accessed July 1, 2024, https://libguides.seminolestate.edu/researchfoundations/informationliteracy#:~:text=The%20term%20%22information%20literacy%22%20describes,and%20acknowledge%20sources%20of%20information.
10. "What are Real-Life Examples of the Application of Big Data Analytics?," *Magnimind*, accessed July 1, 2024, https://magnimindacademy.com/blog/what-are-real-life-examples-of-the-application-of-big-data-analytics/#:~:text=3%2D%20Media%20and%20entertainment%20industry%20The%20media,big%20data%20analytics%20to%20a%20great%20extent.
11. Anvay Bhure and Sharmishta Desai, "Exploring the Intersection of Big Data and Legal Analytics: A Survey of Its Application in the Legal Industry," *Journal of Big Data Technology and Business Analytics* (March 2023): 1, https://doi.org/10.46610/jbdtba.2023.v02i01.002.
12. Giles C. Oatley, "Themes in Data Mining, Big Data, and Crime Analytics," *WIREs Data Mining and Knowledge Discovery* (2022): 5, https://doi.org/10.1002/widm.1432.
13. Rafael Ball, "Big Data and Their Impact on Libraries," *American Journal of Information Science and Technology* 3, no. 1 (2019): 2, https://doi.org/10.11648/j.ajist.20190301.11.
14. Ball, "Big Data and Their Impact on Libraries," 2.
15. "Data Services," University of Michigan Library, accessed July 1, 2024, https://www.lib.umich.edu/research-and-scholarship/data-services.
16. Chee 14, https://repository.ifla.org/bitstream/123456789/1819/1/tilt_newsletterJanuary2022R31Final.pdf.

17. Sze, Kiam, and Yi, "You May Like—How the National Library Board of Singapore use Machine Learning to Recommend Books," 15.
18. Jon Reed, "How the Brooklyn Public Library Used Data Visualization to Build a Better Library," Diginomica, accessed July 1, 2024, https://diginomica.com/how-the-brooklyn-public-library-data-visualization-a-better-library-with-tableau.
19. "Brooklyn Public Library Saves Time, Money, and Headcount with Tableau," Tableau, accessed July 1, 2024, https://www.tableau.com/solutions/customer/brooklyn-public-library-saves-time-money-and-headcount-tableau.
20. Chunli Su, "Big Data Security and Privacy Protection," 2019 International Conference on Virtual Reality and Intelligent Systems (ICVRIS), 87, accessed July 1, 2024, 87, https://doi.org/10.1109/ICVRIS.2019.00030.
21. Su, "Big Data Security and Privacy Protection," 87.
22. Dr. Ajay Lala and Pinkal Jain, "Investigating the Ethics of Big Data and Data Mining," *Data Science: Practical Approach with Python & R* (2023): 86, https://doi.org/10.58532/nbennurch293.
23. Lala and Jain, "Investigating the Ethics of Big Data and Data Mining," 86.
24. Matthew North, *Data Mining for the Masses: With Implementations in RapidMiner,* 3rd ed. (CreateSpace Independent Publishing Platform, September 5, 2018).
25. North, *Data Mining for the Masses*, 11–13.
26. Nel Duffield and Jaime Royals, "The People Side of Change: Applying Change Management Principles in Academic Libraries," in *Chandos Information Professional Series, Technology, Change and the Academic Library*, ed. Jeremy Atkinson (Cambridge, MA: Chandos Publishing, 2021), 33–42, https://doi.org/10.1016/B978-0-12-822807-4.00003-8.
27. Dolores Sucozhañay et al., "Transformational Leadership and Stakeholder Management in Library Change," *LIBER Quarterly: The Journal of the Association of European Research Libraries* 24, no. 2 (2014): 65–67, https://doi.org/10.18352/lq.9583.
28. "Data Science—MLIS Career Pathway," SJSU School of Information, accessed July 1, 2024, https://ischool.sjsu.edu/data-science.
29. "Data Science," Catholic University of America, Department of Information Sciences, accessed July 1, 2024, https://lis.catholic.edu/academics/courses-of-study/data-science/index.html.
30. "Library and Information Science, MLIS," University of Pittsburgh, School of Computing and Information, accessed July 1, 2024, https://www.sci.pitt.edu/academics/masters-degrees/library-and-information-science-mlis.
31. Bipin Bihari Jayasingh, M. R. Patra, and D. Bhanu Mahesh, "Security Issues and Challenges of Big Data Analytics and Visualization," in *International Conference on Contemporary Computing and Informatics,* Noida, India, 2016, Amity University, IEEE-USA, Institute of Electrical and Electronics Engineers Uttar Pradesh Section, and Institute of Electrical and Electronics Engineers, 2016. *Proceedings of the 2016 2nd International Conference on Contemporary Computing and Informatics (IC3I): 14–17 December 2016*, Noida, India. Edited by S. K. Niranjan and V. N. Manjunatha Aradhya (Piscataway, NJ: IEEE, 2016). https://doi.org/10.1109/IC3I39298. accessed July 1, 2024, 206.
32. Danda B. Rawat, Ronald Doku, and Moses Garuba, "Cybersecurity in Big Data Era: From Securing Big Data to Data-Driven Security," *IEEE Transactions on Services Computing* 14, no. 6 (November–December 2021): 6, https://doi.org/10.1109/TSC.2019.2907247.
33. Rawat, Doku, and Garuba, "Cybersecurity in Big Data Era: From Securing Big Data to Data-Driven Security," 12.
34. "Artificial Intelligence (AI) and Data Analytics Solutions," Altair, accessed July 1, 2024, https://altair.com/altair-rapidminer.
"Dataiku at a Glance: The Universal AI Platform," Data Iku, accessed July 1, 2024, https://pages.dataiku.com/interactive-data-sheet?utm_id=14139326388--125114850603--537236723194--dataiku&utm_source=nam-adwords&utm_medium=paid-search&utm_campaign=GLO%20CONTENT%20Interactive%20Data%20Sheet&gad_source=1&gclid=CjwKCAjw4f6zBhBVEiwATEHFVlGQZu7fQYtfdNtMYDHuzoc-QxdJeNSAV1-CfRTahFu1bJRct65WsBoCX9gQAvD_BwE.
35. "Apache Hadoop," Apache Software Foundation, accessed July 1, 2024, https://hadoop.apache.org/.

36. "Top Big Data Consultants, Companies, Services, and Consulting Firms," *Jake Jorgovan*, accessed July 1, 2024. https://jake-jorgovan.com/blog/big-data-consultants-companies-services-consulting-firms.
37. Casey Duncan, "Collection Development," in *Academic Law Libraries Within the Changing Landscape of Legal Education: A Primer for Deans and Provosts,* eds. Michelle M. Wu, Scott B. Pagel, and Joan S. Holland (New York: William S. Hein & Co., Inc., 2020), 110.
38. Annette Day and Hilary Davis, "Collection Intelligence: Using Data Driven Decision Making in Collection Management," in *Proceedings of the Charleston Library Conference,* 81, accessed July 1, 2024, http://dx.doi.org/10.5703/1288284314822.
39. "Introducing JSON," accessed July 1, 2024, https://www.json.org/json-en.html; "Why CouchDB?," accessed July 1, 2024, https://docs.couchdb.org/en/stable/intro/why.html.
40. "Introducing JSON."
41. "Why Big Data Matters: Perspectives from the Libraries," International Federation of Library Associations and Institutions (IFLA), https://www.ifla.org/news/why-big-data-matters-perspectives-from-the-libraries/.
42. "Why Big Data Matters: Perspectives from the Libraries."
43. Emmanouel Garoufallou and Panorea Gaitanou, "Big Data: Opportunities and Challenges in Libraries, a Systematic Literature Review," *College & Research Libraries*, Vol. 82, No. 3 (2021): 7–8.

19

Data on the Horizon

Involvement and Impact of Law Librarians in Big Data Projects

Erik Adams and Kristen Naik

"I don't ask you to put yourself anywhere. I ask you to be where you are."

- Anne Leckie, *Ancillary Mercy*

Law librarians are awash in data. Some of it is generated within the libraries themselves, as in traditional library measurements like the number of reference requests handled or the number of books loaned out. Some of it is institutional, as with the docket sheets generated by courts or the remote corners of university libraries housing volumes of law and treatises so old and obscure that no one has yet bothered to convert them to electronic form. And there is a lot of data externally available, gathered by government agencies or by private companies who are happy to sell that data for a price.

Law librarianship as a profession is inherently multi-disciplinary, like data science. While data science combines statistics, computer science, and domain expertise, law librarianship combines knowledge of law and civics; a deep understanding of how information about the law is gathered, searched, and presented; and the most traditional librarian role of making information available to our user populations in the form they need. With that description in mind, big data is the latest evolution in librarian history that has moved from physical books to electronic databases and from lengthy treatises to shorter encyclopedia-style articles. The growing importance of data is both the latest step in that evolution and a somewhat new category of information in its rawest form.

Librarians may see themselves as facilitators of access to all forms of data, but whether or not their institutions recognize that role is a different question, one that we are investigating in this chapter. We ask the question: "What role in big data projects are law librarians fulfilling, and where do they want to be?" To determine this, we have taken a survey of librarians in several different kinds of law libraries and interviewed a select group of librarians in several different institutions. One thing has become very clear: most of us feel we can do more.

METHODOLOGIES

Aptly, the scope of this chapter was too wide to consider only one form of data. To encapsulate a broader view of big data within law librarianship, we decided to conduct two-fold research. This research was conducted in the form of surveys sent to a mass audience and interviews targeted at key individuals within law librarianship. Since law librarianship is a wide term, we included colleagues who have knowledge or knowledge management in their title as well, as much of this work is related to libraries and the practice of librarianship.

Survey Methodology

To gather information about the current state of Big Data in respect to law librarianship, we conducted a survey. The survey questions were categorized into four sections: Basic Details, Your Law Library and Big Data, Challenges and Opportunities with Big Data in Your Law Library, and a Follow Up. The responses were anonymous with the option of including their name at the end if they chose.

The basic details section included information about the participants: what type of law institution they work for, their role within the library, service population size, and the size of the law library staff. This was followed up by more specific questions about their institution and their data including the number of staff dedicated to data projects, the role of the library within data efforts, types of data used by the library, if they pay for data and what type, how data is used at their institution, how data is used in the law library, and what data visualization tools are used.

Next, we asked about the challenges and opportunities law librarians face in regards to data. These questions covered common challenges and opportunities, as well as specific questions about if and how AI is being used by the respondents. Finally, we inquired if any participant would be interested in being interviewed for this chapter, where we found several of our interviewees.

This survey was distributed on several library listservs including American Association of Law Librarians (AALL), Special Libraries Association (SLA), as well as targeted sub-committees and local chapters of these institutions.

Interview Methodology

In addition to reaching out to individuals who had self-identified in the previous survey, we also reached out to some key figures within the profession. We identified additional interview subjects through recognition via law librarianship accolades (members of the FastCase 50, published work on this topic, etc.). We worked to get diverse experiences within this group, making sure to cover different United States geographic regions, types of institutions, and sizes of institutions. In total, we interviewed eight professionals on this subject over the course of several weeks. Due to the geographic diversity of this group, interviews were conducted over Zoom by both co-authors.

Most interviewees were given the same set of questions, which were used as a starting point for discussion. Questions ranged from personal history with data, involvement in their institution's data efforts, the role of law librarianship with data efforts, to a very speculative "If you had unlimited access and funds, what would you want to create with data?"

These interviews touched on questions about the interviewees' experience in the field, changes they've seen in the profession, current and dream data efforts, the role of big data within law libraries, as well as challenges and opportunities with data and law librarianship. We received a wide range of responses and noted some key trends, which we discuss in the next section.

RESULTS

Survey Results

We received fifty responses to our survey from a range of academic, government, law firm, and public libraries. Our results were split almost evenly between director, managerial, or equivalent director roles and those in an analyst, researcher, or librarian role.

Table 19.1 Types of Law Libraries and Role of Survey Respondents

Type of Library	*Librarian Role (Includes Analyst and Research Roles)*	*Managerial Role*	*Total*
Academic	7	4	11
Government	5	13	18
Law firm	8	12	20
Public	1	0	1
Total	21	29	50

Table 19.2 Type of Law Libraries and Library Staff

		Library Staff				
		1–5	*6–15*	*16–25*	*26–35*	*More than 35*
Type of Library	Academic	1	7	1	1	1
	Government	8	4	3	4	2
	Law firm	8	9	2	1	0
	Public	1	0	0	0	0
	Total	18	20	6	3	3

We also had a variety of responses regarding the size of library staff, although the vast majority of respondents had fifteen or fewer library staff members at their institution. Most law libraries do not have any staff dedicated to data projects, but it is a near even split with 54 percent not having any staff members dedicated to data projects and 46 percent having some staff dedicated to data. Forty percent of respondents have at least one full-time staff member dedicated to data projects.

Interview Results

We were fortunate enough to have willing responses to our call for interviews to be able to identify themes analyzed in the next section. These conversations highlight the state of data within the law librarianship profession, the data skills and experience of law librarians, the relationship between libraries and their greater institutions, and the role of law libraries within greater data conversations within the law library and beyond. Eight librarians were interviewed: four who work for law firms, two who work for law school libraries, one librarian at a court, and one vendor.

There were several common themes in our conversations. One of the most frequently mentioned topics was the value of institutional support in libraries' data efforts. Ed Walters, chief strategy officer at vLex, went so far as to observe that he thought law firms should have a budget specifically for research and development, and that the budget for that effort should sit in the library. While none of our interviewees' institutions had quite gone that far, there had been recognition that librarians could have a role in data projects, and they were involved.

Librarians mentioned that with this support they were able to make concrete contributions to the efforts of their organizations. Librarians have always used statistics to justify purchase decisions, and using modern analysis on our classic problem has yielded real results. Michelle Trovillo, director of information resources at Baker Hostetler, observed, "we've proved time and time again that value in contract negotiations by using data."[1] But in addition to justifying management decisions, these projects prove that librarians are able to gather data, present it in a usable form, and determine important metrics like return on investment and impacts on researcher activities.

Table 19.3 Types of Law Libraries and Data Staff

		Data Staff			
		None	*1 part-time staff*	*1 full-time staff*	*More than 1 full-time staff*
Type of Library	Academic	6	2	1	2
	Government	10	1	4	3
	Law firm	10	0	5	5
	Public	1	0	0	0
	Total	27	3	10	10

However, there were also librarians whose institutional support was less enthusiastic. One librarian told us that even though there was a recognition of the importance of skills with statistics and analytics, her organization expected librarians to be generalists, and technology or data skills were not part of the mix, though perhaps they should be. Joy Shoemaker, branch librarian at the Ninth Circuit Court of Appeals, observed "[data is] not going away . . . it's just going to become more and more integral in the legal industry."[2] Other librarians noted that if the institution didn't see the value of involving librarians in data projects, those projects wouldn't go away: they simply go to a different part of the organization. Joe Cera, digital initiatives and scholarly communications librarian at the University of California, Berkeley, was blunt. "You know, whoever asks for reference questions, if they ask data questions, and we say, 'I don't know, but I know somebody you can ask that's outside of the library.' I think that places the library outside of data conversations. And that's a terrible future. Because I think that those conversations belong in the library as much as any other research related thing."[3]

Related to institutional support were staffing levels. Just as our survey data suggests that institutions are not always adding staff specifically for data projects, our interviewees reported that they often took on the tasks for the simple reason that they were the only people with the necessary skills and the wherewithal to engage. Lisa Lee, knowledge and innovation manager at the law firm O'Melveny and Meyers, described how her role grew out of an earlier position as an electronic resources librarian: "the data part came in sort of gradually, because my job specifically was in electronic resources. So, as we are comprehensively managing all electronic resources out of one place . . . we really needed to understand how people are using our resources. So data came in."[4] Work with internal data led naturally to working with data externally.

Several librarians mentioned that they were envious of the efforts at other organizations. One academic mentioned how another law school had created a data catalog, and they wished they had time to develop a similar product at their own institution. A librarian at a medium-sized law firm expressed a desire for the resources available to librarians and analysts at larger law firms. Interestingly, even librarians whose work was, in the authors' opinion, truly cutting edge, there was dissatisfaction with aspects of it and had a keen desire to do more.

Most of the librarians we spoke to felt that there has been a shift over the last several years toward a greater integration of data in the work we do. Attorneys at law firms are looking for analytics reports on the habits of judges; students at universities are keen to get data for research projects. A recurring challenge that was mentioned was managing expectations: increasingly, there is an assumption that data will be easily available in electronic form and presented in a user-friendly way, which often is not the case.

Several of our librarians discussed the problem of the quality of data. Users think that numbers are free from bias and that data will be self-documenting. Cera used the phrase, "the myth of neutrality of numbers" to describe this phenomenon.[5] Data might be tainted in a variety of subtle and complicated ways, and it takes time and domain expertise to understand those issues. Other librarians addressed the question of transparency of data: vendors developing large language models for

Generative AI systems are often not open about the source of data that feeds into the system, which raises real concerns about quality, bias, and the ability to comply with local laws.

Several interviewees suggested that there is a need for a new form of information literacy, specific to big data, statistics, and artificial intelligence. It was observed that young students and professionals are less critical of the data they find in their research and seem to be unaware that data itself can be biased.

In response to our speculative question, many respondents had exactly the same answer: easier and better access to the dockets and documents filed in state courts. Walters summarized the issue nicely: "The House has passed, and the Senate has ratified a version of a bill that would make PACER data free. That would be a revolution. That's a huge deal. And not just for litigation. There is just a mountain of historical insight . . . that we can't see it's not unanswerable. It's just unanswered."[6]

ANALYSIS

Meet Us Where We Are: The Nexus of Profession and Institution

In recent years, with the rise of new technologies and workplace environments, the law librarian role has expanded. Many of our interviewees described a distinct increase in questions involving data and its analysis directed to the library. This role of law librarians as data stewards and interpreters is, as one interviewee described, "ever increasing. It's not going away."[7] When asked the question: "What role does the law library play in data efforts?" only 14 percent of our survey takers did not answer this question, suggesting their library does not take on this role. Or, perhaps, that it is such a minor role they are not aware of. Unsurprisingly, these are the same respondents that identify as having no data staff at their institution.

Per our survey, law libraries are now taking on a plethora of roles with data in their institutions, indicating that this rise in data is not unique to our interviewees. The most common of these data responsibilities is analysis and report generation, which 66 percent of respondents identified as part of the law libraries' role at their institution. Additionally, law libraries serve a key role in the acquisition of data, primarily as facilitators of data, wherein the library finds data to meet research needs (66 percent) but also as purchasers of data (44 percent), managers of data contracts (40 percent), and/or advisers on procurement of data (40 percent).

Most librarians surveyed used Microsoft Excel, a commonly available spreadsheet tool for their data work (82 percent), and almost a third of these law librarians use Excel exclusively for their data work. However, Excel lacks key functionality available with more complex tools such as PowerBI and Tableau (used by 20 percent of survey takers), which allow one to create custom conditional fields and groupings. This severely limits the type of work that can be completed and the projects that can be undertaken by these institutions. Only 18 percent of survey takers identified as using Python, Ruby, or other coding languages to aid in their data work, which would allow for the most complex data projects. Many fall in the middle, using tools like Microsoft Access (16 percent) or Google Analytics (20 percent). For those who use data tools, most use more than one; however, one-third of respondents reported only one tool being used at their institution.

This work with data and connecting users to data is a natural progression of the librarian role in the modern age. Many of our interviewees see this as a natural outgrowth and, in fact, their duty as librarians to understand and familiarize themselves with data and its associated analysis and technologies. That task in itself, however, can prove challenging.

There Are No Athenas: Data Expertise within Law Librarianship

One of the striking themes from our cohort was the happenstance that led these librarians to take on data and data analytics as part of their work. When asked how they got involved with data and law librarianship, almost all of our interviewees described a sort of falling into their data responsibilities, which always followed their path into law libraries. "No one else wanted it, which was great for me." Cera, an academic law librarian, described how he came to data analytics in law librarianship.[8] Some volunteered for these new responsibilities, interested in the opportunities it seemed to offer. Unsurprisingly, those we interviewed were still working with data, for some as much as fifteen years since they first took on the responsibilities.

No one arrives at this specialty with their skills fully formed, like Athena from the head of Zeus. Most of the data training these librarians received was self-taught and/or on the job. Without guidance, it is easy to get overwhelmed with the tools, terms, and data itself. After all, as referenced previously, data is not neutral and comes with its own inherent limitations. For those who have embraced this opportunity, the learning curve can be steep. Often, the first step in any data project is familiarizing oneself with the data, or as one of our interviewees described it, becoming a "data wrangler."[9]

It takes a lot of time to wrangle data, as anyone who works in this specialty can tell you, and it often involves much trial and error before reaching success. This can deter newcomers from trying their hand at data and statistics, a subject not often covered in library school. One of our interviewees, who wished to remain anonymous, described their contemporaries as "afraid of data," a sentiment echoed by many of those we interviewed. Furthermore, the pace of the addition of data responsibilities into these librarians' roles varied widely. Some describe being thrown into the deep end, being given a project and told to run with it, while others describe this process as more gradual. For those facing a more abrupt entrance into the data sphere, it can prove disheartening. For those who do take on this challenge, the rewards are plentiful, though easier to reap if you have some technical expertise.

Even for those who take on this new mantle confidently, many feel as if they are working alone or, at the very least, not part of the data team. Depending on the institution, the role of data teams and the library can be terribly split, which we will discuss more in later sections. Indeed, the most common data-related challenge identified by our survey was a lack of staff time or expertise, with 74 percent of responses identifying this as an issue from all types of libraries. One survey respondent even added that there is a "lack of willingness to learn and embrace big data" at their institution, which they identified as a government law library. Other challenges included concerns about the quality (60 percent), cost (40 percent), format (48 percent), and integrity of the data (50 percent), as well as licensing restrictions (34 percent).

Even when there is that desire and experience, some librarians have described a lack of bandwidth to complete data projects and grow their own data skills. This is unsurprising, as per our survey, only 20 percent of respondents have more than one staff member dedicated to data projects, and most do not have staff dedicated to data at all (54 percent). If you don't have staff that are trained and available to work on data requests, how can the library pursue data projects?

Institutional Support: DIY Data to Data Lake Houses

Institutional support is key to a law library's big data efforts and directly impacts the scope and ambition of such projects. In institutions where there is active support, data efforts thrive and the value is recognized. In organizations where support is unenthusiastic, data projects are still encountered and must be more homespun.

This simple fact was clear in our survey data. In organizations where there are no staff dedicated to data, such projects tend to be limited to those necessary for the management of the library: contract management and staffing decisions. On the other hand, in organizations that have dedicated staff to data projects (full or part-time), the library is able to take on a wider variety of projects, including purchasing data, finding data to meet research needs, analysis, and report generation.

Software used for data also correlated with institutional support. In organizations with dedicated staff and more projects, there was a greater variety and sophistication of software used in data projects. In organizations with less support for library data projects, there was almost no software used besides Excel. Although we did not specifically ask in our survey or interviews about the use of data warehouse or data lake products, several of our interviewees mentioned that their organizations are using them and that they were an important part of their data projects.

Our interviewees reinforced this pattern. Michelle Pearse, senior research and data librarian at Harvard Law School Library, reported how her institution recognized several years ago that there was a need for someone to handle student-led research projects, and she was given that role.[10] Other interviewees reported that because data projects had not been made a priority, there was no dedicated staff, and projects were handled by people who were also responsible for other essential library functions like research. Several of our interviewees mentioned using data warehouse and data lake products and looking toward newer developments. This stark difference shows the immense effect institutional support has on the data projects able to be accomplished.

A Seat at the Table: Law Librarianship and Data Conversations

Multiple interviewees stressed the importance of librarians being active participants in the projects at their organizations. Cera stressed this importance, "These conversations belong in the library as much as any other research."[11] Trovillo described her role as the result of a process: showing the value of librarians in data projects first via data-driven management decisions for traditional library projects like contract negotiations. This demonstrated her staff's abilities and rigor and opened the door to other projects.

Sadly, our survey data suggests that not everyone is participating in these discussions. Six of our fifty respondents reported that the library has no role, at all, in their organizations' data projects; one suggesting that to the best of their knowledge, no such projects were underway. Fortunately, more than two-thirds reported having a role either in finding data, managing contracts with outside vendors, or purchasing data.

Dreams Abound: Data Utopias

Many of those we interviewed had lofty ideas for ideal data projects. These ranged from the creation of specific research tools to the creation of new organizational entities. Others desired better infrastructure at their institutions, allowing them to handle these projects more easily. One thing is certain—data has much potential in law librarianship, if only we tapped into it.

The most popular of these was a fully searchable state and federal courts docket—a problem long plaguing the law librarianship field. This project would be immensely beneficial indeed, with implications across all law libraries and jurisdictions within the United States. Those who suggested this dream project emphasized that this tool would be publicly available for all to use—unsurprising from a group of law librarians.

Having staff and data available to explore more data projects was another recurring dream. An academic describes his version of this dream as creating a "space" for libraries to "provide data services," which includes data literacy initiatives and support for libraries with their data projects.[12] Another prong of this dream includes an R&D center, focused on data projects within the law library space. This would serve as a consortium for all libraries, sharing the results from these data efforts. In his interview with us, Walters also talked about this desire for an R&D data department, not as a dream, but as a required investment, and as a one law firms should seriously consider.[13]

One private law librarian had a similar dream: a data lake house. In addition to this wonderful store of data, there would be a staff to work with it. This staff would have an understanding of not only data analytics but the tools associated with this discipline. And along with this understanding, "more readily available data" for these experts to use for their data projects. "Having more staff . . . would be a pie in the sky," she describes, smiling with her hands splayed open, as if indicating her willingness to receive such a workforce.[14] This desire for staff versed in data is at the core of most of these dreams—after all, what is a consortium without experts?

Much like utopias themselves, to our knowledge, these dreams currently do not exist at any institution. These dreams demonstrate the appetite for data projects within law librarianship, and true visionaries are already in the field thinking about these subjects. The only thing that remains is finding our way there.

WHERE DO WE GO FROM HERE? RECOMMENDATIONS

Advocacy of Data Analytics within Law Libraries

Data discussions are happening at our institutions; there is no doubt about that. The only question is if the library is involved in these conversations. "It's a mistake to not be involved," Cera warned when we broached this topic during our interview.[15] As outlined above, law libraries make a practical partner in these discussions, as we are well versed in research and its associated activities and could provide key insight and support to these activities.

In some cases, to be a part of these conversations, we must seek them out. If not already, we must make data a priority in our libraries and for the institutions we serve. Not only does this help solidify our value within these organizations, but it also showcases our adeptness with this type of analytics and research. This requires us to be engaged with these issues not only at a local or institutional level but also at a professional level. Law librarianship should be prepared to evolve and acquire these skills if we are to solidify and grow our value to our institutions.

Data Professional Development Opportunities

As the results from our surveys and interviewees demonstrate, data skills, or the lack thereof, among law librarians are a key barrier to realizing the full potential of data work in law libraries. The increasing prevalence of data in research will only grow, and current law librarianship coursework does not provide the data literacy lessons needed to meet this growing demand. Rather than relegating these questions to other departments, this is an opportunity for the law librarianship profession to embrace this new type of information and educate ourselves on its intricacies.

This would require the intentional development of this skillset within the law library profession. This could be accomplished through the engagement of law library associations (AALL comes to mind) to offer these trainings for their members, allowing law librarians to grow these skills as part of their professional development. This also could be tackled even earlier—library schools should offer data science for librarians as an elective to complete one's degree. Data literacy should be offered, and at the minimum, discussed so that new librarians are prepared to face this data-driven future.

Law librarians need to become as comfortable with data as they are with any other legal resource. This requires that law librarians (or at least a good portion of them) be able to understand, analyze, and manipulate datasets, as well as explain these details to their service population, should the need arise. There is a gap in this information service currently, which presents an opportunity for law librarians to adapt and grow to meet this need.

Furthermore, as data gurus at our respective institutions, we can help demonstrate and provide clear statistical evidence of the value and potential role of law libraries. The more we advocate for ourselves in this manner, there will be more confidence in our abilities not only with data but also to adapt and grow as a profession. This is an increasingly needed skill, as technology is advancing at an unprecedented rate and will continue to do so.

For those of you reading this chapter who are involved with data at your law library, continue the work you are doing. The more successful data projects the library completes, the easier will be the justification. For those of you not involved with data but would like to be, we urge you to seek out educational opportunities on this topic. You can start small, using internal data sources and Excel.[16] For those of you in managerial or higher positions, we implore you to seek out ways in which the library can provide data services not only to better understand the law library but also to better serve your patrons.

The Science of Data and Law Librarianship

Over the past twenty years, we have seen the development of a new interdisciplinary field called Data Science. IBM describes Data Science as the combination of "math and statistics, specialized programming, advanced analytics, artificial intelligence, and machine learning with specific subject matter expertise."[17] Most top library schools offer some coursework in Data Science; Rutgers even has it as a concentration within their Master of Information program.[18]

Many law schools offer coursework in Data Science. For example, Georgia State University has a joint JD and Master of Science in Data Science and Analytics program.[19] However, these classes are usually offered either as part of a program toward a JD or as part of a separate Masters of Law program.

That said, we could find no library school that specifically offered a data science program or class with an emphasis on the special needs of the legal community. Our research suggests that this is a shortcoming of the library educational system, as there clearly is a need for the blend of skills and knowledge characteristic of data science but applied to the complex and specialized needs of legal research communities.

DATA IN LAW LIBRARIANSHIP: A NEW PERSPECTIVE

Data are multifaceted. It can serve as an impetus, an obstacle, a justification, a tool. It can provide narratives, tell of problems near and far, and even, at times, predict them. Like data, law librarians are multifaceted as well, with skills in analysis, domain expertise, reference, metadata, and experience with a plethora of information sources. But our silver bullet is not these skills alone but rather that librarians are particularly skillful at learning new types of research and analysis, as we have had to do many times over the course of the profession (those who have survived the dot-com bust can tell stories of another time of rapid change, in the not-so-distant past). This adaptability will need to be used once again, to take on this great opportunity before us.

The possibilities with data and the skillset that librarians inherently possess make an ideal match between law libraries and data. In fact, many of us have already taken on this role, even if in small ways. It is up to us, the purchasers, managers, facilitators, researchers, advisers, and analysts of data, to advocate for data and the role of it within the law library. For those at institutions less awash in data, we have the opportunity to become agents of change and foster a new culture in organizations that are resisting or not recognizing the importance of data. We must not only prepare ourselves but also prepare our libraries and host institutions for this future that is fast approaching.

"Almost everything is a point of data," Nina Rosenblum, senior researcher and research Trainer at Silberberg and Knupp LLP, started our interview.[20] And she is right; data is everywhere, if you have the skills and know how to look. It is this mentality that law librarianship must embrace if we wish to expand our roles and meet this new, increasingly data-driven future. Data is on the horizon, and we, law librarians, must prepare for it.

NOTES

1. Michelle Trovillo, in discussion with the authors, May 31, 2024.
2. Joy Shoemaker, in discussion with the authors, June 13, 2024.

3. Joe Cera, in discussion with the authors, June 10, 2024.
4. Lisa Lee, in discussion with the authors, June 25, 2024.
5. Cera, in discussion with the authors, June 10, 2024.
6. Ed Walters, in discussion with the authors, May 17, 2024.
7. Shoemaker, in discussion with the authors, June 13, 2024.
8. Cera, in discussion with the authors, June 10, 2024.
9. Shoemaker, in discussion with the authors, June 13, 2024.
10. Michelle Pearse, in discussion with the authors, June 21, 2024.
11. Cera, in discussion with the authors, June 10, 2024.
12. Cera, in discussion with the authors, June 10, 2024.
13. Walters, in discussion with the authors, May 17, 2024.
14. Trovillo, in discussion with the authors, May 31, 2024.
15. Cera, in discussion with the authors, June 10, 2024.
16. For more on this, see Erik Adams et al., "DIY Analytics: Beyond Excel," *AALL Spectrum*, November/December (2021): 12–15, accessed July 1, 2024, https://aallspectrum.aallnet.org/html5/reader/production/default.aspx?pubname=&edid=4f936bb4-a5b9-4b39-884a-667d1ad8402b.
17. "What is Data Science?," IBM, accessed July 1, 2024, https://www.ibm.com/topics/data-science.
18. "Data Science," Master of Information: Data Science, Rutgers-New Brunswick School of Communication and Information, accessed July 1, 2024, https://comminfo.rutgers.edu/graduate-programs/master-information/concentrations/data-science.
19. "J.D. & M.S.A. in Data Science and Analytics," College of Law: Student Experience, Georgia State University, accessed July 1, 2024, https://law.gsu.edu/student-experience/academics/jd-curriculum/j-d-master-of-science-in-analytics/.
20. Nina Rosenblum, in discussion with the authors, June 13, 2024.

Part III

Law Library Challenges and Opportunities

20

Advancing the Impact of Legal Information

Challenges and Opportunities in Law Firm Libraries

Scott Bailey

It is difficult to imagine the current state of law firm libraries without referencing at the outset two major phenomena that have become staples of strategic law firm library management thought in recent years—remote work and the advent of Generative AI. These forces create the challenges and opportunities that could very well define our professional value for decades. While there are many other factors influencing challenges and opportunities in law firm libraries, these two have created a truly unprecedented urgency and visibility for our profession.

VISION 20/20 INTERRUPTED

In late 2019, the staff in the Research & Knowledge Services department at Eversheds Sutherland were preparing to roll out a new "Vision 20/20" program in the newly minted Washington, DC Resource Center that had just been redesigned. An open house showcasing the new team and their dynamic capabilities was in the works. Visibility, accessibility, and collaboration were goals in the design. Engaging with a cutting-edge architectural firm and incorporating the latest in collaborative office concepts, they adopted a design for the resource center that would bring research analysts together with customers in a collaborative setting that brought them physically closer. Gone were the partitions between offices, and walls were replaced with more tech. Fewer barriers, more meaningful interactions. Larger screens and open spaces were meant to encourage more meetings, education, and working through problems together in person. Unveiling such an exciting new facility and strategy naturally included an open house event with refreshments to encourage a gathering. There were even custom cookies baked for the occasion, which needed to be consumed in person in a social atmosphere, symbolizing plans that were put on hold that centered around a physical presence in the research center, a collaborative space where lawyers and business professionals could work on common projects and learn about resources and technology . . . in person. Needless to say at this point, but this would be the last event of its kind. By March, all of the firm's staff were working remotely and did not know when or if they would return to that setting.

CHANGE ONE: REMOTE AND HYBRID WORK

The law firm library was more of an actual "place" before 2020, and many left the physical office never (or seldom) to return. But now we had the opportunity and a mandate to transform our roles to serve our clients and colleagues more effectively. Digitizing our collections, migrating to online services, and securely organizing data for remote accessibility became crucial to the safe operation of our businesses. Many of us left print library collections in the process of being transformed and returned slowly (if at all) to a physical library that was almost entirely maintained online to support our businesses and clients. If only a new technology would come along that could revolutionize the delivery of this internal and external data and combine it all to create new insights.

CHANGE TWO: GAI

Enter the second seismic impact: Generative AI. Imagine (if you will) it is December 2022. The buzz starts with a few well-placed phone calls between colleagues and friends of the profession. The network comes alive. What's a ChatGPT? What's an LLM? No longer a Master of Laws degree? Do tell. With the advent of ChatGPT and large language models, law firm libraries and the leadership capabilities of law firm librarians have been thrust into the spotlight in a way that few could have imagined. This is our story and the way we saw it unfold.

CHALLENGES ACCEPTED: NEW TEAMS, MORE CHANGES, NEW METRICS, NEW TOOLS

Law firm libraries witnessed the intersection of remote work and emerging technologies first-hand, which represented a new array of challenges and opportunities. This confluence of change and innovation required a new kind of team. The emerging teams formed in this alchemy would measure success with different benchmarks, but what would they be?

1) Interactions
2) GAI feedback

Interactions and AI at Eversheds Sutherland

Remote and hybrid work raised the bar on visibility, and the team at Eversheds Sutherland sought to document our increasing familiarity with our internal customer base at the firm. Documenting significant interactions with our colleagues on a regular basis revealed that we were already working with a baseline of over 60 percent of the firm. Whether our internal customers are lawyers or business professionals and whether our projects were internal or client-facing, we wanted to know what our customers wanted to know. In fact, this gave rise to our new (possibly a tad cheesy) slogan:

We Want to Know What You Want to Know!

Picture an anchor desk with a news team signing off with that tagline. This is how we rolled out our new team approach with an actual video commercial touting our engagement and improving our visibility. With this mindset, and using firm interactions as a key metric, we are able to demonstrate how much of the firm relies on us for valuable insight. Perhaps more importantly, we are able to demonstrate how that value is increasing.

AI testing and evaluation was a critical new way for our team to prove their value and capturing the firm's feedback in new GAI test groups turned out to be more problematic than first expected. Like many other well-intentioned efforts, people who are gathering GAI feedback around pilots and alpha and beta tests should be aware that feedback will be more difficult to gather than they might expect. After the sensible hurdles of intense security review and responsible documentation are cleared, it might be assumed that gathering feedback would be the easy part but carving out a valuable practitioner's time in an hourly business is always a challenge.

Our experienced team has recognized three main areas of service: research, outreach, and access have been the mainstays of our contributions, and we have organized and cross-trained our team to facilitate this successfully. Research analysts, who may also have other primary responsibilities such as training or managing access to online or digital collections, relish the variety of their roles and deliver tremendous value. Whether we are onboarding new lawyers remotely or setting up self-service access to databases, the new post-2020 team is prepared to make a practice-enhancing impact. In addition to team alignment with practices, resources are aligned with practices as well. Digital collections of resources by practice help bring the relevant resources to our users via our intranet, but future developments could likely make it even easier for our practices to gain access to relevant tools and data.

Teams, Service Orientation, and Access: Meeting the Customer Where They Are

The law firm library professional of the past five years has faced changes that has required nimble resilience. Teams by definition need to work together to provide next-level service, and the ideal team is built with diverse and insightful professionals who bring a corresponding variety of insights to the table. From journalism to publishing to technology to finance, understanding of a variety of business and legal challenges has required transcending the old models of the past. Beyond "traditional" librarianship, the new research analyst must be prepared to face new content, new technologies, and new projects with an open mind.

Immediately apparent to the professional research team today is the need to collaborate and with that has come a host of new demands and capabilities. Of course, the explosion of remote productivity has required that the research professional of the "now" attend meetings more spontaneously on Microsoft Teams, Zoom, or a variety of other platforms, and their accessibility is key. Being available and having healthy boundaries around availability is important. Setting realistic expectations of service hours and then delivering excellent service during those hours increases the law firm's confidence in our team and has led to higher value projects. Be prepared to manage expectations around success.

Feedback, Hackathons, and Future Service Visions: Client-Centered Ideas

Conducting hackathons with client participation can be a great source of opportunity and challenging ideas. With hundreds of online research options available to law firms, a chatbot that helps guide a user to the right tool would be a valuable contribution, particularly when paired or knowledge-mapped to an insightful and experienced research analyst.

FUTURE OF PRACTICE ALIGNMENT

The practice group has arguably been the central, traditional structure for large and midsize law firm management for well over a century. Aligning departmental services with practice groups is nothing new or revolutionary and we certainly have the successful business development professional model to follow. Observing seats at the table reserved for business development professionals over decades, many research and technology professionals have aligned their services with the practices and gained insights that they can apply to add value to their services. Increasingly aligning research analysts with practice groups is a force multiplier when dealing with remote practitioners and practices that want to evaluate the benefits of generative AI to their practice.

Practice-by-practice AI interviews with all of a law firm's major practice groups can result in hours of engaged and well-documented discussion, which the library's research and technology teams could cull for ideas that could be transformed into practice. This includes evaluating use cases driven by practice and searching for technology acquisitions that deliver on their promised value. Through these interviews in a practice-by-practice setting, a firm's lawyers would be able to share confidently with like-minded professionals about their perceived benefits of future GAI implementations. Without fear of "wrong answers," these practices could provide valuable brainstorming sessions with teams, calling out pain points and challenges while envisioning innovative tech solutions. This practice-by-practice approach would reveal far more about the objectives of each group than librarians would be aware of through conducting meetings across practice areas with hundreds of lawyers. The practice area structure continues to provide a good testing ground for common challenges and opportunities. Research & Knowledge Services professionals, aligned in this way, can gather honest and verifiable feedback around the potential GAI tools of the future.

NEW ROLES: TESTING AND VALIDATION

As GAI research tools evolved and gained a more prominent place in law firms since late 2022, law firm library professionals have evolved as leaders in the testing and validation of GAI results. Searching for promised efficiency, law firms have tested and adopted these tools at an explosive rate, and law firm library professionals have been there every step of the way. Conducting vendor tests and managing practice evaluation groups is a new major responsibility for our teams. Coordinating with professional responsibility leadership and technology and security teams and committees to manage the risk and appropriately contract and document our vendor relationships is a high-value way to contribute. With this high value and visibility comes the appropriate responsibility to communicate early and often with management and the appropriate leadership to develop and enforce policies and manage risks associated with GAI. Collaboration with technology teams, data teams, practice groups, AI committees, professional responsibility teams, risk management, and data security personnel is essential to a well-communicated and responsible testing process.

BUDGETING, GOVERNANCE, RISK MANAGEMENT, AND JUSTIFICATION

While law firm librarians and associated professionals have been deploying intelligent justifications for resources over decades, a new level of expense and scrutiny around these tools from a risk perspective, as well as financial justification from a value perspective, has challenged us to have a more active role in the negotiation with vendors and engagement of approval through firm leadership. It is incumbent upon us, as responsible managers, to hold vendors accountable to their promises and efficiency claims around this new technology and engage our data science, knowledge management, as well as our analytical and legal expertise to enlist appropriate counsel and colleagues to review agreements and results as these new tools have complicated implications for data privacy and copyright protection among many other risks. While this may initially present as a foreboding challenge, it can be an opportunity for your team to engage leadership, follow developments, and inform committees and teams about the latest developments in ethics, governance, and regulatory frameworks surrounding the deployment of this technology in your firm.

CROSS TEAM COLLABORATION

Importantly, law firm libraries should not ever be alone in tackling these challenges and opportunities. Like the budget justification outlined above, so must the technical conversations involve technology team members, and leadership must be involved to champion proper policies, responsible use, and risk management. A quick list of collaborative teams to tackle the challenges presented by remote work and GAI exploration might very well be the entire organization. Take care to communicate, involve, and consider, for example, if applicable, the following people:

- Litigation Support
- Business Development
- Practice Leadership
- Power Users of Research and Technology
- Legal Technology
- Litigation Technology
- Finance and Accounting
- AI Committees
- Technology Working Groups
- Paralegals
- C Suite
- Executive Committee
- Pricing and Value
- Recruiting
- Operations
- Helpdesk
- Knowledge Lawyers
- Practice Support Lawyers
- Training and Professional Development
- New Arrivals
- Departing Professionals
- Unknown Users, Mystery Users, Non-Users, Phantoms, and Ghosts

The value of outreach cannot be underestimated, particularly to those in your organization who are not already on your radar screen. As research professionals, it is recommended that you not only document your interactions with people across the firm but also those who are NOT your customers. Imagine building an opportunity list of people that your law firm library has not worked with and study the why of that. It is just as valuable for your law firm library and associated professionals to know who is using them and why as it is to know who is not using you and why not.

Often, this kind of internal engagement inventory can be conducted via a combination of user statistics (from vendors or a third-party monitoring application) and the firm directory. While time may be short for valuable research professionals, a study of the engagement of your user populations is extremely high value and worth investigating, even if it is time-consuming. Project managing the entire life cycle of a legal professional in your organization can pay tremendous dividends to the firm. Do not just survey or interact with users as they arrive, but check in and involve them at regular intervals and even at exit. They will be glad you did, and so will you.

AI CONVERSATIONS

Legal Technology, Client and Practice Development, and Research and Knowledge Services joined forces to actively listen and record dozens of practice group use cases in anticipation of testing emerging GAI technologies at Eversheds Sutherland. These early conversations with each practice group produced dozens of potential use cases that could be tested in current and future GAI offerings. In some cases, these ideas could be put into practice with a tool that was already implemented by the firm. Either way, these conversations proved valuable as a creative exercise, as an awareness campaign, and to gain familiarity with our customers.

AI OFFICE HOURS

Law firm libraries may consider creating and offering drop-in AI Office Hours. In the style of an Apple Store Genius Bar, business professionals and attorneys from across the firm can test their use cases across a select set of vetted tools.

AI TRAINING AND PROMPT GUIDANCE

Another opportunity presented by the proliferation of AI tools is prompt education or training. A staple of the above Office Hours, questions about AI prompts will dominate early training sessions, so be sure to leave time for open-ended questions. How do we get the best results from these tools? Traditional legal research methods using terms and connectors or Boolean search are being challenged by these new platforms, and it is up to law library professionals to test new prompt techniques and educate users about their effectiveness. While some searches may be more appropriate for more traditional methods of searching, users may find a more contextual search using specific prompting techniques to garner more valuable results from these GAI products. For instance, to generate an outline for this article, a law firm librarian might identify themselves and their specific need (writing a chapter for a book) and receive something like the below.

MICROSOFT COPILOT DEPLOYMENT AND TESTING

As part of our exploration and testing of GAI, we have asked it to summarize documents, create timelines, draft memos, and identify clauses. Microsoft Copilot, for instance, can be very good at distilling concepts and creating outlines.

MICROSOFT COPILOT'S CHALLENGES AND OPPORTUNITIES IN LAW FIRM LIBRARIES

As an example, Microsoft Copilot offers the following when prompted about the current challenges and opportunities in law firm libraries.

1. Evolving Role of Law Firm Library Business Professionals:
   - The COVID-19 pandemic significantly impacted law firm libraries. Suddenly thrust into a remote working environment, these libraries gained visibility. Law firm leaders recognized the mission-critical function of library support and services.
   - Firms responded by investing more in staffing and resources. *In 2021, there was a 43 percent increase in researchers and a 65 percent increase in electronic services librarians.*

- The transition to electronic resources accelerated as physical access to volumes diminished. Print budgets decreased, emphasizing the shift toward digital spending.
- Law firm libraries now focus on providing remote access to resources and staff, adapting to the digital era.

2. Importance of Building Library Services and Value:
   - Law librarians play a key role beyond traditional functions. They curate newsletters, handle competitive intelligence, and manage conflicts/new business intake.
   - Demonstrating value involves delivering tangible benefits to both the business and practice of law within the firm.
   - Modernizing libraries for anytime, anywhere access is crucial.
3. Impact and Visibility:
   - Law firms increasingly rely on researchers and electronic services librarians as internal information demands rise.
   - As product and practice needs evolve, legal information professionals continually reassess resources to meet their practice groups' requirements.
   - The future success of law firm libraries depends on role evolution and adaptability.

In summary, law firm libraries have transformed to meet the demands of the digital era, emphasizing accessibility, value, and impact.

II. Challenges

These are some of the challenges that we, as law firm librarians, are facing today.

1. Remote Work Transition
   - Sudden Shift to Remote Work: The COVID-19 pandemic forced law firms to rapidly transition to remote work. Law firm libraries had to adapt to support attorneys, paralegals, and staff working from home.
   - Increased Visibility: With remote work, the importance of law firm library services became more evident. These departments gained visibility as critical resources for legal research and information.
   - Seamless Remote Access: Providing seamless access to legal databases, research materials, and electronic resources posed challenges. Ensuring secure, reliable remote access was crucial.
   - Building the Right Research Team: Law firm libraries needed to assemble a research team capable of addressing remote work challenges. Skills like digital literacy, virtual collaboration, and efficient resource management became essential.
2. Balancing Print and Digital Collections
   - Decline of Print: Print collections faced a decline due to cost, space constraints, and the shift toward digital resources. Law firms had to rethink their reliance on physical volumes.
   - Managing Digitization: Strategies for digitizing existing print materials were necessary. Prioritizing digitization efforts while maintaining access to essential legal materials required careful planning.
   - Access to Essential Legal Materials: Balancing print and digital collections means ensuring access to critical legal resources. Law firm libraries have to curate digital collections effectively.

3 Technology and AI Integration
   - Surge in Legal Technology: The legal industry witnessed a surge in technology adoption. Law firm libraries needed to integrate legal tech tools effectively.

- Balancing Traditional Research with AI Tools: Librarians faced the challenge of incorporating AI-driven research tools alongside traditional methods. Finding the right balance was essential.
- Risk Management and Data Privacy: When using Generative AI tools, law firm libraries had to address risk management and data privacy concerns. Ensuring compliance with ethical guidelines was crucial.

In summary, law firm libraries navigated challenges related to remote work, collection management, and technology integration. Their adaptability and strategic planning were key to overcoming these obstacles.

III. Opportunities

1. Investment in Staffing and Resources
    - Increased Investments: Statistics reveal a surge in investments in research, specialized analysts, and data librarians within law firm libraries. Firms recognize the value of robust library services.
    - Anticipated Budget Increases: Law firm leaders anticipate budget increments for library departments. These funds support critical functions and enhance research capabilities.
    - Leadership Support: Law firm leaders play a pivotal role in supporting library functions. Their advocacy ensures that libraries receive the necessary resources and recognition.
2. Generative AI and Modernization of Library Services
    - Accessible, Anytime-Anywhere Libraries: The need for accessible legal libraries and services has never been greater. Generative AI can facilitate seamless access to legal resources, regardless of location or time.
    - Supporting Remote Work: Innovative approaches are essential to support attorneys and staff working remotely. Generative AI tools can assist with efficient information retrieval and research tasks.
    - Collaborative Evaluation: Law firm libraries can collaborate with AI experts to evaluate and integrate generative AI resources effectively.
3. Client-Centric Approach
    - Aligning with Client Needs: Law firm libraries should align their services with client requirements. Understanding client industries, legal challenges, and business opportunities enables tailored support.
    - Business Development: Libraries contribute to building business for the firm. By providing curated resources and specialized services, they enhance client satisfaction and loyalty.
    - Customized Research Support: Practice groups benefit from customized research assistance. Law librarians can offer targeted insights, contributing to successful client outcomes.

Clearly, law firm libraries have exciting opportunities to evolve, embrace technology, and enhance client value.

IV. Conclusion

In this exploration of law firm libraries, we've encountered both challenges and exciting opportunities.

- Challenges: Law firm libraries navigated the sudden shift to remote work, balanced print and digital collections, and integrated technology. These hurdles required adaptability and strategic planning.

- Opportunities: The investment in staffing and resources, the promise of generative AI, and a client-centric approach offer paths for growth. Law librarians can enhance services, support remote work, and align with client needs.

As law firm libraries continue to evolve, let's embrace the call to action:

- Continuous Adaptation: Stay agile and responsive to changing demands. The legal landscape evolves, and libraries must evolve with it.
- Effective Teaming: Collaborate with colleagues, technology experts, and clients. Together, we can create innovative solutions.
- Commitment to Improvement: Strive for excellence. Whether through training, technology adoption, or client-focused initiatives, let's keep improving.

The journey of law firm libraries is ongoing—a dynamic blend of tradition and innovation.

CONCLUSION: "A DYNAMIC BLEND OF TRADITION AND INNOVATION?"

It is important to recognize the traditional roles and professional responsibilities that guide the governance and framework for deploying responses to these challenges and opportunities in law firm libraries. Acknowledging the clarity and promise that these new tools bring to these challenges is essential, but we must also acknowledge the risks and limitations. We must now, as experienced research professionals, distill the fact from fiction and the hype from the actual value.

The Copilot outline and GAI writing above contain clear, high-level identification of some of the major challenges and opportunities for law firm libraries, librarians, and associated professionals in today's ever-changing landscape. The above outline validates our experience and approach, but I hope that the real-life (IRL), authentic intelligence represented by our experience underscores the human value of our contributions and the increasing need for our services.

While each opportunity for remote work and generative AI represented here has associated challenges, human law firm librarians and their professional teams are stepping up to ensure that the validation of results and careful, responsible testing and selection of tools increase their impact and multiply the value of their contributions as a result.

Our role in the strategic and careful deployment of GAI coupled with a client-centered service that meets our customers where they are is the key to our long-term success in law firm libraries. While we may not fill as many seats in stadiums across the world as Taylor Swift, we are poised to contribute great value to our firms, our clients, and our community.

21

Challenges and Opportunities in Government Law Libraries

Holly Grimes

Welcome to the insightful exploration of challenges and opportunities within government law libraries. As curators of legal knowledge in the public sector, government law libraries navigate a dynamic landscape shaped by evolving legal frameworks, technological advancements, and societal demands. This chapter delves into the complex world of government law libraries, examining the complexities they face, ranging from budgetary constraints to the transformation of legal research due to technological advancements. Amid these challenges, we uncover the numerous opportunities for innovation, collaboration, and enhanced access to legal resources, reaffirming the crucial role of government law libraries in facilitating informed decision-making and upholding the principles of justice and democracy.

OPPORTUNITIES

Community Outreach

Government law librarians agree that a government law library needs to interact with its community. This community may look different depending on the law library. For example, the Virginia State Law Library is only open to government officials, attorneys, and judges. And this library mainly works with appellate judges and staff attorneys.[1] However, the Alabama Supreme Court and State Law Library works with both people in the legal community and the general public. Most county law libraries are also open to the public. Some government law libraries may have a demographic of mostly solo practitioners or attorneys from small law firms who visit in order to do their legal research because they may not have as many resources at the law library associated with their firm, if they have a law firm library.[2] Other county law libraries may have a demographic that is almost 80 percent general public. These could be people who are merely asking for directions, but in many cases, they are pro se litigants and need to do legal research.[3] Due to this, many government law libraries have reference librarians that are able to assist patrons with their needs, and they may have computers set up with HeinOnline or Westlaw available for public access. The Alabama Supreme Court and State Law Library, for instance, has multiple librarians who can assist with reference questions as well as computers available for public use.

Government law librarians also agree that it is important for them to have a relationship with local judges, attorneys, and the state bar. There are many times when an attorney may not know that there is a government law library of any kind in their area until the first time they need one.[4] However, once an attorney or judge knows there is one close by, they may visit the law library more often. If the law library is open to the public, attorneys or judges may send patrons to the law library as well. Having a presence with judges is not only important for this reason but also for networking. If a judge sees what a government law library is doing, they may be convinced that having such a library is important and, hopefully, will want to help it stay open. They may also want to help increase the library's funding so that it can continue to provide such great services.[5]

Information Literacy Instruction

Some government law libraries host continuing legal education courses (CLEs) for local attorneys. In many cases, the government law library that is hosting the event will also provide food as a way to bring in people.[6] There are also times when the government law library that is hosting will get permission from the state bar to host the CLE for free. That way, any attorney who wants to attend the event will not have to pay for it. For example, the Alabama Supreme Court and State Law Library hosted a free CLE in 2023 and provided food for those who attended. Hosting these types of events is a great way to introduce attorneys to their local government law library that many of them may not even realize is around. Other government law libraries may not host CLEs themselves but may provide CLE credit materials that others can look at to learn how to set up a similar event.[7]

Professional Development

Another way that government law librarians can stay in touch with their community is to host events that the local legal community can attend. During National Library Week, the Alabama Supreme Court and State Law Library hosted a coffee and donut break for people who work in the Heflin-Torbert Judicial Building. The people who attended this event included appellate judges, justices, staff attorneys, and others who work in the building. Doing this brought people together and gave them a chance to ask questions about the library. Also during National Library Week, the Virginia State Law Library hosted a book drive where they partnered with a local children's hospital and had people from the building donate books that the library then donated to the hospital. Those who donated to the book drive received a raffle ticket, and at the end of National Library Week, the library selected a winner. The Virginia State Law Library also hosts a book club that is open to everyone in the building. The book club serves as a way to build relationships with people who work in the same building, but may not see each other on a regular basis since they all do not work in the same department.[8]

Partnerships

Outreach for government law librarians does not have to be limited to those coming into the law library. Having a good relationship with the local public library can be beneficial to a government law librarian for several reasons. For starters, if you know your public librarians, they may allow you to leave flyers and business cards in areas where patrons in the public library may be looking for legal materials.[9] Learning that there is a county law library close by may be beneficial to those patrons. Another reason knowing your community as a government law librarian is important is because there may be people in your community who need a place to meet. They could be attorneys who need to meet with a client or a local law school student who needs a place to study. In either situation, people need a quiet place where they can go. A public government law library may have rooms that can be used by the public for situations such as these.[10]

Equal Access to Information

Most government law libraries offer free access to proprietary databases and print collections that the public would otherwise not have access to. Most government law libraries have computers that are available for public use. These computers may have access to legal databases such as Westlaw, LexisNexis, and HeinOnline. Without these computers, patrons would not be able to access the information they need. Government law libraries also have a wide range of legal treatises as well as access to state codes and federal government publications that are available for public use. The patron demographic of several government law libraries is pro se litigants, or people who are self-represented. These databases and print collections help provide the information these people need to educate themselves on how the courts work as well as give them equal access to legal information.

Several government law libraries are a part of Access to Justice. Access to Justice is an agency in the federal government that believes in providing equal access to legal information to all communities and works on implementing access to justice policies in the U.S. Department of Justice and the executive branch. The overarching principles that guide Access to Justice are: 1) expanding access to legal systems, 2) accelerating innovation, and 3) safeguarding integrity.[11]

Generative AI Opportunities

Generative AI (GAI) is a form of artificial intelligence that presents many learning and job opportunities for government law librarians. GAI is a computer technology that can generate, or create, content from text, images, or audio from training data.[12] This means that GAI applications, such as ChatGPT, create what seems like new information based on what the user plugs into the program. In the legal field, many of the online legal research platforms have come out with their own forms of GAI to assist legal researchers.

Ways GAI is beneficial to government law librarians:

1. Understands natural language
2. Saves time when researching
3. Increases productivity

With GAI being a new type of application in the legal world, there are several learning opportunities for government law librarians that can help them navigate these programs. Many webinars that are hosted by the American Association of Law Libraries (AALL) have focused on GAI, how it can be used in the legal world, what some of the risks associated with GAI are, and why law librarians should use GAI. These webinars can help a government law librarian not only with their own research purposes but can also provide tools to assist patrons who may have questions about Westlaw Precision or ChatGPT.

GAI is very beneficial, in that it expands beyond traditional search methods since a researcher can type in a question instead of trying to figure out the best query to meet their needs. This benefits government law librarians because, when serving patrons, government law librarians can be faced with difficult research topics and using a GAI platform may help them jump start their research and better assist their patrons.

Lastly, many states have started putting together GAI task forces. These task forces work on making sure that their states are using GAI in an ethical way. Not every state has a task force. However, many of those that do are looking at the ethical and legal ramifications associated with GAI, and in some of these states, a government law librarian is on the task force. A government law librarian can give insight into how GAI can be used as a productivity tool for employees and as a research tool for legal researchers. *Responsible AI in Legal Services* (RAILS) is a website at https://rails.legal that focuses on bringing people in the legal community together to aid in ethical and responsible uses of

GAI in the legal field.[13] Their website also shows the current orders different courts have regarding Generative AI. Some of these orders are from state courts and some are from federal courts.[14] Overall, RAILS tries to keep the legal community up to date on the changes going on with GAI.

CHALLENGES

Generative AI Challenges

While artificial intelligence is not new to law libraries, GAI is a newer form of artificial intelligence that government law libraries are struggling with due to the challenges with the technology. Since GAI is very new, there are not many guidelines in place regarding how the technology is to be used in the legal field. Also, the legal databases that government law libraries subscribe to have already incorporated GAI into their software. With this update, it brings more challenges and questions to government law librarians, such as:

1. Should they purchase these new packages that include GAI?
2. If they purchase a package with GAI, who is going to have access to it?
3. If they choose not to purchase a package including GAI, what repercussions will they face in the future?
4. Does the library's budget allow for the purchase of a legal database with GAI?
5. What ethical concerns does the library need to consider before purchasing a legal database with GAI?

Another factor that government law librarians must consider when it comes to GAI is whether it can be trusted. Since GAI creates information, government law librarians are concerned about hallucinations (the creation of falsified evidence). Due to accuracy issues associated with GAI, many federal judges have issued standing orders putting guidelines on how GAI is to be used in legal research. Many people view these orders as a positive way to educate users and protect them from potential risks since some users, including attorneys and pro se litigants, may not understand that GAI can produce false information.[15]

Government law libraries are concerned that because GAI learns based on what the user prompts the program that the applications, mainly the free public ones like ChatGPT, will learn the wrong things and produce hallucinations. Due to this, and other factors, many government law libraries have not incorporated GAI platforms into their libraries. Government law librarians are still learning GAI and want to better understand what they will be using and how it should be used before bringing the technology to their libraries.

Staffing: Having a Cross-Generational Workforce

A cross-generational workforce is something that is common in most government law libraries. Since the COVID-19 pandemic (COVID), the workforce has seen a drop in the working-age population, typically ages 16–65. This may be due to the fact that many older staffers retired or were let go during COVID, and there have not been enough younger people entering the workforce to fill these roles. These senior staff members take with them the institutional memories, expertise, and loyalty they carried with them. Therefore, many employers, including law library directors, are doing what they can to retain their older workers while also bringing in young people.[16]

Since there is now a wider age range of employees in government law libraries, librarians are having to learn how to communicate and work together in this kind of environment. For example, an older law librarian may prefer hard copies of everything and want to talk about everything in person, whereas a younger law librarian may prefer digital copies of everything and to talk through email. The differences in how people work may cause friction from time to time; however, in government law libraries, staff members function best when they work as a team. Therefore, when everyone respects each other and tries to learn from each other, relationships between older and younger coworkers can be built. And when coworkers realize that everyone can learn from each other, they tend to be more willing to work together and listen to each other. In many government law libraries, there are more older staff members than younger staff members. Something that helps bridge the gap between the generations is when the library sets up some kind of mentor/mentee program where the older librarians mentor the younger librarians. Most of the time, the younger law librarians are appreciative of that mentorship from an older law librarian.[17]

On the flip side, there are times when a younger law librarian can mentor an older law librarian. This can happen with new technologies such as generative AI that younger staff members may understand better.[18] There are many cases now where a younger person may supervise older staff. While this can be a very beneficial work experience, when the young person first becomes the director or supervisor of their institution, there may be some friction involved while everyone gets used to the new dynamic.[19] Another tactic that can benefit everyone in the workplace is organizing social events, such as holidays and birthday parties. During events like these, coworkers can get together and enjoy themselves in a relaxed setting. This may also benefit morale among remote and hybrid workers.

Limited Funding

A challenge every government law library faces is how to deal with budgets and budget cuts. No one likes a budget cut, but government law libraries are expensive. When an institution needs to cut a department's budget, the law library can be one of the first to get cut, especially if the librarians who work there do not advocate for their library. Unfortunately, no two government law libraries operate the same way. Therefore, their budgeting challenges are not going to be the same, making it almost impossible to find any uniform solutions to funding and budgeting challenges.[20]

Most county law libraries in Oregon receive the majority of their budget from court fees that are supposed to go into a library fund. However, not all counties bring in the same amount of money, which can make what the county law library is getting from those fees very small. Some of these counties do not even have enough of a budget to hire a full-time county law librarian. Due to budgeting issues, most, if not all, Oregon county law libraries have not had the funding to implement legal database updates that include GAI. Some of the county law librarians are getting together to create a survey of the county law libraries in Oregon to see what the county law libraries need, where their funding could use improvements, and so on.[21] In Alabama, county law libraries also receive their funding from court filing fees that are collected by the county treasurer to be deposited into a library fund. There are state statutes that determine how much the county law library receives from the filing fees. Therefore, budgeting is everything for county law libraries because it takes an amendment to the statute in order to increase the amount received, which is easier said than done. Not all counties receive the same amount from filing fees because the amount put into the library fund per month from the treasurer's office changes due to the number of fees paid. It is extremely important for the county law librarian to make sure that their monthly expenses are within the library's means because they never know what the next month will bring. One approach that law librarians can take is negotiating contracts with legal databases/publishers. While costs continue to rise each year, it is the job of the law librarian to negotiate the prices of databases with publishers to keep prices somewhat reasonable for the law library. It is also important for budgeting within a county law library to always leave enough room for price increases when making budgeting predictions for the following year.[22]

As stated earlier, not all government law libraries have the same budgeting and funding issues. In Virginia, the state law library is funded through the General Assembly. While they do not have a huge budget, the budget is enough to cover books and digital resources. Also, they are not the ones responsible for purchasing LexisNexis, and funding for the judges' libraries comes from a different budget. However, like all government law libraries, they do face budgeting issues such as having a static budget that has not changed even though legal database/publisher prices continue to increase.[23] For federal law libraries, budgets have flatlined; however, they do have more of a solid budget than other government law libraries. Like county law libraries, federal law libraries receive part of their funding from court fees, but they also receive part of their funding from Congress through general appropriations because the judicial branch presides over the federal law libraries. The judicial branch is the one who requests the new budget every year and determines what the federal law libraries will receive in funding for the year. With the flatlining in budgets comes some challenges such as having to choose which digital resources they can purchase. According to Anna Russell, Alaska Branch Librarian, U.S. Courts, budget is not the only factor in why most federal law libraries do not have access to GAI platforms, like LexisNexis+AI; however, the budget is one of the factors. A flatlined or decreased budget can also make productivity difficult because a library must have the budget to do the work.[24] Things are more expensive than they used to be, and government law libraries should have a budget that reflects those increased prices. However, government law libraries do not always get those kinds of budgets and have had to learn how to make do with what they have.

The budget and funding of a government law library also affect staffing. Government law libraries are limited when it comes to hiring specialized librarians due to budget limitations. Many government law libraries are run by a very small staff. For example, the Virginia State Law Library has a staff of six people.[25] And other government law libraries, such as the county law libraries of Oregon, mainly have part-time staff members.[26] With teams this small, it is almost impossible for government law librarians to specialize in one area of the library. Also, having a small staff requires most, if not all, librarians on staff to be in the library, meaning that there are not many opportunities for government law librarians to work hybrid or completely remote.

Unauthorized Practice of Law

A significant challenge for government law libraries that are open to the public is making sure that they are not overstepping their boundaries and entering unauthorized practice of law (or providing legal advice). Government law librarians who work with the public must be very careful about how they word things to patrons because patrons listen to what a librarian tells them and, if a librarian is not careful, what they say may be taken as legal advice or seen as practicing law. If the state bar were to hear that a law library is practicing unauthorized law, then they can also come after the law library or the librarian.[27] Unauthorized practice of law is something that law librarians who work with the public see as a challenge because, as a librarian you want to help your patrons, but you also want to do things the right way. Therefore, it is very important as a government law librarian to show your patrons multiple resources and let them do their own research and conclude what they should do on their own. Some tips that may help when assisting patrons are:

1. Start the conversation with "I am not a lawyer."
2. Focus on resources and not answers.
3. If a patron asks you a yes or no question, respond with something similar to "Maybe, but I'm not sure about that. How about doing some research and seeing what the research says."[28]
4. Never tell a patron they should use a specific statute, case, regulation, and so on.[29]

Remember that pro se litigants have probably never set foot in any kind of law library and do not know anything about legal research. They are going to ask the law librarian assisting them a lot of questions, and the law librarian needs to be equipped to answer those questions. If a patron comes into a government law library, the librarian can, and should, assist the patron to the best of their ability. This can be showing a patron where to find information or suggesting resources. The librarian is simply helping the patron find the best or most relevant information. However, this needs to be done by only showing the patron how to use the source (i.e., how to look up a statute).[30] Unauthorized practice of law is a challenge for librarians, and there have been cases where law librarians have overstepped that boundary, but if a law librarian knows their library and is careful with their words, then answering questions without crossing that boundary can be done easily.

CONCLUSION

Overall, government law libraries play a major role as custodians of legal knowledge within the public sector. Navigating a dynamic landscape shaped by evolving legal frameworks, technological advancements, and societal demands, these libraries face several different challenges—from budgetary constraints to changes in technology that alter how legal research is done. However, within these challenges lie abundant opportunities for innovation, collaboration, and improved access to legal resources. Government law libraries remain pivotal in facilitating informed decision-making and upholding the principles of justice and democracy.

NOTES

1. Interview with Alexis Fetzer Sharp, State Law Librarian, Virginia State Law Library, Supreme Court of Virginia, Richmond, Virginia, June 11, 2024.
2. Interview with Amanda "Mandy" Haddin, Electronic Services Librarian, Alabama Supreme Court and State Law Library, May 12, 2024.
3. Interview with Brittany Young, Law Librarian/Program Supervisor, Lane County Law Librarian, Eugene, Oregon, May 31, 2024.
4. Interview with Mandy Haddin.
5. Interview with Brittany Young.
6. Interview with Mandy Haddin.
7. Interview with Brittany Young.
8. Interview with Alexis Fetzer Sharp.
9. Interview with Mandy Haddin.
10. Interview with Brittany Young.
11. Office for Access to Justice, "About ATJ," last updated March 5, 2024, accessed August 13, 2024, https://www.justice.gov/atj/about-atj.
12. Stefan Feurriegel, Jochen Hartmann, Christian Janiesch, and Patrick Zschech, "Generative AI," *Business & Information Systems Engineering* 66, no. 1 (September 12, 2023): 111–126, https://link.springer.com/content/pdf/10.1007/s12599-023-00834-7.pdf.
13. Responsible AI in Legal Services, "About Rails," last updated April 2, 2024, accessed April 10, 2024, https://rails.legal/about-rails/.
14. Responsible AI in Legal Services, "AI in Courts Tracker," last updated March 14, 2024, accessed April 10, 2024, https://airtable.com/appKUCriCQDI1BxIV/shrfIAPpNKaNMnacR/tblNmp6mff8CzLuQD.
15. Sarah Martinson, "Judges and Law Scholars Divided Over AI Standing Orders," *Law360 Pulse*, March 22, 2024, https://www.law360.com/pulse/articles/1810715/judges-and-law-scholars-divided-over-ai-standing-orders.
16. Debra Sabatini Hennelly and Bradley Schurman, "Bridging Generational Divides in Your Workplace," Harvard Business Review, accessed April 24, 2024, https://hbr.org/2023/01/bridging-generational-divides-in-your-workplace.
17. Interview with Brittany Young.
18. Interview with Brittany Young.
19. Interview with Alexis Fetzer Sharp.

20. Laureen Adams and Regina Smith, "The Evolution of Public Law Libraries," AALL Spectrum, accessed April 24, 2024, updated March 2006, https://www.aallnet.org/wp-content/uploads/2017/11/pub_sp0603_Evolution.pdf.
21. Interview with Brittany Young.
22. Interview with Mandy Haddin.
23. Interview with Alexis Fetzer Sharp.
24. Interview with Anna Russell, Alaska Branch Librarian, US Courts Library, James M. Fitzgerald Courthouse, Anchorage, Alaska, June 3, 2024.
25. Interview with Alexis Fetzer Sharp.
26. Interview with Brittany Young.
27. Teresa M. Miguel-Stearns, Zanada Joyner, Cas Laskowski, Aamir Shahnawaz Abdullah, Kaylan Ellis, Heather J. E. Simmons, Susan David deMaine, et al. *Introduction to Law Librarianship.* Creative Commons Attribution 4.0 International License, except where otherwise noted: 2021. https://pressbooks.pub/app/uploads/sites/4509/2021/07/Introduction-to-Law-Librarianship-20210920.pdf.
28. Interview with Brittany Young.
29. Interview with Mandy Haddin.
30. Interview with Mandy Haddin.

22

Using Scenario Planning to Discover Challenges and Opportunities in Academic Law Libraries

Debbie Ginsberg

The list of challenges and opportunities facing academic law librarians today is endless. From budgets to personnel, from access policies to metadata schema, each of us academic law librarians could probably name dozens of hurdles we face every day, let alone those we might face in the coming years. Is there even a place where we can get started?

SCENARIO PLANNING

To pare down the list to something manageable, here are four scenarios, each focusing on a possible future. Each scenario focuses on a specific set of challenges and opportunities to explore, along with a list of relevant resources. These scenarios provide a structured framework to help navigate the complexities of the issues facing academic law librarianship.

Scenario planning encourages librarians to imagine possible futures or outcomes and then ask questions about what these scenarios mean for librarianship. This chapter uses a form of scenario planning that asks, "What do we do now?" These scenarios analyze how librarians might respond to particular future environments. Other forms of scenario planning ask, "How did we get here?" They seek to discover the decisions that led to particular future outcomes, helping librarians identify which might be beneficial and which should be avoided.

Scenario planning is a powerful strategic planning technique. Some scenarios may be relatively simple ("What if one of our reference librarians leaves in the next 12 months?"). Others may require more in-depth planning ("What if another pandemic hits?"). Developing the factors behind each of these stories helps librarians consider current and future resources, risks, and responses.

The scenarios shouldn't be exclusively negative. By considering best-case, medium-case, and worst-case scenarios, law libraries will be best prepared for possible contingencies. This chapter features two "best-case" scenarios (one where we don't have to worry about budgets and one where our institutions unequivocally support equity), one "medium-case" (what if AI takes over research and teaching), and one "worst-case" (what if our budgets get even smaller). Each scenario will feature part of the story and an analysis of what the scenario means for academic law libraries.

Scenario Planning Resources

- "Scenario Planning: Our Ultimate Guide | i-Nexus," April 26, 2023, https://blog.i-nexus.com/scenario-planning.
- "The 5-Box Scenario Planning Tool (and Sample)," The Management Center, November 29, 2021, https://www.managementcenter.org/resources/5-box-scenario-planning-tool/.

CHALLENGES AND OPPORTUNITIES IN LIBRARY SPACE AND STAFFING

We will start with one of the best-case scenarios. It is not easy to imagine what we would do if we could do anything, if resources and budgets were not limited. By generating ideas about how we would design and run our libraries if money were no object, we can set goals for what we wish to see in our own spaces.

Scenario 1: What If Money and Resources Weren't an Issue?

Meet Malia, the director of Big State School of Law Library. In Malia's future, we have solved most economic problems. Resources are readily available and easily affordable. Malia can obtain whatever they need. They don't about budgets.

Malia has been asked to design a new library building. What could this building look like using limitless resources?

Academic Law Librarians as Accessibility Advocates

Challenge: Library spaces are difficult for those with disabilities to navigate.
Opportunity: Improve access to all library users.

Scenario 1, Part 1: Designing a library from scratch is difficult no matter what resources are available. Malia's staff has struggled with how to start their planning. They decide to begin by focusing on a core value: accessibility. With this value in mind, Malia's staff creates a list of needs for exterior access, public service desk features, lighting, desk height, shelf placement, and other universal design elements. The building will be accessible to all regardless of ability.

Analysis: Most of us won't design new libraries, but all of us must plan for accessibility. Often, our work is reactive, fixing problems as they arise. By considering a scenario that is proactive, we can create a "wish list" of what our libraries need to best serve all users.

Librarians can prioritize these lists, taking advantage of opportunities when they arise, even if those opportunities are incremental. We may choose to start with relatively inexpensive options, such as providing noise-canceling headphones for check-out. We then might feature more costly and long-term projects in our strategic plans, such as redesigning existing elevators to accommodate all wheelchair types. By adopting a flexible and adaptive approach, we can ensure continuous improvement in our library services and facilities.

Accessibility and Design Resources

- Jessica de Perio Wittman, "Moving Beyond the Basics of the ADA and Section 504: Opportunities for Equitable and Inclusive Access to Law Libraries, Collections, and Services"[1]
- ALA's accessibility resources: https://www.ala.org/advocacy/diversity/accessibility
- ACRL Building Design Guide: https://acrl.libguides.com/buildingresources

Academic Law Librarians and Staffing

Challenge: Hiring new staff.
Opportunity: Creating optimal work environments.

Scenario 1, Part 2: Malia is hiring a new librarian. In Malia's resource-rich future, salary isn't a big pull. Instead, Malia attracts new staff by offering incentives for personal and professional development. They offer schedule flexibility, work-at-home options, paid research sabbaticals, and time to pursue educational development. Malia also encourages her staff to integrate their interests into their work, giving them the freedom to pursue their own individual plans and goals.

Analysis: Back in the "real world," many libraries are challenged to replace workers (assuming the positions aren't lost entirely to attrition). Searches are not going well. There are not enough new librarians to replace those retiring or moving to other workspaces.

In no small part, this is because the price of becoming a law librarian, not to mention remaining one, is unreachable for many potential employees. The two degrees required by many academic libraries are expensive. We have long struggled to welcome new people to our profession, particularly librarians of color who can often find much better positions elsewhere.

If our salaries covered student debt and adequate daily expenses, perhaps the degrees would be worth their cost. But salaries often barely cover the cost of living (or entirely fail to cover it). The situation is worse for staff who are not librarians.

In 2025, we can improve our hiring chances by taking opportunities to offer similar incentives to Malia's—schedule flexibility, work-from-home options, time to pursue our own research, and access to professional development resources. But we will need more than these incentives to attract new academic law librarians. Realistically, we need higher wages and salaries. We cannot hire new librarians when they must spend more than half their monthly take-home pay to afford rent.[2]

Employee Hiring Resources

- Teresa M. Miguel-Stearns and Casandra Laskowski provide many suggestions in "Democratizing Law Librarianship: Reducing Barriers to Entry through Alternative Pathways to the Profession and Increased Support to Students. A Call to Action."[3]
- AALL Salary Survey: https://www.aallnet.org/resources-publications/publications/salary-survey/

REFERENCE, RESEARCH, INSTRUCTION: WORKING WITH GENERATIVE AI

While there is currently a lot of hype about AI's potential in legal research and instruction, the results so far have been underwhelming. AI is great at summarizing information but has difficulty with common tasks like finding the most recent cases on a particular issue. Whether AI will become an effective research tool is still under debate. Even if it does become effective, academic law librarians will remain important, making this a "medium-case" scenario.

Scenario 2: What If AI Takes over Research and Instruction?

Meet Kay, a reference librarian for New Law School University a few years from now. In Kay's future, AI has developed enough to handle traditional knowledge work. This has changed library work in fundamental ways. The AI tools have access to extensive knowledge and are rarely wrong in their assessments. AI catalogs can direct users to valuable resources. AI research databases answer in-depth questions without extensively formatted prompts. Most skills instruction is handled by flexible AI teachers. Even so, Kay is still a necessary member of her academic law library team.

Academic Law Librarians as Legal Information Experts

Challenge: Technology replacing librarian skills.
Opportunity: Establish technology and resource expertise in our organization.

Scenario 2, Part 1: Kay is helping Jay, a 2L, with a seminar paper. Jay found most of what they required using the AI research catalog and the AI legal databases. But they now needs information not available in conventional resources and the AI catalog hasn't been able to help them. Kay meets with Jay, who locates and demonstrates the specialized databases Jay needs.

Analysis: AIs can only analyze the information they have access to. That statement will be as true in Kay's time as it is now. Kay has access to a powerful AI catalog, but even a futuristic AI catalog cannot have access to every item in every database. It has only a general idea of the resources in individual library databases. Because Kay has granular knowledge of the legal databases they've personally worked with for years, they can make connections the AI cannot.

As AI becomes more sophisticated, academic law librarians may find that users need certain aspects of their expertise less—using the catalog, locating common materials, researching articles. However, librarians will still know the best databases for a given research task, particularly for niche research areas. They will be the experts in evaluating and teaching how to use these tools, just as they do now with our current set of research resources.

Additionally, academic law librarians will be instrumental in building AI research tools. They will participate in institutional efforts such as designing AI catalogs, providing feedback to vendors about AI products, and developing benchmarking resources to test AI research tools. We librarians are in the optimal position to know what will be best for our users" research needs.

Academic Law Librarians as Library Service Designers

Challenge: Users do not understand the limitations of online resources.
Opportunity: Design new services incorporating or working alongside AI and online resources.

Scenario 2, Part 2: Gee just started a research assistant project for a professor. The information the professor is looking for is obscure. Kay uses their library's Print Access Service to determine that Gee will need to consult older print materials and resources available only on microfiche.

Analysis: One of the biggest information blind spots for AI in any era is materials that haven't been digitized—the giant catalog of materials available only in print, microfiche, or other analog media. These materials include historical court dockets and documents, older materials from federal, state, and local agencies, and obsolete municipal regulations.

These items will remain only in print for decades because digitization is slow and expensive.[4] Items are digitized when materials are fragile or breaking, or when access is needed by many researchers (among other reasons). Because many documents are fragile, unique, and not all the same size, the digitization process itself must be done manually. We academic law librarians are—and will remain—experts in knowing which materials are available only in print, as well as determining how to prioritize those items for digitization. We will continue to educate users about which items are not digitized and how to access them.

Academic law librarians will develop services to help users best access these and other materials. These services will directly incorporate AI tools for translation, research, OCR, and more. By showcasing our expertise in emerging technologies such as AI, we will continue to be a vital part of every law school.

Designing New Services Resources

- The Services Portfolio of an Academic Library: A Framework: https://sr.ithaka.org/blog/the-services-portfolio-of-an-academic-library-a-framework/ (a typology of service types)
- Chatting about ChatGPT: How may AI and GPT impact academia and libraries? (SSRN: https://papers.ssrn.com/sol3/papers.cfm?abstract_id=4333415)[5]

Academic Law Librarians as Teachers

Challenge: Teaching students legal research skills in the age of AI.
Opportunity: Librarians as information literacy experts.

Scenario 2, Part 3: The 1Ls at Kay's school use AI to learn legal research fundamentals. The AI matches the pace of individual students, analyzes weak spots, and matches learning styles. Kay supplements the AI with live instruction. Kay demonstrates how different AI databases do not search the same data, how students will need to check more than one resource to make sure their research is complete, and how to carefully evaluate which database they choose as well as review the results produced.

Analysis: The introduction of AI into legal research tools does not eliminate the need for librarians in legal research instruction—it demands their participation. For example, in her blog post, "Information Literacy: A Path Forward for AI Legal Research?" Stephanie Farne explores how BRASS Framework Standards could be used to teach information literacy about AI research tools in law schools (BRASS is the Business Research and Services Section of the ACRL). Among other standards, Farne explores how, in the age of AI, academic law librarians will need to teach students to be critical of sources, to determine the value of information, and to review results for accuracy (among other skills). Librarians will continue to design and update information standards, as well as continue to be responsible for teaching students how to evaluate and select research tools effectively.

Teaching AI Legal Research Resources

- Stephanie Farne, Information Literacy: A Path Forward for AI Legal Research?: https://ripslawlibrarian.wordpress.com/2024/06/25/information-literacy-a-path-forward-for-ai-legal-research/.[6]
- MIT AI Teaching Resources: https://mitsloanedtech.mit.edu/ai/teach/

MATERIALS ACQUISITION: CREATING EQUITABLE COLLECTIONS

Let's visit another "best-case" scenario—a future in which equity is valued by all. In this future, academic institutions enthusiastically dedicate resources to libraries to ensure collections are balanced and accessible. Libraries employ equity specialists to develop equitable collections that reflect the experiences and needs of their students, faculty, and community.

Scenario 3: What If Institutions Prioritized Equitable Collections?

Sasha is the equity services librarian at Free City Law School. He ensures the library's collection reflects the diversity of the law school, the local community, and the country at large. He's been working at Free City for eight years. He has made much progress during that time, but there is still more to do.

Academic Law Librarians as Selectors

Challenge: Creating an equitable collection.
Opportunity: Engaging community expertise.

Scenario 3, Part 1: Recently, a student affinity group asked the library to include materials from an underrepresented community. Sasha agrees that the current collection doesn't fully represent that community and its intersection with the law. However, he is not familiar with this group or its related materials. Fortunately, Sasha has developed a cohort of experts within the local and library communities to help him discover new materials.

Sasha reaches out to his cohort. He learns that a local librarian and a specialist group in a neighboring town can assist. Working together, they build a collection to close the gap the students identified.

Analysis: For most of us in the current world, the imperative to create an equitable collection faces stiff competition with other organizational needs and issues. These include shrinking budgets, insufficient staff to select and process materials, competing law school initiatives, and politics. But we can still create balanced collections.

Sasha used local expertise to bridge collection gaps—those same experts are also available to us. We may also find that while our institutions may not specifically prioritize equitable collection development, they may have other projects and goals that would benefit from a balanced collection. We can leverage those other goals to provide incentives for developing law library collections.

Resources for Collection Equity

- "Leading by Diversifying Collections," *Ithaka S+R* (blog), accessed June 19, 2024, https://sr.ithaka.org/publications/leading-by-diversifying-collections/.
- Diversity, Equity, Inclusion, and Belonging in Library Collections Toolkit: https://www.nellco.org/page/deibtoolkit

Academic Law Librarians Enabling Online Accessibility

Challenge: Providing accessible collections.
Opportunity: Ensuring access to users regardless of abilities or limitations.

Scenario 3, Part 2: A student with low sight needs to access a digital collection. This collection was digitized a long time ago, in the early 2000s. Sasha discovers the collection isn't accessible to screen readers in its current state. Free City's administration wants to make this collection accessible as soon as possible. The collection belongs to a student group, so student services will fund the project. The accessibility office has the best software, so they will handle the conversion. The student will be able to use the collection in time to finish their paper.

Analysis: Despite the ADA and other laws, an unacceptable amount of content cannot be read with traditional screen readers. Some vendors have improved their content, but change is slow.[7] And although accessibility issues may be caused by vendor recalcitrance, academic institutions may still be sued for offering resources that are not available to all.

The library is often the first point of contact when a student experiences accessibility issues. Sometimes, the issue lies within the library. For example, a library may work with a vendor to ensure accessibility.

Other times, the library is asked to help but does not have the resources. Law libraries cannot digitize materials for all students who require them for accessibility reasons (e.g., they may lack funds and necessary expertise). However, assisting with accessibility issues can be a great opportunity for academic law libraries to establish connections within the law school community. Even if the library isn't the correct resource for a given issue, we can use these connections to help our users find the right person for their needs.

Online Accessibility Resources

- ACRL Universal Accessibility Interest Group Library: https://connect.ala.org/acrl/viewdocument/introductory-resources-for-web-acce
- Big Ten Library Accessibility Resources: https://btaa.org/library/programs-and-services/reports

Academic Law Librarians and Metadata

Challenge: Defining equitable metadata.
Opportunity: Creating equitable metadata.

Scenario 3, Part 3: Sasha recommends the replacement of a biased Library of Congress Subject Heading (LCSH). Because he lives in an equitable society, the biased heading is soon replaced.

Analysis: Library of Congress Subject Headings contain and perpetuate bias.[8] Several institutions are working to improve the LCSH on a local level. Yet the list of biased terms grows as critical librarianship becomes more widespread and new issues are discovered.[9]

Committing to change means committing to the discussion. Law librarians are ideal participants, especially since "legal language" has been an excuse to keep biased terms in the LCSH. When librarians and many other stakeholders requested that the Library of Congress remove "Illegal Alien" from the subject heading list, the change was refused. Part of the reason for the refusal was that the term "illegal alien" was used in the US Code.[10] If primary legal sources are used as excuses for continuing bias in the LCSH, we law librarians are uniquely suited to refute these arguments.

Metadata and Cataloging Resources

- Cataloging Lab: https://cataloginglab.org/welcome/
- Critcat (critical cataloging resources): https://critcat.org/

BUDGETS AND RESOURCES: DOING LESS WITH LESS

We'll end with a "worst-case" scenario, a world where academic law libraries receive almost no resources. Our budgets can barely support the most necessary resources, let alone staff and facilities. Everything is stretched to the absolute limit.

Scenario 4: What If We Had Almost No Financial Resources?

Meet Alex. In his thirty-year career as a law librarian, Alex has pretty much seen and done it all. He has loved nearly every aspect of being a law librarian, except his helplessness to forestall the decline of academic law libraries.

Academic Law Librarians Working Collaboratively

Challenge: Academic law libraries cannot afford access to necessary databases.
Opportunity: Active participation in law library and other consortia; negotiation.

Scenario 4, Part 1: Alex is working with the law school to start a new "bioengineering and the law" program. Alex has been combing through his budget to purchase a database the program needs, but it's too expensive and the vendor won't negotiate with him.

Alex's library participates in several library consortia. Through one of them, Alex learns that other libraries are also interested in this database. The consortium's staff works with the vendors to offer affordable access.

Analysis: Many of us must negotiate with vendors for even basic access to resources. These negotiations take a lot of time and energy. To some extent, this is because we are often working with vendors who do not work with academic libraries. A large part of our negotiations involves basic explanations of what academic law libraries are and how they function.

AALL's antitrust policy limits our ability to work collectively with vendors.[11] But law library consortia such as NELLCO and LLMC have been able to provide us access to discounted resources that we otherwise could not afford. If we cannot work within our professional organizations to negotiate access, consortia provide another avenue.

Collaborative and Negotiation Resources

- NELLCO: https://www.nellco.org/
- AALL, Principles & Practices for Licensing Electronic Resources, https://www.aallnet.org/advocacy/vendor-relations/criv-tools/principles-practices-for-licensing-electronic-resources/
- Negotiation resources: "ONEAL Curriculum," SPARC, accessed July 2, 2024, https://sparcopen.org/our-work/negotiation-resources/oneal/oneal-curriculum/.[12]

Academic Law Librarians Using Time as a Resource

Challenge: Libraries asked to do "more with less".
Opportunity: Establish boundaries around doing "more with less".

Scenario 4, Part 2: KU's dean has a problem—the adjunct who teaches the legal technology course is not available next fall. The dean wants one of Alex's librarians, Dom, to teach this class. But Dom's current duties do not give her time for extra projects.

Dom declines to teach the class. Dom was going to say "yes" because they hate upsetting people. Alex has demonstrated time and again through his own actions that it's okay to make others upset. Dom is not responsible for everyone else's feelings. Alex's dean is upset, but Alex arranges a meeting with the three of them to brainstorm. They learn that Dom has a lawyer friend who would be great for the class, but the friend will be on vacation for part of the semester. After reaching out to the friend, they all work out a solution. The friend will teach the class, and Dom and Alex will each substitute once.

Analysis: Libraries can be a "dumping ground" for tasks and projects that no one else can or will take on. Our service orientation and sense of professionalism will often have us saying "yes" just this "one last time." By helping, we can show our value, make connections within our communities, and sometimes even be compensated.

But agreeing to take on everything isn't sustainable in the long run. All of us only have so much time, resources, and energy. Just as we negotiate with vendors, we must also must negotiate with our law school community to best serve the needs of our faculty, our staff, our students, and ourselves.[13]

CONCLUSION: ACADEMIC LAW LIBRARIANS AND OUR PROFESSIONAL IDENTITY

Ours is a profession that sits at the nexus of many spaces. We function in the worlds of law, legal practice, legal research, law schools, and academia. We develop relationships with our publishers and vendors. Some of these are specialized in law, others have a more general focus. Our expertise must run the gamut from finding the oldest, most obscure print materials to teaching students how to work with AI-based legal research tools. We are like other academic libraries in our concerns about creating robust and equitable collections amid shrinking budgets, spaces, and staff. But the scope of our collections is generally focused within specific letters of the Library of Congress classification system. We work with many of the same publishers as our law firm and governmental law librarians, but our specific needs are varied. We are concerned about access to justice, but we can offer very few resources for our communities' vast unmet legal needs.

And yet, there are many opportunities for us to take charge, to set the tone going forward. We will:

- Develop the skills important to law librarians—not just legal research, but selecting collections, investigating new technologies, evaluating resources, teaching law students, researching faculty projects, locating obscure materials, digitizing new collections, managing student workers and library staff, developing new library spaces, budgeting, and much more.

- Work with law librarians, other academic librarians, professors, students, staff, and community members to develop equitable and relevant collections.
- Continuously adapt our libraries' services and collection to best to meet the needs of our law school and community.
- Showcase the expertise of library workers and encourage administrations to pay them salaries sufficient for them to thrive in their communities (and pay off student debts).
- Imagine all the possibilities in our libraries, even if current resources can't support our most loftiest goals.

We will write our own scenarios.

NOTES

1. Jessica de Perio Wittman, "Moving Beyond the Basics of the ADA and Section 504: Opportunities for Equitable and Inclusive Access to Law Libraries, Collections, and Services," *Legal Reference Services Quarterly* 42, no. 3–4 (October 2, 2023): 272–298, https://doi.org/10.1080/0270319X.2023.2264690.
2. The median salary for an academic reference librarian living in the Boston area in 2023 was about $112,000. This is insufficient to afford the average Boston-area rent of about $3,500/month for a one-bedroom. While Boston is an outlier, it is not unique. Rent inflation outpaces wage increases in many cities in the United States.
3. Teresa M. Miguel-Stearns and Casandra Laskowski, "Democratizing Law Librarianship: Reducing Barriers to Entry through Alternative Pathways to the Profession and Increased Support to Students. A Call to Action," *Legal Reference Services Quarterly* 43, no. 1–2 (April 2, 2024): 104–135, https://doi.org/10.1080/0270319X.2024.2331867.
4. Region of Peel Archives, "Why Don't Archivists Digitize Everything?," *Peeling the Past*, May 31, 2017, https://peelarchivesblog.com/2017/05/31/why-dont-archivists-digitize-everything/.
5. Brady D. Lund and Ting Wang, "Chatting about ChatGPT: How May AI and GPT Impact Academia and Libraries?," *Library Hi Tech News* 40, no. 3 (2023): 26–29, https://doi.org/10.1108/LHTN-01-2023-0009.
6. Stephanie Farne, "Information Literacy: A Path Forward for AI Legal Research?," *RIPS Law Librarian Blog*, June 25, 2024, https://ripslawlibrarian.wordpress.com/2024/06/25/information-literacy-a-path-forward-for-ai-legal-research/.
7. See Suffolk's guide detailing which databases are accessible. It doesn't include all vendors. Sarah Smith, "LibGuides: Screen Reading and Library Resources: A Guide for ADA Accessibility: Full List of Accessible Library Databases," accessed July 1, 2024, https://suffolk.libguides.com/c.php?g=654172&p=4590096.
8. Grace Lo, "'Aliens' vs. Catalogers: Bias in the Library of Congress Subject Heading," *Legal Reference Services Quarterly* 38, no. 4 (October 2, 2019): 170–196, https://doi.org/10.1080/0270319X.2019.1696069.
9. See "Problem LCSH—Cataloging Lab," accessed July 2, 2024, https://cataloginglab.org/problem-lcsh/.
10. Lo, footnote 6.
11. "Antitrust Compliance Policy," AALL, accessed July 2, 2024, https://www.aallnet.org/about-us/what-we-do/policies/antitrust-compliance-policy/.
12. "ONEAL Curriculum," SPARC, accessed July 2, 2024, https://sparcopen.org/our-work/negotiation-resources/oneal/oneal-curriculum/.
13. See Christine Park, "A Small Moment of Growth," *RIPS Law Librarian Blog*, March 5, 2024, https://ripslawlibrarian.wordpress.com/2024/03/05/a-small-moment-of-growth/.8/8/24

23

How Law Libraries Can Reimagine Diversity, Equity, and Inclusion (DEI) in an Anti-DEI Climate

Monique Gonzalez and Phebe Huderson-Poydras

Law libraries have long served as custodians of knowledge and access to justice, yet they now find themselves challenged to uphold their commitment to Diversity, Equity, Inclusion, and Accessibility (DEIA) amid a shifting societal landscape. DEIA efforts aim to create holistic environments where every individual has equitable opportunities to succeed while feeling valued for who they are. Libraries play a crucial role in promoting community and creating welcoming environments where everyone feels safe regardless of their background. This chapter explores strategies that law libraries can adopt to reimagine Diversity, Equity, and Inclusion (DEI) efforts in an anti-DEI climate. By leveraging their unique position within the legal ecosystem, law libraries can continue to champion inclusivity and equity while navigating these new obstacles.

TRADITIONAL DEI INITIATIVES IN LAW LIBRARIES

Because law libraries' primary mission is to meet their faculty and students' academic and research needs, they inherently operate with a commitment to DEI initiatives. This commitment supports a holistic understanding of the community the law library serves. Demographics indicate that "in 2022, one-third of all students pursuing a juris doctor degree (33 percent) were students of color."[1] In the 2022–2023 academic year, statistics indicate an increasing enrollment of women outpacing men.[2] Based on the LESSE survey, 17 percent of law students identify as LGBTQ+.[3] Therefore, the community that law libraries serve is a very diverse population with understandably various perspectives and expectations. Law libraries create inclusive collections, promote equity in access, and encourage staff diversity to ensure their patron base is appropriately served.

Recognizing that the community they serve is diverse and has diverse interests, law libraries strive to build inclusive collections representing a wide range of voices and perspectives within the legal field, including materials by and about underrepresented groups such as racial and ethnic minorities, women, LGBTQ+ individuals, and those with disabilities. The American Libraries Association ("ALA") asserts:

> Collection development should reflect the philosophy inherent in Article I of the *Library Bill of Rights*: "Books and other library resources should be provided for the interest, information,

and enlightenment of all people of the community the library serves. Materials should not be excluded because of the origin, background, or views of those contributing to their creation."[4]

Consequently, law library collections focus on expanding the perception and understanding of law students and encouraging transformative scholarship from faculty. Additionally, it helps law students prepare for practice since they must be ready to encounter real-world legal issues upon graduation or while clerking. The law library's collections must be responsive to the current transformations and controversies in the law. Collection efforts include curating collections that cover areas of law impacting marginalized communities, such as civil rights, immigration law, Indigenous law, and gender studies, ensuring that students and researchers have access to a comprehensive range of legal scholarship.

Law libraries often maintain special collections that document the legal history of marginalized groups, providing valuable resources for researchers studying the evolution of legal rights and social justice movements. Another critical aspect of DEI efforts in law libraries is developing and preserving oral histories, personal papers, and records of legal organizations that focus on civil rights and social justice issues. The goal is to provide "content by and about a wide array of people and cultures to authentically reflect a variety of ideas, information, stories, and experiences."[5] Grappling with the past histories is essential to understanding the evolution of law today. Listening to oral histories and reading personal papers and records of legal organizations helps support faculty research and provides context to the challenges marginalized groups have faced.

Libraries traditionally host events and workshops celebrating different cultures and histories, such as Black History Month or LGBTQ+ Pride events. These actions ensure that all groups are considered relevant to society and that their stories merit showcasing. Cultural programming emphasizing marginalized communities creates a sense of belonging, a key component of DEI efforts.

The pandemic magnified equity in access issues for law schools and law libraries. Recognizing that patrons are no longer relegated to brick-and-mortar law schools and that some patrons have physical challenges, law libraries have redefined the delivery of information and resources. Law libraries ensure all users can access legal resources regardless of background or abilities. This assurance includes providing materials in accessible formats, such as digital resources compatible with screen readers, and offering assistive technologies within the library. Law libraries have also established digital collections where patrons have access 24/7 from the comfort of their homes. Law libraries have recognized the need for dedicated staff to assist those taking courses through distance education, understanding that those students need the same support as those physically present in law school. Libraries may also offer tailored support for students and researchers facing barriers to access, such as non-native English speakers, first-generation law students, and low-income students. This additional support levels the playing field by giving disadvantaged students a more equitable start to success.

Law libraries seek to engage their entire patron base by offering brown bag series to demonstrate how to use resources. They also engage in outreach to diverse student populations, offering orientations, workshops, and research assistance tailored to the unique needs of different groups, including international students, students of color, and those interested in social justice lawyering. Law libraries also survey their community to ensure that resources and services meet the needs of all. Likewise, they collaborate with student organizations, such as affinity groups (e.g., Black Law Students Association, Women in Law), allowing the library to understand better and address these communities' needs. These measures aim to ensure that law libraries are responsive and representative of their community.

Another critical component of DEI initiatives in law libraries is recruiting and retaining diverse staff. "Diversity benefits the law library's culture, as well as the development of the profession as a whole, by bringing a wide range of perspectives, backgrounds, and talent to the table."[6] Efforts are made to diversify law library staff, mainly to recruit individuals from underrepresented backgrounds into roles across all library levels, including leadership positions. Hiring personnel and administrators also understand that a diverse staff may allow patrons of similar backgrounds to seek help from those they identify with when needed. Developing retention strategies that create a supportive and inclusive work environment is crucial, including offering professional development opportunities focusing on DEI.

Professional development opportunities for all staff focusing on DEI principles help staff understand the potential impact that isolation or microaggression may have on the mindset of individuals experiencing such actions. Library staff must receive ongoing diversity, equity, and inclusion training. Training should include cultural competency training, workshops on implicit bias, and education on marginalized communities' specific legal challenges. Law libraries may also provide training on recognizing and addressing microaggressions in the workplace and ensure that staff are equipped to provide equitable service to all users. These efforts have helped to shape a culturally competent, non-toxic workplace.

HISTORY OF DIVERSITY, EQUITY, AND INCLUSION

Diversity, Equity, and Inclusion, often expanded to include accessibility as Diversity, Equity, Inclusion and Accessibility, has deep historical roots in the United States.[7] A significant milestone occurred as early as 1948 with President Harry S. Truman's signing of Executive Order No. 9981, which banned racial discrimination within the armed forces.[8] This landmark Executive Order mandated the desegregation of the armed forces. Truman's action marked a critical step toward equality with one of the nation's most pivotal institutions and set a precedent for broader societal changes. The principles and practices of DEI and DEIA initiatives continue to evolve to create more equitable environments where diverse populations are valued, and individuals have access to opportunities regardless of background or identity.

The Civil Rights Movement, a social justice movement from 1954 to 1968 in the United States, served as the catalyst for major legislation and Executive Orders addressing discrimination which was pervasive throughout American society.[9] On March 6, 1961, President John F. Kennedy signed Executive Order No. 10925 establishing the President's Committee on Equal Employment Opportunity to "permanently remove from Government employment and work performed for the Government every trace of discrimination because of race, creed, color or place of national origin."[10] The Executive Order also required government contractors to take "affirmative action" to ensure applicants and employees were not discriminated against based on race, color, creed, or national origin.[11] Significant legislation included the *Equal Pay Act of 1963,* which prohibited gender-based discrimination in pay when performing jobs that require the substantially same skill and working conditions among men and women.[12] Title VII of the *Civil Rights Act of 1964* prohibited discrimination in employment on the basis of race, color, religion, sex, or national origin.[13] The *Age Discrimination in Employment Act of 1967* protected employees and applicants at least forty years of age from age-based discrimination.[14] President Lyndon B. Johnson signed the landmark civil rights legislation of the 1960s into law. *Title IX,* which focused on gender equity in educational settings, was signed into law in 1972.[15] The *Americans with Disabilities Act (ADA),* which prohibits discrimination against people with disabilities, was signed into law on July 26, 1990.[16] Throughout the years, these laws have undergone various amendments while retaining their original intent to prohibit discrimination and promote equality.

Affirmative action policies were often introduced after other means failed to correct inequalities and entrenched discrimination. Some of the policies implemented included expanding employment opportunities for women and other disadvantaged groups; protections for individuals with disabilities; the use of race and sex as a factor in choosing among qualified applicants; and race-conscious efforts such as outreach designed to eliminate racial imbalance and prevent future discrimination in the workforce.

Early DEI initiatives evolved from affirmative action programs and equal employment legislation aimed at addressing racial discrimination. These initiatives were formalized in many institutions over the past fifty years. Modern DEI considers intersectionality and expanded identifiers, which include gender, sexual orientation, religion, ethnicity, race, and so on. DEI is viewed as a fundamental part of most organizations' success. According to Pew Research, in 2023, 30 percent of employees reported that DEI is a priority, and 54 percent reported that their organizations are continuing to emphasize DEI programming.[17]

Starbucks was an early leader in DEI. As early as 1988, it became one of the first employers to foster a diverse workforce by offering full health benefits to all employees, including coverage for same-sex domestic partners.[18] In today's corporate settings, programs focused on DEI are widely accepted. These initiatives are recognized for their ability to boost financial outcomes, enhance the quality of decision-making, and increase employee loyalty and retention. Adopting DEI initiatives is seen as essential for fostering a workplace where employees feel safe and valued. While DEI efforts aim to improve opportunities for disadvantaged groups, they often fall short of their goals due to various challenges.[19] Opposition from advantaged groups, stemming from perceived threats to resources and values, can hinder DEI implementation.[20] Recent research suggests that focusing on inclusion and equity before diversity may lead to more successful outcomes.[21] Despite ongoing efforts, disparities persist, highlighting the need for continued work.

On June 29, 2023, the Supreme Court issued its decisions in *Students for Fair Admissions, Inc. v. President & Fellows of Harvard College* (600 U.S. 181) and *Students for Fair Admissions, Inc. v. University of North Carolina (collectively SFFA Decision)*. The court held that Harvard University and the University of North Carolina at Chapel Hill violated the Equal Protection Clause of the Fourteenth Amendment and Title VI of the *Civil Rights Act of 1964* by using race-conscious admissions processes.[22] It appears that concurring opinions would prefer to ban all affirmative action; however, the majority opinion authored by Chief Justice Roberts focused on apparent deficiencies in these particular admissions programs.[23] The majority opinion did not claim to overrule other significant decisions on affirmative action.

OVERVIEW OF ANTI-DEI EFFORTS

Anti-DEI efforts have increased following the SFFA decision. To date, twenty-eight states have considered or approved new laws targeting DEI initiatives.[24] These efforts have been led or influenced by the Claremont Institute, a conservative California-based think tank that formed about three years ago with the goal of weakening "the leftist social justice revolution."[25] Their broader opposition to anti-discrimination laws can be seen in works they have authored. In a statement for a *New York Times* article, the group stated it was "proud to be a leader in the fight against DEI., since the ideology from which it flows conflicts with America's Founding principles, constitutional government and equality under the law. Those are the things we believe in. Without them there is no America. You cannot have those things with DEI."[26]

Claremont's ideals elevate patriarchy and Eurocentrism. Their anti-DEI campaigns have gained the most traction in Republican-leaning states, and they have claimed credit for helping to pass some of the most far-reaching DEI bans in Florida and Texas. Texas now bans the use of state-appropriated funds for DEI efforts, including diversity, equity, and inclusion offices and staff; diversity statements; giving preference based on characteristics such as race or sex; and mandatory diversity training at public colleges.[27] Similar to Texas, Florida has enacted legislation prohibiting public colleges from spending state or federal funds on DEI efforts unless required by federal law.[28]

A study examining over 4,400 students at nine public universities found that interacting with diverse peers enhanced cognitive abilities such as analytical problem-solving, socio-cognitive skills like cultural awareness, and democracy-related skills like civic engagement.[29] Furthermore, national studies indicate negative interactions such as racial exclusion, being treated as a token representative, and stereotypes are frequently linked to decreased civic engagement, diminished self-esteem, and reduced ethical decision-making.[30] The benefits of diverse academic environments carry over to the workplace.

Corporations and law firms are not exempt from anti-DEI efforts. America First Legal, under the leadership of president Donald Trump adviser Stephen Miller, has argued DEI programs are illegal under Title VII of the 1964 Civil Rights Act. The group has filed at least fifteen lawsuits and sent over thirty letters asking the Equal Employment Opportunity Commission to investigate corporations. It has raised $44 million to fund its cause. The American Alliance for Equal Rights, led by conservative activist Edward Blum, has relied on Section 1981 of the 1866 Civil Rights Act, which affirmed all citizens are equally protected by the law.[31] This group has targeted the DEI efforts of law firms and nonprofits. Interestingly, Blum is also the founder of Students for Fair Admissions, which brought the case that successfully challenged affirmative action in higher education.[32] Some law firms have removed references to gender and race in their diversity fellowship eligibility criteria due to the American Alliance for Equal Rights legal challenges. According to a Leopard Solutions report, diverse hiring has declined since the work of the American Alliance for Equal Rights and America First Legal, which has implications for recent gains in representation in the legal profession.[33]

CHANGES FOR LAW LIBRARIES TO CONSIDER IN THE CURRENT CLIMATE

DEI efforts have recently been challenged by various state legislatures. The question arises regarding how law libraries will adapt to the changing climate and provide inclusive service. A possible response is that law libraries must navigate legal constraints, align DEI programming, reframe DEI language, and acknowledge the intersection of DEI and access to justice.

Law libraries must be strategic in ensuring their policies and practices align with new legal requirements while maintaining a commitment to DEI. Additionally, law libraries must understand the legal risks associated with continuing specific DEI initiatives and how to mitigate them. Although some states have not established policies against DEI initiatives, some states have set a course of action to reduce or eliminate DEI initiatives, so there is yet to be a definitive solution to the DEI challenges. Perhaps adapting DEI programs to focus on a broader definition of inclusion may be helpful in this current climate. For instance, shifting from ethnic, race, or gender-specific initiatives to programs emphasizing universal access and inclusion, potentially including socioeconomic status, geographic diversity, and age, may demonstrate programming appropriate for the entire community.

Another critical aspect that may help in adapting DEI programs is working with local organizations, community groups, and other institutions to continue DEI efforts in a more legally permissible manner. Additionally, state legislatures should be contacted for their views and concerns with DEI programming. As a constituent, it is worth asking for an explanation of the problems surrounding the opposing viewpoint concerning DEI programming. Perhaps, any confusion can be addressed by seeking an answer from those advocating for such legislation.

Another response to the changing climate is to adjust the language or wording used in DEI initiatives to be more inclusive. Law libraries have been relatively successful in this response because DEI initiatives in law libraries are efforts to help library patrons learn more about cultures and groups. However, if the language indicates or is perceived as preferential treatment, the language used in DEI initiatives may warrant revision, making it more inclusive and less likely to draw legal scrutiny. Emphasizing the benefits of DEI in terms of community engagement, access to information, and educational enrichment will unilaterally help the law school since it helps groups understand each other and encourages cultural competency.

The challenges to DEI will impact many people's access to justice. A reduction in DEI initiatives will ultimately impact access to justice.

> To address the gradual decline of . . . DEI initiatives, a robust call to action is essential, advocating for the seamless and organic integration of Diversity, Equity, Inclusion, and Accessibility (DEIA) competencies throughout all facets of academic and professional environments. This approach not only upholds justice, but also cultivates a society where diversity is naturally celebrated, and inclusion emerges as a genuine, shared commitment rather than a forced effort.[34]

DEI's origins are in the inception of Civil Rights Laws, and its ultimate purpose was to remedy inequities that anti-discrimination laws have failed to do.[35] Blatant acts of discrimination have spurred community groups to advocate for social justice. Over the past twenty years, social justice initiatives have substantially increased attention to the economic, cultural, social, and legal ramifications of discrimination in America.[36] Law libraries have joined this challenge by creating research guides, displays, and legal research sessions to demonstrate available resources. Additionally, some law libraries have aided the general public in researching various legal issues concerning their rights while ensuring that they are not violating the unauthorized practice of law (UPL).

IMPORTANCE OF DEI AND CONTINUING INITIATIVES IN LAW LIBRARIES

Law libraries are fundamental to the study and practice of law, where principles of justice, fairness, and equity are paramount. Upholding DEI within the library ensures equitable access to legal information and resources and fosters an environment where diverse perspectives are represented and respected. Promoting DEI is not only an ethical obligation but also aligns with the professional responsibilities of legal educators and practitioners to support diversity and inclusion within the legal profession. Many law schools have explicit commitments to DEI as part of their mission to educate future lawyers who are prepared to serve a diverse society. The law library plays a critical role in advancing these goals by offering resources, services, and programs that reflect and support the school's DEI commitments. Libraries must ensure that their DEI efforts are integrated with broader law school initiatives, contributing to a cohesive and inclusive academic and professional environment.

DEI initiatives in law libraries expand the scope of legal education and research by ensuring that collections, databases, and resources include a wide range of perspectives, including those from historically marginalized communities. This enriches the academic discourse and prepares students for practice in a diverse and complex legal landscape. Inclusive library practices foster a supportive learning environment for all law students, enhancing their educational experiences and contributing to their success in law school and beyond. Law libraries are integral to creating an inclusive law school culture. By continuing to prioritize DEI, law libraries help to build a community where all students, regardless of background, feel supported and empowered in their legal studies. Law libraries also serve as hubs for critical discussions on issues related to diversity, equity, and inclusion in the legal field, offering spaces for events, symposia, and workshops that promote dialogue and understanding among students, faculty, and legal professionals.

As the legal profession increasingly emphasizes diversity and inclusion, law libraries must adapt to meet the needs of a diverse student body and faculty. DEI initiatives ensure that law libraries remain relevant and responsive to these evolving demands, preparing students for successful careers in a globalized and diverse legal environment. Emphasizing DEI also positions the law library as a leader in fostering inclusive legal scholarship and practice, ensuring that the library continues to be a vital resource for legal education and professional development.

ADVOCACY AND LEADERSHIP

Effective leadership in a law library requires knowledge and understanding of not only the state of the profession but also the community (i.e., their sphere of influence). Law library leaders must strongly advocate for DEI within the library, law school, and the broader legal community, emphasizing the critical role that diverse perspectives play in legal education, research, and practice. They must demonstrate the benefits of DEI in a high-functioning work environment and provide empirical data and support for these programs in the law school curriculum. For instance, according to the 2024–2025 Standards and Rules of Procedure for Approval of Law Schools standard 303(c), "a law school shall provide education to law students on bias, cross-cultural competency, and racism: (1) at the start of the program of legal education, and (2) at least once again before graduation."[37] Since law libraries support the mission of law schools, they should have materials, resources, and services that support this mission. Leaders should work to secure funding and resources for DEI initiatives, demonstrating a commitment to these values and ensuring the sustainability of DEI efforts in the face of external challenges.

Finally, law libraries should form alliances with other libraries, educational institutions, and advocacy groups to support and protect DEI initiatives. Partnering with other organizations may strengthen their position and give credence to the objectives that are being advocated. Law librarians should be aware of the stances taken by their professional organizations to ensure that they have sufficient support for strategic undertakings. For instance, the American Library Association,[38] Association of College and Research Libraries,[39] and the American Association of Law Libraries[40] have all taken strong positions against policies that adversely impact diversity. By leveraging these partnerships and aligning with established professional organizations, law libraries can more effectively champion inclusive practices within their communities.

NOTES

1. American Bar Association, "ABA Profile of the Legal Profession - Legal Education," 2023, accessed September 6, 2024, https://www.abalegalprofile.com/legaled.html.
2. Id at 4.
3. "Satisfaction—LSSSE," 2024, accessed September 6, 2024, https://lssse.indiana.edu/tag/satisfaction/#:~:text=That%20year%2C%2093%25%20of%20law,law%20students%20identified%20as%20heterosexual.
4. American Library Association, "Equity, Diversity, Inclusion: An Interpretation of the Library Bill of Rights," July 5, 2017, accessed August 29, 2024, https://www.ala.org/advocacy/intfreedom/librarybill/interpretations/EDI.
5. American Library Association, "Equity, Diversity, Inclusion: An Interpretation of the Library Bill of Rights," July 5, 2017, accessed August 29, 2024, https://www.ala.org/advocacy/intfreedom/librarybill/interpretations/EDI.
6. Alyssa Thurston, "Addressing the "Emerging Majority": Racial and Ethnic Diversity in Law Librarianship in the Twenty-First Century," *Law Library Journal* 104, no. 3 (Summer 2012): 359–382.
7. *History of DE&I*, U.S. Department of Labor, effective December 15, 2023, https://www.dol.gov/agencies/olms/deia/history.
8. *Establishing the President's Committee on Equality of Treatment and Opportunity in the Armed Services*, 13 Federal Reporter 4313 (July 26, 1948).
9. *Civil Rights Movement*, History.com, effective May 14, 2024, https://www.history.com/topics/black-history/civil-rights-movement#jim-crow-laws.
10. *Establishing the President's Committee on Equal Employment Opportunity*, 26 Federal Reporter 1977 (March 6, 1961).
11. *Establishing the President's Committee on Equal Employment Opportunity*, 26 Federal Reporter 1977 (March 6, 1961).

12. *Affirmative Action Policies Throughout History*, American Association for Access, Equity, and Diversity, accessed September 10, 2024, https://www.aaaed.org/aaaed/History_of_Affirmative_Action.asp.
13. *Affirmative Action Policies Throughout History*, American Association for Access, Equity, and Diversity, accessed September 10, 2024, https://www.aaaed.org/aaaed/History_of_Affirmative_Action.asp.
14. *Affirmative Action Policies Throughout History*, American Association for Access, Equity, and Diversity, accessed September 10, 2024, https://www.aaaed.org/aaaed/History_of_Affirmative_Action.asp.
15. *Affirmative Action Policies Throughout History*, American Association for Access, Equity, and Diversity, accessed September 10, 2024, https://www.aaaed.org/aaaed/History_of_Affirmative_Action.asp.
16. *Affirmative Action Policies Throughout History*, American Association for Access, Equity, and Diversity, accessed September 10, 2024, https://www.aaaed.org/aaaed/History_of_Affirmative_Action.asp.
17. Ariam Tesfaye, "What is DEI? A Closer Look at DEI Strategies Throughout History," *Cooleaf*, January 24, 2023, https://www.cooleaf.com/blog/a-history-of-corporate-dei-strategies.
18. Ariam Tesfaye, "What is DEI? A Closer Look at DEI Strategies Throughout History," *Cooleaf*, January 24, 2023, https://www.cooleaf.com/blog/a-history-of-corporate-dei-strategies.
19. Karin Hellerstedt, Timur Uman, and Karl Wennberg, "Fooled by Diversity? When Diversity Initiatives Exacerbate Rather Than Mitigate Bias and Inequality," *Academy of Management Perspectives* 38, no. 1 (2024): 27, https://doi.org/10.5465/amp.2021.0206.
20. Aarti Iyer, "Understanding Advantaged Groups' Opposition to Diversity, Equity, and Inclusion (DEI) Policies: The Role of Perceived Threat," *Social and Personality Psychology Compass* 16 (2022): e12666.
21. Michelle Russen and Mary Dawson, "Which Should Come First? Examining Diversity, Equity and Inclusion," *International Journal of Contemporary Hospitality Management* 36 (2023): 27.
22. *Students for Fair Admissions, Inc. v. President & Fellows of Harvard Coll.*, 600 U.S. 181 (2023).
23. *Students for Fair Admissions, Inc. v. President & Fellows of Harvard Coll.*, 600 U.S. 181 (2023).
24. *DEI Legislation Tracker*, The Chronicle of Higher Education, effective August 30, 2024, https://www.chronicle.com/article/here-are-the-states-where-lawmakers-are-seeking-to-ban-colleges-dei-efforts.
25. "America is Under Attack: Inside the Anti-D.E.I. Crusade," *The New York Times*, January 20, 2024, https://www.nytimes.com/interactive/2024/01/20/us/dei-woke-claremont-institute.html.
26. "America is Under Attack: Inside the Anti-D.E.I. Crusade," *The New York Times*, January 20, 2024, https://www.nytimes.com/interactive/2024/01/20/us/dei-woke-claremont-institute.html.
27. *DEI Legislation Tracker*, The Chronicle of Higher Education, effective August 30, 2024, https://www.chronicle.com/article/here-are-the-states-where-lawmakers-are-seeking-to-ban-colleges-dei-efforts.
28. *DEI Legislation Tracker*, The Chronicle of Higher Education, effective August 30, 2024, https://www.chronicle.com/article/here-are-the-states-where-lawmakers-are-seeking-to-ban-colleges-dei-efforts.
29. New York State Bar Association, *Report and Recommendations of the New York State Bar Association Task Force on Advancing Diversity* (New York: New York State Bar Association, 2023).
30. New York State Bar Association, *Report and Recommendations of the New York State Bar Association Task Force on Advancing Diversity* (New York: New York State Bar Association, 2023).
31. Tatyana Monnay, "Conservative Duo Fights Against DEI One Bias Claim at a Time," *Bloomberg Law News*, June 4, 2024.
32. Monnay, "Conservative Duo Fights Against DEI One Bias Claim at a Time," 3.
33. Tatyana Monnay, "Law Firms Boost Diversity Defenses After Conservative Backlash," *Bloomberg Law News*, March 22, 2024.
34. LeAnne Salazar Montoya, "Equity, Diversity, and Inclusion: What Is in a Name?," *Seattle Journal for Social Justice* 22, no. 3 (2024): 621–672.
35. Todd J. Clark, "Reversing DEI: The Consequence – "IED" Indoctrination and Elimination of Diversity," *University of Toledo Law Review* 55, no. 2 (Winter 2024): 169–194 55 U. Tol. L. Rev. 169, 175.
36. Id.
37. ABA Standards for Accreditation, "2024-2025 Standards and Rules of Procedure for Approval of Law Schools," ABA, last modified September 7, 2024, https://www.americanbar.org/groups/legal_education/resources/standards/.

38. American Library Association, "Equity, Diversity, Inclusion: An Interpretation of the Library Bill of Rights," July 5, 2017, accessed August 29, 2024, https://www.ala.org/advocacy/intfreedom/librarybill/interpretations/EDI.
39. The ACRL Racial and Ethnic Diversity Committee, 2012 October 1. "Diversity Standards: Cultural Competency for Academic Librarians: Approved by the ACRL Board of Directors, April 2012," *College & Research Libraries News* [Online] 73:9.
40. AALL, "Diversity, Equity, and Inclusion Policy - AALL," August 8, 2022, https://www.aallnet.org/about-us/what-we-do/policies/dei-policy/#:~:text=Create%20spaces%20where%20all%20are,%2C%20economic%2C%20and%20political%20divides.

24

Access to Justice

Latia Ward and Rebecca Katz

In 2014, a special committee of the American Association of Law Libraries (AALL) presented a report on "Law Libraries and Access to Justice." In this chapter, we expand on this report, first considering what "access to justice" means for law librarians, and then explore the challenges and opportunities that have arisen since the 2014 report for law librarians interested in pursuing and participating in access to justice initiatives. For the purposes of this chapter, we define the term access to justice as the ability to achieve a fair resolution when bringing your case to court or when advocating for your legal rights outside of court.[1]

HISTORY OF THE TERM "ACCESS TO JUSTICE"

The meaning of the phrase "access to justice" is a product of the time in which it is used. In the 1930s, the words "equal justice under law" were inscribed on the Supreme Court building.[2] By 1962, this ideal was being expressed as "equal access to justice." In an article published that year using this phrase in its title, attorney Orison Marden connected access to justice with access to attorney representation; he wrote, "the specific problem which I venture to discuss is how best to assure competent legal advice and representation for the millions among us—and there are millions—who need the services of a lawyer but cannot pay his reasonable charges."[3] A 1989 conference on access to justice recommended conducting a nationwide survey on what came to be known as the "justice gap."[4] By 2005, with the Legal Services Corporation's first report on the "justice gap," the phrase "access to justice" had become nearly synonymous with efforts to close the justice gap. Sociologist Rebecca Sandefur, whose research on access to justice is essential reading, validated this assertion in 2018 when she noted that "one common operational definition of access to justice in top-down studies holds that access to justice means the availability or affordability of lawyers."[5]

The meaning of the term is also a product of the background of the individual using it. The definitions in the previous paragraph are those of lawyers; other professionals define the phrase more broadly. Mauro Cappelletti and Bryant Garth, the authors of an early scholarly work on access to justice, acknowledged the difficulty in identifying a single definition for the phrase.[6] Nevertheless, their non-definition is instructive: "First," they wrote, "the system must be equally accessible to all; second, it must lead to results that are individually and socially just."[7] This statement suggests that there is an important distinction between bridging the "justice gap" and "access to justice." The 2014 AALL report on law librarians and access to justice presumes this distinction, asserting that the goal of the access to justice movement is to "improve the quality of participation in the justice system by all."[8] On a practical level, access to justice is the ability of a person to engage in daily activities of life without facing legal barriers. These activities include traditionally "legal" matters such as renting or buying a home, navigating through family law matters, or starting or winding down a business, as well as ordinary activities like shopping, traveling, and working. Access to justice "is more than a mere admission ticket to the formal legal process; it is a 'basic political resource' allowing for other opportunities."[9]

The United States Department of Justice includes considerations in addition to expanded access to attorneys in the guiding principles of its Office for Access to Justice:

- Expanding Access. We expand access to legal systems by increasing the availability of legal assistance, supporting public defense, and eliminating barriers that exclude people based on economic, demographic, or geographic factors.
- Accelerating Innovation. We support research, data, and innovative strategies to improve fairness and efficiency in legal systems and to ensure Justice Department services and programs incorporate modern, evidence-based practices to further equal access to justice.
- Safeguarding Integrity. We promote policies and reforms that improve the accountability, fiscal responsibility, and integrity of legal systems and process.[10]

Another definition, from Maryland's Thurgood Marshall State Law Library, is more succinct: "Access to Justice is, generally speaking, the ability of people to seek and obtain fair, accessible, and equitable assistance in reaching an outcome under the law."[11] The use of the phrase "under the law" rather than "in court" is a reminder that legal issues can be resolved both inside and outside of official court proceedings, as Ward's definition suggests.[12]

WHAT ACCESS TO JUSTICE MEANS FOR THOSE WHO CANNOT HIRE AN ATTORNEY

The inability to hire an attorney, due to financial or other factors, can have grave consequences. In 2021, the Legal Services Corporation (LSC) surveyed over 5,000 adults about their civil legal needs.[13] Nearly half of those surveyed who did not pursue legal assistance said that cost was a barrier to seeking legal help.[14] Another reason for not pursuing legal assistance is distrust of the legal system; among those with higher income who were surveyed by the LSC, over half believed that the civil legal system will guard their rights, while only 39 percent of lower-income people believed this.[15] For these individuals who do not have access to an attorney, what does access to justice mean?

Critical to access to justice for those without an attorney is access to legal information. In expressing his excitement about the possibilities of generative artificial intelligence, Jim Sandman, former president of the Legal Services Corporation, stated that the "access to justice problem is an access to information problem."[16] Despite the close relationship between these two concepts, the groups working on these two issues frequently overlook each other. For example, Bob Ambrogi, a lawyer and legal journalist who operates the blog LawSites, noted that in early 2024, leaders of the access to law movement held a conference at Harvard University at the same time that leaders of the access to justice movement held a conference at the American Academy of Arts and Sciences. The conferences were held only a half mile away from each other. Ambrogi learned of the access to justice conference while he attended the conference at Harvard University and asserted that the attendees of these two conferences were "oblivious to each other," while noting that the goals of the two movements are "inextricably intertwined" and imagining the value "if the two groups knew of each other's meeting and had spent even an hour cross-pollinating ideas and strategies."[17] Ambrogi recognizes that accessing the law is very much a part of accessing justice; those who represent themselves are placed at a disadvantage when they do not have a way to access relevant court opinions or statutes and will therefore not have access to justice.

Carl Malamud, founder of the nonprofit organization Public.Resource.Org,[18] which operates Law.Resource.Org, a website to make laws freely available,[19] suggests that the solution to the access to law problem is for the United States Congress to legislate a requirement that all local, state, and federal governments place their laws with the U.S. Government Publishing Office, which would then make the laws freely available.[20] However, even when a government makes the law freely available, if the law is not organized and published in a user-friendly way, the law will still be inaccessible.[21] Similarly, as Angela Jaffee from vLex said at the Harvard access to law event celebrating the launch of the Caselaw Access Project, "it's difficult for the public to access [primary law] because there are so many agencies. You have to know what you're looking for to be able to find it."[22]

WHAT LAW LIBRARIANS CAN DO TO SUPPORT ACCESS TO JUSTICE

As a community, law librarians are passionate about access to justice, as exemplified by the inclusion of this chapter in this book, as well as by numerous conference sessions and symposia with access to justice themes.[23] Unfortunately, we are often prevented from participating in solutions by outside factors. We explore here the challenges to law librarian participation, followed by a discussion of existing programs involving law librarians and opportunities for further engagement.

Challenges

Finding the Line between Legal Information and Legal Advice

The most significant challenge faced by law librarians who want to support access to justice by providing legal reference is how to avoid the unauthorized practice of law. Much has been written about the provision of reference services in the library and avoiding the unauthorized practice of law.[24]

For law librarians, the relevant question of what constitutes the practice of law is where the line is between legal information and legal advice. This question is not new; the vagueness of what constitutes the unauthorized practice of law has been ingrained in the system following a 1934 entreaty from John G. Jackson that "it is important [that] [statutes imposing penalties on the unauthorized practice of law] . . . should not undertake to define the practice of law, for definitions undertaking this have been universally found to be self-limiting and to invite evasion."[25] Unfortunately, this refusal to define the practice of law has resulted in a near monopoly for lawyers and risk aversion for law librarians.

In 1979, Mills wrote about "Reference Service vs. Legal Advice: Is it Possible to Draw the Line?"[26] In the forty-six years since, we have gotten no closer to a "yes" answer to this question. Complicating the conversation is the fact that while every state regulates the practice of law, the specifics of those regulations vary widely, and there hasn't been the capacity among law librarians to consider the question of unauthorized practice of law on a state-by-state basis. Instead, conversations happen at the association level in groups including the AALL Legal Information Services for the Public Special Interest Section (SIS), the AALL Government Law Librarians SIS, and the Self-Represented Litigation Network. Law Librarian, and—despite librarians' concern for information literacy—often include conclusions based on hearsay and rulings handed down by the strictest of states. Even the expert in the study of unauthorized practice of law for law librarians, Paul D. Healey, whose PhD dissertation on uncertainty management centered on the lack of clarity around unauthorized practice of law,[27] does not explore how differences across states can and should lead to different roles for law librarians where state regulation of the practice of law is less stringent.

Law librarians working in court libraries face additional complexities. John M. Greacen, former director of the Administrative Office of the Courts of New Mexico, was the first to write about legal information versus legal advice in the context of the work of court personnel in 1995. In some courts, law librarians have been granted specific authority by the chief judge to perform tasks that might otherwise constitute unauthorized practice of law. In other courts, librarians have been granted authority to perform tasks while working shifts in the court self-help center that they are not authorized to perform while working in the court library.

In law libraries that are open to the public, such as the libraries of many public schools of law and courthouse law libraries, librarians and other staff may face questions from the public that may require more than an answer about where to find resources. Given the lack of a single, clear definition of the practice of law, law librarians serving members of the public often steer clear from the practice of law by noting what they are permitted to do and not permitted to do and staying squarely on the side of legal information. According to Frederick Schauer and Virginia J. Wise, legal information consists of the sources of law such as statutory codes, court opinions, treatises, journal articles, and other similar sources.[28] However, this list excludes valuable resources that are relied upon by laypeople. Are self-help resources considered legal advice by virtue of having been created for laypeople rather than attorneys, or do they fall within the category of legal information? Does a research guide that compiles primary and secondary sources as well as forms for use by nonlawyers constitute legal information, or legal advice?

What is "legal advice"? There is not one clear answer to this question. Greacen has written that there is no "inherent meaning, or even core meaning," in the phrase "legal advice."[29] In one example of an attempt to distill a definition, Ward defines "legal advice" as the application of law to the facts of a person's particular situation, while "legal information" is general knowledge about the law. For example, providing a listing or access to resources on landlord-tenant law even with a summary of what they contain is legal information. On the other hand, telling library patrons whether they have valid claims for rent abatement and assisting them in preparing these claims constitutes legal advice.[30] Greacen asserts that court personnel should steer clear of answering the "should" questions as in "What should I do?"[31]

In 1995, Greacen suggested replacing the term "legal advice" or the prohibition against legal advice with five principles that court personnel can implement. This guidance for court staff includes:

1. Requires explaining court procedure
2. Requires instruction on how to bring a case before the court
3. Prohibits recommending specific actions
4. Reminds staff to remain impartial, and
5. Cautions staff to avoid communication that could be considered *ex parte*[32]

If librarians are not court employees, they may view his principles differently than court employees would. The five principles that Greacen enumerates are an extension of the work of court clerks, which consists of being an asset to the administration of justice. For example, Greacen notes that most court clerks are prohibited from practicing law because their relationship with the court, combined with their practice of law, could give their clients an unfair advantage.[33] Revisiting the topic in 2001, Greacen noted that the prohibition against court staff giving legal advice or answering certain questions is to prevent the unauthorized practice of law by court staff. However, court staff acting as authorized by the court's direction are by definition not engaging in the unauthorized practice of law.[34] In 2022, Greacen did address the work of intermediaries, who are community members from different walks of life and include librarians.[35] These intermediaries should be included in the protection of safe harbor laws and policies that would allow them to assist others with their legal needs without fear of discipline or other negative consequences.[36] For example, court volunteers in Illinois and legal document preparers in Arizona are protected by safe harbor provisions in their respective states.[37]

Avoiding the Unauthorized Practice of Law

Because the line between legal advice and legal information is so blurry, librarians providing reference services to nonlawyers must make situation-specific judgment calls. Librarians serving the public must consider the laws of their state, the policies of their employer, the chances of being misunderstood by the patron, and to what extent the information being shared is known by people outside the legal field. Librarians promote access to justice through initiatives such as self-help centers, periodically updated research guides that are made freely available, and other self-help legal information. Are these resources, with their disclaimers or other annotations, enough to serve the needs of self-represented litigants? For some, these resources will be enough; others will need the assistance of a qualified attorney. However, the research that self-represented litigants do on their own and corresponding resources in the access to justice field are positive steps in educating the general public about the legal system, even in situations where public patrons will need to hire an attorney. Access to justice programs and resources are not universally welcomed across libraries.[38] Moreover, legal resources for laypeople may not be held in high regard by those in the academy: "As a law student you shouldn't rely on materials written for the lay public. Those sources have a very different focus from texts directed to lawyers and law students. They may oversimplify legal doctrine and may simply be wrong."[39] Nevertheless, serving laypeople has a place in law libraries that are open to the public. What follows is a description of two situations at opposite ends of the spectrum that illustrate challenges and opportunities in serving laypeople.

Academic, law firm, and government law librarians can all promote access to justice initiatives. For law libraries that are open to the public, generally academic law libraries and government law libraries such as courthouse law libraries, librarians may encounter patrons who are seeking legal advice, which most librarians are prohibited from giving.

- Situation One: A patron requests that the librarian read the law over the telephone.
  While it might seem clearly unproblematic to comply with this request, in fact it may require a judgment call. For information that is short in length (again, whether information is short or extensive is another judgment call), librarians may have no problem with reading it over the telephone. However, there may be situations in which librarians choose to avoid the confusion that can come from the possibility of accidentally skipping text, complex outline structure, or varied auditory signals when reading lengthy statutes or court opinions over the telephone so that the hearer will not have to distinguish between the actual law and the actual words of the librarian. Another solution would be to provide a written copy of the law by email or text message following the call.
- Situation Two: A patron requests that librarians read giant stacks of files that the patron has brought to the library.
  This situation, unlike the first, seems at first glance to be obviously on the legal advice side of the information-advice divide, not to mention requiring resources (in the form of time) that most librarians do not have. Sometimes, however, reviewing the papers brought by a patron can serve the same purpose as a reference interview. Reviewing files to double-check citations to documents or sources of law may also be permissible in the provision of legal information. However, librarians should be sure to avoid raising patrons' levels of expectation that the librarian will complete court forms or interpret court documents on their behalf.

Both situations above present opportunities for law librarians, especially those who work outside of self-help centers, to share the names and locations of self-help resources available in the jurisdiction and share a list of lawyer referral services in addition to the legal information resources on site at the library. Being clear about what the librarians are permitted and not permitted to do saves the time of the patron and can be done with tact.

After avoiding the unauthorized practice of law, the second challenge faced by law librarians in the pursuit of access to justice is being overlooked by other professionals, as exemplified by this quote from a December 2020 episode of the Legal Services Corporation's *Talk Justice* podcast: "You wouldn't naturally think, 'wow, the American Association of Law Librarians and civil legal aid.'"[40] This failure by groups outside of the law library community to recognize the value that law librarians can play hinders our ability to engage in solutions. The 1998 Working Group on the Use of Nonlawyers "sought to explore how the use of nonlawyers might expand access to justice for low-income individuals [footnotes omitted]" without any reference to libraries or librarians.[41] Richard Zorza, founder of the Self-Represented Litigation Network, and David Udell, founder of the National Center for Access to Justice, suggested "New Roles for Non-Lawyers to Increase Access to Justice," also with no reference to libraries or librarians.[42] Jim Sandman, former president of the Legal Services Corporation and a strong advocate for access to justice, recommends broad collaboration including "people beyond the conventional access to justice community," a group in which he includes public librarians but not law librarians.[43] A keyword search of the *Maryland Bar Journal*, 1968–2022, for the word "librarian" generated only twenty-four results, and only one of those very few results is related to access to justice, in an article about the Maryland People's Law Library.

This oversight is detrimental to systemic approaches to improving access to justice. Access to justice requires access to information,[44] and librarians are critical to ensuring that this access is effective. Initiatives like the Caselaw Access Project[45] and Public.Resources.Org are valuable for making legal information freely available, but availability is not the same as access. By failing to include librarians in these initiatives, concerns such as the organization and findability of information are not prioritized. Connecting people with information is the goal of librarians, and connecting people with legal information is the goal of law librarians.

Few state access to justice commissions include law librarians. From a review conducted in September 2023, only seven commissions that identify the affiliations of their members on the commission website listed law librarians among their members. The absence of law librarians is a loss for the remaining states' access to justice initiatives; law librarians who serve on two of these seven commissions have spoken informally about the value of librarian involvement on the commission, saying that their commissions have benefited from the different ways in which librarians interact with members of the public, librarians' knowledge of different resources, and an increased receptiveness to innovation.[46]

The third challenge faced by law librarians interested in supporting access to justice is the fact of limited resources in combination with library missions prioritizing specific patron groups over members of the public. Academic law libraries have to prioritize their students and faculty; court law libraries generally prioritize judges and court staff. Further contributing to this challenge is the fact that members of the public tend to require greater assistance than patrons with some degree of legal training.[47]

The fourth challenge, an additional challenge that Katz has heard raised by law firm librarians seeking to participate in access to justice programming, is that legal research database contracts limit the distribution of search results. Therefore, they do not have the ability to use the law firm resources that attorneys use for their pro bono cases for what might be considered pro bono librarian work.

The availability of funding for librarians engaged in access to justice work is an additional challenge in some jurisdictions. In some jurisdictions, access to justice grant funds are available only to organizations that provide direct legal services. For example, District of Columbia law provides funding for grants to "nonprofit organizations that deliver civil legal services to low-income and underserved District residents, or support to their nonprofit organization partners, including funds for a shared legal interpreter bank."[48] A law library supporting lawyers might be eligible for a grant under this law; a law library supporting members of the public is not.

Opportunities

Most of the challenges identified above come with corresponding opportunities for research and advocacy to counter the current situation.

The first challenge above is that of unauthorized practice of law. Law librarians are well positioned to conduct research on their own states' regulations and ethics opinions in order to propose specific recommendations for colleagues within their states. Where those recommendations permit a broader range of activity than that which has traditionally been allowed by institutions in the state, there is an opportunity to advocate for loosening the restrictions imposed by those institutions.

The second challenge above is that librarians are overlooked in broader access to justice initiatives and collaborations. One opportunity to improve this situation is to become involved in state access to justice commissions, ideally by becoming members of the commissions, or alternatively by attending commission meetings as guests. Another opportunity is for law librarians to submit articles to state bar publications.

Where state law requires using access to justice funding for direct legal services only, law librarians can advocate for amendments that would expand the permitted uses of the funding.

Existing Programs

One example of law librarians actively contributing to access to justice is that of JusticeAccess, an independent law library founded in 2021 for the primary purpose of providing legal reference services to patrons in a manner designed to counter barriers to accessing traditional law libraries.[49] JusticeAccess serves patrons online through a "virtual reference desk" hosted on a secure video chat platform, in person at existing service points in the community such as public libraries, and by mail and email for incarcerated patrons. JusticeAccess engages law librarians throughout the country as volunteers to staff the virtual reference desk.

Another successful example of law library access to justice efforts is the *Guide to Virginia Legal Information Resources*[50] created by the Virginia Association of Law Libraries (VALL) Access to Justice Committee. The Committee intentionally focused on resources that were available free of charge, at low cost, or available via public libraries to reduce monetary barriers.[51] Removing the cost barrier so that legal materials may be accessed free of charge or at low cost is one thing that is doable and measurable, but being able to understand the law can remain a major challenge for self-represented litigants who cannot understand the materials on their own or do not have access to someone who can provide advice. The VALL Access to Justice Committee initially intended the *Guide* to be used by public librarians as they managed their collections of self-help legal resources, but the Committee believes that the *Guide* should be available to and can be used by library patrons.[52] Not every law library has dedicated space or time for access to justice initiatives, yet a research guide can make a world of difference for patrons. Other law librarians have established programs to expand the capacity of public librarians to assist members of the public who come to them with legal reference questions. The University of South Carolina School of Law's law librarians created the Circuit Riders Outreach Program in 2007 "to teach basic legal research skills to public and academic librarians."[53] Other law school libraries offer similar programs, including a program on "Hands-On Legal Reference for Public Librarians" presented by the University of Connecticut School of Law and Connecticut Judicial Branch Law Library Services Unit.[54]

GENERATIVE AI AND ACCESS TO JUSTICE

Another issue impacting research and the practice of law is generative artificial intelligence (AI). Generative AI tools are impacting legal research and the drafting of legal documents for practitioners and laypeople. These generative AI tools have the potential to save both time and effort in the preparation of legal documents.

Professors Maura R. Grossman and Paul W. Grimm (a retired judge) see the potential of AI to increase access to justice for self-represented litigants by assisting self-represented litigants with evaluating whether legal claims have a likelihood of success.[55] However, Grossman and Grimm say that instructors of law students should teach law students not to relinquish their issue-spotting, critical thinking, and problem-solving to generative AI tools.[56] But self-represented litigants who did not attend law school also need to engage in issue-spotting, critical thinking, and problem-solving skills without the training in how to use these skills. If attorneys need to use their critical thinking skills with the imperfect output of generative AI tools, then surely, laypeople will have to use their critical thinking skills with the imperfect output of generative AI tools. In addition to noting that generative AI tools have the potential to advance access to justice,[57] Grossman, Grimm, and Daniel Brown (a professor of computer science) note that generative AI tools are trained on datasets to predict the words that should come next in the text that these tools are generating and that citations to items (e.g., court cases) that do not exist occur because the generative AI tools are trained to imitate the writing of humans with the newly created text and not necessarily to be accurate at all times.[58] Moreover, Grossman, Grimm, and Brown believe that requiring self-represented litigants to disclose their use of generative AI tools in drafting court filings is a good practice.[59] Many generative AI tools for solving legal problems that have been made available within the last two years are cost-prohibitive for those outside Big Law.[60] Even still, lawyers who work in the field of access to justice are finding ways to make generative AI work for themselves and their clients. Sateesh Nori, an attorney who has been representing tenants in housing disputes for approximately twenty years, has developed AI tools that can answer routine questions of telephone callers to legal aid organizations. Andrew Perlman, dean and professor of law at Suffolk University Law School, has created the Legal Aid Navigator in the ChatGPT store (which leads people to resources in their geographic location) and is collaborating with courts throughout the United States on a "Turbotax of legal documents" which would allow people to file automated legal documents directly with the courts.[61] Moreover, law students can solve access to justice problems through legal technology. Since 2017, at Brigham Young University Law School, law students in the LawX program have created products for use in access to justice work. A recent product that the students have created is Order Up, a platform for creating financial declarations in divorce cases.[62] Paul Hankin, who has worked in information technology in an AmLaw 200 law firm, has opined that more people could have access to justice through new technologies and that now and likely continuing into the future, people will trust answers from generative AI more than answers from seasoned professionals.[63] According to a LexisNexis survey, over half of AmLaw 200 law firms have purchased Legal AI tools and nearly half are using these Legal AI tools. In the long run, will self-represented litigants and others who are interested in access to justice find these tools useful?[64] Perhaps a more salient question is whether librarians who help self-represented patrons access legal information are willing and have the resources to teach and assist these patrons in the use of these new and emerging generative AI tools.

HOPE FOR THE FUTURE

Despite challenges such as the exclusion of law librarians from some discussions on access to justice and the limited availability of grant funding for access to justice initiatives spearheaded by libraries, there is reason to be cautiously optimistic. Access to justice is and remains a priority across the United States, with increasing inclusion of nonlawyer professionals in efforts to pursue solutions. Programs that were established to address social-distancing requirements during the peak of the COVID-19 pandemic, such as court hearings held over video, are continuing because the benefits to self-represented litigants were seen and understood.[65]

In 1977, Cappelletti and Garth called for "far-reaching reforms and for new creativity."[66] It took nearly thirty years, but these reforms and creative initiatives have been introduced and are being studied in many states. While calling for "far-reaching reforms" would require the writing of another book let alone another book chapter, we call for "new creativity" that includes technology in the provision of access to justice initiatives and facilitates the taking of steps that are doable by pro se litigants yet does not provide additional cost barriers or oversimplify the issues faced by those who seek to represent themselves in legal matters.

NOTES

1. Latia Ward, "What Can Librarians Do to Facilitate Access to Justice," *YouTube video*, June 6, 2019, https://www.youtube.com/watch?v=vbsr8WshRcU, https://web.archive.org/web/20200603063928/https://www.youtube.com/watch?v=vbsr8WshRcU.
2. See Supreme Court of the United States, "Building Features," n.d., https://www.supremecourt.gov/about/buildingfeatures.aspx, https://perma.cc/W79U-UM8X.
3. Orison S. Marden, "Equal Access to Justice - The Challenge and the Opportunity," *Washington and Lee Law Review* 19, no. 2 (1962): 153-164, https://heinonline.org/HOL/P?h=hein.journals/waslee19&i=159.
4. "American Bar Association, *Legal Needs and Civil Justice: A Survey of Americans—Major Findings from the Comprehensive Legal Needs Study* (Chicago: American Bar Association, 1994), https://www.wisbar.org/aboutus/membership/Documents/WisTAFApp_J_ABA_Legal_need_study.pdf.
5. Rebecca L. Sandefur, "Access to Civil Justice and Race, Class, and Gender Inequality," *Annual Review of Sociology* 34 (2008): 339-358, 344, https://www.jstor.org/stable/29737794.
6. Mauro Cappelletti and Bryant Garth, "Access to Justice: The Newest Wave in the Worldwide Movement to Make Rights Effective," *Buffalo Law Review* 27, no. 2 (1978 1977): 181-292, at 182, https://heinonline.org/HOL/P?h=hein.journals/buflr27&i=193. ("The words 'access to justice' are admittedly not easily defined, but they serve to focus on two basic purposes of—the legal system—the system by which people may vindicate their rights and/or resolve their disputes under the general auspices of the state.")
7. *Id.* at 182.
8. American Association of Law Libraries, "Law Libraries and Access to Justice: A Report of the American Association of Law Libraries Special Committee on Access to Justice," July 2014, https://www.aallnet.org/wp-content/uploads/2018/01/AccessToJusticeSpecialCommittee2014LawLibrariesAndAccessToJustice.pdf.
9. Estelle Hurter, "Access to Justice: To Dream the Impossible Dream?," *The Comparative and International Law Journal of Southern Africa* 44, no. 3 (2011): 408-427, https://www.jstor.org/stable/24027059.
10. "Guiding Principles," U.S. Department of Justice Office for Access to Justice, accessed April 12, 2024, https://www.justice.gov/atj, https://perma.cc/7HHY-DZ3G.
11. "Element 1: Access to Justice and the Public Library," Thurgood Marshall State Law Library, 2024, https://www.mdcourts.gov/lawlib/using-library/for-librarians/legal-reference-training/PLR-access-to-justice, https://perma.cc/BF2W-FZDU.
12. Ward, *supra* note 1.
13. "The Justice Gap Report: Executive Summary," Legal Services Corporation, 2022, https://justicegap.lsc.gov/resource/executive-summary/, https://perma.cc/X5KF-3C3U.
14. *Id.*
15. *Id.*
16. Washington Council of Lawyers, "Best Practices in Pro Bono: The Role of Artificial Intelligence in Pro Bono and Access to Justice," event held on May 23, 2024, at Fried Frank, Washington, D.C., https://wclawyers.org/240523/.
17. Bob Ambrogi, "Access to Justice Requires Access to Law. So Why Aren't the Advocates of Each More Closely Aligned?," *LawSites (blog)*, March 11, 2024, https://www.lawnext.com/2024/03/access-to-justice-requires-access-to-law-so-why-arent-the-advocates-of-each-more-closely-aligned.html, https://perma.cc/6Y79-CBJ8. Ambrogi also states, "Maybe these are, in some ways, different battlefronts, but they are fighting the same war. The end goal is that everyone in the United States should have access to the law—including both the literal law and the justice system that applies and enforces it."
18. Caralee Adams, "2022 Internet Archive Hero Award: Carl Malamud," *Internet Archive Blogs (blog)*, October 19, 2022, https://blog.archive.org/2022/10/19/2022-internet-archive-hero-award-carl-malamud/, https://perma.cc/U2KQ-KMB2.

19. Public.Resource.org., n.d., "Welcome to Public.Resource.Org!," accessed April 16, 2024, https://public.resource.org/index.html, https://perma.cc/C5BP-YS3G.
20. Ambrogi, *supra* note 17.
21. *Id.*
22. Clea Simon, "Caselaw Access Project Conference Marks Full Release of Digitized Decisions," *Harvard Law School*, accessed June 4, 2024, https://hls.harvard.edu/today/caselaw-access-project-conference-marks-full-release-of-digitized-decisions/.
23. In 2022 and 2023, access to justice was a central subject of meetings of the American Association of Law Libraries (2022 annual meeting theme "Advancing Justice for All"), Northern California Association of Law Libraries (2022 spring institute theme "Expanding Access to Knowledge in Difficult Times"), Southeastern Chapter of the American Association of Law Libraries (2023 pre-meeting Institute), the Western Pacific Chapter of the American Association of Law Libraries (2023 meeting does not have a theme but access to justice is the subject of one program block), and the Virginia Association of Law Libraries (similar to the Western Pacific Chapter, the 2023 meeting did not have a theme but included one program block on access to justice).
24. For discussions on ethics in the provision of reference services and avoiding the unauthorized practice of law, the following works are of interest: Yvette Brown, "From the Reference Desk to the Jail House: Unauthorized Practice of Law and Librarians," *Legal Reference Services Quarterly* 13, no. 4 (1994): 31–46; Paul Jerome McLaughlin, Jr., "Wanting to Do More But Bound to Do Less: A Law Librarian's Dilemma," *The Reference Librarian*, 56, no. 2 (2015): 119–132, https://doi.org/ 10.1080/02763877.2014.982316; Charles J. Condon, "How to Avoid the Unauthorized Practice of Law at the Reference Desk," *Legal Reference Services Quarterly* 19, no. 1-2 (2001): 165–179, https://doi.org/ 10.1300/J113v19n01_11; Southern California Association of Law Libraries Public Access to Legal Information (PALI) Committee, "Legal Reference v. Legal Advice," in *Locating the Law* (PALI Committee, 2016), 46–53, https://scallnet.org/publications/; Wendi Arant and Brian Carpenter, "Where is the Line? Legal Reference Service and the Unauthorized Practice of Law (UPL)—Some Guides That Might Help," *Reference & User Services Quarterly* 38, no. 3 (Spring 1999): 235–239, https://www.jstor.org/stable/20863554; and Lisha Gerber, "Ethical Problems Surrounding the Practice of Legal Reference Service" (Mater's Paper, UNC Chapel Hill, 2001), https://cdr.lib.unc.edu/concern/masters_papers/nc580r423.
25. John G. Jackson, "Foreword," *Unauthorized Practice of Law: A Handbook for Lawyers and Laymen* 1 (1934): 3–12, 5, https://heinonline.org/HOL/P?h=hein.beal/unauplaw0001&i=3.
26. Robin K. Mills, "Reference Service vs. Legal Advice: Is It Possible to Draw the Line," *Law Library Journal* 72, no. 2 (1979): 179–193, https://heinonline.org/HOL/P?h=hein.journals/llj72&i=197.
27. See Paul Healey, *UNCERTAINTY MANAGEMENT IN REFERENCE INTERACTIONS WITH PRO SE LAW LIBRARY USERS*, 2010, https://core.ac.uk/download/pdf/4826762.pdf, https://perma.cc/T7LH-CQ8R.
28. Frederick Schauer and Virginia J. Wise, "Nonlegal Information and the Delegalization of Law," *The Journal of Legal Studies* 29 (2000): 498–499.
29. John M. Greacen, "No Legal Advice from Court Personnel - What Does That Mean," *Judges' Journal* 34, no. 1 (Winter 1995): 10.
30. Latia Ward, "Accessing Justice," *American Libraries Magazine* 53, no. 56 (June 2022): 56, https://digital.americanlibrariesmagazine.org/html5/reader/production/default.aspx?pubname=&edid=4c7068a3-ff3b-4eda-b277-65dfbc7ece87.
31. Greacen, *supra* note 29 at 15.
32. *Id.* at 14–15. The five principles are: "Court staff have an obligation to explain court processes and procedures to litigants, the media, and other interested citizens," Court staff have an obligation to inform litigants, and potential litigants, how to bring their problems before the court for resolution," "Court staff cannot advise litigants whether to bring their problems before the court, or what remedies to seek," "Court staff must always remember the absolute duty of impartiality. They must never give advice or information for the purpose of giving one party an advantage over another. They must never give advice or information to one party that they would not give to an opponent," and "Court staff should be mindful of the basic principle that counsel may not communicate with the judge *ex parte*. Court staff should not let themselves be used to circumvent that principle, or fail to respect it, in acting on matters delegated to them for decision."

33. *Id.* at 12.
34. John M. Greacen, "Legal Information vs. Legal Advice: Developments during the Last Five Years," *Judicature* 84, no. 4 (January-February 2001): 203.
35. John M. Greacen, "Legal Information vs. Legal Advice: A 25 Year Retrospective," *Judicature* 106, no. 2 (June 2022): 56–57, https://judicature.duke.edu/wp-content/uploads/2022/09/GREACEN_Summer2022.pdf.
36. *Id.*
37. *Id.* at 57 citing Illinois Supreme Court, *Illinois Supreme Court Policy On Assistance to Court Patrons by Circuit Clerks, Court Staff, Law Librarians, and Court Volunteers ("Safe Harbor Policy")* (originally effective April 2015, amended November 2018), (IL: Illinois Supreme Court, originally effective April 2015, amended November 2018, amended January 2024), https://www.illinoiscourts.gov/Resources/33fb071a-03e1-44a9-8e28-5d41ab25b73e/Safe_Harbor_Policy.pdf, https://perma.cc/9C3F-395K and "Legal Document Preparer Program," Arizona Judicial Branch (2022), https://www.azcourts.gov/cld/Legal-Document-Preparer-Program, https://perma.cc/T9HP-7NHS.
38. Tawnya K. Plumb, "Legal Research on the Road," video, 35:04, 35:24, March 2, 2022, https://drive.google.com/file/d/1am_McX-Jhc2qFwWcRRowf_VLioz4UB50/view. In the webinar, Plumb stated that there were representatives of libraries who were resistant to the idea of other librarians assisting with the provision of legal research and access to justice information for their patrons. Plumb traveled to libraries throughout Wyoming to speak about legal research and access to justice and noted that there were "four cancellations from one public library," and at another library "the response to everything I wanted to talk about was 'I already know that'"
39. Terrill Pollman, Jeanne Frazier Price, and Linda L. Berger, *Legal Research Examples & Explanations* (New York: Wolters Kluwer, 2017), 129. Pollman, Price, and Berger state the following about self-help legal materials, "As a law student you shouldn't rely on materials written for the lay public. Those sources have a very different focus from texts directed to lawyers and law students. They may oversimplify legal doctrine and may simply be wrong."
40. LSC—Legal Services Corporation: America's Partner for Equal Justice, "Talk Justice: Episode Nine," December 17, 2020, https://www.lsc.gov/media/podcasts/talk-justice/talk-justice-episode-nine, https://perma.cc/GM4G-J27X
41. Derek A. Denckla, "Report of the Working Group on the Use of Nonlawyers Special Issue: Conference on the Delivery of Legal Services to Low-Income Persons: Professional and Ethical Issues," *Fordham Law Review* 67, no. 5 (1998–1999): 1813–1818, https://heinonline.org/HOL/P?h=hein.journals/flr67&i=1829.
42. Richard Zorza and David Udell, "New Roles for Non-Lawyers to Increase Access to Justice," *Fordham Urban Law Journal* 41, no. 4 (March 19, 2016): 1259, https://ir.lawnet.fordham.edu/ulj/vol41/iss4/8, https://perma.cc/7YRW-ZDNQ.
43. James Sandman, "Five Requirements for Realizing Technology's Potential to Improve Access to Justice," LSC - Legal Services Corporation: America's Partner for Equal Justice, January 16, 2020, https://www.lsc.gov/spotlight-blog/five-requirements-realizing-technologys-potential-improve-access-justice, https://perma.cc/BZT8-CYZR.
44. Deborah K. Hackerson, "Access to Justice Starts in the Library: The Importance of Competent Research Skills and Free/Low-Cost Research Resources Symposium - Accessing Justice in Hard Times: Lessons from the Field, Looking to the Future," *Maine Law Review* 62, no. 2 (2010): 473–486, at 478, https://heinonline.org/HOL/P?h=hein.journals/maine62&i=479.
45. "Our Data," Case Law Access Project, last modified 2024, https://case.law/, https://perma.cc/46TF-TQW6.
46. Unrecorded conversations at the 2023 meeting of the Southeast Chapter of the American Association of Law Libraries, March 10, 2023.
47. We state this fact without judgment, although some sources suggest that pro se patrons are "difficult" (e.g., see Robert T. Begg, "The Reference Librarian and the Pro Se Patron," *Law Library Journal* 69, no. 1 (1976): 26–32, https://heinonline.org/HOL/P?h=hein.journals/llj69&i=40) or "problems" (e.g., see John Greacen, "Services for Self-Represented Litigants in Arkansas: A Report to the Arkansas Access to Justice Commission," 2013, at 4. "Many of the Judges, Lawyers and Court Staff with Whom We Met

in the Course of This Study Consistently Link the Terms 'Self-Represented (or pro se) Litigants' and 'Problem'," https://arkansasjustice.org/wp-content/uploads/2017/04/Arkansas-Final-Report-7-26-13-1.pdf, https://perma.cc/QG57-FYW9). We understand that patrons who have no background in the law will naturally need more assistance simply by virtue of needing the addition of basic instruction.

48. D.C. Official Code § 4-1703.01(a).
49. One of the co-authors of this chapter, Rebecca Katz, is the founder of JusticeAccess.
50. Virginia Association of Law Libraries Access to Justice Committee, "Guide to Virginia Legal Information Resources," October 2, 2023, https://www.vacourts.gov/courtadmin/library/virginia_legal_information_resources.pdf, https://web.archive.org/web/20240416201821/https://www.vacourts.gov/courtadmin/library/virginia_legal_information_resources.pdf.
51. Latia Ward, "Self-Help Legal Information Resources in Virginia," *LISP/SR Blog (blog)*, November 1, 2023, https://lispsr.wordpress.com/2023/11/01/self-help-legal-information-resources-in-virginia/, https://perma.cc/HJ8Y-J96A.
52. One of the co-authors, Latia Ward, serves on the Virginia Association of Law Libraries Access to Justice Committee and collaborated with the other committee members in creating the *Guide to Virginia Legal Information Resources.*
53. Rebecca Plevel, "LibGuides: Circuit Riders: Basic Legal Research: Home," accessed June 11, 2024, https://guides.law.sc.edu/CircuitRiders/intro.
54. Email from Anne Rajotte to Rebecca Katz, August 11, 2023.
55. Cary Coglianese, Maura R. Grossman, and Paul W. Grimm, "Legal Information vs. Legal Advice: A 25 Year Retrospective," *Judicature* 107, no. 3 (2024): 66, https://judicature.duke.edu/wp-content/uploads/2024/03/PCP-Grimm-et-al-Vol-107-No-3.pdf, https://perma.cc/S8LF-JQKB.
56. *Id.* at 71.
57. Maura R. Grossman, Paul W. Grimm, and Daniel G. Brown, "Is Disclosure and Certification of the Use of Generative AI Really Necessary?," *Judicature* 107, no. 2 (2023): 69, https://judicature.duke.edu/wp-content/uploads/2023/10/AIOrders_Vol107No2.pdf, archived at https://perma.cc/KJ6S-GUDT.
58. *Id.* at 72–73. "This inability [to separate fact from fiction] becomes especially problematic when one attempts to perform legal research using GenAI tools not built for that purpose. ChatGPT 3.5 routinely cites irrelevant or nonexistent cases, alongside relevant or real ones, because it is trying to fit the pattern of how one writes about the law; it is not necessarily trying to tell a true story."
59. Grossman, Grimm, and Brown, *supra* note 57 at 76.
60. Cassandre Coyer, "Could Gen AI Be a 'Pivotal Moment' for the Legal Aid Market?," *Legaltech® News (blog)*, April 10, 2024, https://www.law.com/legaltechnews/2024/04/10/could-gen-ai-be-a-pivotal-moment-for-the-legal-aid-market/ citing Cassandre Coyer, "Behind the Prices: Is Generative AI Legal Tech Cheaper to Buy or Build?," *Legaltech® News (blog)*, October 12, 2023, https://www.law.com/legaltechnews/2023/10/12/behind-the-prices-is-generative-ai-legal-tech-cheaper-to-buy-or-build/.
61. *Id.*
62. Bob Ambrogi, "Law Students in BYU Law's LawX Program Develop Two Applications Targeting Access to Justice," *LawSites (blog)*, April 12, 2024, https://www.lawnext.com/2024/04/law-students-in-byu-laws-lawx-program-develop-two-applications-targeting-access-to-justice.html, https://perma.cc/5ZKE-VLHN.
63. Paul Hankin, "How Long Before People Trust AI More Than They Trust You?," *Legaltech® news (blog)*, April 22, 2024, https://www.law.com/legaltechnews/2024/04/22/how-long-before-people-trust-ai-more-than-they-trust-you/. Hankin describes a situation in which one new employee trusted the information about software capability from an AI tool and used the AI tool to confirm what an experienced colleague had said. Hankin states, "This incident isn't an isolated anomaly; it's a harbinger of a paradigm shift where AI is increasingly seen as more reliable than even the most experienced professionals."
64. Geoffrey D. Ivnik, "AI vs. Legal AI, What's The Difference?," *LawSites (blog)*, April 23, 2024, https://www.law.com/legaltechnews/2024/04/23/ai-vs-legal-ai-whats-the-difference/, https://perma.cc/T8G7-5ZXU citing "2024 Investing in Legal Innovation Survey," LexisNexis, 2024, https://www.lexisnexis.com/pdf/genai-report.pdf, https://perma.cc/2LYF-T9SH.

65. See, e.g., Victor D. Quintanilla, Kurt Hugenberg, Ryan Hutchings, and Nedim Yel, "Accessing Justice with Zoom: Experiences and Outcomes in Online Civil Courts," 2023, https://law.indiana.edu/research/Accessing-Justice-with-Zoom-Experiences-and-Outcomes-in-Online-Civil-Courts-October-2023.pdf, https://perma.cc/WH2N-Q946.
66. Cappelletti and Garth, *supra* note 6 at 182.

ADDITIONAL RESOURCES

American Association of Law Libraries, "Law Libraries and Access to Justice: A Report of the American Association of Law Libraries Special Committee on Access to Justice," July 2014, https://www.aallnet.org/wp-content/uploads/2018/01/AccessToJusticeSpecialCommittee2014LawLibrariesAndAccessToJustice.pdf, https://perma.cc/SQ8L-KD73.

"Law Librarians Working Group," Self-Represented Litigation Network, last modified 2024, https://www.srln.org/LawLibrariansWorkingGroup, https://perma.cc/JN98-XWF6.

Yolanda Patrice Jones, "Bringing the Law to the Library: The Importance of Librarian Mediation in Access to Justice Services," *Legal Reference Services Quarterly* 37, no. 1 (January 2, 2018): 11–37, https://doi.org/10.1080/0270319X.2018.1493812.

25

Law Library Partnerships

Kris Turner

One of the most fortunate positions a law library may find itself in is a fruitful partnership. To meaningfully connect with a colleague or forge new working relationships provides the library, the library staff, and the library's users with a stronger base of service and expands both the library's reach and capability. As libraries continue to evolve, it is incumbent on all staff members, but especially administrators, to seek out potential partners and projects that will keep the library fully engaged with stakeholders and patrons. A proper partnership will not only give library patrons an added benefit, but it will also showcase why a library is a good investment and an integral part of the organization's operations.

Truly, law libraries thrive in partnerships. That doesn't mean it comes as second nature to form long-term relationships or seek out partners. Common sense dictates that locating like-minded colleagues or organizations can strengthen the ability to support patrons and users, but to create a fully realized partnership that pays dividends requires more work beyond simply reaching out and asking to work together. Advanced planning is frequently required, and not just about the project being worked on. Determining how possible partnerships will grow and be maintained must be considered. A series of questions about how to forge closer connections with partners and their leadership may play a role in how the library takes on partners. Cost and staff time will always be line items that cannot be overlooked, especially when the staff or money may go toward projects that may not be focused on core values of the library's mission.

Regardless of these valid concerns, partnerships are increasingly becoming indispensable for today's law libraries and "it is incumbent upon us to actively embrace collaboration and form strategic partnerships with other law libraries"[1] and other partners beyond law library colleagues. Going it alone and waiting for others to approach to ask for services and support is a good way to become forgotten as many researchers become more competent with digitized research or simply are not accustomed to asking for librarian assistance. By connecting with like-minded partners, librarians will likely complete more complex projects that result in unique resources that consequently thrust library staff, space, and services to the forefront of the dean's, judge's, or partner's mind. This chapter will provide a blueprint for locating potential partners for law libraries of all types and strategies for ensuring that partnerships endure, emphasize the library's value, and align with the library's strategic goals and central mission.

PLANNING FOR AND FORMING PARTNERSHIPS

As with many relationships, it is not advisable to enter the law library partnership without forethought. It may seem as simple as agreeing to a coordinated effort to make resources more accessible or to share the workload on complicated requests. But to enter into an agreement without thinking more deeply about it may shortchange the library's ability to take full advantage of what the partnership has to offer, or worse, shackle the library to unintended work that diverts time and energy from central services. Instead, opportunities must be considered deeply. This is even more fundamental to the planning process when the project will take years or may be ongoing.

Often, partnerships begin with a need or a request. That need may be identified by the law library, such as a gap in research coverage or service, or one that a user suggests, such as generative AI-focused technology and information literacy training. A law library must be open to and able to rise to these new needs to often move on to the next step of forming a partnership that fills the need. Passivity is rarely a trait that will encourage either potential partners to seek out the library to suggest additional services. Instead, presenting the library as a dynamic entity that is willing or at least able to explore new avenues of service is critical. Fostering staff interest and encouraging further professional development are the most direct ways to keep the library forward-facing, though cost can interfere with this at-times lofty goal. However, a low-cost and parallel requirement to discarding the outdated viewpoint of libraries being passive and quiet homes for dusty ideas and books is to advocate. When opportunities present themselves to discuss library services with stakeholders, take them.[2] They may not (and probably won't) be aware of what the library can offer without being told. Encourage them to suggest needs and requests and be prepared to suggest outreach and partnerships as the solutions to filling those needs. Keeping the pipeline of questions and requests coming into the library will lead to more opportunities to reach out to potential partners, as those questions and challenges the library has now may not be answerable on its own. An important caveat when advocating for library use and suggestions is to keep the library's boundaries in mind. If asked for a highly technical website redesign, then suggest the appropriate partner to answer that request. Librarians as a whole love to say "yes," but it is not healthy for librarians to take on all projects that come their way.

Once law libraries have both advocated for themselves and established themselves as forward-facing problem-solvers, they can they begin to think more deeply about how partners could assist in answering these new questions. Whether the need has arisen from an external source, like a stakeholder or patron, or was a gap identified by the law library staff, the initial steps must consider what types of resources the library could dedicate to the project and whether a partnership makes sense, even before identifying possible partners. As with any project, library staff must ask these questions to keep the goals and commitment in mind:

- What staff members are best suited to work on this problem/project? *Are there necessary skills not represented on the library staff? Who would oversee the project?*
- *Do staff have the appropriate time to dedicate to it?* If not, could some of their responsibilities be shifted elsewhere?
- Will this project affect the library's budget? *Could the cost be outsourced in some way?*
- How long will it take to complete this project? Is it ongoing? What kind of upkeep or oversight will it require? *Could the project be completed more quickly with the assistance and skills of others outside the Law Library?*
- What does the final project look like? *How would a law library market the outcome to users, stakeholders, or colleagues? Would the initiating library be willing to share the work with other libraries or departments so they could replicate it or enhance it?*
- Who does this project most benefit? *Are there other organizations whose stakeholders could also benefit? Are there other departments the library could strengthen ties with by working on this project together?*

The italicized questions, if all answered affirmatively, would strongly suggest that the library's project is one that would benefit from a partner. Importantly, note that while the completion of the project is paramount in debating whether to take on a partner, libraries can also consider whether they can leverage the project to further tighten a working relationship with another department or with a community partner. Perhaps a project can forge closer ties with Career Services or the Dean's office in the law school or with a group of attorneys that had previously not utilized the library's services. This could also simply be a chance to strengthen the library's position within professional organizations. An early-career librarian on staff may benefit from working with more seasoned colleagues from other libraries, or promoting cross-library work may give more power to consortia that the library belongs to. While the gap, need, or project may drive the initial question about how and if to provide a new service, the potential benefits of a partnership should enter the discussion relatively early in the planning process.

If library staff have reviewed these questions and found that a partnership would be beneficial, it is now time to start determining which partner would be the best fit. This step may be simpler than it appears. On its face, the project may clearly require partnership with a specific person or organization. Building a website or repository will likely require partnering with IT staff, whereas conducting research into the history of the library's law firm will require partnerships and outreach with retired partners and community members (and perhaps even oral historians or archivists). If it is not clear, then first ascertain whether the partnership should be internal to the organization or require external partners. Next, consider the time and cost commitment of any partners the library would seek out. There may be an ideal partner, but they could be a one-person department or library that cannot spare time or money to join the partnership. Finally, start crafting the initial outreach to potential partners. Consider these factors when first contacting potential partners:

- What is the goal for the partnership? What will the partner get out of the relationship?
- What is the specific task of the partner? Are there specific staff or skills needed to make the partnership succeed?
- What are their financial and time commitments?
- When will the partnership conclude, if at all? How will it be maintained over time? Which people in the initiating library are best positioned to create and maintain the relationships over time?[3]

Most of these factors parallel the initial considerations for creating a partnership in the first place. While there is no need to go through these factors point-by-point, it does pay to keep answers to each in mind, especially if the project is a permanent one. If a library staff member has consciously thought through these questions already, it is probable that the proposed partner will see the benefits immediately. Some projects may involve Memorandums of Understanding or other contractual agreements, but this chapter will focus on the more informal but still professionally necessary requirements of a partnership. Once the prospective partner has agreed to the idea of working together, an initial meeting where details are more fully fleshed out should be set up with all partners represented. This meeting, especially if the partners haven't worked together before, is important for setting the tenor of the partnership. Collegiality and organization ensure a positive beginning to the partnership and further the library's own internal goal of building stronger relationships with new colleagues or internal organization departments. Deliberately approaching projects with an eye toward partnerships creates more productive services and eventually will build a deep bench of partners for the library to consider for future projects or needs.[4]

POTENTIAL PARTNERS: CONNECTING WITH OTHER SKILLED PROFESSIONALS

If library staff or administrators were to write down a list of law library partners, most might be surprised by how long the list would grow. Once the library has decided to take on a project that would be best completed with a partner, the list can then be culled down to the most appropriate partners. Fortunately, the partners will almost always be staffed with skilled professionals who complement the initiating library's own skills or allow for the project to be completed more rapidly with an increased number of librarians. By considering the needs and goals of the new project, libraries can identify partners and begin to cement the new working relationships.

Internal Partners: Reaching Out to Departments and Colleagues within the Institution

Often, the first place to check for potential partners is entirely internal to the library's parent organization. This will shorten the amount of time needed to vet potential partners, deepen internal relationships that will strengthen library services and support, and likely save the library (and the parent organization) money. There are several departments that frequently produce positive results. Working with IT professionals to build better websites, digital collections, or test out new technology all make for strong long-term partnerships that allow for deep collaboration. Digital collections may only be maintained through a strong partnership of library and IT staff and will require input from both departments for a maximally effective resource. IT and library staff both commonly work in the background, and a front-facing project can help further cement the quality and competency of both departments' work.[5] While some librarians have fundamental coding and web design skills, an IT partnership can provide a higher level of security and continued support to digital initiatives.[6]

A second potential partner for law libraries is marketing or external affairs departments. Libraries are well positioned to create content that can encourage engagement with potential clients, students, or the public. If the project features institutional history, marketing can mold the raw findings into a press release, website, or even celebration of an anniversary. In a time when law firm marketing, scholarly visibility, and government transparency are all more important than ever, external affairs is a critical partner in elevating the work that the law library does to make the larger organization work. Many academic law libraries are central to providing data and insights into how and where faculty publish or posting the work itself to various outlets that garner citations and page views. Creating an ongoing partnership with external affairs that forms a pipeline for these postings is a simple and effective manner to cement the library at the center of an increasingly important aspect of law schoolwork.[7] Government and court libraries can ensure that their work is more easily discovered and well-used by their patrons by either developing in-house marketing experience or seeking out partnerships with government publishers. Finally, law firm librarians can work closely with their marketing departments to create attractive histories of the firm itself. Law libraries are an obvious repository of institutional memory and can use these archives and artifacts to make a firm more approachable and memorable, especially if the firm itself has been in existence for decades or longer. These partnerships can also be used to create anniversary material that instills a stronger connection between the firm and the staff, especially new associates who would otherwise be unaware of the history. The marketing and wordsmithing skills that many external affairs professionals possess mesh well with librarian skill sets and fundamentally illustrate how partners should complement each other and fill in knowledge gaps.

Leadership and administrative staff are another group of potential partners that law libraries may overlook. A partnership with a dean of another law school department, such as faculty or student services, can give that leader a better understanding of the services the law library can provide and forge a deeper connection with a diverse set of stakeholders in the building. Partners and government officials present similar opportunities for other law library types. These types of partnerships may not be as permanent in the same sense as working with marketing or IT departments due to the nature of the projects that are necessary to create the partnership but still should be seriously considered because of the chance to work with leaders that may control library staffing or budgetary questions. These partnerships may result in presentations where the library is supporting a goal of the administration, advocating for a particular resource purchase, or creating space that accommodates a shift in collections or institutional need. These partnerships may require the library to approach administration with a more fully developed proposal for the partnership and its goals to ensure that the partnership is worth the busy administrator's time and fully showcases the value of the project and, by extension, the library. This type of partnership brings with it another unique aspect: an imprimatur of high-level approval and value. Not only is the library solving a need or answering a request via a properly vetted partnership, but it is also communicating value and skill to the partner in the process. However, remember that while the library may be getting something of special value out of this partnership, the administrator or partner will also be looking for that special value. Approaching the project and partnership with a high degree of care and communication is important and can lead to more productive partnerships of the same type in the future. By providing a blueprint and clear-eyed goal for the partnership, law libraries can break new ground and find allies in higher places.

There are other internal departments that could provide libraries with valuable partners, ranging from firm working groups or committees to student organizations or staff attorneys that provide different viewpoints for the project. The advantages of internal partnerships are obvious. Law libraries likely already have a relationship with the department and "speak the same language," meaning library staff know the people and are working toward the same institutional goals. Since the staff are familiar, so will be the skills that are available to assist with the partnership and the availability of staff. This insider knowledge will make the initial process of determining whether a partnership is worth forming easier. However, the library must also be aware of limitations. When partnering internally, the library may save time and money but may also limit itself to known entities when instead an external partner might be a better fit for the project. There may also be longer histories, for better or worse, when working with internal colleagues that could make partnerships harder to form and maintain. Regardless, an internal partnership not only grows closer connections with those who the library already supports but also creates more opportunities to burnish the library's reputation among what may be the primary set of library users while also allowing library staff to easily identify which potential partner will fit the project's need.

External Partners: Discovering and Establishing New Connections to Accomplish New Goals

Beyond the walls of the law library lies a wealth of potential partners of all stripes. What they often require is more legwork and networking outside of one's typical siloes.[8] Some of these partners may have once been internal partners who have moved on or represent entirely different organization that is also looking for a partner. As law libraries consider their specific needs, it can be helpful to remember that some organizations are in "partnership deserts," meaning they do not often receive requests to partner with others. Again, this presents an opportunity but also may signal the need to provide guidance for what is expected of a partnership. When searching for external partners, libraries must simultaneously cast a wide net by searching across different types of organizations and peer institutions while specifically targeting potential partners that are not only available and willing to partner but can be equal partner in the undertaking by providing the necessary skill and experience for the project. This requires not only clear planning but also continued check-ins as the partnership inevitably evolves over the course of the project.

Peer Law Libraries

The first external partner to investigate is peer law libraries, meaning libraries that are of the same type as the initiating library, be it academic, firm, or government. The challenges and shared patron bases closely align between similar library types, which results in a group of highly trained professionals who are all working toward the same general goals. While the broad strokes are alike, the details are where differences may occur. Some law libraries may have different funding or staffing models, which may require more frequent partnerships just to meet daily goals. Consortia and other professional groups are excellent places to begin forming these partnerships and find like-minded colleagues. Regardless, even if the potential partners are of similar minds regarding project goals[9] and timelines, it is still important to bring some detailed proposals for the actual partnership workflows, particularly division of labor. As busy law librarians, we already know how easy it is to lose track of obligations and priorities, and sometimes external partnerships may fall far down the rungs of importance. This can be particularly frustrating for the initial organizer of the partnership. Setting staggered meetings and guideposts that allow for the timely completion of particular segments of the partnership will make this aspect of the partnership easier and pave the way for continued cordial relations between peer libraries.

Forging Partnerships across Different Types of Law Libraries

Creating partnerships that straddle different types of libraries has the potential to be even more productive than peer partnerships since day-to-day responsibilities differ significantly enough to create diverse skill sets and closer relationships with a number of patron types (students, faculty, partners, judges, legislators). These partnerships expand patron networks, encouraging students to visit State Law Libraries or attorneys to use an academic library's resources.

Librarians in these partnerships also grow professionally. It's important for academic law librarians to understand the challenges their students will face at the firm or in the courts and government. Firm librarians better grasp what type of training their associates and interns receive in law school, and government librarians can gain a deeper understanding of their judicial or legislative patrons as their backgrounds are likely in firm work or academia. These partnerships also provide more opportunities for resource sharing. Pooling resources, and subsequently saving money, will be top of mind for partners, and if an academic law library's resources can help others, all the better. This is not meant to advocate for partnerships as altruism; instead, it can be another benefit for partners to enter long-term partnerships. All partners aim to get something of use for their institution or users from their partnerships, and at times that means employing the resources that are at hand for one partner but not another. This can come to the fore most especially with staffing and collections. Harnessing the cross-library partnership potential creates closer connections, staff who have a greater understanding of the legal profession, and hopefully an end project that can be maintained over time by perpetuating continually closer growth as the project ties the partners together.

External Partners beyond Law Libraries

Public Libraries

There are actors outside of the law library world who also create dynamic partnerships. First among these numbers are public librarians. Universes of partnership possibilities open up with this group of colleagues, particularly regarding outreach and technology. These partnerships create pipelines to one hard-to-reach patron group: public patrons and local communities.[10] Creating standing programs with local public libraries (or with their staff for in-service days) are powerful partnerships that ensure critical legal research skills and basic understanding of both information literacy and the legal system can be widely shared. While many law librarians already work closely with other legal professionals via national and regional organizations, fewer are involved in other organizations that also include other library types, such as public or academic libraries. These organizations can potentially strengthen the law library's own outreach and provide a new pool of partners. Membership is usually low cost, but presenting at a public library conference can also provide inroads to finding partners for providing new services or ongoing educational events.

Alumni Organizations

For academic law libraries, alumni organizations are also fertile partnerships. After spending time supporting and advocating for students, it is very likely that law libraries are already well positioned to reconnect with alumni as they start to practice. These new practitioners will soon become involved in bar organizations and as partners. County and state bars are often in need of partners for ongoing education, content creation, or for archival assistance. Any of these types of projects align with many library goals and strategic plans and can be made even easier with an enthusiastic partner that is already aware of the library's value. Once these connections have been made, other existing partnerships can be leveraged to make an even stronger multi-partner relationship. Academic law librarians may already have pre-existing relationships with firm or government librarians, who can then also work closely with alums (either at their firms, in their government offices, or beyond). The further afield a library goes to create partners, the more opportunity there is to create an interconnected web of partners that can further connect librarians with new and reliable partners, which in turn create the ability to complete complicated projects that would otherwise not be possible.

Government and Nonprofits

The final group of external organizations to investigate is governmental offices and nonprofit organizations. Government law libraries are well positioned to partner with these groups, but any law library may do so. Housing essential resources, governmental bodies may be interested in expanding access to older materials, backing up their primary websites, or even sharing expertise and resources across different organizations. Perhaps more than any other type of partnership, this type is an opportunity to share resources, either financial or managerial. Nonprofits will have particular goals in mind and the ability to provide financial support for large projects or grant-writing skills, while libraries and governmental organizations have access to unique sets of data and content and very specialized and trained staff. To find partnerships with these groups, libraries can, after first establishing that a partnership is the way to accomplish their goal as outlined above, check with stakeholders that may already have a connection in the nonprofit or governmental world. Many lawyers and faculty already work in these areas and may have insight into what groups are open to partnering. Nonprofits may also reach out to libraries directly in the hope of collaboration. It is critical to be alert to these connections when they happen. As discussed in the case study below, sometimes a small introduction can lead to large results, albeit not without a significant amount of work in the interim.

External partnerships open doors that simply do not otherwise exist. Even more than partnerships with internal departments, skill gaps are filled, responsibilities can be equitably divided, and financial/staff burdens shared. For libraries looking to expand their reach, these partnerships can be invaluable, especially to community partners such as public libraries or local government or state bar offices. Law libraries can also create more dynamic and engaging digital and physical collections via these partnerships as these groups may have access to information that is simply not as widely available as it could be with library intervention and collaboration. Nearly as important as leveraging these partnerships to meet the library's goals is the inherent opportunity to mold how non-library organizations perceive law libraries. Law library value will only grow as alumni, government actors, lawyers, and their professional organizations see the library's work in action and see how integral the work is to the information and legal professions. The law library will use the partnership to grow not only collections or services but also to enhance the standing of the law library in the partner's eyes.

Case Study: Partnerships and the Digital Publication of Tribal Laws[11]

Big partnerships can start in small ways. The Digital Publication of Tribal Law Pilot Project, which required an enduring partnership between two law libraries, an open access publisher, faculty and staff of a law school, and numerous tribal governments, began with simple connections. Bonnie

Shucha, the associate dean for Library and Information Services and director of the University of Wisconsin Law Library, notes that the seed of the partnership was planted when she was a law student. Dean Shucha took a course on tribal law with Professor Richard Monette, a nationally known tribal law expert and founder of the Great Lakes Indigenous Law Center at the University of Wisconsin Law School. Professor Monette's course was a transformational experience for Dean Shucha, giving her a deeper understanding of tribal governance and sovereignty and the integral role of tribal law in the American legal system.

At the same time, David Griesen, the founder and CEO of the 501(c)(3) open access publisher Open Law Library, was busy making his own connections. One of his employees, while visiting the home of a tribal elder in Wisconsin, learned of the tribe's intent to be awarded a grant to publish a print code. This inspired Mr. Griesen to learn more about the needs of tribes and subsequently "cold email" Professor Monette. The connection grew from there, with Professor Monette creating an opportunity for Dean Shucha and Mr. Griesen to meet and begin planning for the project.

Professor Monette also connected the group with Bridget Swanke, an attorney in the legal department of the Stockbridge-Munsee Community, a federally recognized tribe with a written code of tribal law. The group was soon introduced to the final partner via a referral from an attorney who knew Mr. Griesen: The National Indian Law Library (NILL). A well-respected and well-connected resource, NILL is an online portal to numerous tribal resources and supports visitors with Indian law-related research needs.

The group has a clear shared goal—to address the challenges Native Nations face in making their laws accessible. The group decided the best way to accomplish this goal was to build an online tool that allows tribes to add, update, and share their code, which could be integrated into existing platforms already maintained by the law libraries for further accountability and reliability as well as cross-jurisdictional research. Even with a shared goal, each partner gained something from participating. The Stockbridge-Munsee Community's Tribal Council, having already decided to put their code online, gained a functional tool with powerful search and cross-referencing capabilities. Open Law Library would provide technical expertise and build deeper connections with potential future tribal partners. The Great Lakes Indigenous Law Center would gain a resource that their tribal partners and law students have often requested. The UW Law Library and NILL would further enrich their own digital resources and provide more support to their own users in search of tribal code that was previously more difficult to digitally research or locate. In sum, the pilot project would focus on developing a customized platform that enables tribes to openly publish their laws while retaining full ownership and control over the content. Librarians and developers would work closely with Native Nations throughout the project to ensure the platform meets their unique needs and respects their sovereignty.

While each partner could provide staff and expertise, funding was still necessary. Dean Shucha and the UW Law Library were awarded a grant from the Institute of Museum and Library Services in 2020 that allowed for the collaborative effort to proceed. The grant process required a detailed explanation of the project, and each partner had their role to play. Open Law Library would develop the platform and provide technical support to the tribes and libraries. Stockbridge Munsee Community would provide the code and detailed feedback on what they (and potential future tribal partners) needed. The Great Lakes Indigenous Law Center created further inroads with tribal partners and served as the primary point of advocacy and outreach about the project. UW Law Library and NILL provided their own expertise and outreach, such as input on necessary metadata tagging for searching within digital frameworks and presenting at national and local conferences.

Over the next several years, an enormous amount of work was undertaken to make this goal a reality. Standing monthly meetings were established to discuss progress and check in on noted guideposts along the way. Tribal codes were gathered, organized, and reviewed. Computer code was written, tested, and rewritten. Library platforms were built and modified. Continued outreach to new partners was undertaken. Even as new staff members from the different partners rotated on and off the project, the monthly meetings and shared vision stayed constant. The delineation of responsibilities between the partners was clearly laid out and expectations and deadlines set monthly. During the implementation of the project, numerous presentations, papers, websites, and outreach efforts were collaboratively worked on. With the initial pilot phase and grant funding ending in the summer 2024, the project is considered a significant success, with six tribes publishing their laws using the platform and several others in the process of doing so.

Reflecting on the development of the project and the partnership that blossomed alongside it, the participants are satisfied and proud of the final result. Dean Shucha explains that

> the partnerships formed through the Digital Publication of Tribal Laws Pilot Project have significantly strengthened the University of Wisconsin Law Library's ability to serve tribal leaders, members, attorneys, and others seeking tribal law. The project has expanded access to tribal law and supported the right to know the law, which is essential to protect and promote due process, access to justice, and self-governance. These partnerships have enabled the UW Law Library to contribute to making tribal laws more accessible, strengthening the ability of tribes to govern effectively and promoting a better understanding of tribal sovereignty and legal systems.
>
> As part of the project, the UW Law Library developed the Great Lakes Tribal Law Collection in the UW Law School Digital Repository. This collection is a compilation of tribal law documents shared with permission from select Indigenous Nations within Wisconsin and the broader Great Lakes region. The repository encompasses a range of materials and continually grows as tribes revise and update their documents, further enhancing the ability to serve those seeking tribal law resources.
>
> These partnerships have also strengthened the UW Law Library's connection within the law school. Through its collaboration with the Great Lakes Indigenous Law Center on this project, the library is now regarded as a partner in the law school's strategic objectives to expand its presence in Indigenous law and deepen collaborations with Native nations. By working together on these and other projects, the library and GLILC are better able to serve the needs of tribal communities and those engaged in the study and practice of Indian law.

Anne Lucke, the library director at NILL, echoes Dean Shucha's sentiment:

> NILL's Access to Tribal Law Project has benefited directly through the development of the library platform by streamlining the maintenance of our Tribal Law Gateway. A significant amount of staff time is dedicated to reviewing the laws available through our Gateway, updating content, and correcting errors. The library platform developed through this partnership requires less time and is more accurate than our current manual system, allowing our small staff to focus on other services our library provides. In addition, our partners have brought new tribes to our platform who we did not have relationships with before. We have been able to do the same, by referring tribes to Open Law Library when the support they needed to publish their laws was more than NILL could provide.

While the formal partnership of the initial phase is ending, all the partners plan to continue outreach to more tribal communities in the hopes of publishing codes and court opinions online. The partnerships between like-minded organizations who were already invested in and working on similar goals were able to enhance the partnership and lead to an entirely new digital platform that promises to grow further in the coming years.[12]

THE FUTURE OF LAW LIBRARIANSHIP PRACTICE AND THE IMPACT OF EFFICIENT PARTNERSHIPS

As the Digital Publication of Tribal Codes Pilot Project illustrates, amazing outcomes result from partnerships, particularly partnerships that create outcomes that align with the larger goals of the library or its home institution. However, as the case study also emphasizes, the outcomes do not happen without a significant amount of outreach, collaboration, patience, and foresight. This means that the earliest steps in forming partnerships—connecting with and vetting partners, understanding the roles of each partner, and fleshing out the scope of the project that requires the partnership—take on more importance.

The evaluation and development of partnerships are integral to the future of law librarianship practice. Formal partnerships, such as MALLCO, NELLCO, and other similar consortia, provide financial benefits (shared costs for subscriptions and print depositories) and a more unified front for professional development and advocacy. These same benefits filter down to partnerships that librarians can form for either short-term or ongoing projects. With the continuing shift from print to digital resources, technology and digital preservation are areas ripe with partnership potential. Technology in general, especially generative AI, also makes for a compelling project that could include tech companies or other external partners wishing to expand their AI-generated datasets or improve search and research capabilities. Law librarians can also leverage these partnerships to emphasize the central role that they play in their organization. If a library is a vital partner in creating and completing projects, stakeholders will remember this when staffing and budgeting decisions must be made. It can also leave a positive impression on patrons or users. A law library that has proactively reached out to established or growing companies or peer libraries to solve a long-standing problem (or just to create a better workflow or resource) is proving their value while also accomplishing its essential goals. Going it alone or hoping that another organization will reach out is not enough—take reasonable chances and be prepared to take the next step when the partnership search bears fruit.

Regardless of the importance that uncovering and cementing partnerships is to the library's mission, projects, and future, it can still be a daunting task, even to established law library administrators. The points listed below are designed to answer common concerns that arise when seeking out partnerships, and just as importantly, when working to maintain them.

- *Sometimes, serendipity is essential to the formation of successful partnerships.* A social encounter at the parent organization's holiday party or at a conference can break the ice and get library staff talking to others outside of the library's normal sphere of contacts. Introverts and extroverts alike can glean insights from these conversations that libraries can then either connect to the library's larger goals or to a particular project that has been on the backburner for want of support or expertise. As illustrated in the case study, a discussion with the right people can lead to successful partnerships but only if the library follows up and connects those people with other partners. Libraries should stay aware of these opportunities when staff are chatting with new colleagues and also be sure to follow up if there is partnership potential.
- *Understand the limitations of the library's skills and time constraints.* Committing to a long-term partnership is equal parts exhilarating and stressful. If a library staff member is the primary contact or director of the partnership, they must understand the amount of time staff will dedicate to the project. Similarly, if staff are assigned to a project by a director, honest communication about how much time can be dedicated to the project is essential to ensuring that the careful partnership building that has gone into this project is not wasted when expectations do not match the promises of a partner. Critically, this is not a static concept—time and skill dedication will change as a project continues, and staff members are likely to rotate on and off through the months or years. Keep all the partners in the loop about changes that will affect the project's workflow. Honest

and consistent communication between partners about staff capacity will go a long way toward keeping all partners happy and working well together.

- *Create sunsetting procedures for when a partnership has run its course and to preserve the work.* Some partnerships end unexpectedly or suddenly, threatening the stability and integrity of the project. Once again, open and regular communication with partners will help allay the collapse, but there are also times when the partnership is no longer viable. This could be due to the inability of one or more partners to continue their commitment, or the lack of demand for the project that required the project in the first place. Regular meetings of key partners will remove the specter of a sudden ending, but they can also provide a chance to discuss how a project will wrap up or how to ramp down an ongoing project so that the work is properly archived. If the project revolves around a database or repository, determining who could host it long term after the work is completed should be decided early in the process. If the project focused on outreach or creating new content, a primary "owner" could be set to ensure that if the project restarts, the institutional knowledge is maintained. This relatively simple step that is often forgotten will allow future librarians and their partners to build off the library's already substantial work.
- *Look to the future when investigating potential partnerships.* Legal technology startups are gathering more capital as generative AI continues to evolve. If the law library is involved in this sphere, consider a partnership with a company that may need input on their product in a real-world environment or needs to get their product in front of potential customers. Use these needs to create advantages for students, lawyers, or users that may gain better experience and exposure to what could become the next big legal tech tool. Even if the technology does not pan out, the patrons have had a chance to see the potential benefits and to think deeply about how the legal profession can change with the implementation of these new technology concepts.
- *Win hearts and minds with strategic partnerships.* A deeply thought-out partnership serves many purposes. The primary goal is to accomplish a particular goal that will serve the library's mission and provide better services or resources to patrons, students, or staff. However, an important secondary goal is to put the library in the middle of the action. A partnership with a variety of internal partners will strengthen library ties within the organization and encourage these groups to remember the library's services and willingness to work together to accomplish institutional goals. Reaching out to peer libraries will strengthen the library's professional reputation and likely put the library staff in a better position to succeed professionally as colleagues from all walks of law library life recognize the work the library has put into connecting with like-minded colleagues on important projects. Finally, connecting with new organizations such as technology startups, nonprofits, or government offices further expands the library's reach and puts the library's services at the forefront of minds that may not otherwise consider a library as an active or potential player in that space. Partnerships are opportunities in many ways, but one particular opportunity is to spread the gospel about the central and ongoing importance of the law library to both new and established users. Don't miss the chance to advocate for the library via partnerships.

Creating and fostering partnerships is not a skill that library hiring committees will seek out nor is it a characteristic that rises to the top of one's mind when compiling the necessary skills for a law librarian. However, this downplays the foundational importance of building sturdy partnerships with a diverse set of partners. Thoughtful and deliberate consideration of when and how to seek out partners is the essential first step, but this is only the first step. As with any relationship, a law library partnership asks that each partner keep up honest communication about their needs and abilities to contribute to a successful project. Scheduling regular check-ins and establishing markers along the way will give all partners a clear view of what is to be accomplished and by whom. Multiple-partner projects, such as the Digital Publication of Tribal Codes Pilot Project, are not only possible but preferable when a goal requires more support, and the outcomes promise a previously unimagined answer to a complicated problem. Partnerships, by definition, expand the connections and capabilities of the law library and grow the skills of the staff involved, and just as importantly, provide a springboard for the law library to remain a viable partner for a diverse set of departments, companies, and government entities as the legal research landscape continues to evolve. Consider the library's partners and accompanying projects carefully but embrace the chances to grow connections that will place the law library in the enviable position of establishing a successful partnership that will pay dividends.

NOTES

1. Lindsey Carpino, Annie Mentkowski, and Clanitra Stewart Nejdl, "Building Strategic Partnerships through Collaboration between Law Libraries," *AALL Spectrum* 24, no. 4 (March/April 2020): 17.
2. Kris Turner, "Aggressive Helpfulness: A Case Study of Innovative Outreach to Special Library Patrons," *Public Services Quarterly* 15, no. 1 (January 2019): 73–84.
3. Tasha Squires, *Library Partnerships: Making Connections Between School and Public Libraries* (Medford, MA: Information Today, Inc., 2009).
4. For ideas and concepts for successful partnerships, albeit public library-centric ones, see Karen Ellis, ed., *Partnerships and Collaborations in Public Library Communities: Resources and Solutions* (Hershey, PA: IGI Global, 2011).
5. For an example of a successful IT/Library partnership, see "The Wisconsin Briefs Collection," University of Wisconsin Law School, accessed June 28, 2024, https://repository.law.wisc.edu/s/uwlaw/page/wisconsin-briefs.
6. For additional insight into the benefits and potential pitfalls of IT/Library partnerships, see Bethany Latham, "A Perspective on Collaborative Partnerships to Expand Campus Buy-in for Digital Collections," *Digital Library Perspectives* 38, no. 4 (September 2021): 529–530.
7. For additional academic library partnerships focused on scholarly visibility and more, see Bradford Lee Eden, ed., *Partnerships and New Roles in the 21st-Century Academic Library: Collaborating, Embedding, and Cross-Training for the Future* (Lanham, MD: Rowman & Littlefield Publishers, 2015).
8. Carpino et al., "Building Strategic Partnerships."
9. For an interesting examination of what happens when partners do not align in their shared goals and purpose of partnership and the failure that can follow, see Tom Chrisp and Stuart Macdonald, "Acknowledging the Purpose of Partnership," *Journal of Business Ethics* 59, no. 4 (July 2005): 307–371, https://doi.org/10.1007/s10551-004-3235-5.
10. For an excellent example of how law libraries and public libraries can work together, see Sara V. Pic, "Bridging the Gap between Public Libraries & Law Libraries to Improve Access to Justice," *AALL Spectrum* 25, no. 4 (March/April 2021): 20–23.
11. This case study is a synthesis of the author's experience and electronic interviews with several other librarians and partners who are heavily involved in the project. Participants are noted in the text, and quotes are from their interviews.
12. The Stockbridge Munsee Community's tribal code can be viewed on their own website (built in partnership with the Open Law Library) here: https://law.mohican.com/us/nsn/mohican/council/code. The NILL version can be viewed here: https://www.narf.org/nill/triballaw/us/nsn/mohican/council/index.html. The UW Law Library version can be viewed here: https://repository.law.wisc.edu/s/uwlaw/page/tribal-law.

26

Working in the Field without an MLIS

Don Boman

Many people are successfully working in the law library field without an MLIS degree. This chapter will discuss what new and ongoing roles exist in today's law libraries that do not necessitate a library degree, as well as how to navigate the field without one. Some questions to be answered include: What kinds of jobs are out there? What are the requirements for education and previous experience? Can skills be transferable to a law library from another type of library or another industry? Where are the jobs? Is there on-the-job training, and are there opportunities for continuing education?

PARAPROFESSIONAL ROLES

The American Association of Law Libraries defines professional and non-professional positions in its biennial salary survey: "Professionals are defined as those whose roles typically require the MLS degree (or equivalent) while paraprofessional roles are positions that do not typically require an MLS degree (or equivalent)."[1] Traditional law library paraprofessional roles can be found in a few general areas: technical services—including acquisitions, serials, and cataloging; general public services such as circulation and interlibrary loan; as specialists in government documents; and in administrative functions such as executive assistants.[2] E-resources management has steadily become another kind of focus area for many paraprofessionals in the law library, one that touches and/or subsumes technical services and interlibrary loan, at the very least.[3] Some law libraries are also staffed with IT specialists and computer technicians who handle the often complex digital infrastructure. Others have positions for those engaging in research and knowledge management work. Law library paraprofessional roles can vary from one organization to another, and any one task could be the primary focus of a paraprofessional or merely one of many that the staff member is required to perform as part of their job. "Generalizations about [library support staff] are difficult to make, and to find an all-encompassing job description, nearly impossible"[4] A list of some traditional and more modern law library paraprofessional roles, that is, those that can be performed without an MLIS, can be found below.

- Library Assistant/Technician: Assists with daily library operations, including shelving books, maintaining records, and helping patrons find materials.
- Circulation Clerk: Manages the lending and return of library materials, maintains patron records, and handles overdue accounts.
- Research Assistant: Supports legal research by gathering and organizing relevant information and resources under the guidance of librarians or legal professionals.

- Technical Services Assistant: Helps with cataloging, processing new materials, and managing electronic resources.
- Administrative Assistant: Provides general administrative support, including scheduling, correspondence, and clerical duties.
- Document Delivery Specialist: Manages interlibrary loans and document delivery services, ensuring patrons receive the needed materials from other libraries.
- Library IT Support: Provides technical assistance and support for library systems, databases, and software applications.
- Knowledge Management Specialist: Focuses on organizing and managing the law firm's or library's knowledge base, ensuring information is easily accessible and up-to-date.
- Digital Asset Manager: Manages the library's digital collections, including e-books, online databases, and digital archives.
- Legal Information Analyst: Analyzes legal information and trends to provide insights and support decision-making processes.
- Compliance Officer: Ensures the library or firm adheres to legal and regulatory standards, particularly in data privacy and information management.
- Content Curator: Selects and organizes relevant content for the library's digital platforms, such as websites, social media, and intranets.
- Data Librarian: Manages and curates datasets used in legal research, ensuring they are properly stored, cataloged, and accessible.
- Legal Technology Specialist: Supports the integration and use of legal tech tools and software in the library, such as AI-driven research platforms and e-discovery tools.
- Information Security Analyst: Protects the library's digital information from security threats and ensures data integrity and confidentiality.

With so many types of jobs, it's no wonder that many paraprofessionals have said that their positions are far more challenging than they used to be.[5,6] In just one role, a paraprofessional could be expected to answer routine reference questions and otherwise assist patrons, teach patrons how to use databases and other resources, and even compile bibliographies and put together current awareness materials on relevant subjects of interest to their individual library.[7] This could be a function of "upskilling" and the shifting of responsibilities that used to be primarily under the purview of librarians over to paraprofessionals, or it could just be the result of advances in technology and the nature of the work.[8] The job description of a law library paraprofessional may now also include the responsibilities of liaising with stakeholders within their organization, evaluating and reporting the usage of current products, considering new acquisitions, working with vendors, following up with publishers, troubleshooting resource access issues, and budget monitoring, just to name a few.[9]

QUALIFICATIONS AND REQUIREMENTS

There are several pathways that can lead to a career in law librarianship besides obtaining an MLIS. In some cases, other advanced degrees (such as a Juris Doctor (JD)) combined with relevant experience can be acceptable substitutes for an MLIS. Continuing education and professional development opportunities can also enhance qualifications and career prospects in law librarianship. Alternative routes often involve a combination of relevant education, professional experience, and specialized training.

Some qualifications can provide different skills than those obtained with an MLIS or at least provide them in different ways. A law degree can impart an understanding of legal systems, procedures, and research methods and can often be suitable for legal research librarians, reference librarians, or legal information specialists, especially in academic and law firm libraries. A bachelor's degree in a related field such as legal studies, political science, or information science might also compensate for the lack of an MLIS. Paralegals and legal assistants often have strong research skills and familiarity with legal resources; transitioning to a law library role can be facilitated by leveraging this practical experience. There are also opportunities for those with other types of advanced degrees, including those in information science or knowledge management, which can provide skills applicable to managing legal information and resources. Job skills gained in other types of libraries are often transferable to a law library, for example, information management, cataloging, and reference services. Additionally, industry-specific workshops, seminars, and training sessions can also enhance knowledge and skills relevant to law library roles.

Specific educational requirements for law library jobs can vary depending on the type of law library and the role in question. While an MLIS is often preferred, and sometimes required, for many positions in law libraries, it is not always mandatory. Examples of law library job postings for roles in law firm, court, and academic settings, including their minimum education requirements, can be found in table 26.1. Typical educational requirements by library type are below.

- Academic: In academic law libraries, especially those affiliated with larger universities, there are many roles that do require an MLIS degree, some of which may additionally require a JD degree, per academic and accreditation standards. However, there are paraprofessional roles in academic law libraries just as there are in other academic library settings.
- Law Firm: While an MLIS is often preferred, it is not always a strict requirement. Some law firm libraries may prioritize candidates with a JD, while others may weigh legal research or knowledge management skills more heavily. Many law firm libraries value practical experience and may accept candidates with a combination of relevant experience and other degrees, such as a bachelor's degree in a related field.
- Government: These libraries may have varied requirements. Some positions may require an MLIS, while others may prioritize legal expertise or experience in a specific area of law. Like law firm libraries, practical experience and specialized knowledge are highly valued.

In addition to minimum education requirements, some law library positions may also have experience requirements or combinations and ratios of education and experience. If the job seeker does not have library experience at all, gaining some without a formal job can be achieved through various channels, including volunteering in libraries, internships in libraries, freelance work, and participation in library-related projects. Skills and knowledge transfer, even if they are achieved outside of normal channels.

Salaries and Hiring

Several organizations and institutions conduct surveys to gather information on staffing in law libraries. These surveys provide insights into staffing trends, salary data, and the overall state of law library employment. The American Association of Law Libraries publishes a comprehensive biannual salary survey for library staff across all levels and in all three types of law libraries: academic, government, and law firm.[10] Table 26.2 shows median salaries for representative job categories that do not require an MLIS in each type of library. The educational requirements for each of these categories are below.

- Computer/IT Technician/Specialist
    - Requirements: BA, BS, or associate degree in a computer or technical field; relevant experience may sometimes substitute for college degree; some organizations may require network certification or experience with specific types of platforms, programming languages, or hardware.

Table 26.1 Examples of Job Minimum Education Requirements

Title and Employer	*Minimum Education Requirements*
Research Coordinator Arnold & Porter Kaye Scholer LLP Location: Western United States (remote/local office) Annual Salary: $60,000-$72,000	Bachelor's degree
Library Research Specialist Goldberg Segalla LLP Location: Buffalo, NY Annual Salary: $45,011.20-$49,920.00	Associate's degree and one year of library/research experience
Law Library Clerk The New York State Unified Court System—Binghamton Law Library Location: Binghamton, NY Annual Salary: $50,410	High school diploma or the equivalent and two years of clerical experience in a library
Law Library Clerk The County of Hidalgo Location: Edinburg, TX Annual Salary: $20,800 (part-time)	Graduation from a high school or equivalent (GED)
Library Assistant II Rutgers University—Camden Law Library Location: Camden, NJ Annual Salary: $42,904.22	Requires a high school/vocational school education and three years of general library, library-related, or clerical experience; two years of college study and one year of library, database management, or information systems experience may be substituted for the three years of library experience requirement
Digital Initiatives and Archives Assistant Yale University Law Library Location: New Haven, CT Annual Salary: $59,065.50	Six years of related work experience, four of them in the same job family at the next lower level, and high school level education; or four years of related work experience and an associate's degree; or little or no work experience and a bachelor's degree in a related field; or an equivalent combination of education and related experience

Sources: Colorado Association of Law Libraries (CoALL), Indeed.com.

Table 26.2 Law Library Median Salaries

Position	*Academic Law Libraries*	*Law Firm Libraries*	*Government Law Libraries*
Computer Technician / IT Specialist	$61,734	-	$55,000
Administrative Assistant[a]	$51,935	-	-
Library Clerk	$48,830	-	$44,789
Library Assistant / Technician / Specialist	$46,734	$56,000	$47,122
Senior Library Assistant[b]	-	$69,510	-

Source: American Association of Law Libraries *2023 Biennial Salary Survey & Organizational Characteristics*.
Note: Not all positions were represented in all library types.
[a]The Administrative Assistant position was only recorded for academic law libraries.
[b]The Senior Library Assistant position was only recorded for law firm libraries.

- Administrative Assistant
  - Requirements: BA, BS, or associate degree.
- Library Clerk
  - Requirements: BA, BS, or associate degree.
- Library Assistant/Technician/Specialist
  - Requirements: BA, BS, or associate degree; in some organizations, relevant experience may substitute for college degree.
- Senior Library Assistant
  - Requirements: BA/BS with significant paraprofessional experience.

Also included in the AALL survey is a breakdown of the average number of library staff members by law library type. Their data on the staffing ratios between librarians and paraprofessionals suggest that there are quite a lot of paraprofessional positions in the law library field, specifically in firm/corporate law libraries and government law libraries: "The ratio of professional to paraprofessional staff at Firm/Corporate Law Libraries was 1:4.34 in 2023, while the 2023 ratio for Government Law Library respondents was 1:2.66."[11]

In addition to the AALL survey, some other resources for obtaining compensation information include the Special Libraries Association (SLA) salary surveys, industry-specific compensation data, job boards such as Indeed and Glassdoor (salary estimates for specific job titles based on current job listings and user-reported data), the Occupational Outlook Handbook published by the Bureau of Labor Statistics (data on salaries, job outlook, and employment statistics for librarians, including those in specialized roles like law libraries), industry reports and surveys conducted by Library Journal (annual salary surveys and reports that include data on various types of libraries and librarian positions), the American Library Association-Allied Professional Association (ALA-APA) Library Salary Survey (detailed salary information for library professionals), professional groups on LinkedIn, and specialized recruitment firms.

Job Searching

Finding a job in a law firm library without an MLIS can be challenging but achievable with the right strategy. Something a job seeker may want to consider is why they want to work in a law library. This can help them tailor their search more effectively. What is interesting about the field? Is it the challenging work? Perhaps a candidate believes "law libraries [are] at the cutting edge of information development in terms of e-information and knowledge management," as James O'Brien wrote in an essay on why he sought a role in the profession.[12] After further looking into the field of law librarianship, considering interests and affinities for particular types of roles, and deciding to move forward in a job search, the prospective paraprofessional should then make a strategic plan for success and start looking for their new role.

To get started, one can go online to get an idea of the types of jobs that don't require an MLIS currently available. This can sometimes be a good way for the job seeker to determine their success plan. Table 26.3 lists job search sites with descriptions of each. Next, creating a great resume is extremely important as it must represent the job seeker and is typically the first impression a potential employer will get. It should highlight one's skills and be tailored for the law library job search. Having a well-developed professional online profile, such as on LinkedIn, could also be utilized for success. Additionally, networking through professional organizations like AALL and SLA can offer insights into the profession, help with navigating the job market, and can sometimes even lead to unadvertised opportunities. Taking online courses or attending workshops focused on legal research, information science, or digital information management could also be part of a good strategy. They should also determine if any of their experience and skills can be leveraged in their job search, that

Table 26.3 Job Search Sites

Website Name and URL	*Description*
American Association of Law Libraries (AALL) Career Center https://careers.aallnet.org/	A dedicated platform for jobs in law libraries and legal information management.
Indeed https://www.indeed.com/	Job search engine where one can find listings for both traditional law library roles and newer types of roles with specific job titles like "Knowledge Management Specialist" or "Legal Technology Specialist."
LinkedIn https://www.linkedin.com/	Provides job listings, networking opportunities, and company insights. Filters can narrow down job searches to specific roles and industries.
Glassdoor https://www.glassdoor.com/	Offers job listings, company reviews, and salary information. It can also provide insight into company culture and employee experiences.
SimplyHired https://www.simplyhired.com/	Job search engine that collects listings from the web, including company career pages, job boards, and niche job websites, including those in law libraries. Includes a salary estimator.
Special Libraries Association (SLA) https://careers.sla.org/	Lists job opportunities for specialized librarians, including those in legal settings.
American Library Association (ALA) JobLIST https://joblist.ala.org/	Features a wide range of library job listings, including roles in law libraries.
Library Jobline https://www.libraryjobline.org/	Contains listings of library job opportunities, including law library positions.
Professional Networking Groups and Forums	Groups related to law libraries and legal information management on platforms like LinkedIn or Facebook often post open positions.
Law Firm Websites	Many large law firms have dedicated career pages listing positions in their libraries or knowledge management departments.
Universities and Law Schools	The career pages of universities with law schools often have law libraries with relevant job openings.

is, legal backgrounds and/or library experience. If a job seeker is just starting out in the profession, entry-level positions such as library assistants or technicians should be researched. Another way to find roles is through recruiters who work with law libraries and can match the prospective paraprofessional with opportunities that match their skills and background.

CONTINUING EDUCATION

With the constant updates to workflows, increases in the complexity of tasks, and more responsibilities for law library paraprofessionals, there are many ways to train and engage in continuing education for their ever-evolving roles. "Training of support staff is an ongoing function of the law library. Staff must not only be current on policies and procedures but must understand and implement the latest technologies available."[13] Professional development is as important for paraprofessionals as it is for librarians with MLIS degrees. Trainings and awareness programs conducted by librarians within the organization or bespoke sessions with outside vendors customized for the individual law library (e.g., on research databases, ILS software, etc.) can be effective in getting a law library's paraprofessional(s) up to date on current law library trends, introducing new ideas into the organization, updating and training the staff on new internal policies and workflows, and so on. Additionally, there are numerous outside associations that have both synchronous and asynchronous courses and on-demand, one-off sessions on various topics within the field. AALL, SLA, and local/regional chapters of those groups are good places to start. One should note that on-the-job learning is recognized as highly important by current and/or future employers and allows the paraprofessional to move forward in their career.[14]

> A law library is like a science laboratory, where the books are the tools one uses to discover the answers. Legal research is a skill that must be learned in order to find the law. . . . You must have some understanding of how the various sets of books in the law library relate, and how they are used. As the staff learn more about how to find the law they can accommodate patrons' requests more easily.[15]

Those paraprofessionals who conduct legal research can supplement their skills by taking advantage of some of the suggestions below, which include various educational resources, networking opportunities, and volunteering options. These suggestions can also be used as an entry point for prospective paraprofessionals who have found it difficult to develop proficiencies in legal research without currently working in a law library.

- Coursera, edX, and LinkedIn Learning offer courses in legal research and information management, often including practical exercises with legal databases.
- Westlaw, LexisNexis, and Bloomberg Law are major legal research platforms that offer free and paid online tutorials, webinars, and certification programs.
- Fastcase and Casetext are two other research platforms that both offer free access and training resources.
- Cornell Legal Information Institute (LII) provides legal information and guidance.
- Workshops and seminars conducted and/or hosted by professional associations (e.g., American Association of Law Libraries (AALL), SLA, and local bar associations) frequently include webinars, workshops, and conferences that provide legal research training.
- Volunteering at law libraries, legal aid organizations, or nonprofits that provide legal services can provide hands-on experience conducting legal research.

CONCLUSION

"Perhaps I had led a sheltered life, but I didn't know such a role existed," O'Brien wrote.[16] The field of law librarianship does exist and has many dynamic roles and career paths for paraprofessionals without an MLIS. There are challenges and opportunities. And there are many ways to enter the field for qualified individuals coming from both traditional library backgrounds as well as for those with non-typical trajectories. Technology continues to change and law libraries continue to adapt, and there seem to be few limits to what paraprofessionals may be called on to do in the future. This opens the door to having even more types of paraprofessional roles in the law library, potentially desiring other types of educational backgrounds.

NOTES

1. American Association of Law Libraries, *2023 Biennial Salary Survey & Organizational Characteristics* (Chicago: American Association of Law Libraries, 2023).

2. American Association of Law Libraries, *2023 Biennial Salary Survey & Organizational Characteristics.*
3. Rachel Erb and Brian Erb, "The Use of Paraprofessionals in Electronic Resources Management: Results of a Survey," *The Journal of Academic Librarianship* 41, no. 4 (2015): 394–415, https://doi.org/10.1016/j.acalib.2015.05.006.
4. American Library Association, "Overview of Library Support Staff," March 29, 2007, https://www.onetonline.org/link/summary/25-4031.00.
5. Suzanne L. Sager, "Library Support Staff Today and How it Has Changed," *OLA Quarterly* 20, no. 3 (2014): 4–6, https://doi.org/10.7710/1093-7374.1768.
6. Erb and Erb, "Use of Paraprofessionals."
7. Bureau of Labor Statistics, U.S. Department of Labor, *Occupational Outlook Handbook: Library Technicians and Assistants,* https://www.bls.gov/ooh/education-training-and-library/library-technicians-and-assistants.htm.
8. Erb and Erb, "Use of Paraprofessionals."
9. Lynne Howarth, "The Role of the Paraprofessional in Technical Services in Libraries," *Library Trends* 46 (1998): 526.
10. AALL, *2023 Biennial Salary Survey.*
11. AALL, *2023 Biennial Salary Survey.*
12. James O'Brien, "Finding a Role in the Profession," *Library & Information Update* 5, no. 6 (2016): 36–37.
13. Andrew Laurence, "Support Staff & the Law Libraries," *Library Mosaics* 4 (1993): 8–10.
14. Erb and Erb, "Use of Paraprofessionals."
15. Laurence, "Support Staff."
16. O'Brien, "Finding a Role."

27

The Professional Law Librarian Today

Malika Lipscomb and Nicholas Lamb

With a profession that is constantly in flux and with recent factors of great impact such as the Digital Revolution, the COVID-19 pandemic, and now the rise of generative artificial intelligence, what can profitably be said of the professional law librarian today? Much, we believe, can be said; we therefore endeavor to provide this sketch of the professional law librarian, both in firm and in academic contexts, that we hope will be widely useful.

WHAT IS A LAW LIBRARIAN?

Law librarians support the research needs of legal professionals in a variety of ways and in various settings. Whether they work at a law firm, in a law school, court, government agency, or public library, law librarians are professionals who skillfully find and assess information relevant to specific law practices. Imperative to the role of law librarians are the tools they have at their disposal. As such, one of the many responsibilities of law librarians includes acquiring and maintaining widely helpful resources. That, however, is scratching the surface. Below is a comprehensive list of some of the most prominent duties of the professional law librarian today.[1]

- Acquisitions: Find and develop a collection of print and electronic materials. Books, periodicals, treatises, statutes, regulations, and case law are items that can be accessed in print or electronic format. Law librarians gather these types of materials accordingly.
- Cataloging/Classification: Create and maintain bibliographic records using cataloging standards and classification systems. Law librarians organize library catalogs in a way that is easily accessible to their patrons, whether online or in stacks in-person.
- Research: Perform timely and efficient research upon request using expert knowledge of the best resources for any question at hand.
- Electronic Resources Coordination: Oversee subscriptions to online legal databases. Electronic resources require unique maintenance compared to print resources. Maintenance includes choosing the appropriate subscription levels, disseminating accessibility (usernames and passwords), and troubleshooting technical issues.
- User/LibGuides: Create step-by-step guides that explain how to use specific resources. These are often stored in a document management system and shared for reference.

- Training: Through live demonstrations, teach users what the best resources are for different types of legal research and explain how to use them. This often includes fielding on-demand questions. Training sessions are often recorded for future reference.
- Outreach: Build a pipeline into the profession through mentorship and recruitment. Also, work with colleagues in other departments, including attorneys, professors, paralegals, judges, and business development specialists, to find out how the library department can help with their needs.
- Administration: Manage resources (i.e., handle invoices for resources and subscriptions) and supervise staff.
- Professional Development: Stay on top of the latest technologies and trends within the field of law librarianship. Participate in professional organizations, such as the American Association of Law Libraries, and attend conferences.

LAW LIBRARIAN CAREER PATHS

Although not the historic focus of library schools, law librarians can find ample career opportunities in several areas of the profession. The professional law librarian today can be any of the following:

- Law Firm Librarian: Works in a law firm supporting attorneys and even paralegals and other legal staff through research, training, and access to legal materials.
- Academic Law Librarian: Works in a law school, helping law students and faculty learn how to perform legal research and find the best informational resources.
- Government Law Librarian: Works in a government agency (i.e., Library of Congress) supporting the research needs of government attorneys, policymakers, and other government officials. Legal collections include, but are not limited to, statutes, regulations, and administrative decisions.
- Court Law Librarian: Works in a state or federal court. Has similar duties and responsibilities to those of a paralegal. Experts on court-specific rules.
- Public Law Librarian: Works at a law library that is open to the public. Supports the research needs of fellow legal professionals or anyone with an interest in the field of law. Public law librarians must exercise great caution to avoid actually practicing law if they do not have a license to do so.

These are just five examples of the different types of law librarians today. Yet, the profession is wider still. Other types of law librarians include Special Collections Law Librarians, Foreign/International Law Librarians, and Corporate Law Librarians, just to name a few.[2]

THE PROFESSIONAL LAW FIRM LIBRARIAN

Up until early 2020, before the onset of the COVID-19 pandemic, law firm librarians worked largely with print materials. There was a relatively slow arc toward digital resources across the field, but the idea of relying mainly (or even solely) on online resources in place of print resources seemed somewhat far-fetched. The pandemic represented something of a seismic shift, leaving law firm librarians little-to-no choice but to accept the rapid adoption of digital resources to support their law firm counterparts.

According to a post-pandemic survey of twenty-five law librarians in the New York metropolitan area regarding this shift in resources, the following held true:

- Every survey respondent said that their library canceled at least some of its print subscriptions as a result of the pandemic.

- Most survey respondents said that their library reduced/canceled between 20 percent and 40 percent of their entire print collections; some survey respondents said their library reduced/canceled at least 75 percent of theirs, which is a significant amount of library materials by any standard.
- Eight percent of survey respondents said that their library did not intend to make reinstations of print subscriptions—underscoring the likely permanence of this seismic shift.
- Although most survey respondents (88 percent) said that the availability of electronic resources increased in their libraries, a few said that the usage of electronic resources declined.
- In the short-term, survey respondents noted that a great deal of funds were saved by canceling subscriptions to printed materials; in the long-term, however, these savings were offset by an increase in the prices of electronic resources.
- Some survey respondents noted that their library substituted traditional circulation of printed materials with curbside pickup, mail-at-home services, and limited in-person access; on the other hand, some survey respondents noted that their library was not able to offer any printed materials at all during the pandemic-induced shutdown—not even in electronic form at.

In May 2024, another survey was conducted for this chapter, and the most salient results underscore the changes that occurred:

- There are now more electronic resources in law firm library collections than there are print materials.
- Fifteen out of twenty-five survey respondents said that subscriptions to electronic resources have become significantly more expensive since 2021–2022.
- The circulation of print materials in most law firm libraries decreased over the same period, though some libraries noticed no significant difference.
- At least one law firm library eliminated most, or all, print materials before the onset of the COVID-19 pandemic.
- Tangible efforts are being made at most of the law firm libraries to not only decrease print materials but also to increase electronic resources within collections.
- Lack of space is still an issue in some law firm libraries and was another cause of the decrease in print collections.

These survey results are informative for this chapter. Post pandemic, the professional law firm librarian finds something of a different era where even the sometimes slow-to-change business of law is profoundly evolving, and thus so is the law firm library along with it. Not only are firm libraries now maintaining virtual spaces in addition to the more familiar physical spaces, but they are oftentimes able to do so in a fully digital and remote fashion.

The word "library" itself often evokes images of bricks and mortar, physical books, and sometimes even public libraries. Law firm librarians, especially those operating on a fully remote basis are, in some ways, still trying to navigate what the word "library" fully means today. For example, as noted in a 2022 Reuters article, "How Law Firm Librarians are Reinventing Themselves," the title "librarian" itself sounds outdated to some and thus no longer reflects the services and solutions offered by such professionals.[3] Likewise, in "The Increasingly Essential Role of the Law Librarian," Robert Ambrogi, a nationally noted journalist on legal topics and legal technology, discusses the whys and hows of law librarians serving as gatekeepers, guides, ethicists, and interpreters in all sorts of contexts.[4] For reasons like these, alternative titles to "librarian" were coined and have been used in any number of contexts. Some law firm librarians, for example, now have formal titles that are thought to be more indicative of their more modern primary roles, as opposed to the traditional "librarian" nomenclature. Some examples of these types of modern titles are:[5]

- Competitive Intelligence Analyst
- Chief Knowledge Officer
- Law Professor
- Law Library Director

Law librarians in other settings have skillfully navigated these changes as well, but as shown, there are certain unique considerations within the law firm space. Given this, it is likewise useful to briefly sketch a bit of law firm librarian history here: In the early 1900s, Covington & Burling hired renowned firm librarian Elizabeth Finley, who revolutionized the library at that firm during her tenure. In Finley's book, *Recollections of a Mid-Twentieth-Century Law Firm Librarian*, she discussed how she did so. For example, through "old files and conversations with old-timers," she learned of interoffice memos that had been circulated between partners about the acquisition of books.[6]

> Those same notes also contained candid conversations about the library before her arrival there: "One dated September 3, 1934, from Charles P. Light, Jr. suggested the acquisition of Harper on Torts and the Explanatory Notes to the various tentative drafts of the Restatements. . . . He also complained of the glass panel in the library door, and that the 'lighting in the library is bad.'"[7] Another memo that Finley found pre-dating her arrival stated outright that a librarian should be hired, followed by a list of 14 responsibilities which included what she described as extracurricular duties. Finley noted that the firm had stated that it wanted a librarian for "[proofreading] and [handling] printing of briefs, Shepardizing cases, checking citations, and [keeping] time records for work spent on cases for all men in the office."[8]

Not daunted, Finley went right to work. A great deal changed for the firm's library once Finley settled into her role there as librarian. No longer was it the partners' responsibility to acquire materials, nor were books only shelved in one room or organized by color. Describing her contributions to the firm's library in her own words, Finley wrote:

> When I arrived, there were thirty-four on the legal staff, and the firm occupied all of the seventh floor and the sixth floor as far as Mr. Gesell's room. The understanding had been that this was too small a domain to occupy all of my time, so I was also supposed to be "office manager." This I never was, but I did take on some housekeeping chores. I took over the buying of supplies . . . and also equipment-which was not so simple during the war shortages. I supervised the periodic room switches and looked after office maintenance in general, including trying to keep the air conditioners neither too cold nor too hot. . . . For the first few months, I felt that I was living in a vacuum. The library office was not cut through into the library proper, so I worked in solitude. The lawyers gave me a wide berth, as if I were some strange dog in the neighborhood. It never occurred to them to ask me for help. . . . I took over the few volumes of memoranda of law that Mr. Meck had collected and indexed them. I wrote countless memos on what the library needed and why, and began being active in the local library associations. By the time the entrance to the library was changed, and I was in, not of, the library, the strangeness began to wear off.[9]

The firm's collection and physical library space grew significantly, and the library even held training courses for the secretaries to teach them how to problem-solve using legal materials.[10] Note the fundamentals of the profession sketched by Finley, which, in some ways, remain true even today. Law firm librarians everywhere still "wear many hats," all while managing budgets and space as best possible.

To return to the situation as it is today, it is possible to add "translators" to Ambrogi's aforementioned list of characteristics that law librarians possess. Having the ability to break down language barriers between their counterparts in the field of law (i.e., attorneys, marketing professionals, students, and faculty) is another important facet of the law librarian in any setting. Indeed, law librarians are very much "multilingual" professionals as they are learning to speak the language of generative artificial intelligence.

In the context of law firm librarians, we put three artificial intelligence platforms to the test for this chapter: CoCounsel, Westlaw's Generative AI-Assisted Research, and OpenAI's ChatGPT, asking the following question: "What does the future hold for law firm librarians?" The responses from each of them held an uncanny resemblance to some of the previous discussions in this chapter above. For example, "The future of law firm librarians is uncertain, but it seems that they will need to adapt to changes in the legal industry in order to remain relevant," offered CoCounsel.[11] Similarly, AI-Assisted Research stated:

> The future of law firm librarians appears to be evolving towards a requirement for more specialized training and qualifications, particularly in legal research and possibly legal knowledge. . . . This could mean that the future for law firm librarians involves a greater integration with the academic and practical aspects of law, potentially leading to roles that are more central in the legal research and education process within law firms.[12]

ChatGPT offered more specifics, including potential developments such as client-facing roles and adapting to remote work.[13] ChatGPT also offered this:

> In essence, while the role of law firm librarians is evolving with technology and changing client demands, their expertise in legal research, information management, and knowledge sharing remains critical. Adaptation to new technologies and an understanding of how to leverage them effectively will be key to their continued relevance and impact within law firms.[14]

We must agree. And, as it stands today, it is undoubtedly an exciting time to be a professional law librarian.

THE PROFESSIONAL ACADEMIC LAW LIBRARIAN

Academic law libraries historically have endeavored to align their missions with the missions of their respective universities. This has historically shaped the contours of the professional academic law librarian. Yet, aligning academic law libraries' missions with their parent universities' missions has proved to be no easy task today because the very same changes that have been impacting academic law libraries also have been impacting colleges and universities. Colleges and universities have been reassessing not only their delivery of services but also their missions to some degree, making it that much more challenging for academic law libraries to align their own delivery of services and, indeed, their respective missions, with their parent institutions.[15]

These factors as well as the Digital Revolution, the COVID-19 pandemic, and now the rise of generative artificial intelligence, have made academic law librarians the modes and models of library services on campuses nationwide. As a result, academic law librarians have been exploring new avenues for providing library and information services and have displayed a great deal of nimbleness in doing so.

Over the last few decades, and certainly accelerating during and post pandemic, there has been a general shift in academic law library services toward the digital and the virtual.[16] These modes of delivery differ considerably from those which "traditionally" have been identified with academic library services: mainly brick-and-mortar library services. Still, even with these shifts in the landscape, most academic law libraries are rooted on their respective campuses, perhaps a bit more than firm libraries might be today. This is undoubtedly connected to the in-person nature of the vast majority of JD, LLM, SJD, and related programs, in which being on campus and interacting with professors and fellow students both inside and outside of the classroom is considered a mainstay of the degree experience and professional preparation. Academic law librarians have been and remain an integral part of this degree experience and, professional preparation.

Perhaps it goes without saying that teaching, learning, and research lie at the heart of law schools. With the various changes noted above, however, these core modalities are likewise shifting themselves, while, at the same time, questions of "value" are increasingly being brought to the forefront on campuses nationwide.[17] Increased flexibility in the delivery of library services on campuses, as well as the offering of more and new types of library services to increased and diverse populations across campuses, have enabled academic law libraries to both accommodate changes as well as maintain and increase "value."[18] As one scholar aptly notes, academic libraries of all kinds have served as a kind of "great leveler" on their respective campuses, in that all have access to the campus libraries for any number of purposes.[19] We believe that in this way, academic law libraries can both continue to best serve all members of their respective campus communities and sketch the contours of the profession today, and for the future.

As virtual library services become increasingly accepted and perhaps even dominant in the academic library environment, the concepts of the library both as a space and as a partner on campus are becoming more and more important at the same time. These are interwoven concepts. As law libraries—and law librarians—increasingly work with campus partners across their universities and law schools on projects like collection development, resource sharing, and outreach, new ways of leveraging library spaces are emerging. New demands such as the increased need for collaboration spaces, instructional spaces and information labs, and "Zoom rooms" likewise are informing discussions of space in academic law libraries. These discussions are providing academic law libraries with the renewed ability and impetus to foster essential relationships across law schools and university campuses.[20] One recent study, in parsing this out, explored various ways that academic libraries could reach out to and partner, for example, with campus veterans groups; veterans, who account for approximately 10 percent of the United States population, historically have been underserved by their respective academic libraries.[21] The academic law librarian today is without a doubt central to these campus discussions and the thoughtful implementation of these new library services and spaces.

With new services and spaces come new and increased costs for academic law libraries. As in firm settings, budgetary pressures in academic settings are continually pressing, in both good and bad economic environments. As one scholar points out, "Universities are increasingly operating a business culture of management and this impacts the way that professional support services are provided."[22] As another treatise further points out, "No law library has the budget to provide all things to all users."[23] And this is in the best of times too. Resources are tighter, budgets must be trimmed, and costs watched with vigilance. The phrase "doing more with less" is no longer heard only in corporate environments; across campuses too, academic law libraries are becoming increasingly proficient at juggling priorities and finding creative solutions to the various challenges that arise in all sorts of economic conditions. Among so many other areas, the academic law librarian today must be literate in budgets, line items, and leveraging this information to make the case across campus for all of the services and spaces that the law library provides.

Given the breadth and depth of proficiencies required by today's academic law librarians, creativity, nimbleness, and expertise will remain the qualities that enable academic law librarians to continue meeting the complex and changing needs of students, professors, and researchers, who, despite all of this change in the library space, continue, to seek out library services as trusted and informed information experts on their respective campuses. The current and next generation of campus library patrons continue and will continue to view academic law libraries as relevant and robust—the "great levelers" on their campuses. Academic law librarians, like their counterparts in firms, deserve much credit for their adaptability and creativity in ensuring this and that it will remain so.

CONCLUDING THOUGHTS

As all of the developments discussed in this chapter continue to impact and shape the profession both in firm and in academic contexts, the importance of using creativity to translate the physical library into the virtual library—without "losing anything in translation"—is becoming especially critical.[24] For example, a recent Cornell University doctoral dissertation cautions librarians against the total "assimilation" into the virtual.[25] To counteract any such "loss in translation," library outreach likely must become an increasingly vital library service.[26] Lacking a physical space, either completely or very nearly so, many law libraries, going forward, will rely on outreach for "visibility." This outreach is and likely will increasingly be focused on driving engagement and on developing connections with library users and with potential library users. These efforts, therefore, also could be paired profitably with thoughtful library marketing efforts. It is again important to note that law librarians are "multilingual" professionals, and many are already engaging in this important work for their respective law libraries.

As some law library services grow and realign, other law library services will become less essential or less effective (consider, for example, the once widespread practice of routing periodicals). Even as these trends continue to develop, it is possible, nonetheless, to distinguish the essential fundamentals of the law library field, even if the exact boundaries remain blurry at times—as they perhaps long have been.

As we have seen, law libraries of all kinds comprise a field in which change has been the primary constant over time. Professional law librarians in firm and academic settings are at the forefront of these developments. As we continue to embrace this change, the resources and services offered and those that will be offered likewise reflect this ethos of change in a myriad of ways, including lessening the professional boundaries between us and our counterparts, rethinking how we speak about what we do among our colleagues, and building a wider pipeline into the profession through outreach and mentorship. This chapter's observations aim to provide something of a guiding framework—although certainly not dispositive—to assist in understanding better and thus navigating better the currents facing the profession today.

NOTES

1. CareerExplorer, "What Does a Law Librarian Do?," accessed July 29, 2024, https://www.careerexplorer.com/careers/law-librarian/#what-is-a-law-librarian.
2. CareerExplorer, "What Does a Law Librarian Do?"
3. Jenna Greene, "How Law Firm Librarians are Reinventing Themselves," *Reuters*, February 18, 2022, https://www.reuters.com/legal/legalindustry/how-law-firm-librarians-are-reinventing-themselves-2022-02-18/.
4. Robert Ambrogi, "The Increasingly Essential Role of the Law Librarian," *Above the Law*, July 13, 2020, https://abovethelaw.com/2020/07/the-increasingly-essential-role-of-the-law-librarian/.
5. AALL, "About the Profession," Careers, accessed July 29, 2024, https://www.aallnet.org/careers/about-the-profession/.
6. Elizabeth Finley and David S. Mao, "Recollections of a Mid-Twentieth-Century Law Firm Librarian," *Law Library Journal* 97, no. 3 (Summer 2005): 568, https://heinonline.org/HOL/P?h=hein.journals/llj97&i=563.
7. Finley and Mao, "Recollections," 568.
8. Finley and Mao, "Recollections," 568.
9. Finley and Mao, "Recollections," 569–570.
10. Finley and Mao, "Recollections," 572.
11. "CoCounsel: Legal Research Memo," Casetext, accessed June 17, 2024, https://casetext.com/v2/ai-assistant.
12. "Westlaw AI-Assisted Research," Westlaw Precision, accessed June 17, 2024, https://next.westlaw.com/.

13. "ChatGPT," ChatGPT, accessed June 17, 2024, https://chatgpt.com/.
14. "ChatGPT," ChatGPT.
15. Cf. Anne Llewellyn, "Innovations in Learning and Teaching in Academic Libraries: A Literature Review," *New Review of Academic Librarianship* 25, no. 2/4 (2019): 129–149.
16. Julius J. Marke, et al., *Legal Research and Law Library Management* (New York: Law Journal Press, 2020), note 26 at 2.01, 3.0. See also Ciara McCaffrey, "Transforming the University Library One Step at a Time: A Ten Year LibQUAL+ Review," *New Review of Academic Librarianship* 25, no. 1 (2019): 2–3. See generally Frank Baudino and Carolyn Johnson, eds., *Brick and Click Libraries: An Academic Library Conference* (Mayville, ND: Northwest Missouri State University, 2015).
17. Mousin Omar Saib, et al., "Digital Pedagogies for Libraries in Higher Education: A Systematic Review of Literature," *Information Discovery and Delivery* 51, no. 1 (2022): 13–25.
18. Rosemary Bodolay et al., "Moving from Co-location to Cooperation to Collaboration: Redefining a Library's Role within the University," in Brian Doherty, ed. *Space and Organizational Considerations in Academic Library Partnerships and Collaborations* (Hershey, PA IGI Global, 2016).
19. Bruce E. Massis, "The Academic Library Becomes the Academic Learning Commons," *New Library World* 111, no. 3/4 (2010): 161–163.
20. Ursula Gorham and Paul T. Jaeger, "The Law School Library or the Library at the Law School: How Lessons from Other Types of Libraries Can Inform the Evolution of the Academic Law Library in the Digital Age," *Law Library Journal* 109, no. 1 (Winter 2017): 60–65.
21. J. J. Pionke, "Veteran Views of the Library," *Reference & User Services Quarterly* 58, no. 4 (2019): 227–234.
22. Llewellyn, "Innovations," 131.
23. Marke, "Legal Research," ¶¶ 2.01. See also, Martha Kyrillidou, "Library Value May Be Proven, If Not Self-Evident," *Research Libraries: A Bimonthly Report from ARL, CNI, and SPARC* 271, no. 1 (August 2010): 1–3.
24. Magdalena Wójcik, "How to Design Innovative Information Services at the Library?," *Library Hi Tech* 37, no. 2 (2019): 138–154.
25. Carl Jay Lagoze, *Lost Identity: The Assimilation of Digital Libraries into the Web* (Ithaca, NY: Cornell University, 2010: UMI no. 3396228).
26. L. Cindy Dabney, et al., "Marketing and Outreach in Law Libraries: A White Paper," *Law Library Journal* 105, no. 4 (Fall 2013): 525–538.

28

The Law Library as a Center for Innovation

Kenton Brice

WHAT IS INNOVATION?

Innovation. Over the past few decades, the use of the word has increased more and more toward true buzzword status. Law libraries are not immune to this trend. With more and more institutions touting their "innovation" initiatives, the meaning of the word has seemingly been diluted to mean anything and nothing at the same time. This chapter hopes to recapture some of the essence and substantial nature that innovation, as encapsulated by those cultures, projects, and people attempting to move the legal profession forward, is playing out and can be played out in a modern law library. As used in this chapter, the notion of innovation should be read to align with the hallmarks of innovation from before the 1990s, which would include curious and change-oriented leadership and strategies in hopes of facilitating value creation for themselves, their stakeholders and patrons, and for society as a whole.

Innovation can take various forms and degrees. With any attempt at innovating, context and objectives are key drivers for these forms and degrees. Innovation can be incremental, radical, disruptive, transformative, or all of these at once in a spark of ingenuity or in stages according to a systematic process. Innovation can also be based on different types of knowledge, such as scientific, technological, organizational, social, or artistic. Innovation can occur at different levels, such as individual, group, organizational, sectoral, regional, national, or global. Innovation can involve different actors, such as researchers, entrepreneurs, managers, professionals, customers, citizens, or policymakers. And innovation can have different impacts, such as economic, social, environmental, cultural, or legal. For law libraries, innovation can have different meanings, effects, and shapes depending on how much and who it affects by changing the current situation, and sometimes, it can reveal something that has always been part of its culture.

THE EVOLUTION OF LAW LIBRARIES AS CENTERS FOR INNOVATION

Law libraries have long been an essential component of legal education and practice, providing access to a vast collection of books, journals, and other sources of legal information. However, the role of law libraries has changed significantly in the past few decades, as digital technologies have transformed the way that legal information is created, stored, accessed, and used. Law libraries are no longer merely repositories of physical materials but rather dynamic service providers that support the diverse and evolving needs of their users. The ever-evolving needs of the legal profession are all centered around the creation, curation, discovery, dissemination, and preservation of legal information.

Since the turn of the nineteenth century to the twentieth, and then the twenty-first, centuries law libraries and law librarians have always been the mediators between what has been, what is, and what is possible in the legal profession. This mediation is the hallmark of innovation: law libraries making the connections and building bridges of possibility to drive the legal profession forward. Even the foundational model for modern legal practice, with a nod toward the resulting foundational model of legal education and licensure, started with a librarian and the need to understand how to better utilize legal information. The "Cravath method," named after an immensely innovative lawyer, Paul Cravath, started with a librarian. One of Paul Cravath's realizations and first orders of innovation for his method of legal practice in the modern era during the early 1900s was to hire a librarian for his small firm, a practice that no other law firm had a model for at that time. Now, over 100 years later, law libraries have grown their services, and the time for continued innovation is needed now more than ever.

CONTINUING TO INNOVATE: THE IMPERATIVE FOR CHANGE

As our patrons, parent institutions, and the practice of law continue to move forward into a more digital and artificially intelligent-infused world, it is imperative for law libraries to not just "keep up," but to lead. Leading as innovators, especially now, will not be easy. Law libraries face new challenges and opportunities that require them to rethink their roles and strategies due to some of the key realities of the modern legal environment. The growth of legal data, maturing principles of knowledge management, developments in artificial intelligence, and the variety of other emerging technologies that affect how information is created, consumed, or presented are calling on law libraries to become the centers for innovation in their institutions.

A Modern Data Explosion

The amount and variety of legal information available have been growing and continue to grow exponentially due to the online nature of the practice of law, making it harder for users to find, evaluate, and use relevant and reliable sources. Law libraries must provide data-informed solutions that can help users navigate, filter, and work through the information overload to find actionable solutions and value from such a glut of data. Law libraries need to help their patrons generate and manage knowledge from various sources and formats, such as books, journals, databases, websites, social media, videos, and podcasts.

Law libraries have the expertise to create the metadata, taxonomies, ontologies, indexes, search engines, and recommender systems necessary to harness this data while also providing the tools and skills for data analysis, visualization, and storytelling, such as data mining, text mining, sentiment analysis, network analysis, and dashboard creation. Law libraries are needed now more than ever to innovate their own services and product offerings to help the legal profession utilize reliable and actionable data-informed solutions.

Developments in Artificial Intelligence

Artificial intelligence (AI) is transforming the practice and delivery of legal services, creating new possibilities and risks for all members of the legal profession. From law students to lawyers and from paralegals to the public, law libraries must continue to investigate innovative solutions to provide fundamental understandings of information literacy and leverage AI tools in a new environment, such as natural language processing, machine learning, predictive analytics, and document automation. Law libraries also need to educate and advise their patrons on the ethical, legal, and social implications of using AI in legal contexts. Doing so is possible as long as law libraries harness innovative mindsets and find ways to systematically engage with new possibilities.

Harnessing a Variety of Technologies

Law libraries need to continue to lead as centers for innovation by harnessing a variety of technologies and empowering their patrons to take advantage of them. Law libraries need to expose their patrons to what is possible, such as blockchain, smart contracts, virtual reality, augmented reality, and gamification. Law libraries also need to design and implement programs that foster creativity, collaboration, and problem-solving, such as design thinking sprints, hackathons, and developing legal-centric makerspaces.

The Educational Mandate: Preparing Future Lawyers for a Tech-Driven World

All law libraries educate their patrons and stakeholders in one form or another. Law libraries are poised to be centers for education on what is possible, providing people those safe spaces to learn about and be exposed to the modern technologies that are useful to the legal profession. For academic law libraries, the educational mandate is more pressing. The current era of technology and its unique challenges require law librarians to work through what legal research and legal skills instruction look like. By upskilling themselves, law librarians can ensure that they have the ability to expand what is possible in their institutions through heightened digital literacy and competencies. All of these realities in a modern law library call for them to embrace their role as a center of innovation.

WHAT CONSTITUTES INNOVATION IN A LAW LIBRARY?

Hopefully by now it is clear that law libraries are faced with the imperative to be centers for innovation in their institutions; however, hard questions persist on what this may mean. Although different contexts for the variety of law libraries in the legal ecosystem necessitate calls for different approaches to innovation, there are some recent examples of law libraries embracing their roles as centers for innovation to create value for their institutions and their patrons.

Creating Educational Programs and Workshops on Existing and Legal Technologies

One of the ways law libraries can act as centers for innovation is by creating educational programs and workshops on existing and emerging legal technologies. These programs can help students, faculty, and practitioners develop the skills and knowledge they need to use technology effectively and ethically in legal practice. Law libraries can also provide access to various technological tools and platforms, such as artificial intelligence, virtual reality, and augmented reality, and facilitate their integration into the curriculum and research. By doing so, law libraries can enhance the quality of legal education and prepare future lawyers for the challenges and opportunities of the digital age.

University of Oklahoma College of Law Library

One example is the University of Oklahoma College of Law Library's Digital Initiative. Launched in 2014, the Digital Initiative integrates technology into legal education through a comprehensive, non- and co-curricular program built around four pillars: a common technology platform in Apple iPad and Pencil, a law practice-oriented technology curriculum, technology-forward facilities, and access to emerging technologies. Each student receives an iPad to support their learning, and the curriculum includes mandatory tech-training courses on all aspects of technology's effect on the legal profession so as to ensure graduates are proficient with modern legal tools. Additionally, the Digital Initiative focuses on engaging with emerging technologies, including artificial intelligence, blockchain, drones, virtual reality, and augmented reality, all to explore and prepare students to lead in an evolving legal landscape. Recognized by Bloomberg Law and Apple, the OU Law Digital Initiative not only enhances the educational experience but also sets a standard for integrating technology into legal practice, demonstrating the critical role law libraries play in fostering technological competence and innovation in the legal profession.

BYU Law Library's Legal Tech Initiative

The BYU Law Library's Legal Tech Initiative is another example of a law library that serves as a center for innovation. Launched in 2017, the initiative aims to expose students to the latest developments and opportunities in legal technology and provide courses, workshops, and events that teach students how to use and create legal tech solutions. By providing students and faculty with the skills, tools, and resources to engage with legal technology, the BYU Law Library's Legal Tech Initiative fosters a culture of innovation and prepares future lawyers to meet the challenges and opportunities of the digital age.

Creating Opportunities for Everyone to Engage with Legal Information

Another innovation opportunity is to help democratize the law: to make the law more accessible to all in a more permanent form by leveraging modern technologies. This includes efforts, as noted below, to digitize and make freely accessible all published U.S. court decisions in an attempt to provide comprehensive and user-friendly access to legal information.

Harvard Law Library Innovation Lab: Perma.cc and Caselaw Access Project

The Harvard Law Library Innovation Lab is a center for innovation that aims to foster creative and collaborative solutions to challenges in the legal domain. One of its projects is Perma.cc, a web archiving service that helps authors and publishers preserve online sources and prevent link rot. Perma.cc allows users to create permanent links to web pages that will always be accessible, even if the original page changes or disappears. This enhances the reliability and verifiability of legal scholarship and journalism, as well as the preservation of digital history.

Another project of the Harvard Law Library Innovation Lab is the Caselaw Access Project, which digitizes and makes freely available the entire collection of U.S. case law from the Harvard Law Library. The Caselaw Access Project provides access to over 6.4 million cases dating back to 1658, covering federal courts and state courts from all fifty states and territories. The project also offers an API and bulk data downloads for researchers and developers who want to explore and analyze the corpus of U.S. case law. The Caselaw Access Project democratizes access to legal information and enables new forms of legal research and education.

Georgia State University's Legal Analytics & Innovation Initiative

The Legal Analytics & Innovation Initiative at Georgia State University is another example of a law library that fosters innovation and engagement with legal information. The initiative leverages data science, machine learning, and natural language processing to create new tools and methods for legal analysis and problem-solving. The initiative also offers courses, workshops, and events to educate students, faculty, and the public on how to use legal analytics and technology in their practice and research. The initiative collaborates with various partners, such as law firms, courts, and legal aid organizations, to provide innovative solutions to real-world legal challenges and improve access to justice.

Harris County Law Library's LAWPod

One example of a law library innovating in ways to connect others with legal information and make it accessible is the Harris County Law Library's LAWPod. The LAWPod, which stands for Legal Access

Workspace, is a mobile unit that provides self-help legal resources and guidance to residents of Harris County, Texas. The LAWPod is located at a public library branch, where it can reach people who may not have access to the internet or transportation to visit the law library downtown. The LAWPod offers free access to computers, printers, scanners, and legal databases, as well as assistance from trained staff and volunteers. The LAWPod also hosts workshops and clinics on various legal topics, such as family law, immigration, expunctions, and landlord-tenant issues. The LAWPod aims to bridge the justice gap by empowering people to resolve their legal problems and exercise their rights. The LAWPod is a collaborative project between the Harris County Law Library and the Harris County Public Library, as well as other community partners, such as legal aid organizations, bar associations, and pro bono attorneys. The LAWPod was launched in 2024, coinciding with the Law Day theme of "Voices of Democracy," which celebrates the principles of democracy and the rule of law. The LAWPod embodies these values by ensuring that legal information and services are accessible and affordable to all members of the community, regardless of background or circumstance. The LAWPod is an innovative example of how law libraries can leverage technology and partnerships to expand their reach and impact and to promote access to justice for all.

Transforming Spaces to Foster Collaboration

One of the core identities that a law library holds is its space. For most law libraries, the space, or its place, whether digital or physical, is where community building and other initiatives can flourish. Law libraries have incredible opportunities to think innovatively about their space, whether large or small, to enhance library services for its institution.

OU Law's CLC and ALC Renovations

One major example of innovative renovation of library space is at the University of Oklahoma College of Law Library. As part of the Digital Initiative, as noted above, the law library has reimagined its facilities to serve as hubs of innovation and technology-driven education through the establishment of the Inasmuch Foundation Collaborative Learning Center, the Chickasaw Nation Active Learning Classroom, and the Digital Initiative Lab. These state-of-the-art spaces are integral to community development and engaging technology deeply into the law school curriculum. Built in 2016, the Inasmuch Foundation Collaborative Learning Center provides a dynamic environment where students can collaborate using the latest technological tools, fostering a hands-on approach to learning. Similarly, the Chickasaw Nation Active Learning Classroom and Digital Initiative Lab, completed in 2020, are designed to facilitate interactive and immersive learning experiences, equipped with advanced technological resources.

These facilities ensure that OU Law students are not only proficient in traditional legal skills but are also adept at using modern technology, preparing them to lead in a rapidly evolving legal landscape. The law library's innovative reimagining of its spaces underscores its commitment to providing a cutting-edge legal education and exemplifies how law libraries can be central to technological and educational advancements.

HOW TO CULTIVATE AN ENVIRONMENT OF INNOVATION

Innovation in law libraries does not just happen by accident. It takes institutional buy-in and culture-building that come from visionary leadership. It also comes about by understanding resources, resources that must be utilized at whatever scope or scale exists for a law library. Finally, it comes down to creating environments for experimentation and systematic process building, all aimed at having a center for innovation.

Figure 28.1 The University of Oklahoma College of Law Chickasaw Active Learning Classroom. *Source*: Created by author.

Leadership

Any innovation effort starts with leadership and culture building within a law library. This is probably the hardest part of a law library adopting an identity as a center for innovation. Most law libraries, as storied institutions (libraries) within other storied institutions (legal entities), while innovative in the past, have fallen into patterns of doing things a certain way. When asked why, responses could range from "just because" and "it is how we have always done it" to complaints about resource issues or lack of talent to accomplish new, innovative projects. While bold decisions and actions are a definite must to tackle these potential barriers, nothing is possible unless leaders are willing to adopt principles and strategies of leadership to propel a library into a new identity as a center of innovation.

Thankfully, there has been considerable work done to discover the leadership competencies needed to help create robust, successful organizations. Law library leadership should look to the core leadership principles as identified by Kouzes and Posner in their work, "The Leadership Challenge," now in its sixth edition.[1] They have identified five leadership principles that modern leaders can leverage to encourage their teams toward success: Model the Way, Inspire a Shared Vision, Challenge the Process, Enable Others to Act, and Encourage the Heart. While all five principles are key in leading in the modern era, two of these principles are highlighted here, and their relation to the other principles, for law library leadership to embrace to see their law library become a center for innovation: Inspire a Shared Vision and Challenge the Process.

Inspire a Shared Vision

To "Inspire a Shared Vision" for a law library as a center for innovation, law librarian leadership must craft and communicate a compelling vision of the library that aligns with what is possible if the library were to step out into a project, or multiple projects, that would create value in a new or adjusted manner for all stakeholders, including faculty, students, and the broader legal community. This vision should highlight the library's role in advancing legal education, research, and practice through innovative approaches and technologies. Law library leadership should then share this vision with the library team, soliciting their input, feedback, and ideas. By doing so, leaders can foster a sense of ownership and commitment among the team, as well as tap into their diverse perspectives and experiences to refine and finalize the vision.

Once the vision is cast, leaders should then communicate that vision clearly and consistently, using stories, examples, and metaphors that resonate with the team and other institutional stakeholders. By doing so, leaders can create a compelling narrative that motivates the team to pursue the vision and overcome the challenges along the way.

For instance, envisioning the library as a hub for cutting edge, artificially intelligent legal research to foster greater access to legal information can galvanize the library's internal and external communities to support and engage with the library's initiatives. With this vision clearly communicated, a leader can then allocate resources to gain small wins internally, or point to other examples externally, that show how transformative this technology can be. Then, by regularly sharing success stories on how AI has been leveraged to benefit patrons, through meetings, informal conversations, social media posts, and formal press releases, these leaders can further embed this vision in the institutional culture, fostering a collective commitment to innovation and continuous improvement.

Challenge the Process

"Challenging the Process" involves encouraging a culture of experimentation and risk-taking, which is crucial for driving innovation in the law library. Acknowledging another leadership principle, law librarian leadership must "Model the Way," or in other words, "lead by example," promoting their own iterative process improvements and leveraging new technologies to enhance library services and operations. Leadership should question traditional practices and seek novel solutions in hopes of moving the library forward, as well as inspiring staff to think creatively and embrace change. Borrowing from yet another leadership principle, once leadership models itself challenging the existing status quo, it should then "Enable Others to Act," allowing the law library the freedom to experiment on their own.

Encouraging Experimentation and Risk-Taking

Encouraging experimentation and risk-taking within law libraries is crucial for fostering an innovative culture. In recent years, there has been a notable emphasis on integrating new technologies within the legal field, which has simultaneously increased anxiety among those tasked with implementing these changes. To counter this, it is essential for leaders to cultivate a positive culture that embraces experimentation as a pathway to innovation.

For over the past ten years at the University of Oklahoma College of Law a "culture of yes" has been pivotal in encouraging innovation. This culture, created by former associate dean and director of the Law Library, Darin Fox, and continued to this day, emphasizes openness to new ideas and a willingness to explore unconventional solutions. Such a culture supports law librarians in experimenting with new technologies and methodologies, thus driving the library's evolution as a center for innovation. By creating a supportive environment where failure is viewed as a learning opportunity, law libraries can transform anxiety about change into enthusiasm for new possibilities.

Resources

It is said that "insanity is doing the same thing over and over again and expecting different results."[2] One of the starkest realities for law libraries is that they are traditional entities within traditional institutions, and thus, have tradition and history wrapped into how they approach two major resource categories that fuel their work: money and talent. Relatedly, and as explored below, law library budgets are traditionally allocated for two large buckets: collection development and salaries. In the colloquial sense, if a law library does not intend to approach its budget or its talent in an innovative way, then any endeavor for a law library to become a center for innovation is insane. It takes incredible vision, tenacity, and yes, sometimes "strategic greediness," to break free from these historical realities and move a law library forward as a leader in innovation for its institution.

Building a Budget for Innovation Spending

To be a center for innovation, a law library must spend money on the tools and resources necessary for its staff and patrons to experiment with what is possible. However, either through a lack of institutional vision, inherent inertia in budgeting processes, the fallacy of sunk costs, or the inability to just ask for something new or different from administrative or executive leadership, law libraries generally have a difficult time "finding" the funds to make purchases that would fuel an innovation initiative.

Instead of working to find funds, law libraries should work toward finding easy wins in their budget. One example would be to review, at least yearly, spending amounts on collection development or maintenance and asking fundamental questions about the cost-benefits of certain resources. This will lead to questions surrounding traditional library spending that may have carried over from the past two to three decades. Asking these fundamental and hard questions will illuminate some sacred cows that either library staff, patrons, or other stakeholders may have. Some sample questions to ask when looking to free up budget to invest in the future:

- Does a library really need two or three different legal periodical indices in the modern era?
- How many duplicative databases or secondary content are there in the collection and why?
- What percentage of spending is toward renewals, serials, or standing orders that a library has continued for over a decade? Why?
- What usage statistics are available for any databases or electronic resources that the law library has been licensing or purchasing for over five years?
- What is the mission, vision, and values of the law library and its parent institution? Is there a strategic plan in place? How has spending drifted away from those core identifiers for collection development?

While these questions surround collection development strategies, they highlight areas where a law library could improve its spending efficiency and, therefore, find funds to facilitate innovative projects. Additionally, they highlight where spending has drifted from the strategies or mission of the institution, allowing for correction back to spending opportunities that align with the value propositions that the institution seeks.

Not all innovation spending is earth-shatteringly expensive or cumbersome. Most spending on innovation projects starts with a small sample or trial group to allow experimentation to see what is possible. For instance, ChatGPT, an incredible tool leveraging foundational LLM technology for Generative AI, is only $20/month for a Plus account and $25/month for a Team account. If a law library purchases this for a small pilot team of ten people, the maximum spend for a law library is $3,000 per year, which is a fraction of the cost of some legal databases and can be equal to a treatise.[3] This trial, for less than the cost of a treatise, could open the doors to amazing possibilities and provide proofs-of-concepts that could build momentum and institutional buy-in for smarter or greater spending. As with most innovative culture-building initiatives, starting small will have compounding effects over time to build toward larger-scale projects and, hopefully, a culture of innovation.

Additionally, working with vendors that are on the bleeding edge of legal technologies is much more approachable than most think. A little diplomacy, and the ability to ask for discounts where no one ever has before in the law library space, can open a world of possibilities for a law library. For example, the University of Oklahoma College of Law was able to negotiate the first-ever LiquidText site license for all of the faculty, staff, and students at the college. After informing LiquidText of the realities of a law school's usage and budget, and asking for an incredible discount, the site license was possible, giving faculty and staff a new experimentation tool.

Developing Talent for Innovation in Law Libraries

Creating a robust culture of continuous learning and adaptability within a law library requires a commitment to staff training and professional development, especially in non-traditional competencies. As the legal information and technology landscape continues to evolve, law libraries that aspire to be centers of innovation must expand the skill sets of their staff beyond traditional legal research, reference services, collection development, and archival. Developing these future-oriented competencies can be achieved by either engaging in external or internal professional development opportunities tailored to the specific needs of the law librarians.

Externally, there are a variety of levels of engagement and costs to help develop a team's ability to engage in an innovative way. At the higher end of resource intensity are full-blown degree or certification regimes for certain competencies, such as developing expertise in data analytics, computer science, Lean Six Sigma process improvement, and project management. At the lower end of resource intensity for professional development might include general and continuing education webinars, taking advantage of online courses or developing skills through sources such as LinkedIn Learning or even YouTube. In the middle are a host of opportunities for large-scale legal technology and knowledge management conferences, such as the ABA TECHSHOW, ILTACON, InspireKM, CLOC Global Institute, or LegalWeek, and other targeted professional development activities, such as weekend seminars or offerings from the American Association of Law Libraries.

Internal professional development could come from internally hosted workshops or even leveraging content provided by human resources and technology trainers within certain organizations. Additionally, when exploring innovative solutions that include a technology product, vendors are usually more than willing to provide targeted training that goes beyond the normal demonstration webinar to ensure that their technology is implemented and adopted successfully.

In combination with external and internal professional development opportunities, and as noted above about Enabling Others to Act as part of Challenging the Process, experimentation is a vital strategy for building competencies needed for innovation. Experimentation involves trying different methods and activities to discover their effects. This hands-on approach helps shift law librarians from unconscious incompetence, where they are unaware of their knowledge gaps, to conscious competence, where they understand and can deliberately apply their skills in a new and innovative manner. Providing safe spaces for staff, and even patrons, to tinker with new technologies, such as advanced legal research tools or AI-driven applications, can significantly enhance their proficiency and confidence in using these tools effectively to great effect.

Ultimately, embracing experimentation and risk-taking within law libraries not only supports the professional development of staff but also drives the institution's mission to advance legal education and practice through innovation. This approach aligns with the broader goal of fostering a culture of continuous learning and adaptability, ensuring that law libraries remain pivotal resources in the ever-evolving legal information and technology landscape, thereby realizing their potential as centers for innovation.

ADOPTING AN INNOVATION TOOLKIT

Along with leadership and resources, and in tandem with the freedom to experiment, law libraries should adopt a toolkit to create a systematic process for innovation. While experimentation allows for free discovery and competency-building, a toolkit provides a law library with a foundation to build innovative initiatives on, reducing the uncertainty that can breed fear of failure within a traditional entity such as a law school or a law firm. Implementing a toolkit ensures that innovations are not only creative but also aligned with the strategic goals of the library and its parent institution, enhancing its effectiveness and encouraging repeatable "wins" within an institution. In short, having a toolkit provides a "method," or a systematic and predictable way of doing something, to what others may see as innovation "madness," or experimentation.

Fortunately, other industries and thought leadership have been developing systematic methods for creating solutions to problems or enhancing work processes. By combining and leveraging concepts from human-centered design[4] and Lean Six Sigma,[5] below is a proposed innovation toolkit incorporating a five-step process that law librarians can use to facilitate process improvements or the creation of new offerings that will enhance their services and support their users.

Step 1—Propose an Area for Improvement

The first step in the innovation toolkit involves identifying the new opportunities that exist for a law library to create an innovative solution, either by improving an existing process, developing a new service or product, or implementing a new technology. In this stage, at the outset of any innovative initiative, it is crucial to consider the impact of whatever is being proposed on the operational efficiency and potential value to the institution and its stakeholders. The proposed innovation should enhance patron or institutional satisfaction, loyalty, or retention, reduce costs and resource usage, and enable the creation of new or improved solutions for clients. Ensuring the proposed improvement is Specific, Measurable, Achievable, Relevant, and Time-bound (SMART) is essential. This involves clearly defining the objectives, measurement criteria, resource availability, alignment with strategic goals, and the expected completion timeframe. Doing all this hard work at the outset of an innovation effort will provide more traditional stakeholders with measurable impacts of the initiative, which evidences the value of innovation.

Step 2—Define the Problem to Be Solved

Probably the most difficult step in the toolkit is defining the problem to be solved. In most scenarios, especially when there are historical and traditional ways of performing work, it is easy to propose an improvement and jump to a solution without actually understanding the problem that the solution is actually supposed to solve. This method of creating solutions actually stifles innovation, and this step of the innovative toolkit is a systematic effort to help traditional institutional cultures transform their work to become truly innovative culture. Additionally, when innovation efforts are seen just as experimentation efforts alone, they tend to be dismissed as one-offs or disconnected from actual problems that need solving. Again, as emphasized throughout this chapter, the goal is for a library to be seen as a center for innovation or a trusted partner to help move the legal profession forward.

This step, defining the problem to be solved, focuses on empathizing with clients or users to understand their needs, pain points, expectations, and motivations in designing new innovative offerings to solve an actual problem. For most law libraries that do not have unlimited resources or unfettered administrative latitude, innovation for innovation's sake is usually a costly mistake. Understanding underlying problems to be solved and how they connect with the ultimate users of the potential solutions helps to alleviate this problem and develop trust among even the most skeptical

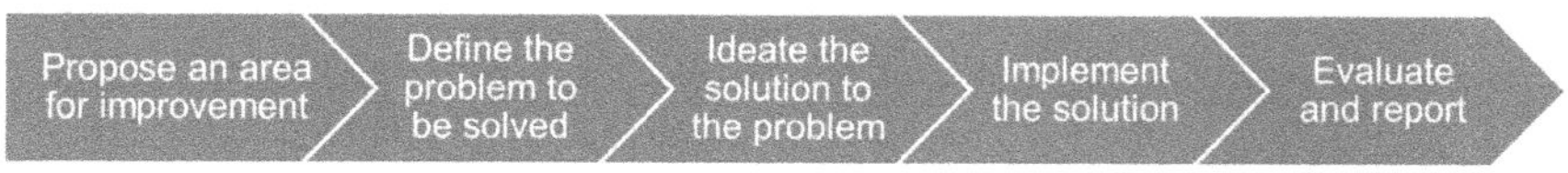

Figure 28.2 Five-Step Process for the Creation of New Offerings That Will Enhance Library Services and Support Users. *Source*: Created by author.

stakeholders. Tools like user personas, user journey maps, and process mapping can help create a detailed profile of the target audience and map their interactions with whatever solutions that are being implemented.

In this stage, identifying the root causes of the problem to be solved is crucial. Asking the "5 Whys" is a technique from Lean methodology that helps to identify the root cause of a problem by repeatedly asking why the problem occurred. This technique can help law librarians be innovative because it allows them to uncover the underlying issues and assumptions behind their current work and challenge them with evidence and data. By asking the five Whys, law librarians can avoid superficial or quick fixes that do not address the core of the problem and instead create solutions that are more effective, efficient, and user-centered. Asking the five Whys can also help law librarians to learn from their mistakes, failures, or feedback, and to continuously improve their performance and quality. By using this technique, law librarians can foster a culture of curiosity, inquiry, and problem-solving that drives innovation for the future.

Step 3—Ideate the Solution to the Problem

In this step, generating and evaluating possible solutions to the defined problem is key. Methods such as brainstorming and mind-mapping can be employed to generate a variety of ideas addressing the current challenges with the problem to be solved.

For a brainstorming exercise to discover potential solutions to a problem, the whole team should be involved, and this should be a fast-paced exercise. Post-It Notes are a great technology for this stage, where team members create ideas and then post their ideas on a board. Using the "yes, and . . . " technique in brainstorming is a great method to foster further innovative ideas without prejudging any potential solutions. Once the brainstorming exercise is completed, which should usually take an hour or less, the team should then categorize all the ideas and vote on which one seems to be the most viable or realistic option to solve the problem at issue.

Evaluating the feasibility and benefits of these ideas using tools like decision matrices or cost-benefit analysis helps select the most promising solution. Prototyping the solution, which involves creating low-fidelity or high-fidelity versions for testing and refinement, is then essential so that everyone on the team can "see" the proposed solution before actual implementation.

As with most innovation projects, technology might be at the core of any potential solution. If this is the case, then the team should go through a selection of technology platforms, using any requirements that the team has gathered through the ideation stage and any restrictions from the host institution to evaluate potential technology solutions. Demos and trials can be an immense aid from technology vendors in this evaluation process, which may take some time.

Once a solution is decided on, the team should define the scope of the innovation project and create a "work breakdown structure," which outlines the boundaries, requirements, and tasks, ensuring a structured approach to implementation. Finally, responsibilities for the different tasks should be delegated appropriately, and then the team can move on to implementation.

Step 4—Implement the Solution

Executing the chosen solution requires following the defined scope and work breakdown structure, within the roles and responsibilities assigned to team members. Progress should be tracked using predefined success metrics, and any issues or risks should be reported. Starting with a pilot phase allows for testing the solution on a small scale, collecting feedback, and making necessary adjustments before broader implementation, which is definitely key to a successful implementation. While implementation may take much longer than the first three steps and can be somewhat frustrating, this approach helps refine the solution based on real-world data and client feedback, ensuring a more successful rollout.

Step 5—Evaluate and Report

Assessing the results and outcomes of the implemented solution is crucial. Measuring the impact and value of the solution for clients and the organization's operational efficiency and innovation potential will provide the law library team with either success stories and narratives for future innovation buy-in or hard lessons to identify areas for further improvement. Transparent and honest communication of findings and recommendations, using tools such as dashboards, charts, and reports, ensures stakeholders are informed and engaged in the innovation process. All of this data provides valuable insights for future initiatives, with the hopes to build more innovation projects in the future.

CONCLUSION

Law libraries, as they have historically done, will continue to need to innovate to deal with new difficulties and possibilities in the modern legal profession. Leaders who can cast vision and challenge the status quo while using existing and new resources can create law libraries that are centers of innovation within their institutions. The time is now for law libraries to continue to innovate as partners for a better future for the legal profession and the people it serves.

NOTES

1. James M. Kouzes, and Barry Z. Posner, *The Leadership Challenge : How to Make Extraordinary Things Happen in Organizations,* 6th ed. (Somerset: John Wiley & Sons, Incorporated, 2017).
2. Attributed to Albert Einstein; however, it is common knowledge that this cannot be verified.
3. For reference, the current list price for Kuntz, A Treatise on the Law of Oil and Gas, a LexisNexis publication, is $3,064.00. The current list price for Summers Oil and Gas, 3d Ed., a Thomson Reuters publication, is $3,067.00.
4. Human-centered design is a powerful methodology and mindset to create new and innovative solutions to problems. It focuses on understanding the needs, behaviors, and experiences of people to create solutions that truly resonate with them. The process involves five "steps": empathizing with users, defining problems from their perspective, ideating innovative solutions, prototyping, and testing these solutions to refine them based on user feedback. This iterative approach ensures that the solutions developed are practical, effective, and user-friendly. To learn more about HCD and what is possible in developing skills in HCD, see Stanford's d.school offerings at https://dschool.stanford.edu.
5. Lean Six Sigma is a process improvement methodology that combines the principles from Lean to eliminate waste and inefficiencies in processes with the principles from Six Sigma to optimize the value and quality of the outputs of a process. While not initially intuitive due to the founding nature and application of Lean Six Sigma—manufacturing—law librarians can nevertheless apply a variety of tools and strategies from Lean Six Sigma in their efforts to innovate.

Bibliography

"4.9 Law School Policy on Generative AI," *University of Chicago Law School*, November 8, 2023, https://www.law.uchicago.edu/students/handbook/academicmatters/generative-ai.

"2022 Americans on Cybersecurity," PC Matic, 2022, https://www.pcmatic.com/news/USACyber-Survey/ [https://perma.cc/G86H-VGE2].

"2024 Data Breach Investigations Report," Verizon, 7. https://www.verizon.com/business/resources/reports/2024-dbir-data-breach-investigations-report.pdf.

"2024 Data Breach Investigations Report," Verizon, 21. https://www.verizon.com/business/resources/reports/2024-dbir-data-breach-investigations-report.pdf.

"2024 Data Breach Investigations Report," Verizon, 2024, 43, https://www.verizon.com/business/resources/reports/dbir/2024/dbir-report/ [https://perma.cc/2C6V-XQTL].

AALL Career Center, "Law Library Jobs," n.d., https://careers.aallnet.org.

"Accessibility Statement," Boston University School of Law, https://www.bu.edu/law/libraries/about/accessibility-statement/.

"AI Adoption and Risk Report," Cyberhaven Labs, Q2 2024, 9–10, https://www.cyberhaven.com/lp/lp-eb-data-report-q2-2024 [https://perma.cc/5L5J-DVSW].

"AI-Powered Legal Research: Where Legal Research Meets Generative AI," *Thomson Reuters Law Blog*, December 1, 2023, https://legal.thomsonreuters.com/blog/legal-research-meets-generative-ai/.

"Antitrust Compliance Policy," AALL, accessed July 2, 2024, https://www.aallnet.org/about-us/what-we-do/policies/antitrust-compliance-policy/.

"Apache Hadoop", Apache Software Foundation, https://hadoop.apache.org/.

"Apply to the JD Program," *University of Michigan Law School*, https://michigan.law.umich.edu/admissions/apply-jd-program#.

"Artificial Intelligence (AI) and Data Analytics Solutions," Altair. https://altair.com/data-analytics.

"ASU Law to Permit Use of Generative AI in Applications," *ASU*, July 27, 2023, https://law.asu.edu/newsroom/asu-law-permit-use-generative-ai-applications.

"Big Data Analytics in the Tourism and Travel Industry," Epam, accessed July 14, 2024, https://start-ups.epam.com/blog/big-data-in-tourism-and-travel.

"Bootstrap Get Started," W3 Schools, https://www.w3schools.com/bootstrap/bootstrap_get_started.asp.

"Brooklyn Public Library Saves Time, Money, and Headcount with Tableau," Tableau, accessed July 1, 2024, https://www.tableau.com/solutions/customer/brooklyn-public-library-saves-time-money-and-headcount-tableau.

"Cecilia AI," *DISCO's Generative AI-Powered Legal Solutions,* accessed June 17, 2024, https://csdisco.com/offerings/cecilia.

"Charles N. and Hilda H.M. Mason Law Library," University of the District of Columbia David A. Clarke School of Law, https://udclaw.libguides.com/home.

"ChatGPT," ChatGPT, https://chatgpt.com/.

"CIS Benchmarks," Center for Internet Security, https://www.cisecurity.org/cis-benchmarks-overview [https://perma.cc/D48Q-HEWG].

"CIS Critical Security Controls® Version 8.1," Center for Internet Security, June 2024, https://learn.cisecurity.org/cis-controls-download-v8 [https://perma.cc/2B4E-YLCY].
"Cocounsel," *Casetext*, December 22, 2023, https://casetext.com/.
"CoCounsel: Legal Research Memo," Casetext, https://casetext.com/v2/ai-assistant.
"Collection Development Policies," American Association of Law Libraries (AALL) Academic Law Libraries Special Interest Section, https://www.aallnet.org/allsis/resources-publications/academiclawlibcoldevpolicies/.
"Collection Development Policies," American Association of Law Libraries (AALL) Government Documents Special Interest Section, https://www.aallnet.org/gllsis/resources-publications/toolkit/collection-development/.
"Communications and Branding," Oklahoma City University School of Law, https://law.okcu.edu/communications-and-branding/.
"Computer Security Resource Center," National Institute of Standards and Technology, accessed June 24, 2024, https://csrc.nist.gov/ [https://perma.cc/QL5B-26DY].
"Conduct on Library Premises," Library of Congress, https://www.loc.gov/rr/conduct.html.
"Cost of a Data Breach Report 2023," IBM, 2023, 20, https://www.ibm.com/reports/data-breach [https://perma.cc/6RVF-J3SL].
"Cultural Proficiencies for Racial Equity: A Framework - 2.4 Policies, Procedures and Norms," Joint ALA/ARL Building Cultural Proficiencies for Racial Equity Framework Task Force, https://www.ala.org/sites/default/files/advocacy/content/diversity/ALA%20ARL%20Cultural%20Proficiencies%20for%20Racial%20Equity%20Framework.pdf.
"Current Publications – SP 800," NIST Computer Security Resource Center, https://csrc.nist.gov/publications/sp800 [https://perma.cc/7N55-Q3Y4].
"Cybersecurity Basics," Federal Trade Commission Cybersecurity for Small Business, , https://www.ftc.gov/business-guidance/small-businesses/cybersecurity/basics [https://perma.cc/822M-3BAP].
"Cybersecurity for Small Business," Protecting Small Businesses, Federal Trade Commission, accessed June 24, 2024, https://www.ftc.gov/business-guidance/small-businesses/cybersecurity [https://perma.cc/24A2-TDDX].
"Data Protection and Privacy Legislation Worldwide," UNCTAD, accessed June 20, 2024, https://unctad.org/page/data-protection-and-privacy-legislation-worldwide [https://perma.cc/72QJ-7LXM].
"Data Science," Catholic University of America, Department of Information Sciences, accessed July 1, 2024, https://lis.catholic.edu/academics/courses-of-study/data-science/index.html.
"Data Science," Master of Information: Data Science, Rutgers-New Brunswick School of Communication and Information, https://comminfo.rutgers.edu/graduate-programs/master-information/concentrations/data-science.
"Data Science—MLIS Career Pathway," SJSU School of Information, accessed July 1, 2024, https://ischool.sjsu.edu/data-science.
"Data Security Laws: State Government," National Conference of State Legislatures, https://www.ncsl.org/technology-and-communication/data-security-laws-state-government [https://perma.cc/M4JZ-6EKA].
"Data Services," University of Michigan Library, https://www.lib.umich.edu/research-and-scholarship/data-services.
"Dataiku at a Glance: The Universal AI Platform," Data Iku, https://pages.dataiku.com/interactive-data-sheet?utm_id=14139326388--125114850603--537236723194--dataiku&utm_source=nam-adwords&utm_medium=paid-search&utm_campaign=GLO%20CONTENT%20Interactive%20Data%20Sheet&gad_source=1&gclid=CjwKCAjw4f6zBhBVEiwATEHFVIGQZu7fQYtfdNtMYDHuzoc-QxdJeNSAV1-CfRTahFu1bJRct65WsBoCX9gQAvD_BwE.
"Defining Insider Threats," CISA, https://www.cisa.gov/topics/physical-security/insider-threat-mitigation/defining-insider-threats [https://perma.cc/MHG9-G8KC].

"Definition of 'Policy,'" *The Britannica Dictionary Online*, https://www.britannica.com/dictionary/policy.
"Digital Collections," Rutgers Law School, https://njlaw.rutgers.edu/.
"Does Working From Home Make Employees More Productive?," *The Economist*, December 27, 2020, https://www.economist.com/graphic-detail/2020/12/27/does-working-from-home-make-employees-more-productive?.
"Element 1: Access to Justice and the Public Library," Thurgood Marshall State Law Library, 2024, https://www.mdcourts.gov/lawlib/using-library/for-librarians/legal-reference-training/PLR-access-to-justice, https://perma.cc/BF2W-FZDU.
"FDLP: Free Document Dissemination through the Federal Depository Library Program," U.S. Government Printing Office, https://www.gpo.gov/how-to-work-with-us/agency/services-for-agencies/federal-depository-library-program.
"Federal Information Processing Standards Publications (FIPS Pubs)," NIST Information Technology Laboratory, https://www.nist.gov/itl/publications-0/federal-information-processing-standards-fips [https://perma.cc/TPG2-FBBU].
"Fee-Based Services," *Columbia Law School*, https://guides.law.columbia.edu/fbs/subscriptionservice/faqs.
"FIPS 200: Minimum Security Requirements for Federal Information and Information Systems," National Institute of Standards and Technology Computer Security Resource Center, March 2006, https://doi.org/10.6028/NIST.FIPS.200.
"(General-23-09) Updates to the Gramm-Leach-Bliley Act Cybersecurity Requirements," Federal Student Aid, February 9, 2023, https://fsapartners.ed.gov/knowledge-center/library/electronic-announcements/2023-02-09/updates-gramm-leach-bliley-act-cybersecurity-requirements [https://perma.cc/YGN6-5BGL].
"Generative AI for Library and Information Professionals," International Federation of Library Associations and Institutions Artificial Intelligence Special Interest Group, April 1, 2024, https://www.ifla.org/g/ai/generative-ai/.
"Generative AI for Professional Services," Harvey, accessed June 17, 2024, https://www.harvey.ai/.
"Generative AI Resources," *Berkeley Law Library*, https://www.law.berkeley.edu/library/legal-research/chatgpt/.
"Glossary: Malware," NIST Computer Security Resource Center, https://csrc.nist.gov/glossary/term/malware [https://perma.cc/8CZN-DCPA].
"Glossary: Misconfiguration," NIST Computer Security Resource Center, https://csrc.nist.gov/glossary/term/misconfiguration [https://perma.cc/WVN2-AJC4].
"Glossary: Zero Day Attack," NIST Computer Security Resource Center, https://csrc.nist.gov/glossary/term/zero_day_attack [https://perma.cc/A5QU-3V8B].
"Guidelines for Policy Development at UW-Madison," UW-Madison Policy Library, University of Wisconsin-Madison, https://development.policy.wisc.edu/.
"Guiding Principles," U.S. Department of Justice Office for Access to Justice, accessed April 12, 2024, https://www.justice.gov/atj, https://perma.cc/7HHY-DZ3G.
"Homepage," Sacramento County Public Law Library, https://saclaw.org/.
"Homepage," University of Washington Gallagher Law Library, https://lib.law.uw.edu/home.
"Honor Code and Procedure for Law Students," *Washburn University School of Law*, https://www.washburnlaw.edu/policies/honorcode.html.
"How Much Data is Created Every Day in 2024?" Tech Jury, https://techjury.net/blog/how-much-data-is-created-every-day/.
"How Passkeys Work," FIDO Alliance, https://fidoalliance.org/how-fido-works/ [https://perma.cc/U52K-EFS5].
"HTML Basics," MDN Web Docs, https://developer.mozilla.org/en-US/docs/Learn/Getting_started_with_the_web/HTML_basics.

"Implementing Phishing-Resistant MFA," Cybersecurity & Infrastructure Security Agency, October 2022, https://www.cisa.gov/sites/default/files/2023-01/fact-sheet-implementing-phishing-resistant-mfa-508c.pdf [https://perma.cc/XRX2-AL2J].

"International Counter Ransomware Initiative Members Come Together to Strongly Discourage Ransomware Payments," Singapore National Police Force, January 29, 2024, https://counter-ransomware.org/briefingroom/8ed7d1de-1a74-4a36-a2df-d5950624ebd8.

"Intranet." Merriam-Webster, 2024, accessed June 6, 2024, https://www.merriam-webster.com/dictionary/intranet.

"Introducing JSON," https://www.json.org/json-en.html.

"Is it a Policy, Procedure, or Guideline?," UW–Madison Policy Library, https://development.policy.wisc.edu/2022/06/01/is-it-a-policy-procedure-or-guideline/.

"J.D. & M.S.A. in Data Science and Analytics," College of Law: Student Experience, Georgia State University, accessed July 1, 2024, https://law.gsu.edu/student-experience/academics/jd-curriculum/j-d-master-of-science-in-analytics/.

"JavaScript Tutorial," W3 Schools, https://www.w3schools.com/js/default.asp.

"Known Exploited Vulnerabilities Catalog," Cybersecurity & Infrastructure Security Agency, https://www.cisa.gov/known-exploited-vulnerabilities-catalog.

"Law Library," Cornell University Library, accessed June 26, 2024, https://law.library.cornell.edu/.

"Learning Lessons from the Cyber-Attack: British Library Cyber Incident Review," British Library, March 8, 2024, 6, 14, https://www.bl.uk/home/british-library-cyber-incident-review-8-march-2024.pdf [https://perma.cc/AK7J-ZEXY].

"Legal Needs and Civil Justice: A Survey of Americans," Consortium on Legal Services and the Public, 1994. https://www.wisbar.org/aboutus/membership/Documents/WisTAFApp_J_ABA_Legal_need_study.pdf.

"LibGuides & LibGuides CMS," Springshare, https://springshare.com/libguides/.

"Library and Information Science, MLIS," University of Pittsburgh, School of Computing and Information, accessed July 1, 2024, https://www.sci.pitt.edu/academics/masters-degrees/library-and-information-science-mlis

"Members Program Borrowing Rules," *LALAWLIBRARY*, https://www.lalawlibrary.org/pdfs/Members%20Borrowing%20Rules%2012_1_2021.pdf.

"Navigating Cyberthreats and Strengthening Defenses in the Era of AI," Microsoft Threat Intelligence Cyber Signals, February 2024, 4–5, https://www.microsoft.com/en-us/security/business/security-insider/wp-content/uploads/2024/02/cyber-signals-issue-6.pdf [https://perma.cc/Y2F8-273K].

"NISA and CISA Red and Blue Teams Share Top Ten Cybersecurity Misconfigurations," Cybersecurity & Infrastructure Security Agency Cybersecurity Advisory, October 5, 2023, https://www.cisa.gov/news-events/cybersecurity-advisories/aa23-278a [https://perma.cc/8QXD-2DZL].

"ONEAL Curriculum," SPARC, accessed July 2, 2024, https://sparcopen.org/our-work/negotiation-resources/oneal/oneal-curriculum/.

"Our Data," Case Law Access Project, last modified 2024, https://case.law/, https://perma.cc/46TF-TQW6.

"PALMPrint Law Library Consortium, Inc.," *NELLCO*, accessed August 18, 2024, https://www.nellco.org/page/palmprint.

"PCI Security Standards Overview," PCI Security Standards Council, https://www.pcisecuritystandards.org/standards/ [https://perma.cc/W8P5-QEFZ].

"Pennsylvania Courts' Cyber Attack Update," The Unified Judicial System of Pennsylvania News, February 12, 2024, https://www.pacourts.us/news-and-statistics/news/news-detail/1166/pennsylvania-courts-cyber-attack-update [https://perma.cc/Z9YQ-NE23].

"Program Basics," FedRAMP, accessed June 25, 2024, https://www.fedramp.gov/program-basics/ [https://perma.cc/BUP4-DX9Q].

"Q&A: What Is Remote Work?," Indeed, https://www.indeed.com/career-advice/finding-a-job/remote-work.
"Ransomware: What It Is & What to Do About It," CISA, https://www.cisa.gov/sites/default/files/2021-01/NCIJTF%20Ransomware_Fact_Sheet.pdf [https://perma.cc/82JT-2ZGZ].
"Remote Workers Work Longer, Not More Efficiently," *The Economist*, June 10, 2021, https://www.economist.com/business/2021/06/10/remote-workers-work-longer-not-more-efficiently?
"Research Foundations: Information Literacy," Seminole State College of Florida, https://libguides.seminolestate.edu/researchfoundations/informationliteracy#:~:text=The%20term%20%22information%20literacy%22%20describes,and%20acknowledge%20sources%20of%20information.
"Research Guides & Videos," Harvard Law School, https://hls.harvard.edu/library/research-services/research-guides-videos/.
"Research Libraries Guiding Principles for Artificial Intelligence," Association of Research Libraries, April 2024, https://doi.org/10.29242/principles.ai2024.
"Resource Guides Copyright for Libraries: General Information," American Library Association, https://libguides.ala.org/copyright.
"Resource Guides Copyright for Libraries: Special Topics," American Library Association, https://libguides.ala.org/copyright/special-topics.
"Rule 1.6: Confidentiality of Information" in Center for Professional Responsibility (American Bar Association). 2013. "Model Rules of Professional Conduct." https://www.americanbar.org/groups/professional_responsibility/publications/model_rules_of_professional_conduct/.
"Rule 3.3: Candor Toward the Tribunal" in Center for Professional Responsibility (American Bar Association). 2013. "Model Rules of Professional Conduct." https://www.americanbar.org/groups/professional_responsibility/publications/model_rules_of_professional_conduct/.
"Satisfaction – LSSSE," 2024, https://lssse.indiana.edu/tag/satisfaction/#:~:text=That%20year%2C%2093%25%20of%20law,law%20students%20identified%20as%20heterosexual.
"Save Time and Money with Donotpay!" *DoNotPay*, accessed June 17, 2024, https://donotpay.com/.
"Secure Our World," Cybersecurity & Infrastructure Security Agency Cybersecurity Best Practices, https://www.cisa.gov/secure-our-world [https://perma.cc/5ZB6-RDDE].
"Self-Represented Litigant Guide to Legal Research," Harris County Robert W. Hainsworth Law Library, https://www.harriscountylawlibrary.org/self-represented-litigant-guide-to-legal-resources.
"SP 800-53 Rev. 5: Security and Privacy Controls for Information Systems and Organizations," September 2020, https://doi.org/10.6028/NIST.SP.800-53r5.
"Start Here: Quick Guides to Library Resources and Websites on a Given Topic," Wisconsin State Law Library, https://wilawlibrary.gov/learn/starthere/index.html.
"State Privacy Laws Regarding Library Records," American Library Association, https://www.ala.org/advocacy/privacy/statelaws.
"Structured and Unstructured Data," Imperva. https://www.imperva.com/learn/data-security/structured-and-unstructured-data/.
"Survey of Business Uncertainty, Monthly Report: December 2023," Federal Reserve Bank of Atlanta, released December 2023, https://www.atlantafed.org/-/media/documents/datafiles/research/surveys/business-uncertainty/chart-pack/2023/2023-12.pdf.
"The Justice Gap Report: Executive Summary," Legal Services Corporation, 2022, https://justicegap.lsc.gov/resource/executive-summary/, https://perma.cc/X5KF-3C3U.
"The State of Ransomware in Education 2023," SOPHOS, July 2023, 7, https://assets.sophos.com/X24WTUEQ/at/j74v496cfwh4qsvgqhs4pmw/sophos-state-of-ransomware-education-2023-wp.pdf [https://perma.cc/PZ8Q-UUHL].
"The Top 11 Legal Industry Cyber Attacks," *Artic Wolf Blog*, April 30, 2024, https://arcticwolf.com/resources/blog/top-legal-industry-cyber-attacks/ [https://perma.cc/H8FT-MN5M].

"Top Big Data Consultants, Companies, Services, and Consulting Firms," Jake Jorgovan, accessed July 1, 2024, https://jake-jorgovan.com/blog/big-data-consultants-companies-services-consulting-firms.
"Trends," American Library Association, last modified August 8, 2014, accessed June 27, 2024, https://www.ala.org/future/trends.
"Tutorials," Georgetown Law Library, https://guides.ll.georgetown.edu/home/tutorials.
"Types of Law Libraries," American Association of Law Libraries, https://www.aallnet.org/careers/about-the-profession/types-of-law-libraries/.
"Unauthorized Practice of Law," *Eisner Gorin LLP,* accessed June 17, 2024, https://www.egattorneys.com/unauthorized-practice-of-law-bpc-6125.
"Understanding Denial-of-Service Attacks," *Cybersecurity & Infrastructure Security Agency Blog*, February 1, 2021, https://www.cisa.gov/news-events/news/understanding-denial-service-attacks [https://perma.cc/MYT5-LARM].
"Understanding Patches and Software Updates," *Cybersecurity & Infrastructure Security Agency Blog*, February 23, 2023, https://www.cisa.gov/news-events/news/understanding-patches-and-software-updates [https://perma.cc/53H6-8SJ4].
"Updated Advisory on Potential Sanctions Risks for Facilitating Ransomware Payments," United States Department of the Treasury, September 21, 2021, https://ofac.treasury.gov/media/912981/download [https://perma.cc/NC2M-TQ4E].
"Usability and User Studies," American Association of Law Libraries, https://www.aallnet.org/allsis/resources-publications/marketing-outreach-toolkit/usability-user/.
"Use Strong Passwords," Cybersecurity & Infrastructure Security Agency Secure Our World, accessed June 24, 2024, https://www.cisa.gov/secure-our-world/use-strong-passwords [https://perma.cc/27T3-8B29].
"Vendor Security," Federal Trade Commission Cybersecurity for Small Business, accessed June 24, 2024, https://www.ftc.gov/business-guidance/small-businesses/cybersecurity/vendor-security [https://perma.cc/J5NT-B2VA].
"Videos and Tutorials," Alameda County Bernard E. Witkin Law Library, https://lawlibrary.acgov.org/videos-and-tutorials/#.
"We're All in this Together: A Year in Review of Zero-Days Exploited In-the-Wild in 2023," *Google*, March 2024, 4, https://storage.googleapis.com/gweb-uniblog-publish-prod/documents/Year_in_Review_of_ZeroDays.pdf [https://perma.cc/4C8B-KM72].
"Web Content Accessibility Guidelines (WCAG) 2.2," World Wide Web Consortium, https://www.w3.org/TR/WCAG22/.
"Westlaw AI-Assisted Research," Westlaw Precision, https://next.westlaw.com/.
"What are Real-Life Examples of the Application of Big Data Analytics?," Magnimind, accessed July 1, 2024, https://magnimindacademy.com/blog/what-are-real-life-examples-of-the-application-of-big-data analytics/#:~:text=3%2D%20Media%20and%20entertainment%20industry%20The%20media,big%20data%20analytics%20to%20a%20great%20extent.
"What Is Cybersecurity?," *Cybersecurity & Infrastructure Security Agency Blog*, February 1, 2021, https://www.cisa.gov/news-events/news/what-cybersecurity [https://perma.cc/7QF2-X53X].
"What is Data Science?," IBM, https://www.ibm.com/topics/data-science.
"Why Big Data Matters: Perspectives from the Libraries," International Federation of Library Associations and Institutions (IFLA), https://www.ifla.org/news/why-big-data-matters-perspectives-from-the-libraries/.
"Why CouchDB?" accessed July 1, 2024, https://docs.couchdb.org/en/stable/intro/why.html.
"Why Using a Polite Tone with AI Matters," *Microsoft*, https://www.microsoft.com/en-us/worklab/why-using-a-polite-tone-with-ai-matters.
"Work Smarter with Ai Legal Assistants," *LawDroid*, June 14, 2024, https://lawdroid.com/.
"X-Force Threat Intelligence Index 2024," IBM, 2024, 4, https://www.ibm.com/reports/threat-intelligence [https://perma.cc/PAC5-EAKF].

16 C.F.R. § 314.1 (2024); Federal Trade Commission, Bureau of Consumer Protection, "Advisory Opinion on Application of Title V, Subtitle A, of the G-L-B Act, and of the Commission's Privacy Rule to Attorneys at Law," April 8, 2002, https://www.ftc.gov/sites/default/files/documents/advisory_opinions/application-title-v-subtitle-g-l-b-act-and-commissions-privacy-rule-attorneys-law/hirshon-beales020408.pdf [https://perma.cc/DT7V-RVWN].

20 U.S.C. § 1232g; 34 C.F.R. pt. 99 (2023).

45 C.F.R. § 160.103(1)(ii) (2023).

2024 Threat Report, Arctic Wolf Labs, 2024, 10, https://arcticwolf.com/resource/aw/arctic-wolf-labs-2024-threat-report?lb-mode=overlay [https://perma.cc/7AYF-75XP].

A. H. Kuzucuoglu, "Risk Management in Libraries, Archives, and Museums," *IIB International Refereed Academic Social Sciences Journal* 5, no. 15 (2014): 277–294, https://www.proquest.com/scholarly-journals/risk-management-libraries-archives-museums/docview/1647083539/se-2.

AALL, "About the Profession," Careers, https://www.aallnet.org/careers/about-the-profession/.

AALL, "Diversity, Equity, and Inclusion Policy – AALL," August 8, 2022, https://www.aallnet.org/about-us/what-we-do/policies/dei-policy/#:~:text=Create%20spaces%20where%20all%20are,%2C%20economic%2C%20and%20political%20divides.

AALL Digital White Paper, "Defining ROI: Law Library Best Practices," https://www.aallnet.org/wp-content/uploads/2016/01/AALL-ROI-Whitepaper-2016_FINAL.pdf.

Aaron Mok, "A Stressed Out Rookie Lawyer Says He Got Fired after He Used ChatGPT to Do His Job," *Business Insider*, accessed June 17, 2024, https://www.businessinsider.com/young-lawyer-fired-using-chatgpt-job-work-hallucinations-errors-2023-11.

Aaron Schmidt and Amanda Etches, *Useful, Usable, Desirable: Applying User Experience Design to Your Library* (Chicago, IL: American Library Association, 2014).

Aarti Iyer, "Understanding Advantaged Groups' Opposition to Diversity, Equity, and Inclusion (DEI) Policies: The Role of Perceived Threat," *Social and Personality Psychology Compass* 16 (2022): e12666.

ABA Committee on Ethics & Professional Responsibility, Formal Opinion 477R, revised May 22, 2017, https://www.americanbar.org/content/dam/aba/administrative/professional_responsibility/ethics-opinions/aba-formal-opinion-477.pdf.

ABA Committee on Ethics & Professional Responsibility, Formal Opinion 483, October 17, 2018, https://www.americanbar.org/content/dam/aba/administrative/professional_responsibility/ethics-opinions/aba-formal-op-483.pdf.

ABA Committee on Ethics & Professional Responsibility, Formal Opinion 498, March 10, 2021, https://www.americanbar.org/content/dam/aba/administrative/professional_responsibility/ethics-opinions/aba-formal-opinion-498.pdf.

ABA, "Model Rules of Professional Conduct Rule 1.6, Comment [18]," https://www.americanbar.org/groups/professional_responsibility/publications/model_rules_of_professional_conduct/rule_1_6_confidentiality_of_information/comment_on_rule_1_6/.

ABA, "Model Rules of Professional Conduct Rule 1.9, Comment [7]," https://www.americanbar.org/groups/professional_responsibility/publications/model_rules_of_professional_conduct/rule_1_9_duties_of_former_clients/comment_on_rule_1_9/.

ABA, "Model Rules of Professional Conduct Rule 1.15," https://www.americanbar.org/groups/professional_responsibility/publications/model_rules_of_professional_conduct/rule_1_15_safekeeping_property/.

ABA, "Model Rules of Professional Conduct Rule 5.3, Comment [3]", https://www.americanbar.org/groups/professional_responsibility/publications/model_rules_of_professional_conduct/rule_5_3_responsibilities_regarding_nonlawyer_assistant/comment_on_rule_5_3/.

ABA Standards for Accreditation, "2024-2025 Standards and Rules of Procedure for Approval of Law Schools," ABA, last modified September 7, 2024, https://www.americanbar.org/groups/legal_education/resources/standards/.

Abigail Potter, "Introducing the LC Labs Artificial Intelligence Planning Framework," *The Signal*, November 15, 2023, https://blogs.loc.gov/thesignal/2023/11/introducing-the-lc-labs-artificial-intelligence-planning-framework/.

Above the Law & Arctic Wolf, "Law Firm Cybersecurity in the New Reality," 8, 2024, https://info.abovethelaw.com/hubfs/2024%20Artic%20Wolf%20Report/ATL_ArticWolf_LawFirm_Cybersecurity_Report_2023.pdf [https://perma.cc/4HUT-HNJP].

Adrienne Watt, *Project Management* (BCcampus Open Education, 2014), https://opentextbc.ca/projectmanagement/.

Affirmative Action Policies Throughout History, American Association for Access, Equity, and Diversity, accessed September 10, 2024, https://www.aaaed.org/aaaed/History_of_Affirmative_Action.asp.

Ahmadian, Chandrashekara, and Marjaei, "Study of Library Policies in Universities." https://digitalcommons.unl.edu/libphilprac/2324/.

AI.Law, "Legal AI Like Nothing Else on the Market." *AI.Law*, June 8, 2024, https://www.ai.law/.

ALA, "Library Bill of Rights," adopted June 19, 1939 and last amended January 29, 2019, https://www.ala.org/advocacy/intfreedom/librarybill [https://perma.cc/L9F2-2SCP].

ALA, *Library Privacy Guidelines for Library Management Systems,* https://www.ala.org/advocacy/privacy/guidelines/library-management-systems.

ALA, *Resource Guide for Library Safety and Preparedness,* https://www.ala.org/advocacy/resource-guide-library-safety-and-preparedness.

ALA Intellectual Freedom Committee, "Privacy: An Interpretation of the Library Bill of Rights," adopted June 19, 2002 and last amended June 24, 2019, https://www.ala.org/advocacy/intfreedom/librarybill/interpretations/privacy [https://perma.cc/X5U5-LAG6].

Alicia Solow-Niederman, "Administering Artificial Intelligence," *Southern California Law Review* 93, no. 4 (2020): 633.

Aliyu Nasiru Muhammad, Rufai Clis Misau, and Yerima Muhammad, "Budgeting in Public Libraries," *Journal of Accounting and Financial Management* 3, no. 1 (2017): 2–3.

Alyssa Thurston, "Addressing the "Emerging Majority": Racial and Ethnic Diversity in Law Librarianship in the Twenty-First Century," *Law Library Journal* 104, no. 3 (Summer 2012): 359–382.

Amanda B. Albert, "Communicating Library Value – The Missing Piece of the Assessment Puzzle," *Journal of Academic Librarianship* 40 (2014): 634–637.

Amanda Watson, Amanda Karel, Amanda Runyon, and Leslie Street, "Demonstrating Law Library Value Through Mission-Centered Assessment," *Law Library Journal* 115, no. 40 (2023): 10.

Amatriain Xavier, "Prompt Design and Engineering: Introduction and Advanced Methods," arXiv.org, January 24, 2024, https://arxiv.org/abs/2401.1442.

"Amendment Law," *U.C. Davis Law Review* 51, no. 2 (December 2017) 589.

"America is Under Attack: Inside the Anti-D.E.I. Crusade," *The New York Times,* January 20, 2024, https://www.nytimes.com/interactive/2024/01/20/us/dei-woke-claremont-institute.html.

American Association of Law Libraries, "Ethical Principles," Approved by the AALL Membership August 30, 2019, https://www.aallnet.org/advocacy/government-relations/recommended-guidelines/aall-ethical-principles/ [https://perma.cc/VER3-82TS].

American Association of Law Libraries, https://www.aallnet.org/.

American Association of Law Libraries, "Law Libraries and Access to Justice: A Report of the American Association of Law Libraries Special Committee on Access to Justice," July 2014, https://www.aallnet.org/wp-content/uploads/2018/01/AccessToJusticeSpecialCommittee2014LawLibrariesAndAccessToJustice.pdf.

American Association of Law Libraries, "Marketing and Outreach Toolkit," https://www.aallnet.org/allsis/resources-publications/marketing-outreach-toolkit/mktgtools/.

American Association of Law Libraries, "The Economic Value of Law Libraries," 2015, last visited June 27, 2024, https://www.aallnet.org/wp-content/uploads/2018/01/EconomicValue-ofLawLibrariesFinalReport.pdf.

American Association of Law Libraries, *2023 Biennial Salary Survey & Organizational Characteristics* (American Association of Law Libraries, 2023).
American Association of Law Libraries. *Law Libraries and Access to Justice: A Report of the American Association of Law Libraries Special Committee on Access to Justice.* July 2014. https://www.aallnet.org/wp-content/uploads/2018/01/AccessToJusticeSpecialCommittee2014LawLibrariesAndAccessToJustice.pdf.
American Bar Association, "ABA Profile of the Legal Profession - Legal Education," 2023, https://www.abalegalprofile.com/legaled.html.
American Bar Association, "Model Rules of Professional Conduct Rule 1.1, Comment [8]," https://www.americanbar.org/groups/professional_responsibility/publications/model_rules_of_professional_conduct/rule_1_1_competence/comment_on_rule_1_1/.
American Libraries, "Realizing Potential," *American Libraries,* March 1, 2024, https://americanlibrariesmagazine.org/2024/03/01/realizing-potential/.
American Library Association, "ALA Code of Ethics," adopted 1939 and last amended June 29, 2021, https://www.ala.org/tools/ethics [https://perma.cc/3737-RTMQ].
American Library Association, "Equity, Diversity, Inclusion: An Interpretation of the Library Bill of Rights," July 5, 2017, https://www.ala.org/advocacy/intfreedom/librarybill/interpretations/EDI.
American Library Association, "Overview of Library Support Staff," March 29, 2007, https://www.onetonline.org/link/summary/25-4031.00.
American Library Association, "State Privacy Laws Regarding Library Records," ALA Privacy, https://www.ala.org/advocacy/privacy/statelaws [https://perma.cc/C7FL-6G89].
Andrew Cox, "How Artificial Intelligence Might Change Academic Library Work: Applying the Competencies Literature and the Theory of the Professions," *Journal of the Association for Information Science and Technology* 74, no. 3 (2023): 367.
Andrew Folks, "US State Privacy Legislation Tracker," International Association of Privacy Professionals' Research Center, June 17, 2024, https://iapp.org/resources/article/us-state-privacy-legislation-tracker/# [https://perma.cc/49XK-7GC6].
Andrew Laurence, "Support Staff & the Law Libraries." *Library Mosaics* 4 (1993): 8–10.
Andrew M. Cox, Stephen Pinfield, and Sophie Rutter, "The Intelligent Library: Thought Leaders' Views on the Likely Impact of Artificial Intelligence on Academic Libraries," *Library Hi Tech* 37, no. 3 (2019) 418.
Anemona Hartocollis, "Yale and Harvard Law Schools Withdraw From the U.S. News Rankings," *The New York Times,* November 16, 2022.
Anne Robbins, "LibGuides: AI and Law Teaching: Introduction," *libguides.law.illinois.edu,* November 28, 2023, https://libguides.law.illinois.edu/AILegalTeaching.
Annette Day and Hilary Davis, "Collection Intelligence: Using Data Driven Decision Making in Collection Management," in *Proceedings of the Charleston Library Conference,* 2010, 81, http://dx.doi.org/10.5703/1288284314822.
Anvay Bhure and Sharmishta Desai, "Exploring the Intersection of Big Data and Legal Analytics: A Survey of It's Application in the Legal Industry," *Journal of Big Data Technology and Business Analytics* (March 2023): 1, https://doi.org/10.46610/jbdtba.2023.v02i01.002.
Ariam Tesfaye, "What is DEI? A Closer Look at DEI Strategies Throughout History," *Cooleaf,* January 24, 2023, https://www.cooleaf.com/blog/a-history-of-corporate-dei-strategies.
Arnold Hirshon, *Integrated Library Information Systems in ARL Libraries* (Washington, DC: Association of Research Libaries,1983).
Australian Law Librarians' Association, https://www.austlawlib.org/.
Barbara Kawecki, "Transforming Library Vendor Relations: Turning Relationships into Partnerships," *Against the Grain* 30, no. 2 (January 1, 2018), https://doi.org/10.7771/2380-176X.8034.
Benjamin L. W. Sobel, "Artificial Intelligence's Fair Use Crisis," *Columbia Journal of Law & the Arts* 41, no. 1 (2017): 45.

Benjamin Weiser, "Here's What Happens When Your Lawyer Uses ChatGPT," *The New York Times*, May 27, 2023, https://www.nytimes.com/2023/05/27/nyregion/avianca-airline-lawsuit-chat-gpt.html.

Bethany Latham, "A Perspective on Collaborative Partnerships to Expand Campus Buy-in for Digital Collections," *Digital Library Perspectives* 38, no. 4 (September 2021): 529–530.

Billy Perrigo, "OpenAI Used Kenyan Workers on Less than $2 per Hour: Exclusive," *Time*, January 18, 2023, https://time.com/6247678/openai-chatgpt-kenya-workers/.

Bipin Bihari Jayasingh, M. R. Patra, and D. Bhanu Mahesh, "Security Issues and Challenges of Big Data Analytics and Visualization," *International Conference on Contemporary Computing and Informatics*, Noida, India, Amity University, IEEE-USA, Institute of Electrical and Electronics Engineers Uttar Pradesh Section, and Institute of Electrical and Electronics Engineers, *Proceedings of the 2016 2nd International Conference on Contemporary Computing and Informatics (IC3I)*: 14–17 December 2016, Noida, India. Edited by S. K. Niranjan and V. N. Manjunatha Aradhya. Piscataway, NJ: IEEE, 2016. https://doi.org/10.1109/IC3I39298.2016.

Bob Ambrogi, "Access to Justice Requires Access to Law. So Why Aren't the Advocates of Each More Closely Aligned?," *LawSites*, March 11, 2024, https://www.lawnext.com/2024/03/access-to-justice-requires-access-to-law-so-why-arent-the-advocates-of-each-more-closely-aligned.html, https://perma.cc/6Y79-CBJ8.

Bob Ambrogi, "Law Students in BYU Law's LawX Program Develop Two Applications Targeting Access to Justice," *LawSites*, April 12, 2024, https://www.lawnext.com/2024/04/law-students-in-byu-laws-lawx-program-develop-two-applications-targeting-access-to-justice.html, https://perma.cc/5ZKE-VLHN.

Bootstrap, "Bootstrap Homepage," Bootstrap, accessed August 15, 2024, https://getbootstrap.com.

Brady D. Lund and Ting Wang, "Chatting about ChatGPT: How May AI and GPT Impact Academia and Libraries?," *Library Hi Tech News* 40, no. 3 (2023): 26–29, https://doi.org/10.1108/LHTN-01-2023-0009.

Brennan Center for Justice, *States Take the Lead on Regulating Artificial Intelligence* (Washington, DC, 2023), https://www.brennancenter.org/our-work/research-reports/states-take-lead-regulating-artificial-intelligence.

British and Irish Association of Law Libraries, 2024, https://biall.org.uk/.

Bruce E. Massis, "The Academic Library Becomes the Academic Learning Commons," *New Library World* 111, no. 3/4 (2010): 161–163.

Bruce M. Kennedy, *Confidentiality of Library Records: A Survey of Problems, Policies, and Laws*, 1989.

Bureau of Labor Statistics, U.S. Department of Labor, "Library Technicians and Assistants," Occupational Outlook Handbook, April 17, 2024, https://www.bls.gov/ooh/education-training-and-library/library-technicians-and-assistants.htm.

Cal. Civil Code §§ 1798.100 to1798.199.100 (Deering, Lexis current through 2024 Reg. Sess. Ch. 22).

Camilla J. Martinez and Tiffani A. Mezitis, "Harvard Business School Partners With BCG on AI Productivity Study," *News | the Harvard Crimson*, October 13, 2023, https://www.thecrimson.com/article/2023/10/13/jagged-edge-ai-bcg/.

Canadian Association of Law Libraries/Association Canadienne Des Bibliothèques De Droit, 2024, https://www.callacbd.ca/.

Caralee Adams, "2022 Internet Archive Hero Award: Carl Malamud," *Internet Archive Blogs*, October 19, 2022, https://blog.archive.org/2022/10/19/2022-internet-archive-hero-award-carl-malamud/, https://perma.cc/U2KQ-KMB2.

CareerExplorer, "What Does a Law Librarian Do?," https://www.careerexplorer.com/careers/law-librarian/#what-is-a-law-librarian.

Carl Jay Lagoze. 2010. "Lost Identity : The Assimilation of Digital Libraries into the Web." Dissertation.

Carlos A. Cuadra, "Are Computer Service Agencies Responding to the Needs of Libraries," *Law Library Journal* 64, no. 2 (May 1974): 126.

Cary Coglianese, Maura R. Grossman, and Paul W. Grimm, "Legal Information vs. Legal Advice: A 25 Year Retrospective," *Judicature* 107, no. 3 (2024): 66, https://judicature.duke.edu/wp-content/uploads/2024/03/PCP-Grimm-et-al-Vol-107-No-3.pdf, https://perma.cc/S8LF-JQKB.
Casey Duncan, "Collection Development," in *Academic Law Libraries Within the Changing Landscape of Legal Education: A Primer for Deans and Provosts,* eds. Michelle M. Wu, Scott B. Pagel, and Joan S. Holland (New York: William S. Hein & Co., Inc., 2020), 110.
Cassandre Coyer, "Could Gen AI Be a 'Pivotal Moment' for the Legal Aid Market?," *Legaltech® News,* April 10, 2024, https://www.law.com/legaltechnews/2024/04/10/could-gen-ai-be-a-pivotal-moment-for-the-legal-aid-market/ citing Cassandre Coyer, "Behind the Prices: Is Generative AI Legal Tech Cheaper to Buy or Build?," *Legaltech® News,* October 12, 2023, https://www.law.com/legaltechnews/2023/10/12/behind-the-prices-is-generative-ai-legal-tech-cheaper-to-buy-or-build/.
CatalogerGPT, accessed June 17, 2024, https://chatgpt.com/g/g-8ymg1Ftwo-catalogergpt.
Cathy Anderson, "Is 'The Great Resignation' Contagious?'" *LinkedIn News,* 2022, https://www.linkedin.com/posts/linkedin-news_is-the-great-resignation-contagious-activity6889270475533381632-WzTU?utm_source=share&utm_medium=member_desktop.
Cf. Anne Llewellyn, "Innovations in Learning and Teaching in Academic Libraries: A Literature Review," *New Review of Academic Librarianship* 25, no. 2/4 (2019): 129–149.
Charles J. Condon, "How to Avoid the Unauthorized Practice of Law at the Reference Desk," *Legal Reference Services Quarterly* 19, no. 1–2 (2001) 165--180.
Chickasaw Nation Law Library, Oklahoma City University School of Law, https://libguides.okcu.edu/lawlibraryhome/home.
Christine Bowersox and Sheri H. Lewis, "Collection Building in the Twenty-First Century: Law Firm and Academic Perspectives," *AALL Spectrum* 21, no. 6 (July/August 2017) 48–52.
Christine Park, "A Small Moment of Growth," *RIPS Law Librarian Blog,* March 5, 2024, https://ripslawlibrarian.wordpress.com/2024/03/05/a-small-moment-of-growth/.
Chunli Su, "Big Data Security and Privacy Protection," in 2019 International Conference on Virtual Reality and Intelligent Systems (ICVRIS), 87, accessed July 1, 2024, https://doi.org/10.1109/ICVRIS.2019.00030.
Ciara McCaffrey, "Transforming the University Library One Step at a Time: A Ten Year LibQUAL+ Review," *New Review of Academic Librarianship* 25, no. 1 (2019): 2–3.
Civil Rights Movement, History.com, effective May 14, 2024, https://www.history.com/topics/black-history/civil-rights-movement#jim-crow-laws.
Claire M. Germain, "Digital Legal Information: Here Today, Gone Tomorrow?" *AALL Spectrum* 2, no. 8 (May 1998) 27.
Clea Simon, "Caselaw Access Project Conference Marks Full Release of Digitized Decisions," Harvard Law School, https://hls.harvard.edu/today/caselaw-access-project-conference-marks-full-release-of-digitized-decisions/.
Common Crawl, https://commoncrawl.org/.
Coursera Staff, "CHATGPT-3.5 vs. 4: What's the Difference?" *Coursera,* accessed June 17, 2024, https://www.coursera.org/articles/chat-gpt-3-vs-4.
Cyber Safety Review Board, "Review of the Summer 2023 Microsoft Exchange Online Intrusion," Cybersecurity & Infrastructure Agency, 17, March 20, 2024, https://www.cisa.gov/sites/default/files/2024-04/CSRB_Review_of_the_Summer_2023_MEO_Intrusion_Final_508c.pdf [https://perma.cc/P3SJ-2K7M].
Cybersecurity Risk Management, Strategy, Governance, and Incident Disclosure, 88 Fed. Reg. 51896, August 4, 2023.
Dahlia Allwyn Riberio and Arti D. Kalro, "Four Decades of Negative Word-of-Mouth and Negative Electronic Word-of-Mouth: A Morphological Analysis," *International Journal of Consumer Studies* 47, no. 6 (2023): 2528–2552.

Danda B. Rawat, Ronald Doku, and Moses Garuba, "Cybersecurity in Big Data Era: From Securing Big Data to Data-Driven Security," *IEEE Transactions on Services Computing* 14, no. 6 (November-December 1, 2021): 6, https://doi.org/10.1109/TSC.2019.2907247.

Daryl Lim, "AI & IP: Innovation & Creativity in an Age of Accelerated Change," *Akron Law Review* 52, no. 3 (2018) 813.

David Badertscher, "Introduction," *Law Library Journal* 64, no. 2 (May 1974): 113.

David Lehr and Paul Ohm, "Playing *with the Data: What Legal Scholars Should Learn About Machine Learning,*" *U.C. Davis Law Review* 51, no. 2 (2017) 653.

de Perio Wittman, "Moving beyond the Basics," 275-77 (discussing the promise and ultimately weak results of Section 504 of the Rehabilitation Act of 1973, which at least prevented law schools from denying admission to students with disabilities).

Deborah K. Hackerson, "Access to Justice Starts in the Library: The Importance of Competent Research Skills and Free/Low-Cost Research Resources Symposium – Accessing Justice in Hard Times: Lessons from the Field, Looking to the Future," *Maine Law Review* 62, no. 2 (2010), https://heinonline.org/HOL/P?h=hein.journals/maine62&i=479.

Debra Cassens Weiss, "Use of ChatGPT to Support Fee Bid Is 'Utterly and Unusually Unpersuasive' Federal Judge Says," *ABA Journal*, February 27, 2024, https://www.abajournal.com/news/article/use-of-chatgpt-to-support-fee-bid-is-utterly-and-unusually-unpersuasive-federal-judge-says#google_vignette.

Debra Sabatini Hennelly and Bradley Schurman, "Bridging Generational Divides in Your Workplace," *Harvard Business Review*, accessed April 24, 2024, https://hbr.org/2023/01/bridging-generational-divides-in-your-workplace.

DEI Legislation Tracker, The Chronicle of Higher Education, August 30, 2024, https://www.chronicle.com/article/here-are-the-states-where-lawmakers-are-seeking-to-ban-colleges-dei-efforts.

Derek A. Denckla, "Report of the Working Group on the Use of Nonlawyers Special Issue: Conference on the Delivery of Legal Services to Low-Income Persons: Professional and Ethical Issues," *Fordham Law Review* 67, no. 5 (1998–1999): 1813–1818, https://heinonline.org/HOL/P?h=hein.journals/flr67&i=1829.

Devorah Kletenik et al., "From Awareness to Action: Teaching Software Accessibility for Neurodiverse Users," *SIGCSE 2024: Proceedings of the 55th ACM Technical Symposium on Computer Science Education* 1 (March 2024): 687, 691, https://doi.org/10.1145/3626252.3630859.

Dolores Sucozhañay et al., "Transformational Leadership and Stakeholder Management in Library Change," *LIBER Quarterly: The Journal of the Association of European Research Libraries* 24, no. 2 (2014): 65–67, https://doi.org/10.18352/lq.9583.

Dr. Ajay Lala and Pinkal Jain, "Investigating the Ethics of Big Data and Data Mining," *Data Science: Practical Approach with Python & R* (2023), 85, https://doi.org/10.58532/nbennurch293.

Dr. Gleb Tsipursky, "Is The End Of Remote Work Jobs Approaching?," *Forbes*, updated February 6, 2023, https://www.forbes.com/sites/glebtsipursky/2023/02/06/the-future-of-remote-work-is-here-to-stay/.

E. Shepherd, A. Stevenson, and A. Flinn, "The Impact of Freedom of Information on Records Management and Record Use in Local Government: A Literature Review," *Journal of the Society of Archivists* 30, no. 2 (2009): 227–248, https://doi.org/10.1080/00379810903445000.

Eden, Bradford Lee, ed. *Partnerships and New Roles in the 21st-Century Academic Library: Collaborating, Embedding, and Cross-Training for the Future* (Blue Ridge Summit, PA: Rowman & Littlefield Publishers, Incorporated, 2015).

Edward M. Corrado, "Artificial Intelligence: The Possibilities for Metadata Creation," *Technical Services Quarterly* 38, no. 4 (2021): 395.

Edward Segal, "Must Surveyed Americans Lack Confidence in Government to Protect them from Cyberattacks," August 12, 2021, https://www.forbes.com/sites/edwardsegal/2021/08/12/most-surveyed-americans-lack-confidence-in-government-to-protect-them-from-cyberattacks/ [https://perma.cc/6XNA-2A6N].

Elaine McArdle, "HLS Students Harness Artificial Intelligence to Revolutionize How Lawyers Draft and Manage Contracts," *Harvard Law Today,* December 20, 2017, https://hls.harvard.edu/today/evisort/.

Elizabeth Finley and David S. Mao, "Recollections of a Mid-Twentieth-Century Law Firm Librarian," *Law Library Journal* 97, no. 3 (Summer 2005): 568, https://heinonline.org/HOL/P?h=hein.journals/llj97&i=563.

Elizabeth G. Adelman, et al., "Academic Law Library Director Status since the Great Recession: Strengthened, Maintained, or Degraded?," *Law Library Journal* 112, no. 1 (Winter 2020) 117–134.

Ellyssa Kroski, "Card Sorting," PB Works, http://cardsorting.pbworks.com/w/page/14591705/FrontPage.

Emma W., "The Problems with Patching," *National Cyber Security Centre Blog*, July 10, 2019, https://www.ncsc.gov.uk/blog-post/the-problems-with-patching [https://perma.cc/Q43C-QYFM].

Emmanouel Garoufallou and Panorea Gaitanou, "Big Data: Opportunities and Challenges in Libraries: A Systematic Literature Review," *College & Research Libraries* 82, no. 3 (2021): 7–8.

Eric Martínez, "Re-Evaluating GPT-4's Bar Exam Performance," *Artificial Intelligence and Law*, March 30, 2024, https://doi.org/10.1007/s10506-024-09396-9.

Erik Adams, Martin Korn, and Cassie Laskowski, "DIY Data Analytics: Beyond Excel," *AALL Spectrum* November/December (2021): 12–15, accessed July 1, 2024, https://aallspectrum.aallnet.org/html5/reader/production/default.aspx?pubname=&edid=4f936bb4-a5b9-4b39-884a-667d1ad8402b.

Establishing the President's Committee on Equal Employment Opportunity, 26 Federal Reporter 1977 (March 6, 1961).

Establishing the President's Committee on Equality of Treatment and Opportunity in the Armed Services, 13 Federal Reporter 4313 (July 26, 1948).

Estelle Hurter, "Access to Justice: To Dream the Impossible Dream?," *The Comparative and International Law Journal of Southern Africa* 44, no. 3 (2011): 408–427, https://www.jstor.org/stable/24027059.

Etai Mizrahi, "4 Common Metadata Standards To Follow," *Seconda,* May 2, 2024, https://www.secoda.co/blog/4-common-metadata-standards-to-follow.

Ex Libris [Clarivate], *Aleph*, https://exlibrisgroup.com/products/aleph-integrated-library-system/.

Ex Libris [Clarivate], "Change is the Name of the Interlibrary Loan Game. Are You Ready?," https://exlibrisgroup.com/blog/change-is-the-name-of-the-interlibrary-loan-game-are-you-ready/.

Ex Libris [Clarivate], *Rapido*, https://exlibrisgroup.com/products/rapido-library-resource-sharing/.

F.T.C. v. Wyndham Worldwide Corp., 799 F.3d 236 (3d Cir. 2015).

Fahimeh Ahmadian, M. Chandrashekara, and Seyedhadi Marjaei, "Study of Library Policies in Universities," *Library Philosophy and Practice,* March 2019, https://digitalcommons.unl.edu/libphilprac/2324/.

Family Educational Rights & Privacy Act, 20 U.S.C. § 1232g.

Federal Information Security Modernization Act of 2014, Pub. L. No. 113–283, 128 Stat. 3073 (2014).

Frank Baudino and Carolyn Johnson, eds., *Brick and Click Libraries: An Academic Library Conference* (Mayville, ND: Northwest Missouri State University, 2015).

Frank Martens and Larry Rittenberg, *Risk Appetite-Critical to Success: Using Risk Appetite to Thrive in a Changing World* (Research, COSO, 2020), https://www.worldcomplianceassociation.com/noticias/noticia_doc_wca__seg_220520_243166.pdf

Frederick E. Smith, "Computer Application to Legal Documentation: What Is Not Being Done," *Law Library Journal* 64, no. 2 (May 1974) 114-118.

Frederick Schauer and Virginia J. Wise, "Nonlegal Information and the Delegalization of Law," *The Journal of Legal Studies* 29 (2000): 498–499.

Gabriele Aroni, "Games as Authorial Platforms? An Exploration of the Legal Status of User-created Content from Digital Games," *International Journal for the Semiotics of Law-Revue* 36, no. 5 (2023): 2021.

Gao Linna, "The Impact of ChatGPT on Enterprise Competitive Intelligence Systems," *Information Systems and Economics* 4, no. 9 (January 1, 2023), https://doi.org/10.23977/infse.2023.040909.

GDPR arts. 33, 34, https://eur-lex.europa.eu/legal-content/EN/TXT/PDF/?uri=CELEX:32016R0679.

General Data Protection Regulation, Regulation (EU) 2016/679.

Geoffrey D. Ivnik, "AI vs. Legal AI, What's The Difference?," *LawSites*, April 23, 2024, https://www.law.com/legaltechnews/2024/04/23/ai-vs-legal-ai-whats-the-difference/, https://perma.cc/T8G7-5ZXU citing "2024 Investing in Legal Innovation Survey," LexisNexis, 2024, https://www.lexisnexis.com/pdf/genai-report.pdf, https://perma.cc/2LYF-T9SH.

George Bradt, "Why You Should Outsource All Your Support Functions," *Forbes*, 2017, https://www.forbes.com/sites/georgebradt/2017/07/03/why-you-should-outsource-all-your-support-functions/.

George M. Eberhart, "Why Artificial Intelligence Matters," *American Libraries*, June 26, 2018, https://americanlibrariesmagazine.org/blogs/the-scoop/ai-lab-library/.

George Machovec, "Consortial Partnerships with Libraries and Vendors," *Against the Grain* 30, no. 2 (January 1, 2018), https://doi.org/10.7771/2380-176X.8039.

George Pike, "The Academic Law Library Budget," in *Academic Law Libraries Within the Changing Landscape of Legal Education: A Primer for Deans and Provosts*, eds. Michelle Wu, Scott B. Pagel, and Joan S. Howland (Getsville, NY: William S. Hein & Co., Inc., 2020) 20–21.

Georgie Donovan, "The Myth of the Tough Negotiator," *Against the Grain* 30, no. 2 (January 1, 2018), https://doi.org/10.7771/2380-176X.8037.

Ggaliwango Marvin, Nakayiza Hellen, Daudi Jjingo, and Joyce Nakatumba-Nabende, "Prompt Engineering in Large Language Models," *Algorithms for Intelligent Systems* (2024): 387–402, https://doi.org/10.1007/978-981-99-7962-2_30.

Giles C. Oatley, "Themes in Data Mining, Big Data, and Crime Analytics," *WIREs Data Mining and Knowledge Discovery* (2022): 5, https://doi.org/10.1002/widm.1432.

GitHub, "Library of Congress AI Framework," https://github.com/LibraryOfCongress/labs-ai-framework/tree/main.

Grace Lo, "'Aliens' vs. Catalogers: Bias in the Library of Congress Subject Heading," *Legal Reference Services Quarterly* 38, no. 4 (October 2, 2019): 170–196, https://doi.org/10.1080/0270319X.2019.1696069.

Greg Lambert, "Who Leads the Law Library? How About Law Librarians?, # *Geeks and A law Blog*, https://www.geeklawblog.com/2017/03/who-leads-law-library-how-about-law.html.

Greg Noone, "Generative AI Banned at Over a Quarter Of Firms, While Two-Thirds Have Imposed Stringent Guardrails," *Tech Monitor* 30, updated January 26, 2024, https://techmonitor.ai/technology/ai-and-automation/firms-generative-ai-ban [https://perma.cc/U6V5-K6FJ].

Hao Yu, "Reflection on Whether Chat GPT Should be Banned by academia from the Perspective of Education and Teaching," *Frontiers in Psychology* 14 (2023): 1181712.

Have I Been Pwned, https://haveibeenpwned.com/.

Heiner Stuckenschmidt and Frank van Harmelen, *Information Sharing on Th Semantic Web* (Heidelberg: Springer, 2005).

Helen Georgas, "Google vs. the Library (Part II): Student Search Patterns and Behaviors When using Google and a Federated Search Tool," *portal: Libraries and the Academy* 14, no. 4 (2014): 503.

History of DE&I, U.S. Department of Labor, December 15, 2023 https://www.dol.gov/agencies/olms/deia/history.

HIVE Systems, "Are Your Passwords in the Green?" *HIVE Blog*, https://www.hivesystems.com/blog/are-your-passwords-in-the-green [https://perma.cc/NN93-F2LH].

https://airtable.com/appKUCriCQDI1BxlV/shrfIAPpNKaNMnacR/tblNmp6mff8CzLuQD.

https://altair.com/altair-rapidminer;

https://rails.legal/about-rails/.

https://repository.ifla.org/bitstream/123456789/1819/1/tilt_newsletterJanuary2022R31Final.pdf

https://www.imperva.com/learn/data-security/structured-and-unstructured-data/#:~:text=Structured%20data%20is%20usually%20easier,it%20in%20a%20relational%20database.
https://www.juliemorgenstern.com/
Ifeoma Ajunwa, "The Paradox of Automation as Anti-Bias Intervention," *Cardozo Law Review* 41, no. 5 (2020): 1671.
IFLA, "IFLA Statement on Cybersecurity," February 2022, https://repository.ifla.org/handle/123456789/1912.
IFLA Document Delivery and Resource Sharing (DDRS) Section, "Can Artificial Intelligence Lead Us to a Smarter ILL Future or Other Library Services?" [webinar description], https://www.ifla.org/news/can-artificial-intelligence-lead-us-to-a-smarter-ill-future-or-other-library-services/.
Independent Information Professionals Reads, https://aiip.org/Discover/IIP-Reading-List.
Ingeborg Fredlund, "Loose Leaf Law Reports," *Law Library Journal* 3 (1911): 44.
Institute of Museum and Library Services [grant LG-252349-OLS-22], https://www.imls.gov/sites/default/files/project-proposals/LG-252349-OLS-22-preliminary-proposal.pdf.
International Association of Law Libraries, https://iall.org/.
International Federation of Library Associations and Institutions (IFLA), "IFLA Code of Ethics for Librarians and Other Information Workers (Full Version)," approved August 2012, https://repository.ifla.org/handle/123456789/1850.
Isaiah Michael Omame and Juliet C. Alex-Nmecha, "Artificial Intelligence in Libraries," in *Managing and Adapting Library Information Services for Future Users*, ed. Nkem Ekene Osuigwe (Hershey, PA: IGI Global, 2020), 129, https://doi.org/10.4018/978-1-7998-1116-9.
J. J. Pionke, "Veteran Views of the Library," *Reference & User Services Quarterly* 58, no. 4 (2019): 227–234.
J. Thompson and Carol Seiler, "Library-Vendor Partnerships – An Overview of Our Symbiotic Relationships," *Against the Grain* 30, no. 2 (January 1, 2018), https://doi.org/10.7771/2380-176X.8035.
James Heller, "Do Androids Dream of Electric Books? Thoughts on Legal Content Dissemination and Consumption in the Digital Environment," *AALL Spectrum* 18, no. 1 (September/October 2013) 23, 24.
James O'Brien, "Finding a Role in the Profession." *Library & Information Update* 5, no. 6 (2016): 36–37.
James Sandman, "Five Requirements for Realizing Technology's Potential to Improve Access to Justice," LSC – Legal Services Corporation: America's Partner for Equal Justice, January 16, 2020, https://www.lsc.gov/spotlight-blog/five-requirements-realizing-technologys-potential-improve-access-justice, https://perma.cc/BZT8-CYZR.
James Vincent, "How Much Electricity Does AI Consume?" *The Verge*, February 16, 2024, https://www.theverge.com/24066646/ai-electricity-energy-watts-generative-consumption.
Jan Hatzius, Joseph Briggs, Devesh Kodnani, and Griovanni Pierdomenico, "The Potentially Large Effects of Artificial Intelligence on Economic Growth," *Global Economics Analyst*, March 25, 2023, https://www.gspublishing.com/content/research/en/reports/2023/03/27/d64e052b-0f6e-45d7-967b-d7be35fabd16.html.
Jasmin Hollingum, "Collection Development Policies in Law Firm Libraries: Do We Need Them?" *Legal Information Management* 13, no. 1 (2013), https://doi.org/10.1017/S147266961300011X.
Jean Godby, Karen Smith-Yoshimura, Bruce Washburn, Kalan Knudson Davis, Karen Detling, Christine Fernsebner Eslao, Steven Folsom, Xiaoli Li, Marc McGee, Karen Miller, Honor Moody, Craig Thomas, and Holly Tomren, *Creating Library Linked Data with Wikibase: Lessons Learned from Project Passage* (Dublin, OH: OCLC Research, 2019), https://doi.org/10.25333/faq3-ax08.
Jean M. Wegner, Montell Davenport, Carolyn Hayes, and David Sanborne, "Using Metrics to Showcase Value," AALL Digital White Paper. Defining ROI: Law Library Best Practices, 2016, https://www.aallnet.org/wp-content/uploads/2016/01/AALL-ROI-Whitepaper-2016_FINAL.pdf.
Jeff Kosseff, *Cybersecurity Law*, 3rd ed. (Hoboken, NJ: John Wiley & Sons, Inc., 2023).

Jeff Kosseff, *Cybersecurity Law*, 46, Appendix B; "Security Breach Notification Laws," National Conference of State Legislatures, updated January 17, 2022, https://www.ncsl.org/technology-and-communication/security-breach-notification-laws [https://perma.cc/7BFF-ZUEN].

Jean Godby, Karen Smith-Yoshimura, Bruce Washburn, Kalan Knudson Davis, Karen Detling, Christine Fernsebner Eslao, Steven Folsom, Xiaoli Li, Marc McGee, Karen Miller, Honor Moody, Craig Thomas, and Holly Tomren, *Creating Library Linked Data with Wikibase: Lessons Learned from Project Passage* (Dublin, OH: OCLC Research, 2019), https://doi.org/10.25333/faq3-ax08.

Jenay Robert, "Student Data Privacy and Security: A Call for Transparent Practices," *Educause*, October 3, 2022, https://www.educause.edu/ecar/research-publications/2022/student-data-privacy-and-security-a-call-for-transparent-practices/trusting-institutions [https://perma.cc/BZ2T-4Z7F].

Jenna Greene, "How Law Firm Librarians are Reinventing Themselves," *Reuters*, February 18, 2022, https://www.reuters.com/legal/legalindustry/how-law-firm-librarians-are-reinventing-themselves-2022-02-18/.

Jennifer Soper, "Internal vs. External Recruitment: A Guide for Small Businesses," https://fitsmallbusiness.com/internal-vs-external-recruiting/.

Jerome Becquart, "PKI and FIDO2: The Dynamic Duo of Authentication," *Axiad Blog*, accessed June 24, 2024, https://www.axiad.com/blog/pki-and-fido2/ [https://perma.cc/H8JS-GXRK].

Jessica Almeida and Nicole P. Dyszlewski, "Marketing and Outreach," in *Introduction to Law Librarianship*, eds. Zanada Joyner and Cas Laskowski (Mountain View, CA: Press Books, 2021).

Jessica de Perio Wittman, "Moving Beyond the Basics of the ADA and Section 504: Opportunities for Equitable and Inclusive Access to Law Libraries, Collections, and Services," *Legal Reference Services Quarterly* 42, no. 3–4 (October 2, 2023): 272–298, https://doi.org/10.1080/0270319X.2023.2264690.

Joe Regalia, "ChatGPT and Legal Writing: The Perfect Union?" *Write.law*, accessed June 17, 2024, https://write.law/blog/chatgpt-and-legal-writing-the-perfect-union.

John Eye, "Improving Contract Negotiations for Library Collections through Open Records Requests," *College & Research Libraries* 84, no. 6 (2023), https://crl.acrl.org/index.php/crl/article/view/26101/34023.

John G. Jackson, "Foreword," *Unauthorized Practice of Law: A Handbook for Lawyers and Laymen* 1 (1934): 3–12, 5. https://heinonline.org/HOL/P?h=hein.beal/unauplaw0001&i=3.

John M. Greacen, "Legal Information vs. Legal Advice: A 25 Year Retrospective," *Judicature* 106, no. 2 (June 2022): 56–57, https://judicature.duke.edu/wp-content/uploads/2022/09/GREACEN_Summer2022.pdf.

John M. Greacen, "Legal Information vs. Legal Advice: Developments during the Last Five Years," *Judicature* 84, no. 4 (January–February 2001): 203.

John M. Greacen, "No Legal Advice from Court Personnel – What Does That Mean," *Judges' Journal* 34, no. 1 (Winter 1995): 10.

John Simek, "2023 Cybersecurity TechReport," *ABA TechReport 2023*, December 18, 2023, https://www.americanbar.org/groups/law_practice/resources/tech-report/2023/2023-cybersecurity-techreport/.

Jon Reed, "How the Brooklyn Public Library Used Data Visualization to Build a Better Library," *Diginomica*, accessed July 1, 2024, https://diginomica.com/how-the-brooklyn-public-library-data-visualization-a-better-library-with-tableau.

Jonathan Greig, "An Inside Look into States' Efforts to Ban Gov't Ransomware Payments," August 22, 2022, https://therecord.media/an-inside-look-into-states-efforts-to-ban-govt-ransomware-payments [https://perma.cc/BG3T-AAKV].

Jonathan Greig and Suzanne Smalley, "CISA Forced to Take Two Systems Offline Last Month After Ivanti Compromise," *The Record*, March 8, 2024, https://therecord.media/cisa-takes-two-systems-offline-following-ivanti-compromise [https://perma.cc/Z8HY-2U64].

Joseph Esposito, *What if Walmart Ran a Library,* https://quod.lib.umich.edu/j/jep/3336451.0009.104?view=text;rgn=main.
Joseph Landau, "School of Law Memorandum on Academic Integrity," Fordham University, https://www.fordham.edu/school-of-law/life-at-fordham-law/student-life/office-of-student-affairs/conduct-and-grievance-policy/academic-integrity/.
Josh Farley, "The Thinker & the Doer," *AALL Spectrum* 28, no. 3 (January 2024), https://aallspectrum.aallnet.org/html5/reader/production/default.aspx?pubname=&edid=e43d1447-80e9-4753-9db1-ff7f18c86736&pnum=43.
Joshua A. T. Fairfield, *Owned: Property, Privacy, and the New Digital Serfdom* (New York: Cambridge University Press, 2017).
Joshua Lenon, "A List of All the Ethics Opinions on Cloud Computing for Lawyers," *CLIO Blog*, https://www.clio.com/blog/cloud-computing-lawyers-ethics-opinions/ [https://perma.cc/3DPE-YG8W].
Julia Angwin, Jeff Larson, Surya Mattu, and Lauren Kirchner, "Machine Bias," *ProPublica*, May 23, 2016, https://www.propublica.org/article/machine-bias-risk-assessments-in-criminal-sentencing.
Julie E. Cohen, "Law for the Platform Economy," *U.C. Davis Law Review* 51, no. 1 (2017): 133.
Julius J. Marke, et al., *Legal Research and Law Library Management* (New York: Law Journal Press, 2020), note 26 at 2.01, 3.0.
Kalin Hristov, "Artificial Intelligence and the Copyright Dilemma," *IDEA: The Journal of the Franklin Pierce Center for Intellectual Property* 57, no. 3 (2017) 431.
Karen Ellis, ed. *Partnerships and Collaborations in Public Library Communities: Resources and Solutions* (Hershey, PA: IGI Global, 2011).
Karin Hellerstedt, Timur Uman, and Karl Wennberg, "Fooled by Diversity? When Diversity Initiatives Exacerbate Rather Than Mitigate Inequality," *Academy of Management Perspectives* 38 (2023): 27.
Karl Manheim and Lyric Kaplan, "Artificial Intelligence: Risks to Privacy and Democracy," *Yale Journal of Law and Technology* 21 (2019): 108.
Kate Crawford, "Generative AI's Environmental Costs Are Soaring – And Mostly Secret," *Nature News*, February 20, 2024, https://www.nature.com/articles/d41586-024-00478-x.
Kaylan Ellis, Heather J. E. Simmons, Susan David deMaine, et al., *Introduction to Law Librarianship.* Creative Commons Attribution 4.0 International License, except where otherwise noted: 2021, https://pressbooks.pub/app/uploads/sites/4509/2021/07/Introduction-to-Law-Librarianship-20210920.pdf.
Keith Courtney, "Library/Vendor Relations: An Academic Publisher's Perspective," *Journal of Library Administration* 44, no. 3–4 (August 31, 2006): 57–68, https://doi.org/10.1300/J111v44n03_06.
Keith Day, "ChatGPT Blocked for NARA Usage," *National Archives Employee Communications*, May 1, 2024, https://www.archives.gov/files/foia/2024.05.01-nara-employee-communications-blocking-chatgpt.docx.pdf.
Kelly Kunsch, "Natural Born Killers: An Argument against Teaching Natural Language Searching," *AALL Spectrum* 1, no. 2 (1996): 16.
Kenneth Crews, *Copyright Law for Librarians and Educators* (Chicago: American Library Association, 2020).
Kenneth Olmstead and Aaron Smith, "Americans and Cybersecurity," *Pew Research Center*, January 26, 2017, https://www.pewresearch.org/internet/wp-content/uploads/sites/9/2017/01/Americans-and-Cyber-Security-final.pdf [https://perma.cc/SZ2K-34C3].
Kevin Schaul, Szu Yu Chen, and Nitasha Tiku, "Inside the Secret List of Websites That Make AI Like ChatGPT Sound Smart," *Washington Post*, April 19, 2023, https://www.washingtonpost.com/technology/interactive/2023/ai-chatbot-learning/.
Kevin Werbach, "Trust, but Verify: Why the Blockchain Needs the Law," *Berkeley Technology Law Journal* 33, no. 2 (2018): 487.

Kirsten Ostergaard and Doralyn Rossmann, "There's Work to Be Done: Exploring Library-Vendor Relations," *Technical Services Quarterly* 34, no. 1 (January 2, 2017): 13–33, https://doi.org/10.1080/07317131.2017.1238196.

Kris Turner, "Aggressive Helpfulness: A Case Study of Innovative Outreach to Special Library Patrons," *Public Services Quarterly* 15, no. 1 (January 2019): 73–84.

Krishna Ronanki, Beatriz Cabrero-Daniel, and Christian Berger, "Prompt Smells: An Omen for Undesirable Generative AI Outputs," January 23, 2024, https://doi.org/10.1145/3644815.3644982.

Kristin Delaney, "Introducing Ask Practical Law AI on Practical Law: Generative AI Meets Legal How-to," *Thomson Reuters Law Blog*, January 24, 2024, https://legal.thomsonreuters.com/blog/legal-how-to-meets-generative-ai/.

L. Cindy Dabney, et al., "Marketing and Outreach in Law Libraries: A White Paper," *Law Library Journal* 105, no. 4 (Fall 2013): 525–538.

Latia Ward, "Accessing Justice," *American Libraries Magazine* 53, no. 56 (June 2022): 56, https://digital.americanlibrariesmagazine.org/html5/reader/production/default.aspx?pubname=&edid=4c7068a3-ff3b-4eda-b277-65dfbc7ece87.

Latia Ward, "Self-Help Legal Information Resources in Virginia," *LISP/SR Blog*, November 1, 2023, https://lispsr.wordpress.com/2023/11/01/self-help-legal-information-resources-in-virginia/, https://perma.cc/HJ8Y-J96A.

Laureen Adams and Regina Smith, "The Evolution of Public Law Libraries." AALL Spectrum, accessed April 24, 2024, updated March 2006, https://www.aallnet.org/wp-content/uploads/2017/11/pub_sp0603_Evolution.pdf.

Laurel Sammonds Crawford and Allyson Rodriguez, "Evolving Ethos and Etiquette," in *Library Technical Services*, ed. Stacey Marien, 399–416. Adapting to a Changing Environment (Purdue University Press, 2020), https://doi.org/10.2307/j.ctvs1g8h5.29.

Lauren Coffee, "Universities Boost Spending to Curb Cyber Attacks," *Inside Higher Ed.*, April 25, 2024, https://www.insidehighered.com/news/quick-takes/2024/04/25/colleges-spending-more-ever-cybersecurity-efforts# [https://perma.cc/79Z8-228S].

Lauren Leffer, "The AI Boom Could Use a Shocking Amount of Electricity," *Scientific American*, October 13, 2023, https://www.scientificamerican.com/article/the-ai-boom-could-use-a-shocking-amount-of-electricity/.

Law Library Journal, "Current Comments," *Law Library Journal* 55, no. 2 (May 1962): 123 ("The Council has allocated $162,258 for the study, the initial phase of which is expected to be completed in October 1962.")

LeAnne Salazar Montoya, "Equity, Diversity, and Inclusion: What Is in a Name?," Seattle Journal for Social Justice 22, no. 3 (2024): 621–672.

Lee F. Peoples, "Designing a Law Library to Encourage Learning," *Journal of Legal Education* 63, no. 4 (May 2014): 612.

Leo Appleton, "AI and Academic Libraries: What's All the Fuss About?" *New Review of Academic Librarianship* 30, no. 1 (2024): 1.

Lesley Ellen Harris, *Licensing Digital Content: A Practical Guide for Librarians* (Chicago, IL: American Library Association, 2002).

Lesley Ellen Harris, "Licensing Digital Content for Your Library," *AALL Spectrum 5*, no. 5 (February 2001): 28–30.

LexisNexis, "Lexis+ Ai: Ai Legal Assistant by LexisNexis," *Lexis+ AI | AI Legal Assistant by LexisNexis,* accessed June 17, 2024, https://www.lexisnexis.com/en-us/products/lexis-plus-ai.page.

LexisNexis Practical Guidance. Policy on AI Use. LexisNexis Practical Guidance, 2023, https://www.lexisnexis.com/pdf/practical-guidance/ai/pgexpert-annotated-form-ai-driven-tools-in-the-workplace.pdf.

Libin Han, et al., "The Effect of Commuting Time on Quality of Life: Evidence from China," *International Journal of Environmental Research and Public Health* 20, no. 1 (2023): 573, https://www.ncbi.nlm.nih.gov/pmc/articles/PMC9819363/.

LibLime, "Revolutionizing Library Cataloging with Artificial Intelligence (AI)," *LinkedIn,* December 4, 2023, https://www.linkedin.com/pulse/revolutionizing-library-cataloging-artificial-intelligence-ai-coo9c/

Lindsey Carpino, Annie Mentkowski, and Clanitra Stewart Nejdl, "Building Strategic Partnerships through Collaboration between Law Libraries," *AALL Spectrum* 24, no. 4 (March/April 2020): 17.

Loida Garcia-Febo, "Exploring AI," *American Libraries Magazine,* March 1, 2019.

Lounsberry, "Troubleshooting Electronic Resources," 223; see also Margaret A. Leary, "Creating One Library at the University of Michigan Law Library," *Trends in Law Library Management and Technology* 18 (2008): 12.

LSC - Legal Services Corporation: America's Partner for Equal Justice, "Talk Justice: Episode Nine," December 17, 2020, https://www.lsc.gov/media/podcasts/talk-justice/talk-justice-episode-nine, https://perma.cc/GM4G-J27X.

Lynne Howarth, "The Role of the Paraprofessional in Technical Services in Libraries," *Library Trends* 46 (1998): 526.

M. Kathleen Price, "Setting the Legal Information Agenda for the Year 2000: Preliminary Report of the National Legal Resources Committee," *Law Library Journal* 81, no. 2 (1989): 349.

M. M. Kessler, *TIP System Report* (Cambridge, MA: Massachusetts Institute of Technology Technical Information Project, 1967).

Maaike Oldemans and Jennifer Kronenbitter, "Technical Metamorphosis by Design," in *Library Technical Services*, ed. Stacey Marien, 323–332. Adapting to a Changing Environment (Purdue University Press, 2020), https://doi.org/10.2307/j.ctvs1g8h5.24.

Magdalena Wójcik, "How to Design Innovative Information Services at the Library?," *Library Hi Tech* 37, no. 2 (2019): 138–154.

Malcolm Brown, Mark McCormack, Jaime Reeves, D. Christopher Brook, Susan Grajek, Bryan Alexander, Maha Bali, Stephanie Bulger, Shawna Dark, Nicole Engelbert, Kevin Gannon, Adrienne Gauthier, David Gibson, Rob Gibson, Brigitte Lundin, George Veletsianos, and Nicole Weber, *2020 Educause Horizon Report Teaching and Learning Edition* (Louisville, CO: EDUCAUSE), 6, https://www.learntechlib.org/p/215670/.

Manasi Vartak, "Responsible AI Explained," *Built In,* May 18, 2023, https://builtin.com/artificial-intelligence/responsible-ai.

Marc Schubhan, Maximilian Altmeyer, Dominic Buchheit, and Pascal Lessel, "Investigating User-created Gamification in an Image Tagging Task," in CHI Conference Online, Regina Bernhaupt, Florian Mueller, Joanna McGrenere, Andy Cockburn, SIGCHI (Group: U.S.), and Association for Computing Machinery. CHI'20: Proceedings of the 2020 CHI Conference on Human Factors in Computing Systems: April 25–30, Honolulu, HI. New York: Association for Computing Machinery, 2020. https://doi.org/10.1145/3313831.

Marco Poggio, "Gen AI Shows Promise - And Peril - For Pro Se Litigants," *Law360,* May 3, 2024, https://www.law360.com/articles/1812918/gen-ai-shows-promise-and-peril-for-pro-se-litigants.

Marco Tulio Ribeiro, Sameer Singh, and Carlos Guestrin, "'Why Should I Trust You?' Explaining the Predictions of Any Classifier," in *International Conference on Knowledge Discovery & Data Mining*, San Francisco, CA, Balaji Krishnapuram, ACM Digital Library, Association for Computing Machinery Special Interest Group on Management of Data, and Association for Computing Machinery Special Interest Group on Knowledge Discovery & Data Mining. *KDD'16: Proceedings of the 22nd ACM SIGKDD International Conference on Knowledge Discovery and Data Mining*: August 13–17, 1135, San Francisco, CA. New York: Association for Computing Machinery, 2016. https://doi.org/10.1145/2939672.

Margaret Maher Krause, "Look Beyond LEXIS and WESTLAW: Other Computer Applications in the Practice of Law," *Law Library Journal* 85, no. 3 (1993): 575.

Margot E. Kaminski, "Authorship, Disrupted: AI Authors in Copyright and First Amendment Law," *U.C. Davis Law Review* 51, no. 2 (December 2017): 589

Marie Keen Shaw and Hali R. Keeler, *Supervision and Management: An Introduction for Support Staff* (Lanham, MD: Rowman and Littlefield, 2019).

Marke, "Legal Research," 2.01. See also, Martha Kyrillidou, "Library Value May Be Proven, If Not Self-Evident," *Research Libraries: A Bimonthly Report from ARL, CNI, and SPARC* 271, no. 1 (August 2010): 1–3.

Marshall Breeding, "Libraries Under Cyberattack," *Computers in Libraries* 44, no. 2 (March 2024), https://librarytechnology.org/document/29866/library-tech-trends-2024.

Massachusetts Institute of Technology, *News Office Records* (AC-0069) (Cambridge, MA: Massachusetts Institute of Technology), https://cdn.libraries.mit.edu/dissemination/diponline/AC0069_NewReleases/NewsRelease_1960/AC0069_1964/AC0069_196412_012.pdf.

Massachusetts Institute of Technology, *Press Release* (Cambridge, MA: Office of Public Relations of the Massachusetts Institute of Technology, December 11, 1964).

Massachusetts Institute of Technology Libraries, *Collection Overview, Fernando J. Corbató Papers* (Cambridge, MA: MIT Libraries, MIT), https://archivesspace.mit.edu/repositories/2/resources/866.

Massachusetts Institute of Technology Libraries, *Collection Overview, Myer M. Kessler Papers* (Cambridge, MA: MIT Libraries, MIT), https://archivesspace.mit.edu/repositories/2/resources/1008.

Mata v. Avianca, Inc. (United States District Court Southern District of New York June 22, 2023) No. 1:2022cv01461 - Document 54.

Matt O'Brien and Hannah Fingerhut, "Artificial Intelligence Technology behind ChatGPT Was Built in Iowa - With a Lot of Water," *AP News*, September 9, 2023, https://apnews.com/article/chatgpt-gpt4-iowa-ai-water-consumption-microsoft-f551fde98083d17a7e8d904f8be822c4.

Matthew B. Kugler and Carly Pace, "Deepfake Privacy: Attitudes and Regulation," *Northwestern University Law Review* 116, no. 3 (2021): 611.

Matthew Dahl, Varun Magesh, Mirac Suzgun, and Daniel E Ho, "Hallucinating Law: Legal Mistakes with Large Language Models Are Pervasive," *Law Regulation and Policy*, January 11, 2024, https://hai.stanford.edu/news/hallucinating-law-legal-mistakes-large-language-models-are-pervasive.

Matthew North. *Data Mining for the Masses: With Implementations in RapidMiner*. 3rd ed. (CreateSpace Independent Publishing Platform, September 5, 2018): 11–13.

Maungwa and Laughton, "The Use of Theories in Competitive Intelligence: A Systematic Literature Review," *Journal of Intelligence Studies in Business* 13, no. 2 (2023), https://repository.up.ac.za/bitstream/handle/2263/95327/Maungwa_Use_2023.pdf?sequence=1&isAllowed=y(up.ac.za).

Maura R. Grossman, Paul W. Grimm, and Daniel G. Brown, "Is Disclosure and Certification of the Use of Generative AI Really Necessary?," Judicature 107, no. 2 (2023): 69, https://judicature.duke.edu/wp-content/uploads/2023/10/AIOrders_Vol107No2.pdf, archived at https://perma.cc/KJ6S-GUDT.

Mauro Cappelletti and Bryant Garth, "Access to Justice: The Newest Wave in the Worldwide Movement to Make Rights Effective," *Buffalo Law Review* 27, no. 2 (1978 1977): 181–292, at 182, https://heinonline.org/HOL/P?h=hein.journals/buflr27&i=193.

Max Eddy and Thorin Klosowski, "The Best Two-Factor Authentication App," *New York Times Wirecutter*, updated April 12, 2024, https://www.nytimes.com/wirecutter/reviews/best-two-factor-authentication-app/ [https://perma.cc/6FDP-MHUD].

Megan Lounsberry, "Troubleshooting Electronic Resources from an Interlibrary Loan Perspective," *Technical Services Quarterly* 37, no. 3 (2020): 223.

Michael D. Murray, "Generative and AI Authored Artworks and Copyright Law," *Hastings Communications and Entertainment Law Journal* 45, no. 1 (Winter 2023): 27.

Michael M. Grynbaum and Ryan Mac, "The Times Sues OpenAI and Microsoft over AI Use of Copyrighted Work," *The New York Times*, December 27, 2023, https://www.nytimes.com/2023/12/27/business/media/new-york-times-open-ai-microsoft-lawsuit.html.

Mendez, Michael. *The Missing Link: An Introduction to Web Development and Programming* (Geneseo, NY: Published by Open SUNY Textbooks, Milne Library, State University of New York at Geneseo, 2014). https://torl.biblioboard.com/content/417626ca-ced4-4bad-8291-5f16e13e52e7

Michele I. Dalehite, "Vendor-Supplied Automated Authority Control: What It Is and How to Get It," *Law Library Journal* 81, no. 1 (1989) 117–130.
Michelle M. Wu, "Restoring the Balance of Copyright: Antitrust, Misuse, and Other Possible Paths to Challenge Inequitable Licensing Practices," *Law Library Journal* 114, no. 2 (Spring 2022): 131, 152–153.
Michelle M. Wu, "Why Print and Electronic Resources Are Essential to the Academic Law Library," *Law Library Journal* 97, no. 2 (Spring 2005): 233, 242.
Michelle Russen and Mary Dawson, "Which Should Come First? Examining Diversity, Equity and Inclusion," *International Journal of Contemporary Hospitality Management* 36 (2023): 27.
Microsoft Learn, "Understanding LLMs," May 9, 2024, https://learn.microsoft.com/en-us/ai/playbook/technology-guidance/generative-ai/getting-started/use-case-recommend.
Mona J. E. Danner, et al., *Using Focus Groups to Listen, Learn, and Lead in Higher Education*, 1st ed. (Sterling, VA: Routledge, 2018).
Morris L. Cohen, "President's Page: Technology and Law Librarianship," *Law Library Journal* 64, no. 2 (May 1974): 111–112.
Mousin Omar Saib, et al., "Digital Pedagogies for Libraries in Higher Education: A Systematic Review of Literature," *Information Discovery and Delivery* 51, no. 1 (2022): 13–25.
Mubashir Hassan, et al., "Innovations in Genomics and Big Data Analytics for Personalized Medicine and Health Care: A Review," *International Journal of Molecular Sciences* (April 22, 2022): 23, https://doi.org/10.3390/ijms23094645.
Nancy J. Campbell, *Writing Effective Policies and Procedures: A Step-by-Step Resource for Clear Communication* (New York: American Management Association, 1998).
Nathan A. Delmar, and Theresa K. Tarves, "Policy Development & Strategic Planning." In *Introduction to Law Librarianship*, edited by Zanada Joyner and Cas Laskowski, 49–62 (Tucson, AZ: Daniel F. Cracchiolo Law Library, 2021).
National Academies of Sciences, Engineering, and Medicine. *The Owner's Role in Project Risk Management* (Washington, DC: The National Academies Press, 2005). https://doi.org/10.17226/11183. 41.
National Conference of State Legislatures, *Artificial Intelligence 2024 Legislation* (Washington, DC, June 3, 2024), https://www.ncsl.org/technology-and-communication/artificial-intelligence-2024-legislation.
Nel Duffield and Jaime Royals, "The People Side of Change: Applying Change Management Principles in Academic Libraries," in *Chandos Information Professional Series, Technology, Change and the Academic Library*, ed. Jeremy Atkinson (Cambridge, MA: Chandos Publishing, 2021), 33–42, https://doi.org/10.1016/B978-0-12-822807-4.00003-8.
NELLCO, ALLStAR, https://www.nellco.org/page/allstar#:~:text=Allstar%20is%20NELLCO's%20data%2Dsharing,analyze%20data%20about%20their%20libraries.
New York State Bar Association. *Report and Recommendations of the New York State Bar Association Task Force on Advancing Diversity* (New York: New York State Bar Association, 2023).
Nonlawyer Assistance and 5.5: Unauthorized Practice of Law" in Center for Professional Responsibility (American Bar Association). 2013. "Model Rules of Professional Conduct." https://www.americanbar.org/groups/professional_responsibility/publications/model_rules_of_professional_conduct/.
Office for Access to Justice, "About ATJ," last updated March 5, 2024, https://www.justice.gov/atj/about-atj.
Oguz A. Acar, "AI Prompt Engineering Isn't the Future," *Harvard Business Review*, June 8, 2023, https://hbr.org/2023/06/ai-prompt-engineering-isnt-the-future.
OpenAI, "GPT-4," March 14, 2023, https://openai.com/index/gpt-4-research/.
OpenAI, "Introducing GPT-4O and More Tools to ChatGPT Free Users," accessed June 17, 2024, https://openai.com/index/gpt-4o-and-more-tools-to-chatgpt-free/.
OpenAI, "March 20 Chat GPT Outage: Here's What Happened," March 24, 2023, https://openai.com/index/march-20-chatgpt-outage/.

Orison S. Marden, "Equal Access to Justice--The Challenge and the Opportunity," *Washington and Lee Law Review* 19, no. 2 (1962): 153–164, https://heinonline.org/HOL/P?h=hein.journals/waslee19&i=159.
Oscar M. Trelles, "Automation in Law Libraries: The State of the Art," *Law Library Journal* 68, no. 3 (August 1975): 209–233.
"Overview," *Jenkins Law Library*, https://www.jenkinslaw.org/membership/overview.
Park v. Kim, No. 22-2057 (2d Cir. 2024).
Patrick J. Lynch and Sarah Horton, "Page Structure," in *Web Style Guide*, 4th ed. (New Haven, CT: Yale University Press, 2016), https://webstyleguide.com/6-page-structure.html.
Paul Bischoff, "A Recent History of US Government Breaches – Can You Trust Them with Your Data?," *Comparitech*, November 28, 2023, https://www.comparitech.com/blog/vpn-privacy/us-government-breaches/ [https://perma.cc/PU6C-4B3G].
Paul Hankin, "How Long Before People Trust AI More Than They Trust You?," *Legaltech® News*, April 22, 2024, https://www.law.com/legaltechnews/2024/04/22/how-long-before-people-trust-ai-more-than-they-trust-you/.
Paul Healey, *Uncertainty Management in Reference Interactions with Pro Se Law Library Users*, 2010, https://core.ac.uk/download/pdf/4826762.pdf, https://perma.cc/T7LH-CQ8R.
Paul W. Grimm, Maura R. Grossman, and Gordon V. Cormack, "Artificial Intelligence as Evidence," *Northwestern Journal of Technology and Intellectual Property* 19, no. 1 (2021): 9.
Paula M. Singer, with Gail Griffith, *Succession Planning in the Library: Developing Leaders, Managing Change* (New York: ALA, 2010).
Peggy Johnson, *Fundamentals of Collection Development and Management*, 2nd ed. (Chicago, IL: American Library Association, 2009).
Perplexity, "How Does Perplexity Work?," https://www.perplexity.ai/hub/faq/how-does-perplexity-work.
Perplexity, "What is Perplexity Pro?," https://www.perplexity.ai/hub/faq/what-is-perplexity-pro.
"Personal Identity Verification Card 101," IDManagement, https://www.idmanagement.gov/university/piv/ [https://perma.cc/L4ZZ-H3ZY].
Personal Information Protection Law of the People's Republic of China, arts.3, 51, updated December 29, 2021, http://en.npc.gov.cn.cdurl.cn/2021-12/29/c_694559.htm [https://perma.cc/68D4-AESC] (unofficial translation).
Peter Griffiths, *Managing Your Internet and Intranet Services: The Information and Library Professional's Guide to Strategy* (London: Library Association Publishing, 2000).
Peter Lloyd and Paula Boyle, *Web-Weaving: Intranets, Extranets and Strategic Alliances* (Woburn, MA: Butterworth-Heinemann, 1998).
Peter Nycum, "Looking Ahead--Law and the New Technology," *Law Library Journal* 64, no. 2 (May 1974): 123 ("The National Science Foundation is a sponsor of 17 different regional computing networks.").
Peter W. Martin, "Neutral Citation, Court Web Sites, and Access to Authoritative Case Law," *Law Library Journal* 99, no. 2 (Spring 2007) 329–330.
"Policies and Laws," *Law Library Journal* 81, no. 4 (Fall 1989): "State Privacy Laws Regarding Library Records," American Library Association, last updated November 2021, https://www.ala.org/advocacy/privacy/statelaws.
Provost & Chief Academic Officer, "Student Generative AI Usage Guidance," *UNC Chapel Hill*, February 13, 2024, https://provost.unc.edu/student-generative-ai-usage-guidance/.
Public.Resource.org., n.d., "Welcome to Public.Resource.Org!," https://public.resource.org/index.html, https://perma.cc/C5BP-YS3G.
Rachel Erb and Brian Erb, "The Use of Paraprofessionals in Electronic Resources Management: Results of a Survey," *The Journal of Academic Librarianship* 41, no. 4 (2015): 394–415, https://doi.org/10.1016/j.acalib.2015.05.006.

Rafael Ball, "Big Data and Their Impact on Libraries," *American Journal of Information Science and Technology* 3, no. 1 (2019): 2, https://doi.org/10.11648/j.ajist.20190301.11.
Ramishah Maruf, "Lawyer Apologizes for Fake Court Citations from ChatGPT," *CNN Business,* May 28, 2023, https://www.cnn.com/2023/05/27/business/chat-gpt-avianca-mata-lawyers/index.html.
Rebecca L. Sandefur, "Access to Civil Justice and Race, Class, and Gender Inequality," *Annual Review of Sociology* 34 (2008): 339–358, 344, https://www.jstor.org/stable/29737794.
Rebecca Plevel, "LibGuides: Circuit Riders: Basic Legal Research: Home," accessed June 11, 2024, https://guides.law.sc.edu/CircuitRiders/intro.
Region of Peel Archives, "Why Don't Archivists Digitize Everything?," *Peeling the Past*, May 31, 2017, https://peelarchivesblog.com/2017/05/31/why-dont-archivists-digitize-everything/.
Regulation 2016/679 of The European Parliament and of the Council of 27 April 2016 on the Protection of Natural Persons with Regard to the Processing of Personal Data and on the Free Movement of such Data (GDPR), 2016 O.J. (L 119), art. 5, https://eur-lex.europa.eu/legal-content/EN/TXT/PDF/?uri=CELEX:32016R0679.
Relativity, "Relativity Announces Expansions to Relativity Air Its Suite of Generative AI Solutions at Legalweek 2024," *PR Newswire*, January 29, 2024, https://www.prnewswire.com/news-releases/relativity-announces-expansions-to-relativity-air-its-suite-of-generative-ai-solutions-at-legalweek-2024-302046049.html.
Responsible AI in Legal Services, "About Rails," Llast updated April 2, 2024, Aaccessed onApril 10, 2024, https://rails.legal/about-rails/.
Responsible AI in Legal Services, "AI in Courts Tracker," lLast updated March 14, 2024, Aaccessed on April 10, 2024, https://airtable.com/appKUCriCQDI1BxIV/shrfIAPpNKaNMnacR/tblNmp6mff8CzLuQD.
Responsible AI in Legal Services, "AI Use in Courts Tracker," April 3, 2024, https://airtable.com/appKUCriCQDI1BxIV/shrfIAPpNKaNMnacR/tblNmp6mff8CzLuQD.
Rhonda Y. Kauffman and Martina S. Anderson, "Diversity, Inclusion, and Social Justice in Library Technical Services," in *Library Technical Services.* Adapting to a Changing Environment, ed. Stacey Marien, 213–236 (Purdue University Press, 2020), https://doi.org/10.2307/j.ctvs1g8h5.17.
Richard A. Danner, "From the Editor: Public Access to the Law," *Law Library Journal* 79, no. 2 (Spring 1987) 163.
Richard Zorza and David Udell, "New Roles For Non-Lawyers To Increase Access To Justice," *Fordham Urban Law Journal* 41, no. 4 (March 19, 2016): 1259, https://ir.lawnet.fordham.edu/ulj/vol41/iss4/8, https://perma.cc/7YRW-ZDNQ.
Rick Battle and Teja Gollapudi, "The Unreasonable Effectiveness of Eccentric Automatic Prompts," *arXiv.org*, February 20, 2024, https://arxiv.org/abs/2402.10949.
Rifqah Olufunmilayo Okunlaya, Norris Syed Abdullah, and Rose Alinda Alias, "Artificial Intelligence (AI) Library Services Innovative Conceptual Framework for the Digital Transformation of University Education," *Library Hi Tech* 40, no. 6 (2022): 1869.
Robert Ambrogi, "The Increasingly Essential Role of the Law Librarian," *Above the Law*, July 13, 2020, https://abovethelaw.com/2020/07/the-increasingly-essential-role-of-the-law-librarian/.
Robert D. Stueart and Barbara B. Moran, *Library and Information Center Management*, 7th ed. (Westport, CT: Libraries Unlimited, 2007).
Robert M. Fano, *Project MAC Progress Report V, July 1967-1968* (Cambridge, MA: Massachusetts Institute of Technology, 1968).
Robert T. Begg, "The Reference Librarian and the Pro Se Patron," *Law Library Journal* 69, no. 1 (1976): 26–32, https://heinonline.org/HOL/P?h=hein.journals/llj69&i=40).
Robert Iger, *The Ride of a Lifetime: Lessons Learned from 15 Years as CEO of the Walt Disney Company* (New York: Random House, 2019).
Robin K. Mills, "Reference Service vs. Legal Advice: Is It Possible to Draw the Line," *Law Library Journal* 72, no. 2 (1979): 179–193, https://heinonline.org/HOL/P?h=hein.journals/llj72&i=197.

Robyn Rebollo, "One More Look at Shepard's Citation Service: A Private Law Librarian's Perspective," *LLRX.com*, September 1, 1999, https://web.archive.org/web/20160321204657/http://www.llrx.com/features/shepards.htm.

Rory Van Loo, "The Missing Regulatory State: Monitoring Businesses in an Age of Surveillance," *Vanderbilt Law Review* 72, no. 5 (2019): 1563.

Rosemary Bodolay et al., "Moving from Co-location thelp_outlineo Cooperation to Collaboration: Redefining a Library's Role within the University," in Doherty, Brian, ed. *Space and Organizational Considerations in Academic Library Partnerships and Collaborations* (Hershey, PA: IGI Global, 2016).

Rudi Keller, "Missouri Appeals Court Fines Litigant after Finding Fake AI-Generated Cases Cited in Filings," *Missouri Independent*, February 13, 2024, https://missouriindependent.com/2024/02/13/missouri-appeals-court-fines-litigant-after-finding-fake-ai-generated-cases-cited-in-filings.

Sally Alexander, Mary Breighner, and Jeanne Drewes, eds. *Risk Management and Insurance Manual for Libraries* (ALA Editions: Core Publishing, 2021), https://alastore.ala.org/sites/default/files/book_samples/9780838948019_sample.pdf.

Sam Brooks, "Introduction: The Importance of Open Communication Between Libraries and Vendors." *Journal of Library Administration* 44, no. 3–4 (August 31, 2006): 1–4, https://doi.org/10.1300/J111v44n03_01.

Sam Cook, "US Schools Leaked 37.6 Million Records in 3,713 Data Breaches," *Comparitech*, May 14, 2024, https://www.comparitech.com/blog/vpn-privacy/us-schools-data-breaches/ [https://perma.cc/XL6J-9DVU].

Sandra Nelson and June Garcia for the Public Library Association, *Creating Policies for Results: From Chaos to Clarity* (Chicago, IL: American Library Association, 2003).

Sandra S. Nelson, June Garcia, and Public Library Association. *Creating Policies for Results: From Chaos to Clarity* (Chicago: American Library Association, 2003).

Sara Merken, "Legal AI Startup Donotpay Reaches Settlement in Customer Class Action," *Reuters*, June 6, 2024, https://www.reuters.com/legal/legalindustry/legal-ai-startup-donotpay-reaches-settlement-customer-class-action-2024-06-06.

Sara V. Pic, "Bridging the Gap between Public Libraries & Law Libraries to Improve Access to Justice," *AALL Spectrum* 25, no. 4 (March/April 2021): 20–23.

Sarah Martinson, "Judges and Law Scholars Divided Over AI Standing Orders," *Law360 Pulse,* March 22, 2024, https://www.law360.com/pulse/articles/1810715/judges-and-law-scholars-divided-over-ai-standing-orders.

Sarah Smith, "LibGuides: Screen Reading and Library Resources: A Guide for ADA Accessibility: Full List of Accessible Library Databases," accessed July 1, 2024, https://suffolk.libguides.com/c.php?g=654172&p=4590096.

Sawdah Bhaimiya, "Samsung Bans Employees from Using AI Tools like ChatGPT and Google Bard after an Accidental Data Leak Report Says," *Business Insider*, May 2, 2023, https://www.businessinsider.com/samsung-chatgpt-bard-data-leak-bans-employee-use-report-2023-5.

Scott Bennett, *Libraries Designed for Learning* (Washington, DC: Council on Library and Information Resources, 2003).

Scott Bennett, *Righting the Balance, in Library as Place: Rethinking Roles, Rethinking Space* (Washington, DC: Council on Library and Information Resources, 2005), II.

Scott F. Burson, "A Reconstruction of Thamus: Comments on the Evaluation of Legal Information Retrieval Systems," *Law Library Journal* 79, no. 1 (1987): 133–144.

Shanee Dawkins and Jody Jacobs, "NIST Phish Scale User Guide," NIST, November 2023, https://doi.org/10.6028/NIST.TN.2276.

Sheila S. Intner and Peggy Johnson, *Fundamentals of Technical Services Management* (Chicago, IL: American Library Association, 2008).

Sheilla E. Desert, "WESTLAW Is Natural v. Boolean Searching: A Performance Study," *Law Library Journal* 85, no. 4 (1993): 713

Shlomit Yanisky-Ravid, "Generating Rembrandt: Artificial Intelligence, Copyright, and Accountability in the 3A Era: The Human-like Authors Are Already Here: A New Model," *Michigan State Law Review* 2017, no. 4 (2017): 659.

South David Saffo Laura, Olga Vitek, Cody Dunne, and Michelle A. Borkin, "Effective Use of Likert Scales in Visualization Evaluations: A Systematic Review," *Computer Graphics Forum* 41, no. 3 (2022): 43–55.

Stanford University Human Centered Artificial Intelligence, "Artificial Intelligence Index Report 2024," 64, https://aiindex.stanford.edu/wp-content/uploads/2024/04/HAI_AI-Index-Report-2024.pdf.

State of New Jersey, "Interim Guidance on Responsible Use of Generative AI," 2023, https://www.nj.gov/circulars/23-oit-007.pdf.

Stefan Baack, "A Critical Analysis of the Largest Source for Generative AI Training Data: Common Crawl," in *FAccT '24: Proceedings of the 2024 ACM Conference on Fairness, Accountability, and Transparency*, June 2024, pp. 2199–2208, https://doi.org/10.1145/3630106.3659033.

Stefan Feurriegel, Jochen Hartmann, Christian Janiesch, and Patrick Zschech, "Generative AI," *Business & Information Systems Engineering* 66, no. 1 (September 12, 2023), https://link.springer.com/content/pdf/10.1007/s12599-023-00834-7.pdf.

Stephanie Farne, "Information Literacy: A Path Forward for AI Legal Research?," *RIPS Law Librarian Blog*, June 25, 2024, https://ripslawlibrarian.wordpress.com/2024/06/25/information-literacy-a-path-forward-for-ai-legal-research/.

Steve Lastres, "Law Libraries ... By the Numbers: Demonstrate the Value of Your Library to Drive Optimal Legal Services," AALL Digital White Paper. Defining ROI: Law Library Best Practices, 2016, https://www.aallnet.org/wp-content/uploads/2016/01/AALL-ROI-Whitepaper-2016_FINAL.pdf.

Steven Bell, Lorcan Dempsey, Barbara Fister, and Nancy Allen, eds., "New Roles for the Road Ahead: Essays Commissioned for ACRL's 75th Anniversary," Association of Research Libraries, Chicago, IL, 2015, https://alair.ala.org/bitstream/handle/11213/17196/new_roles_75th.pdf?sequence=1&isAllowed=y.

Steven P. Anderson, "ROI for Government Law Libraries," AALL Digital White Paper. Defining ROI: Law Library Best Practices, 2016, https://www.aallnet.org/wp-content/uploads/2016/01/AALL-ROI-Whitepaper-2016_FINAL.pdf.

Students for Fair Admissions, Inc. v. President & Fellows of Harvard Coll., 600 U.S. 181 (2023).

Subject Cataloger, accessed June 17, 2024, https://chatgpt.com/g/g-Eg4pSebTH-subject-cataloger.

Supreme Court of the United States, "Building Features," n.d., https://www.supremecourt.gov/about/buildingfeatures.aspx, https://perma.cc/W79U-UM8X.

Survey on the usage of chat reference among academic law libraries in 2022, Jingwei Zhang, Survey of chat reference ABA Law Schools (updated 08_2022), https://doi.org/10.7282/00000413.

Susan Gaultier, Teresa Miguel-Stearns, Sarah Ryan, and Fang Wang, "More than a Bunch of Old Books: Perspectives from Rare Book School," *AALL Spectrum* 19, no. 5 (March 2015) 27.

Susanne Markgren, "Challenging the Status Quo," in *Library Technical Services*, ed. Stacey Marien, 295–308. Adapting to a Changing Environment. Purdue University Press, 2020, https://doi.org/10.2307/j.ctvs1g8h5.22.

Suzanne L. Sager, "Library Support Staff Today and How it Has Changed," *OLA Quarterly* 20, no. 3 (2014): 4–6, https://doi.org/10.7710/1093-7374.1768.

Syd Stephenson, "Government/Non-Profit Law Library Website Survey Data," https://scholarship.law.okcu.edu/work/ns/bfe58409-eb2e-4040-9972-39bcf8406d69.

Tan Wen Sze, Lim Chee Kiam, and Chow Ying Yi, "You May Like—How the National Library Board of Singapore Use Machine Learning to Recommend Books," *Trends in Issues in Library Technology, Special Big Data Issue* (January 2022): 14.

Tasha Squires, *Library Partnerships: Making Connections Between School and Public Libraries* (Medford, OR: Information Today, Inc., 2009).

Tatyana Monnay, "Conservative Duo Fights Against DEI One Bias Claim at a Time," *Bloomberg Law News*, June 4, 2024.
Tatyana Monnay, "Law Firms Boost Diversity Defenses After Conservative Backlash," *Bloomberg Law News*, March 22, 2024.
Tawnya K. Plumb, "Access to Justice in the Age of AI," in *Law Librarianship in the Age of AI*, ed. E. Kroski (Chicago, IL: ALA Editions, 2019), 125.
Tawnya K. Plumb, "Legal Research on the Road," video, 35:04, 35:24, March 2, 2022, https://drive.google.com/file/d/1am_McX-Jhc2qFwWcRRowf_VLioz4UB5O/view.
Teresa M. Miguel-Stearns and Casandra Laskowski, "Democratizing Law Librarianship: Reducing Barriers to Entry through Alternative Pathways to the Profession and Increased Support to Students. A Call to Action," *Legal Reference Services Quarterly* 43, no. 1–2 (April 2, 2024): 104–135, https://doi.org/10.1080/0270319X.2024.2331867.
Teresa M. Miguel-Stearns, Zanada Joyner, Cas Laskowski, Aamir Shahnawaz Abdullah, Kaylan Ellis, Heather J. E. Simmons, Susan David deMaine, et al. Introduction to Law Librarianship. Creative Commons Attribution 4.0 International License, except where otherwise noted: 2021. https://pressbooks.pub/app/uploads/sites/4509/2021/07/Introduction-to-Law-Librarianship-20210920.pdf.
Teresa M. Miguel-Stearns and Casandra Laskowski, "Democratizing Law Librarianship: Reducing Barriers to Entry through Alternative Pathways to the Profession and Increased Support to Students. A Call to Action," *Legal Reference Services Quarterly* 43, no. 1–2 (April 2, 2024): 104–135, https://doi.org/10.1080/0270319X.2024.2331867.
Teresa M. Miguel-Stearns and Sarah E. Ryan, "The Empirical Research Law Librarian Part 1: Making the Case and Filling the Role," *Trends in Law Library Management & Technology* 24, no. 1 (2014): 1.
Terrill Pollman, Jeanne Frazier Price, and Linda L. Berger, *Legal Research Examples & Explanations* (New York: Wolters Kluwer, 2017), 129.
The 62 Books People in Power Found Essential This Year, https://www.bloomberg.com/news/newsletters/2023-12-14/best-books-of-2023-picked-by-ceos-and-wall-street-leaders.
The ACRL Racial and Ethnic Diversity Committee, "Diversity Standards: Cultural Competency for Academic Librarians: Approved by the ACRL Board of Directors, April 2012," *College & Research Libraries News* 73, no. 9 (October 1, 2012) 551-561.
The Council of State Governments, *Artificial Intelligence in the States: Emerging Legislation* (Washington, DC, December 6, 2023), https://www.csg.org/2023/12/06/artificial-intelligence-in-the-states-emerging-legislation/.
The Library's Legal Answer Book (Chicago, IL: American Library Association, 2003).
The NILL, https://www.narf.org/nill/triballaw/us/nsn/mohican/council/index.html.
The NIST Cybersecurity Framework (CSF) 2.0, National Institute of Standards and Technology, February 26, 2024, https://doi.org/10.6028/NIST.CSWP.29.
The Seattle Public Library, "Statement on Ransomware Event Impacting Library Services," *Shelf Talk Blog*, May 28, 2024, https://shelftalkblog.wordpress.com/statement/ [https://perma.cc/F54P-HH6D].
The Stockbridge Munsee Community's tribal code can be viewed on their own website (built in partnership with the Open Law Library), https://law.mohican.com/us/nsn/mohican/council/code.
The UW Law Library, https://repository.law.wisc.edu/s/uwlaw/page/tribal-law.
"The Wisconsin Briefs Collection," University of Wisconsin Law School, https://repository.law.wisc.edu/s/uwlaw/page/wisconsin-briefs.
Thomas Sneed, "The Effect of COVID-19 on Law Libraries: Are These Changes Temporary or a Sign of the Future?," *Washburn Law Journal* 60, no. 1 (2020): 107–129, 111.
Thomson Reuters, "Westlaw Precision Now Has Generative AI," *Thomson Reuters*, accessed June 22, 2024, https://legal.thomsonreuters.com/en/c/westlaw/westlaw-precision-now-with-generative-ai.
Todd J. Clark, "Reversing DEI: The Consequence – "IED" Indoctrination and Elimination of Diversity," *University of Toledo Law Review* 55, no. 2 (Winter 2024): 169–194, 175.

Tom Chrisp and Stuart Macdonald, "Acknowledging the Purpose of Partnership," *Journal of Business Ethics* 59, no. 4 (July 2005): 307–371, https://doi.org/10.1007/s10551-004-3235-5.
Tomas A. Lipinski, ed., *Libraries, Museums, and Archives: Legal Issues and Ethical Challenges in the New Information Era* (Lanham, MD: Scarecrow Press, 2002).
Trudi Bellardo Hahn, "Pioneers of the Online Age," *Information Processing & Management* 32, no. 1 (1996) 33–48.
Tyson Greer, *Understanding Intranets* (Redmond, WA: Microsoft Press, 1998).
U.S. District Court for the Eastern District of Pennsylvania, *Standing Order Re: Artificial Intelligence ("AI") In Cases Assigned to Judge Baylson*, June 6, 2023, https://www.paed.uscourts.gov/sites/paed/files/documents/procedures/Standing%2520Order%2520Re%2520Artificial%2520Intelligence%25206.6.pdf.
UNC-Chapel Hill Law Libraries, "On the Books: Jim Crow and the Algorithms of Resistance," https://onthebooks.lib.unc.edu/.
University of North Texas Libraries, "Leveraging Existing Bibliographic Metadata," 1.
University of Washington School of Law, "Honor Code," UW School of Law - Academic Policies, https://www.law.washington.edu/students/academics/honorcode.aspx.
Ursula Gorham and Paul T. Jaeger, "The Law School Library or the Library at the Law School: How Lessons from Other Types of Libraries Can Inform the Evolution of the Academic Law Library in the Digital Age," *Law Library Journal* 109, no. 1 (Winter 2017): 60–65.
Varun Magesh, Faiz Surani, Matthew Dahl, Mirac Suzgun, Christopher D. Manning, and Daniel E. Ho, "Hallucination-Free? Assessing the Reliability Leading AI Legal Research Tools," May 30, 2024, https://dho.stanford.edu/wp-content/uploads/Legal_RAG_Hallucinations.pdf.
Vicki L. Gregory, *Collection Development and Management For 21st Century Library Collections: An Introduction*, 2nd ed. (Chicago, IL: ALA Neal-Schuman, 2019).
Victor D. Quintanilla, Kurt Hugenberg, Ryan Hutchings, and Nedim Yel, "Accessing Justice with Zoom: Experiences and Outcomes in Online Civil Courts," 2023, https://law.indiana.edu/research/Accessing-Justice-with-Zoom-Experiences-and-Outcomes-in-Online-Civil-Courts-October-2023.pdf, https://perma.cc/WH2N-Q946.
Virginia Association of Law Libraries Access to Justice Committee, "Guide to Virginia Legal Information Resources," October 2, 2023, https://www.vacourts.gov/courtadmin/library/virginia_legal_information_resources.pdf, https://web.archive.org/web/20240416201821/https://www.vacourts.gov/courtadmin/library/virginia_legal_information_resources.pdf.
Vishnu Pendyala, *Veracity of Big Data: Machine Learning and Other Approaches to Verifying Truthfulness* (San Jose, CA: Apress, 2018), 5–9.
W. Michael Schuster, "Artificial Intelligence and Patent Ownership," *Washington and Lee Law Review* 75, no. 4 (Fall 2018): 1945.
Ward, Latia, "What Can Librarians Do to Facilitate Access to Justice," *YouTube Video*, June 6, 2019, https://www.youtube.com/watch?v=vbsr8WshRcU, https://web.archive.org/web/20200603063928/https://www.youtube.com/watch?v=vbsr8WshRcU.
Washington Council of Lawyers, "Best Practices in Pro Bono: The Role of Artificial Intelligence in Pro Bono and Access to Justice," event held on May 23, 2024, at Fried Frank, Washington, D.C., https://wclawyers.org/240523/.
Wendi Arant and Brian Carpenter, "Where is the Line? Legal Reference Service and the Unauthorized Practice of Law (UPL)—Some Guides That Might Help," *Reference & User Services Quarterly* 38, no. 3 (Spring 1999): 235–239.
Wilding, "Figure 11-1, 11-2, 11-3," 3, https://archive.org/details/figures-11-1-11-2-11-3-color-law-librarianship-practice.
Wilhelmina Randtke, "Long Term Financial Costs of Maintaining a Digital Collection," *Technical Services Law Librarian* 43, no. 3 (March 2018): 11, 12.
William J. Rothwell, *Effective Succession Planning* (New York: Amacom, 2010).

William Morriss, "Who Owns AI Created Content? The Surprising Answer and What to Do about It," *Reuters*, December 14, 2023, https://www.reuters.com/legal/legalindustry/who-owns-ai-created-content-surprising-answer-what-do-about-it-2023-12-14/.

William R. Fair, "The Corporate CIA—A Prediction of Things to Come," *Management Science* 12, no. 10 (June 1, 1966): B-503, https://doi.org/10.1287/mnsc.12.10.b489.

Young Sam Cho, "From Code to Cure: Unleashing the Power of Generative Artificial Intelligence in Medicine," *International Neurourology Journal* 27, no. 4 (December 2023): 225–226, https://doi.org/10.5213/inj.2323edi06.

Yumin Jiang and Georgia Briscoe, "The Wise Researcher: One Library's Experience Implementing a Federated Search Product," *AALL Spectrum,* November 2008.

Ziwei Xu, Sanjay Jain, and Mohan Kankanhalli, "Hallucination Is Inevitable: An Innate Limitation of Large Language Models," *arXiv.org*, January 22, 2024, https://arxiv.org/abs/2401.11817.

Index

About the Editor

Ellyssa Kroski is the Director of Innovation & Engagement at the New York Law Institute and an award-winning editor and author of seventy-seven books, showcasing her vast expertise in the library and information science field. As an adjunct faculty member at San Jose State University and a celebrated international conference speaker, Kroski is known for her insights into innovation and technology within librarianship. Her contributions extend beyond her leadership roles, influencing both the academic and professional spheres. Discover more about her work at http://www.amazon.com/author/ellyssa, where her publications reflect her dedication to advancing the library profession.

About the Contributors

Erik Adams is the Director of Library Digital Technology at Sidley Austin and Chief of Technology of Golden Arrow Publishing. He has more than twenty years' experience working in law firms and high-tech startups. He contributed a chapter to the book *Law Librarianship in the Age of AI*, is a co-author of the AALL Spectrum article "DIY Analytics: Beyond Excel," and has spoken at several conferences on the use of technology in law libraries. He is a dot-com survivor, having worked for several years at the kinds of companies that had a foosball table in the break room. He received his master's in Library and Information Science from UCLA back when gopher was more popular than www.

Crystal Alberthal is the Head of Collections, Resource & Information Management at the University of Washington Gallagher Law Library. In her current role, she oversees Technical Services, Circulation, and Collections, managing the entire acquisition-to-discovery lifecycle, including budget management, licensing, contract negotiations, and related privacy considerations. Crystal actively participates in professional organizations such as American Association of Law Libraries (AALL), LLOPS, NASIG, and New England Law Library Consortium (NELLCO), volunteers on committees and task forces for these organizations, and contributes to the professional discourse through presentations and publications.

Scott Bailey is the Director of Research & Knowledge Services at Eversheds Sutherland. There are five guiding values, and Scott is building a service that resonates with them: Collaborative, Creative, Professional, Inclusive, and Open. As a champion of success through authentic intelligence and building a knowledge community, Scott is one of those people who works collaboratively with a variety of professionals within and beyond the legal industry. He believes in creatively fostering situations where aligning the right people, data, and resources leads to multiplied value for everyone involved. Scott shares actively by publishing and exploring AI, legal research, and knowledge at the American Association of Law Libraries and other conferences. He recently moved to Moon, Virginia, by the Chesapeake Bay with his family and is possibly contemplating chickens.

Iain Barksdale is the Law Technology Services Librarian at the Bounds Law Library at the University of Alabama School of Law. Iain manages library technology and assists with reference and research requests from all our patron groups. He served as Electronic Services Librarian for the Rogers College of Law at the University of Arizona, and as the Assistant Director for Information Technology and Assistant Professor of Library Services at the Chase College of Law, as well as Adjunct Professor of History and Anthropology at Northern Kentucky University.

He received his BA in Anthropology and Psychology from the University of California at Santa Barbara, his MPhil in Archaeology from the University of Glasgow, his JD from the Louis D. Brandeis School of Law at the University of Louisville, and his master's in Information Resources and Library Science from the University of Arizona.

Susan Boland is the Associate Director for the University of Cincinnati Robert S. Marx Law Library. She teaches legal research, offers reference and research support services to all law library users, and is responsible for the library's online presence. Prior to joining the University of Cincinnati, she was the Head of Information Services for the Ruth Lilly Law Library at the Robert H. McKinney School of Law and the Research & Instructional Services librarian at Northern Illinois University College of Law, where she also served as webmaster for the law school. She has also held positions at a public library and community college library and served as a judicial clerk for the Iowa District Court for the Fifth Judicial District. She is a member of various professional associations both regionally and nationally and served as Chair of the Computing Services Special Interest Section of the American Association of Law Libraries (now known as the Legal Innovation & Technology Special Interest Society) and President of the Mid-America Association of Law Libraries. She has presented at regional and national conferences, as well as at continuing legal education programs. Her publications include annotated bibliographies on the death penalty and election law, as well as articles on legal research, technology, and teaching.

Don Boman is currently the Research & Knowledge Resources Manager at Skadden, Arps, Slate, Meagher & Flom in New York. Originally from Mobile, AL, he graduated from The University of Southern Mississippi with a bachelor's degree in Journalism and a master's in Library and Information Science. He has worked in various legal and non-legal library technical services, research, and knowledge management positions. He lives in Brooklyn, NY.

Kenton Brice is the Director of the Law Library and Associate Professor of Law at the University of Oklahoma College of Law. After practicing law for six years, he began his academic career at OU Law in 2015 as the Law Library's first Digital Resources Librarian before becoming the college's first director of Technology Innovation in 2017. With a focus on building and expanding the College-Wide Digital Initiative, he created the OU Law Center for Technology & Innovation in Practice, establishing OU Law as a leader in innovation in legal education. Thanks to Kenton's efforts, the college was the first law school in the world to receive the Apple Distinguished School award and has been listed as in Top 20 Most Innovative Law Schools multiple times. Kenton has a BBA in Marketing from Northeastern State University, a JD from the University of Oklahoma, and a master's in Science in Library Science from the University of North Texas. Kenton is a member of the 2018 class of the Fastcase 50, a former member of the Texas Bar's Pro Bono College, a former Texas Appellate Lawyer of the Week, a member of the Order of Barristers, a founding member of the Northeastern State University Rugby Team, and an avid woodworker.

Marcia L. Burris is a distinguished leader in the field of law librarianship, with over thirty years of experience in managing and optimizing library services within prominent law firms. Currently serving as the Director of Research and Knowledge Management at Womble Bond Dickinson (US) LLP, Marcia has a proven track record of aligning knowledge services with organizational goals, implementing innovative technology solutions, and leading strategic initiatives to improve service delivery and efficiency. Marcia is committed to the advancement of law librarianship and has been recognized for her innovative contributions. An active member of the American Association of Law Libraries and the Private Law Librarians & Information Professionals Special Interest Section, she has held various leadership roles and served on numerous committees within AALL and PLLIP-SIS. Marcia aspires to foster the professional growth of others and actively mentors emerging professionals in the field, as well as presenting frequently on topics related to law librarianship and knowledge management.

Amy Carr has worked in diverse library and library-adjacent settings for over twenty-five years, including law firms, public institutions, academic libraries, and legal tech. She's currently the Senior

Manager of Knowledge Management at Bowman and Brooke LLP. She's a solo librarian responsible for all aspects of research and knowledge management at the firm.

Amy has been a speaker or has moderated sessions on a number of topics—remote work, orientation and onboarding, developing your leadership potential, and, most recently, succession planning. She's actively involved in her local AALL chapter, LLAGNY, where she serves on both the Corporate Sponsorship and Membership committees. Amy has a BA in Sociology from Oklahoma State University and an MLIS from the University of Pittsburgh.

Jim Curie has over twenty years of experience in corporate and law firm competitive intelligence and has been CI Manager at Norton Rose Fulbright since 2013. Jim has been a featured speaker on several panels and webinars, including sessions such as How to Write a Useful CI Report (PLLIP-SIS), Law Firm AI and CI: A Conversation (PLLIP-SIS), and Applying Ethics and the Code of Professional Responsibility to Research (ARK Group). In addition to his MBA from NYU Stern, Jim holds a BA in Philosophy from Binghamton University, where he specialized in the philosophy of artificial intelligence. Jim currently serves as Vice-President/President-elect of LLAGNY, the Law Library Association of Greater New York.

Suzanne Miner Darais is the Director of the James E. Faust Law Library at the University of Utah S. J. Quinney College of Law and Associate Dean of University Libraries. She received her BS from the University of Utah, her JD from Brigham Young University Law School, and her MLS from the University of Washington. Professor Darais is admitted to the bar in Utah and is an active member of the American Association of Law Libraries (AALL). She teaches basic and advanced legal research courses as a professor at the College of Law and has published and presented on multiple topics, including legal research, formative assessment hacks, and using games to enhance active learning in the classroom.

John J. DiGilio is an accomplished legal information professional, educator, and advocate. He is also an award-winning author in the fields of legal research and law librarianship. Currently the Firmwide Director of Library Services at Sidley Austin LLP, John has held roles at Reed Smith, K&L Gates, Thomson Reuters, and Carlow University. As an information professional, John has received numerous awards and recognition over the years for his work as an author and speaker. In his teaching capacity, he has designed and delivered undergraduate and graduate courses in business law, e-commerce, ethics, fair employment practices, and applied research methodologies. John received his MLIS from the University of Pittsburgh and was awarded a JD by Pepperdine University School of Law. He is currently serving as President of the Special Libraries Association (2024), where he has also been named a fellow.

Josh Farley is Senior Competitive Intelligence Coordinator at Norton Rose Fulbright U.S. LLP. He holds a Bachelor of Arts from The Ohio State University and is currently pursuing a master's degree in information science. Beyond his professional and academic commitments, Josh volunteers as a Court Appointed Special Advocate (CASA) for CASA of Galveston County, serving as a member of the Legislative Advocacy Team, Youth Rights Committee, and advocating for children brought before the court for reasons of abuse, neglect, or refusal to accept parental responsibility. Additionally, Josh is the author of "The Thinker and the Doer," published in AALL Spectrum, January/February 2024.

Debbie Ginsberg is the Faculty Services Manager at Harvard Law School Library, where she supervises faculty research and scholarship support. She joined Harvard in 2021 after working at Chicago-Kent College of Law, where she served as an Educational Technology Librarian. Debbie has a BA from Brown University, a BFA from the Art Institute of Chicago, a JD from the University of Illinois, Urbana-Champaign, and an MLIS from Dominican University. She is active in AALL and her local law library organization. Her research interests include AI's effects on legal research, the intersection of blockchain, the law, and AI, and leveraging technology as an efficient and effective law librarian.

Monique Gonzalez, JD, MLIS, is currently the Assistant Dean and Director for Library and Information Technology Services at Paul M. Herbert Law Center, Louisiana State University, where she oversees the law library, information technology services, and instructional technology, as well as teaches in the legal research program. She holds a master's in Library and Information Science degree from the University of North Texas and a Juris Doctor from Thurgood Marshall School of Law, Texas Southern University. Her experience as both an attorney and law librarian brings a unique perspective to law librarianship. Having served as a law librarian in both law firm and academic settings, she has become well-regarded for her practical approach to teaching and the innovative use of technology. Her contributions to the field extend beyond her professional role. She was most recently President of Houston Area Law Librarians (HALL), her local professional association. She is also an active member of the American Association of Law Librarians (AALL), where she has been appointed to several key committees such as the Committee on Vendor Relations, Council of Chapter Presidents, and the State of the Profession Report Committee. She hopes to continue to inspire and lead in the ever-evolving landscape of legal information management, advocate for the integration of cutting-edge technology in legal education, and provide the highest level of service.

Rachel Gordon is the Director of Library Services and Lecturer in Legal Research at the Lillian Goldman Law Library at Yale Law School. Ms. Gordon has a JD from the University of Tennessee, an MBA from Mercer University, an MLS from Drexel University, and BAs in International Studies, and Diplomacy and Foreign Affairs from Miami University. Ms. Gordon was formerly the Associate Director for Public Services and Senior Lecturing Fellow at the J. Michael Goodson Law Library at Duke Law School. She has more than twenty years' experience teaching legal research, and her writing has been published in monographs, the *Tennessee Law Review*, *Transactions: The Tennessee Journal of Business Law*, *Public Services Quarterly*, and *AALL Spectrum*.

Holly Grimes is the Circulation Librarian for the Alabama Supreme Court & State Law Library. She has been in this position for 2.5 years, beginning in October 2021. She has a master's in Library and Information Sciences with a concentration in archives from the University of Alabama and a Bachelor of Arts in History from the University of Montevallo.

Justin Huckaby is the Director of the Law Library and Assistant Professor of Law at the University of Mississippi Grisham Law Library in Oxford, Mississippi. He received his Doctor of Jurisprudence from Mississippi College School of Law. Huckaby graduated with his Bachelor of Arts in Religious Studies and Music from Millsaps College and his Master of Science in Library and Information Science from Drexel University. He teaches within the legal research curriculum, focusing on Advanced Legal Research and International Legal Research. He also teaches Professional Identity Formation within the first-year curriculum. Prior to joining the University of Mississippi School of Law, Huckaby served as a teaching librarian and the Director of the Judicial Data Project and the Legislative History Project at Mississippi College School of Law. Huckaby's research focuses on legal research pedagogy regarding the integration of bibliographic instruction with process learning as well as the legislative process. He has actively participated in numerous professional organizations, including serving as the National Chair of the American Association of Law Libraries Committee on Continuing Status and Tenure.

Phebe Huderson-Poydras is the Director of library services and serves on the faculty at the Southern University Law Center, where she is responsible for the overall management of the library and its staff. She has taught Professionalism, Advanced Legal Research, Advanced Legal Writing, Legal Research, Legal Bibliography, and Legal Methods. Poydras received a master's in education with a concentration in Higher Education Administration in 2024 from Louisiana State University, a master's in Library and Information Science from Louisiana State University in 1998, and a Juris Doctor from the Southern University Law Center in 1995.

Rebecca Katz is a lawyer and information professional with a commitment to using her skills to make society better and a specific passion for access to justice. Prior to founding JusticeAccess, a nonprofit law library based in Washington, DC, she was a member of the Harvard Legal Aid Bureau, a staff attorney for University Legal Services, and state archivist for the District of Columbia. She earned her undergraduate degree from Washington University, her law degree from Harvard Law School, and her library degree from Catholic University of America.

Nicholas Lamb is the Information Research Specialist in Learning Technology at Baker Library, Harvard Business School, specializing in library instruction. Over the years, Nicholas has worked in academic, corporate, and special libraries. He studied Classical Studies at Harvard College, the University of Oxford, and Columbia University. He also studied law, receiving his law degree from the College of William and Mary School of Law. He enjoys writing, blogging, occasionally making artworks inspired by his love of the Mediterranean, as well as keeping in touch with friends and colleagues.

Cas Laskowski is a veteran, librarian, gamer, teacher, Latina, techie, comic book nerd, and empiricist in perpetual beta. Currently the Head of Research, Data, & Instruction at the University of Arizona, she regularly engages in AI initiatives nationally. She was a founding fellow of the University of Tennessee Library's inaugural IDEA Institute on Artificial Intelligence and the only librarian of any type to be selected for the 2022 Summer Conference on Applied Data Science at North Carolina State University, where she leveraged machine learning summarization methods to design a prototype system that would aid intelligence analysts in efficiently identifying relevant audio files.

She is currently a member of the AI and Access to Justice Subgroup of the Arizona Steering Committee on Artificial Intelligence and the Courts, a member of the University Libraries AI Working Group, and co-lead of the Making AI Generative for Higher Education UA steering committee team, a national two-year cross-institution research project with Ithaka S+R. She previously co-led two teams for the University's AI Access and Integrity Working Group. She is also pursuing her PhD in Information at the University of Arizona, focusing on legal information infrastructures.

Sheri Lewis has worked as a librarian in law schools for over thirty years. Spending most of her career as a library manager, she has been the Director of the D'Angelo Law Library and a Lecturer in Law at the University of Chicago Law School since 2013. Ms. Lewis holds a Bachelor of Arts from Northwestern University, a Juris Doctor from New York University School of Law, and a Master of Library and Information Science from Rosary College (now Dominican University).

Malika Lipscomb is a Research & Training Librarian at Fisher Phillips, LLP. She obtained a Bachelor of Arts degree in English from Brooklyn College at the City University of New York (CUNY) and a master's degree in Library Science from Queens College (CUNY). Malika began her library career as a part-timer at the Brooklyn Public Library, where she also held roles as Office Administrator and Technology Resource Specialist. She briefly worked as Systems Administrator in an academic library (The New School) before becoming Electronic Resources and Acquisitions Librarian at a global Am Law 100 firm. After relocating to Raleigh, North Carolina, in 2022, Malika now works remotely and enjoys spending time with family and traveling.

Kerry Lohmeier is the Associate Dean of Library and Information Services and an assistant professor at the University of Akron School of Law. Before joining Akron Law, she served as a librarian and adjunct faculty member at the University of Utah College of Law and as a librarian and assistant professor at Concordia University School of Law. She received her BS from Iowa State University, her JD with distinction from the University of Iowa College of Law, and her MS from the University of Tennessee-Knoxville. Dean Lohmeier is admitted to the bar in New Mexico and is an active member of the American Association of Law Libraries. She teaches classes on legal research, foreign and international research, technology, and administrative law. She has published and presented on topics related to legal research, formative assessments, using games to enhance active learning, and teaching asynchronous courses.

Pearl McCrea is the Collection Management Librarian at the University of Washington Gallagher Law Library. Holding a Master of Library and Information Science degree from the University of Washington Information School, Pearl plays a pivotal role in shaping the law library's strategic direction. She oversees collection development, acquisitions, archival digitization, and resource sharing, emphasizing the modernization of workflows and enhancing library operations through collaboration with vendor partners. Pearl's dedication to access to justice and open access is evident in her leadership of the law library's recent project to digitize court briefs related to the Boldt Decision, making these documents freely accessible to support legal research, education, and public understanding. Her insights are invaluable in discussions on integrating technology in law libraries and promoting transparency and access to information.

Kristen Naik has an MLIS from Simmons University. Over the past decade, she has worked in a variety of library institutions, primarily focusing on digital resources, technologies, and data analytics. As part of these duties, Kristen completed the IMLS-funded CARLI Counts program, where she received in-depth training on data gathering, analytics, and advocacy in the context of academic libraries. In her current role at Sidley Austin LLP, Kristen gathers, refines, analyzes, and presents data to various departments within the firm. Her work also includes data visualizations, automation of data processes, and ad hoc data analytics. In addition to her work with data, she also assesses and implements new technologies, including intranets, artificial intelligence, and other emerging technologies.

Michelle Rodenburg is the Law and Technology Librarian at the Kathrine R. Everett Law Library at the University of North Carolina at Chapel Hill School of Law. She teaches the Law Practice Technologies course and manages the law library's electronic databases. Michelle earned her law degree from the University of Minnesota, her MIS from Florida State University, and her BA in anthropology from Florida Gulf Coast University. She is licensed to practice law in North Carolina, Minnesota, Florida, Pennsylvania, and New York.

Abigail Ellsworth Ross is an information professional, professor, and author with over twenty-five years of professional legal research and management experience. She is the Founder and Principal of RoFinCo, LLC, a legal and corporate research and library management company in Washington, DC. RoFinCo, LLC, helps firms and companies leverage legal, financial, competitive intelligence, industry, and expert witness data in their research analysis projects. Her sophisticated research services to administrators and librarians change a perceived black hole of revenue into a tool that demonstrates meaningful ROI for every organization. Information is power, and RoFinCo, LLC, leads the pack. Ross speaks regularly at conferences and events across the country, including the American Association of Law Libraries and Special Libraries Association. She is an adjunct professor at Catholic University and a regular guest lecturer at George Mason University School of Law. Ross holds a Master of Library Science from the University of Maryland and a BSLA from Georgetown University.

Sarah Ryan is the Director of the Law Librarianship program at the University of North Texas. She previously served as the Head of Empirical Legal Research Services at Yale Law School. Sarah serves on the editorial board for the *Law Library Journal* and on the AALL Scholarship Awards Jury. In 2018–19, she clerked for Hon. Victor A. Bolden (D. Conn). In 2020–2021, Sarah's article on judicial resentencing authority under the First Step Act was cited in briefs to the Supreme Court and reported in *The New York Times*. Sarah's previous scholarship includes articles in law librarianship and social science journals and a co-edited book, *Dialogues Across Diasporas: Women Writers, Scholars, and Activists of Africana and Latina Descent in Conversation*.

Sabrina Sondhi became a law librarian in 2008. She has worked at Columbia Law School, Fordham Law School, and Cornell Law School, and has been the Director of the Law Library and a Professor of Legal Research at Penn State Dickinson Law since 2021. Sabrina has been the Chair of AALL's Academic Law Libraries Section, served on several strategic planning committees, and co-chaired LLAGNY's Education Committee with Amy Carr. She has spoken on or moderated sessions on a number of topics, including capturing institutional knowledge and succession planning. Sabrina received her JD from Cornell Law School and her MLIS from the University of Washington. Prior to becoming a librarian, she worked as a litigator in California.

Syd Stephenson (they/them) is the Electronic Services & Systems Librarian and a guest lecturer at Oklahoma City University School of Law. They received their MLIS from the University of Oklahoma in 2022, as well as a Bachelor of Arts in LGBTQ+ Studies from the University of Oklahoma in 2020. They have worked in academic libraries for six years. They are an active member of the American Association of Law Libraries and the Oklahoma Library Association.

Victoria Swindle is the Library Technology Specialist at Steptoe & Johnson PLLC, where she handles research cost recovery, account creation, the library catalog, and technology support. She earned a Bachelor's Degree in Information Science with minors in Museum Studies and English Literature (2021) and a Master's in Library and Information Science (2022), both from the University of Pittsburgh. Victoria is the President of the Western Pennsylvania Law Librarian Association (WPLLA) and a writer for the AALL's Legal Innovation & Technology SIS Blog Committee. In her spare time, she is the President of Green Tree Public Library's Board of Trustees and a member of the Council of the Metropolia of the Ukrainian Orthodox Church of the USA.

Kris Turner is the Associate Director of Public Services at the University of Wisconsin Law Library, where he oversees the reference and circulation departments, as well as the development of the Law Library's website and digital repository. He also teaches Law Practice Technologies and co-teaches Advanced Legal Research, which were selected as a Bloomberg Law finalist for Law School Innovation in 2024. Kris has served as the President of the Wisconsin Library Association, the Law Librarians Association of Wisconsin, and has held a number of committee and programming roles for the American Association of Law Libraries. He has written articles focused on library outreach, the law of libraries, space and contracts law, and leadership transitions. Before joining UW Law, he worked at Madison Public Library and the Forest Products Laboratory Library.

Latia "Tia" Ward is Research Librarian at the Arthur J. Morris Law Library at the University of Virginia School of Law. Her previous employment includes working as a librarian in academic law libraries and at the Law Library of Congress. Ward graduated from the University of North Carolina at Chapel Hill with a Bachelor of Arts in English and a Master of Science in Library Science. She graduated from Wake Forest University School of Law with a Juris Doctor and is a member of the North Carolina State

Bar. In addition, Ward is a member of the American Association of Law Libraries and is the current chair of the Virginia Association of Law Libraries Access to Justice Committee.

Ronald E. Wheeler serves as the Associate Dean of the Fineman & Pappas Law Libraries and Associate Professor of Law & Legal Research at the Boston University School of Law, where he has been since 2016. Prior to moving to Boston, Professor Wheeler served in various law library management roles at law schools across the country, including Suffolk University Law School, the University of San Francisco School of Law, the Georgia State University College of Law, and the University of New Mexico School of Law. He is a recognized leader in the areas of legal research instruction, legal research techniques, law library management, and Diversity, Equity, Inclusion, and Belonging. Wheeler has taught 1L legal research in numerous formats and permutations, including as a standalone course, as a "by invitation" component of 1L legal writing, as an upper-division-only course, and now at BU as a truly integrated course that weaves legal research into the assignments given in the year-long course called Lawyering Skills, which is co-taught by a law librarian and a member of the legal writing faculty. Wheeler has also taught numerous seminar courses, including Queer Legal Scholarship, Critical Race Theory, and Critical Thinking. He will teach Critical Legal Research in the Spring of 2025. Professor Wheeler served as president of the AALL in 2016–2017 making him the first Black male president of AALL. He was appointed to chair AALL's Inclusion, Diversity, & Equity Awareness Special Committee, whose work from 2020 to 2022 resulted in AALL's adoption of several recommendations proposed by the Special Committee. Wheeler received the AALL Minority Leadership Development Award in 2005 and the Distinguished Alumnus Award from the Wayne State University School of Library & Information Science in 2016. Wheeler is an active member of the Law Librarians of New England (LLNE), the International Association of Law Libraries (IALL), the British & Irish Association of Law Libraries, and the Association of Boston Law Librarians (ABLL). Professor Wheeler serves on the executive boards of the NELLCO, the Boston Academic Law Library Collective (BALLCO), and the Law Library Microform Consortium (LLMC). He is a proud, home-owning resident of the City of Providence in the great, small, and beautiful state of Rhode Island.

Marci Wilding is Public Services Law Librarian at the Grisham Law Library and Assistant Professor of the practice of law at the University of Mississippi School of Law. She holds a JD from the University of Mississippi, an MHED from the University of Mississippi, and a nursing degree from the University of Western Kentucky. She creates and teaches law courses in risk management and compliance, and she teaches a research course in intermediate legal research. She serves as the faculty adviser for the Student Health Law Association and serves as coach and judge for moot court and negotiation board teams. In addition to her academic contributions, Marci has been recognized with the faculty diversity award for 2024 and was a graduate of the inaugural cohort of the Leadership for Equity and Inclusive Excellence program at the University of Mississippi. She has over ten years of healthcare experience in which she served as the Director of Risk. She has published in the areas of equity and access in higher education and libraries.

Jennifer Wondracek is the *Director of the Law Library and Professor of Legal Research & Writing* at Capital University Law School. She has extensive experience in law librarianship and legal technology. Wondracek has held positions in the law libraries at Barry University, Elon University, the University of Florida, and UNT Dallas. While at UNT Dallas, she became the Founding Director of the Legal Educational Technology department. Wondracek's research focus includes VR, 360 photography, legal ethics, generative AI, and technology competence. A frequent speaker at conferences and CLE events, Wondracek was recognized as an ABA LTRC Women of Legal Tech Honoree and Fastcase50 member in 2021.

Jingwei Zhang is the reference and student services librarian at Rutgers Law School Library in Camden, NJ. She provides reference services both in person and through virtual chat to support the research needs of the Rutgers Law School community. She also works as the library liaison to assigned law faculty members and law student journal editors. Jingwei received her LLB from Fudan University in Shanghai, China, LLM from Cornell Law School, and her MLS from Rutgers University.

www.ingramcontent.com/pod-product-compliance
Ingram Content Group UK Ltd.
Pitfield, Milton Keynes, MK11 3LW, UK
UKHW051932150926
475560UK00005B/354

9 781538 199732